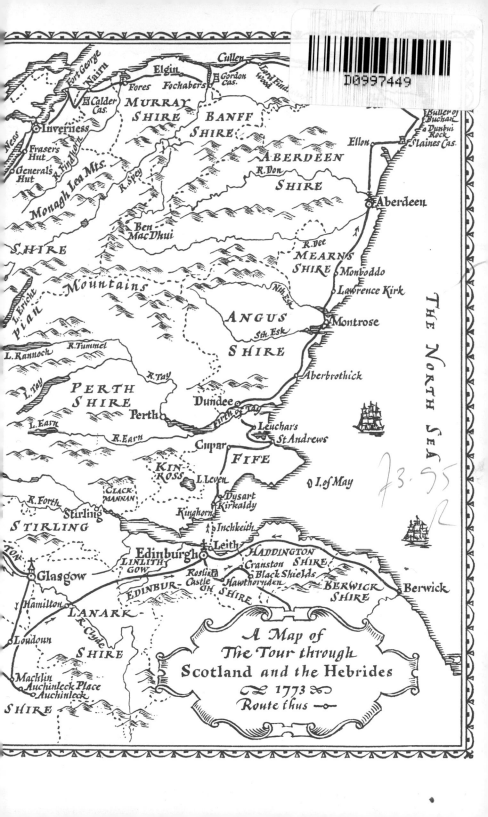

A Map of
The Tour through
Scotland and the Hebrides
1773
Route thus

EVERYBODY'S BOSWELL

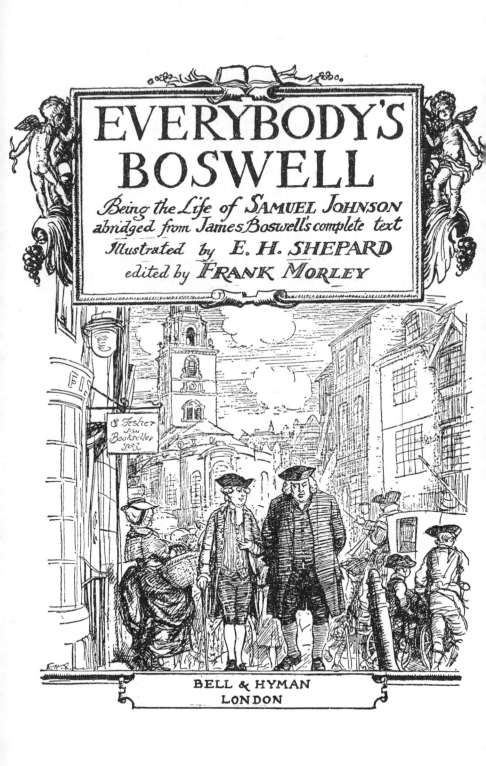

EVERYBODY'S BOSWELL

Being the Life of SAMUEL JOHNSON
abridged from James Boswell's *complete text*

Illustrated by E. H. SHEPARD

edited by FRANK MORLEY

BELL & HYMAN
LONDON

Published by
BELL & HYMAN LIMITED
Denmark House
37-39 Queen Elizabeth Street
London SE1 2QB

First published in 1930 by
G. Bell & Sons Ltd
Reprinted six times
Reissued 1980

Abridgement and introduction
© Bell & Hyman Limited 1980
Illustrations © The Executors of
the late Ernest H. Shepard 1980

ISBN 0 7135 1237 7

Printed in Great Britain by
REDWOOD BURN LIMITED
Trowbridge & Esher

CONTENTS

LIST OF ILLUSTRATIONS

INTRODUCTION

"Friendship, the wine of life, should be renewed," says this immortal book, quite early on; this I have taken to be true, not only in the life that leads us, but in the larger life of reading. And so, without depending on such other references as might be brought forward, I take it that neither Johnson nor Boswell would object to one more edition, nor to the kind of abridgement I have here attempted. This is a shorter version of Boswell's writings about Johnson, in that what seems to me comparatively dead wood is removed; but in no respect, save that of length, is it distorted. I have, I hope, allowed no single taboo of temporary taste or distaste to influence the choice of episode; it is within its scale a full projection; whatever the two friends talked about is represented in these pages. And what good talk it is, needs no impertinent proof from me.

The one man, Johnson, was in his fifties when the other, a very young gentleman of twenty-three, deliberately sought him out. "Dictionary" Johnson's fame was by that time solid. He had emerged unaided from cold obscurity to the position of a Sage; he was now not the leader of a clique but an acknowledged universal Great Cham of Literature. But that position, earned by genius and exertion, was not kept up without a struggle in which there is something more than mere buffalo-like buttings at possible rivals. The tension which found expression in sudden groans and beatings of the breast and lonely, meditated prayers—all faithfully recorded here by Boswell—was fundamentally due to a discordance between his rôle of public moralist and what he looked upon as dreadful weaknesses in his own life. It was this strain which caused such bellowings when Boswell prodded him, or when, more often, his honest searching spirit probed itself. I do not in the least doubt that Johnson's sins were real; not to recognise that is surely to do less than justice to his victory. He was victorious; and the last scene of all, when after life-long dread of death he gained composure, is not far from sublime.

He has been charged with lack of humour; but after all humour is only a way of coming to terms with life, a dissipating and incom-

plete solution, and Johnson fought to conquer, not to draw. But
as with many great men the side-skirmishes are full of comedies.
Among them one of the least is that he became (I think) the pro-
totype of Sherlock Holmes. I often hoped to ask Sir Arthur Conan
Doyle that question; not only, which is obvious, are many of Dr.
Watson's characteristics found in Boswell, not only is the very
name Dr. Watson found in Boswell's *Life*, but quite a number of
Sherlock Holmes's early traits are discovered in Johnson's affection for London, for driving rapidly in post-chaises, for black-letter
books, for writing prescriptions in technical characters. This perhaps is ardent fancy; yet it is worth pointing out that a host of
qualities will be found in Johnson, such as have been diluted and
displayed elsewhere in fiction to permanent delight.

Boswell's mind, like Pepys's, was always at the window, and there
are other similarities between the characters. To me Boswell is the
more interesting; his private, personal conduct could be more coarse
than that of Pepys, but he was not so hard, so self-reliant. The Keynote
of this elder son of a respected Scottish judge is not, as one might
think at first glance, ordinary vanity. It is true that Boswell loved to
bask in reflected glory. He revelled in the pleasure of being familiar
with great men. Doctor Johnson, General Paoli, Voltaire, Hume,
Rousseau—anyone who had a name was like a candle to a moth. But
as well as this type of ambition there was in him a constant aspiration
simply to be a good man. His warm imagination, while he was young,
always looked forward with great complacency to the sobriety, health-
fulness and worth of his future years. Frequent were his misconducts
and humiliations, and various (as with Pepys) were the methods for
bolstering his hopes. Sometimes he prayed, sometimes took vows, but
mostly took great men. In his fidelity to Johnson there is a great deal
of this desire for self-help; and indeed all the hints in this volume that
he would go to pieces if left to himself were later on painfully fulfilled. Not the least of the astonishments of this extraordinary
biography, so cunningly written and so luminous, with gifts of
genius (far beyond Pepys's) strikingly displayed, is the fact that
much of it was put together when Boswell was, except for these
memories, a completely broken man. But of himself as pictured,
of himself when young, there is scarcely anything here which is not
vivacious and charming; even the vanity is of an innocuous kind,
and much of it artfully exposed in order to enlarge the stature of
his friend. The shifts at disguising his identity when he makes
remarks which prove fatuous, are often noticeable and are always

amusing, though sometimes they are merely there for the sake of variety. Boswell is a masterly interrogator, and very deft with indirect methods of exposition. What he can do in direct narrative is shown in the description of the storm towards the end of the *Tour to the Hebrides*, which is bound up here with the *Life*. It is interesting to compare the *Tour* with the *Life*, and it is in the *Tour* that Boswell (as a younger man) lets himself go with that naive exuberance which one regards as particularly attractive. It is there that he is far from malice, and has so much good humour, that it seems scarce a virtue.

A word as to the London and the England and Scotland of that day. They are obliterated. The extraordinary alterations produced by the application of capital to inventions, and by the activity of humanitarians and reformers, had scarcely begun. London, which seemed so large to Johnson, had less than three quarters of a million people in it. The narrow cobble-stoned streets, without curbs and with gutters down the middle, remained as intricate, as dirty, and at night-time almost as ill-lighted as they had been in the reign of Queen Anne. Scavengers appointed by each ward considered their work done when they removed the night-soil half a mile from the Town; and in hot weather other scavengers appraised the city's refuse—the kites that flew over London then were the real ones Cowper speaks of, not the paper toys to which they gave their name. The words "reform" and "change" were not yet in good repute; what one was born to, one lived with, and made the best of. What one was born to, in London, included: ordure left lying in the streets, broken pavements, ruinous houses, the driving of bullocks through the city, the prevalence of mad dogs, the gin-shops, the swarms of beggars, the deluge of profanity and street-cries.

To appreciate life then we have to rid ourselves of more than a century of incessant alteration and reform; and to appreciate the philosophy of life which still ruled then, we have to rid ourselves of the fixed ideas of "progress" and "evolution." We, who have been nurtured on these ideas (which would have seemed to Johnson fantastic, and which indeed may be so), are unlikely to be able to overdo the ridding process. But without making the effort, it is perhaps impossible to sympathise with Johnson's grand scheme of "subordination"—the fixed idea of his time—implying not the equality but the harmony of classes. In his lifetime, however, that grand scheme was breaking down; the very clarity with which the ideal was elucidated, shows that it was losing its grip on life. It was impressed upon the age, not its expression. For underneath, in domestic as in foreign affairs, life was very much in movement, and working in an incalculable direction. London was like Watt's steam-kettle; the city was boiling, though the gentry, by and large, were sitting on the lid. So one comes round at the end of a description to contradict the beginning; and rightly, for it was a very complex period, turbulent and interesting; a period of preoccupation with moral problems, of exploration and invention; of indefinable and yet definite difference of opinion between young men and old; and that is what lends another interest to the pair here pictured.

But it is not as material for history that the book has its most lasting merit; as said above it is because these two unusual men found a lively comfort in companionship, and because one of them, the lesser in all else, had the great talent to communicate it.

1980   FRANK MORLEY

PRINCIPAL CHARACTERS

Dr. Samuel Johnson. (1709–1784.) *The subject of this biography.*

James Boswell. (1740–1795.) *The author of this biography.*

A son of Alexander Boswell (Lord Auchinleck) a distinguished Scottish judge who owned a large estate which had been in the family since 1505. James was educated at Edinburgh High School and University, and studied Civil Law at Glasgow. Possessed of a great desire to know distinguished people and record their sayings, he started to keep a journal as a boy. When he was seventeen he met David Hume the historian; when he was twenty-three he met Johnson, who was thirty-one years his senior; and during the next few years when he toured the Continent after studying law at Utrecht, he met Rousseau, Voltaire, and Gen. Paoli (who suspected him for a spy when he saw him making notes of the interview) and resumed his acquaintance with John Wilkes. On his return he published his *Account of Corsica* (1768). After various love affairs, notably with the vivacious Isabella de Zuylen (Zélide), who had a good deal in common with him, Boswell married his cousin Margaret Montgomery in 1769; they had six children.

In 1773 Boswell realised two ambitions, being admitted a member of the *Literary Club*, and persuading Johnson to undertake with him the tour to the Hebrides, which lasted over three months.

Boswell loved London life, and though he was called to the Bar in Edinburgh in 1766 and eventually became Laird of Auchinleck with estates worth £1600 a year, he spent as much of his time in London as possible, particularly in the company of Johnson and his circle. In 1786, two years after Johnson's death, he was called to the English Bar.

Boswell's wife died in 1789, and he himself survived Johnson only eleven years. After Johnson's death his occasional fits of hypochondria increased, and he drank more heavily. But it was during this period that he published the two works that brought him immediate and enduring fame. *The Journal of a Tour to the Hebrides* was published in 1785, and *The Life of Samuel Johnson* in 1791.

Rev. William Adams. (1706–1789.)

While a young man at Pembroke College, Oxford, made the acquaintance of Johnson during the latter's period of residence (1728–29). Fellow and Tutor of Pembroke till 1755 when he became rector of Counde. In 1775 he was elected Master of his old College, where he frequently entertained Johnson at the lodge.

Topham Beauclerk. (1739–1780.)

Only son of Lord Sydney Beauclerk, and grandson of the first Duke of St. Albans. Educated at Trinity College, Oxford, where he formed a close friendship with Bennet Langton (*q.v.*). Of refined taste, and interested in many intellectual pursuits, he "made a conquest" of Johnson, who seems to have had a great affection for him. Beauclerk married in 1768 Lady Diana Spencer, divorced wife of the second Viscount Bolingbroke.

EDMUND BURKE. (1729–1797.)

Second son of Richard Burke, an attorney of Dublin. Educated at Trinity College, Dublin, and the Middle Temple. Became a member of *The Club* (1764), and shortly after, being elected M.P. for Wendover embarked on a brilliant political career, his talent for oratory being so amazing that he was known as "the British Cicero." He was offered a peerage by George III., but declined it on account of the death of his beloved son Richard Burke.

DR. CHARLES BURNEY. (1726–1814.)

Educated at Chester School. His early proficiency and interest in music attracted the attention of Dr. Arne, who, in 1744, took him as a pupil to London, where he studied and gave lessons. Organist at St. Dionis Backchurch (1749); Lynn Church (1751–1760); Chelsea Hospital (1783). Produced an opera at Drury Lane (1766). Travelled widely on the Continent, collecting material for his *History of Music* (4 vols., 1776–89), and published amusing anecdotes of his foreign tours. His wit, geniality, and hospitality made him welcome in the literary circles led by Dr. Johnson, Sir Joshua Reynolds, etc., and the fame of his daughter Fanny (Mme. d'Arblay), the authoress of *Evelina, Cecilia*, etc., still more enlarged the circle of his acquaintances, most of whom appear frequently in Boswell's pages.

EARL OF CHESTERFIELD. (1694–1773.)

Philip Dormer Stanhope, son of the third Earl, succeeded his father in 1726. He was a bitter opponent of Sir Robert Walpole. Ambassador at The Hague in 1728 and 1745: Lord-Lieutenant of Ireland (1746) and Secretary of State (1746). In 1755 occurred the famous dispute with Johnson over the dedication of the *Dictionary*. In 1768 the son for whom Chesterfield's famous *Letters to his Son* had been penned, died, and the Earl, overcome with grief, retired into obscurity. He had a great reputation among his contemporaries for oratory, elegant manners, and culture.

EDWARD DILLY (1732–1779) and CHARLES DILLY (1739–1807).

Carried on a bookselling business in the Poultry, London, and published Boswell's *Corsica*. They were hospitably disposed to authors, and frequently entertained Johnson and Boswell at their excellent dinner parties. Charles Dilly, after his brother's death, published Boswell's *Tour to the Hebrides* (1785), and the first three editions of his *Life of Dr. Johnson* (1791–99).

DAVID GARRICK. (1717–1779.)

Third son of Captain Peter Garrick, who was of French Protestant descent. Educated at Lichfield Grammar School, and for a short time under the tuition of Johnson at Edial. With Johnson he went to London to seek his fortune. After unsuccessful attempts to set up in business, he took to the stage, for which he always had a leaning, and first appeared on the boards in March, 1741. His success was instantaneous, and for nearly thirty years he was the leading English actor and theatrical producer. He was buried in Westminster Abbey.

OLIVER GOLDSMITH. (1728–1774.)

Second son of Charles Goldsmith, an Irish schoolmaster. Born at Pallas, Co. Longford. Whilst Oliver was a child his father obtained the living of Kilkenny, Co. Meath, and Oliver was educated in the village school, and in neighbouring grammar schools. In 1744 he went as a sizar to Trinity College, Dublin, where he lived in great poverty. After his father's death (1749) he wandered about Ireland, studied medicine at Edinburgh, rambled as a vagrant flute-player through Belgium, France, and Switzerland, and after 1756 continued to exist precariously on his wits in London, where he eventually became a bookseller's hack. Though the work he turned out for the bookseller was of little value, his style and his personality brought him into contact with men of position in the literary world, notably Johnson, Burke, and Reynolds. He was one of the original members of *The Club*.

His poem *The Traveller*, published in 1764, was his first work of real merit, and this was followed in 1766 by *The Vicar of Wakefield*, which established his reputation for all time. Turning to the drama he increased his reputation, and at length earned money with his *Good Natur'd Man* (1768), *She Stoops to Conquer* (1773), and received good payment for his slight but admirably condensed histories of Rome, England, and Greece. Always erratic, frivolous, and improvident, and his own worst enemy, he died comparatively young in 1774.

MRS. SAMUEL JOHNSON. (1689–1752.)

Elizabeth Jervis, married (1) Henry Porter, a mercer; (2) Samuel Johnson. Johnson met Mrs. Porter and her husband when he was living in Birmingham in 1733. After the death of Mr. Porter, who left two sons and a daughter, Johnson married the widow, in 1736, when he was twenty-seven and she was forty-seven. It was, he told Beauclerk, "a love marriage on both sides." Johnson set up a school at Edial, but this did not pay and he went to London to seek his fortune, leaving his wife at Lichfield. In 1737 he took her to London. Possibly her health began to give trouble, for in 1748 Johnson took her to Tunbridge Wells for a visit, and later on we read that "for the sake of country air" she had lodgings in Hampstead for a time. In March, 1752, she died, to Johnson's deep and lasting distress. She was buried in the Parish Church of Bromley, Kent; and in 1784 Johnson had an inscription in Latin inscribed on her tombstone.

BENNET LANGTON. (1737–1801.)

Son of George Langton, of Langton, Lincs. When young he obtained on his own initiative an introduction to Johnson. Educated at Trinity College, Oxford, where his chief friend was Topham Beauclerk (*q.v.*). Johnson visited him at Langton in 1759. In 1764 he was elected an original member of *The Club*. His friendship with Johnson was close and lifelong. He succeeded Johnson as Professor of Ancient Literature at the Royal Academy (1788).

DONALD MACLEAN, the young Laird of Col.

Col Maclean was called "the young Laird" or "Young Col" although his father was still alive, and in fact survived him. Boswell and Johnson met Col at the house of his uncle, Macleod of Talisker on their tour of the Hebrides; and from that day (24th Sept., 1773) until 19th October, he took charge of the party, escorting them to several islands. Boswell and Johnson became fond of young

Col, who was a sportsman, a progressive landlord, and a good-natured companion; and they were very grieved to hear of his death the next year (1774) when he was drowned in the Sound between Ulva and Mull.

REV. DONALD M'QUEEN.

A Minister of Skye, well known for his antiquarian lore and literary knowledge. When Johnson and Boswell were touring the Hebrides, he was an elderly man. Hearing that he was "the most intelligent man in Sky," Boswell obtained a letter of introduction and arranged to meet him at Rasay; and he accompanied them from the 8th until the 25th September on their visits to various parts of Skye. They were impressed by his vigour of mind and learning, and wanted him to write a book on Skye.

PASQUALE PAOLI. (1725–1807.)

Corsican patriot, and leader of the islanders against Genoese overlordship of the island. When Corsica was ceded by the Genoese to France, Paoli resisted all attempts of the French to subdue the island for two years, but eventually had to flee and seek asylum in England (1769), where his fame had preceded him. During his stay in England, he was introduced to Johnson by Boswell, and won the Doctor's regard. In 1789 he was made Governor of Corsica by the French Constituent Assembly, but during the excesses of the French Revolution he again led a national rising. When this failed he returned once more to England (1796), where he remained till his death.

LUCY PORTER. (1716–1786.)

Daughter, by her first husband, of Dr. Johnson's wife. When Mrs. Johnson died in 1752, her daughter was thirty-six—only seven years younger than the Doctor. She lived for many years with Johnson's mother at Lichfield, and eventually, coming into a considerable sum of money, built herself a comfortable house in that town. Though not always on the best of terms with his stepdaughter, the Doctor frequently visited her, and a number of his letters to her are to be found in the following pages.

SIR JOSHUA REYNOLDS. (1723–1792.)

The famous painter. Born at Plympton-Earl's, Devonshire. He was one of Johnson's earliest friends in London, and at his house was to be met all the best intellectual society of the period. At his suggestion *The Club* was founded in 1764. In 1768 he was elected first President of the newly founded Royal Academy, and was knighted by George III.

REV. JOHN TAYLOR. (1711–1788.)

Son of Thomas Taylor of Ashbourne, Derbyshire. Educated at Lichfield School (when he began a life-long friendship with Johnson) and at Christchurch, Oxford. After 1736 he was ordained, and in 1740 was presented to Market Bosworth rectory, which he held to his death. He also held simultaneously other preferments. He resided mainly at Ashbourne, where his wealth enabled him to live the life of a country gentleman, and to breed fine cattle. He was often visited by Johnson, and in 1776 Boswell also made a short stay at his house.

HESTER LYNCH THRALE (afterwards MRS. PIOZZI). (1741–1821.)

Daughter of John Salusbury. Married (1) in 1763 Henry Thrale, a wealthy brewer, after whose death she shocked most of her friends, including Johnson, by marrying in 1784 (2) a Mr. Piozzi, an Italian musician. Johnson was introduced to the Thrales by Arthur Murphy, in 1765, and their acquaintance ripened into one of the most intimate friendships in Johnson's life. He passed much of his time at their home in Streatham, and visited Paris with them.

Mrs. Piozzi, retaining her vivacity and wit to the last, died at Clifton in 1821, having lived since her second marriage for the most part in Italy and Wales. Her *Recollections* and *Anecdotes* and *Letters to and from Dr. Johnson* rank only below Boswell's great *Life* as our best source of information regarding the Lexicographer.

JOHN WILKES. (1727–1797.)

Had a stormy political career. M.P. for Aylesbury in 1759 and 1761; in 1762 he founded a paper called *The North Briton*, in opposition to *The Briton* which supported Bute's government. In No. 45 of the *North Briton* he attacked the King's speech at the opening of Parliament, and in consequence was arrested on a general warrant. Though he was discharged and ultimately obtained damages for illegal arrest, he was expelled from Parliament and outlawed. When in exile he met Boswell in Italy. The outlawry was reversed, but he was again expelled from Parliament for libel in 1769, and three times re-elected for Middlesex ("for Wilkes and Liberty"), the election in each case being annulled. His case was supported by Junius, the Government's by Dr. Johnson. He became Sheriff of London and Middlesex in 1771, and was again returned for Parliament, this time being allowed to take his seat. He was Lord Mayor of London in 1774.

Johnson said in 1763 that Wilkes ought to be well ducked, in 1769 described him as "a retailer of sedition and obscenity," "a criminal from a gaol," and in 1773 was still violently against him. It was therefore no mean triumph when (in 1776) Boswell, with delicate diplomacy, induced Johnson to be a fellow-guest with Wilkes at dinner at the Dillys. The gay, good-humoured Wilkes bore no malice against his opponent.

MRS. ANNA WILLIAMS. (1706–1783.)

Daughter of Zachariah Williams, a scientific inventor and medical practitioner, who died in London in 1755, after a life of hardship and poverty. When he was an inmate of the Charterhouse (as a poor pensioner) he became acquainted with Dr. Johnson and his wife, and the Doctor taking pity on Anna, who had lost her sight in 1752, gave her lodging in his house. Though she was of a peevish disposition, "her prompt elocution, universal curiosity, and comprehensive knowledge" appealed to Johnson, who always stood up for her against critics of his curious household. She published a collection of *Miscellanies* in 1766, to which Johnson himself and Mrs. Thrale contributed. In 1756 Garrick gave a benefit performance of Aaron Hill's *Mérope* on her behalf.

THE LIFE OF
SAMUEL JOHNSON, LL.D.

THE LIFE OF

SAMUEL JOHNSON, LL.D.

To write the life of him who excelled all mankind in writing the lives of others, and who, whether we consider his extraordinary endowments, or his various works, has been equalled by few in any age, is an arduous, and may be reckoned in me a presumptuous task.

Had Dr. Johnson written his own Life, in conformity with the opinion which he has given, that every man's life may be best written by himself; had he employed in the preservation of his own history, that clearness of narration and elegance of language in which he has embalmed so many eminent persons, the world would probably have had the most perfect example of biography that was ever exhibited. But although he at different times, in a desultory manner, committed to writing many particulars of the progress of his mind and fortunes, he never had persevering diligence enough to form them into a regular composition. Of these memorials a few have been preserved; but the greater part was consigned by him to the flames, a few days before his death.

As I had the honour and happiness of enjoying his friendship for upwards of twenty years; as I had the scheme of writing his life constantly in view; as he was well apprised of this circumstance, and from time to time obligingly satisfied my inquiries, by communicating to me the incidents of his early years; as I acquired a facility in recollecting, and was very assiduous in recording, his conversation, of which the extraordinary vigour and vivacity constituted one of the first features of his character; and as I have spared no pains in obtaining materials concerning him, from every quarter where I could discover that they were to be found, and have been favoured with the most liberal communications by his friends; I flatter myself that few biographers have entered upon such a work as this, with more advantages; independent of literary abilities, in which I am not vain enough to compare myself with some great names who have gone before me in this kind of writing.

Instead of melting down my materials into one mass, and constantly speaking in my own person, I produce, wherever it is in my power, his own minutes, letters, or conversation, being convinced that this mode is more lively, and will make my readers better acquainted with him, than even most of those were who actually knew him, but could know him only partially. Indeed, I cannot conceive a more perfect mode of writing any man's life, than not only relating all the most important events of it in their order, but interweaving what he privately wrote, and said, and thought; by which mankind are enabled as it were to see him live, and to "live o'er each scene" with him, as he actually advanced through the several stages of his life. Had his other friends been as diligent and ardent as I was, he might have been almost entirely preserved. As it is, I will venture to say, that he will be seen in this work more completely than any man who has ever yet lived.

And he will be seen as he really was; for I profess to write not his panegyric, which must be all praise, but his life; which, great and good as he was, must not be supposed to be entirely perfect. To be as he was, is indeed subject of panegyric enough to any man in this state of being; but in every picture there should be shade as well as light; and when I delineate him without reserve, I do what he himself recommended, both by his precept and his example.

Samuel Johnson was born at Lichfield, in Staffordshire, on the 18th of September, N.S., 1709. His father was Michael Johnson, a native of Derbyshire, of obscure extraction, who settled in Lichfield as a bookseller and stationer. His mother was Sarah Ford, descended of an ancient race of substantial yeomanry in Warwickshire. They were well advanced in years when they married, and never had more than two children, both sons; Samuel, their first born, and Nathaniel, who died in his twenty-fifth year.

Mr. Michael Johnson was forced by the narrowness of his circumstances to be very diligent in business, not only in his shop, but by occasionally resorting to several towns in the neighbourhood, some of which were at a considerable distance from Lichfield. At that time booksellers' shops in the provincial towns of England were very rare, so that there was not one even in Birmingham, in which town old Mr. Johnson used to open a shop every market-day. He was a pretty good Latin scholar, and a citizen so creditable as to be made one of the magistrates of Lichfield; and, being a man of good sense, and skill in his trade, he acquired a reasonable share of wealth, of which, however, he afterwards lost the greatest part, by engaging unsuccessfully in a manufacture of parchment.

Johnson's mother was a woman of distinguished understanding. Her piety was not inferior; and to her must be ascribed those early impressions of religion upon the mind of her son, from which the world afterwards derived so much benefit. He told me, that he remembered distinctly having had the first notice of heaven, "a place to which good people went," and hell, "a place to which bad people went," communicated to him by her, when a little child in bed with her; and that it might be the better fixed in his memory, she sent him to repeat it to Thomas Jackson, their man-servant.

In following so very eminent a man from his cradle to his grave, every minute particular which can throw light on the progress of his mind is interesting. It is certainly unwise to pay too much attention to incidents which the credulous relate with eager satisfaction, and the more scrupulous or witty inquirer considers only as topics of ridicule: yet there is a traditional story of the infant Hercules of Toryism, so curiously characteristic, that I shall not withhold it.[1]

When Dr. Sacheverel was at Lichfield, Johnson was not quite three years old. My grandfather Hammond observed him at the cathedral perched upon his father's shoulders, listening and gaping at the much celebrated preacher. Mr. Hammond asked Mr. Johnson how he could possibly think of bringing such an infant to church, and in the midst of so great a crowd. He answered, because it was impossible to keep him at home; for, young as he was, he believed he had caught the public spirit and zeal for Sacheverel, and would have staid for ever in the church, satisfied with beholding him.

Nor can I omit a little instance of that jealous independence of spirit, and impetuosity of temper, which never forsook him. One day, when the servant who used to be sent to school to conduct him home had not come in time, he set out by himself, though he was then so near-sighted, that he was obliged to stoop down on his hands and knees to take a view of the kennel before he ventured to step over it. His schoolmistress, afraid that he might miss his way, or fall into the kennel, or be run over by a cart, followed him at some distance. He happened to turn about and perceive her. Feeling her careful attention as an insult to his manliness, he ran

1 Communicated to Boswell by Miss Adye of Lichfield.

back to her in a rage, and beat her, as well as his strength would permit. Of the power of his memory, for which he was all his life eminent to a degree almost incredible, the following early instance was told me. When he was a child in petticoats, and had learnt to read, Mrs. Johnson one morning put the common prayer-book into his hands, pointed to the collect for the day, and said, "Sam, you must get this by heart." She went upstairs, leaving him to study it: but by the time she had reached the second floor, she heard him following her. "What's the matter?" said she. "I can say it," he replied; and repeated it distinctly, though he could not have read it more than twice.

Young Johnson had the misfortune to be much afflicted with the scrofula, or king's evil, which disfigured a countenance naturally well formed, and hurt his visual nerves so much, that he did not see at all with one of his eyes, though its appearance was little different from that of the other. There is amongst his prayers, one inscribed "*When my* EYE *was restored to its use*," which ascertains a defect that many of his friends knew he had, though I never perceived it. I supposed him to be only near-sighted; and indeed I must observe, that in no other respect could I discern any defect in his vision; on the contrary, the force of his attention and perceptive quickness made him see and distinguish all manner of objects with a nicety that is rarely to be found. And the ladies with whom he was acquainted agree, that no man was more nicely and minutely critical in the elegance of female dress.

It has been said, that he contracted this grievous malady from his nurse. His mother, yielding to the superstitious notion, which prevailed so long, as to the virtue of the regal touch, carried him to London, where he was actually touched by Queen Anne. Johnson used to talk of this very frankly; being asked, if he could remember Queen Anne. "He had," he said, "a confused, but somehow a sort of solemn recollection of a lady in diamonds, and a long black hood." This touch, however, was without any effect.

He was first taught to read English by Dame Oliver, a widow, who kept a school for young children in Lichfield. When he was going to Oxford, she came to take leave of him, brought him, in the simplicity of her kindness, a present of gingerbread, and said he was the best scholar she ever had. He delighted in mentioning this early compliment; adding, with a smile, that "this was as high a proof of his merit as he could conceive."

HE WAS ACTUALLY TOUCHED BY QUEEN ANNE

He began to learn Latin with Mr. Hawkins, usher or under-master of Lichfield school, "a man," said he, "very skilful in his little way." With him he continued two years, and then rose to be under the care of Mr. Hunter, the head master, who, according to his account, "was very severe, and wrongheadedly severe. He used," said he, "to beat us unmercifully; and he did not distinguish between ignorance and negligence: for he would beat a boy equally for not knowing a thing, as for neglecting to know it. He would ask a boy a question, and if he did not answer it, he would beat him, without considering whether he had an opportunity of knowing how to answer it. For instance, he would call up a boy and ask him Latin for a candlestick, which the boy could not expect to be asked. Now, sir, if a boy could answer every question, there would be no need of a master to teach him."

It is, however, but justice to mention that Johnson was very sensible how much he owed to Mr. Hunter. Mr. Langton one day asked him, how he had acquired so accurate a knowledge of Latin, in which, I believe, he was exceeded by no man of his time: he said, "My master whipt me very well. Without that, Sir, I should have done nothing." He told Mr. Langton, that while Hunter was flogging his boys unmercifully, he used to say, "And this I do to save you from the gallows." Johnson, upon all occasions, expressed his approbation of enforcing instruction by means of the rod. "I would rather," said he, "have the rod to be the general terror to all, to make them learn, than tell a child if you do thus or thus, you will be more esteemed than your brothers or sisters. The rod produces an effect which terminates in itself. A child is afraid of being whipped, and gets his risk, and there's an end on't; whereas, by exciting emulation and comparisons of superiority, you lay the foundation of lasting mischief; you make brothers and sisters hate each other."

That superiority over his fellows, which he maintained with so much dignity in his march through life, was not assumed from vanity and ostentation, but was the natural and constant effect of those extraordinary powers of mind, of which he could not but be conscious by comparison; the intellectual difference, which in other cases of comparison of characters is often a matter of undecided contest, being as clear in his case as the superiority of stature in some men above others. From his earliest years, his superiority was perceived and acknowledged. He was from the beginning a king of men. His school-fellow, Mr. Hector, assured me that he never knew him corrected at school, but for talking and diverting other boys from their business. He seemed to learn by intuition; for though indolence and procrastination were inherent in his constitution, whenever he made an exertion he did more than any one else.

His favourites used to receive very liberal assistance from him; and such was the submission and deference with which he was treated, such the desire to obtain his regard, that three of the boys, of whom Mr. Hector was sometimes one, used to come in the morning as his humble attendants, and carry him to school. One in the middle stooped, while he sat upon his back, and one on each side supported him; and thus he was borne triumphant. Such a proof of the early predominance of intellectual vigour is very remarkable, and does honour to human nature.

He never joined with the other boys in their ordinary diversions; his only amusement was in winter, when he took a pleasure in being drawn upon the ice by a boy bare-footed, who pulled him along by a garter fixed around him; no very easy operation, as his size was remarkably large. His defective sight, indeed, prevented him from enjoying the common sports; and he once pleasantly remarked to me, "how wonderfully well he had contrived to be idle without them."

Johnson was, at the age of fifteen, removed to the school of Stourbridge, in Worcestershire. He remained at Stourbridge little more than a year, and then returned home, where he passed two years in what he thought idleness, and was scolded by his father for his want of steady application. Yet he read a great deal in a desultory manner. He used to mention one curious instance of his casual reading, when but a boy. Having imagined that his brother had hid some apples behind a large folio upon an upper shelf in his father's shop, he climbed up to search for them. There were no apples; but the large folio proved to be Petrarch, whom he had seen mentioned as one of the restorers of learning. His curiosity having been thus excited, he sat down with avidity and read a great part of the book. What he read during these two years, he told me, was not works of mere amusement, "not voyages and travels, but all literature, Sir, all ancient writers, all manly; though but little Greek, only some of Anacreon and Hesiod: but in this irregular manner," added he, "I had looked into a great many books, which were not commonly known at the universities, where they seldom read any books but what are put into their hands by their tutors; so that when I came to Oxford, Dr.

THUS HE WAS BORNE TRIUMPHANT

Adams, now master of Pembroke College, told me, I was the best qualified for the university that he had ever known come there."

That a man in Mr. Michael Johnson's circumstances should think of sending his son to the expensive university of Oxford, at his own charge, seems very improbable. The subject was too delicate to question Johnson upon: but I have been assured by Dr. Taylor, that the scheme never would have taken place had not a gentleman of Shropshire, one of his schoolfellows, spontaneously undertaken to support him at Oxford, in the character of his companion; though, in fact, he never received any assistance whatever from that gentleman.

He, however, went to Oxford, and was entered a commoner of Pembroke College, on the 31st of October, 1728, being then in his nineteenth year.

The Reverend Dr. Adams, who afterwards presided over Pembroke College with universal esteem, was present, and gave me some account of what passed on the night of Johnson's arrival at Oxford. On that evening, his father, who had anxiously accompanied him, found means to have him introduced to Mr. Jorden, who was to be his tutor. His father seemed very full of the merits of his son, and told the company he was a good scholar, and a poet, and wrote Latin verses. His figure and manner appeared strange to them; but he behaved modestly, and sat silent, till upon something which occurred in the course of conversation, he suddenly struck in and quoted Macrobius; and thus he gave the first impression of that more extensive reading in which he had indulged himself.

His tutor, Mr. Jorden, fellow of Pembroke, was not, it seems, a man of such abilities as we should conceive requisite for the instructor of Samuel Johnson, who gave me the following account of him: "He was a very worthy man, but a heavy man; and I did not profit much by his instructions. Indeed, I did not attend him much. The first day after I came to college I waited for him, and then staid away four. On the sixth, Mr. Jorden asked me why I had not attended. I answered, I had been sliding in Christ Church meadow. And this I said with as much *nonchalance* as I am now talking to you. I had no notion that I was wrong or irreverent to my tutor."—Boswell. "That, Sir, was great fortitude of mind."—Johnson. "No, Sir; stark insensibility." [1]

[1] "When he related to me this anecdote, he laughed very heartily at the recollection of his own insolence, and said they endured it from him with wonderful acquiescence, and a gentleness that, whenever he thought of it, astonished himself."—*Piozzi's Anecdotes*.

He had a love and respect for Jorden, not for his literature, but for his worth. "Whenever," said he, "a young man becomes Jorden's pupil, he becomes his son."

The "morbid melancholy," which was lurking in his constitution, and to which we may ascribe those particularities, and that aversion to regular life, which at a very early period marked his character, gathered such strength in his twentieth year, as to afflict him in a dreadful manner. While he was at Lichfield, in the college vacation of the year 1729, he felt himself overwhelmed with a horrible hypochondria, with perpetual irritation, fretfulness, and impatience; and with a dejection, gloom, and despair, which made existence misery. He was sometimes so languid and inefficient, that he could not distinguish the hour upon the town-clock.

Johnson, upon the first violent attack of this disorder, strove to overcome it by forcible exertions. He frequently walked to Birmingham and back again, and tried many other expedients, but all in vain. His expression concerning it to me was, "I did not then know how to manage it." His distress became so intolerable, that he applied to Dr. Swinfen, physician in Lichfield, his godfather, and put into his hands a state of his case, written in Latin. But let not little men triumph upon knowing that Johnson was an Hypochondriack. Though he suffered severely from it, he was not therefore degraded. The powers of his great mind might be troubled, and their full exercise suspended at times; but the mind itself was ever entire.

The history of his mind as to religion is an important article. I have mentioned the early impressions made upon his tender imagination by his mother, who continued her pious cares with assiduity, but, in his opinion, not with judgment. "Sunday," said he, "was a heavy day to me when I was a boy. My mother confined me on that day, and made me read 'The Whole Duty of Man,' from a great part of which I could derive no instruction. I fell into an inattention to religion, or an indifference about it, in my ninth year. The church at Lichfield, in which we had a seat, wanted reparation, so I was to go and find a seat in other churches; and having bad eyes, and being awkward about this, I used to go and read in the fields on Sunday. This habit continued till my fourteenth year; and still I find a great reluctance to go to church. I then became a sort of lax *talker* against religion, for I did not much *think* against it; and this lasted till I went to Oxford, where it would not be *suffered*. When at Oxford I took up 'Law's Serious

Call to a Holy Life,' expecting to find it a dull book (as such books generally are), and perhaps to laugh at it. But I found Law quite an overmatch for me; and this was the first occasion of my thinking in earnest of religion, after I became capable of rational enquiry."

The particular course of his reading while at Oxford cannot be traced. He told me what he read *solidly* at Oxford was Greek; not the Grecian historians, but Homer and Euripides, and now and then a little Epigram; that the study of which he was the most fond was metaphysics, but he had not read much, even in that way. I always thought that he did himself injustice in his account of what he had read. Dr. Adam Smith once observed to me, that "Johnson knew more books than any man alive." He had a peculiar facility in seizing at once what was valuable in any book, without submitting to the labour of perusing it from beginning to end. He had, from the irritability of his constitution, at all times, an impatience and hurry when he either read or wrote. A certain apprehension arising from novelty made him write his first exercise at college twice over; but he never took that trouble with any other composition; and we shall see that his most excellent works were struck off at a heat, with rapid exertion.

Yet he appears, from his early notes or memorandums in my possession, to have at various times attempted, or at least planned, a methodical course of study, according to computation, of which he was all his life fond, as it fixed his attention steadily upon something without, and prevented his mind from preying upon itself. Thus I find in his handwriting the number of lines in each of two of Euripides's "Tragedies," of the "Georgics" of Virgil, of the first six books of the "Æneid," of Horace's "Art of Poetry," of three of the books of Ovid's "Metamorphoses," of some parts of Theocritus, and of the tenth Satire of Juvenal; and a table, showing at the rate of various numbers a day (I suppose, verses to be read), what would be, in each case, the total amount in a week, month, and year.

No man had a more ardent love of literature, or a higher respect for it, than Johnson. His apartment in Pembroke College was that upon the second floor over the gateway. The enthusiast of learning will ever contemplate it with veneration. One day, while he was sitting in it quite alone, Dr. Panting, then master of the College, whom he called "a fine Jacobite fellow," overheard him uttering this soliloquy in his strong emphatic voice: "Well, I have a mind to see what is done in other places of learning. I'll go and visit the universities abroad. I'll go to France and Italy. I'll go to Padua. And I'll mind my business. For an *Athenian* blockhead is the worst of all blockheads."

Dr. Adams told me that Johnson, while he was at Pembroke College, "was caressed and loved by all about him, was a gay and frolicsome fellow, and passed there the happiest part of his life." But this is a striking proof of the fallacy of appearances, for the truth is, that he was then depressed by poverty, and irritated by disease. When I mentioned to him this account as given me by Dr. Adams, he said, "Ah, Sir, I was mad and violent. It was bitterness which they mistook for frolic. I was miserably poor, and I thought to fight my way by my literature and my wit; so I disregarded all power and all authority."

The Bishop of Dromore observes in a letter to me, "The pleasure he took in vexing the tutors and fellows has been often mentioned. I have heard from some of his contemporaries that he was generally seen lounging at the college gate, with a circle of young students round him, whom he was entertaining with wit, and keeping from their studies, if not spiriting them up to rebellion against the college discipline, which in his maturer years he so much extolled."

I do not find that he formed any close intimacies with his fellow-collegians. But Dr. Adams told me, that he contracted a love and regard for Pembroke College, which he retained to the last. He took a pleasure in boasting of the many eminent men who had been educated at Pembroke. Being himself a poet, Johnson was peculiarly happy in mentioning how many of the sons of Pembroke were poets; adding, with a smile of sportive triumph, "Sir, we are a nest of singing-birds."

He was not, however, blind to what he thought the defects of his own college: and I have, from the information of Dr. Taylor, a very strong instance of that rigid honesty which he ever inflexibly preserved. Taylor had obtained his father's consent to be entered of Pembroke, that he might be with his schoolfellow Johnson. This would have been a great comfort to Johnson. But he fairly told Taylor that he could not, in conscience, suffer him to enter where he knew he could not have an able tutor. He then made inquiry all round the university, and having found that Mr. Bateman, of Christchurch, was the tutor of highest reputation, Taylor was entered of that college. Mr. Bateman's lectures were so excellent, that Johnson used to come and get them at second-hand from Taylor, till his poverty being so extreme, that his shoes were worn

THREW THEM AWAY WITH INDIGNATION

out, and his feet appeared through them, he saw that this humiliating circumstance was perceived by the Christchurch men, and he came no more. He was too proud to accept of money, and somebody having set a pair of new shoes at his door, he threw them away with indignation. How must we feel when we read such an anecdote of Samuel Johnson!

The *res angusta domi* prevented him from having the advantage of a complete academical education. The friend to whom he had trusted for support had deceived him. His debts in college, though not great, were increasing; and his scanty remittances from Lichfield, which had all along been made with great difficulty, could be supplied no longer, his father having fallen into a state of insolvency. Compelled, therefore, by irresistible necessity, he left the college in autumn 1731, without a degree, having been a member of it little more than three years.

And now (I had almost said poor) Samuel Johnson returned to his native city, destitute, and not knowing how he should gain even a decent livelihood. His father's misfortunes in trade rendered him unable to support his son; and for some time there appeared no means by which he could maintain himself. In the December of this year his father died.

The state of poverty in which he died appears from a note in one of Johnson's little diaries of the following year, which strongly displays his spirit and virtuous dignity of mind. "1732, *Julii* 15. *Undecim aureos deposui, quo die quicquid ante matris funus (quod serum sit precor) de paternis bonis sperari licet, viginti scilicet libras, accepi. Usque adeo mihi fortuna fingenda est. Interea, ne paupertate vires animi languescant, nec in flagitia egestas abigat, cavendum.* I layed by eleven guineas on this day, when I received twenty pounds, being all that I have reason to hope for out of my father's effects, previous to the death of my mother; an event which I pray God may be very remote. I now therefore see that I must make my own fortune. Meanwhile, let me take care that the powers of my mind be not debilitated by poverty, and that indigence do not force me into any criminal act."

In the forlorn state of his circumstances, he accepted of an offer to be employed as usher, in the school of Market-Bosworth, in Leicestershire, to which it appears, from one of his little fragments of a diary, that he went on foot, on the 16th of July,—"*Julii* 16. *Bosvortiam pedes petii.*" This employment was very irksome to him in every respect, and he complained grievously of it in his letters to his friend Mr. Hector, who was now settled as a surgeon at Birmingham. Mr. Hector recollects his writing "that the poet had described the dull sameness of his existence in these words, '*Vitam continet una dies*' (one day contains the whole of my life); that it was unvaried as the note of the cuckoo; and that he did not know whether it was more disagreeable for him to teach, or the boys to learn, the grammar rules." After suffering for a few months such complicated misery, he relinquished a situation which all his life afterwards he recollected with the strongest aversion, and even a degree of horror.

Being now again totally unoccupied, he was invited by Mr. Hector to pass some time with him at Birmingham. He made some valuable acquaintances there, amongst whom was Mr. Porter, a mercer, whose widow he afterwards married.

Johnson had, from his early youth, been sensible to the influence of female charms. When at Stourbridge school, he was much enamoured of Olivia Lloyd, a young quaker, to whom he wrote a copy of verses. His juvenile attachments to the fair sex were, however, very transient; and it is certain, that he formed no criminal connection whatsoever. Mr. Hector, who lived with him in his younger days in the utmost intimacy and social freedom, has assured me, that even at that ardent season his conduct was strictly virtuous in that respect; and that, though he loved to exhilarate himself with wine, he never knew him intoxicated but once.

In a man whom religious education has secured from licentious indulgences, the passion of love, when once it has seized him, is exceedingly strong; being unimpaired by dissipation and totally concentrated in one object. This was experienced by Johnson, when he became the fervent admirer of Mrs. Porter, after her first husband's death. Miss Porter told me, that when he was first introduced to her mother, his appearance was very forbidding: he was then lean and lank, so that his immense structure of bones was hideously striking to the eye, and the scars of the scrofula were deeply visible. He also wore his hair, which was straight and stiff, and separated behind; and he often had, seemingly, convulsive starts and odd gesticulations, which tended to excite at once surprise and ridicule. Mrs. Porter was so much engaged by his conversation, that she overlooked all these external disadvantages, and said to her daughter, "This is the most sensible man that I ever saw in my life."

Though Mrs. Porter was double the age of Johnson, and her person and manner were by no means pleasing to others, she must have had a superiority of understanding and talents, as she certainly inspired him with more than ordinary passion; and she having signified her willingness to accept of his hand, he went to Lichfield to ask his mother's consent to the marriage; which he could not but be conscious was a very imprudent scheme, both on account of their disparity of years, and her want of fortune. But Mrs. Johnson knew too well the ardour of her son's temper, and was too tender a parent to oppose his inclinations.

I know not for what reason the marriage ceremony was not performed at Birmingham; but a resolution was taken that it should be at Derby, for which place the bride and bridegroom set out on horseback, I suppose in very good humour. But though Mr. Topham Beauclerk used archly to mention Johnson's having told him, with much gravity, "Sir, it was a love-marriage on both sides," I have had from my illustrious friend the following curious account of their journey to church upon the nuptial morn [9th July]:—"Sir, she had read the old romances, and had got into her head the fantastical notion that a woman of spirit should use her lover like a dog. So, sir, at first she told me that I rode too fast, and she could not keep up with me; and, when I rode a little slower, she passed me, and complained that I lagged behind. I was not to be made the slave of caprice; and I resolved to begin as I meant to end. I therefore pushed on briskly, till I was fairly out of her sight. The road lay between two hedges, so I was sure she could not miss it; and I contrived that she should soon come up with me. When she did, I observed her to be in tears."

This, it must be allowed, was a singular beginning of connubial felicity; but there is no doubt, that Johnson, though he thus showed a manly firmness, proved a most affectionate and indulgent husband to the last moment of Mrs. Johnson's life; and in his "Prayers and Meditations," we find very remarkable evidence that his regard and fondness for her never ceased even after her death.

He now set up a private academy, for which purpose he hired a large house, well situated near his native city. In the "Gentleman's Magazine" for 1736 there is the following advertisement:

At EDIAL, *near Lichfield, in Staffordshire, young gentlemen are boarded and taught the Latin and Greek languages by* SAMUEL JOHNSON.

But the only pupils that were put under his care were the celebrated David Garrick and his brother George, and a Mr. Offely, a
young gentleman of good fortune, who died early.

While we acknowledge the justness of Thomson's beautiful
remark,

> Delightful task! to rear the tender thought,
> To teach the young idea how to shoot!

we must consider that a mind gloomy and impetuous, like that of
Johnson, must be so frequently irritated by unavoidable slowness
and error in the advances of scholars, as to perform the duty,
with little pleasure to the teacher, and no great advantage to
the pupils.

Johnson was not more satisfied with his situation as the master
of an academy, than with that of the usher of a school; we need
not wonder, therefore, that he did not keep his academy above a
year and a half. From Mr. Garrick's account, he did not appear
to have been profoundly reverenced by his pupils. His oddities of
manner, and uncouth gesticulations, could not but be the subject
of merriment to them; and, in particular, the young rogues used
to listen at the door of his bedchamber, and peep through the
key-hole, that they might turn into ridicule his tumultuous and
awkward fondness for Mrs. Johnson, whom he used to name by
the familiar appellation of *Tetty* or *Tetsey*, which, like *Betty* or
Betsey, is provincially used as a contraction for *Elizabeth*, her
Christian name, but which to us seems ludicrous, when applied to
a woman of her age and appearance. Mr. Garrick described her
to me as very fat, with a bosom of more than ordinary protuberance, with swelled cheeks, of a florid red, produced by thick
painting, and increased by the liberal use of cordials; flaring and
fantastic in her dress, and affected both in her speech and her
general behaviour. I have seen Garrick exhibit her, by his exquisite
talent of mimicry, so as to excite the heartiest bursts of laughter;
but he, probably, as is the case in all such representation, considerably aggravated the picture.

While Johnson kept his academy, he wrote a great part of his
tragedy of "Irene." He now thought of trying his fortune in
London, the great field of genius and exertion, where talents of
every kind have the fullest scope and the highest encouragement.
It is a memorable circumstance, that his pupil, David Garrick,
went thither at the same time, with intent to complete his education

USED TO LISTEN AT THE DOOR

and follow the profession of the law, from which he was soon
diverted by his decided preference for the stage.

How Johnson employed himself upon his first coming to London
is not particularly known.[1] He had a little money when he came
to town, and he knew how he could live in the cheapest manner.
His first lodgings were at the house of Mr. Norris, a staymaker, in
Exeter Street, adjoining Catherine Street, in the Strand. "I
dined," said he, "very well for eight-pence, with very good company, at the Pine Apple in New Street, just by. Several of them
had travelled. They expected to meet every day; but did not
know one another's names. It used to cost the rest a shilling, for
they drank wine; but I had a cut of meat for sixpence, and bread
for a penny, and gave the waiter a penny; so that I was quite well
served, nay, better than the rest for they gave the waiter nothing."

He at this time, I believe, abstained entirely from fermented
liquors: a practice to which he rigidly conformed for many years
together, at different periods of his life.

An Irish painter, whom he knew at Birmingham, and who had
practised his own precepts of economy for several years in the
British capital, assured Johnson, "that thirty pounds a year was
enough to enable a man to live there without being contemptible.
He allowed ten pounds for clothes and linen. He said a man might
live in a garret at eighteen-pence a week; few people would inquire
where he lodged; and if they did, it was easy to say, 'Sir, I am to be
found at such a place.' By spending three-pence in a coffee-house,
he might be for some hours every day in very good company; he
might dine for sixpence, breakfast on bread and milk for a penny,
and do without supper. On *clean-shirt-day* he went abroad, and
paid visits." I have heard him more than once talk of his frugal
friend, whom he recollected with esteem and kindness, and did
not like to have one smile at the recital. "This man," said he,
gravely, "was a very sensible man, who perfectly understood
common affairs: a man of a great deal of knowledge of the world,
fresh from life, not strained through books."

Amidst this cold obscurity, there was one brilliant circumstance
to cheer him; he was well acquainted with Mr. Henry Hervey,
one of the branches of the noble family of that name, who had been
quartered at Lichfield as an officer of the army, and had at this
time a house in London, where Johnson was frequently entertained,

---

[1] One curious anecdote was communicated by himself to Mr. John Nichols. Mr. Wilcox, the bookseller, on being informed by him that his intention was to get his livelihood as an author, eyed his robust
frame attentively, and, with a significant look, said, "You had better buy a porter's knot."—*Boswell.*

and had an opportunity of meeting genteel company. Not very long before his death, he mentioned "Harry Hervey" thus: "He was a vicious man, but very kind to me. If you call a dog 'Hervey,' I shall love him."

He told me he had now written only three acts of his "Irene," and that he retired for some time to lodgings at Greenwich, where he proceeded in it somewhat further, and used to compose, walking in the Park. In the course of the summer he returned to Lichfield, where he had left Mrs. Johnson, and there he at last finished his tragedy, which was not executed with his rapidity of composition upon other occasions, but was slowly and painfully elaborated.

Johnson's residence at Lichfield, on his return to it at this time, was only for three months. He removed to London with Mrs. Johnson. His lodgings were for some time in Woodstock Street, near Hanover Square, and afterwards in Castle Street, near Cavendish Square.

His tragedy being by this time, as he thought, completely finished and fit for the stage, he was very desirous that it should be brought forward. Mr. Peter Garrick told me, that Johnson and he went together to the Fountain tavern, and read it over, and that he afterwards solicited Mr. Fleetwood, the patentee of Drury Lane Theatre, to have it acted at his house; but Mr. Fleetwood would not accept it, probably because it was not patronized by some man of high rank; and it was not acted till 1749, when his friend David Garrick was manager of that theatre.

The "Gentleman's Magazine," begun and carried on by Mr. Edward Cave, under the name of Sylvanus Urban, had attracted the notice and esteem of Johnson, in an eminent degree, before he came to London as an adventurer in literature. He told me, that when he first saw St. John's Gate, the place where that deservedly popular miscellany was originally printed, he "beheld it with reverence." His first performance was a copy of Latin verses, in March, 1738, addressed to the editor in so happy a style of compliment, that Cave must have been destitute both of taste and sensibility, had he not felt himself highly gratified.

He was now enlisted as a regular coadjutor, by which he probably obtained a tolerable livelihood. What we know to have been done by him was the debates in both houses of Parliament, under the name of "The Senate of Lilliput," sometimes with feigned denominations of the several speakers, sometimes with denominations formed of the letters of their real names in the manner of what is called anagram, so that they might easily be deciphered. Parliament then kept the press in a kind of mysterious awe, which made it necessary to have recourse to such devices.

But what first displayed his transcendent powers, and "gave the world assurance of the man," was his "London, a Poem, in imitation of the third Satire of Juvenal"; which came out in May this year, and burst forth with a splendour, the rays of which will for ever encircle his name.

It has been generally said, I know not with what truth, that Johnson offered his "London" to several booksellers, none of whom would purchase it. To this circumstance Mr. Derrick alludes in the following lines:

> Will no kind patron Johnson own?
> Shall Johnson friendless range the town?
> And every publisher refuse
> The offspring of his happy muse?

But the worthy, modest, and ingenious Mr. Robert Dodsley had taste enough to perceive its uncommon merit, and thought it creditable to have a share in it. He bargained for the whole property of it, for which he gave Johnson ten guineas. It came out on the same morning with Pope's satire, entitled "1738": so that England had at once its Juvenal and Horace as poetical monitors. Every body was delighted with it; and there being no name to it, the first buzz of the literary circles was, "Here is an unknown poet, greater even than Pope."

Pope, who then filled the poetical throne without a rival, it may reasonably be presumed, must have been particularly struck by the sudden appearance of such a poet; and to his credit let it be remembered, that his feelings and conduct on the occasion were candid and liberal. He requested Mr. Richardson, son of the painter, to endeavour to find out who this new author was. Mr. Richardson, after some inquiry, having informed him that he had discovered only that his name was Johnson, and that he was some obscure man, Pope said, "He will soon be *déterré*."

Though thus elevated into fame, and conscious of uncommon powers, he could not expect to produce many such works as his "London," and he felt the hardships of writing for bread; he was therefore willing to resume the office of a schoolmaster, so as to have a sure, though moderate, income for his life; and an offer being made to him of the mastership of a school, provided he could obtain the degree of Master of Arts, Dr. Adams was applied to, by a common friend, to know whether that could be granted him as a favour from the University of Oxford. But though he had made such a figure in the literary world, it was then thought too great a favour to be asked.

Pope, without any knowledge of him but from his "London," recommended him to Earl Gower, who endeavoured to procure for him a degree from Dublin, by a letter to a friend of Dean Swift. It was, perhaps, no small disappointment to Johnson that this respectable application had not the desired effect.

About this time he made one other effort to emancipate himself from the drudgery of authorship. He applied to Dr. Adams, to consult the Commons, whether a person might be permitted to practise as an advocate there, without a doctor's degree in civil law. "I am," said he, "a total stranger to these studies; but whatever is a profession, and maintains numbers, must be within the reach of common abilities, and some degree of industry." But here, also, the want of a degree was an insurmountable bar.

He was, therefore, under the necessity of persevering in that course, into which he had been forced.

In 1739 his separate publications were, "A Complete Vindication of the Licensers of the Stage, from the malicious and scandalous Aspersions of Mr. Brooke, Author of Gustavus Vasa," being an ironical attack upon them for their suppressions of that Tragedy; and "Marmor Norfolciense; or, an Essay on an ancient prophetical Inscription, in monkish Rhyme, lately discovered near Lynne, in Norfolk, by Probus Britannicus."

As Mr. Pope's note concerning Johnson, alluded to in a former page, refers both to his "London," and his "Marmor Norfolciense," I have deferred inserting it till now. I have transcribed it with minute exactness, that the peculiar mode of writing, and imperfect spelling of that celebrated poet, may be exhibited to the curious in literature. It justifies Swift's epithet of "paper-sparing Pope," [1] for it is written on a slip no larger than a common message-card, and was sent to Mr. Richardson, along with the imitation of Juvenal.

This is imitated by one Johnson who put in for a Public-school in Shropshire, but was disappointed. He has an infirmity of the convulsive kind, that attacks him sometimes, so as to make Him a

---

[1] The original MS. of Pope's "Homer" (preserved in the British Museum) is almost entirely written on the covers of letters and sometimes between the lines of the letters themselves

sad Spectacle. Mr. P. from the merit of This Work which was all the knowledge he had of Him endeavour'd to serve Him without his own application; & wrote to my L^d. gore, but he did not succeed. Mr. Johnson published afterw^{ds}. another Poem in Latin with Notes the whole very Humerous call'd the Norfolk Prophecy.   P.

Johnson had been told of this note; and Sir Joshua Reynolds informed him of the compliment which it contained, but, from delicacy, avoided showing him the paper itself. When Sir Joshua observed to Johnson that he seemed very desirous to see Pope's note, he answered, "Who would not be proud to have such a man as Pope so solicitous in inquiring about him?"

The infirmity to which Mr. Pope alludes, appeared to me also to be of the convulsive kind, and of the nature of that distemper called St. Vitus's dance. Sir Joshua Reynolds, however, was of a different opinion, and favoured me with the following paper.

Those motions or tricks of Dr. Johnson are improperly called convulsions. He could sit motionless, when he was told so to do, as well as any other man. My opinion is that it proceeded from a habit which he had indulged himself in, of accompanying his thoughts with certain untoward actions; and those actions always appeared to me as if they were meant to reprobate some part of his past conduct. Whenever he was not engaged in conversation, such thoughts were sure to rush into his mind; and, for this reason, any company, any employment whatever, he preferred to being alone. The great business of his life (he said) was to escape from himself. This disposition he considered as the disease of his mind, which nothing cured but company.

One instance of his absence of mind and particularity, as it is characteristic of the man, may be worth relating. When he and I took a journey together into the West, we visited the late Mr. Bankes, of Dorsetshire; the conversation turning upon pictures, which Johnson could not well see, he retired to a corner of the room, stretching out his right leg as far as he could reach before him, then bringing up his left leg, and stretching his right still further on. The old gentleman, observing him, went up to him, and in a very courteous manner assured him, though it was not a new house, the flooring was perfectly safe. The Doctor started from his reverie, like a person waked out of his sleep, but spoke not a word.

While we are on this subject, my readers may not be displeased with another anecdote from the relation of Mr. Hogarth.

Johnson used to be a pretty frequent visitor at the house of Mr. Richardson, author of "Clarissa," and other novels of extensive reputation. Mr. Hogarth came one day to see Richardson, soon after the execution of Dr. Cameron for having taken arms for the house of Stuart in 1745–6; and being a warm partisan of George the Second, he observed to Richardson, that certainly there must have been some very unfavourable circumstances lately discovered in this particular case, which had induced the King to approve of an execution for rebellion so long after the time when it was committed, as this had the appearance of putting a man to death in cold blood, and was very unlike his Majesty's usual clemency. While he was talking, he perceived a person standing at a window in the room, shaking his head, and rolling himself about in a strange ridiculous manner. He concluded that he was an idiot, whom his relations had put under the care of Mr. Richardson. To his great surprise, however, this figure stalked forwards to where he and Mr. Richardson were sitting, and all at once took up the argument, and burst out into an invective against George the Second, as one who, upon all occasions, was unrelenting and barbarous; mentioning many instances; particularly, that when an officer of high rank had been acquitted by a court martial, George the Second had, with his own hand, struck his name off the list. In short, he displayed such a power of eloquence, that Hogarth looked at him with astonishment, and actually imagined that this idiot had been at the moment inspired. Neither Hogarth nor Johnson were made known to each other at this interview.

In 1740, Dr. Johnson wrote an "Essay on Epitaphs," and an "Epitaph on Philips, a Musician." This Epitaph has been ascribed to Garrick; but I have heard Mr. Garrick declare, that it was written by Dr. Johnson, and give the following account of the manner in which it was composed. Johnson and he were sitting together; when, amongst other things, Garrick repeated an Epitaph upon this Philips by a Dr. Wilkes, in these words:

> Exalted soul! whose harmony could please
> The love-sick virgin, and the gouty ease;
> Could jarring discord, like Amphion, move
> To beauteous order and harmonious love;
> Rest here in peace, till angels bid thee rise,
> And meet thy blessed Saviour in the skies.

Johnson shook his head at these common-place funeral lines, and said to Garrick, "I think, Davy, I can make a better." Then,

"HE WAS IMPERTINENT TO ME, AND I BEAT HIM"

stirring about his tea for a little while, in a state of meditation, he almost extempore produced the following verses:

> Philips, whose touch harmonious could remove
> The pangs of guilty power or hapless love;
> Rest here, distress'd by poverty no more,
> Here find that calm thou gav'st so oft before;
> Sleep, undisturb'd, within this peaceful shrine,
> Till angels wake thee with a note like thine!

In 1742 he wrote the "Proposals for printing Bibliotheca Harleiana, or a Catalogue of the Library of the Earl of Oxford." His account of that celebrated collection of books cannot fail to impress all his readers with admiration of his philological attainments. He was employed in this business by Mr. Thomas Osborne, the bookseller, who purchased the library for 13,000l. It has been confidently related, with many embellishments, that Johnson one day knocked Osborne down in his shop with a folio, and put his foot upon his neck. The simple truth I had from Johnson himself. "Sir, he was impertinent to me, and I beat him. But it was not in his shop: it was in my own chamber."

In 1743 Johnson had an opportunity of obliging his schoolfellow Dr. James, of whom he once observed, "No man brings more mind to his profession." James published this year his "Medicinal Dictionary," in three volumes folio. Johnson, as I understood from him, had written, or assisted in writing, the proposals for this work; and being very fond of the study of physic, in which James was his master, he furnished some of the articles.

His circumstances were at this time embarrassed; yet his affection for his mother was so warm, and so liberal, that he took upon himself a debt of hers, which, though small in itself, was then considerable to him.[1]

In 1744 he produced one work, fully sufficient to maintain the high reputation which he had acquired. This was "The Life of Richard Savage"; a man of whom it is difficult to speak impartially, without wondering that he was for some time the intimate companion of Johnson; for his character was marked by profligacy, insolence, and ingratitude: yet, as he undoubtedly had a warm and vigorous, though unregulated mind, had seen life in all its varieties, and been much in the company of the statesmen and wits of his time, he could communicate to Johnson an abundant supply

---

[1] The sum was twelve pounds; he asked for two months in which to make payment.

of such materials as his philosophical curiosity most eagerly desired; and as Savage's misfortunes and misconduct had reduced him to the lowest state of wretchedness as a writer for bread, his visits to St. John's Gate naturally brought Johnson and him together.

It is melancholy to reflect, that Johnson and Savage were sometimes in such extreme indigence, that they could not pay for a lodging; so that they have wandered together whole nights in the street. One night in particular, when Savage and he walked round St. James's Square for want of a lodging, they were not at all depressed by their situation; but, in high spirits and brimful of patriotism, traversed the square for several hours, inveighed against the minister,[1] and "resolved they would *stand by their country.*"

I am afraid, however, that by associating with Savage, who was habituated to the dissipation and licentiousness of the town, Johnson, though his good principles remained steady, did not entirely preserve that conduct, for which, in days of greater simplicity, he was remarked by his friend Mr. Hector; but was imperceptibly led into some indulgences which occasioned much distress to his virtuous mind.

Of Johnson's "Life of Savage," Sir Joshua Reynolds told me, that upon his return from Italy he met with it in Devonshire, knowing nothing of its author, and began to read it while he was standing with his arm leaning against a chimney-piece. It seized his attention so strongly, that, not being able to lay down the book till he had finished it, when he attempted to move, he found his arm totally benumbed. The rapidity with which this work was composed is a wonderful circumstance. Johnson has been heard to say, "I wrote forty-eight of the printed octavo pages of the 'Life of Savage' at a sitting; but then I sat up all night."

It is remarkable, that in this biographical disquisition there appears a very strong symptom of Johnson's prejudice against players; a prejudice which may be attributed to the following causes: first, the imperfection of his organs, which were so defective that he was not susceptible of the fine impressions which theatrical excellence produces upon the generality of mankind; secondly, the cold rejection of his tragedy; and, lastly, the brilliant success of Garrick, who had been his pupil, who had come to London at the same time with him, not in a much more prosperous state than

---

[1] This walk must have taken place some years before 1744; the minister was possibly Walpole.

himself, and whose talents he undoubtedly rated low, compared with his own. His being outstripped by his pupil in the race of immediate fame, as well as of fortune, probably made him feel some indignation, as thinking, that whatever might be Garrick's merits in his art, the reward was too great when compared with what the most successful efforts of literary labour could attain. At all periods of his life Johnson used to talk contemptuously of players; but in this work he speaks of them with peculiar acrimony.

His schoolfellow and friend, Dr. Taylor, told me a pleasant anecdote of Johnson's triumphing over his pupil, David Garrick. When that great actor had played some little time at Goodman's Fields, Johnson and Taylor went to see him perform, and afterwards passed the evening at a tavern with him and old Giffard. Johnson, after censuring some mistakes in emphasis, which Garrick had committed in the course of that night's acting, said, "The players, Sir, have got a kind of rant, with which they run on, without any regard either to accent or emphasis." Both Garrick and Giffard were offended at this sarcasm, and endeavoured to refute it; upon which Johnson rejoined, "Well now, I'll give you something to speak, with which you are little acquainted, and then we shall see how just my observation is. That shall be the criterion. Let me hear you repeat the ninth Commandment, 'Thou shalt not bear false witness against thy neighbour.'" Both tried at it, said Dr. Taylor, and both mistook the emphasis, which should be upon *not* and *false witness*. Johnson put them right, and enjoyed his victory with great glee.

In 1745, he published a pamphlet entitled "Miscellaneous Observations on the Tragedy of Macbeth," to which he affixed, "Proposals for a new edition of Shakespeare." But the little encouragement which was given by the public to his anonymous proposals for the execution of a task which Warburton was known to have undertaken, probably damped his ardour. His pamphlet, however, was fortunate enough to obtain the approbation even of the supercilious Warburton himself, who in the Preface to his "Shakspeare," published two years afterwards, thus mentioned it: "As to all those things which have been published under the titles of *Essays, Remarks, Observations,* &c. on Shakspeare, if you except some critical Notes on Macbeth, given as a specimen of a projected edition, and written, as appears, by a man of parts and genius, the rest are absolutely below a serious notice."

Of this flattering distinction shown to him by Warburton, a very grateful remembrance was ever entertained by Johnson, who said, "He praised me at a time when praise was of value to me."

It is somewhat curious, that his literary career appears to have been almost totally suspended in the years 1745 and 1746, those years which were marked by a civil war in Great Britain, when a rash attempt was made to restore the House of Stuart to the throne. That he had a tenderness for that unfortunate House, is well known; and some may fancifully imagine, that a sympathetic anxiety impeded the exertion of his intellectual powers: but I am inclined to think, that he was, during this time, sketching the outlines of his great philological work.

The year 1747 is distinguished as the epoch when Johnson's "DICTIONARY OF THE ENGLISH LANGUAGE," was announced to the world, by the publication of its "Plan" or *Prospectus*.

How long this immense undertaking had been the object of his contemplation, I do not know. I once asked him by what means he had attained to that astonishing knowledge of our language, by which he was enabled to realize a design of such extent and accumulated difficulty. He told me, that "it was not the effect of particular study; but that it had grown up in his mind insensibly." I have been informed by Mr. James Dodsley, that several years before this period, when Johnson was one day sitting in his brother Robert's shop, he heard his brother suggest to him, that a "Dictionary of the English Language" would be a work that would be well received by the public; that Johnson seemed at first to catch at the proposition, but, after a pause, said, in his abrupt, decisive manner, "I believe I shall not undertake it." That he, however, had bestowed much thought upon the subject, before he published his "Plan," is evident from the enlarged, clear, and accurate views which it exhibits.

The booksellers who contracted with Johnson, single and unaided, for the execution of a work, which in other countries has not been effected but by the co-operating exertions of many, were Mr. Robert Dodsley, Mr. Charles Hitch, Mr. Andrew Millar, the two Messieurs Longman, and the two Messieurs Knapton. The price stipulated was fifteen hundred and seventy-five pounds.

The "Plan" was addressed to Philip Dormer, Earl of Chesterfield, then one of his Majesty's Principal Secretaries of State; a nobleman who was very ambitious of literary distinction, and who, upon being informed of the design, had expressed himself in terms

very favourable to its success. There is, perhaps, in every thing of
any consequence, a secret history which it would be amusing to
know, could we have it authentically communicated. Johnson
told me, "Sir, the way in which the plan of my 'Dictionary' came
to be inscribed to Lord Chesterfield, was this; I had neglected to
write it by the time appointed. Dodsley suggested a desire to
have it addressed to Lord Chesterfield. I laid hold of this as a pretext for delay, that it might be better done, and let Dodsley have
his desire. I said to my friend, Dr. Bathurst, 'Now, if any good
comes of my addressing to Lord Chesterfield, it will be ascribed to
deep policy, when, in fact, it was only a casual excuse for laziness.' "
That he was fully aware of the arduous nature of the undertaking
he acknowledges; but he had a noble consciousness of his own
abilities, which enabled him to go on with undaunted spirit.

Dr. Adams found him one day busy at his Dictionary, when the
following dialogue ensued. "ADAMS. This is a great work, Sir. How
are you to get all the etymologies? JOHNSON. Why, Sir, here is a
shelf with Junius, and Skinner, and others; and there is a Welsh
gentleman who has published a collection of Welsh proverbs, who
will help me with the Welsh. ADAMS. But, Sir, how can you do
this in three years? JOHNSON. Sir, I have no doubt that I can do it
in three years. ADAMS. But the French Academy, which consists
of forty members, took forty years to compile their Dictionary.
JOHNSON. Sir, thus it is. This is the proportion. Let me see; forty
times forty is sixteen hundred. As three to sixteen hundred, so is
the proportion of an Englishman to a Frenchman." With so much
ease and pleasantry could he talk of that prodigious labour which
he had undertaken to execute.

No doubt Johnson was wise to avail himself of what had been
done in this country by prior Lexicographers, so far as they went:
but the learned yet judicious research of etymology, the various
yet accurate display of definition, and the rich collection of authorities, were reserved for the superior mind of our great philolo-
gist. For the mechanical part he employed, as he told me, six
amanuenses; and let it be remembered by the natives of North-
Britain, to whom he is supposed to have been so hostile, that five
of them were of that country. There were two Messieurs Macbean;
Mr. Shiels; Mr. Stewart, son of Mr. George Stewart, bookseller of
Edinburgh; and a Mr. Maitland. The sixth of these humble
assistants was Mr. Peyton, who, I believe taught French, and
published some elementary tracts.

To all these painful labourers, Johnson showed a never-ceasing kindness, so far as they stood in need of it. The elder Mr. Macbean afterwards was left without a shilling. Johnson, by the favour of Lord Thurlow, got him admitted a poor brother of the Charter-house. For Shiels, who died of a consumption, he had much tenderness; and it has been thought that some choice sentences in the "Lives of the Poets" were supplied by him. Peyton, when reduced to penury, had frequent aid from the bounty of Johnson, who at last was at the expense of burying him and his wife.

While the Dictionary was going forward, Johnson lived part of the time in Holborn, part in Gough Square, Fleet Street; and he had an upper room fitted up like a counting-house for the purpose, in which he gave to the copyists their several tasks. The words partly taken from other dictionaries, and partly supplied by himself, having been first written down with spaces left between them, he delivered in writing their etymologies, definitions, and various significations. The authorities were copied from the books themselves, in which he had marked the passages with a black-lead pencil, the traces of which could easily be effaced. I have seen several of them, in which that trouble had not been taken; so that they were just as when used by the copyists.

The necessary expense of preparing a work of such magnitude for the press, must have been a considerable deduction from the price stipulated to be paid for the copyright. I understand that nothing was allowed by the booksellers on that account; and I remember his telling me, that a large portion of it having, by mistake, been written upon both sides of the paper, so as to be inconvenient for the compositor, it cost him twenty pounds to have it transcribed upon one side only.

He is now to be considered as "tugging at his oar," as engaged in a steady continued course of occupation, sufficient to employ all his time for some years; and which was the best preventive of that constitutional melancholy which was ever lurking about him, ready to trouble his quiet. But his enlarged and lively mind could not be satisfied without more diversity of employment, and the pleasure of animated relaxation. He therefore formed a club in Ivy Lane, Paternoster Row, with a view to enjoy literary discussion, and amuse his evening hours.

In January, 1749, he published "The Vanity of Human Wishes, being the Tenth Satire of Juvenal, imitated." He, I believe, composed it the preceding year. Mrs. Johnson, for the sake of country

GAVE TO THE COPYISTS THEIR SEVERAL TASKS

air, had lodgings at Hampstead, to which he resorted occasionally, and there the greatest part, if not the whole, of this imitation was written. The fervid rapidity with which it was produced, is scarcely credible. I have heard him say, that he composed seventy lines of it in one day, without putting one of them upon paper till they were finished.

The profits of a single poem, however excellent, appear to have been very small. I have mentioned, upon Johnson's own authority, that for his "London" he had only ten guineas; and now, after his fame was established, he got for his "Vanity of Human Wishes" but five guineas more.

His "Vanity of Human Wishes" has less of common life, but more of a philosophic dignity, than his "London." Garrick observed, "When Johnson lived much with the Herveys, and saw a good deal of what was passing in life, he wrote his 'London,' which is lively and easy; when he became more retired he gave us his 'Vanity of Human Wishes,' which is as hard as Greek: had he gone on to imitate another satire, it would have been as hard as Hebrew."

Garrick being now vested with theatrical power by being manager of Drury Lane Theatre, he kindly and generously made use of it to bring out Johnson's tragedy, which had been long kept back for want of encouragement. But in this benevolent purpose he met with no small difficulty from the temper of Johnson, which could not brook that a drama which he had formed with much study, and had been obliged to keep more than the nine years of Horace, should be revised and altered at the pleasure of an actor. Yet Garrick knew well, that without some alterations it would not be fit for the stage. A violent dispute having ensued between them, Garrick applied to the Reverend Dr. Taylor to interpose. Johnson was at first very obstinate. "Sir," said he, "The fellow wants me to make Mahomet run mad, that he may have an opportunity of tossing his hands and kicking his heels." He was, however, at last, with difficulty, prevailed on to comply with Garrick's wishes, so as to allow of some changes; but still there were not enough.

Dr. Adams was present the first night of the representation of "Irene," and gave me the following account: "Before the curtain drew up, there were catcalls, whistling, which alarmed Johnson's friends. The Prologue, which was written by himself in a manly strain, soothed the audience, and the play went off tolerably, till it came to the conclusion, when Mrs. Pritchard, the heroine of the piece, was to be strangled upon the stage, and was to speak two lines with the bowstring round her neck. The audience cried out '*Murder! murder!*' She several times attempted to speak; but in vain. At last she was obliged to go off the stage alive." This passage was afterwards struck out, and she was carried off to be put to death behind the scenes, as the play now has it.

Notwithstanding all the support of such performers as Garrick, Barry, Mrs. Cibber, Mrs. Pritchard, and every advantage of dress and decoration, the tragedy of "Irene" did not please the public. Mr. Garrick's zeal carried it through for nine nights, so that the author had his three nights' profit; and from a receipt signed by him it appears that his friend, Mr. Robert Dodsley, gave him one hundred pounds for the copy.

When asked how he felt upon the ill success of his tragedy, he replied, "Like the Monument"; meaning that he continued firm and unmoved as a column. And let it be remembered, as an admonition to the *genus irritabile* of dramatic writers, that this great man, instead of peevishly complaining of the bad taste of the town, submitted to its decision without a murmur. He had, indeed, upon all occasions, a great deference for the general opinion: "A man," said he, "who writes a book, thinks himself wiser or wittier than the rest of mankind; he supposes that he can instruct or amuse them, and the public to whom he appeals must, after all, be the judges of his pretensions."

On occasion of this play being brought upon the stage, Johnson had a fancy that, as a dramatic author, his dress should be more gay than what he ordinarily wore: he therefore appeared behind the scenes, and even in one of the side boxes, in a scarlet waistcoat, with rich gold lace, and a gold-laced hat.

His necessary attendance while his play was in rehearsal, and during its performance, brought him acquainted with many of the performers of both sexes, which produced a more favourable opinion of their profession, than he had harshly expressed in his "Life of Savage." With some of them he kept up an acquaintance as long as he and they lived, and was ever ready to show them acts of kindness. He, for a considerable time, used to frequent the *Green-Room*, and seemed to take delight in dissipating his gloom, by mixing in the sprightly chit-chat of the motley circle then to be found there. Mr. David Hume related to me from Mr. Garrick, that Johnson at last denied himself this amusement, from considerations of rigid virtue; saying, "I'll come no more behind your

USED TO FREQUENT THE "GREEN ROOM"

scenes, David; for the silk stockings and white bosoms of your actresses excite my amorous propensities."

In 1750 he came forth in the character for which he was eminently qualified, a majestic teacher of moral and religious wisdom. The vehicle which he chose was that of a periodical paper. Johnson was, I think, not very happy in the choice of his title, "The Rambler," which certainly is not suited to a series of grave and moral discourses. He gave Sir Joshua Reynolds the following account of its getting this name: "What *must* be done, Sir, *will* be done. When I was to begin publishing that paper, I was at a loss how to name it. I sat down at night upon my bedside, and resolved that I would not go to sleep till I had fixed its title. *The Rambler* seemed the best that occurred, and I took it."

With what devout and conscientious sentiments this paper was undertaken, is evidenced by the following prayer, which he composed and offered up on the occasion:

Almighty GOD, the giver of all good things, without whose help all labour is ineffectual, and without whose grace all wisdom is folly: grant, I beseech Thee, that in this undertaking Thy Holy Spirit may not be withheld from me, but that I may promote Thy glory, and the salvation of myself and others: grant this, O Lord, for the sake of Thy Son, JESUS CHRIST. Amen.

The first paper of the "Rambler" was published on Tuesday the 20th of March, 1750; and its author was enabled to continue it, without interruption, every Tuesday and Saturday, till Saturday the 17th of March, 1752, on which day it closed. This is a strong confirmation of the truth of a remark of his, which I have had occasion to quote elsewhere, that "a man may write at any time, if he will set himself doggedly to it"; for, notwithstanding his constitutional indolence, his depression of spirits, and his labour in carrying on his Dictionary, he answered the stated calls of the press twice a week from the stores of his mind during all that time.

Posterity will be astonished when they are told, upon the authority of Johnson himself, that many of these discourses, which we should suppose had been laboured with all the slow attention of literary leisure, were written in haste as the moment pressed, without even being read over by him before they were printed. It can be accounted for only in this way; that, by reading and meditation, and a very close inspection of life, he had accumulated a great fund of miscellaneous knowledge, which, by a peculiar promptitude of mind, was ever ready at his call, and which he had constantly accustomed himself to clothe in the most apt and energetic expression. Sir Joshua Reynolds once asked him, by what means he had attained this extraordinary accuracy and flow of language. He told him, that he had early laid it down as a fixed rule to do his best on every occasion, and in every company: to impart whatever he knew in the most forcible language he could put it in; and that by constant practice, and never suffering any careless expression to escape him, or attempting to deliver his thoughts without arranging them in the clearest manner, it became habitual to him.

Johnson told me, with an amiable fondness, a little pleasing circumstance relative to the "Rambler." Mrs. Johnson, in whose judgment and taste he had great confidence, said to him, after a few numbers of the "Rambler" had come out, "I thought very well of you before; but I did not imagine you could have written any thing equal to this." Distant praise, from whatever quarter, is not so delightful as that of a wife whom a man loves and esteems. Her approbation may be said to "come home to his *bosom*"; and, being so near, its effect is most sensible and permanent.

The "Rambler" has increased in fame as in age. Soon after its first folio edition was concluded, it was published in six duodecimo volumes; and its author lived to see ten numerous editions of it in London, besides those of Ireland and Scotland.

The style of this work has been censured by some shallow critics as involved and turgid, and abounding with antiquated and hard words. It must, indeed, be allowed, that the structure of his sentences is expanded, and often has somewhat of the inversion of Latin; and that he delighted to express familiar thoughts in philosophical language; being in this the reverse of Socrates, who, it is said, reduced philosophy to the simplicity of common life.

Johnson's language must be allowed to be too masculine for the delicate gentleness of female writing. His ladies, therefore, seem strangely formal, even to ridicule; and are well denominated by the names which he has given them, as Misella, Zozima, Properantia, Rhodoclia.[1]

In 1751 we are to consider him as carrying on both his "Dictionary," and "Rambler." Though Johnson's circumstances were at this time far from being easy, his humane and charitable disposition was constantly exerting itself. Mrs. Anna Williams,

---

[1] Burke said that "his ladies were all *Johnsons in petticoats*."

daughter of a very ingenious Welsh physician, and a woman of more than ordinary talents and literature, having come to London in hopes of being cured of a cataract in both her eyes, which afterwards ended in total blindness, was kindly received as a constant visitor at his house while Mrs. Johnson lived; and, after her death, having come under his roof in order to have an operation upon her eyes performed with more comfort to her than in lodgings, she had an apartment from him during the rest of her life, at all times when he had a house.[1]

In 1752 he was almost entirely occupied with his "Dictionary." The last paper of his "Rambler" was published March 2, this year: after which there was a cessation for some time of any exertion of his talents as an essayist. That there should be a suspension of his literary labours will not seem strange, when it is considered that soon after closing his "Rambler," he suffered a loss which, there can be no doubt, affected him with the deepest distress. For on the 17th of March, O.S., his wife died. Why Sir John Hawkins should unwarrantably take upon him even to *suppose* that Johnson's fondness for her was *dissembled* (meaning simulated or assumed), and to assert, that if it was not the case, "it was a lesson he had learned by rote," I cannot conceive; unless it proceeded from a want of similar feelings in his own breast.

The following very solemn and affecting prayer was found after Dr. Johnson's decease, by his servant, Mr. Francis Barber. I present it to the world as an undoubted proof of a circumstance in the character of my illustrious friend, which, though some, whose hard minds I never shall envy, may attack as superstitious, will, I am sure, endear him more to numbers of good men. I have an additional, and that a personal motive for presenting it, because it sanctions what I myself have always maintained and am fond to indulge.

April 26, 1752, being after 12 at Night of the 25th.

O Lord! Governor of heaven and earth, in whose hands are embodied and departed spirits, if thou hast ordained the souls of the dead to minister to the living, and appointed my departed wife to have the care of me, grant that I may enjoy the good effects of

---

[1] Mrs. Williams was remembered by contemporary writers as a pale, shrunken old lady, dressed in scarlet, with a lace cap, which had two stiffened projecting wings at the sides, and a black lace hood over it. She possessed about thirty-five or forty pounds a year. Her apartment in Johnson's house was fitted with her own furniture; her expenses were small, tea and bread and butter being at least half her nourishment. To one who remarked on her facility in moving about the house, searching into drawers, and finding books, without the help of sight, " Believe me," said she, " persons who cannot do these common offices without sight, did but little while they enjoyed that blessing." She was as active as bad health and blindness permitted; though sometimes impatient, for her temper was "marked with Welsh fire."

her attention and ministration, whether exercised by appearance, impulses, dreams, or in any other manner agreeable to thy government. Forgive my presumption, enlighten my ignorance, and however meaner agents are employed, grant me the blessed influences of thy Holy Spirit, through Jesus Christ our Lord. *Amen.*

What actually followed upon this most interesting piece of devotion by Johnson, we are not informed; but I, whom it has pleased God to afflict in a similar manner to that which occasioned it, have certain experience of benignant communication by dreams.

That his love for his wife was of the most ardent kind, and, during the long period of fifty years, was unimpaired by the lapse of time, is evident from other memorials, two of which I select, as strongly marking the tenderness and sensibility of his mind.

March 28, 1753. I kept this day as the anniversary of my Tetty's death, with prayer and tears in the morning. In the evening I prayed for her conditionally, if it were lawful.

April 23, 1753. I know not whether I do not too much indulge the vain longings of affection; but I hope they intenerate my heart, and that when I die like my Tetty, this affection will be acknowledged in a happy interview, and that in the meantime I am incited by it to piety. I will, however, not deviate too much from common and received methods of devotion.

Her wedding-ring, when she became his wife, was, after death, preserved by him, as long as he lived, with an affectionate care, in a little round wooden box, in the inside of which he pasted a slip of paper, thus inscribed by him in fair characters, as follows:

Eheu!
Eliz. Johnson,
Nupta Jul. 9° 1736,
Mortua, eheu!
Mart. 17° 1752.

I have, indeed, been told by Mrs. Desmoulins, who, before her marriage, lived for some time with Mrs. Johnson at Hampstead, that she indulged herself in country air and nice living, at an unsuitable expense, while her husband was drudging in the smoke of London, and that she by no means treated him with that complacency which is the most engaging quality in a wife. But all this is perfectly compatible with his fondness for her, especially when it is remembered that he had a high opinion of her understanding, and that the impressions which her beauty, real or imaginary, had originally made upon his fancy, being continued by habit, had not been effaced, though she herself was doubtless much altered for the worse. The dreadful shock of separation took place in the night; and he immediately despatched a letter to his friend, the Reverend Dr. Taylor, which, as Taylor told me, expressed grief in the strongest manner he had ever read. The letter was brought to Dr. Taylor, at his house in the cloisters, Westminster, about three in the morning; and as it signified an earnest desire to see him, he got up, and went to Johnson as soon as he was dressed, and found him in tears and in extreme agitation. After being a little while together, Johnson requested him to join with him in prayer. He then prayed extempore, as did Dr. Taylor; and thus by means of that piety which was ever his primary object, his troubled mind was, in some degree, soothed and composed.

That his sufferings upon the death of his wife were severe, beyond what are commonly endured, I have no doubt, from the information of many who were then about him, to none of whom I give more credit than to Mr. Francis Barber, his faithful negro servant,[1] who came into his family about a fortnight after the dismal event. These sufferings were aggravated by the melancholy inherent in his constitution; and although he probably was not oftener in the wrong than she was, in the little disagreements which sometimes troubled his married state, during which, he owned to me, that the gloomy irritability of his existence was more painful to him than ever, he might very naturally, after her death, be tenderly disposed to charge himself with slight omissions and offences, the sense of which would give him much uneasiness.

He deposited the remains of Mrs. Johnson in the church of Bromley in Kent,[2] to which he was probably led by the residence of his friend Hawkesworth at that place. The funeral sermon which he composed for her, was never preached.

From Mr. Francis Barber I have had the following authentic and artless account of the situation in which he found him recently after his wife's death: "He was in great affliction. Mrs. Williams was then living in his house, which was in Gough Square. He was

---

[1] Francis Barber was born in Jamaica, and was brought to England in 1750, by Colonel Bathurst, father of Johnson's very intimate friend Dr. Bathurst. The Colonel by his will left him his freedom, and Dr. Bathurst was willing that he should enter into Johnson's service, in which he continued from 1752 till Johnson's death, with the exception of two intervals; in one of which, upon some difference with his master, he went and served an apothecary in Cheapside, but still visited Dr. Johnson occasionally; in another, when he took a fancy to go to sea. Part of the time, indeed, he was, by the kindness of his master, at a school in Northamptonshire, that he might have the advantage of some learning.— Boswell.

[2] It is a blue slate slab, at the west end of the central aisle, in good preservation.

busy with the 'Dictionary.' Mr. Shiels, and some others of the gentlemen who had formerly written for him, used to come about him. He had then little for himself, but frequently sent money to Mr. Shiels when in distress. The friends who visited him at that time, were chiefly Dr. Bathurst, and Mr. Diamond, an apothecary in Cork Street, Burlington Gardens, with whom he and Mrs. Williams generally dined every Sunday. There was a talk of his going to Iceland with him, which would probably have happened had he lived. There were also Mr. Cave, Dr. Hawkesworth, Mr. Ryland, merchant on Tower-hill, Mrs. Masters, the poetess, who lived with Mr. Cave, Mrs. Carter, and sometimes Mrs. Macaulay; also Mrs. Gardiner, wife of a tallow-chandler on Snow-hill, not in the learned way, but a worthy good woman; Mr. (now Sir Joshua) Reynolds; Mr. Millar, Mr. Dodsley, Mr. Bouquet, Mr. Payne, of Paternoster-row, booksellers; Mr. Strahan, the printer; the Earl of Orrery, Lord Southwell, Mr. Garrick."

Many are, no doubt, omitted in this catalogue of his friends, and in particular, his humble friend Mr. Robert Levett, an obscure practiser in physic amongst the lower people, his fees being sometimes very small sums, sometimes whatever provisions his patients could afford him; but of such extensive practice in that way, that his walk was from Houndsditch to Marylebone. It appears, from Johnson's diary, that their acquaintance commenced about the year 1746; and such was Johnson's predilection for him, and fanciful estimation of his moderate abilities, that I have heard him say that he should not be satisfied, though attended by all the College of Physicians, unless he had Mr. Levett with him. Ever since I was acquainted with Dr. Johnson, and many years before, Mr. Levett had an apartment in his house, or his chambers, and waited upon him every morning, through the whole course of his late and tedious breakfast. He was of a strange grotesque appearance, stiff and formal in his manner, and seldom said a word while any company was present.[1]

[1] Robert Levett, though an Englishman by birth, became early in life a waiter at a coffee-house in Paris; where the surgeons who frequented it, finding him of an inquisitive turn, and attentive to their conversation, made a purse for him, and gave him some instructions in their art. They afterwards furnished him with the means of other knowledge, by procuring him free admission to such lectures in pharmacy and anatomy as were read by the ablest professors of that period. Where the middle part of his life was spent is uncertain. He resided about twenty years under Johnson's hospitable roof, who never wished him to be regarded as an inferior, or treated him like a dependent.
In 1762 there was an adventurous interlude. Levett married, when he was near sixty, a woman of the town, who had persuaded him (notwithstanding their place of congress was a small coal shed in Fetter Lane) that she was nearly related to a man of fortune, but was kept by him out of large possessions. Johnson used to say, that, compared with the marvels of this transaction, the Arabian Nights seemed familiar occurrences. Never was a hero more completely duped. He had not been married four months before a writ was taken out against him, for debts contracted by his wife. He was secreted, and his friend then procured him a protection from a foreign minister. In a short time afterwards she ran away

The circle of his friends, indeed, at this time was extensive and various, far beyond what has been generally imagined. To trace his acquaintance with each particular person, if it could be done, would be a task, of which the labour would not be repaid by the advantage. But exceptions are to be made; one of which must be a friend so eminent as Sir Joshua Reynolds, who was truly his *dulce decus*, and with whom he maintained an uninterrupted intimacy to the last hour of his life. When Johnson lived in Castle Street, Cavendish Square, he used frequently to visit two ladies who lived opposite to him, Miss Cotterells, daughters of Admiral Cotterell. Reynolds used also to visit there, and thus they met. Mr. Reynolds, as I have observed above, had from the first reading of his "Life of Savage," conceived a very high admiration of Johnson's powers of writing. His conversation no less delighted him; and he cultivated his acquaintance with the laudable zeal of one who was ambitious of general improvement. Sir Joshua, indeed, was lucky enough, at their very first meeting, to make a remark, which was so much above the common-place style of conversation, that Johnson at once perceived that Reynolds had the habit of thinking for himself. The ladies were regretting the death of a friend, to whom they owed great obligations; upon which Reynolds observed, "You have, however, the comfort of being relieved from a burthen of gratitude." They were shocked a little at this alleviating suggestion, as too selfish; but Johnson defended it in his clear and forcible manner, and was much pleased with the *mind*, the fair view of human nature, which it exhibited, like some of the reflections of Rochefoucauld. The consequence was, that he went home with Reynolds, and supped with him.

His acquaintance with Bennet Langton, Esq., of Langton, in Lincolnshire, another much valued friend, commenced soon after the conclusion of his "Rambler"; which that gentleman, then a youth, had read with so much admiration, that he came to London chiefly with a view of endeavouring to be introduced to its author.[1] By a fortunate chance, he happened to take lodgings in a house where Mr. Levett frequently visited; and having mentioned his wish to his landlady, she introduced him to Mr. Levett, who readily obtained Johnson's permission to bring Mr. Langton to him.

from him, and was tried for picking pockets at the Old Bailey. She pleaded her own cause, and was acquitted; a separation took place: and Johnson then took Levett home, where he continued till his death.

[1] Langton was only fifteen when the "Rambler" was terminated, having been born about 1737. He entered Trinity College, Oxford, July 7, 1757. He was remarkable for his knowledge of Greek, and on Dr. Johnson's death, succeeded him as professor of ancient literature in the Royal Academy.

Mr. Langton was exceedingly surprised when the sage first appeared. He had not received the smallest intimation of his figure, dress, or manner. From perusing his writings, he fancied he should see a decent, well-drest, in short, a remarkably decorous philosopher. Instead of which, down from his bed-chamber about noon, came, as newly risen, a huge uncouth figure, with a little dark wig which scarcely covered his head, and his clothes hanging loose about him. But his conversation was so rich, so animated, and so forcible, and his religious and political notions so congenial with those in which Langton had been educated, that he conceived for him that veneration and attachment which he ever preserved. Johnson was not the less ready to love Mr. Langton, for his being of a very ancient family; for I have heard him say with pleasure, "Langton, Sir, has a grant of free-warren from Henry the Second; and Cardinal Stephen Langton, in King John's reign, was of this family."

Mr. Langton afterwards went to pursue his studies at Trinity College, Oxford, where he formed an acquaintance with his fellow-student, Mr. Topham Beauclerk,[1] who, though their opinions and modes of life were so different, that it seemed utterly improbable that they should at all agree, had so ardent a love of literature, so acute an understanding, such elegance of manners, that they became intimate friends.

Johnson, soon after this acquaintance began, passed a considerable time at Oxford. He at first thought it strange that Langton should associate so much with one who had the character of being loose, both in his principles and practice; but, by degrees, he himself was fascinated. Mr. Beauclerk's being of the St. Albans family, and having, in some particulars, a resemblance to Charles the Second, contributed, in Johnson's imagination, to throw a lustre upon his other qualities; and, in a short time, the moral, pious Johnson, and the gay, dissipated Beauclerk, were companions. "What a coalition!" (said Garrick, when he heard of this;) "I shall have my old friend to bail out of the Round-house." But I can bear testimony that it was a very agreeable association. Beauclerk was too polite, and valued learning and wit too much, to offend Johnson by sallies of infidelity or licentiousness; and Johnson delighted in the good qualities of Beauclerk, and hoped to correct the evil. Innumerable were the scenes in which Johnson was

---

[1] Topham Beauclerk, only son of Lord Sidney Beauclerk, third son of the first Duke of St. Albans, was born in 1739, and entered Trinity College, Oxford, in November, 1757.

JOHNSON MADE SOME ATTEMPTS TO HELP THEM

amused by these young men. Beauclerk could take more liberty with him than any body with whom I ever saw him; but, on the other hand, Beauclerk was not spared by his respectable companion, when reproof was proper. Beauclerk had such a propensity to satire, that at one time Johnson said to him, "You never open your mouth but with intention to give pain; and you have often given me pain, not from the power of what you said, but from seeing your intention." At another time applying to him, with a slight alteration, a line of Pope, he said, "Thy love of folly, and thy scorn of fools. Every thing thou dost shows the one, and every thing thou say'st, the other." At another time he said to him, "Thy body is all vice, and thy mind all virtue." Beauclerk not seeming to relish the compliment, Johnson said, "Nay, Sir, Alexander the Great, marching in triumph into Babylon, could not have desired to have had more said to him."

Johnson was some time with Beauclerk at his house at Windsor, where he was entertained with experiments in natural philosophy. One Sunday, when the weather was very fine, Beauclerk enticed him, insensibly, to saunter about all the morning. They went into a churchyard, in the time of divine service, and Johnson laid himself down at his ease upon one of the tomb-stones. "Now, Sir, (said Beauclerk) you are like Hogarth's Idle Apprentice." When Johnson got his pension, Beauclerk said to him, in the humorous phrase of Falstaff, "I hope you'll now purge, and live cleanly, like a gentleman."

One night when Beauclerk and Langton had supped at a tavern in London, and sat till about three in the morning, it came into their heads to go and knock up Johnson, and see if they could prevail on him to join them in a ramble. They rapped violently at the door of his chambers in the Temple, till at last he appeared in his shirt, with his little black wig on the top of his head, instead of a nightcap, and a poker in his hand, imagining, probably, that some ruffians were coming to attack him. When he discovered who they were, and was told their errand, he smiled, and with great good-humour agreed to their proposal: "What, is it you, you dogs! I'll have a frisk with you." He was soon drest, and they sallied forth together into Covent Garden, where the green-grocers and fruiterers were beginning to arrange their hampers, just come in from the country. Johnson made some attempts to help them; but the honest gardeners stared so at his figure and manner, and odd interference, that he soon saw his services were not relished.

They then repaired to one of the neighbouring taverns, and made a bowl of that liquor called *Bishop*, which Johnson had always liked: while, in joyous contempt of sleep, from which he had been roused, he repeated the festive lines,

> Short, O short then be thy reign,
> And give us to the world again!

They did not stay long, but walked down to the Thames, took a boat, and rowed to Billingsgate. Beauclerk and Johnson were so well pleased with their amusement, that they resolved to persevere in dissipation for the rest of the day: but Langton deserted them, being engaged to breakfast with some young ladies. Johnson scolded him for "leaving his social friends, to go and sit with a set of wretched *un-idea'd* girls." Garrick, being told of this ramble, said, to him smartly, "I heard of your frolic t'other night. You'll be in the Chronicle." Upon which Johnson afterwards observed, "*He* durst not do such a thing. His *wife* would not *let* him!"

He entered upon this year, 1753, with his usual piety, as appears from the following prayer, which I transcribed from that part of his diary which he burnt a few days before his death:

Jan. 1, 1753, N.S.; which I shall use for the future.

Almighty GOD, who hast continued my life to this day, grant that, by the assistance of thy Holy Spirit, I may improve the time which thou shalt grant me, to my eternal salvation. Make me to remember, to thy glory, thy judgments and thy mercies. Make me so to consider the loss of my wife, whom thou hast taken from me, that it may dispose me, by thy grace, to lead the residue of my life in thy fear. Grant this, O LORD, for JESUS CHRIST's sake. *Amen.*

In one of the books of his diary I find the following entry:

Apr. 3, 1753. I began the second vol. of my "Dictionary," room being left in the first for Preface, Grammar, and History, none of them yet begun.

O GOD, who hast hitherto supported me, enable me to proceed in this labour, and in the whole task of my present state; that when I shall render up, at the last day, an account of the talent committed to me, I may receive pardon, for the sake of JESUS CHRIST. *Amen.*

In 1754 the "Dictionary," we may believe, afforded Johnson full occupation. As it approached to its conclusion, he probably worked with redoubled vigour, as seamen increase their exertion and alacrity when they have a near prospect of their haven.

Lord Chesterfield, to whom Johnson had paid the high compliment of addressing the plan of his "Dictionary," had behaved to him in such a manner as to excite his contempt and indignation. He told me, that there never was any particular incident which produced a quarrel between Lord Chesterfield and him; but that his lordship's continued neglect was the reason why he resolved to have no connection with him.

When the "Dictionary" was upon the eve of publication, Lord Chesterfield, who, it is said, had flattered himself with expectations that Johnson would dedicate the work to him, attempted, in a courtly manner, to soothe and insinuate himself with the sage, conscious, as it should seem, of the cold indifference with which he had treated its learned author; and further attempted to conciliate him, by writing two papers in "The World," in recommendation of the work; and it must be confessed, that they contain some studied compliments, so finely turned, that if there had been no previous offence, it is probable that Johnson would have been highly delighted. Praise, in general, was pleasing to him; but by praise from a man of rank and elegant accomplishments, he was peculiarly gratified.

But this courtly device failed of its effect. Johnson despised the honied words, and was even indignant that Lord Chesterfield should, for a moment, imagine that he could be the dupe of such an artifice. His expression to me concerning Lord Chesterfield, upon this occasion, was, "Sir, after making great professions, he had, for many years, taken no notice of me; but when my 'Dictionary' was coming out, he fell a scribbling in 'The World' about it. Upon which, I wrote him a letter expressed in civil terms, but such as might show him that I did not mind what he said or wrote, and that I had done with him."

This is that celebrated letter of which so much has been said, and about which curiosity has been so long excited, without being gratified. I for many years solicited Johnson to favour me with a copy of it, that so excellent a composition might not be lost to posterity. He delayed from time to time to give it me; till at last, in 1781, when we were on a visit at Mr. Dilly's, at Southill in Bedfordshire, he was pleased to dictate it to me from memory. He afterwards found among his papers a copy of it; this he gave to Mr. Langton; adding, that if it were to come into print, he wished it to be from that copy. By Mr. Langton's kindness, I am enabled to enrich my work with a perfect transcript of what the world has so eagerly desired to see.

To The Right Honourable The Earl of Chesterfield

February 7, 1755

MY LORD,

I have been lately informed by the proprietor of "The World," that two papers, in which my "Dictionary" is recommended to the public, were written by your lordship. To be so distinguished, is an honour, which, being very little accustomed to favours from the great, I know not well how to receive, or in what terms to acknowledge.

When, upon some slight encouragement, I first visited your lordship, I was overpowered, like the rest of mankind, by the enchantment of your address, and could not forbear to wish that I might boast myself *Le vainqueur du vainqueur de la terre;*—that I might obtain that regard for which I saw the world contending; but I found my attendance so little encouraged, that neither pride nor modesty would suffer me to continue it. When I had once addressed your lordship in public, I had exhausted all the art of pleasing which a retired and uncourtly scholar can possess. I had done all that I could; and no man is well pleased to have his all neglected, be it ever so little.

Seven years, my lord, have now past, since I waited in your outward rooms, or was repulsed from your door; during which time I have been pushing on my work through difficulties, of which it is useless to complain, and have brought it, at last, to the verge of publication, without one act of assistance, one word of encouragement, or one smile of favour. Such treatment I did not expect, for I never had a patron before.

The shepherd in Virgil grew at last acquainted with Love, and found him a native of the rocks.

Is not a patron, my lord, one who looks with unconcern on a man struggling for life in the water, and when he has reached ground, encumbers him with help? The notice which you have been pleased to take of my labours, had it been early, had been kind; but it has been delayed till I am indifferent, and cannot enjoy it; till I am solitary and cannot impart it; till I am known, and do not want it. I hope it is no very cynical asperity not to confess obligations where no benefit has been received, or to be unwilling that the public should consider me as owing that to a patron, which Providence has enabled me to do for myself.

Having carried on my work thus far with so little obligation to any favourer of learning, I shall not be disappointed though I should conclude it, if less be possible, with less; for I have been long wakened from that dream of hope, in which I once boasted myself with so much exultation, my Lord, your lordship's most humble, most obedient servant,   SAM. JOHNSON

"While this was the talk of the town (says Dr. Adams in a letter to me), I happened to visit Dr. Warburton, who finding that I was acquainted with Johnson, desired me earnestly to carry his compliments to him, and to tell him, that he honoured him for his manly behaviour in rejecting these condescensions of Lord Chesterfield, and for resenting the treatment he had received from him with a proper spirit.   Johnson was visibly pleased with this compliment, for he had always a high opinion of Warburton."

There is a curious minute circumstance which struck me, in comparing the various editions of Johnson's "Imitations of Juvenal." In the tenth Satire one of the couplets upon the vanity of wishes even for literary distinction stood thus:

> Yet think what ills the scholar's life assail,
> Toil, envy, want, the *garret*, and the jail.

But after experiencing the uneasiness which Lord Chesterfield's fallacious patronage made him feel, he dismissed the word *garret* from the sad group, and in all the subsequent editions the line stands

> Toil, envy, want, the *Patron*, and the jail.

That Lord Chesterfield must have been mortified by the lofty contempt, and polite, yet keen, satire with which Johnson exhibited him to himself in this letter, it is impossible to doubt. He, however, with that glossy duplicity which was his constant study, affected to be quite unconcerned. Dr. Adams mentioned to Mr. Robert Dodsley that he was sorry Johnson had written his letter to Lord Chesterfield. Dodsley, with the true feelings of trade, said "he was very sorry too; for that he had a property in the 'Dictionary,' to which his lordship's patronage might have been of consequence. He then told Dr. Adams, that Lord Chesterfield had shown him the letter. "I should have imagined (replied Dr. Adams) that Lord Chesterfield would have concealed it."—"Poh! (said Dodsley), do you think a letter from Johnson could hurt Lord Chesterfield? Not at all, sir. It lay upon his table, where any body might see it. He read it to me; said, 'This man has great powers,' pointed out the severest passages, and observed how well they were expressed." This air of indifference, which imposed upon the worthy Dodsley, was certainly nothing but a specimen of that dissimulation which Lord Chesterfield inculcated as one of the most essential lessons for the conduct of life.

Dr. Adams expostulated with Johnson, and suggested, that his not being admitted when he called on him, was probably not to be imputed to Lord Chesterfield; for his lordship had declared to Dodsley, that "he would have turned off the best servant he ever had, if he had known that he denied him to a man who would have been always more than welcome"; and in confirmation of this, he insisted on Lord Chesterfield's general affability and easiness of access, especially to literary men. "Sir, (said Johnson) that is not Lord Chesterfield; he is the proudest man this day existing."— "No, (said Dr. Adams) there is one person, at least, as proud; I think, by your own account, you are the prouder man of the two." —"But mine (replied Johnson instantly) was *defensive* pride." This, as Dr. Adams well observed, was one of those happy turns for which he was so remarkably ready.

Johnson having now explicitly avowed his opinion of Lord Chesterfield, did not refrain from expressing himself concerning that nobleman with pointed freedom: "This man, (said he) I thought had been a lord among wits: but, I find, he is only a wit among lords!" And when his letters to his natural son were published, he observed, that "they teach the morals of a whore, and the manners of a dancing master."

Johnson this year found an interval of leisure to make an excursion to Oxford, for the purpose of consulting the libraries there. Of his conversation while at Oxford at this time, Mr. Warton preserved and communicated to me the following memorial:

When Johnson came to Oxford in 1754, the long vacation was beginning, and most people were leaving the place. This was the first time of his being there, after quitting the University. The next morning after his arrival, he wished to see his old college, *Pembroke.* I went with him. He was highly pleased to find all the college-servants which he had left there still remaining, particularly a very old butler; and expressed great satisfaction at being recognized by them, and conversed with them familiarly. He waited on the master, Dr. Radcliffe, who received him very coldly. Johnson at least expected that the master would order a copy of his "Dictionary," now near publication; but the master did not choose to talk on the subject, never asked Johnson to dine, nor even to visit him, while he staid at Oxford. After we had left the lodgings, Johnson said to me, "*There* lives a man, who lives by the revenues of literature, and will not move a finger to support it. If I come to live at Oxford, I shall take up my abode at Trinity." We then called on the Reverend Mr. Meeke, one of the fellows, and of Johnson's standing. Here was a most cordial greeting on both sides. On leaving him, Johnson said, "I used to think Meeke had excellent parts, when we were boys together at the college: but, alas!

Lost in a convent's solitary gloom!—

"I remember, at the classical lecture in the Hall, I could not bear Meeke's superiority, and I tried to sit as far from him as I could, that I might not hear him construe."

In an evening we frequently took long walks from Oxford into the country, returning to supper. Once, in our way home, we viewed the ruins of the abbeys of Oseney and Rewley, near Oxford. After at least half an hour's silence, Johnson said, "I viewed them with indignation!"

I forgot to observe before, that when he left Mr. Meeke (as I have told above), he added, "About the same time of life, Meeke was left behind at Oxford to feed on a fellowship, and I went to London to get my living: now, Sir, see the difference of our literary characters!"

The degree of Master of Arts, which, it has been observed, could not be obtained for him at an early period of his life, was now considered as an honour of considerable importance, in order to grace the title-page of his "Dictionary"; and his character in the literary world being by this time deservedly high, his friends thought that, if proper exertions were made, the University of Oxford would pay him the compliment.

To the Rev. Mr. Thomas Warton

[London,] Nov. 28, 1754
DEAR SIR,
    I am extremely obliged to you and to Mr. Wise, for the uncommon care which you have taken of my interest; [1] if you can accomplish your kind design, I shall certainly take me a little habitation among you. . . .

[1] In procuring him the degree of M.A., by diploma. It was conferred in February.

Can I do anything to promoting the diploma? I would not be wanting to co-operate with your kindness; of which, whatever be the effect, I shall be, dear Sir, your most obliged, &c.

SAM. JOHNSON

In 1755 we behold him to great advantage; his degree of Master of Arts conferred upon him, his Dictionary published, his correspondence animated, his benevolence exercised.

Mr. Andrew Millar, bookseller in the Strand, took the principal charge of conducting the publication of Johnson's Dictionary; and as the patience of the proprietors was repeatedly tried and almost exhausted, by their expecting that the work would be completed within the time which Johnson had sanguinely supposed, the learned author was often goaded to dispatch, more especially as he had received all the copy-money, by different drafts, a considerable time before he had finished his task. When the messenger who carried the last sheet to Millar returned, Johnson asked him, "Well, what did he say?"—"Sir (answered the messenger), he said, 'Thank GOD, I have done with him.'" "I am glad (replied Johnson, with a smile,) that he thanks GOD for any thing."

The Dictionary, with a Grammar and History of the English Language, being now at length published, in two volumes folio, the world contemplated with wonder so stupendous a work achieved by one man, while other countries had thought such undertakings fit only for whole academies.

The etymologies, though they exhibit learning and judgment, are not, I think, entitled to the first praise amongst the various parts of this immense work. The definitions have always appeared to me such astonishing proofs of acuteness of intellect and precision of language, as indicate a genius of the highest rank. They, who will make the experiment of trying how they can define a few words of whatever nature, will soon be satisfied of the unquestionable justice of this observation, which I can assure my readers is founded upon much study, and upon communication with more minds than my own.

A few of his definitions must be admitted to be erroneous. A lady once asked him how he came to define *Pastern* the *knee* of a horse: instead of making an elaborate defence, as she expected, he at once answered, "Ignorance, Madam, pure ignorance." His definition of *Network* [1] has been often quoted with sportive ma-

---

[1] Anything reticulated or decussated, at equal distances, with interstices between the intersections.

lignity, as obscuring a thing in itself very plain.   But to these frivolous censures no other answer is necessary than that with which we are furnished by his own Preface:

To explain, requires the use of terms less abstruse than that which is to be explained, and such terms cannot always be found. For, as nothing can be proved but by supposing something intuitively known, and evident without proof, so nothing can be defined but by the use of words too plain to admit of definition. Sometimes easy words are changed into harder, as, *burial*, into *sepulture* or *interment; dry*, into *desiccative; dryness*, into *siccity*, or *aridity; fit*, into *paroxysm;* for the *easiest* word, whatever it be, can never be translated into one more easy.

His introducing his own opinions, and even prejudices, under general definitions of words, while at the same time the original meaning of the words is not explained, as his, *Tory, Whig, Pension, Oats, Excise*,[1] and a few more, cannot be fully defended, and must be placed to the account of capricious and humorous indulgence.

Let it, however, be remembered, that this indulgence does not display itself only in sarcasm towards others, but sometimes in playful allusion to the notions commonly entertained of his own laborious task.   Thus: "*Grub Street*, the name of a street in London, much inhabited by writers of small histories, *dictionaries*, and temporary poems; whence any mean production is called *Grub Street*."—"*Lexicographer*, a writer of dictionaries, *a harmless drudge*."

At the time when he was concluding his very eloquent Preface, Johnson's mind appears to have been in a state of depression.

I (says he) may surely be contented without the praise of perfection, which if I could obtain in this gloom of solitude, what would it avail me?   I have protracted my work till most of those whom I wished to please have sunk into the grave; and success and miscarriage are empty sounds.   I therefore dismiss it with frigid tranquillity, having little to fear or hope from censure or from praise.

[1] TORY [*a cant term, derived, I suppose, from an Irish word, signifying a savage. One who adheres to the ancient constitution of the state and the apostolic hierarchy of the Church of England; opposed to a Whig*].
WHIG [*the name of a faction*].
PENSION [*an allowance made to any one without an equivalent. In England it is generally understood to mean pay given to a state hireling for treason to his country*].
PENSIONER [*a slave of state hired by a stipend to obey his master*].
OATS [*a grain which in England is generally given to horses, but in Scotland supports the people*].
He thus defines *Excise:* "A hateful tax levied upon commodities, and adjudged not by the common judges of property, but wretches hired by those to whom excise is paid." The Commissioners of Excise, being offended by this severe reflection, consulted Mr. Murray, then Attorney-General, to know whether redress could be legally obtained. I am informed, that the import was, that the passage might be considered as actionable; but that it would be more prudent in the board not to prosecute. Johnson never made the smallest alteration in this passage.

It must undoubtedly seem strange, that the conclusion of his Preface should be expressed in terms so desponding, when it is considered that the author was then only in his forty-sixth year. But we must ascribe its gloom to that miserable dejection of spirits to which he was constitutionally subject, and which was aggravated by the death of his wife two years before. I have heard it ingeniously observed by a lady of rank and elegance, that "his melancholy was then at its meridian." It pleased GOD to grant him almost thirty years of life after this time; and once, when he was in a placid frame of mind, he was obliged to own to me that he had enjoyed happier days, and had many more friends, since that gloomy hour, than before.

It is a sad saying, that "most of those whom he wished to please had sunk into the grave"; and his case at forty-five was singularly unhappy, unless the circle of his friends was very narrow. I have often thought, that as longevity is generally desired, and I believe, generally expected, it would be wise to be continually adding to the number of our friends, that the loss of some may be supplied by others. Friendship, "the wine of life," should, like a well-stocked cellar, be thus continually renewed; and it is consolatory to think, that although we can seldom add what will equal the generous *first-growths* of our youth, yet friendship becomes insensibly old in much less time than is commonly imagined, and not many years are required to make it very mellow and pleasant. The proposition which I have now endeavoured to illustrate was, at a subsequent period of his life, the opinion of Johnson himself. He said to Sir Joshua Reynolds, "If a man does not make new acquaintance as he advances through life, he will soon find himself left alone. A man, Sir, should keep his friendship *in constant repair.*"

The celebrated Mr. Wilkes, whose notions and habits of life were very opposite to his, but who was ever eminent for literature and vivacity, sallied forth with a little *Jeu d'Esprit* upon the following passage in his Grammar of the English Tongue, prefixed to the Dictionary: "*H* seldom, perhaps never, begins any but the first syllable." In an essay printed in "The Public Advertiser," this lively writer enumerated many instances in opposition to this remark: for example: "The author of this observation must be a man of a quick *appre-hension*, and of a most *compre-hensive* genius."

This light sally, we may suppose, made no great impression on our Lexicographer; for we find that he did not alter the passage till many years afterwards.[1]

He had the pleasure of being treated in a very different manner by his old pupil Mr. Garrick, in the following complimentary Epigram:

On Johnson's Dictionary

Talk of war with a Briton, he'll boldly advance,
That one English soldier will beat ten of France;
Would we alter the boast from the sword to the pen,
Our odds are still greater, still greater our men:
In the deep mines of science though Frenchmen may toil,
Can their strength be compar'd to Locke, Newton, and Boyle?
Let them rally their heroes, send forth all their powers,
Their verse-men and prose-men, then match them with ours!
First Shakespeare and Milton, like Gods in the fight,
Have put their whole drama and epic to flight;
In satires, epistles, and odes would they cope,
Their numbers retreat before Dryden and Pope;
And Johnson, well arm'd like a hero of yore,
Has beat forty French,[2] and will beat forty more!

In 1756 Johnson found that the great fame of his Dictionary had not set him above the necessity of "making provision for the day that was passing over him." [3] No royal or noble patron extended a munificent hand to give independence to the man who had conferred stability on the language of his country. We may feel indignant that there should have been such unworthy neglect; but we must, at the same time, congratulate ourselves, when we consider, that to this very neglect, operating to rouse the natural indolence of his constitution, we owe many valuable productions, which otherwise, perhaps, might never have appeared.

He had spent, during the progress of the work, the money for which he had contracted to write his Dictionary. We have seen that the reward of his labour was only fifteen hundred and seventy-five pounds: and when the expense of amanuenses, and paper and other articles, are deducted, his clear profit was very inconsiderable. I once said to him, "I am sorry, Sir, you did not get more

---

[1] In the third edition, published in 1773, he left out the words *perhaps never*, and added the following paragraph: "It sometimes begins middle or final syllables in words compounded, as *block-head*, or derived from the Latin, as *compre-hended.*"—*Boswell.*

[2] The number of the French Academy employed in settling their language.—*Boswell.*

[3] He was this year in great pecuniary distress, having been arrested for debt; on which occasion his friend Samuel Richardson became his surety.

for your Dictionary." His answer was, "I am sorry too. But it was very well. The booksellers are generous, liberal-minded men." He, upon all occasions, did ample justice to their character in this respect. He considered them as the patrons of literature; and, indeed, although they have eventually been considerable gainers by his Dictionary, it is to them that we owe its having been undertaken and carried through at the risk of great expense.

His works this year were, an abstract or epitome, in octavo, of his folio "Dictionary," and a few essays in a monthly publication, entitled "THE UNIVERSAL VISITOR." He engaged also to superintend and contribute largely to another monthly publication, entitled "THE LITERARY MAGAZINE, OR UNIVERSAL REVIEW," the first number of which came out in May this year. What were his emoluments from this undertaking, I have not discovered.

Some of his reviews in this Magazine are very short accounts of the pieces noticed, but many of them are examples of elaborate criticism, in the most masterly style. In his review of the "memoirs of the Court of Augustus," he has the resolution to think and speak from his own mind, regardless of the cant transmitted from age to age, in praise of the ancient Romans. Thus: "I know not why any one but a schoolboy in his declamation should whine over the Commonwealth of Rome, which grew great only by the misery of the rest of mankind. The Romans, like others, as soon as they grew rich, grew corrupt; and in their corruption sold the lives and freedoms of themselves, and of one another." Again: "A people, who while they were poor robbed mankind; and as soon as they became rich robbed one another."

His defence of Tea against Mr. Jonas Hanway's violent attack upon that elegant and popular beverage, shows how very well a man of genius can write upon the slightest subject, when he writes, as the Italians say, con amore: I suppose no person ever enjoyed with more relish the infusion of that fragrant leaf than Johnson. The quantities which he drank of it at all hours were so great, that his nerves must have been uncommonly strong, not to have been extremely relaxed by such an intemperate use of it.[1] He assured me, that he never felt the least inconvenience from it; which is a proof that the fault of his constitution was rather a too great ten-

[1] In this review, Johnson describes himself as "a hardened and shameless tea-drinker, who has for many years diluted his meals with only the infusion of this fascinating plant; whose kettle has scarcely time to cool; who with tea amuses the evening, with tea solaces the midnights, and with tea welcomes the morning." This last phrase his friend, Tom Tyers, happily parodied, "te veniente die—te decedente." The Rev. Mr. Parker, of Henley, is in possession of a tea-pot which belonged to Dr. Johnson, and which contains about two quarts.—Croker.

sion of fibres, than the contrary. Mr. Hanway wrote an angry answer to Johnson's review of his "Essay on Tea," and Johnson, after a full and deliberate pause, made a reply to it; the only instance, I believe, in the whole course of his life, when he condescended to oppose anything that was written against him.

This year Mr. William Payne published "An Introduction to the Game of Draughts," to which Johnson contributed a dedication and a preface. Johnson, I believe, did not play at draughts after leaving College; by which he suffered; for it would have afforded him an innocent soothing relief from the melancholy which distressed him so often. I have heard him regret that he had not learnt to play at cards; and the game of draughts we know is peculiarly calculated to fix the attention without straining it. There is a composure and gravity in draughts which insensibly tranquillises the mind; and, accordingly, the Dutch are fond of it, as they are of smoking, of the sedative influence of which, though he himself never smoked, he had a high opinion.[1] Besides, there is in draughts some exercise of the faculties.

He this year resumed his scheme of giving an edition of Shakspeare with notes. He issued Proposals of considerable length, but his indolence prevented him from pursuing it with that diligence which alone can collect those scattered facts, that genius, however acute, penetrating, and luminous, cannot discover by its own force. It is remarkable, that at this time his fancied activity was for the moment so vigorous, that he promised his work should be published before Christmas, 1757. Yet nine years elapsed before it saw the light. His throes in bringing it forth had been severe and remittent; and at last we may almost conclude that the Cæsarian operation was performed by the knife of Churchill, whose upbraiding satire, I dare say, made Johnson's friends urge him to dispatch.

He for subscribers baits his hook,
And takes their cash; but where's the book?
No matter where; wise fear, we know,
Forbids the robbing of a foe;
But what, to serve our private ends,
Forbids the cheating of our friends?[2]

[1] Hawkins heard Johnson say, that insanity had grown more frequent since smoking had gone out of fashion.—*Croker.*

[2] Boswell writes elsewhere: "In the year 1763 a young bookseller waited on him with a subscription to his 'Shakspeare'; and observing that the doctor made no entry in any book, ventured diffidently to ask whether the gentleman's address might be properly inserted in the printed list of subscribers. '*I shall print no list of subscribers,*' said Johnson, with great abruptness; but almost immediately recollecting himself, added, very complacently, 'Sir, I have two very cogent reasons for not printing any list of subscribers: one, that I have lost all the names; the other, that I have spent all the money.'"

In 1758 we find him, it should seem, in as easy and pleasant a state of existence, as constitutional unhappiness ever permitted him to enjoy.

Dr. Burney, who, during a visit to the capital, dined and drank tea with him, has kindly favoured me with the following memorandum: "After dinner, Mr. Johnson proposed to Mr. Burney to go up with him into his garret, which being accepted, he there found about five or six Greek folios, a deal writing-desk, and a chair and a half. Johnson, giving to his guest the entire seat, tottered himself on one with only three legs and one arm. Here he gave Mr. Burney Mrs. Williams's history, and showed him some volumes of Shakspeare already printed, to prove that he was in earnest. Upon Mr. Burney's opening the first volume, at the 'Merchant of Venice,' he observed to him that he seemed to be more severe on Warburton than Theobald. 'O poor Tib! (said Johnson) he was ready knocked down to my hands; Warburton stands between me and him.'—'But, Sir (said Mr. Burney), you'll have Warburton upon your bones, won't you?' 'No, Sir; he'll not come out: he'll only growl in his den.'—'But you think, Sir, that Warburton is a superior critic to Theobald?'—'O, Sir, he'd make two-and-fifty Theobalds cut into slices! The worst of Warburton is, that he has a rage for saying something, when there's nothing to be said.' Mr. Burney asked him if he had seen Warburton's book against Bolingbroke's 'Philosophy'?—'No, Sir; I have never read Bolingbroke's impiety, and therefore am not interested about its confutation.'"

On the fifteenth of April he began a new periodical paper, entitled "THE IDLER," which came out every Saturday in a weekly newspaper, called "The Universal Chronicle, or Weekly Gazette." These essays were continued till April 5, 1760. Of one hundred and three, their total number, twelve were contributed by his friends; of which, Nos. 33, 93, and 96 were written by Mr. Thomas Warton; No. 67 by Mr. Langton; and Nos. 76, 79, and 82 by Sir Joshua Reynolds.

"The Idler" is evidently the work of the same mind which produced the "Rambler," but has less body and more spirit. It has more variety of real life, and greater facility of language. He describes the miseries of idleness, with the lively sensations of one who has felt them; and in his private memorandums while engaged in it, we find, "This year I hope to learn diligence." Many of these excellent essays were written as hastily as an ordinary letter.

Mr. Langton remembers Johnson, when on a visit to Oxford, asking him one evening how long it was till the post went out; and on being told about half an hour, he exclaimed, "then we shall do very well." He upon this instantly sat down and finished an "Idler," which it was necessary should be in London the next day. Mr. Langton having signified a wish to read it, "Sir (said he) you shall not do more than I have done myself." He then folded it up and sent it off.

In 1759, in the month of January, his mother died, at the great age of ninety, an event which deeply affected him; not that "his mind had acquired no firmness by the contemplation of mortality"; [1] but that his reverential affection for her was not abated by years, as indeed he retained all his tender feelings even to the latest period of his life. I have been told, that he regretted much his not having gone to visit his mother, for several years previous to her death. But he was constantly engaged in literary labours which confined him to London; and though he had not the comfort of seeing his aged parent, he contributed liberally to her support.

To Mrs. Johnson, Lichfield

13th Jan. 1759

HONOURED MADAM,
      The account which Miss [Porter] gives me of your health pierces my heart. God comfort and preserve you and save you, for the sake of Jesus Christ.
      I would have Miss read to you from time to time the Passion of our Saviour, and sometimes the sentences in the Communion Service, beginning, *Come unto me, all ye that travail and are heavy laden, and I will give you rest.*
      I have just now read a physical book, which inclines me to think that a strong infusion of the bark would do you good. Do, dear mother, try it.
      Pray, send me your blessing, and forgive all that I have done amiss to you. And whatever you would have done, and what debts you would have paid first, or any thing else that you would direct, let Miss [Porter] put it down; I shall endeavour to obey you.
      I have got twelve guineas [2] to send you, but unhappily am at a loss how to send it to-night. If I cannot send it to-night, it will come by the next post.

---

[1] Hawkin's *Life of Johnson*, p. 365.
[2] Six of these twelve guineas Johnson appears to have borrowed from Mr. Allen, the printer.

Pray, do not omit any thing mentioned in this letter. God bless you for ever and ever.—I am your dutiful son,

SAM. JOHNSON

To the Same

16th Jan. 1759

DEAR HONOURED MOTHER,
Your weakness afflicts me beyond what I am willing to communicate to you. I do not think you unfit to face death, but I know not how to bear the thought of losing you. Endeavour to do all you [can] for yourself. Eat as much as you can.
I pray often for you; do you pray for me. I have nothing to add to my last letter. I am, dear, dear mother, your dutiful son,

SAM. JOHNSON

To the Same

18th Jan. 1759

DEAR HONOURED MOTHER,
I fear you are too ill for long letters; therefore I will only tell you, you have from me all the regard that can possibly subsist in the heart. I pray God to bless you for evermore, for Jesus Christ's sake. Amen.
Let Miss write to me every post, however short.
I am, dear mother, your dutiful son,   SAM. JOHNSON

To Miss Porter, at Mrs. Johnson's, in Lichfield

20th Jan. 1759

DEAR MISS,
I will, if it be possible, come down to you. God grant I may yet [find] my dear mother breathing and sensible. Do not tell her lest I disappoint her. If I miss to write next post, I am on the road. I am my dearest Miss, your most humble servant,

SAM. JOHNSON

On the other side.

20th Jan. 1759

DEAR HONOURED MOTHER,
Neither your condition nor your character make it fit for me to say much. You have been the best mother, and I believe the best woman in the world. I thank you for your indulgence to me, and beg forgiveness of all that I have done ill, and all that I have omitted to do well. God grant you his Holy Spirit, and receive you to everlasting happiness, for Jesus Christ's sake. Amen.

Lord Jesus receive your spirit. Amen.—I am, dear, dear mother, your dutiful son,

SAM. JOHNSON

To Miss Porter, in Lichfield

23rd Jan. 1759 [1]

You will conceive my sorrow for the loss of my mother, of the best mother. If she were to live again, surely I should behave better to her. But she is happy, and what is past is nothing to her; and for me, since I cannot repair my faults to her, I hope repentance will efface them. I return you and all those that have been good to her my sincerest thanks, and pray God to repay you all with infinite advantage. Write to me, and comfort me, dear child. I shall be glad likewise, if Kitty will write to me. I shall send a bill of twenty pounds in a few days, which I thought to have brought to my mother; but God suffered it not. I have not power or composure to say much more. God bless you, and bless us all. I am, dear Miss, your affectionate humble servant,

SAM. JOHNSON

Soon after this event, he wrote his "RASSELAS, PRINCE OF ABYSSINIA." Mr. Strahan the printer told me, that Johnson wrote it, that with the profits he might defray the expense of his mother's funeral, and pay some little debts which she had left. He told Sir Joshua Reynolds, that he composed it in the evenings of one week, sent it to the press in portions as it was written, and had never since read it over. Mr. Strahan, Mr. Johnston, and Mr. Dodsley purchased it for a hundred pounds, but afterwards paid him twenty-five pounds more, when it came to a second edition.

Considering the large sums which have been received for compilations, and works requiring not much more genius than compilations, we cannot but wonder at the very low price which he was content to receive for this admirable performance; which, though he had written nothing else, would have rendered his name immortal in the world of literature. None of his writings has been so extensively diffused over Europe; for it has been translated into most, if not all, of the modern languages. This tale, with all the charms of oriental imagery, and all the force and beauty of which the English language is capable, leads us through the most important scenes of human life, and shows us that this stage of our being is full of "vanity and vexation of spirit." Voltaire's "CANDIDE,"

[1] Mrs. Johnson probably died on the 20th or 21st January, and was buried on the day this letter was written.

written to refute the system of Optimism, which it has accomplished with brilliant success, is wonderfully similar in its plan and conduct to Johnson's "RASSELAS"; insomuch, that I have heard Johnson say, that if they had not been published so closely one after the other that there was not time for imitation, it would have been in vain to deny that the scheme of that which came latest was taken from the other. Though the proposition illustrated by both these works was the same, namely, that in our present state there is more evil than good, the intention of the writers was very different. Voltaire, I am afraid, meant only by wanton profaneness to obtain a sportive victory over religion, and to discredit the belief of a superintending Providence: Johnson meant, by showing the unsatisfactory nature of things temporal, to direct the hopes of man to things eternal.

He now refreshed himself by an excursion to Oxford, of which the following short characteristical notice, in his own words, is preserved:

—— is now making tea for me. I have been in my gown ever since I came here.[1] It was, at my first coming, quite new and handsome. I have swum thrice, which I had disused for many years. I have proposed to Vansittart climbing over the wall, but he has refused me. And I have clapped my hands till they are sore, at Dr. King's speech.

His negro servant, Francis Barber, having left him, and been some time at sea, not pressed as has been supposed, but with his own consent, it appears from a letter to John Wilkes, Esq. from Dr. Smollett, that his master kindly interested himself in procuring his release from a state of life of which Johnson always expressed the utmost abhorrence. Mr. Wilkes applied to his friend Sir George Hay, and Francis Barber was discharged, as he has told me, without any wish of his own. He found his old master in Chambers in the Inner Temple, and returned to his service.

What particular new scheme of life Johnson had in view this year, I have not discovered; but that he meditated one of some sort, is clear from his private devotions, in which we find [24th March] "the change of outward things which I am now to make"; and, "Grant me the grace of thy Holy Spirit, that the course which I am now beginning may proceed according to thy laws, and end in

---

[1] Lord Stowell informs me that he prided himself in being, during his visits to Oxford, accurately academic in all points; and he wore his gown almost *ostentatiously.*—*Croker.*

the enjoyment of thy favour." But he did not, in fact, make any external or visible change. In 1760 I have not discovered a single private letter written by him to any of his friends. It should seem, however, that he had at this period a floating intention of writing a history of the recent and wonderful successes of the British arms in all quarters of the globe; for among his resolutions or memorandums, September 18, there is, "Send for books for Hist. of War." [1] How much is it to be regretted that this intention was not fulfilled! His majestic expression would have carried down to the latest posterity the glorious achievements of his country, with the same fervent glow which they produced on the mind at the time. He would have been under no temptation to deviate in any degree from truth, which he held very sacred, or to take a licence, which he once seemed, in a conversation, jocularly to allow to historians. "There are (said he) inexcusable lies, and consecrated lies. For instance, we are told that on the arrival of the news of the unfortunate battle of Fontenoy, every heart beat and every eye was in tears. Now we know that no man eat his dinner the worse, but there *should* have been all this concern; and to say there *was* (smiling) may be reckoned a consecrated lie."

In 1761 Johnson appears to have done little. He was still, no doubt, proceeding in his edition of Shakspeare; but what advances he made in it cannot be ascertained. He certainly was at this time not active; for in his scrupulous examination of himself on Easter eve, he laments, in his too rigorous mode of censuring his own conduct, that his life, since the communion of the preceding Easter, had been "dissipated and useless." He, however, contributed this year the Preface to "Rolt's Dictionary of Trade and Commerce," in which he displays such a clear and comprehensive

---

[1] The memorandum, made on his birthday in this year, may be quoted as an example of the rules and resolutions which he was in the habit of making, for the guidance of his moral conduct and literary studies:

"Sept. 18. Resolved, D (*eo*) j (*uvante*).
To combat notions of obligation:
To apply to study:
To reclaim imaginations:
To consult the resolves on Tetty's coffin:
To rise early:
To study religion:
To go to church:
To drink less strong liquors:
To keep a journal:
To oppose laziness, by doing what is to be done to-morrow:
Rise as early as I can:
Send for Books for Hist. of War:
Put books in order:
Scheme of life."

knowledge of the subject, as might lead the reader to think that its author had devoted his life to it. I asked him whether he knew much of Rolt, and of his work. "Sir, (said he) I never saw the man, and never read the book. The booksellers wanted a Preface to a Dictionary of Trade and Commerce. I knew very well what such a Dictionary should be, and I wrote a Preface accordingly." Rolt, who wrote a great deal for the booksellers, was, as Johnson told me, a singular character. Though not in the least acquainted with him, he used to say, "I am just come from Sam. Johnson." This was a sufficient specimen of his vanity and impudence.

A lady having at this time solicited him to obtain the Archbishop of Canterbury's patronage to have her son sent to the University,— one of those solicitations which are too frequent, where people, anxious for a particular object, do not consider propriety, or the opportunity which the persons whom they solicit have to assist them,—he wrote to her the following answer:

To Mrs. ——

June 8, 1762

Madam,

I hope you will believe that my delay in answering your letter could proceed only from my unwillingness to destroy any hope that you had formed. Hope is itself a species of happiness, and, perhaps, the chief happiness which this world affords: but, like all other pleasures immoderately enjoyed, the excesses of hope must be expiated by pain; and expectations improperly indulged, must end in disappointment. If it be asked, what is the improper expectation which it is dangerous to indulge, experience will quickly answer, that it is such expectation as is dictated, not by reason, but by desire; expectation raised, not by the common occurrences of life, but by the wants of the expectant; an expectation that requires the common course of things to be changed, and the general rules of action to be broken.

When you made your request to me, you should have considered, Madam, what you were asking. You ask me to solicit a great man, to whom I never spoke, for a young person whom I had never seen, upon a supposition which I had no means of knowing to be true. There is no reason why, amongst all the great, I should choose to supplicate the Archbishop, nor why, among all the possible objects of his bounty, the Archbishop should choose your son. I know, Madam, how unwillingly conviction is admitted, when interest opposes it; but surely, Madam, you must allow, that there is no reason why that should be done by me, which every other man may do with equal reason, and which, indeed, no man can do properly, without some very particular relation both to the Archbishop and to you. If I could help you in this exigence by any proper means, it would give me pleasure; but this proposal is so very remote from usual methods, that I cannot comply with it, but at the risk of such answer and suspicions as I believe you do not wish me to undergo.

I have seen your son this morning; he seems a pretty youth, and will, perhaps, find some better friend than I can procure him; but though he should at last miss the University, he may still be wise, useful, and happy. I am, Madam, your most humble servant,

SAM. JOHNSON

The accession of George the Third to the throne of these kingdoms opened a new and brighter prospect to men of literary merit, who had been honoured with no mark of royal favour in the preceding reign. His present Majesty's education in this country, as well as his taste and beneficence, prompted him to be the patron of science and the arts; and early this year, Johnson having been represented to him as a very learned and good man, without any certain provision, his Majesty was pleased to grant him a pension of three hundred pounds a year. The Earl of Bute, who was then Prime Minister, had the honour to announce this instance of his Sovereign's bounty, concerning which, many and various stories, all equally erroneous, have been propagated; maliciously representing it as a political bribe to Johnson, to desert his avowed principles, and become the tool of a government which he held to be founded in usurpation. I have taken care to have it in my power to refute them from the most authentic information. Lord Bute told me, that Mr. Wedderburne, now Lord Loughborough, was the person who first mentioned this subject to him. Lord Loughborough told me, that the pension was granted to Johnson solely as the reward of his literary merit, without any stipulation whatever, or even tacit understanding that he should write for administration. His Lordship added, that he was confident the political tracts which Johnson afterwards did write, as they were entirely consonant with his own opinions, would have been written by him, though no pension had been granted to him. Sir Joshua Reynolds told me, that Johnson called on him after his Majesty's intention had been notified to him, and said he wished to consult his friends as to the propriety of his accepting this mark of the royal favour, after the definitions which he had given in his "Dictionary" of *pension* and *pensioners*. He said he should not have Sir Joshua's answer till next day, when he would call again, and desired he might think of it. Sir Joshua answered that he was clear to give his opinion then, that there could be no objection to his receiving from the King a reward for literary merit; and that certainly the definitions in his "Dictionary" were not applicable to him. Johnson, it should seem, was satisfied, for he did not call again till he had accepted the pension, and had waited on Lord Bute to thank him. He then told Sir Joshua that Lord Bute said to him expressly, "It is not given you for any thing you are to do, but for what you have done." His Lordship, he said, behaved in the handsomest manner. He repeated the words twice, that he might be sure Johnson heard them, and thus set his mind perfectly at ease. Mr. Sheridan told me that when he communicated to Dr. Johnson that a pension was to be granted him, he replied in a fervour of gratitude, "The English language does not afford me terms adequate to my feelings on this occasion. I must have recourse to the French. I am *pénétré* with his Majesty's goodness." When I repeated this to Dr. Johnson, he did not contradict it.

But I shall not detain my readers longer by any words of my own, on a subject on which I am enabled to present them with what Johnson himself wrote:

To The Right Honourable The Earl of Bute

July 20, 1762

My Lord,

When the bills were yesterday delivered to me by Mr. Wedderburne, I was informed by him of the future favours which his Majesty has by your Lordship's recommendation, been induced to intend for me.

Bounty always receives part of its value from the manner in which it is bestowed; your Lordship's kindness includes every circumstance that can gratify delicacy, or enforce obligation. You have conferred your favours on a man who has neither alliance nor interest, who has not merited them by services, nor courted them by officiousness; you have spared him the shame of solicitation, and the anxiety of suspense.

What has been thus elegantly given, will, I hope, not be reproachfully enjoyed; I shall endeavour to give your Lordship the only recompence which generosity desires,—the gratification of finding that your benefits are not improperly bestowed. I am, my Lord, your Lordship's most obliged, most obedient, and most humble servant,   SAM. JOHNSON [1]

This year his friend, Sir Joshua Reynolds, paid a visit of some weeks to his native county, Devonshire, in which he was accompanied by Johnson, who was much pleased with this jaunt, and declared he had derived from it a great accession of new ideas. He was entertained at the seats of several noblemen and gentlemen in the west of England;[2] but the greatest part of this time was passed at Plymouth, where the magnificence of the navy, the shipbuilding and all its circumstances, afforded him a grand subject of contemplation.

While Johnson was at Plymouth, he saw a great many of its inhabitants, and was not sparing of his very entertaining conversation. It was here that he made that frank and truly original confession that "ignorance, pure ignorance," was the cause of a wrong definition in his "Dictionary" of the word *pastern*, to the no small surprise of the lady who put the question to him.

Sir Joshua Reynolds mentions a very characteristical anecdote of Johnson while at Plymouth. Having observed, that in consequence of the Dock-yard a new town had arisen about two miles off as a rival to the old, he set himself resolutely on the side of the old town, the *established* town, in which his lot was cast, considering it as a kind of duty to *stand by* it. He accordingly entered warmly into its interests, and upon every occasion talked of the *Dockers*, as the inhabitants of the new town were called, as upstarts and aliens. Plymouth is very plentifully supplied with water by a river brought into it from a great distance, which is so abundant that it runs to waste in the town. The Dock, or New Town, being totally

---

[1] The addition of three hundred pounds a year, to what Johnson was able to earn by the ordinary exercise of his talents, raised him to a state of comparative affluence, and afforded him the means of assisting many whose real or pretended wants had formerly excited his compassion. He now practised a rule which he often recommended to his friends, always to go abroad with some loose money to give to beggars.—*Hawkins.*

He loved the poor as I never yet saw any one else do, with an earnest desire to make them happy. What signifies, says some one, giving halfpence to common beggars? they only lay it out in gin or tobacco. "And why (says Johnson) should they be denied such sweeteners of their existence? it is surely very savage to refuse them every possible avenue to pleasure, reckoned too coarse for our own acceptance. Life is a pill which none of us can bear to swallow without gilding; yet for the poor we delight in stripping it still barer, and are not ashamed to show even visible displeasure, if ever the bitter taste is taken from their mouths." In consequence of these principles he nursed whole nests of people in his house, where the lame, the blind, the sick, and the sorrowful found a sure retreat from all the evils whence his little income could secure them.—*Piozzi, Anecdotes.*

When visiting Lichfield, towards the later part of his life, he was accustomed, on his arrival, to deposit with Miss Porter as much cash as would pay his expenses back to London. He could not trust himself with his own money, as he felt himself unable to resist the importunity of the numerous claimants on his benevolence.—*Harwood.—Croker.*

[2] At one of these seats, in order to amuse him till dinner should be ready, he was taken out to walk in the garden. The master of the house, thinking it proper to introduce something scientific into the conversation, addressed him thus: "Are you a botanist, Dr. Johnson?" "No, Sir, (answered Johnson) I am not a botanist; and, (alluding, no doubt, to his near-sightedness,) should I wish to become a botanist, I must first turn myself into a reptile."

destitute of water, petitioned Plymouth that a small portion of the conduit might be permitted to go to them, and this was now under consideration. Johnson affecting to entertain the passions of the place, was violent in opposition; and half laughing at himself for his pretended zeal, where he had no concern, exclaimed, "No, no! I am against the *Dockers;* I am a Plymouth-man. Rogues! let them die of thirst. They shall not have a drop!"

The following letter was found, by the present Earl of Bute, among his father's papers.

To the Right Honourable the Earl of Bute

Temple Lane, Nov. 3, 1762

My Lord,

That generosity, by which I was recommended to the favour of his Majesty, will not be offended at a solicitation necessary to make that favour permanent and effectual.

The pension appointed to be paid me at Michaelmas I have not received, and I know not where or from whom I am to ask it. I beg, therefore, that your Lordship will be pleased to supply Mr. Wedderburne with such directions as may be necessary, which, I believe, his friendship will make him think it no trouble to convey to me.

To interrupt your Lordship, at a time like this, with such petty difficulties, is improper and unseasonable; but your knowledge of the world has long since taught you, that every man's affairs, however little, are important to himself. Every man hopes that he shall escape neglect; and with reason may every man, whose vices do not preclude his claim, expect favour from that beneficence which has been extended to, my Lord, your Lordship's most obliged and most humble servant, Sam. Johnson

This [1763] is to me a memorable year; for in it I had the happiness to obtain the acquaintance of that extraordinary man whose memoirs I am now writing; an acquaintance which I shall ever esteem as one of the most fortunate circumstances in my life. Though then but two and twenty, I had for several years read his works with delight and instruction, and had the highest reverence for their author, which had grown up in my fancy into a kind of mysterious veneration, by figuring to myself a state of solemn elevated abstraction, in which I supposed him to live in the immense metropolis of London. Mr. Gentleman, a native of Ireland, who passed some years in Scotland as a player, and as an instructor in the English language, a man whose talents and worth were depressed by misfortunes, had given me a representation of the figure and manner of DICTIONARY JOHNSON! as he was then called; and during my first visit to London, which was for three months in 1760, Mr. Derrick the poet, who was Gentleman's friend and countryman, flattered me with hopes that he would introduce me to Johnson,—an honour of which I was very ambitious. But he never found an opportunity; which made me doubt that he had promised to do what was not in his power; till Johnson some years afterwards told me, "Derrick, Sir, might very well have introduced you. I had a kindness for Derrick, and am sorry he is dead."

In the summer of 1761, Mr. Thomas Sheridan was at Edinburgh, and delivered lectures upon the English language and Public Speaking to large and respectable audiences. I was often in his company, and heard him frequently expatiate upon Johnson's extraordinary knowledge, talents, and virtues, repeat his pointed sayings, describe his particularities, and boast of his being his guest sometimes till two or three in the morning. At his house I hoped to have many opportunities of seeing the sage, as Mr. Sheridan obligingly assured me I should not be disappointed.

When I returned to London in the end of 1762, to my surprise and regret I found an irreconcileable difference had taken place between Johnson and Sheridan. A pension of two hundred pounds a year had been given to Sheridan. Johnson, who, as has been already mentioned, thought slightingly of Sheridan's art, upon hearing that he was also pensioned, exclaimed, "What! have they given *him* a pension? Then it is time for me to give up mine." Whether this proceeded from a momentary indignation, as if it were an affront to his exalted merit that a player should be rewarded in the same manner with him, or was the sudden effect of a fit of peevishness, it was unluckily said, and, indeed, cannot be justified.

Besides, Johnson should have recollected that Mr. Sheridan taught pronunciation to Mr. Alexander Wedderburne, whose sister was married to Sir Harry Erskine, an intimate friend of Lord Bute, who was the favourite of the king; and surely the most outrageous Whig will not maintain, that, whatever ought to be the principle in the disposal of *offices*, a *pension* ought never to be granted from any bias of court connection. Mr. Macklin, indeed, shared with Mr. Sheridan the honour of instructing Mr. Wedderburne; and though it was too late in life for a Caledonian to acquire the genuine English cadence, yet so successful were Mr. Wedderburne's instructors, and his own unabating endeavours, that he got rid of the coarse part of his Scotch accent, retaining only as much of the "native wood-note wild," as to mark his country; which, if any Scotchman should affect to forget, I should heartily despise him. Notwithstanding the difficulties which are to be encountered by those who have not had the advantage of an English education, he by degrees formed a mode of speaking, to which Englishmen do not deny the praise of elegance. Hence his distinguished oratory has had its fame and ample reward, in much higher spheres. I have dwelt the longer upon this because it affords animating encouragement to other gentlemen of North Britain to try their fortunes in the southern part of the island, where they may hope to gratify their utmost ambition.

Mr. Thomas Davies the actor, who then kept a bookseller's shop in Russell Street, Covent Garden,[1] told me that Johnson was very much his friend, and came frequently to his house, where he more than once invited me to meet him; but by some unlucky accident or other he was prevented from coming to us.

At last, on Monday, the 16th of May, when I was sitting in Mr. Davies's back parlour, after having drunk tea with him and Mrs. Davies, Johnson unexpectedly came into the shop; and Mr. Davies having perceived him, through the glass-door in the room in which we were sitting, advancing towards us, he announced his awful approach to me, somewhat in the manner of an actor in the part of Horatio, when he addresses Hamlet on the appearance of his father's ghost, "Look, my lord, it comes!" I found that I had a very perfect idea of Johnson's figure, from the portrait of him painted by Sir Joshua Reynolds soon after he had published his "Dictionary." Mr. Davies mentioned my name, and respectfully introduced me to him. I was much agitated; and recollecting his prejudice against the Scotch, of which I had heard much, I said to Davies, "Don't tell where I come from."—"From Scotland," cried Davies, roguishly. "Mr. Johnson," said I, "I do indeed come from Scotland, but I cannot help it." I am willing to flatter myself that I meant this as light pleasantry to soothe and conciliate him, and not as an humiliating abasement at the expense of my country. But however that might be, this speech was somewhat unlucky; for he seized the expression "come from Scotland," which

[1] No. 8.—The very place where I was fortunate enough to be introduced to the illustrious subject of this work, deserves to be particularly marked. I never pass by it without feeling reverence and regret. —*Boswell.*

I used in the sense of being of that country; and retorted, "That, Sir, I find, is what a very great many of your countrymen cannot help." This stroke stunned me a good deal; and when we had sat down, I felt myself not a little embarrassed, and apprehensive of what might come next. He then addressed himself to Davies: "What do you think of Garrick? He has refused me an order for the play for Miss Williams, because he knows the house will be full, and that an order would be worth three shillings." Eager to take any opening to get into conversation with him, I ventured to say, "O Sir, I cannot think Mr. Garrick would grudge such a trifle to you." "Sir," said he, with a stern look, "I have known David Garrick longer than you have done: and I know no right you have to talk to me on the subject." Perhaps I deserved this check; for it was rather presumptuous in me, an entire stranger, to express any doubt of the justice of his animadversion upon his old acquaintance and pupil. I now felt myself much mortified, and began to think that the hope which I had long indulged of obtaining his acquaintance was blasted. And, in truth, had not my ardour been uncommonly strong, and my resolution uncommonly persevering, so rough a reception might have deterred me for ever from making any further attempts. Fortunately, however, I remained upon the field not wholly discomfited; and was soon rewarded by hearing some of his conversation, of which I preserved the following short minute, without marking the questions and observations by which it was produced.

"People," he remarked, "may be taken in once, who imagine that an author is greater in private life than other men. Uncommon parts require uncommon opportunities for their exertion.

"In barbarous society, superiority of parts is of real consequence. Great strength or great wisdom is of much value to an individual. But in more polished times there are people to do every thing for money; and then there are a number of other superiorities, such as those of birth, and fortune, and rank, that dissipate men's attention, and leave no extraordinary share of respect for personal and intellectual superiority. This is wisely ordered by Providence, to preserve some equality among mankind.

"The notion of liberty amuses the people of England, and helps to keep off the *tædium vitæ*. When a butcher tells you that *his heart bleeds for his country*, he has, in fact, no uneasy feeling."

I was highly pleased with the extraordinary vigour of his conversation, and regretted that I was drawn away from it by an engagement at another place.   I had, for a part of the evening, been left alone with him, and had ventured to make an observation now and then, which he received very civilly; so that I was satisfied that though there was a roughness in his manner, there was no ill-nature in his disposition.   Davies followed me to the door, and when I complained to him a little of the hard blows which the great man had given me, he kindly took upon him to console me by saying, "Don't be uneasy, I can see he likes you very well."

A few days afterwards I called on Davies, and asked him if he thought I might take the liberty of waiting on Mr. Johnson at his chambers in the Temple.   He said I certainly might, and that Mr. Johnson would take it as a compliment.   So upon Tuesday the 24th of May I boldly repaired to Johnson.   His chambers were on the first floor of No. 1, Inner Temple Lane, and I entered them with an impression given me by the Rev. Dr. Blair of Edinburgh, who described his having "found the Giant in his den"; an expression which, when I came to be pretty well acquainted with Johnson, I repeated to him, and he was diverted at this picturesque account of himself.

He received me very courteously; but it must be confessed, that his apartment, and furniture, and morning dress, were sufficiently uncouth.   His brown suit of clothes looked very rusty; he had on a little old shrivelled unpowdered wig, which was too small for his head; his shirtneck and knees of his breeches were loose; his black worsted stockings ill drawn up; and he had a pair of unbuckled shoes by way of slippers.   But all these slovenly particularities were forgotten the moment that he began to talk.   Some gentlemen, whom I do not recollect, were sitting with him; and when they went away, I also rose; but he said to me, "Nay, don't go."—"Sir," said I, "I am afraid that I intrude upon you.   It is benevolent to allow me to sit and hear you."   He seemed pleased with this compliment, which I sincerely paid him, and answered, "Sir, I am obliged to any man who visits me."—I have preserved the following short minute of what passed this day.

"Madness frequently discovers itself merely by unnecessary deviation from the usual modes of the world.   My poor friend Smart showed the disturbance of his mind by falling upon his knees and saying his prayers in the street, or in any other unusual place.   Now, although, rationally speaking, it is greater madness not to pray at all, than to pray as Smart did, I am afraid there are

HE RECEIVED ME VERY COURTEOUSLY

so many who do not pray, that their understanding is not called in question."

Concerning this unfortunate poet, Christopher Smart, who was confined in a madhouse, he had, at another time, the following conversation with Dr. Burney.—BURNEY. "How does poor Smart do, Sir? is he likely to recover?" JOHNSON. "It seems as if his mind had ceased to struggle with the disease; for he grows fat upon it." BURNEY. "Perhaps, Sir, that may be from want of exercise." JOHNSON. "No, Sir; he has partly as much exercise as he used to have, for he digs in the garden. Indeed, before his confinement, he used for exercise to walk to the ale-house; but he was *carried* back again. I did not think he ought to be shut up. His infirmities were not noxious to society. He insisted on people praying with him; and I'd as lief pray with Kit Smart as any one else. Another charge was, that he did not love clean linen; and I have no passion for it."

Johnson continued. "Mankind have a great aversion to intellectual labour; but even supposing knowledge to be easily attainable, more people would be content to be ignorant than would take even a little trouble to acquire it.

"The morality of an action depends on the motive from which we act. If I fling half a crown to a beggar with intention to break his head, and he picks it up and buys victuals with it, the physical effect is good; but, with respect to me, the action is very wrong. So, religious exercises, if not performed with an intention to please God, avail us nothing. As our Saviour says of those who perform them from other motives, 'Verily, they have their reward.'"

Talking of Garrick, he said, "He is the first man in the world for sprightly conversation."

When I rose a second time, he again pressed me to stay, which I did.

He told me that he generally went abroad at four in the afternoon, and seldom came home till two in the morning. I took the liberty to ask if he did not think it wrong to live thus, and not make more use of his great talents. He owned it was a bad habit. On reviewing, at the distance of many years, my journal of this period, I wonder how, at my first visit, I ventured to talk to him so freely, and that he bore it with so much indulgence.

Before we parted, he was so good as to promise to favour me with his company one evening at my lodgings; and, as I took my leave, shook me cordially by the hand. It is almost needless to add, that I felt no little elation at having now so happily established an acquaintance of which I had been so long ambitious.

My readers will, I trust, excuse me for being thus minutely circumstantial, when it is considered that the acquaintance of Dr. Johnson was to me a most valuable acquisition, and laid the foundation of whatever instruction and entertainment they may receive from my collections concerning the great subject of the work which they are now perusing.

I did not visit him again till Monday, June 13th, at which time I recollect no part of his conversation, except that when I told him I had been to see Johnson [1] ride upon three horses, he said, "Such a man, Sir, should be encouraged; for his performances show the extent of the human powers in one instance, and thus tend to raise our opinion of the faculties of man. He shows what may be attained by persevering application; so that every man may hope, that by giving as much application, although perhaps he may never ride three horses at a time, or dance upon a wire, yet he may be equally expert in whatever profession he has chosen to pursue."

He again shook me by the hand at parting, and asked me why I did not come oftener to him. Trusting that I was now in his good graces, I answered, that he had not given me much encouragement, and reminded him of the check I had received from him at our first interview. "Poh poh!" said he, with a complacent smile, "never mind these things. Come to me as often as you can. I shall be glad to see you."

I had learnt that his place of frequent resort was the Mitre Tavern in Fleet Street, where he loved to sit up late, and I begged I might be allowed to pass an evening with him there soon, which he promised I should. A few days afterwards I met him near Temple Bar, about one o'clock in the morning, and asked if he would then go to the Mitre. "Sir," said he, "it is too late; they won't let us in. But I'll go with you another night with all my heart."

A revolution of some importance in my plan of life had just taken place; for instead of procuring a commission in the foot-guards, which was my own inclination, I had, in compliance with my father's wishes, agreed to study the law, and was soon to set out for Utrecht, to hear the lectures of an excellent civilian in that University, and then to proceed on my travels. Though very desirous of obtaining Dr. Johnson's advice and instructions on the mode of

---

[1] An Irishman, "an active, clever fellow in his way," who exhibited feats of horsemanship.

pursuing my studies, I was at this time so occupied, shall I call it? or so dissipated, by the amusements of London, that our next meeting was not till Saturday, June 25th, when he agreed to meet me in the evening at the Mitre. I called on him, and we went thither at nine. We had a good supper, and port wine, of which he then sometimes drank a bottle. The orthodox high-church sound of the MITRE,—the figure and manner of the celebrated SAMUEL JOHNSON,—the extraordinary power and precision of his conversation, and the pride arising from finding myself admitted as his companion, produced a variety of sensations, and a pleasing elevation of mind, beyond what I had ever before experienced.

Finding him in a placid humour, and wishing to avail myself of the opportunity, I opened my mind to him ingenuously, and gave him a little sketch of my life, to which he was pleased to listen with great attention.

I acknowledged, that though educated very strictly in the principles of religion, I had for some time been misled into a certain degree of infidelity; but that I was come now to a better way of thinking, and was fully satisfied of the truth of the Christian revelation, though I was not clear as to every point considered to be orthodox. Being at all times a curious examiner of the human mind, and pleased with an undisguised display of what had passed in it, he called to me with warmth, "Give me your hand; I have taken a liking to you."

After having given credit to reports of his bigotry, I was agreeably suprised when he expressed the following very liberal sentiment: "For my part, Sir, I think all Christians, whether Papists or Protestants, agree in the essential articles, and that their differences are trivial, and rather political than religious."

Our conversation proceeded. "Your going abroad, Sir, and breaking off idle habits, may be of great importance to you. I would go where there are courts and learned men. There is a good deal of Spain that has not been perambulated. I would have you go thither. A man of inferior talents to yours may furnish us with useful observations upon that country." His supposing me, at that period of life, capable of writing an account of my travels that would deserve to be read, elated me not a little.

I appeal to every impartial reader whether this faithful detail of his frankness, complacency, and kindness to a young man, a stranger, and a Scotchman, does not refute the unjust opinion of the harshness of his general demeanour.

I complained to him that I had not yet acquired much knowledge, and asked his advice as to my studies. He said, "Don't talk of study now. I will give you a plan; but it will require some time to consider of it." "It is very good in you," I replied, "to allow me to be with you thus. Had it been foretold to me some years ago that I should pass an evening with the author of the 'RAMBLER,' how should I have exulted!" What I then expressed, was sincerely from the heart. He was satisfied that it was, and cordially answered, "Sir, I am glad we have met. I hope we shall pass many evenings, and mornings too, together." We finished a couple of bottles of port, and sat till between one and two in the morning.

As Dr. Oliver Goldsmith will frequently appear in this narrative, I shall endeavour to make my readers in some degree acquainted with his singular character. He was a native of Ireland, and a contemporary with Mr. Burke, at Trinity College, Dublin, but did not then give much promise of future celebrity. He, however, observed that "though he made no great figure in mathematics, which was a study in much repute there, he could turn an Ode of Horace into English better than any of them." He afterwards studied physic at Edinburgh, and upon the continent; and, I have been informed, was enabled to pursue his travels on foot, partly by demanding at Universities to enter the lists as a disputant, by which, according to the custom of many of them, he was entitled to the premium of a crown, when, luckily for him, his challenge was not accepted; so that, as I once observed to Dr. Johnson, he *disputed* his passage through Europe. He then came to England, and was employed successively in the capacities of an usher to an academy, a corrector of the press, a reviewer, and a writer for a newspaper. He had sagacity enough to cultivate assiduously the acquaintance of Johnson, and his faculties were gradually enlarged by the contemplation of such a model. To me and many others it appeared that he studiously copied the manner of Johnson, though, indeed, upon a smaller scale.

At this time I think he had published nothing with his name, though it was pretty generally known that *one Dr. Goldsmith* was the author of "An Inquiry into the Present State of Polite Learning in Europe," and of "The Citizen of the World," a series of letters supposed to be written from London by a Chinese. No man had the art of displaying with more advantage, as a writer, whatever literary acquisitions he made. "*Nihil quod tetigit non ornavit.*" His mind resembled a fertile, but thin soil. There was a quick, but not a strong vegetation, of whatever chanced to be thrown upon it. No deep root could be struck. The oak of the forest did not grow there; but the elegant shrubbery and the fragrant parterre appeared in gay succession. It has been generally circulated and believed that he was a mere fool in conversation; but, in truth, this has been greatly exaggerated. He had, no doubt, a more than common share of that hurry of ideas which we often find in his countrymen, and which sometimes produces a laughable confusion in expressing them. From vanity and an eager desire of being conspicuous wherever he was, he frequently talked carelessly without knowledge of the subject, or even without thought. His person was short, his countenance coarse and vulgar, his deportment that of a scholar awkwardly affecting the easy gentleman. Those who were in any way distinguished, excited envy in him to so ridiculous an excess, that the instances of it are hardly credible. When accompanying two beautiful young ladies with their mother on a tour in France, he was seriously angry that more attention was paid to them than to him; and once, at the exhibition of the *Fantoccini* in London, when those who sat next him observed with what dexterity a puppet was made to toss a pike, he could not bear that it should have such praise, and exclaimed with some warmth, "Pshaw! I can do it better myself."

He, I am afraid, had no settled system of any sort, so that his conduct must not be strictly scrutinised; but his affections were social and generous, and when he had money he gave it away very liberally. His desire of imaginary consequence predominated over his attention to truth. He boasted to me at this time of the power of his pen in commanding money, which I believe was true in a certain degree, though in the instance he gave he was by no means correct. He told me that he had sold a novel for four hundred pounds. This was his "Vicar of Wakefield." But Johnson informed me, that he had made the bargain for Goldsmith, and the price was sixty pounds. "And, Sir," said he, "a sufficient price too, when it was sold; for then the fame of Goldsmith had not been elevated, as it afterwards was, by his 'Traveller'; and the bookseller had such faint hopes of profit by his bargain, that he kept the manuscript by him a long time, and did not publish it till after the 'Traveller' had appeared. Then, to be sure, it was accidentally worth more money."

Mrs. Piozzi and Sir John Hawkins have strangely misstated the history of Goldsmith's situation and Johnson's friendly interference when this novel was sold. I shall give it authentically from Johnson's own exact narration:

"I received one morning a message from poor Goldsmith that he was in great distress, and, as it was not in his power to come to me, begging that I would come to him as soon as possible. I sent him a guinea, and promised to come to him directly. I accordingly went as soon as I was dressed, and found that his landlady had arrested him for his rent, at which he was in a violent passion. I perceived that he had already changed my guinea, and had got a bottle of Madeira and a glass before him. I put the cork into the bottle, desired he would be calm, and began to talk to him of the means by which he might be extricated. He then told me that he had a novel ready for the press, which he produced to me. I looked into it, and saw its merit; told the landlady I should soon return; and, having gone to a bookseller, sold it for sixty pounds. I brought Goldsmith the money, and he discharged his rent, not without rating his landlady in a high tone for having used him so ill."

My next meeting with Johnson was on Friday, the 1st of July, when he and I and Dr. Goldsmith supped at the Mitre. I was before this time pretty well acquainted with Goldsmith. He had increased my admiration of the goodness of Johnson's heart, by incidental remarks in the course of conversation: such as, when I mentioned Mr. Levett, whom he entertained under his roof, "He is poor and honest, which is recommendation enough to Johnson"; and when I wondered that he was very kind to a man of whom I had heard a very bad character, "He is now become miserable, and that insures the protection of Johnson."

Goldsmith attempting this evening to maintain, I suppose from an affectation of paradox, "that knowledge was not desirable on its own account, for it often was a source of unhappiness";— JOHNSON. "Why, Sir, that knowledge may in some cases produce unhappiness, I allow. But, upon the whole, knowledge, *per se*, is certainly an object which every man would wish to attain, although, perhaps, he may not take the trouble necessary for attaining it."

He talked very contemptuously of Churchill's poetry, observing, that "it had a temporary currency, only from his audacity of abuse, and being filled with living names, and that it would sink into oblivion." I ventured to hint that he was not quite a fair judge, as Churchill had attacked him violently. JOHNSON. "Nay, Sir, I am a very fair judge. He did not attack me violently till he found I did not like his poetry; and his attack on me shall not prevent me from continuing to say what I think of him, from an apprehension that it may be ascribed to resentment. No, Sir, I called the fellow a blockhead at first, and I will call him a blockhead still. However, I will acknowledge that I have a better opinion of him now than I once had; for he has shown more fertility than I expected. To be sure, he is a tree that cannot produce good fruit: he only bears crabs. But, Sir, a tree that produces a great many crabs is better than a tree which produces only a few."

Let me here apologise for the imperfect manner in which I am obliged to exhibit Johnson's conversation at this period. In the early part of my acquaintance with him, I was so wrapt in admiration of his extraordinary colloquial talents, and so little accustomed to his peculiar mode of expression, that I found it extremely difficult to recollect and record his conversation with its genuine vigour and vivacity. In progress of time, when, my mind was, as it were, *strongly impregnated with the Johnsonian æther*, I could, with much more facility and exactness, carry in my memory and commit to paper the exuberant variety of his wisdom and wit.

At this time *Miss* Williams, as she was then called, though she did not reside with him in the Temple under his roof, but had lodgings in Bolt-court, Fleet-street, had so much of his attention, that he every night drank tea with her before he went home, however late it might be, and she always sat up for him. This, it may be fairly conjectured, was not alone a proof of his regard for *her;* but of his own unwillingness to go into solitude, before that unseasonable hour at which he had habituated himself to expect the oblivion of repose. Dr. Goldsmith, being a privileged man, went with him this night, strutting away, and calling to me with an air of superiority, "I go to Miss Williams." I confess, I then envied him this mighty privilege, of which he seemed so proud; but it was not long before I obtained the same mark of distinction.

On Tuesday the 5th of July, I again visited Johnson. Talking of London, he observed, "Sir, if you wish to have a just notion of the magnitude of this city, you must not be satisfied with seeing its great streets and squares, but must survey the innumerable little lanes and courts. It is not in the showy evolutions of buildings, but in the multiplicity of human habitations which are crowded together, that the wonderful immensity of London consists."

On Wednesday, July 6, he was engaged to sup with me at my lodgings in Downing-street, Westminster. But on the preceding night my landlord having behaved very rudely to me and some company who were with me, I had resolved not to remain another night in his house. I was exceedingly uneasy at the awkward appearance I supposed I should make to Johnson and the other gentlemen whom I had invited, not being able to receive them at home, and being obliged to order supper at the Mitre. I went to Johnson in the morning, and talked of it as of a serious distress. He laughed, and said, "Consider, Sir, how insignificant this will appear a twelvemonth hence. There is nothing," continued he, "in this mighty misfortune; nay, we shall be better at the Mitre." I told him that I had been informed that, though I had taken my lodgings for a year, I might quit them when I pleased, without being under an obligation to pay rent for any longer time than while I possessed them. The fertility of Johnson's mind could show itself even upon so small a matter as this. "Why, Sir," said he, "I suppose this must be the law, since you have been told so in Bow-street. But, if your landlord could hold you to your bargain, and the lodgings should be yours for a year, you may certainly use them as you think fit. So, Sir, you may quarter two life-guards-men upon him; or you may send the greatest scoundrel you can find into your apartments; or you may say that you want to make some experiments in natural philosophy, and may burn a large quantity of assafœtida in his house."

This evening at the Mitre tavern, Goldsmith, as usual, en-deavoured, with too much eagerness, to *shine*, and disputed very warmly with Johnson against the well-known maxim of the British constitution, "the king can do no wrong"; affirming, that "what was morally false could not be politically true; and as the king might, in the exercise of his regal power, command and cause the doing of what was wrong, it certainly might be said, in sense and in reason, that he could do wrong." JOHNSON. "Sir, you are to consider, that in our constitution, according to its true principles, the king is the head, he is supreme; he is above every thing, and there is no power by which he can be tried. Therefore it is, Sir, that we hold the king can do no wrong; that whatever may happen to be wrong in government may not be above our reach, by being ascribed to Majesty. Redress is always to be had against oppres-sion, by punishing the immediate agents. The king, though he should command, cannot force a judge to condemn a man unjustly;

therefore it is the judge whom we prosecute and punish. Political institutions are formed upon the consideration of what will most frequently tend to the good of the whole, although now and then exceptions may occur. Thus it is better in general that a nation should have a supreme legislative power, although it may at times be abused. And then, Sir, there is this consideration, that *if the abuse be enormous, Nature will rise up; and, claiming her original rights, overturn a corrupt political system.*" I mark this animated sentence with peculiar pleasure, as a noble instance of that truly dignified spirit of freedom which ever glowed in his heart, though he was charged with slavish tenets by superficial observers; because he was at all times indignant against that false patriotism, that pretended love of freedom, that unruly restlessness, which is inconsistent with the stable authority of any good government.

"Great abilities," said he, "are not requisite for an historian; for in historical composition all the greatest powers of the human mind are quiescent. He has facts ready to his hand; so there is no exercise of invention. Imagination is not required in any high degree; only about as much as is used in the lower kinds of poetry. Some penetration, accuracy, and colouring, will fit a man for the task, if he can give the application which is necessary.

"Bayle's Dictionary is a very useful work for those to consult who love the biographical part of literature, which is what I love most."

Mr. Ogilvie was unlucky enough to choose for the topic of his conversation the praises of his native country. He began with saying, that there was very rich land around Edinburgh. Goldsmith, who had studied physic there, contradicted this, very untruly, with a sneering laugh. Disconcerted a little by this, Mr. Ogilvie then took new ground, where, I suppose, he thought himself perfectly safe; for he observed, that Scotland had a great many noble wild prospects. JOHNSON. "I believe, Sir, you have a great many. Norway, too, has noble wild prospects; and Lapland is remarkable for prodigious noble wild prospects. But, Sir, let me tell you, the noblest prospect which a Scotchman ever sees, is the high road that leads him to England!" This unexpected and pointed sally produced a roar of applause.

On Saturday, July 9, I found Johnson surrounded with a numerous levée, but have not preserved any part of his conversation. On the 14th we had another evening by ourselves at the Mitre. It happening to be a very rainy night, I made some common-place observations on the relaxation of nerves and depression of spirits which such weather occasioned; adding, however, that it was good for the vegetable creation. Johnson answered, with a smile of ridicule, "Why, yes, Sir, it is good for vegetables, and for the animals who eat those vegetables, and for the animals who eat those animals." This observation of his aptly enough introduced a good supper; and I soon forgot, in Johnson's company, the influence of a moist atmosphere.

Feeling myself now quite at ease as his companion, though I had all possible reverence for him, I expressed a regret that I could not be so easy with my father, though he was not much older than Johnson, and certainly, however respectable, had not more learning and greater abilities to depress me. I asked him the reason of this. JOHNSON. "Why, Sir, I am a man of the world. I live in the world, and I take, in some degree, the colour of the world as it moves along. Your father is a judge in a remote part of the island, and all his notions are taken from the old world. Besides, Sir, there must always be a struggle between a father and son, while one aims at power, and the other at independence."

Talking of those who denied the truth of Christianity, he said, "It is always easy to be on the negative side. If a man were now to deny that there is salt upon the table, you could not reduce him to an absurdity. Come, let us try this a little further. I deny that Canada is taken, and I can support my denial by pretty good arguments. The French are a much more numerous people than we; and it is not likely that they would allow us to take it. 'But the ministry have assured us, in all the formality of the "Gazette," that it is taken.'—Very true. But the ministry have put us to an enormous expense by the war in America, and it is their interest to persuade us that we have got something for our money.—'But the fact is confirmed by thousands of men who were at the taking of it.'—Ay, but these men have still more interest in deceiving us. They don't want that you should think the French have beat them, but that they have beat the French. Now suppose you should go over and find that it really is taken; that would only satisfy yourself; for when you come home we will not believe you. We will say, you have been bribed.—Yet, Sir, notwithstanding all these plausible objections, we have no doubt that Canada is really ours. Such is the weight of common testimony. How much stronger are the evidences of the Christian religion!

"Idleness is a disease which must be combated; but I would not advise a rigid adherence to a particular plan of study. I myself have never persisted in any plan for two days together. A man ought to read just as inclination leads him; for what he reads as a task will do him little good. A young man should read five hours in the day, and so may acquire a great deal of knowledge."

To such a degree of unrestrained frankness had he now accustomed me, that in the course of this evening I talked of the numerous reflections which had been thrown out against him on account of his having accepted a pension from his present Majesty. "Why, Sir (said he with a hearty laugh), it is a mighty foolish noise that they make. I have accepted of a pension as a reward which has been thought due to my literary merit; and now that I have this pension, I am the same man in every respect that I have ever been; I retain the same principles. It is true, that I cannot now curse (smiling) the house of Hanover; nor would it be decent for me to drink King James's health in the wine that King George gives me money to pay for. But, Sir, I think that the pleasure of cursing the house of Hanover, and drinking King James's health, are amply overbalanced by three hundred pounds a year."

There was here, most certainly, an affectation of more Jacobitism than he really had. Yet there is no doubt that at earlier periods he was wont often to exercise both his pleasantry and ingenuity in talking Jacobitism. One day when dining at old Mr. Langton's, where Miss Roberts, his niece, was one of the company, Johnson, with his usual complacent attention to the fair sex, took her by the hand and said, "My dear, I hope you are a Jacobite." Old Mr. Langton, who though a high and steady Tory, was attached to the present royal family, seemed offended, and asked Johnson with great warmth, what he could mean by putting such a question to his niece? "Why, Sir," said Johnson, "I meant no offence to your niece; I meant her a great compliment. A Jacobite, Sir, believes in the divine right of kings. He that believes in the divine right of kings believes in a Divinity. A Jacobite believes in the divine right of bishops. He that believes in the divine right of bishops, believes in the divine authority of the Christian religion. Therefore, Sir, a Jacobite is neither an atheist nor a deist. That cannot be said of a Whig; for *Whiggism is a negation of all principle.*"

I described to him an impudent fellow from Scotland, who affected to be a savage, and railed at all established systems. JOHNSON. "There is nothing surprising in this, Sir. He wants to make himself conspicuous. He would tumble in a hogsty, as long as you looked at him and called to him to come out. But let him alone, never mind him, and he'll soon give it over."

I added, that the same person maintained that there was no distinction between virtue and vice. JOHNSON. "Why, Sir, if the fellow does not think as he speaks, he is lying; and I see not what honour he can propose to himself from having the character of a liar. But if he does really think that there is no distinction between virtue and vice, why, Sir, when he leaves our houses let us count our spoons."

He recommended to me to keep a journal of my life, full and unreserved. He said it would be a very good exercise, and would yield me great satisfaction when the particulars were faded from my remembrance. I had kept such a journal for some time; and it was no small pleasure to me to have this to tell him, and to receive his approbation. He counselled me to keep it private, and said I might surely have a friend who would burn it in case of my death. From this habit I have been enabled to give the world so many anecdotes, which would otherwise have been lost to posterity. I mentioned that I was afraid I put into my journals too many little incidents. JOHNSON. "There is nothing, Sir, too little for so little a creature as man. It is by studying little things, that we attain the great art of having as little misery and as much happiness as possible."

Next morning Mr. Dempster happened to call on me, and was so much struck even with the imperfect account which I gave him of Dr. Johnson's conversation, that to his honour be it recorded, when I complained that drinking port and sitting up late with him, affected my nerves for some time after, he said, "One had better be palsied at eighteen than not keep company with such a man."

On Tuesday, July 19, Mr. Levett showed me Dr. Johnson's library, which was contained in two garrets over his chambers. I found a number of good books, but very dusty and in great confusion. The floor was strewed with manuscript leaves, in Johnson's own handwriting, which I beheld with a degree of veneration, supposing they perhaps might contain portions of the "Rambler," or of "Rasselas." I observed an apparatus for chemical experiments, of which Johnson was all his life very fond. The place seemed to be very favourable for retirement and meditation. Johnson told me, that he went up thither without mentioning it to his servant when he wanted to study, secure from interruption;

for he would not allow his servant to say he was not at home when he really was. "A servant's strict regard for truth,"said he,"must be weakened by such a practice. A philosopher may know that it is merely a form of denial; but few servants are such nice distinguishers. If I accustom a servant to tell a lie for *me*, have I not reason to apprehend that he will tell many lies for *himself?*"

On Wednesday, July 20, Dr. Johnson supped with me at my new chambers at the bottom of Inner Temple Lane. JOHNSON. "Pity is not natural to man. Children are always cruel. Savages are always cruel. Pity is acquired and improved by the cultivation of reason. We may have uneasy sensations from seeing a creature in distress, without pity; for we have not pity unless we wish to relieve them. When I am on my way to dine with a friend, and finding it late, have bid the coachman make haste, if I happen to attend when he whips his horses, I may feel unpleasantly that the animals are put to pain, but I do not wish him to desist: no, Sir, I wish him to drive on."

Rousseau's treatise on the inequality of mankind was at this time a fashionable topic. It gave rise to an observation that the advantages of fortune and rank were nothing to a wise man, who ought to value only merit. JOHNSON. "If man were a savage, living in the woods by himself, this might be true; but in civilised society we all depend upon each other, and our happiness is very much owing to the good opinion of mankind. Now, Sir, in civilised society, external advantages make us more respected. A man with a good coat upon his back meets with a better reception than he who has a bad one. Sir, you may analyse this, and say, What is there in it? But that will avail you nothing, for it is a part of a general system. Pound St. Paul's church into atoms, and consider any single atom; it is, to be sure, good for nothing: but, put all these atoms together, and you have St. Paul's church. So it is with human felicity, which is made up of many ingredients, each of which may be shown to be very insignificant. In civilised society, personal merit will not serve you so much as money will. Sir, you may make the experiment. Go into the street, and give one man a lecture on morality, and another a shilling, and see which will respect you most. If you wish only to support nature, Sir William Petty fixes your allowance at three pounds a year; but as times are much altered, let us call it six pounds. This sum will fill your belly, shelter you from the weather, and even get you a strong lasting coat, supposing it to be made of good bull's hide. Now, Sir, all beyond this is artificial, and is desired in order to obtain a greater degree of respect from our fellow creatures. And, Sir, if six hundred pounds a year procure a man more consequence, and of course, more happiness, than six pounds a year, the same proportion will hold as to six thousand, and so on, as far as opulence can be carried. Perhaps he who has a large fortune may not be so happy as he who has a small one; but that must proceed from other causes than from his having the large fortune: for, *cæteris paribus*, he who is rich, in civilised society must be happier than he who is poor; as riches, if properly used (and it is a man's own fault if they are not), must be productive of the highest advantages. Money, to be sure, of itself is of no use; for its only use is to part with it. Rousseau, and all those who deal in paradoxes, are led away by a childish desire of novelty. When I was a boy, I used always to choose the wrong side of a debate, because most ingenious things, that is to say, most new things, could be said upon it. Sir, there is nothing for which you may not muster up more plausible arguments, than those which are urged against wealth and other external advantages. Why, now, there is stealing; why should it be thought a crime? When we consider by what unjust methods property has been often acquired, and that what was unjustly got it must be unjust to keep, where is the harm in one man's taking the property of another from him? Besides, Sir, when we consider the bad use that many people make of their property, and how much better use the thief may make of it, it may be defended as a very allowable practice. Yet, Sir, the experience of mankind has discovered stealing to be so very bad a thing, that they make no scruple to hang a man for it. When I was running about this town a very poor fellow, I was a great arguer for the advantages of poverty; but I was, at the same time, very sorry to be poor. Sir, all the arguments which are brought to represent poverty as no evil, show it to be evidently a great evil. You never find people labouring to convince you that you may live very happily upon a plentiful fortune. So you hear people talking how miserable a king must be; and yet they all wish to be in his place."

Mr. Dempster having endeavoured to maintain that intrinsic merit *ought* to make the only distinction amongst mankind. JOHNSON. "Why, Sir, mankind have found that this cannot be. How shall we determine the proportion of intrinsic merit? Were that to be the only distinction amongst mankind, we should soon quarrel about the degrees of it. Were all distinctions abolished, the strongest would not long acquiesce, but would endeavour to obtain a superiority by their bodily strength. But, Sir, as subordination is very necessary for society, and contentions for superiority very dangerous, mankind, that is to say, all civilised nations, have settled it upon a plain invariable principle. A man is born to hereditary rank; or his being appointed to certain offices gives him a certain rank. Subordination tends greatly to human happiness. Were we all upon an equality, we should have no other enjoyment than mere animal pleasure."

I said, I consider distinction of rank to be of so much importance in civilised society, that if I were asked on the same day to dine with the first duke in England, and with the first man in Britain for genius, I should hesitate which to prefer. JOHNSON. "To be sure, Sir, if you were to dine only once, and it were never to be known where you dined, you would choose rather to dine with the first man for genius; but to gain most respect, you should dine with the first duke in England. For nine people in ten that you meet with, would have a higher opinion of you for having dined with a duke; and the great genius himself would receive you better, because you had been with the great duke."

He took care to guide himself against any possible suspicion that his settled principles of reverence for rank, and respect for wealth, were at all owing to mean or interested motives; for he asserted his own independence as a literary man. "No man," said he, "who ever lived by literature, has lived more independently than I have done." He said he had taken longer time than he needed to have done in composing his "Dictionary." He received our compliments upon that great work with complacency, and told us that the Academy *della Crusca* could scarcely believe that it was done by one man.

The next night, Mr. Johnson and I supped in a private room at the Turk's Head coffee-house, in the Strand. "I encourage this house," said he, "for the mistress of it is a good civil woman, and has not much business.

"Sir, I love the acquaintance of young people; because, in the first place, I don't like to think myself growing old, in the next place, young acquaintances must last longest, if they do last; and then, Sir, young men have more virtue than old men; they have more generous sentiments in every respect. I love the young dogs of this age; they have more wit and humour and knowledge of life than we had; but then the dogs are not so good scholars. Sir, in my early years I read very hard. It is a sad reflection, but a true one, that I knew almost as much at eighteen as I do now. My judgment, to be sure, was not so good; but I had all the facts. I remember very well, when I was at Oxford, an old gentleman said to me, 'Young man, ply your book diligently now, and acquire a stock of knowlledge; for when years come unto you, you will find that poring upon books will be but an irksome task.'"

He mentioned it to me now, for the first time, that he had been distressed by melancholy, and for that reason had been obliged to fly from study and meditation, to the dissipating variety of life. Against melancholy he recommended constant occupation of mind, a great deal of exercise, moderation in eating and drinking, and especially to shun drinking at night. He said melancholy people were apt to fly to intemperance for relief, but that it sunk them much deeper in misery. He observed, that labouring men, who work hard, and live sparingly, are seldom or never troubled with low spirits.

He again insisted on the duty of maintaining subordination of rank. "Sir, I would no more deprive a nobleman of his respect, than of his money. I consider myself as acting a part in the great system of society, and I do to others as I would have them to do to me. I would behave to a nobleman as I should expect he would behave to me, were I a nobleman and he Sam. Johnson. Sir, there is one Mrs. Macaulay, in this town, a great republican. One day when I was at her house, I put on a very grave countenance, and said to her, 'Madam, I am now become a convert to your way of thinking. I am convinced that all mankind are upon an equal footing; and to give you an unquestionable proof, Madam, that I am in earnest, here is a very sensible, civil, well-behaved fellow citizen, your footman; I desire that he may be allowed to sit down and dine with us.' I thus, Sir, showed her the absurdity of the levelling doctrine. She has never liked me since. Sir, your levellers wish to level *down* as far as themselves; but they cannot bear levelling *up* to themselves. They would all have some people under them; why not then have some people above them?" I mentioned a certain author who disgusted me by his forwardness, and by showing no deference to noblemen into whose company he was admitted. JOHNSON. "Suppose a shoemaker should claim an equality with him, as he does with a lord: how he would stare! 'Why, Sir, do you stare? (says the shoemaker) I do great service to society. 'Tis true, I am paid for doing it; but so are you, Sir: and, I am sorry to say it, better paid than I am, for doing something not so necessary. For mankind could do better without your books, than without my shoes.' Thus, Sir, there would be a perpetual struggle for precedence, were there no fixed invariable rules for the distinction of rank, which creates no jealousy, as it is allowed to be accidental."

We talked of the Western Islands of Scotland, to visit which he expressed a wish, that then appeared to me a very romantic fancy, which I little thought would be afterwards realised. He said, he would go to the Hebrides with me, when I returned from my travels, unless some very good companion should offer when I was absent, which he did not think probable; adding, "There are few people to whom I take so much as to you." And when I talked of my leaving England, he said with a very affectionate air, "My dear Boswell, I should be very unhappy at parting, did I think we were not to meet again."

He maintained, that a boy at school was the happiest of human beings. I supported a different opinion, from which I have never yet varied, that a man is happier: and I enlarged upon the anxiety and sufferings which are endured at school. JOHNSON. "Ah! Sir, a boy's being flogged is not so severe as a man's having the hiss of the world against him. Men have a solicitude about fame; and the greater share they have of it, the more afraid they are of losing it." I silently asked myself, "Is it possible that the great SAMUEL JOHNSON really entertains any such apprehension, and is not confident that his exalted fame is established upon a foundation never to be shaken?"

On Tuesday, July 26, I found Mr. Johnson alone. We talked of the education of children; and I asked him what he thought was the best to teach them first. JOHNSON. "Sir, it is no matter what you teach them first, any more than what leg you shall put into your breeches first. Sir, you may stand disputing which is best to put in first, but in the mean time your breech is bare. Sir, while you are considering which of two things you should teach your child first, another boy has learnt them both."

On Thursday, July 28, we again supped in private at the Turk's Head coffee-house. I again begged his advice as to my method of study at Utrecht. "Come," said he, "let us make a day of it. Let us go down to Greenwich and dine, and talk of it there." The following Saturday was fixed for this excursion.

As we walked along the Strand to-night, arm in arm, a woman of the town accosted us, in the usual enticing manner. "No, no, my girl," said Johnson, "it won't do." He, however, did not treat her with harshness; and we talked of the wretched life of such women, and agreed, that much more misery than happiness, upon the whole, is produced by illicit commerce between the sexes.

On Saturday, July 30, Dr. Johnson and I took a sculler at the Temple-stairs, and set out for Greenwich. I asked him if he really thought a knowledge of the Greek and Latin languages an essential requisite to a good education. JOHNSON. "Most certainly, Sir; for those who know them have a very great advantage over those who do not. Nay, Sir, it is wonderful what a difference learning makes upon people even in the common intercourse of life, which does not appear to be much connected with it." "And yet," said I, "people go through the world very well, and carry on the business of life to good advantage, without learning." JOHNSON. "Why Sir, that may be true in cases where learning cannot possibly be of any use; for instance, this boy rows us as well without learning as if he could sing the song of Orpheus to the Argonauts, who were the first sailors." He then called to the boy, "What would you give, my lad, to know about the Argonauts?" "Sir," said the boy, "I would give what I have." Johnson was much pleased with his answer, and we gave him a double fare. Dr. Johnson then turning to me, "Sir," said he, "a desire of knowledge is the natural feeling of mankind; and every human being, whose mind is not debauched, will be willing to give all that he has, to get knowledge."

We landed at the Old Swan, and walked to Billingsgate, where we took oars and moved smoothly along the silver Thames. It was a very fine day. We were entertained with the immense number and variety of ships that were lying at anchor, and with the beautiful country on each side of the river.

I talked of preaching, and of the great success which those called methodists have. JOHNSON. "Sir, it is owing to their expressing themselves in a plain and familiar manner, which is the only way to do good to the common people, and which clergymen of genius and learning ought to do from a principle of duty, when it is suited to their congregations; a practice, for which they will be praised by men of sense. To insist against drunkenness as a crime, because it debases reason, the noblest faculty of man, would be of no service to the common people: but to tell them that they may die in a fit of drunkenness, and show them how dreadful that would be, cannot fail to make a deep impression. Sir, when your Scotch clergy give up their homely manner, religion will soon decay in that country."

"WHAT WOULD YOU GIVE, MY LAD, TO KNOW ABOUT THE ARGONAUTS?"

I was much pleased to find myself with Johnson at Greenwich, which he celebrates in his "London" as a favourite scene. I had the poem in my pocket, and read the lines aloud with enthusiasm:

> On Thames's banks in silent thought we stood,
> Where Greenwich smiles upon the silver flood:
> Struck with the seat that gave ELIZA birth,
> We kneel and kiss the consecrated earth.

He remarked that the structure of Greenwich Hospital was too magnificent for a place of charity, and that its parts were too much detached, to make one great whole.

Afterwards he entered upon the business of the day, which was to give me his advice as to a course of study. And here I am to mention, with much regret, that my record of what he said is miserably scanty. I recollect with admiration an animating blaze of eloquence, which roused every intellectual power in me to the highest pitch, but must have dazzled me so much, that my memory could not preserve the substance of his discourse; for the note which I find of it is no more than this: "He ran over the grand scale of human knowledge; advised me to select some particular branch to excel in, but to acquire a little of every kind."

We walked in the evening in Greenwich Park. He asked me, I suppose by way of trying my disposition, "Is not this very fine?" Having no exquisite relish of the beauties of nature, and being more delighted with "the busy hum of men," I answered, "Yes, Sir; but not equal to Fleet-street." JOHNSON. "You are right, Sir."

We staid so long at Greenwich, that our sail up the river, in our return to London, was by no means so pleasant as in the morning; for the night air was so cold that it made me shiver. I was the more sensible of it from having sat up all the night before recollecting and writing in my Journal what I thought worthy of preservation; an exertion, which, during the first part of my acquaintance with Johnson, I frequently made. I remember having sat up four nights in one week, without being much incommoded in the day-time.

Johnson, whose robust frame was not in the least affected by the cold, scolded me, as if my shivering had been a paltry effeminacy, saying, "Why do you shiver?" Sir William Scott told me, that when he complained of a headach in the post-chaise, as they were travelling together, Johnson treated him in the same manner: "At your age, Sir, I had no headach."

We concluded the day at the Turk's Head coffee-house very socially. He was pleased to listen to a particular account which I gave him of my family, and of its hereditary estate, as to the extent and population of which he asked questions, and made calculations; recommending, at the same time, a liberal kindness to the tenantry, as people over whom the proprietor was placed by Providence. He took delight in hearing my description of the romantic seat of my ancestors. "I must be there, Sir," said he, "and we will live in the old castle; and if there is not a room in it remaining, we will build one." I was highly flattered, but could scarcely indulge a hope that Auchinleck would indeed be honoured by his presence, and celebrated by a description, as it afterwards was.

After we had again talked of my setting out for Holland, he said, "I must see thee out of England; I will accompany you to Harwich." I could not find words to express what I felt upon this unexpected and very great mark of his affectionate regard.

Next day, Sunday, July 31, I told him I had been that morning at a meeting of the people called Quakers, where I had heard a woman preach. JOHNSON. "Sir, a woman preaching is like a dog's walking on his hind legs. It is not done well; but you are surprised to find it done at all."

On Tuesday, August 2, (the day of my departure from London having been fixed for the 5th,) Dr. Johnson did me the honour to pass a part of the morning with me at my chambers. He said, that "he always felt an inclination to do nothing." I observed, that it was strange to think that the most indolent man in Britain had written the most laborious work, "The English Dictionary."

I had now made good my title to be a privileged man, and was carried by him in the evening to drink tea with Miss Williams, whom, though under the misfortune of having lost her sight, I found to be agreeable in conversation; for she had a variety of literature, and expressed herself well; but her peculiar value was the intimacy in which she had long lived with Johnson, by which she was well acquainted with his habits, and knew how to lead him on to talk.

After tea he carried me to what he called his walk, which was a long narrow paved court in the neighbourhood, over-shadowed by some trees. There we sauntered a considerable time; and I complained to him that my love of London and of his company was such, that I shrunk almost from the thought of going away even to travel, which is generally so much desired by young men. He roused me by manly and spirited conversation. He advised me, when settled in any place abroad, to study with an eagerness after knowledge, and to apply to Greek an hour every day; and when I was moving about, to read diligently the great book of mankind. On Wednesday, August 3, we had our last social evening at the Turk's Head coffee-house, before my setting out for foreign parts. I had the misfortune, before we parted, to irritate him unintentionally. I mentioned to him how common it was in the world to tell absurd stories of him, and to ascribe to him very strange sayings. JOHNSON. "What do they make me say, Sir?" BOSWELL. "Why, Sir, as an instance very strange indeed, (laughing heartily as I spoke,) David Hume told me, you said that you would stand before a battery of cannon to restore the Convocation to its full powers." Little did I apprehend that he had actually said this: but I was soon convinced of my error; for, with a determined look, he thundered out, "And would I not, Sir? Shall the Presbyterian *kirk* of Scotland have its General Assembly, and the Church of England be denied its Convocation?" He was walking up and down the room, while I told him the anecdote; but when he uttered this explosion of high-church zeal, he had come close to my chair, and his eyes flashed with indignation. I bowed to the storm, and diverted the force of it, by leading him to expatiate on the influence which religion derived from maintaining the church with great external respectability.

On Friday, August 5, we set out early in the morning in the Harwich stage-coach. A fat elderly gentlewoman, and a young Dutchman, seemed the most inclined among us to conversation. At the inn where we dined, the gentlewoman said that she had done her best to educate her children; and particularly, that she had never suffered them to be a moment idle. JOHNSON. "I wish, Madam, you would educate me too: for I have been an idle fellow all my life." "I am, sure, Sir," said she, "you have not been idle." JOHNSON. "Nay, Madam, it is very true; and that gentleman there," pointing to me, "has been idle. He was idle at Edinburgh. His father sent him to Glasgow, where he continued to be idle. He then came to London, where he has been very idle; and now he is going to Utrecht, where he will be as idle as ever." I asked him privately how he could expose me so. JOHNSON. "Poh, poh!" said he, "they know nothing about you, and will think of it no more." In the afternoon the gentlewoman talked violently against the Roman Catholics, and of the horrors of the Inquisition. To the utter astonishment of all the passengers but myself, who knew that he could talk upon any side of a question, he defended the Inquisition, and maintained, that "false doctrine should be checked on its first appearance; that the civil power should unite with the church in punishing those who dare to attack the established religion, and that such only were punished by the Inquisition." He had in his pocket "*Pomponius Mela de Situ Orbis*," in which he read occasionally, and seemed very intent upon ancient geography. Though by no means niggardly, his attention to what was generally right was so minute, that having observed at one of the stages that I ostentatiously gave a shilling to the coachman, when the custom was for each passenger to give only sixpence, he took me aside and scolded me, saying that what I had done would make the coachman dissatisfied with all the rest of the passengers, who gave him no more than his due.

Having stopped a night at Colchester, Johnson talked of that town with veneration, for having stood a siege for Charles I. At supper this night he talked of good eating with uncommon satisfaction. "Some people," said he, "have a foolish way of not minding, or pretending not to mind, what they eat. For my part, I mind my belly very studiously, and very carefully; for I look upon it, that he who does not mind his belly will hardly mind anything else." He now appeared to me *Jean Bull philosophe*, and he was for the moment, not only serious, but vehement. Yet I have heard him, upon other occasions, talk with great contempt of people who were anxious to gratify their palates; and the 206th number of his "Rambler" is a masterly essay against gulosity. His practice, indeed, I must acknowledge, may be considered as casting the balance of his different opinions upon this subject; for I never knew any man who relished good eating more than he did. When at table, he was totally absorbed in the business of the moment: his looks seemed rivetted to his plate; nor would he, unless when in very high company, say one word, or even pay the least attention to what was said by others, till he had satisfied his appetite; which was so fierce, and indulged with such intenseness, that while in the act of eating, the veins of his forehead swelled, and generally a strong perspiration was visible. To those whose sensations were delicate, this could not but be disgusting; and it was doubtless not very suitable to the character of a philosopher, who should be distinguished by self-command. But it must be owned, that Johnson, though he could be rigidly *abstemious*, was not a *temperate* man either in eating or drinking. He could refrain, but he could not use moderately. He told me, that he had fasted two days without inconvenience, and that he had never been hungry but once. They who beheld with wonder how much he ate upon all occasions, when his dinner was to his taste, could not easily conceive what he must have meant by hunger; and not only was he remarkable for the extraordinary quantity which he ate, but he was, or affected to be, a man of very nice discernment in the science of cookery. He used to descant critically on the dishes which had been at table where he had dined or supped, and to recollect very minutely what he had liked. I remember when he was in Scotland, his praising *Gordon's palates* (a dish of palates at the Honourable Alexander Gordon's) with a warmth of expression which might have done honour to more important subjects. "As for Maclaurin's imitation of a *made dish*, it was a wretched attempt." He about the same time was so much displeased with the performances of a nobleman's French cook, that he exclaimed with vehemence, "I'd throw such a rascal into the river"; and he then proceeded to alarm a lady at whose house he was to sup, by the following manifesto of his skill: "I, Madam, who live at a variety of good tables, am a much better judge of cookery than any person who has a very tolerable cook, but lives much at home; for his palate is gradually adapted to the taste of his cook; whereas, Madam, in trying by a wider range, I can more exquisitely judge." When invited to dine, even with an intimate friend, he was not pleased if something better than a plain dinner was not prepared for him. I have heard him say on such an occasion, "This was a good dinner enough, to be sure; but it was not a dinner to *ask* a man to." On the other hand, he was wont to express, with great glee, his satisfaction when he had been entertained quite to his mind. One day when he had dined with his neighbour and landlord in Bolt Court, Mr. Allen, the printer, whose old housekeeper had studied his taste in every thing, he pronounced this eulogy: "Sir, we could not have had a better dinner, had there been a *Synod of Cooks*."

While we were left by ourselves, I teased him with fanciful apprehensions of unhappiness. A moth having fluttered round the candle, and burnt itself, he laid hold of this little incident to admonish me; saying, with a sly look, and in a solemn but a quiet tone, "That creature was its own tormentor, and I believe its name was BOSWELL."

Next day we got to Harwich to dinner; and my passage in the packet boat to Helvoetsluys being secured, and my baggage put on board, we dined at our inn by ourselves. I happened to say, it would be terrible if he should not find a speedy opportunity of returning to London, and be confined in so dull a place. JOHNSON. "Don't, Sir, accustom yourself to use big words for little matters. It would *not* be *terrible* though I *were* to be detained some time here."

We went and looked at the church, and having gone into it and walked up to the altar, Johnson, whose piety was constant and fervent, sent me to my knees, saying, "Now that you are going to leave your native country, recommend yourself to the protection of your CREATOR and REDEEMER."

After we came out of the church, we stood talking for some time together of Bishop Berkeley's ingenious sophistry to prove the non-existence of matter, and that every thing in the universe is merely ideal. I observed, that though we are satisfied his doctrine is not true, it is impossible to refute it. I never shall forget the alacrity with which Johnson answered, striking his foot with mighty force against a large stone, till he rebounded from it, "I refute it *thus*."

My revered friend walked down with me to the beach, where we embraced and parted with tenderness, and engaged to correspond by letters. I said, "I hope, Sir, you will not forget me, in my absence." JOHNSON. "Nay, Sir, it is more likely you should forget me, than that I should forget you." As the vessel put out to sea, I kept my eyes upon him for a considerable time, while he remained rolling his majestic frame in his usual manner; and at last I perceived him walk back into the town, and he disappeared.

Early in 1764, Johnson paid a visit to the Langton family, at their seat of Langton in Lincolnshire, where he passed some time much to his satisfaction.

Soon after his return to London, which was in February, was founded that CLUB which existed long without a name, but at Mr. Garrick's funeral became distinguished by the title of THE LITERARY CLUB. Sir Joshua Reynolds had the merit of being the first proposer of it; to which Johnson acceded, and the original members were, Sir Joshua Reynolds, Dr. Johnson, Mr. Edmund Burke, Dr. Nugent, Mr. Beauclerk, Mr. Langton, Dr. Goldsmith, Mr. Chamier, and Sir John Hawkins. They met at the Turk's

WE . . . PARTED WITH TENDERNESS

Head, in Gerrard Street, Soho, one evening in every week, at seven, and generally continued their conversation till a pretty late hour. This club has been gradually increased to its present [1791] number, thirty-five. After about ten years, instead of supping weekly, it was resolved to dine together once a fortnight during the meeting of Parliament. Their original tavern having been converted into a private house, they moved first to Prince's in Sackville Street, then to Le Telier's in Dover Street, and now meet at Parsloe's, St. James's Street.

Not very long after the institution of our club, Sir Joshua Reynolds was speaking of it to Garrick. "I like it much," said he; "I think I shall be of you." When Sir Joshua mentioned this to Dr. Johnson, he was much displeased with the actor's conceit. *"He'll be of us,"* said Johnson, "how does he know we will *permit* him? the first duke in England has no right to hold such language." However, when Garrick was regularly proposed some time afterwards, Johnson, though he had taken a momentary offence at his arrogance, warmly and kindly supported him, and he was accordingly elected.

In this year, except what he may have done in revising Shakspeare, we do not find that Johnson laboured much in literature. The ease and independence to which he had at last attained by royal munificence, increased his natural indolence. In his " Meditations," he thus accuses himself:

Good Friday, April 20, 1764.—I have made no reformation; I have lived totally useless, more sensual in thought, and more addicted to wine and meat.

He then solemnly says, "This is not the life to which heaven is promised"; and he earnestly resolves an amendment.

It was his custom to observe certain days with a pious abstraction: viz., New Year's Day, the day of his wife's death, Good Friday, Easter Day, and his own birthday. He this year says,

I have now spent fifty-five years in resolving; having, from the earliest time almost that I can remember, been forming schemes of a better life. I have done nothing. The need of doing, therefore, is pressing, since the time of doing is short. O God, grant me to resolve aright, and to keep my resolutions, for Jesus Christ's sake. Amen.

Such a tenderness of conscience, such a fervent desire of improvement, will rarely be found.

About this time he was afflicted with a very severe return of the hypochondriac disorder, which was ever lurking about him. He was so ill, as, notwithstanding his remarkable love of company, to be entirely averse to society, the most fatal symptom of that malady. Dr. Adams told me, that, as an old friend, he was admitted to visit him, and that he found him in a deplorable state, sighing, groaning, talking to himself, and restlessly walking from room to room. He then used this emphatical expression of the misery which he felt: "I would consent to have a limb amputated to recover my spirits."

Talking to himself was, indeed, one of his singularities ever since I knew him. I was certain that he was frequently uttering pious ejaculations; for fragments of the Lord's Prayer have been distinctly overheard. He had another particularity, of which none of his friends ever ventured to ask an explanation. It appeared to me some superstitious habit, which he had contracted early, and from which he had never called upon his reason to disentangle him. This was his anxious care to go out or in at a door or passage, by a certain number of steps from a certain point, or at least so as that either his right or his left foot (I am not certain which) should constantly make the first actual movement when he came close to the door or passage. Thus I conjecture: for I have, upon innumerable occasions, observed him suddenly stop, and then seem to count his steps with a deep earnestness; and when he had neglected or gone wrong in this sort of magical movement, I have seen him go back again, put himself in a proper posture to begin the ceremony, and, having gone through it, break from his abstraction, walk briskly on, and join his companion.[1]

That the most minute singularities which belonged to him, and made very observable parts of his appearance and manner, may not be omitted, it is requisite to mention, that, while talking, or even musing as he sat in his chair, he commonly held his head to one side towards his right shoulder, and shook it in a tremulous manner, moving his body backwards and forwards, and rubbing

---

[1] "Mr. Sheridan," says Mr. Whyte, "at one time lived in Bedford Street, opposite Henrietta Street, which ranges with the south side of Covent Garden, so that the prospect lies open the whole way, free of interruption. We were standing together at the drawing-room window, expecting Johnson, who was to dine there. Mr. Sheridan asked me, could I see the length of the Garden? 'No, Sir.' [Mr. Whyte was short-sighted.] 'Take out your opera-glass, Johnson is coming; you may know him by his gait.' I perceived him at a good distance, working along with a peculiar solemnity of deportment, and an awkward sort of measured step. At that time the broad flagging at each side the streets was not universally adopted, and stone posts were in fashion, to prevent the annoyance of carriages. Upon every post, as he passed along, I could observe, he deliberately laid his hand; but missing one of them when he had got at some distance, he seemed suddenly to recollect himself, and immediately returning back, carefully performed the accustomed ceremony, and resumed his former course, not omitting one till he gained the crossing. This, Mr. Sheridan assured me, however odd it might appear, was his constant practice; but why or wherefore he could not inform me."—Whyte, *Miscellanea Nova*.

his left knee in the same direction, with the palm of his hand. In the intervals of articulating he made various sounds with his mouth, sometimes as if ruminating, or what is called chewing the cud, sometimes giving a half-whistle, sometimes making his tongue play backwards from the roof of his mouth, as if clucking like a hen, and sometimes protruding it against his upper gums in front, as if pronouncing quickly, under his breath, *too, too, too;* all this accompanied sometimes with a thoughtful look, but more frequently with a smile. Generally, when he had concluded a period, in the course of a dispute, by which time he was a good deal exhausted by violence and vociferation, he used to blow out his breath like a whale. This, I suppose, was a relief to his lungs; and seemed in him to be a contemptuous mode of expression, as if he had made the arguments of his opponent fly like chaff before the wind.

Early in the year 1765 he paid a short visit to the University of Cambridge, with his friend Mr. Beauclerk. There is a lively picturesque account of his behaviour on this visit in an extract of a letter. "He drank his large potations of tea with me, interrupted by many an indignant contradiction, and many a noble sentiment." —"Several persons got into his company the last evening at Trinity, where, about twelve, he began to be very great; stripped poor Mrs. Macaulay to the very skin, then gave her for his toast, and drank her in two bumpers."

The strictness of his self-examination, and scrupulous Christian humility, appear in his pious meditation on Easter-day this year.

"Since the last Easter I have reformed no evil habit; my time has been unprofitably spent, and seems as a dream that has left nothing behind. *My memory grows confused, and I know not how the days pass over me.* Good Lord, deliver me!"

Trinity College, Dublin, at this time surprised Johnson with a spontaneous compliment of the highest academical honours, by creating him Doctor of Laws. This unsolicited mark of distinction did much honour to the judgment and liberal spirit of that learned body.

This year was distinguished by his being introduced into the family of Mr. Thrale, one of the most eminent brewers in England, and member of Parliament for the borough of Southwark. Foreigners are not a little amazed when they hear of brewers, distillers, and men in similar departments of trade, held forth as persons of considerable consequence. In this great commercial country it is natural that a situation which produces much wealth should be considered as very respectable; and, no doubt, honest industry is entitled to esteem. But, perhaps, the too rapid advance of men of low extraction tends to lessen the value of that distinction by birth and gentility, which has ever been found beneficial to the grand scheme of subordination.

Johnson used to give this account of the rise of Mr. Thrale's father: "He worked at six shillings a week for twenty years in the great brewery, which afterwards was his own. The proprietor of it had an only daughter, who was married to a nobleman. It was not fit that a peer should continue the business. On the old man's death, therefore, the brewery was to be sold. To find a purchaser for so large a property was a difficult matter; and, after some time, it was suggested, that it would be advisable to treat with Thrale, a sensible, active, honest man, who had been employed in the house, and to transfer the whole to him for thirty thousand pounds, security being taken upon the property. This was accordingly settled. In eleven years Thrale paid the purchase money. He acquired a large fortune, and lived to be a member of parliament for Southwark. But what was most remarkable was the liberality with which he used his riches. He gave his son and daughters the best education.

The son, though in affluent circumstances, had good sense enough to carry on his father's trade, which was of such extent, that I remember he once told me, he would not quit it for an annuity of ten thousand a year. Having left daughters only, the property was sold for the immense sum of one hundred and thirty-five thousand pounds: a magnificent proof of what may be done by fair trade in a long period of time.

Mr. Thrale had married Miss Hesther Lynch Salusbury, of good Welsh extraction, a lady of lively talents, improved by education. Johnson accepted of an invitation to dinner at Thrale's, and was so much pleased with his reception, both by Mr. and Mrs. Thrale, and they so much pleased with him, that his invitations to their house were more and more frequent, till at last he became one of the family, and an apartment was appropriated to him, both in their house at Southwark and in their villa at Streatham.

Johnson had a very sincere esteem for Mr. Thrale. "I know no man," said he, "who is more master of his wife and family than Thrale. If he but holds up a finger, he is obeyed. It is a great mistake to suppose that she is above him in literary attainments.

She is more flippant; but he has ten times her learning: he is a regular scholar; but her learning is that of a schoolboy in one of the lower forms." Mr. Thrale was tall, well proportioned, and stately. As for *Madam*, or *my Mistress*, by which epithets Johnson used to mention Mrs. Thrale, she was short, plump, and brisk. She has herself given us a lively view of the idea which Johnson had of her person, on her appearing before him in a dark-coloured gown: "You little creatures should never wear those sort of clothes, however; they are unsuitable in every way. What! have not all insects gay colours?"

Nothing could be more fortunate for Johnson than this connection. He had at Mr. Thrale's all the comforts and even luxuries of life; his melancholy was diverted, and his irregular habits lessened, by association with an agreeable and well-ordered family. He was treated with the utmost respect, and even affection. The vivacity of Mrs. Thrale's literary talk roused him to cheerfulness and exertion, even when they were alone. But this was not often the case; for he found here a constant succession of what gave him the highest enjoyment, the society of the learned, the witty, and the eminent in every way; who were assembled in numerous companies, called forth his wonderful powers, and gratified him with admiration, to which no man could be insensible.

In the October of this year he at length gave to the world his edition of "Shakspeare." In his Preface Johnson treated Voltaire very contemptuously, observing, upon some of his remarks, "These are the petty cavils of petty minds." Voltaire, in revenge, made an attack upon Johnson. Voltaire was an antagonist with whom I thought Johnson should not disdain to contend. I pressed him to answer. He said, he perhaps might; but he never did.

Both in 1764 and 1765 it should seem that he was so busily employed with his edition of Shakspeare, as to have had little leisure for any other literary exertion, or, indeed, even for private correspondence. He did not favour me with a single letter for more than two years. Notwithstanding his long silence, I never omitted to write to him, when I had any thing worthy of communicating. I generally kept copies of my letters to him, that I might have a full view of our correspondence, and never be at a loss to understand any reference in his letters. He kept the greater part of mine very carefully; and a short time before his death was attentive enough to seal them up in bundles, and ordered them to be delivered to me. Amongst them I found one, which I own I read with pleasure at the distance of almost twenty years. It is dated November, 1765, at the palace of Pascal Paoli, in Corte, the capital of Corsica, and is full of generous enthusiasm. After giving a sketch of what I had seen and heard in that island, it proceeded thus: "I dare to call this a spirited tour. I dare to challenge your approbation."

This letter produced the following answer, which I found on my arrival at Paris.

A. M. M. BOSWELL

Chez M. Waters, Banquier, à Paris

Johnson's Court, Fleet Street, Jan. 14, 1766

DEAR SIR,

Apologies are seldom of any use. We will delay till your arrival the reasons, good or bad, which have made me such a sparing and ungrateful correspondent. Be assured, for the present, that nothing has lessened either the esteem or love with which I dismissed you at Harwich. Both have been increased by all that I have been told of you by yourself or others; and when you return, you will return to an unaltered, and, I hope, unalterable friend.

All that you have to fear from me is the vexation of disappointing me. No man loves to frustrate expectations which have been formed in his favour; and the pleasure which I promise myself from your journals and remarks is so great, that perhaps no degree of attention or discernment will be sufficient to afford it.

Come home, however, and take your chance. I long to see you, and to hear you; and hope that we shall not be so long separated again. Come home, and expect such welcome as is due to him, whom a wise and noble curiosity has led, where perhaps no native of this country ever was before.

I have no news to tell you that can deserve your notice; nor would I willingly lessen the pleasure that any novelty may give you at your return. I am afraid we shall find it difficult to keep among us a mind which has been so long feasted with variety. But let us try what esteem and kindness can effect.

As your father's liberality has indulged you with so long a ramble, I doubt not but you will think his sickness, or even his desire to see you, a sufficient reason for hastening your return. The longer we live, and the more we think, the higher value we learn to put on the friendship and tenderness of parents and of friends. Parents we can have but once; and he promises himself too much, who enters life with the expectation of finding many friends. Upon some motive, I hope, that you will be here soon; and am willing to think that it will be an inducement to your return, that it is sincerely desired by, dear Sir, your affectionate humble servant,   SAM. JOHNSON

I returned to London in February, and found Dr. Johnson in a good house in Johnson's Court, Fleet Street, in which he had accommodated Miss Williams with an apartment on the ground floor, while Mr. Levett occupied his post in the garret: his faithful Francis was still attending upon him. He received me with much kindness. The fragments of our first conversation, which I have preserved, are these: I told him that Voltaire, in a conversation with me, had distinguished Pope and Dryden thus: "Pope drives a handsome chariot, with a couple of neat, trim nags; Dryden a coach, and six stately horses." JOHNSON. "Why, Sir, the truth is, they both drive coaches and six; but Dryden's horses are either galloping or stumbling; Pope's go at a steady even trot." He said of Goldsmith's "Traveller," which had been published in my absence, "There has not been so fine a poem since Pope's time."

Talking of education, "People have now-a-days," said he, "got a strange opinion that everything should be taught by lectures. Now, I cannot see that lectures can do so much good as reading the books from which the lectures are taken. I know nothing that can be best taught by lectures, except where experiments are to be shown. You may teach chymistry by lectures: you might teach making of shoes by lectures!"

At night I supped with him at the Mitre tavern, that we might renew our social intimacy at the original place of meeting. But there was now a considerable difference in his way of living. Having had an illness, in which he was advised to leave off wine, he had, from that period, continued to abstain from it, and drank only water, or lemonade.

Dr. Johnson was very kind this evening, and said to me, "You have now lived five-and-twenty years, and you have employed them well." "Alas, Sir," said I, "I fear not. Do I know history? Do I know mathematics? Do I know law?" JOHNSON. "Why, Sir, though you may know no science so well as to be able to teach it, and no profession so well as to be able to follow it, your general mass of knowledge of books and men renders you very capable to make yourself master of any science, or fit yourself for any profession."

I talked of the mode adopted by some to rise in the world, by courting great men, and asked him whether he had ever submitted to it. JOHNSON. "Why, Sir, I never was near enough to great men, to court them. You may be prudently attached to great men, and yet independent. You are not to do what you think wrong; and, Sir, you are to calculate, and not pay too dear for what you get. You must not give a shilling's worth of court for sixpence worth of good. But if you can get a shilling's worth of good for sixpence worth of court, you are a fool if you do not pay court."

Our next meeting at the Mitre was on Saturday the 15th of February. I having mentioned that I had passed some time with Rousseau in his wild retreat, and having quoted some remark made by Mr. Wilkes, with whom I had spent many pleasant hours in Italy, Johnson said, sarcastically, "It seems, Sir, you have kept very good company abroad,—Rousseau and Wilkes!" Thinking it enough to defend one at a time, I answered with a smile, "My dear Sir, you don't call Rousseau bad company. Do you really think *him* a bad man?" JOHNSON. "Sir, if you are talking jestingly of this, I don't talk with you. If you mean to be serious, I think him one of the worst of men; a rascal, who ought to be hunted out of society, as he has been. Three or four nations have expelled him: and it is a shame that he is protected in this country." BOSWELL. "I don't deny, Sir, but that his novel may, perhaps, do harm; but I cannot think his intention was bad." JOHNSON. "Sir, that will not do. We cannot prove any man's intention to be bad. You may shoot a man through the head, and say you intended to miss him; but the judge will order you to be hanged. An alleged want. of intention, when evil is committed, will not be allowed in a court of justice. Rousseau, Sir, is a very bad man. I would sooner sign a sentence for his transportation, than that of any felon who has gone from the Old Bailey these many years. Yes, I should like to have him work in the plantations." BOSWELL. "Sir, do you think him as bad a man as Voltaire?" JOHNSON. "Why, Sir, it is difficult to settle the proportion of iniquity between them."

On his favourite subject of subordination, Johnson said, "So far is it from being true that men are naturally equal, that no two people can be half an hour together, but one shall acquire an evident superiority over the other."

I mentioned the advice given us by philosophers to console ourselves, when distressed or embarrassed, by thinking of those who are in a worse situation than ourselves. This, I observed, could not apply to all, for there must be some who have nobody worse than they are. JOHNSON. "Why, to be sure, Sir, there are; but they don't know it. There is no being so poor and so contemptible, who does not think there is somebody still poorer, and still more contemptible."

One evening, when a young gentleman teased him with an account of the infidelity of his servant, who, he said, would not believe the scriptures, because he could not read them in the original tongues, and be sure that they were not invented, "Why, foolish fellow," said Johnson, "has he any better authority for almost every thing that he believes?" BOSWELL. "Then the vulgar, Sir, never can know they are right, but must submit themselves to the learned." JOHNSON. "To be sure, Sir. The vulgar are the children of the State, and must be taught like children." BOSWELL. "Then Sir, a poor Turk must be a Mahometan, just as a poor Englishman must be a Christian?" JOHNSON. "Why, yes, Sir; and what then? This, now, is such stuff as I used to talk to my mother, when I began to think myself a clever fellow; and she ought to have whipt me for it."

Another evening Dr. Goldsmith and I called on him, with the hope of prevailing on him to sup with us at the Mitre. We found him indisposed, and resolved not to go abroad. "Come, then," said Goldsmith, "we will not go to the Mitre to-night, since we cannot have the big man with us." Johnson then called for a bottle of port, of which Goldsmith and I partook, while our friend, now a water-drinker, sat by us. GOLDSMITH. "I think, Mr. Johnson, you don't go near the theatres now. You give yourself no more concern about a new play, than if you had never had anything to do with the stage." JOHNSON. "Why, Sir, our tastes greatly alter. The lad does not care for the child's rattle, and the old man does not care for the young man's whore." GOLDSMITH. "Nay, Sir; but your Muse was not a whore." JOHNSON. "Sir, I do not think she was. But as we advance in the journey of life we drop some of the things which have pleased us; whether it be that we are fatigued, and don't choose to carry so many things any farther, or that we find other things which we like better." BOSWELL. "But, Sir, why don't you give us something in some other way?" GOLD-SMITH. "Ay, Sir, we have a claim upon you." JOHNSON. "No, Sir, I am not obliged to do any more. No man is obliged to do as much as he can do. A man is to have part of his life to himself. If a soldier has fought a good many campaigns, he is not to be blamed if he retires to ease and tranquillity. A physician, who has practised long in a great city, may be excused if he retires to a small town, and takes less practice. Now, Sir, the good I can do by my conversation bears the same proportion to the good I can do by my writings, that the practice of a physician, retired to a small town, does to his practice in a great city." BOSWELL. "But I wonder, Sir, you have not more pleasure in writing than in not writing." JOHNSON. "Sir, you *may* wonder."

Such specimens of the easy and playful conversation of the great Dr. Samuel Johnson are, I think, to be prized; as exhibiting the little varieties of a mind so enlarged and so powerful when objects of consequence required its exertions, and as giving us a minute knowledge of his character and modes of thinking.

After I had been some time in Scotland, I complained of irresolution, and mentioned my having made a vow as a security for good conduct. I wrote to him again without being able to move his indolence: nor did I hear from him till he had received a copy of my inaugural Exercise, or Thesis in Civil Law, which I published at my admission as an Advocate, as is the custom in Scotland.

In February, 1767, there happened one of the most remarkable incidents of Johnson's life, which gratified his monarchical enthusiasm, and which he loved to relate with all its circumstances, when requested by his friends. This was his being honoured by a private conversation with his Majesty, in the library at the Queen's house. He had frequently visited those splendid rooms and noble collection of books, which he used to say was more numerous and curious than he supposed any person could have made in the time which the King had employed. Mr. Barnard, the librarian, took care that he should have every accommodation that could contribute to his ease and convenience, while indulging his literary taste in that place; so that he had here a very agreeable resource at leisure hours.

His Majesty having been informed of his occasional visits, was pleased to signify a desire that he should be told when Dr. Johnson came next to the library. Accordingly, the next time that Johnson did come, as soon as he was fairly engaged with a book, on which, while he sat by the fire, he seemed quite intent, Mr. Barnard stole round to the apartment where the King was, and in obedience to his Majesty's commands, mentioned that Dr. Johnson was then in the library. His Majesty said he was at leisure, and would go to him; upon which Mr. Barnard took one of the candles that stood

GEORGE III. IN THE ROYAL LIBRARY

upon the King's table, and lighted his Majesty through a suite of rooms, till they came to a private door into the library, of which his Majesty had the key. Being entered, Mr. Barnard stepped forward hastily to Dr. Johnson, who was still in a profound study, and whispered him, "Sir, here is the King." Johnson started up, and stood still. His Majesty approached him, and at once was courteously easy.

His Majesty began by observing, that he understood he came sometimes to the library; and then mentioning his having heard that the Doctor had been lately at Oxford, asked him if he was not fond of going thither. To which Johnson answered, that he was indeed fond of going to Oxford sometimes, but was likewise glad to come back again. The King then asked him what they were doing at Oxford. Johnson answered, he could not much commend their diligence, but that in some respects they were mended, for they had put their press under better regulations, and were at that time printing Polybius. He was then asked whether there were better libraries at Oxford or Cambridge. He answered, he believed the Bodleian was larger than any they had at Cambridge; at the same time adding, "I hope, whether we have more books or not than they have at Cambridge, we shall make as good use of them as they do."

His Majesty inquired if he was then writing any thing. He answered, he was not, for he had pretty well told the world what he knew, and must now read to acquire more knowledge. The King, as it should seem with a view to urge him to rely on his own stores as an original writer, and to continue his labours, then said, "I do not think you borrow much from any body." Johnson said, he thought he had already done his part as a writer. "I should have thought so too," said the King, "if you had not written so well." Johnson observed to me, upon this, that "No man could have paid a handsomer compliment; and it was fit for a King to pay. It was decisive." When asked by another friend, at Sir Joshua Reynolds's, whether he made any reply to this high compliment, he answered, "No, Sir. When the King had said it, it was to be so. It was not for me to bandy civilities with my Sovereign."

His Majesty having observed to him that he supposed he must have read a good deal; Johnson answered, that he thought more than he read; that he had read a great deal in the early part of his life, but having fallen into ill health, he had not been able to read much, compared with others: for instance, he said he had not read much, compared with Dr. Warburton. Upon which the King said, that he heard Dr. Warburton was a man of such general knowledge, that you could scarce talk with him on any subject on which he was not qualified to speak; and that his learning resembled Garrick's acting, in its universality. His Majesty then talked of the controversy between Warburton and Lowth, which he seemed to have read, and asked Johnson what he thought of it. Johnson answered, "Warburton has most general, most scholastic learning; Lowth is the more correct scholar. I do not know which of them calls names best." The King was pleased to say he was of the same opinion, adding, "You do not think then, Dr. Johnson, that there was much argument in the case." Johnson said, he did not think there was. "Why, truly," said the King, "when once it comes to calling names, argument is pretty well at an end."

During the whole of this interview, Johnson talked to his Majesty with profound respect, but still in his firm manly manner, with a sonorous voice, and never in that subdued tone which is commonly used at the levée and in the drawing-room. After the King withdrew, Johnson showed himself highly pleased with his Majesty's conversation, and gracious behaviour. He said to Mr. Barnard, "Sir, they may talk of the King as they will; but he is the finest gentleman I have ever seen."

At Sir Joshua Reynolds's, where a circle of Johnson's friends was collected round him to hear his account of this memorable conversation, Dr. Joseph Warton, in his frank and lively manner, was very active in pressing him to mention the particulars. "Come now, Sir, this is an interesting matter; do favour us with it." Johnson, with great good-humour, complied. During all the time in which Dr. Johnson was employed in relating what passed between the King and him, Dr. Goldsmith remained unmoved upon a sofa at some distance, affecting not to join in the least in the eager curiosity of the company. He assigned as a reason for his gloom and seeming inattention, that he apprehended Johnson had relinquished his purpose of furnishing him with a Prologue to his play, with the hopes of which he had been flattered; but it was strongly suspected that he was fretting with chagrin and envy at the singular honour Dr. Johnson had lately enjoyed. At length, the frankness and simplicity of his natural character prevailed. He sprung from the sofa, advanced to Johnson, and in a kind of flutter, from imagining himself in the situation which he had just been hearing described, exclaimed, "Well, you acquitted yourself in this conversation better than I should have done; for I should have bowed and stammered through the whole of it."

It appears from his notes of the state of his mind, that Johnson suffered great perturbation and distraction in 1768. Nothing of his writings was given to the public this year, except the Prologue to Goldsmith's comedy of "The Good-natured Man."

In the spring of this year, having published my "Account of Corsica,[1] with the Journal of a Tour to that Island," I returned to London, very desirous to see Dr. Johnson, and hear him upon the subject. I found he was at Oxford, with his friend Mr. Chambers. I was impatient to be with him, and therefore followed him. I found he had sent a letter to me to Scotland, and that I had nothing to complain of but his being more indifferent to my anxiety than I wished him to be.

His prejudice against Scotland appeared remarkably strong at this time. When I talked of our advancement in literature, "Sir," said he, "you have learnt a little from us, and you think yourselves very great men. Hume would never have written history, had not Voltaire written it before him. He is an echo of Voltaire." BOSWELL. "But, Sir we have lord Kames." JOHNSON. "You *have* lord Kames. Keep him; ha, ha, ha! We don't envy you him. Do you ever see Dr. Robertson?" BOSWELL. "Yes, Sir." JOHNSON. "Does the dog talk of me?" BOSWELL. "Indeed, Sir, he does, and loves you." Thinking that I now had him in a corner, and being solicitous for the literary fame of my country, I pressed him for his opinion on the merit of Dr. Robertson's History of Scotland. But to my surprise, he escaped.—"Sir, I love Robertson, and I won't talk of his book."

An essay, written by a divine of the Church of England, maintaining the future life of brutes, was mentioned, and the doctrine insisted on by a gentleman who seemed fond of curious speculation; Johnson, who did not like to hear of anything concerning a future state which was not authorised by the regular canons of orthodoxy, discouraged this talk; and being offended at its continuation, he watched an opportunity to give the gentleman a blow of reprehen-

---

[1] "Mr. Boswell's book I was going to recommend to you when I received your letter; it has pleased and moved me strangely, all (I mean) that relates to Paoli. He is a man born two thousand years after his time! The pamphlet proves what I have always maintained, that any fool may write a most valuable book by chance, if he will tell us what he heard and saw with veracity. Of Mr. Boswell's truth I have not the least suspicion, because I am sure he could invent nothing of this kind. The true title of this part of his work is, a Dialogue between a Green-Goose and a Hero."—Gray to Horace Walpole, Feb. 25, 1768. "The attention of London Society had been attracted to Corsica by a well-timed book of travels; for Boswell, who had been sent abroad to study law, had found his way to Paoli's head-quarters, and returning home with plenty to tell, had written what is still by far the best account of the island that has ever been published."—Trevelyan's Early History of Charles James Fox, 1880.

sion. So, when the poor speculatist, with a serious metaphysical pensive face, addressed him, "But really, Sir, when we see a very sensible dog, we don't know what to think of him"; Johnson, rolling with joy at the thought which beamed in his eye, turned quickly round, and replied, "True, Sir: and when we see a very foolish *fellow*, we don't know what to think of *him*." He then rose up, strided to the fire, and stood for some time laughing and exulting.

I told that I had several times, when in Italy, seen the experiment of placing a scorpion within a circle of burning coals; that it ran round and round in extreme pain; and finding no way to escape, retired to the centre, and, like a true Stoic philosopher, darted its sting into its head, and thus at once freed itself from its woes. "*This must end 'em.*" I said, this was a curious fact, as it showed deliberate suicide in a reptile. Johnson would not admit the fact. He said, Maupertuis was of opinion that it does not kill itself, but dies of the heat; that it gets to the centre of the circle, as the coolest place; that its turning its tail in upon its head is merely a convulsion, and that it does not sting itself. He said he would be satisfied if the great anatomist Morgagni, after dissecting a scorpion on which the experiment had been tried, should certify that its sting had penetrated into its head.

He seemed pleased to talk of natural philosophy. "That woodcocks," said he, "fly over the northern countries is proved, because they have been observed at sea. Swallows certainly sleep all the winter. A number of them conglobulate together, by flying round and round, and then all in a heap throw themselves under water and lie in the bed of a river." He told us, one of his first essays was a Latin poem upon the glow-worm; I am sorry I did not ask where it was to be found.

He talked of the heinousness of the crime of adultery, by which the peace of families was destroyed. He said, "Confusion of progeny constitutes the essence of the crime; and therefore a woman who breaks her marriage vows is much more criminal than a man who does it. A man, to be sure, is criminal in the sight of God; but he does not do his wife a very material injury, if he does not insult her; if, for instance, from mere wantonness of appetite, he steals privately to her chamber-maid. Sir, a wife ought not greatly to resent this. I would not receive home a daughter who had run away from her husband on that account. A wife should study to reclaim her husband by more attention to please him. Sir, a man will not, once in a hundred instances, leave his wife and go to a harlot, if his wife has not been negligent of pleasing."

I asked him if it was not hard that one deviation from chastity should so absolutely ruin a young woman. JOHNSON. "Why no, Sir; it is the great principle which she is taught. When she has given up that principle, she has given up every notion of female honour and virtue, which are all included in chastity."

At this time I observed upon the dial-plate of his watch a short Greek inscription, taken from the New Testament, νύξ γὰρ ἔρχεται, being the first words of our Saviour's solemn admonition to the improvement of that time which is allowed us to prepare for eternity; "*the night cometh* when no man can work." He some time afterwards laid aside this dial-plate; and when I asked him the reason, he said, "It might do very well upon a clock which a man keeps in his closet; but to have it upon his watch, which he carries about with him, and which is often looked at by others, might be censured as ostentatious."

He remained at Oxford a considerable time. I was obliged to go to London, where I received this letter.

To James Boswell, Esq.

Oxford, March 23, 1768

MY DEAR BOSWELL,

I have omitted a long time to write to you, without knowing very well why. I could now tell why I should not write; for who would write to men who publish the letters of their friends, without their leave? [1] Yet I write to you in spite of my caution, to tell you that I shall be glad to see you, and that I wish you would empty your head of Corsica, which I think has filled it rather too long. But, at all events, I shall be glad, very glad, to see you. I am, Sir, yours affectionately,

SAM. JOHNSON

I answered thus:

To Mr. Samuel Johnson

London, April 29, 1768

MY DEAR SIR,

I have received your last letter, which, though very short, and by no means complimentary, yet gave me real pleasure, be-

---

[1] Boswell, in his Journal of a Tour in Corsica, had printed the second and third paragraphs of Johnson's letter to him of January 14, 1766. See p. 106.

cause it contains these words, "I shall be glad, very glad to see you."—Surely you have no reason to complain of my publishing a single paragraph of one of your letters; the temptation to it was so strong. An irrevocable grant of your friendship, and your signifying my desire of visiting Corsica with the epithet of "a wise and noble curiosity," are to me more valuable than many of the grants of kings.

But how can you bid me "empty my head of Corsica"? My noble-minded friend, do you not feel for an oppressed nation bravely struggling to be free? Consider fairly what is the case. The Corsicans never received any kindness from the Genoese. They never agreed to be subject to them. They owe them nothing, and when reduced to an abject state of slavery, by force, shall they not rise in the great cause of liberty, and break the galling yoke? And shall not every liberal soul be warm for them? Empty my head of Corsica? Empty it of honour, empty it of humanity, empty it of friendship, empty it of piety. No! while I live, Corsica, and the cause of the brave islanders, shall ever employ much of my attention, shall ever interest me in the sincerest manner. . . . I am, &c.,   JAMES BOSWELL

Upon his arrival in London in May, he surprised me one morning with a visit at my lodging in Halfmoon Street, was quite satisfied with my explanation, and was in the kindest and most agreeable frame of mind. As he had objected to a part of one of his letters being published, I thought it right to take this opportunity of asking him explicitly whether it would be improper to publish his letters after his death. His answer was, "Nay, Sir, when I am dead, you may do as you will."

Soon afterwards, he supped at the Crown and Anchor tavern in the Strand, with a company whom I collected to meet him. He was this evening in remarkable vigour of mind, and eager to exert himself in conversation, which he did with great readiness and fluency. When I called upon Dr. Johnson next morning, I found him highly satisfied with his colloquial prowess the preceding evening. "Well," said he, "we had good talk." BOSWELL. "Yes, Sir; you tossed and gored several persons."

The late Alexander Earl of Eglintoune had a great admiration of Johnson; but, from the remarkable elegance of his own manners, was perhaps too delicately sensible of the roughness which sometimes appeared in Johnson's behaviour. One evening about this time, when his lordship did me the honour to sup at my lodgings, he regretted that Johnson had not been educated with more refinement, and lived more in polished society. "No, no, my lord," said Signor Baretti, "do with him what you would, he would always have been a bear." "True," answered the earl, with a smile, "but he would have been a *dancing* bear."

To obviate all the reflections which have gone round the world to Johnson's prejudice, by applying to him the epithet of a *bear*, let me impress upon my readers a just and happy saying of my friend Goldsmith, who knew him well: "Johnson, to be sure, has a roughness in his manner; but no man alive has a more tender heart. *He has nothing of the bear but his skin.*"

In 1769, His Majesty having the preceding year instituted the Royal Academy of Arts in London, Johnson had now the honour of being appointed Professor in Ancient Literature.

I came to London in the autumn; and having informed him that I was going to be married in a few months, I wished to have as much of his conversation as I could before engaging in a state of life which would probably keep me more in Scotland, and prevent me seeing him so often as when I was a single man; but I found he was at Brighthelmstone with Mr. and Mrs. Thrale. I was very sorry that I had not his company with me at the Jubilee, in honour of Shakspeare, at Stratford-upon-Avon. Johnson's connection both with Shakspeare and Garrick founded a double claim to his presence; and it would have been highly gratifying to Mr. Garrick. Upon this occasion I particularly lamented that he had not that warmth of friendship for his brilliant pupil, which we may suppose would have had a benignant effect on both. When almost every man of eminence in the literary world was happy to partake in this festival of genius, the absence of Johnson could not but be wondered at and regretted.[1]

After his return to town, we met frequently, and I continued the practice of making notes of his conversation, though not with so much assiduity as I wish I had done. At this time, indeed, I had a sufficient excuse for not being able to appropriate so much time to my journal; for General Paoli,[2] after Corsica had been overpowered by the monarchy of France, was now no longer at the head of his brave countrymen; but, having with difficulty escaped from his

---

[1] Boswell appeared at the Jubilee masquerade in the character of an armed Corsican chief, with the words CORSICA BOSWELL in large letters round his hat.

[2] Pascal Paoli, born in 1726, was appointed by his countrymen Chief Magistrate and General in their resistance to the Genoese. After an honourable, and for a time successful defence, he was at last overpowered by the French, and sought refuge in England in 1769, where he resided, till the French revolution seeming to afford an opportunity to liberate his country from the yoke of France, he went thither, and was a principal promoter of its short-lived union to the British Crown. When this was dissolved, Paoli returned to England, where he resided till his death in 1807.

native island, had sought an asylum in Great Britain; and it was my duty, as well as my pleasure, to attend much upon him. Such particulars of Johnson's conversations at this period as I have committed to writing, I shall here introduce, without any strict attention to methodical arrangement.

On the 30th of September we dined together at the Mitre. I attempted to argue for the superior happiness of the savage life, upon the usual fanciful topics. JOHNSON. "Sir, there can be nothing more false. The savages have no bodily advantages beyond those of civilised men. They have not better health; and as to care or mental uneasiness, they are not above it, but below it, like bears. No, Sir; you are not to talk such paradox: let me have no more on't. It cannot entertain, far less can it instruct. Lord Monboddo, one of your Scotch judges, talked a great deal of such nonsense. I suffered *him;* but I will not suffer *you.*" BOSWELL. "But, Sir, does not Rousseau talk such nonsense?" JOHNSON. "True, Sir; but Rousseau *knows* he is talking nonsense, and laughs at the world for staring at him." BOSWELL. "How so, Sir?" JOHNSON. "Why, Sir, a man who talks nonsense so well, must know that he is talking nonsense. But I am *afraid* (chuckling and laughing) Monboddo does *not* know that he is talking nonsense." BOSWELL. "Is it wrong, then, Sir, to affect singularity, in order to make people stare?" JOHNSON. "Yes, if you do it by propagating error: and, indeed, it is wrong in any way. There is in human nature a general inclination to make people stare; and every wise man has himself to cure of it, and does cure himself. If you wish to make people stare, by doing better than others, why, make them stare till they stare their eyes out. But consider how easy it is to make people stare, by being absurd. I may do it by going into a drawing-room without my shoes. You remember the gentleman in the 'Spectator,' who had a commission of lunacy taken out against him for his extreme singularity, such as never wearing a wig, but a night-cap. Now, Sir, abstractedly, the night-cap was best: but, relatively, the advantage was over-balanced by making the boys run after him."

Talking of a London life, he said, "The happiness of London is not to be conceived but by those who have been in it. I will venture to say, there is more learning and science within the circumference of ten miles from where we now sit, than in all the rest of the kingdom." BOSWELL. "The only disadvantage is the great distance at which people live from one another." JOHNSON. "Yes,

Sir; but that is occasioned by the largeness of it, which is the cause of all the other advantages." BOSWELL. "Sometimes I have been in the humour of wishing to retire to a desert." JOHNSON. "Sir, you have desert enough in Scotland."

Although I had promised myself a great deal of instructive conversation with him on the conduct of the married state, of which I had then a near prospect, he did not say much upon that topic. He maintained to me, contrary to the common notion, that a woman would not be the worse wife for being learned; in which, from all that I have observed, I humbly differed from him.

When I censured a gentleman of my acquaintance for marrying a second time, as it showed a disregard of his first wife, he said, "Not at all, Sir. On the contrary, were he not to marry again, it might be concluded that his first wife had given him a disgust to marriage; but by taking a second wife he pays the highest compliment to the first, by showing that she made him so happy as a married man, that he wishes to be so a second time." And yet, on another occasion, he owned that he once had almost asked a promise of Mrs. Johnson that she would not marry again, but had checked himself. Indeed I cannot help thinking, that in his case the request would have been unreasonable; for if Mrs. Johnson forgot, or thought it no injury to the memory of her first love— the husband of her youth and the father of her children—to make a second marriage, why should she be precluded from a third, should she be so inclined? In Johnson's persevering fond appropriation of his *Tetty*, even after her decease, he seems totally to have overlooked the prior claim of the honest Birmingham trader. I presume that her having been married before had, at times, given him some uneasiness; for I remember his observing upon the marriage of one of our common friends, "He has done a very foolish thing, Sir; he has married a widow, when he might have had a maid."

I had last year the pleasure of seeing Mrs. Thrale at Dr. Johnson's one morning, and had conversation enough with her to show her that I was as Johnsonian as herself. Dr. Johnson had probably been kind enough to speak well of me, for he delivered me a very polite card from Mr. Thrale and her, inviting me to Streatham.

On the 6th of October I complied with this obliging invitation; and found, at an elegant villa, six miles from town, every circumstance that can make society pleasing. Johnson, though quite at home, was yet looked up to with an awe, tempered by affection, and seemed to be equally the care of his host and hostess. I rejoiced at seeing him so happy.

He played off his wit against Scotland with a good-humoured pleasantry, which gave me, though no bigot to national prejudices, an opportunity for a little contest with him. I having said that England was obliged to us for gardeners, almost all their good gardeners being Scotchmen:—JOHNSON. "Why, Sir, that is because gardening is much more necessary amongst you than with us, which makes so many of your people learn it. It is *all* gardening with you. Things which grow wild here, must be cultivated with great care in Scotland. Pray now (throwing himself back in his chair, and laughing), are you ever able to bring the *sloe* to perfection?"

Mrs. Thrale disputed with him on the merit of Prior. He attacked him powerfully; said he wrote of love like a man who had never felt it; his love verses were college verses: and he repeated the song, "Alexis shunn'd his fellow swains," &c. in so ludicrous a manner, as to make us all wonder how any one could have been pleased with such fantastical stuff. Mrs. Thrale stood to her guns with great courage, in defence of amorous ditties, which Johnson despised, till he at last silenced her by saying, "My dear lady, talk no more of this. Nonsense can be defended but by nonsense."

Mrs. Thrale then praised Garrick's talents for light gay poetry; and, as a specimen, dwelt with peculiar pleasure on this line:

I'd smile with the simple, and feed with the poor.

JOHNSON. "Nay, my dear lady, this will never do. Poor David! Smile with the simple!—what folly is that? And who would feed with the poor that can help it? No, no; let me smile with the wise, and feed with the rich." I repeated this sally to Garrick, and wondered to find his sensibility as a writer not a little irritated by it. To soothe him, I observed, that Johnson spared none of us; and I quoted the passage in Horace, in which he compares one who attacks his friends for the sake of a laugh to a pushing ox, that is marked by a bunch of hay put upon his horns: "*fœnum habet in cornu.*" "Ay," said Garrick, vehemently, "he has a whole *mow* of it."

I know not from what spirit of contradiction he burst out into a violent declamation against the Corsicans, of whose heroism I talked in high terms. "Sir," said he, "what is all this rout about the Corsicans? They have been at war with the Genoese for upwards of twenty years, and have never yet taken their fortified towns. They might have battered down their walls, and reduced them to powder in twenty years. They might have pulled the walls in pieces, and cracked the stones with their teeth in twenty years." It was in vain to argue with him upon the want of artillery: he was not to be resisted for the moment.

On the evening of October 10, I presented Dr. Johnson to General Paoli. I had greatly wished that two men, for whom I had the highest esteem, should meet. They met with a manly ease, mutually conscious of their own abilities, and of the abilities of each other. The General spoke Italian, and Dr. Johnson English, and understood one another very well, with a little aid of interpretation from me, in which I compared myself to an isthmus which joins two great continents. Upon Johnson's approach, the General said, "From what I have read of your works, Sir, and from what Mr. Boswell has told me of you, I have long held you in great veneration." The General talked of languages being formed on the particular notions and manners of a people, without knowing which, we cannot know the language. We may know the direct signification of single words; but by these no beauty of expression, no sally of genius, no wit is conveyed to the mind. All this must be by allusion to other ideas. "Sir," said Johnson, "you talk of language, as if you had never done any thing else but study it, instead of governing a nation." The General said, "*Questo è un troppo gran complimento*"; this is too great a compliment. Johnson answered, "I should have thought so, Sir, if I had not heard you talk." The General asked him what he thought of the spirit of infidelity which was so prevalent. JOHNSON. "Sir, this gloom of infidelity, I hope, is only a transient cloud passing through the hemisphere, which will soon be dissipated, and the sun break forth with his usual splendour." "You think then," said the General, "that they will change their principles like their clothes." JOHNSON. "Why, Sir, if they bestow no more thought on principles than on dress, it must be so." The General said, that "a great part of the fashionable infidelity was owing to a desire of showing courage. Men who have no opportunities of showing it as to things in this life, take death and futurity as objects on which to display it." JOHNSON. "That is mighty foolish affectation. Fear is one of the passions of human nature, of which it is impossible to divest it. You remember that the Emperor Charles V., when he read upon the tombstone of a Spanish nobleman, 'Here lies one who never knew fear,' wittily said, 'Then he never snuffed a candle with his fingers.' "

Dr. Johnson went home with me, and drank tea till late in the night. He said, "General Paoli had the loftiest port of any man he had ever seen." He denied that military men were always the best bred men. "Perfect good breeding," he observed, "consists in having no particular mark of any profession, but a general elegance of manners; whereas, in a military man, you can commonly distinguish the *brand* of a soldier, *l'homme d'épée.*"

Dr. Johnson shunned to-night any discussion of the perplexed question of fate and free-will, which I attempted to agitate: "Sir," said he, "we *know* our will is free, and *there's* an end on't."

He honoured me with his company at dinner on the 16th of October, at my lodgings in Old Bond Street. Garrick played round him with a fond vivacity, taking hold of the breasts of his coat, and, looking up in his face with a lively archness, complimented him on the good health he seemed to enjoy; while the sage, shaking his head beheld him with a gentle complacency. One of the company not being come at the appointed hour, I proposed, as usual, upon such occasions, to order dinner to be served; adding, "Ought six people to be kept waiting for one?" "Why, yes," answered Johnson, with a delicate humanity, "if the one will suffer more by your sitting down, than the six will do by waiting." Goldsmith, to divert the tedious minutes, strutted about, bragging of his dress, and I believe was seriously vain of it, for his mind was wonderfully prone to such impressions. "Come, come," said Garrick, "talk no more of that. You are, perhaps, the worst—eh, eh!"—Goldsmith was eagerly attempting to interrupt him, when Garrick went on, laughing ironically, "Nay, you will always *look* like a gentleman; but I am talking of being well or *ill drest.*" "Well, let me tell you," said Goldsmith, "when my tailor brought home my bloom-coloured coat, he said, 'Sir, I have a favour to beg of you. When any body asks you who made your clothes, be pleased to mention John Filby, at the Harrow, in Water Lane.' " JOHNSON. "Why, Sir, that was because he knew the strange colour would attract crowds to gaze at it, and thus they might hear of him, and see how well he could make a coat, even of so absurd a colour."

After dinner our conversation first turned upon Pope. Johnson said, his characters of men were admirably drawn, those of women not so well. He repeated to us, in his forcible, melodious manner,

"YOU WILL ALWAYS 'LOOK' LIKE A GENTLEMAN"

the concluding lines of the "Dunciad." While he was talking loudly in praise of those lines,—one of the company ventured to say, "Too fine for such a poem:—a poem on what?" JOHNSON (with a disdainful look), "Why on *dunces*. It was worth while being a dunce then. Ah, Sir, hadst *thou* lived in those days! It is not worth while being a dunce now, when there are no wits."

On Thursday, October 19, I passed the evening with him at his house. He advised me to complete a Dictionary of words peculiar to Scotland, of which I showed him a specimen. "Sir," said he, "Ray has made a collection of north-country words. By collecting those of your country, you will do a useful thing towards the history of the language." He bade me also go on with collections which I was making upon the antiquities of Scotland. "Make a large book; a folio." BOSWELL. "But of what use will it be, Sir?" JOHNSON. "Never mind the use; do it."

I mentioned to him that I had seen the execution of several convicts at Tyburn two days before, and that none of them seemed to be under any concern. JOHNSON. "Most of them, Sir, have never thought at all." BOSWELL. "But is not the fear of death natural to man?" JOHNSON. "So much so, Sir, that the whole of life is but keeping away the thoughts of it." He then, in a low and earnest tone, talked of his meditating upon the awful hour of his own dissolution, and in what manner he should conduct himself upon that occasion: "I know not," said he, "whether I should wish to have a friend by me, or have it all between GOD and myself."

Talking of our feeling for the distresses of others:—JOHNSON. "Why, Sir, there is much noise made about it, but it is greatly exaggerated. No, Sir, we have a certain degree of feeling to prompt us to do good; more than that Providence does not intend. It would be misery to no purpose." BOSWELL. "But suppose now, Sir, that one of your intimate friends were apprehended for an offence for which he might be hanged." JOHNSON. "I should do what I could to bail him, and give him any other assistance: but if he were once fairly hanged, I should not suffer." BOSWELL. "Would you eat your dinner that day, Sir?" JOHNSON. "Yes, Sir; and eat it as if he were eating with me. Why, there's Baretti,[1] who is to be tried for his life to-morrow, friends have risen up for

[1] On the 3rd of October, as Giuseppe Marc' Antonio Baretti, an Italian miscellaneous writer, who had lived and taught in England since 1751, was going hastily up the Haymarket, he was accosted by a woman, who behaving with great indecency, he was provoked to give her a blow on the hand; upon which three men immediately interfering, and endeavouring to push him from the pavement, with a view to throwing him into a puddle, he was alarmed for his safety, and rashly struck one of them with a knife (which he constantly wore for the purpose of carving fruit and sweetmeats), and gave him a wound, of which he died the next day.—*European Magazine.*

him on every side; yet if he should be hanged, none of them will eat a slice of pudding the less. Sir, that sympathetic feeling goes a very little way in depressing the mind."

I told him that I had dined lately at Foote's, who showed me a letter which he had received from Tom Davies, telling him that he had not been able to sleep from the concern he felt on account of *"this sad affair of Baretti,"* begging of him to try if he could suggest any thing that might be of service; and, at the same time, recommending to him an industrious young man who kept a pickle shop. JOHNSON. "Ay, Sir, here you have a specimen of human sympathy; a friend hanged and a cucumber pickled. We know not whether Baretti or the pickle-man has kept Davies from sleep; nor does he know himself. And as to his not sleeping, Sir; Tom Davies is a very great man; Tom has been upon the stage, and knows how to do those things: I have not been upon the stage, and cannot do those things." BOSWELL. "I have often blamed myself, Sir, for not feeling for others as sensibly as many say they do." JOHNSON. "Sir, don't be duped by them any more. You will find these very feeling people are not very ready to do you good. They *pay* you by *feeling.*"

BOSWELL. "Foote has a great deal of humour." JOHNSON. "Yes, Sir." BOSWELL. "He has a singular talent of exhibiting character." JOHNSON. "Sir, it is not a talent, it is a vice; it is what others abstain from. It is not comedy, which exhibits the character of a species, as that of a miser gathered from many misers: it is farce, which exhibits individuals." BOSWELL. "Did not he think of exhibiting you, Sir?" JOHNSON. "Sir, fear restrained him; he knew I would have broken his bones. I would have saved him the trouble of cutting off a leg; I would not have left him a leg to cut off." BOSWELL. "Pray, Sir, is not Foote an infidel?" JOHNSON. "I do not know, Sir, that the fellow is an infidel; but if he be an infidel, he is an infidel as a dog is an infidel; that is to say, he has never thought upon the subject."

Next day, October 20, he appeared, for the only time I suppose in his life, as a witness in a court of justice, being called to give evidence to the character of Mr. Baretti, who, having stabbed a man in the street, was arraigned at the Old Bailey for murder. Never did such a constellation of genius enlighten the awful Sessions-house, emphatically called Justice-hall; Mr. Burke, Mr. Garrick, Mr. Beauclerk, and Dr. Johnson: and undoubtedly their favourable testimony had due weight with the court and jury.

Johnson gave his evidence in a slow, deliberate, and distinct
manner, which was uncommonly impressive. Mr. Baretti was
acquitted.

On the 26th of October, we dined together at the Mitre tavern.
I found fault with Foote for indulging his talent of ridicule at the
expense of his visitors, which I colloquially termed making fools of
his company. JOHNSON. "Sir, he does not make fools of his company; they whom he exposes are fools already; he only brings them
into action."

Talking of trade, he observed, "It is a mistaken notion that a
vast deal of money is brought into a nation by trade. It is not so.
Commodities come from commodities; but trade produces no
capital accession of wealth. However, though there should be
little profit in money, there is a considerable profit in pleasure, as
it gives to one nation the productions of another, as we have wines
and fruits, and many other foreign articles, brought to us." Bos-
WELL. "Yes, Sir, and there is a profit in pleasure, by its furnishing
occupation to such numbers of mankind." JOHNSON. "Why, Sir,
you cannot call that pleasure, to which all are averse, and which
none begin but with the hope of leaving off; a thing which men
dislike before they have tried it, and when they have tried it."
BOSWELL. "But, Sir, the mind must be employed, and we grow
weary when idle." JOHNSON. "That is, Sir, because others being
busy, we want company; but if we were all idle, there would be no
growing weary; we should all entertain one another. There is,
indeed, this in trade;—it gives men an opportunity of improving
their situation. If there were no trade, many who are poor would
always remain poor. But no man loves labour for itself."

We went home to his house to tea. Mrs. Williams made it with
sufficient dexterity, notwithstanding her blindness, though her
manner of satisfying herself that the cups were full enough, appeared to me a little awkward; for I fancied she put her finger down
a certain way, till she felt the tea touch it. In my first elation at
being allowed the privilege of attending Dr. Johnson at his late
visits to this lady, which was like being *e secretioribus consiliis*, I
willingly drank cup after cup, as if it had been the Heliconian
spring. But as the charm of novelty went off, I grew more fastidious; and besides, I discovered that she was of a peevish temper.

There was a pretty large circle this evening. Dr. Johnson was in
very good humour, lively, and ready to talk upon all subjects.
Mr. Ferguson told him of a new-invented machine which went

without horses: a man who sat in it turned a handle, which worked a spring that drove it forward. "Then, Sir," said Johnson, "what is gained is, the man has his choice whether he will move himself alone, or himself and the machine too." Dominicetti being mentioned, he would not allow him any merit. "There is nothing in all this boasted system. No, Sir; medicated baths can be no better than warm water: their only effect can be that of tepid moisture." One of the company took the other side, maintaining that medicines of various sorts, and some too of most powerful effect, are introduced into the human frame by the medium of the pores; and, therefore, when warm water is impregnated with salutiferous substances, it may produce great effects as a bath. This appeared to me very satisfactory. Johnson did not answer it; but talked for victory, and determined to be master of the field. He turned to the gentleman, "Well, Sir, go to Dominicetti, and get thyself fumigated; but be sure that the steam be directed to thy *head*, for *that* is the *peccant part*." [1] This produced a triumphant roar of laughter from the motley assembly of philosophers, printers, and dependents, male and female.

I know not how so whimsical a thought came into my mind, but I asked, "If, Sir, you were shut up in a castle, and a new-born child with you, what would you do?" JOHNSON. "Why, Sir, I should not much like my company." BOSWELL. "But would you take the trouble of rearing it?" He seemed, as may well be supposed, unwilling to pursue the subject: but upon my persevering in my question, replied, "Why yes, Sir, I would; but I must have all conveniences. If I had no garden, I would make a shed on the roof, and take it there for fresh air. I should feed it, and wash it much, and with warm water to please it, not with cold water to give it pain." BOSWELL. "But, Sir, does not heat relax?" JOHNSON. "Sir, you are not to imagine the water is to be very hot. I would not *coddle* the child. No, Sir, the hardy method of treating children does no good. I'll take you five children from London, who shall cuff five Highland children. Sir, a man bred in London will carry a burthen, or run, or wrestle, as well as a man brought up in the hardest manner in the country." BOSWELL. "Good living, I suppose, makes the Londoners strong." JOHNSON. "Why, Sir, I don't know that it does. Our chairmen from Ireland, who are as strong men as any, have been brought up upon potatoes. Quantity

---

[1] The "gentleman" was Boswell himself, whose way of relating Johnson's wit without confessing that he was the object of it was well known to his contemporaries and much amused them. Dominicetti was a quack, famed for his medicated baths.

makes up for quality." BOSWELL. "Would you teach this child that I have furnished you with, any thing?" JOHNSON. "No, I should not be apt to teach it." BOSWELL. "Would not you have a pleasure in teaching it?" JOHNSON. "No, Sir, I should *not* have a pleasure in teaching it." BOSWELL. "Have you not a pleasure in teaching men? *There* I have you. You have the same pleasure in teaching men, that I should have in teaching children." JOHNSON. "Why, something about that."

BOSWELL. "Do you think, Sir, that what is called natural affection is born with us? It seems to me to be the effect of habit, or of gratitude for kindness. No child has it for a parent whom it has not seen." JOHNSON. "Why, Sir, I think there is an instinctive natural affection in parents towards their children."

"The London Chronicle," which was the only newspaper he constantly took in, being brought, the office of reading it aloud was assigned to me. I was diverted by his impatience. He made me pass over so many parts of it, that my task was very easy.

I had hired a Bohemian as my servant while I remained in London; and being much pleased with him, I asked Dr. Johnson whether his being a Roman Catholic should prevent my taking him with me to Scotland. JOHNSON. "Why no, Sir. If *he* has no objection, you can have none." BOSWELL. "So, Sir, you are no great enemy to the Roman Catholic religion." JOHNSON. "No more, Sir, than to the Presbyterian religion." BOSWELL. "You are joking." JOHNSON. "No, Sir, I really think so. Nay, Sir, of the two, I prefer the Popish." BOSWELL. "How so, Sir?" JOHNSON. "Why, Sir, the Presbyterians have no church, no apostolical ordination." BOSWELL. "And do you think that absolutely essential, Sir?" JOHNSON. "Why, Sir, as it was an apostolical institution, I think it is dangerous to be without it. And, Sir, the Presbyterians have no public worship; they have no form of prayer in which they know they are to join. They go to hear a man pray, and are to judge whether they will join with him." BOSWELL. "But, Sir, their doctrine is the same with that of the Church of England. Their confession of faith, and the thirty-nine articles, contain the same points, even the doctrine of predestination." JOHNSON. "Why, yes, Sir; predestination was a part of the clamour of the times, so it is mentioned in our articles, but with as little positiveness as could be." BOSWELL. "Is it necessary, Sir, to believe all the thirty-nine articles?" JOHNSON. "Why, Sir, that is a question which has been much agitated. Some have thought it necessary that they should all be believed; others have considered them to be only articles of peace, that is to say, you are not to preach against them." BOSWELL. "It appears to me, Sir, that predestination, or what is equivalent to it, cannot be avoided, if we hold an universal prescience in the Deity." JOHNSON. "Why, Sir, does not God every day see things going on without preventing them?" BOSWELL. "True, Sir; but if a thing be *certainly* foreseen, it must be fixed, and cannot happen otherwise; and if we apply this consideration to the human mind, there is no free will, nor do I see how prayer can be of any avail." I did not press it further, when I perceived that he was displeased, and shrunk from any abridgment of an attribute usually ascribed to the Divinity, however irreconcileable in its full extent with the grand system of moral government.

I proceeded: "What do you think, Sir, of Purgatory, as believed by the Roman Catholics?" JOHNSON. "Why, Sir, it is a very harmless doctrine. They are of opinion that the generality of mankind are neither so obstinately wicked as to deserve everlasting punishment, nor so good as to merit being admitted into the society of blessed spirits; and therefore that God is graciously pleased to allow of a middle state, where they may be purified by certain degrees of suffering. You see, Sir, there is nothing unreasonable in this." BOSWELL. "But then, Sir, their masses for the dead?" JOHNSON. "Why, Sir, if it be once established that there are souls in purgatory, it is as proper to pray for *them*, as for our brethren of mankind who are yet in this life." BOSWELL. "The idolatry of the mass?"—JOHNSON. "Sir, there is no idolatry in the mass. They believe God to be there, and they adore him." BOSWELL. "The worship of saints?" JOHNSON. "Sir, they do not worship saints; they invoke them; they only ask their prayers. I am talking all this time of the *doctrines* of the Church of Rome. I grant you that, in *practice*, purgatory is made a lucrative imposition, and that the people do become idolatrous as they recommend themselves to the tutelary protection of particular saints. I think their giving the sacrament only in one kind is criminal, because it is contrary to the express institution of Christ, and I wonder how the Council of Trent admitted it." BOSWELL. "Confession?" JOHNSON. "Why, I don't know but that is a good thing. The Scripture says, 'Confess your faults one to another,' and the priests confess as well as the laity. Then it must be considered that their absolution is only upon repentance, and often upon penance also. You think your sins may be forgiven without penance, upon repentance alone."

I thus ventured to mention all the common objections against the Roman Catholic church, that I might hear so great a man upon them. What he said is here accurately recorded. But it is not improbable that, if one had taken the other side, he might have reasoned differently.

I must however mention, that he had a respect for "*the old religion,*" as the mild Melancthon called that of the Roman Catholic church, even while he was exerting himself for its reformation in some particulars. Sir William Scott informs me, that he heard Johnson say, "A man who is converted from Protestantism to Popery, may be sincere: he parts with nothing: he is only superadding to what he already had. But a convert from Popery to Protestantism gives up so much of what he has held as sacred as any thing that he retains—there is so much *laceration of mind* in such a conversion—that it can hardly be sincere and lasting."

When we were alone, I introduced the subject of death, and endeavoured to maintain that the fear of it might be got over. I told him that David Hume said to me, he was no more uneasy to think he should *not be* after this life, than that he *had not been* before he began to exist. JOHNSON. "Sir, if he really thinks so, his perceptions are disturbed; he is mad: if he does not think so, he lies. He may tell you, he holds his finger in the flame of a candle without feeling pain; would you believe him? When he dies, he at least gives up all he has." BOSWELL. "Foote, Sir, told me, that when he was very ill he was not afraid to die." JOHNSON. "It is not true, Sir. Hold a pistol to Foote's breast, or to Hume's breast, and threaten to kill them; and you'll see how they behave." BOSWELL. "But may we not fortify our minds for the approach of death?"—Here I am sensible I was in the wrong, to bring before his view what he ever looked upon with horror; for although, when in a celestial frame of mind, in his "Vanity of Human Wishes," he has supposed death to be "kind Nature's signal for retreat" from this state of being to "a happier seat," his thoughts upon this awful change were in general full of dismal apprehensions. His mind resembled the vast amphitheatre, the Coliseum at Rome. In the centre stood his judgment, which, like a mighty gladiator, combated those apprehensions that, like the wild beasts of the *arena*, were all around in cells, ready to be let out upon him. After a conflict he drives them back into their dens; but not killing them, they were still assailing him. To my question, whether we might not fortify our minds for the approach of death, he answered, in a passion, "No, Sir, let it alone. It matters not how a man dies, but how he lives. The act of dying is not of importance, it lasts so short a time." He added (with an earnest look), "A man knows it must be so, and submits. It will do him no good to whine."

I attempted to continue the conversation. He was so provoked, that he said,—"Give us no more of this"; and was thrown into such a state of agitation, that he expressed himself in a way that alarmed and distressed me; showed an impatience that I should leave him, and when I was going away, called to me sternly, "Don't let us meet to-morrow."

I went home exceedingly uneasy. All the harsh observations which I had ever heard made upon his character crowded into my mind; and I seemed to myself like the man who had put his head in the lion's mouth a great many times with perfect safety, but at last had it bit off.

Next morning [27th October], I sent him a note, stating that I might have been in the wrong, but it was not intentionally; he was therefore, I could not help thinking, too severe upon me. That notwithstanding our agreement not to meet that day, I would call on him in my way to the city, and stay five minutes by my watch. "You are," said I, "in my mind, since last night, surrounded by cloud and storm. Let me have a glimpse of sunshine, and go about my affairs in serenity and cheerfulness."

Upon entering his study, I was glad that he was not alone, which would have made our meeting more awkward. There were with him, Mr. Steevens and Mr. Tyers, both of whom I now saw for the first time. My note had, on his own reflection, softened him, for he received me very complacently; so that I unexpectedly found myself at ease, and joined in the conversation.

I whispered him, "Well, Sir, you are now in good humour." JOHNSON. "Yes, Sir." I was going to leave him, and had got as far as the staircase. He stopped me, and smiling, said, "Get you gone in"; a curious mode of inviting me to stay, which I accordingly did for some time longer.

This little incidental quarrel and reconciliation must be esteemed as one of many proofs which his friends had, that though he might be charged with *bad humour* at times, he was always a *good-natured* man; and I have heard Sir Joshua Reynolds, a nice and delicate observer of manners, particularly remark, that when upon any occasion Johnson had been rough to any person in company, he took the first opportunity of reconciliation, by drinking to him, or addressing his discourse to him; but if he found his dignified indirect overtures sullenly neglected, he was quite indifferent, and considered himself as having done all that he ought to do, and the other as now in the wrong.

Being to set out for Scotland on the 10th of November, I went to him at Streatham early in the morning. "Now," said he, "that you are going to marry, do not expect more from life than life will afford. You may often find yourself out of humour, and you may often think your wife not studious enough to please you; and yet you may have reason to consider yourself as upon the whole very happily married."

I was volatile enough to repeat to him a little epigrammatic song of mine,[1] on matrimony, which Mr. Garrick had, a few days before, procured to be set to music.

A Matrimonial Thought

In the blithe days of honey-moon,
　　With Kate's allurements smitten,
I loved her late, I loved her soon,
　　And called her dearest kitten.

But now my kitten's grown a cat,
　　And cross like other wives;
Oh! by my soul, my honest Mat,
　　I fear she has nine lives.

My illustrious friend said, "It is very well, Sir; but you should not swear." Upon which I altered "Oh! by my soul," to "Alas, alas!"

He was so good as to accompany me to London, and see me into the post-chaise which was to carry me on my road to Scotland.

In 1770 the following minute describes his state:

June 1, 1770. Every man naturally persuades himself that he can keep his resolutions, nor is he convinced of his imbecility but by length of time and frequency of experiment. This opinion of our own constancy is so prevalent, that we always despise him who suffers his general and settled purpose to be overpowered by an occasional desire. They, therefore, whom frequent failures have made desperate, cease to form resolutions; and they who are become cunning, do not tell them. Those who do not make them are very few, but of their effect little is perceived; for scarcely any man persists in a course of life planned by choice, but as he

---

[1] In convivial society Boswell used to sing songs of his own composition.

is restrained from deviation by some external power. He who may live as he will, seldom lives long in the observation of his own rules.

During this year,there was a total cessation of all correspondence between Dr. Johnson and me, without any coldness on either side, but merely from procrastination, continued from day to day; and, as I was not in London, I had no opportunity of enjoying his company and recording his conversation. To supply this blank, I shall present my readers with some *Collectanea*, obligingly furnished to me by the Rev. Dr. Maxwell, of Falkland, in Ireland, some time assistant preacher at the Temple, and for many years the social friend of Johnson, who spoke of him with a very kind regard.

My acquaintance with that great and venerable character commenced in the year 1754. His general mode of life, during my acquaintance, seemed to be pretty uniform. About twelve o'clock I commonly visited him, and frequently found him in bed, or declaiming over his tea, which he drank very plentifully. He generally had a levée of morning visitors, chiefly men of letters, and sometimes learned ladies; particularly I remember a French lady of wit and fashion doing him the honour of a visit. He seemed to me to be considered as a kind of public oracle, whom everybody thought they had a right to visit and consult; and doubtless they were well rewarded. I never could discover how he found time for his compositions. He declaimed all the morning, then went to dinner at a tavern, where he commonly stayed late, and then drank his tea at some friend's house, over which he loitered a great while, but seldom took supper. I fancy he must have read and wrote chiefly in the night, for I can scarcely recollect that he ever refused going with me to a tavern, and he often went to Ranelagh, which he deemed a place of innocent recreation.

Two young women from Staffordshire visited him when I was present, to consult him on the subject of Methodism, to which they were inclined. "Come," said he, "you pretty fools, dine with Maxwell and me at the Mitre, and we will talk over that subject"; which they did, and after dinner he took one of them upon his knee, and fondled her for half an hour together.

Upon a visit to me at a country lodging near Twickenham, he asked what sort of society I had there. I told him, but indifferent; as they chiefly consisted of opulent traders, retired from business. He said he never much liked that class of people: "For, Sir," said he, "they have lost the civility of tradesmen, without acquiring the manners of gentlemen."

Johnson was much attached to London: he observed, that a man

HE OFTEN WENT TO RANELAGH

stored his mind better there, than any where else; and that in remote situations a man's body might be feasted, but his mind was starved, and his faculties apt to degenerate, from want of exercise and competition. "No place," he said, "cured a man's vanity or arrogance, so well as London; for no man was either great or good *per se*, but as compared with others not so good or great, he was sure to find in the metropolis many his equals, and some his superiors." He observed, that a man in London was in less danger of falling in love indiscreetly, than any where else; for there the difficulty of deciding between the conflicting pretensions of a vast variety of objects, kept him safe. He told me, that he had frequently been offered country preferment, if he would consent to take orders; but he could not leave the improved society of the capital, or consent to exchange the exhilarating joys and splendid decorations of public life, for the obscurity, insipidity, and uniformity of remote situations.

He loved, he said, the old black-letter books; they were rich in matter, though their style was inelegant; wonderfully so, considering how conversant the writers were with the best models of antiquity.

Burton's "Anatomy of Melancholy," he said, was the only book that ever took him out of bed two hours sooner than he wished to rise.

He had great compassion for the miseries and distresses of the Irish nation, particularly the Papists; and severely reprobated the barbarous debilitating policy of the British government, which, he said, was the most detestable mode of persecution. To a gentleman who hinted such policy might be necessary to support the authority of the English government, he replied by saying, "Let the authority of the English government perish, rather than be maintained by iniquity. Better would it be to restrain the turbulence of the natives by the authority of the sword, and to make them amenable to law and justice by an effectual and vigorous police, than to grind them to powder by all manner of disabilities and incapacities. Better," said he, "to hang or drown people at once, than by an unrelenting persecution to beggar and starve them." The moderation and humanity of the present times have, in some measure, justified the wisdom of his observations.

When exasperated by contradiction, he was apt to treat his opponents with too much acrimony: as, "Sir, you don't see your way through that question":—"Sir, you talk the language of ignorance." On my observing to him, that a certain gentleman had remained silent the whole evening, in the midst of a very brilliant and learned society, "Sir," said he, "the conversation overflowed, and drowned him."

His philosophy, though austere and solemn, was by no means morose and cynical, and never blunted the laudable sensibilities of his character, or exempted him from the influence of the tender passions. Want of tenderness, he always alleged, was want of parts, and was no less a proof of stupidity than depravity.

Speaking of Mr. Hanway, who published "An Eight Days' Journey from London to Portsmouth," "Jonas," said he, "acquired some reputation by travelling abroad, but lost it all by travelling at home."

Of the passion of love he remarked, that its violence and ill effects were much exaggerated; for who knows any real sufferings on that head, more than from the exorbitancy of any other passion?

He observed, that the influence of London now extended every where, and that from all manner of communication being opened, there shortly would be no remains of the ancient simplicity, or places of cheap retreat to be found.

He used frequently to observe, that there was more to be endured than enjoyed, in the general condition of human life; and frequently quoted those lines of Dryden:

Strange cozenage! none would live past years again,
Yet all hope pleasure from what still remain.

For his part, he said, he never passed that week in his life which he would wish to repeat, were an angel to make the proposal to him.

He was of opinion, that the English nation cultivated both their soil and their reason better than any other people; but admitted that the French, though not the highest, perhaps, in any department of literature, yet in every department were very high. Intellectual pre-eminence, he observed, was the highest superiority; and that every nation derived their highest reputation from the splendour and dignity of their writers.

In a Latin conversation with the Père Boscovich, at the house of Mrs. Cholmondely, I heard him maintain the superiority of Sir Isaac Newton over all foreign philosophers, with a dignity and eloquence that surprised that learned foreigner. It being observed to him, that a rage for every thing English prevailed much in France after Lord Chatham's glorious war, he said, he did not wonder at it, for that we had drubbed those fellows into a proper reverence for us, and that their national petulance required periodical chastisement.

Somebody observing that the Scotch Highlanders, in the year 1745, had made surprising efforts, considering their numerous wants and disadvantages; "Yes, Sir," said he, "their wants were

numerous: but you have not mentioned the greatest of them all—
the want of law."

Speaking of the *inward light*, to which some Methodists pretended, he said, it was a principle utterly incompatible with social
or civil security. "If a man," said he, "pretends to a principle
of action of which I can know nothing, nay, not so much as that
he has it, but only that he pretends to it; how can I tell what that
person may be prompted to do? When a person professes to be
governed by a written ascertained law, I can then know where to
find him."

Speaking of a dull, tiresome fellow, whom he chanced to meet,
he said, "That fellow seems to me to possess but one idea, and
that is a wrong one."

Much inquiry having been made concerning a gentleman, who
had quitted a company where Johnson was, and no information
being obtained, at last Johnson observed, that "he did not care
to speak ill of any man behind his back, but he believed the gentleman was an *attorney*."

A gentleman who had been very unhappy in marriage, married
immediately after his wife died: Johnson said, it was the triumph
of hope over experience.

He observed, that a man of sense and education should meet a
suitable companion in a wife. It was a miserable thing when the
conversation could only be such as, whether the mutton should
be boiled or roasted, and probably a dispute about that.

He did not approve of late marriages, observing that more was
lost in point of time, than compensated for by any possible advantages. Even ill-assorted marriages were preferable to cheerless
celibacy.

He observed, "it was a most mortifying reflection for any man
to consider, *what he had done*, compared with what *he might have
done*."

He said few people had intellectual resources sufficient to forego
the pleasures of wine. They could not otherwise contrive how to
fill the interval between dinner and supper.

He went with me, one Sunday, to hear my old master, Gregory
Sharpe, preach at the Temple. In the prefatory prayer, Sharpe
ranted about *liberty*, as a blessing most fervently to be implored,
and its continuance prayed for. Johnson observed, that our *liberty*
was in no sort of danger:—he would have done much better to
pray against our *licentiousness*.

He observed, a principal source of erroneous judgment was
viewing things partially and only on *one side*; as for instance,
fortune-hunters when they contemplated the fortunes *singly* and
separately, it was a dazzling and tempting object; but when they

came to possess the wives and their fortunes *together*, they began to suspect they had not made quite so good a bargain.

He advised me, if possible, to have a good orchard. He knew, he said, a clergyman of small income, who brought up a family very reputably, which he chiefly fed with apple dumplings.

Speaking of a certain prelate, who exerted himself very laudably in building churches and parsonage houses; "however," said he, "I do not find that he is esteemed a man of much professional learning, or a liberal patron of it;—yet, it is well where a man possesses any strong positive excellence. Few have all kinds of merit belonging to their character. We must not examine matters too deeply. No, Sir, a *fallible being will fail somewhere.*"

We dined *tête-à-tête* at the Mitre, as I was preparing to return to Ireland, after an absence of many years. I regretted much leaving London, where I had formed many agreeable connections; "Sir," said he, "I don't wonder at it: no man, fond of letters, leaves London without regret. But remember, Sir, you have seen and enjoyed a great deal;—you have seen life in its highest decorations, and the world has nothing new to exhibit. No man is so well qualified to leave public life as he who has long tried it and known it well. We are always hankering after untried situations, and imagining greater felicity from them than they can afford. No, Sir, knowledge and virtue may be acquired in all countries, and your local consequence will make you some amends for the intellectual gratifications you relinquish." Then he quoted the following lines with great pathos:

> He who has early known the pomps of state,
> (For things unknown 'tis ignorance to condemn;)
> And having view'd the gaudy bait,
> Can boldly say, the trifle I contemn;
> With such a one contented could I live,
> Contented could I die.

In 1771, Mr. Strahan, the printer, who had been long in intimacy with Johnson, who was at once his friendly agent in receiving his pension for him, and his banker in supplying him with money when he wanted it; who was himself now a member of parliament, and who loved much to be employed in political negotiation; thought he should do eminent service, both to government and Johnson, if he could be the means of his getting a seat in the House of Commons. With this view, he wrote a letter to one of the Secretaries of the Treasury.

This recommendation, we know, was not effectual; but how, or

for what reason, can only be conjectured.[1] It is not to be believed
that Mr. Strahan would have applied, unless Johnson had approved
of it. I never heard him mention the subject; but at a later period
of his life, when Sir Joshua Reynolds told him that Mr. Edmund
Burke had said, that if he had come early into parliament, he
certainly would have been the greatest speaker that ever was
there, Johnson exclaimed, "I should like to try my hand now."

I at length renewed a correspondence which had been too long
discontinued.

I gave him an account of my comfortable life as a married
man[2] and a lawyer in practice at the Scotch bar; invited him to
Scotland, and promised to attend him to the Highlands and
Hebrides.

To James Boswell, Esq.

London, June 20, 1771

Dear Sir,

If you are now able to comprehend that I might neglect to
write without diminution of affection, you have taught me, likewise, how that neglect may be uneasily felt without resentment.
I wished for your letter a long time, and when it came, it amply
recompensed the delay. I never was so much pleased as now with
your account of yourself; and sincerely hope, that between public
business, improving studies, and domestic pleasures, neither melancholy nor caprice will find any place for entrance. Whatever
philosophy may determine of material nature, it is certainly true
of intellectual nature, that it *abhors a vacuum:* our minds cannot
be empty; and evil will break in upon them, if they are not pre-
occupied by good. My dear Sir, mind your studies, mind your
business, make your lady happy, and be a good Christian. . . .

If we perform our duty, we shall be safe and steady, "*Sive per,*"
&c. whether we climb the Highlands, or are tossed among the
Hebrides; and I hope the time may come when we may try our

---

[1] Mr. Thrale made a like attempt. He had two meetings with the minister, who, at first, seemed
inclined to find him a seat; but, whether upon conversation he doubted his fitness for the purpose, or
that he thought himself in no need of his assistance, the project failed. Johnson was a little soured
at this disappointment: he spoke of Lord North in terms of severity.

   Lord Stowell added, that it was understood amongst Johnson's friends that "Lord North was afraid
that Johnson's *help* (as he himself said of Lord Chesterfield's) might have been sometimes *embarrassing*.
He perhaps thought, and not unreasonably, that, like the elephant in the battle, he was quite as likely
to trample down his friends as his foes."

[2] Boswell had married, in November, 1769, Miss Margaret Montgomerie, of the family of the Mont-
gomeries of Lainshawe, who were baronets, and claimed the peerage of Lyle. Dr. Johnson says of this
lady to Mrs. Thrale: "Mrs. B. has the mien and manner of a gentlewoman, and such a person and mind
as would not in any place either be admired or condemned. She is in a proper degree inferior to her
husband: she cannot rival him, nor can he ever be ashamed of her."

powers both with cliffs and water. . . . I am this day going into Staffordshire and Derbyshire for six weeks. I am, dear Sir, your most affectionate and most humble servant,

SAM. JOHNSON

In his religious record of this year we observe that he was better than usual, both in body and mind, and better satisfied with the regularity of his conduct. But he is still "trying his ways" too rigorously. He charges himself with not rising early enough; yet he mentions what was surely a sufficient excuse for this: "One great hindrance is want of rest; my nocturnal complaints grow less troublesome towards morning; and I am tempted to repair the deficiencies of the night." Alas! how hard would it be, if this indulgence were to be imputed to a sick man as a crime. In his retrospect on the following Easter-eve, he says, "When I review the last year, I am able to recollect so little done, that shame and sorrow, though perhaps too weakly, come upon me." Had he been judging of any one else in the same circumstances, how clear would he have been on the favourable side. How very difficult, and in my opinion almost constitutionally impossible, it was for him to be raised early, even by the strongest resolutions, appears from a note in one of his little paper-books (containing words arranged for his "Dictionary"), written, I suppose, about 1753: "I do not remember that, since I left Oxford, I ever rose early by mere choice, but once or twice at Edial, and two or three times for the 'Rambler.' " I think he had fair ground enough to have quieted his mind on the subject, by concluding that he was physically incapable of what is at best but a commodious regulation.

In 1772 he was altogether quiescent as an author; but it will be found, from the various evidences which I shall bring together, that his mind was acute, lively, and vigorous.

To Dr. Johnson

MY DEAR SIR,

It is hard that I cannot prevail on you to write to me oftener. But I am convinced that it is in vain to expect from you a private correspondence with any regularity. I must, therefore, look upon you as a fountain of wisdom, from whence few rills are communicated to a distance, and which must be approached at its source, to partake fully of its virtues. . . .

I am coming to London soon, and am to appear in an appeal

from the Court of Session in the House of Lords. A schoolmaster in Scotland was, by a court of inferior jurisdiction, deprived of his office, for being somewhat severe in the chastisement of his scholars. The Court of Session, considering it to be dangerous to the interest of learning and education, to lessen the dignity of teachers, and make them afraid of too indulgent parents, instigated by the complaints of their children, restored him. His enemies have appealed to the House of Lords, though the salary is only twenty pounds a year. I was counsel for him here. I hope there will be little fear of a reversal; but I must beg to have your aid in my plan of supporting the decree. It is a general question, and not a point of particular law. . . . I am, &c.,

JAMES BOSWELL

To James Boswell, Esq.

March 15, 1772

DEAR SIR,
    That you are coming so soon to town I am very glad; and still more glad that you are coming as an advocate. I think nothing more likely to make your life pass happily away, than that consciousness of your own value, which eminence in your profession will certainly confer. If I can give you any collateral help, I hope you do not suspect that it will be wanting. My kindness for you has neither the merit of singular virtue, nor the reproach of singular prejudice. Whether to love you be right or wrong, I have many on my side: Mrs. Thrale loves you, and Mrs. Williams loves you, and, what would have inclined me to love you, if I had been neutral before, you are a great favourite of Dr. Beattie. . . . [1]
    The ejection which you come hither to oppose, appears very cruel, unreasonable, and oppressive. I should think there could not be much doubt of your success.
    My health grows better, yet I am not fully recovered. I believe it is held, that men do not recover very fast after threescore. I have not given up the western voyage. But however all this may be or not, let us try to make each other happy when we meet, and not refer our pleasure to distant times or distant places.
    How comes it that you tell me nothing of your lady? I hope to see her some time, and till then shall be glad to hear of her. I am, dear Sir, &c.,   SAM. JOHNSON

    On the 21st of March, I was happy to find myself again in my friend's study, and was glad to see my old acquaintance, Mr.

---

[1] Professor of Moral Philosophy at Aberdeen who had been furnished by Boswell in July 1771 with a letter of introduction to Johnson.

Francis Barber, who was now returned home. Dr. Johnson received me with a hearty welcome; saying, "I am glad you are come, and glad you are come upon such an errand": (alluding to the cause of the schoolmaster). BOSWELL. "I hope, Sir, he will be in no danger. It is a very delicate matter to interfere between a master and his scholars: nor do I see how you can fix the degree of severity that a master may use." JOHNSON. "Why, Sir, till you can fix the degree of obstinacy and negligence of the scholars, you cannot fix the degree of severity of the master. Severity must be continued until obstinacy be subdued, and negligence be cured." He mentioned the severity of Hunter, his own master. "Sir," said I, "Hunter is a Scotch name: so it should seem this schoolmaster, who beat you so severely, was a Scotchman. I can now account for your prejudice against the Scotch." JOHNSON. "Sir, he was not Scotch; and, abating his brutality, he was a very good master."

We talked of his two political pamphlets, "The False Alarm," and "Thoughts concerning Falkland's Islands." JOHNSON. "Well, Sir, which of them did you think the best?" BOSWELL. "I liked the second best." JOHNSON. "Why, Sir, I liked the first best. Sir, there is a subtlety of disquisition in the first, that is worth all the fire of the second." BOSWELL. "Pray, Sir, is it true that Lord North paid you a visit, and that you got two hundred a year in addition to your pension?" JOHNSON. "No, Sir. Except what I had from the bookseller, I did not get a farthing by them. And, between you and me, I believe Lord North is no friend to me." BOSWELL. "How so, Sir?" JOHNSON. "Why, Sir, you cannot account for the fancies of men. Well, how does Lord Elibank? and how does Lord Monboddo?" BOSWELL. "Very well, Sir. Lord Monboddo still maintains the superiority of the savage life." JOHNSON. "What strange narrowness of mind now is that, to think the things we have not known, are better than the things which we have known." BOSWELL. "Why, Sir, that is a common prejudice." JOHNSON. "Yes, Sir, but a common prejudice should not be found in one whose trade it is to rectify error."

He spoke of St. Kilda, the most remote of the Hebrides. I told him, I thought of buying it. JOHNSON. "Pray do, Sir. We will go and pass a winter amid the blasts there. We shall have fine fish, and we will take some dried tongues with us, and some books. We will have a strong-built vessel, and some Orkney men to navigate her. We must build a tolerable house: but we may carry with us a wooden house ready made, and requiring nothing but to be put up. Consider, Sir, by buying St. Kilda, you may keep the people from falling into worse hands. We must give them a clergyman, and he shall be one of Beattie's choosing. He shall be educated at Marischal College. I'll be your Lord Chancellor, or what you please." BOSWELL. "Are you serious, Sir, in advising me to buy St. Kilda? for if you should advise me to go to Japan, I believe I should do it." JOHNSON. "Why yes, Sir, I am serious." BOSWELL. "Why then, I'll see what can be done."

He was engaged to dine abroad, and asked me to return to him in the evening, at nine, which I accordingly did.

We drank tea with Mrs. Williams, who told us a story of second sight, which happened in Wales, where she was born. He listened to it very attentively, and said he should be glad to have some instances of that faculty well authenticated. His elevated wish for more and more evidence for spirit, in opposition to the grovelling belief of materialism, led him to a love of such mysterious disquisitions. He justly observed, that we could have no certainty of the truth of supernatural appearances, unless something was told us which we could not know by ordinary means, or something done which could not be done but by supernatural power; that Pharaoh in reason and justice required such evidence from Moses; nay, that our Saviour said, "If I had not done among them the works which none other man did, they had not had sin."

I mentioned the petition to parliament for removing the subscription to the Thirty-nine Articles. JOHNSON. "It was soon thrown out. Sir, they talk of not making boys at the University subscribe to what they do not understand; but they ought to consider, that our Universities were founded to bring up members for the Church of England, and we must not supply our enemies with arms from our arsenal. No, Sir, the meaning of subscribing is, not that they fully understand all the articles, but that they will adhere to the Church of England. Now, take it in this way, and suppose that they should only subscribe their adherence to the Church of England, there would be still the same difficulty; for still the young men would be subscribing to what they do not understand. For if you should ask them, what do you mean by the Church of England? Do you know in what it differs from the Presbyterian church? from the Romish church? from the Greek church? from the Coptic church? they could not tell you. So, Sir, it comes to the same thing." BOSWELL "But, would it not be sufficient to subscribe the Bible?" Johnson. "Why, no, Sir; for all sects will subscribe the Bible; nay, the Mahometans will subscribe the Bible; for the Mahometans acknowledge Jesus Christ, as well as Moses, but maintain that God sent Mahomet as a still greater prophet than either."

In the morning we had talked of old families, and the respect due to them. Johnson. "Sir, you have a right to that kind of respect, and are arguing for yourself. I am for supporting the principle, and am disinterested in doing it, as I have no such right." Boswell. "Why, Sir, it is one more incitement to a man to do well." Johnson. "Yes, Sir, and it is a matter of opinion, very necessary to keep society together. What is it but opinion, by which we have a respect for authority, that prevents us, who are the rabble, from rising up and pulling down you who are gentlemen from your places, and saying, 'We will be gentlemen in our turn'? Now, Sir, that respect for authority is much more easily granted to a man whose father has had it, than to an upstart, and so society is more easily supported." Boswell. "Perhaps, Sir, it might be done by the respect belonging to office, as among the Romans, where the dress, the *toga*, inspired reverence." Johnson. "Why, we know very little about the Romans. But, surely, it is much easier to respect a man who has always had respect, than to respect a man who we know was last year no better than ourselves, and will be no better next year. In republics there is no respect for authority, but a fear of power." Boswell. "At present, Sir, I think riches seem to gain most respect." Johnson. "No, Sir, riches do not gain hearty respect; they only procure external attention. A very rich man, from low beginnings, may buy his election in a borough; but, *cæteris paribus*, a man of family will be preferred. People will prefer a man for whose father their fathers have voted, though they should get no more money, or even less. That shows that the respect for family is not merely fanciful, but has an actual operation. If gentlemen of family would allow the rich upstarts to spend their money profusely, which they are ready enough to do, and not vie with them in expense, the upstarts would soon be at an end, and the gentlemen would remain; but if the gentlemen will vie in expense with the upstarts, which is very foolish, they must be ruined."

On Monday, March 23, I found him busy, preparing a fourth edition of his folio "Dictionary." Mr. Peyton, one of his original amanuenses, was writing for him. He seemed also to be intent on some sort of chemical operation. I was entertained by observing how he contrived to send Mr. Peyton on an errand, without seeming to degrade him: "Mr. Peyton, Mr. Peyton, will you be so good as to take a walk to Temple-Bar? You will there see a chemist's shop, at which you will be pleased to buy for me an ounce of oil of vitriol; not spirit of vitriol, but oil of vitriol. It will cost three halfpence." Peyton immediately went, and returned with it, and told him it cost but a penny.

I then reminded him of the Schoolmaster's cause, and proposed to read to him the printed papers concerning it. "No, Sir," said he, "I can read quicker than I can hear." So he read them to himself. I said, "I am afraid, Sir, it is troublesome." "Why, Sir," said he, "I do not take much delight in it; but I'll go through it."

We went to the Mitre, and dined in the room where he and I first supped together. He gave me great hopes of my cause. "Sir," said he, "the government of a schoolmaster is somewhat of the nature of military government; that is to say, it must be arbitrary, —it must be exercised by the will of one man, according to particular circumstances. You must show some learning upon this occasion. You must show that a schoolmaster has a prescriptive right to beat; and that an action of assault and battery cannot be admitted against him unless there is some great excess, some barbarity. This man has maimed none of his boys. They are all left with the full exercise of their corporeal faculties. In our schools in England, many boys have been maimed; yet I never heard an action against a schoolmaster on that account. Puffendorf, I think, maintains the right of a schoolmaster to beat his scholars."

On Saturday, March 27, I introduced to him Sir Alexander Macdonald. Sir Alexander observed, "I have been correcting several Scotch accents in my friend Boswell. I doubt, Sir, if any Scotchman ever attains to a perfect English pronunciation." JOHNSON. "Why, Sir, few of them do, because they do not persevere after acquiring a certain degree of it."

Upon another occasion I talked to him on this subject, having myself taken some pains to improve my pronunciation, by the aid of the late Mr. Love, of Drury Lane theatre, when he was a player at Edinburgh, and also of old Mr. Sheridan. Johnson said to me, "Sir, your pronunciation is not offensive." With this concession I was pretty well satisfied; and let me give my countrymen of North Britain an advice not to aim at absolute perfection in this respect. A small intermixture of provincial peculiarities may, perhaps, have an agreeable effect.

I again visited him at night. Finding him in a very good humour, I ventured to lead him to the subject of our situation in a future state, having much curiosity to know his notions on that point. JOHNSON. "Why, Sir, the happiness of an unembodied spirit will consist in a consciousness of the favour of God, in the contemplation of truth, and in the possession of felicitating ideas." BOSWELL. "But, Sir, is there any harm in our forming to ourselves conjectures as to the particulars of our happiness, though the Scripture has said but very little on the subject? 'We know not what we shall be.'" JOHNSON. "Sir, there is no harm. What philosophy suggests to us on this topic is probable: what Scripture tells us is certain. Dr. Henry More has carried it as far as philosophy can. You may buy both his theological and philosophical works, in two volumes folio, for about eight shillings." BOSWELL. "One of the most pleasing thoughts is, that we shall see our friends again." JOHNSON. "Yes, Sir: but you must consider, that when we are become purely rational, many of our friendships will be cut off. Many friendships are formed by a community of sensual pleasures: all these will be cut off. We form many friendships with bad men, because they have agreeable qualities, and they can be useful to us; but, after death, they can no longer be of use to us. We form many friendships by mistake, imagining people to be different from what they really are. After death, we shall see every one in a true light. Then, Sir, they talk of our meeting our relations; but then all relationship is dissolved; and we shall have no regard for one person more than another, but for their real value. However, we shall either have the satisfaction of meeting our friends, or be satisfied without meeting them." BOSWELL. "Yet, Sir, we see in Scripture, that Dives still retained an anxious concern about his brethren." JOHNSON. "Why, Sir, we must either suppose that passage to be metaphorical, or hold, with many divines and all the Purgatorians, that departed souls do not all at once arrive at the utmost perfection of which they are capable." BOSWELL. "I think, Sir, that is a very rational supposition." JOHNSON. "Why yes, Sir; but we do not know it is a true one. There is no harm in believing it: but you must not compel others to make it an article of faith; for it is not revealed." BOSWELL. "Do you think, Sir, it is wrong in a man who holds the doctrine of Purgatory, to pray for the souls of his deceased friends?" JOHNSON. "Why no, Sir." BOSWELL. "I have been told, that in the liturgy of the episcopal church of Scotland, there was a form of prayer for the dead."

JOHNSON. "Sir, it is not in the liturgy which Laud framed for the episcopal church of Scotland: if there is a liturgy older than that, I should be glad to see it." BOSWELL. "As to our employment in a future state, the sacred writings say little. The Revelation, however, of St. John gives us many ideas, and particularly mentions music." JOHNSON. "Why, Sir, ideas must be given you by means of something which you know: and as to music, there are some philosophers and divines who have maintained, that we shall not be spiritualised to such a degree, but that something of matter, very much refined, will remain. In that case, music may make a part of our future felicity."

BOSWELL. "I do not know whether there are any well-attested stories of the appearance of ghosts. You know there is a famous story of the appearance of Mrs. Veal, prefixed to 'Drelincourt on Death.'" JOHNSON. "I believe, Sir, that is given up. I believe the woman declared upon her death-bed that it was a lie."[1] BOSWELL. "This objection is made against the truth of ghosts appearing: that if they are in a state of happiness, it would be a punishment to them to return to this world; and if they are in a state of misery, it would be giving them a respite." JOHNSON. "Why, Sir, as the happiness or misery of unembodied spirits does not depend upon place, but is intellectual, we cannot say that they are less happy or less miserable by appearing upon earth."

We went down between twelve and one to Mrs. Williams' room, and drank tea.

On Tuesday, March 31, he and I dined at General Paoli's. A question was started, whether the state of marriage was natural to man. JOHNSON. "Sir, it is so far from being natural for a man and woman to live in a state of marriage, that we find all the motives which they have for remaining in that connection, and the restraints which civilized society imposes to prevent separation, are hardly sufficient to keep them together." The General said, that in a state of nature a man and woman uniting together would form a strong and constant affection, by the mutual pleasure each would receive; and that the same causes of dissension would not arise between them, as occur between husband and wife in a civilized state. JOHNSON. "Sir, they would have dissensions enough, though of another kind. One would choose to go a hunting in this wood, the other in that; one would choose to go a fishing in this

---

[1] This fiction was invented by Daniel Defoe, and was added to the second edition of the English translation of Drelincourt's work (which was originally written in French), to make it sell.

lake, the other in that; or, perhaps, one would choose to go a hunting, when the other would choose to go a fishing; and so they would part. Besides, Sir, a savage man and a savage woman meet by chance: and when the man sees another woman that pleases him better, he will leave the first."

We then fell into a disquisition, whether there is any beauty independent of utility. The General maintained there was not. Dr. Johnson maintained that there was; and he instanced a coffee cup which he held in his hand, the painting of which was of no real use, as the cup would hold the coffee equally well if plain; yet the painting was beautiful.

Dr. Johnson went home with me to my lodgings in Conduit Street and drank tea, previous to our going to the Pantheon, which neither of us had seen before.

He said, "Goldsmith's 'Life of Parnell' is poor; not that it is poorly written, but that he had poor materials; for nobody can write the life of a man, but those who have eat and drunk and lived in social intercourse with him."

I said, that if it was not troublesome and presuming too much, I would request him to tell me all the little circumstances of his life; what schools he attended, when he came to Oxford, when he came to London, &c. &c. He did not disapprove of my curiosity as to these particulars; but said, "They'll come out by degrees, as we talk together."

We talked of the proper use of riches. JOHNSON. "If I were a man of great estate, I would drive all the rascals whom I did not like out of the county, at an election."

I asked him, how far he thought wealth should be employed in hospitality. JOHNSON. "You are to consider that ancient hospitality, of which we hear so much, was in an uncommercial country, when men, being idle, were glad to be entertained at rich men's tables. But in a commercial country, a busy country, time becomes precious, and therefore hospitality is not so much valued. No doubt there is still room for a certain degree of it; and a man has a satisfaction in seeing his friends eating and drinking around him. But promiscuous hospitality is not the way to gain real influence. You must help some people at table before others; you must ask some people how they like their wine oftener than others. You therefore offend more people than you please. You are like the French statesman, who said, when he granted a favour, '*J'ai fait dix mécontents et un ingrat.*' Besides, Sir, being entertained ever so well at a man's table, impresses no lasting regard or esteem. No, Sir, the way to make sure of power and influence is, by lending money confidentially to your neighbours at a small interest, or perhaps at no interest at all, and having their bonds in your possession." We then walked to the Pantheon. The first view of it did not strike us so much as Ranelagh,[1] of which he said, "the *coup d'œil* was the finest thing he had ever seen." I said there was not half a guinea's worth of pleasure in seeing this place. JOHNSON. "But, Sir, there is half a guinea's worth of inferiority to other people in not having seen it." BOSWELL. "I doubt, Sir, whether there are many happy people here." JOHNSON. "Yes, Sir, there are many happy people here. There are many people here who are watching hundreds, and who think hundreds are watching them."

Happening to meet Sir Adam Ferguson, I presented him to Dr. Johnson. Sir Adam expressed some apprehension that the Pantheon would encourage luxury. "Sir," said Johnson, "I am a great friend to public amusements; for they keep people from vice. You now," addressing himself to me, "would have been with a wench, had you not been here. Oh! I forgot you were married."

Sir Adam suggested, that luxury corrupts a people, and destroys the spirit of liberty. JOHNSON. "Sir, that is all visionary. I would not give half a guinea to live under one form of government rather than another. It is of no moment to the happiness of an individual. Sir, the danger of the abuse of power is nothing to a private man. What Frenchman is prevented from passing his life as he pleases?" SIR ADAM. "But, Sir, in the British constitution it is surely of importance to keep up a spirit in the people, so to preserve a balance against the crown." JOHNSON. "Sir, I perceive you are a vile Whig. Why all this childish jealousy of the power of the crown? The crown has not power enough. When I say that all governments are alike, I consider that in no government power can be abused long. Mankind will not bear it. If a sovereign oppresses his people to a great degree, they will rise and cut off his head. There is a remedy in human nature against tyranny, that will keep us safe under every form of government. Had not the people of France thought themselves honoured in sharing in the brilliant

[1] *Ranelagh*, so called because its site was that of a villa of Viscount Ranelagh, near Chelsea, was a place of entertainment, of which the principal room was a *Rotunda* of great dimensions, with an orchestra in the centre, and tiers of boxes all round. The chief amusement was *promenading*, as it was called, round and round the circular area below, and taking refreshments in the boxes, while the orchestra executed different pieces of music. The *Pantheon*, in Oxford Street, was built in 1772, after Wyatt's designs, as a kind of *town Ranelagh*, but partook more of the shape of a theatre. The original Pantheon was burned down in 1792, but was rebuilt on a more moderate scale. In 1834, the building was converted into a bazaar.

actions of Louis XIV, they would not have endured him; and we may say the same of the King of Prussia's people." Sir Adam introduced the ancient Greeks and Romans. JOHNSON. "Sir, the mass of both of them were barbarians. The mass of every people must be barbarous where there is no printing, and consequently knowledge is not generally diffused. Knowledge is diffused among our people by the newspapers." Sir Adam mentioned the orators, poets, and artists of Greece. JOHNSON. "Sir, I am talking of the mass of the people. We see even what the boasted Athenians were. The little effect which Demosthenes' orations had upon them shows that they were barbarians."

On Sunday, April 5, after attending divine service at St. Paul's church, I found him alone. I mentioned a cause in which I had appeared as counsel at the bar of the General Assembly of the Church of Scotland, where a *Probationer* (as one licensed to preach, but not yet ordained, is called) was opposed in his application to be inducted, because it was alleged that he had been guilty of fornication five years before. JOHNSON. "Why, Sir, if he has repented, it is not a sufficient objection. A man who is good enough to go to heaven, is good enough to be a clergyman." I told him, that by the rules of the Church of Scotland, in their "Book of Discipline," if a *scandal*, as it is called, is not prosecuted for five years, it cannot afterwards be proceeded upon, "unless it be *of a heinous nature*, or again become flagrant"; and that hence a question arose, whether fornication was a sin of a heinous nature. JOHNSON. "No, Sir, it is not a heinous sin. A heinous sin is that for which a man is punished with death or banishment." BOSWELL. "But, Sir, after I had argued that it was not a heinous sin, an old clergyman rose up, and repeating the text of scripture denouncing judgment against whoremongers, asked, whether, considering this, there could be any doubt of fornication being a heinous sin." JOHNSON. "Why, Sir, observe the word *whoremonger*. Every sin, if persisted in, will become heinous. Whoremonger is a dealer in whores, as ironmonger is a dealer in iron. But as you don't call a man an ironmonger for buying and selling a penknife; so you don't call a man a whoremonger for getting one wench with child."

On Monday, April 6, I dined with him at Sir Alexander Macdonald's, where was a young officer in the regimentals of the Scots Royal, who talked with a vivacity, fluency, and precision so uncommon, that he attracted particular attention. He proved to be the Honourable Thomas Erskine.

On Friday, April 10, I dined with him at General Oglethorpe's, where we found Dr. Goldsmith.

I started the question, whether duelling was consistent with moral duty. The brave old general fired at this, and said, with a lofty air, "Undoubtedly a man has a right to defend his honour." GOLDSMITH (turning to me). "I ask you first, Sir, what would you do if you were affronted?" I answered, I should think it necessary to fight. "Why then," replied Goldsmith, "that solves the question." JOHNSON. "No, Sir, it does not solve the question. It does not follow, that what a man would do is therefore right." I said, I wished to have it settled, whether duelling was contrary to the laws of Christianity. Johnson immediately entered on the subject, and treated it in a masterly manner; and so far as I have been able to recollect, his thoughts were these: "Sir, as men become in a high degree refined, various causes of offence arise; which are considered to be of such importance, that life must be staked to atone for them, though in reality they are not so. A body that has received a very fine polish may be easily hurt. Before men arrive at this artificial refinement, if one tells his neighbour—he lies, his neighbour tells him—he lies; if one gives his neighbour a blow, his neighbour gives him a blow; but in a state of highly polished society, an affront is held to be a serious injury. It must, therefore, be resented, or rather a duel must be fought upon it; as men have agreed to banish from society one who puts up with an affront without fighting a duel. Now, Sir, it is never unlawful to fight in self-defence. He, then, who fights a duel does not fight from passion against his antagonist, but out of self-defence; to avert the stigma of the world, and to prevent himself from being driven out of society. I could wish there was not that superfluity of refinement; but while such notions prevail, no doubt a man may lawfully fight a duel.

"Let it be remembered, that this justification is applicable only to the person who *receives* an affront. All mankind must condemn the aggressor."[1]

The General told us, that, when he was a very young man, I think only fifteen, serving under Prince Eugene of Savoy, he was sitting in a company at table with a prince of Wirtemberg. The prince took up a glass of wine, and, by a fillip, made some of it fly in Oglethorpe's face. Here was a nice dilemma. To have challenged him instantly, might have fixed a quarrelsome character

---

[1] Boswell's eldest son, Sir Alexander, was killed in a duel, arising from a political dispute, on the 26th of March, 1822, by Mr. Stuart, of Dunearn. This conversation on duelling was quoted on Mr. Stuart's trial by his counsel, Mr. Jeffrey, afterwards Lord Jeffrey.

upon the young soldier: to have taken no notice of it, might have been considered as cowardice. Oglethorpe, therefore, keeping his eye upon the prince, and smiling all the time, as if he took what his highness had done in jest, said "*Mon Prince,—*" (I forget the French words he used; the purport however was) "That's a good joke; but we do it much better in England"; and threw a whole glass of wine in the prince's face. An old general, who sat by, said, "*Il a bien fait, mon prince, vous l'avez commencé*": and thus all ended in good humour.

Dr. Johnson said, "Pray, General, give us an account of the siege of Belgrade." Upon which the general, pouring a little wine upon the table, described every thing with a wet finger: "Here we were; here were the Turks," &c. &c. Johnson listened with the closest attention.

A question was started, how far people who disagree in a capital point can live in friendship together. Johnson said they might. Goldsmith said they could not, as they had not the *idem velle atque idem nolle*—the same likings and the same aversions. JOHNSON. "Why, Sir, you must shun the subject as to which you disagree. For instance, I can live very well with Burke: I love his knowledge, his genius, his diffusion and affluence of conversation; but I would not talk to him of the Rockingham party." GOLDSMITH. "But, Sir, when people live together who have something as to which they disagree, and which they want to shun, they will be in the situation mentioned in the story of Bluebeard: 'You may look into all the chambers but one.' But we should have the greatest inclination to look into that chamber, to talk of that subject." JOHNSON (with a loud voice). "Sir, I am not saying that *you* could live in friendship with a man from whom you differ as to some point; I am only saying that *I* could do it."

Goldsmith told us, that he was now busy in writing a Natural History;[1] and, that he might have full leisure for it, he had taken lodgings at a farmer's house, near to the six mile-stone, on the Edgeware-road, and had carried down his books in two returned post-chaises. He said, he believed the farmer's family thought him an odd character. Mr. Mickle, the translator of "The Lusiad," and I, went to visit him at this place a few days afterwards. He was not at home; but, having a curiosity to see his apartment, we went in, and found curious scraps of descriptions of animals, scrawled upon the wall with a black-lead pencil.

[1] Published, in 1774, under the title of *A History of the Earth and Animated Nature.*

THREW A WHOLE GLASS OF WINE IN THE PRINCE'S FACE

The subject of ghosts being introduced, Johnson repeated what he had told me of a friend of his [Cave], an honest man, and a man of sense, having asserted to him that he had seen an apparition. Goldsmith told us, he was assured by his brother, the Reverend Mr. Goldsmith, that he also had seen one. General Oglethorpe told us, that Prendergast, an officer in the Duke of Marlborough's army, had mentioned to many of his friends, that he should die on a particular day. That upon that day a battle took place with the French; that after it was over, and Prendergast was still alive, his brother officers, while they were yet in the field, jestingly asked him, where was his prophecy now? Prendergast gravely answered, "I shall die, notwithstanding what you see." Soon afterwards, there came a shot from a French battery, to which the orders for a cessation of arms had not yet reached, and he was killed upon the spot.

On Saturday, April 11, Johnson appointed me to come to him in the evening, when he should be at leisure to give me some assistance for the defence of Hastie, the schoolmaster, for whom I was to appear in the House of Lords. When I came, I found him unwilling to exert himself. I pressed him to write down his thoughts upon the subject. He said, "There's no occasion for my writing: I'll talk to you." He was, however, at last prevailed on to dictate to me, while I wrote.

The charge is, that he has used immoderate and cruel correction. Correction in itself is not cruel; children, being not reasonable, can be governed only by fear. To impress this fear is, therefore, one of the first duties of those who have the care of children. It is the duty of a parent; and has never been thought inconsistent with parental tenderness. It is the duty of a master, who is in his highest exaltation when he is *loco parentis*. Yet, as good things become evil by excess, correction, by being immoderate, may become cruel. But when is correction immoderate? When it is more frequent or more severe than is required *ad monendum et docendum*, for reformation and instruction. No severity is cruel which obstinacy makes necessary; for the greatest cruelty would be, to desist, and leave the scholar too careless for instruction, and too much hardened for reproof. Locke, in his treatise of education, mentions a mother, with applause, who whipped an infant eight times before she subdued it; for had she stopped at the seventh act of correction, her daughter, says he, would have been ruined. The degrees of obstinacy in young minds are very different: as different must be the degrees of persevering severity. A stubborn scholar must be corrected till he is subdued. The discipline of a school is military. There must be either unbounded licence or absolute authority. The master, who punishes, not only consults the future happiness of him who is the immediate subject of correction, but he propagates obedience through the whole school, and establishes regulatory by exemplary justice. The victorious obstinacy of a single boy would make his future endeavours of reformation or instruction totally ineffectual. Obstinacy, therefore, must never be victorious. Yet it is well known, that there sometimes occurs a sullen and hardy resolution, that laughs at all common punishment, and bids defiance to all common degrees of pain. Correction must be proportionate to occasions. The flexible will be reformed by gentle discipline, and the refractory must be subdued by harsher methods. The degrees of scholastic as well as of military punishment, no stated rules can ascertain. It must be enforced till it overpowers temptation; till stubbornness becomes flexible, and perverseness regular. Custom and reason have, indeed, set some bounds to scholastic penalties. The schoolmaster inflicts no capital punishments; nor enforces his edicts by either death or mutilation. The civil law has wisely determined, that a master who strikes at a scholar's eye shall be considered as criminal. But punishments, however severe, that produce no lasting evil, may be just and reasonable, because they may be necessary. Such have been the punishments used by the respondent. No scholar has gone from him either blind or lame, or with any of his limbs or powers injured or impaired. They were irregular, and he punished them: they were obstinate, and he enforced his punishment. But however provoked, he never exceeded the limits of moderation, for he inflicted nothing beyond present pain; and how much of that was required, no man is so little able to determine as those who have determined against him—the parents of the offenders. It has been said, that he used unprecedented and improper instruments of correction. Of this accusation the meaning is not very easy to be found. No instrument of correction is more proper than another, but as it is better adapted to produce present pain without lasting mischief. Whatever were his instruments, no lasting mischief has ensued; and therefore, however unusual, in hands so cautious they were proper. It has been objected, that the respondent admits the charge of cruelty by producing no evidence to confute it. Let it be considered, that his scholars are either dispersed at large in the world, or continue to inhabit the place in which they were bred. Those who are dispersed cannot be found; those who remain are the sons of his prosecutors, and are not likely to support a man to whom their fathers are enemies. If it be supposed that the enmity of their fathers proves the justness of the charge, it must be considered how often experience shows us, that men who are angry on one ground will accuse one another; with how little kindness, in a town of low trade, a man who lives by learning is regarded; and how implicitly, where the inhabitants are not very rich, a rich man is hearkened to and followed. In a place like Campbelltown, it is easy for one of the principal inhabitants to make a party. It is easy for that party to heat themselves with imaginary grievances. It is easier for them to oppress a man poorer than themselves, and natural to assert the dignity of riches, by persisting in oppression. The argument which attempts to prove the impropriety of restoring him to the school, by alleging that he has lost the confidence of the people, is not the subject of juridical consideration; for he is to suffer, if he must suffer, not for their judgment, but for his own actions. It may be convenient for them to have another master; but it is a convenience of their own making. It would be likewise convenient for him to find another school; but this convenience he cannot obtain. The question is not what is now convenient, but what is generally right. If the people of Campbelltown be distressed by the restoration of the respondent, they are distressed only by their own fault; by turbulent passions and unreasonable desires; by tyranny, which law has defeated, and by malice, which virtue has surmounted.

"This, Sir," said he, "you are to turn in your mind, and make the best use of it you can in your speech."

Of our friend Goldsmith he said, "Sir, he is so much afraid of being unnoticed, that he often talks merely lest you should forget that he is in the company." BOSWELL. "Yes, he stands forward." JOHNSON. "True, Sir; but if a man is to stand forward, he should wish to do it, not in an awkward posture, not in rags, not so as that he shall only be exposed to ridicule." BOSWELL. "For my part, I like very well to hear honest Goldsmith talk away carelessly." JOHNSON. "Why, yes, Sir; but he should not like to hear himself."

On Tuesday, April 14, the decree of the court of sessions in the schoolmaster's cause was reversed in the House of Lords, after a very eloquent speech by Lord Mansfield, who showed himself an adept in school discipline, but I thought was too rigorous towards my client. On the evening of the next day I supped with Dr. Johnson, at the Crown and Anchor tavern, in the Strand. I repeated a sentence of Lord Mansfield's speech: "My Lords, severity is not the way to govern either boys or men." "Nay," said Johnson, "it is the way to *govern* them. I know not whether it be the way to *mend* them."

I talked of the recent expulsion of six students from the University of Oxford, who were methodists, and would not desist from publicly praying and exhorting. JOHNSON. "Sir, that expulsion was extremely just and proper. What have they to do at an university, who are not willing to be taught, but will presume to teach? Where is religion to be learnt but at an university? Sir, they were examined, and found to be mighty ignorant fellows." BOSWELL. "But, was it not hard, Sir, to expel them; for I am told they were good beings?" JOHNSON. "I believe they might be good beings; but they were not fit to be in the University of Oxford. A cow is a very good animal in the field; but we turn her out of a garden."

Mr. Langton told us he was about to establish a school upon his estate; but it had been suggested to him, that it might have a tendency to make the people less industrious. JOHNSON. "No, Sir; while learning to read and write is a distinction, the few who have that distinction may be the less inclined to work; but when every body learns to read and write, it is no longer a distinction. A man who has a laced waistcoat is too fine a man to work; but if every body had laced waistcoats, we should have people working in laced waistcoats. There are no people whatever more industrious, none who work more, than our manufacturers; yet they have all learnt to read and write. Sir, you must not neglect doing a thing immediately good, from fear of remote evil; from fear of its being abused. A man who has candles may sit up too late, which he would not do if he had not candles; but nobody will deny that the art of making candles, by which light is continued to us beyond the time that the sun gives us light, is a valuable art, and ought to be preserved." BOSWELL. "But, Sir, would it not be better to follow nature, and go to bed and rise just as nature gives us light or withholds it?" JOHNSON. "No, Sir; for then we should have no kind of equality in the partition of our time between sleeping and waking. It would be very different in different seasons and in different places. In some of the northern parts of Scotland how little light is there in the depth of winter!"

At this time, it appears, from his "Prayers and Meditations," that he had been more than commonly diligent in religious duties, particularly in reading the Holy Scriptures. It was Passion Week, that solemn season which the Christian world has appropriated to the commemoration of the mysteries of our redemption, and during which, whatever embers of religion are in our breasts, will be kindled into pious warmth.

I paid him short visits both on Friday and Saturday; and, seeing his large folio Greek Testament before him, beheld him with a reverential awe, and would not intrude upon his time. While he was thus employed to such good purpose, and while his friends in their intercourse with him constantly found a vigorous intellect and a lively imagination, it is melancholy to read in his private register, "My mind is unsettled and my memory confused. I have of late turned my thoughts with a very useless earnestness upon past incidents. I have yet got no command over my thoughts: an unpleasing incident is almost certain to hinder my rest."

On Sunday April 19, being Easter-day, General Paoli and I paid him a visit before dinner. Talking on the subject of taste in the arts, he said, that difference of taste was, in truth, difference of skill. BOSWELL. "But, Sir, is there not a quality called taste, which consists merely in perception or in liking? for instance, we find people differ much as to what is the best style of English composition. Some think Swift's the best; others prefer a fuller and grander way of writing." JOHNSON. "Sir, you must first define what you mean by style, before you can judge who has a good taste in style, and who has a bad. The two classes of persons whom you have mentioned, don't differ as to good and bad. They both agree that Swift has a good neat style; but one loves a neat style, another loves a style of more splendour. In like manner, one loves a plain coat, another loves a laced coat; but neither will deny that each is good in its kind."

While I remained in London this spring, I was with him at several other times, both by himself and in company.

I regretted the reflection, in his preface to Shakspeare, against Garrick, to whom we cannot but apply the following passage: "I collated such copies as I could procure, and wished for more, but have not found the collectors of these rarities very communicative." I told him, that Garrick had complained to me of it, and had vindicated himself by assuring me, that Johnson was made welcome to the full use of his collection, and that he left the key of it with a servant, with orders to have a fire and every convenience for him. I found Johnson's notion was, that Garrick wanted to be courted for them, and that, on the contrary, Garrick should have courted him, and sent him the plays of his own accord. But, indeed, considering the slovenly and careless manner in which books were treated by Johnson, it could not be expected that scarce and valuable editions should have been lent to him.[1]

A gentleman having, to some of the usual arguments for drinking, added this: "You know, Sir, drinking drives away care, and makes us forget whatever is disagreeable. Would not you allow a man to drink for that reason?" JOHNSON. "Yes, Sir, if he sat next *you*."

When one of his friends endeavoured to maintain that a country gentleman might contrive to pass his life very agreeably, "Sir," said he, "you cannot give me an instance of any man who is permitted to lay out his own time, contriving not to have tedious hours."

A learned gentleman, who, in the course of conversation, wished to inform us of this simple fact, that the counsel upon the circuit of Shrewsbury were much bitten by fleas, took, I suppose, seven or eight minutes in relating it circumstantially. He in a plenitude of phrase told us, that large bales of woollen cloth were lodged in the town-hall; that by reason of this, fleas nestled there in prodigious numbers; that the lodgings of the counsel were near the town-hall; and that those little animals moved from place to place with wonderful agility. Johnson sat in great impatience till the gentleman had finished his tedious narrative, and then burst out (playfully however), "It is a pity, Sir, that you have not seen a lion; for a flea has taken you such a time, that a lion must have served you a twelvemonth."

He would not allow Scotland to derive any credit from Lord Mansfield; for he was educated in England. "Much," said he, "may be made of a Scotchman, if he be *caught* young."

He said, "I am very unwilling to read the manuscripts of authors, and give them my opinion. If the authors who apply to me have money, I bid them boldly print without a name; if they have written in order to get money, then to go to the booksellers and make the best bargain they can." BOSWELL. "But, Sir, if a bookseller should bring you a manuscript to look at?" JOHNSON. "Why, Sir, I would desire the bookseller to take it away."

Before leaving London this year, I renewed my solicitations that Dr. Johnson would accomplish his long-intended visit to Scotland.

In 1773, his only publication was an edition of his folio "Dictionary," with additions and corrections.

---

[1] Cooke records an instance of Johnson's treating Garrick's library very roughly—opening the books so wide as to crack the backs, and throwing them on the floor, to Garrick's very natural displeasure.

To James Boswell, Esq.

London, Feb. 22, 1773

DEAR SIR,

. . . A new edition of my great "Dictionary" is printed, from a copy which I was persuaded to revise; but, having made no preparation, I was able to do very little. Some superfluities I have expunged, and some faults I have corrected, and here and there have scattered a remark; but the main fabric of the work remains as it was. I had looked very little into it since I wrote it; and, I think, I found it full as often better, or worse, than I expected.

Baretti and Davies have had a furious quarrel; a quarrel, I think, irreconcileable. Dr. Goldsmith has a new comedy, which is expected in the spring. No name is yet given it. The chief diversion arises from a stratagem by which a lover is made to mistake his future father-in-law's house for an inn. This, you see, borders upon farce. The dialogue is quick and gay, and the incidents are so prepared as not to seem improbable.[1] . . .

My health seems in general to improve; but I have been troubled for many weeks with a vexatious catarrh, which is sometimes sufficiently distressful. I have not found any great effects from bleeding and physic; and I am afraid that I must expect help from brighter days and softer air.

Write to me now and then; and whenever any good befalls you, make haste to let me know it; for no one will rejoice at it more than, dear Sir, your most humble servant,   SAM. JOHNSON

You continue to stand very high in the favour of Mrs. Thrale.

While a former edition of my work was passing through the press, I was unexpectedly favoured with a packet from Philadelphia, from Mr. James Abercrombie, a gentleman of that country, who is pleased to honour me with very high praise of my "Life of Dr. Johnson." To have the fame of my illustrious friend, and his faithful biographer, echoed from the New World, is extremely flattering; and my grateful acknowledgments shall be wafted across the Atlantic. Mr. Abercrombie has politely conferred on me a considerable additional obligation, by transmitting to me copies of two letters from Dr. Johnson to American gentlemen. "Gladly, Sir," says he, "would I have lent you the originals; but being the only relics of the kind in America, they are considered by

---

[1] "She Stoops to Conquer, or the Mistakes of a Night," was performed, for the first time, at Covent Garden, on the 15th of March.

the possessors of such inestimable value, that no possible consideration would induce them to part with them. In some future publication of yours relative to that great and good man, they may perhaps
be thought worthy of insertion."

To Mr. B——d [1]

London, Johnson's Court, Fleet Street,
March 4, 1773

SIR,
That in the hurry of a sudden departure you should yet find
leisure to consult my convenience, is a degree of kindness, and
an instance of regard, not only beyond my claims, but above
my expectation. You are not mistaken in supposing that I set
a high value on my American friends, and that you should confer
a very valuable favour upon me by giving me an opportunity of
keeping myself in their memory.

I have taken the liberty of troubling you with a packet, to which
I wish a safe and speedy conveyance, because I wish a safe and
speedy voyage to him that conveys it. I am, Sir, your most humble
servant,   SAM. JOHNSON

To Rev. Mr. White [2]

Johnson's Court, March 4, 1773

DEAR SIR,
Your kindness for your friends accompanies you across the
Atlantic. It was long since observed by Horace, that no ship
could leave care behind: you have been attended in your voyage
by other powers,—by benevolence and constancy; and I hope
care did not often show her face in their company.

I received the copy of Rasselas. The impression is not magnificent,
but it flatters an author, because the printer seems to have expected
that it would be scattered among the people. The little book has
been well received, and is translated into Italian, French, German,
and Dutch. It has now one honour more by an American edition.

I know not that much has happened since your departure that
can engage your curiosity. Of all public transactions the whole
world is now informed by the newspapers. Opposition seems to
despond; and the dissenters, though they have taken advantage of

---

[1] Probably a Mr. Richard Bland, of Virginia, a public character of considerable dignity.
[2] Now Dr. White, and Bishop of the Episcopal Church in Pennsylvania. During his first visit to
England in 1771, as a candidate for holy orders, he was several times in company with Dr. Johnson, who
expressed a wish to see the edition of Rasselas, which Dr. White told him had been printed in America.
Dr. White, on his return, immediately sent him a copy.—*Boswell.*

unsettled times, and a government much enfeebled, seem not likely to gain any immunities.

Dr. Goldsmith has a new comedy in rehearsal at Covent Garden, to which the manager predicts ill success. I hope he will be mistaken. I think it deserves a very kind reception.

I shall soon publish a new edition of my large Dictionary. I have been persuaded to revise it, and have mended some faults, but added little to its usefulness.

No book has been published since your departure, of which much notice is taken. Faction only fills the town with pamphlets, and greater subjects are forgotten in the noise of discord.

Thus have I written, only to tell you how little I have to tell. Of myself I can only add, that having been afflicted many weeks with a very troublesome cough, I am now recovered.

I take the liberty which you give me of troubling you with a letter, of which you will please to fill up the direction. I am, Sir, you most humble servant,　　　　　　　　　SAM. JOHNSON

On Saturday, April 3, the day after my arrival in London this year, I went to his house late in the evening, and sat with Mrs. Williams till he came home. I found in the "London Chronicle," Dr. Goldsmith's apology to the public for beating Evans, a bookseller, on account of a paragraph in a newspaper published by him, which Goldsmith thought impertinent to him and to a lady of his acquaintance. The apology was written so much in Dr. Johnson's manner, that both Mrs. Williams and I supposed it to be his; but when he came home, he soon undeceived us. When he said to Mrs. Williams, "Well, Dr. Goldsmith's *manifesto* has got into your paper"; I asked him if Dr. Goldsmith had written it, with an air that made him see I suspected it was his, though subscribed by Goldsmith. JOHNSON. "Sir, Dr. Goldsmith would no more have asked me to write such a thing as that for him, than he would have asked me to feed him with a spoon, or to do any thing else that denoted his imbecility. I as much believe that he wrote it, as if I had seen him do it. Sir, had he shown it to any one friend, he would not have been allowed to publish it. He has, indeed, done it very well; but it is a foolish thing well done. I suppose he has been so much elated with the success of his new comedy, that he has thought every thing that concerned him must be of importance to the public." BOSWELL. "I fancy, Sir, this is the first time that he has been engaged in such an adventure." JOHNSON. "Why, Sir, I believe it is the first time he has *beat*, he may have *been beaten* before. This, Sir, is a new plume to him."

At Mr. Thrale's, in the evening, Lord Chesterfield being mentioned, Johnson remarked, that almost all of that celebrated nobleman's witty sayings were puns. He, however, allowed the merit of good wit to his lordship's saying of Lord Tyrawley and himself, when both very old and infirm: "Tyrawley and I have been dead these two years; but we don't choose to have it known."

On Thursday, April 8, I sat a good part of the evening with him, but he was very silent. Though he was not disposed to talk, he was unwilling that I should leave him; and when I looked at my watch, and told him it was twelve o'clock, he cried, "What's that to you and me?" and ordered Frank to tell Mrs. Williams that we were coming to drink tea with her, which we did. It was settled that we should go to church together next day.

On the 9th of April, being Good Friday, I breakfasted with him on tea and cross-buns; *Doctor* Levett, as Frank called him, making the tea. He carried me with him to the church of St. Clement Danes, where he had his seat; and his behaviour was, as I had imaged to myself, solemnly devout. I never shall forget the tremulous earnestness with which he pronounced the awful petition in the Litany: "In the hour of death, and at the day of judgment, good Lord deliver us."

We went to church both in the morning and evening. In the interval between the two services we did not dine; but he read in the Greek New Testament, and I turned over several of his books.

To my great surprise he asked me to dine with him on Easter Day. I never supposed that he had a dinner at his house; for I had not then heard of any one of his friends having been entertained at his table. He told me, "I generally have a meat pie on Sunday: it is baked at a public oven, which is very properly allowed, because one man can attend it; and thus the advantage is obtained of not keeping servants from church to dress dinners."

April 11, being Easter Sunday, after having attended divine service at St. Paul's, I repaired to Dr. Johnson's. I had gratified my curiosity much in dining with JEAN JACQUES ROUSSEAU, while he lived in the wilds of Neufchâtel: I had as great a curiosity to dine with DR. SAMUEL JOHNSON, in the dusky recess of a court in Fleet Street. I supposed we should scarcely have knives and forks, and only some strange, uncouth, ill-drest dish: but I found every thing in very good order. We had no other company but Mrs. Williams and a young woman whom I did not know. As a dinner here was considered as a singular phenomenon, and as I was frequently interrogated on the subject, my readers may perhaps be desirous to know our bill of fare. Foote, I remember, in allusion to Francis, the *negro*, was willing to suppose that our repast was *black broth*. But the fact was, that we had a very good soup, a boiled leg of lamb and spinach, a veal pie, and a rice pudding.

I put a question to him upon a fact in common life, which he could not answer, nor have I found any one else who could. What is the reason that women servants, though obliged to be at the expense of purchasing their own clothes, have much lower wages than men servants, to whom a great proportion of that article is furnished, and when in fact our female house-servants work much harder than the male?

He told me that he had twelve or fourteen times attempted to keep a journal of his life, but never could persevere. He advised me to do it. "The great thing to be recorded," said he, "is the state of your own mind; and you should write down every thing that you remember, for you cannot judge at first what is good or bad; and write immediately while the impression is fresh, for it will not be the same a week afterwards."

On Tuesday, April 13, he and Dr. Goldsmith and I dined at General Oglethorpe's. Goldsmith expatiated on the common topic, that the race of our people was degenerated, and that this was owing to luxury. JOHNSON. "Sir, in the first place, I doubt the fact. I believe there are as many tall men in England now, as ever there were. But, secondly, supposing the stature of our people to be diminished, that is not owing to luxury; for, Sir, consider to how very small a proportion of our people luxury can reach. Our soldiery, surely, are not luxurious, who live on sixpence a day; and the same remark will apply to almost all the other classes. Luxury, so far as it reaches the poor, will do good to the race of people; it will strengthen and multiply them. Sir, no nation was ever hurt by luxury; for, as I said before, it can reach but to a very few. I admit that the great increase of commerce and manufactures hurts the military spirit of a people; because it produces a competition for something else than martial honours,—a competition for riches. It also hurts the bodies of the people; for you will observe, there is no man who works at any particular trade, but you may know him from his appearance to do so. One part or the other of his body being more used than the rest, he is some degree deformed: but, Sir, that is not luxury. A tailor sits cross-legged; but that is not luxury." GOLDSMITH. "Come, you're just going to the same place by another road." JOHNSON. "Nay, Sir, I say that is not *luxury*. Let us take a walk from Charing Cross to White-chapel, through, I suppose, the greatest series of shops in the world; what is there in any of these shops (if you except gin-shops) that can do any human being any harm?" GOLDSMITH. "Well, Sir, I'll accept your challenge. The very next shop to Northumberland House is a pickle-shop." JOHNSON. "Well, Sir; do we not know that a maid can in one afternoon make pickles sufficient to serve a whole family for a year? nay, that five pickle-shops can serve all the kingdom? Besides, Sir, there is no harm done to any body by the making of pickles, or the eating of pickles."

We drank tea with the ladies; and Goldsmith sang Tony Lumpkin's song in his comedy, "She Stoops to Conquer," and a very pretty one, to an Irish tune, which he had designed for Miss Hardcastle; but as Mrs. Bulkeley, who played the part, could not sing, it was left out. Dr. Johnson, in his way home, stopped at my lodgings in Piccadilly, and sat with me, drinking tea a second time, till a late hour.

I told him that Mrs. Macaulay said, she wondered how he could reconcile his political principles with his moral: his notions of inequality and subordination with wishing well to the happiness of all mankind, who might live so agreeably, had they all their portions of land, and none to domineer over another. JOHNSON. "Why, Sir, I reconcile my principles very well, because mankind are happier in a state of inequality and subordination. Were they to be in this pretty state of equality, they would soon degenerate into brutes; they would become Monboddo's nation; their tails would grow. Sir, all would be losers, were all to work for all: they would have no intellectual improvement. All intellectual improvement arises from leisure; all leisure arises from one working for another."

On Thursday, April 15, I dined with him and Dr. Goldsmith at General Paoli's. We found here Signor Martinelli of Florence, author of a History of England in Italian, printed at London.

I spoke of Allan Ramsay's "Gentle Shepherd," in the Scottish dialect, as the best pastoral that had ever been written; not only abounding with beautiful rural imagery, and just and pleasing sentiments, but being a real picture of manners; and I offered to teach Dr. Johnson to understand it. "No, Sir," said he, "I won't learn it. You shall retain your superiority by my not knowing it."

It having been observed that there was little hospitality in

GOLDSMITH SANG TONY LUMPKIN'S SONG

London: JOHNSON. "Nay, Sir, any man who has a name, or who has the power of pleasing, will be very generally invited in London. The man Sterne, I have been told, has had engagements for three months." GOLDSMITH. "And a very dull fellow." JOHNSON. "Why, no, Sir."

We talked of the king's coming to see Goldsmith's new play. "I wish he would," said Goldsmith: adding, however, with an affected indifference, "Not that it would do me the least good." JOHNSON. "Well then, Sir, let us say it would do *him* good (laughing). No, Sir, this affectation will not pass;—it is mighty idle. In such a state as ours, who would not wish to please the chief magistrate?" GOLDSMITH. "I *do* wish to please him. I remember a line in Dryden—

And every poet is the monarch's friend.

It ought to be reversed." JOHNSON. "Nay, there are finer lines in Dryden on this subject:

For colleges on bounteous Kings depend,
And never rebel was to arts a friend."

General Paoli observed, that successful rebels might. MARTINELLI. "Happy rebellions." GOLDSMITH. "We have no such phrase." GENERAL PAOLI. "But have you not the *thing?*" GOLDSMITH. "Yes; all our *happy* revolutions. They have hurt our constitution, and will hurt it, till we mend it by another HAPPY REVOLUTION."
—I never before discovered that my friend Goldsmith had so much of the old prejudice in him.

A person was mentioned, who it was said could take down in short-hand the speeches in parliament with perfect exactness. JOHNSON. "Sir, it is impossible. I remember one Angel, who came to me to write for him a preface or dedication to a book upon short-hand, and he professed to write as fast as a man could speak. In order to try him, I took down a book, and read while he wrote; and I favoured him, for I read more deliberately than usual. I had proceeded but a very little way, when he begged I would desist, for he could not follow me."

On Monday, April 19, he called on me with Mrs. Williams, in Mr. Strahan's coach, and carried me out to dine. A printer having acquired a fortune sufficient to keep his coach, was a good topic for the credit of literature. Mrs. Williams said, that another printer, Mr. Hamilton, had not waited so long as Mr. Strahan, but had kept his coach several years sooner. JOHNSON. "He was in the right. Life is short. The sooner that a man begins to enjoy his wealth, the better."

He this day again defended duelling, and put his argument upon what I have ever thought the most solid basis; that if public war be allowed to be consistent with morality, private war must be equally so. Indeed we may observe what strained arguments are used to reconcile war with the Christian religion. But, in my opinion, it is exceedingly clear that duelling, having better reasons for its barbarous violence, is more justifiable than war, in which thousands go forth without any cause of personal quarrel, and massacre each other.

On Wednesday, April 21, I dined with him at Mr. Thrale's. A gentleman attacked Garrick for being vain. JOHNSON. "No wonder, Sir, that he is vain; a man who is perpetually flattered in every mode that can be conceived. So many bellows have blown the fire, that one wonders he is not by this time become a cinder." BOSWELL. "And such bellows too! Lord Mansfield with his cheeks like to burst: Lord Chatham like an Æolus. I have read such notes from them to him, as were enough to turn his head." JOHNSON. "True. When he whom every body else flatters, flatters me, I then am truly happy." MRS. THRALE. "The sentiment is in Congreve, I think." JOHNSON. "Yes, Madam, in 'The Way of the World':

> If there's delight in love, 'tis when I see
> That heart which others bleed for, bleed for me.

No, Sir, I should not be surprised though Garrick chained the ocean and lashed the winds."

The various views with which men travel in quest of new scenes having been talked of, a learned gentleman expatiated on the happiness of a savage life; and mentioned an instance of an officer who had lived for some time in the wilds of America, of whom, when in that state, he quoted this reflection with an air of admiration: "Here am I, free and unrestrained, amidst the rude magnificence of Nature, with this Indian woman by my side, and this gun, with which I can procure food when I want it: what more can be desired for human happiness?" JOHNSON. "Do not allow yourself, Sir, to be imposed upon by such gross absurdity. It is sad stuff; it is brutish. If a bull could speak, he might as well exclaim,—Here am I with this cow and this grass; what being can enjoy greater felicity?"

We talked of the melancholy end of a gentleman who had destroyed himself. JOHNSON. "It was owing to imaginary difficulties in his affairs, which, had he talked of with any friend, would soon have vanished." BOSWELL. "Do you think, Sir, that all who commit suicide are mad?" JOHNSON. "Sir, they are often not universally disordered in their intellects, but one passion presses so upon them, that they yield to it, and commit suicide, as a passionate man will stab another." He added, "I have often thought, that after a man has taken the resolution to kill himself, it is not courage in him to do any thing, however desperate, because he has nothing to fear." GOLDSMITH. "I don't see that." JOHNSON. "Nay, but, my dear Sir, why should you not see what every one else sees?" GOLDSMITH. "It is for fear of something that he has resolved to kill himself: and will not that timid disposition restrain him?" JOHNSON. "It does not signify that the fear of something made him resolve; it is upon the state of his mind, after the resolution is taken, that I argue. Suppose a man, either from fear, or pride, or conscience, or whatever motive, has resolved to kill himself; when once the resolution is taken, he has nothing to fear. He may then go and take the king of Prussia by the nose, at the head of his army. He cannot fear the rack, who is resolved to kill himself. When Eustace Budgel was walking down to the Thames, determined to drown himself, he might, if he pleased, without any apprehension of danger, have turned aside, and first set fire to St. James's Palace."

On Tuesday, April 27, Mr. Beauclerk and I called on him in the morning. As we walked up Johnson's Court, I said, "I have a veneration for this court"; and was glad to find that Beauclerk had the same reverential enthusiasm. We found him alone. He said, "Goldsmith should not be for ever attempting to shine in conversation: he has not temper for it, he is so much mortified when he fails. Sir, a game of jokes is composed partly of skill, partly of chance; a man may be beat at times by one who has not the tenth part of his wit. Now Goldsmith's putting himself against another, is like a man laying a hundred to one, who cannot spare the hundred. It is not worth a man's while. A man should not lay a hundred to one, unless he can easily spare it, though he has a hundred chances for him: he can get but a guinea, and may lose a hundred. Goldsmith is in this state. When he contends, if he gets the better, it is a very little addition to a man of his literary reputation: if he does not get the better, he is miserably vexed."

Johnson's own superlative powers of wit set him above any risk of such uneasiness. Garrick had remarked to me of him, a few days before, "Rabelais and all other wits are nothing compared with him. You may be diverted by them; but Johnson gives you a forcible hug, and shakes laughter out of you, whether you will or no."

Goldsmith, however, was often very fortunate in his witty contests, even when he entered the lists with Johnson himself. Sir Joshua Reynolds was in company with them one day, when Goldsmith said, that he thought he could write a good fable, mentioned the simplicity which that kind of composition requires, and observed, that in most fables the animals introduced seldom talk in character. "For instance," said he, "the fable of the little fishes, who saw birds fly over their heads, and, envying them, petitioned Jupiter to be changed into birds. The skill," continued he, "consists in making them talk like little fishes." While he indulged himself in this fanciful reverie, he observed Johnson shaking his sides, and laughing. Upon which he smartly proceeded, "Why, Dr. Johnson, this is not so easy as you seem to think: for if you were to make little fishes talk, they would talk like WHALES."

On Thursday, April 29, I dined with him at General Oglethorpe's, where were Sir Joshua Reynolds, Mr. Langton, Dr. Goldsmith, and Mr. Thrale. I was very desirous to get Dr. Johnson absolutely fixed in his resolution to go with me to the Hebrides this year; he now talked in such a manner of his long intended tour, that I was satisfied he meant to fulfil his engagement.

The custom of eating dogs at Otaheite being mentioned, Goldsmith observed, that this was also a custom in China; that a dog-butcher is as common there as any other butcher; and that when he walks abroad all the dogs fall on him. JOHNSON. "That is not owing to his killing dogs, Sir. I remember a butcher at Lichfield, whom a dog that was in the house where I lived, always attacked. It is the smell of carnage which provokes this, let the animals he has killed be what they may." GOLDSMITH. "Yes, there is a general abhorrence in animals at the signs of massacre. If you put a tub full of blood into a stable, the horses are like to go mad." JOHNSON. "I doubt that." GOLDSMITH. "Nay, Sir, it is a fact well authenticated." THRALE. "You had better prove it before you put it into your book on natural history. You may do it in my stable if you will." JOHNSON. "Nay, Sir, I would not have him prove it. If he is content to take his information from others, he may get through his book with little trouble, and without much endangering his reputation. But if he makes experiments for so comprehensive a book as his, there would be no end to them; his erroneous assertions would then fall upon himself; and he might be blamed for not having made experiments as to every particular."

Dr. Goldsmith's new play, "She Stoops to Conquer," being mentioned;—Johnson. "I know of no comedy for many years that has so much exhilarated an audience, that has answered so much the great end of comedy—making an audience merry."

Goldsmith having said, that Garrick's compliment to the Queen, which he introduced into the play of "The Chances," which he had altered and revised this year, was mean and gross flattery;—Johnson. "Why, Sir, I would not *write*, I would not give solemnly under my hand, a character beyond what I thought really true; but a speech on the stage, let it flatter ever so extravagantly, is formular. It has always been formular to flatter kings and queens: so much so, that even in our church-service we have 'our most religious king,' used indiscriminately, whoever is king. Nay, they even flatter themselves;—'we have been graciously pleased to grant.' No modern flattery, however, is so gross as that of the Augustan age, where the emperor was deified. And as to meanness"—(rising into warmth) "how is it mean in a player—a showman—a fellow who exhibits himself for a shilling, to flatter his queen? The attempt, indeed, was dangerous; for if it had missed, what became of Garrick, and what became of the queen? As Sir William Temple says of a great general, it is necessary not only that his designs be formed in a masterly manner, but that they should be attended with success. Sir, it is right, at a time when the royal family is not generally liked, to let it be seen that the people like at least one of them." Sir Joshua Reynolds. "I do not perceive why the profession of a player should be despised; for the great and ultimate end of all the employments of mankind is to produce amusement. Garrick produces more amusement than any body." Boswell. "You say, Dr. Johnson, that Garrick exhibits himself for a shilling. In this respect he is only on a footing with a lawyer, who exhibits himself for his fee, and even will maintain any nonsense or absurdity, if the case require it. Garrick refuses a play or a part which he does not like: a lawyer never refuses." Johnson. "Why, Sir, what does this prove? only that a lawyer is worse. Boswell is now like Jack in the Tale of a Tub, who, when he is puzzled by an argument, hangs himself. He thinks I shall cut him down, but I'll let him hang"—(laughing vociferously).

On Friday, April 30, I dined with him at Mr. Beauclerk's, where were Lord Charlemont, Sir Joshua Reynolds, and some more members of the LITERARY CLUB, whom he had obligingly invited to meet me, as I was this evening to be balloted for as candidate for admission into that distinguished society. Johnson had done me the honour to propose me, and Beauclerk was very zealous for me.

Goldsmith being mentioned;—JOHNSON. "It is amazing how little Goldsmith knows. He seldom comes where he is not more ignorant than any one else." SIR JOSHUA REYNOLDS. "Yet there is no man whose company is more liked." JOHNSON. "To be sure, Sir. When people find a man of the most distinguished abilities as a writer, their inferior while he is with them, it must be highly gratifying to them. What Goldsmith comically says of himself is very true—he always gets the better when he argues alone; meaning, that he is master of a subject in his study, and can write well upon it; but when he comes into company, grows confused, and unable to talk. Take him as a poet, his 'Traveller' is a very fine performance; ay, and so is his 'Deserted Village,' were it not sometimes too much the echo of his 'Traveller.' Whether, indeed, we take him as a poet—as a comic writer—or as an historian, he stands in the first class." BOSWELL. "An historian! My dear Sir, you surely will not rank his compilation of the Roman History with the works of other historians of this age?" JOHNSON. "Why, who are before him?" BOSWELL. "Hume—Robertson—Lord Lyttelton." JOHNSON (his antipathy to the Scotch beginning to rise). "I have not read Hume; but, doubtless, Goldsmith's History is better than the *verbiage* of Robertson, or the foppery of Dalrymple." BOSWELL. "Will you not admit the superiority of Robertson, in whose History we find such penetration, such painting?" JOHNSON. "Sir, you must consider how that penetration and that painting are employed. It is not history, it is imagination. He who describes what he never saw, draws from fancy. Robertson paints minds as Sir Joshua paints faces in a history-piece: he imagines an heroic countenance. You must look upon Robertson's work as romance, and try it by that standard. History it is not. Besides, Sir, it is the great excellence of a writer to put into his book as much as his book will hold. Goldsmith has done this in his History. Now Robertson might have put twice as much into his book. Robertson is like a man who has packed gold in wool: the

I SAT IN A STATE OF ANXIETY

wool takes up more room than the gold. No, Sir; I always thought
Robertson would be crushed by his own weight—would be buried
under his own ornaments. Goldsmith tells you shortly all you
want to know: Robertson detains you a great deal too long. No
man will read Robertson's cumbrous detail a second time; but
Goldsmith's plain narrative will please again and again. I would
say to Robertson what an old tutor of a college said to one of his
pupils: 'Read over your compositions, and wherever you meet with
a passage which you think is particularly fine, strike it out.'
Goldsmith's abridgment is better than that of Lucius Florus or
Eutropius; and I will venture to say, that if you compare him with
Vertot, in the same places of the Roman History, you will find
that he excels Vertot. Sir, he has the art of compiling, and of saying
every thing he has to say in a pleasing manner. He is now writing
a Natural History, and will make it as entertaining as a Persian
tale."

JOHNSON. "I remember once being with Goldsmith in Westminster Abbey. While we surveyed the Poet's Corner, I said to
him,

'Forsitan et nostrum nomen miscebitur istis.'

When we got to Temple Bar he stopped me, pointed to the heads [1]
upon it, and slily whispered me,

'Forsitan et nostrum nomen miscebitur ISTIS.'" [2]

Johnson praised John Bunyan highly. "His 'Pilgrim's Progress'
has great merit, both for invention, imagination, and the conduct
of the story; and it has had the best evidence of its merit, the
general and continued approbation of mankind. Few books, I
believe, have had a more extensive sale. It is remarkable, that it
begins very much like the poem of Dante; yet there was no translation of Dante when Bunyan wrote. There is reason to think that he
had read Spenser."

The gentlemen went away to their club, and I was left at Beauclerk's till the fate of my election should be announced to me. I
sat in a state of anxiety which even the charming conversation of
Lady Di Beauclerk could not entirely dissipate. In a short time I
received the agreeable intelligence that I was chosen. I hastened

---

[1] The heads of Fletcher and Townley, executed for the rebellion of 1745—and possibly others—were
placed on Temple Bar.
[2] In allusion to Dr. Johnson's supposed political principles, and perhaps his own.

to the place of meeting, and was introduced to such a society as can seldom be found. Mr. Edmund Burke, whom I then saw for the first time, and whose splendid talents had long made me ardently wish for his acquaintance; Dr. Nugent, Mr. Garrick, Dr. Goldsmith, Mr. (afterwards Sir William) Jones, and the company with whom I had dined. Upon my entrance, Johnson placed himself behind a chair, on which he leaned as on a desk or pulpit, and with humorous formality gave me a *charge*, pointing out the conduct expected from me as a good member of this club.

Much pleasant conversation passed, which Johnson relished with great good humour. But his conversation alone, or what led to it, or was interwoven with it, is the business of this work.

On Saturday, May 1, we dined by ourselves at our old rendezvous, the Mitre tavern. He was placid, but not much disposed to talk. He observed, that "the Irish mix better with the English than the Scotch do; their language is nearer to English; as a proof of which, they succeed very well as players, which Scotchmen do not. Then, Sir, they have not that extreme nationality which we find in the Scotch. I will do you, Boswell, the justice to say, that you are the most *unscottified* of your countrymen. You are almost the only instance of a Scotchman that I have known, who did not at every other sentence bring in some other Scotchman."

On Friday, May 7, I breakfasted with him at Mr. Thrale's in the Borough. While we were alone, I endeavoured as well as I could to apologise for a lady [1] who had been divorced from her husband by act of parliament. I said that he had used her very ill, had behaved brutally to her, and that she could not continue to live with him without having her delicacy contaminated; that all affection for him was thus destroyed; that the essence of conjugal union being gone, there remained only a cold form, a mere civil obligation; that she was in the prime of life, with qualities to produce happiness; that these ought not to be lost; and, that the gentleman on whose account she was divorced had gained her heart while thus unhappily situated. Seduced, perhaps, by the charms of the lady in question, I thus attempted to palliate what I was sensible could not be justified; for when I had finished my harangue, my venerable friend gave me a proper check: "My dear Sir, never accustom your mind to mingle virtue and vice. The woman's a ——, and there's an end on't."

---

[1] No doubt Lady Diana Spencer, daughter of Charles Duke of Marlborough, born in 1734, married in 1757 to Viscount Bolingbroke, from whom she was divorced in 1768, and married immediately after to Mr. Topham Beauclerk.

He did not give me full credit when I mentioned that I had carried on a short conversation by signs with some Esquimaux, who were then in London, particularly with one of them, who was a priest. He thought I could not make them understand me. No man was more incredulous as to particular facts which were at all extraordinary; and therefore no man was more scrupulously inquisitive, in order to discover the truth.

I dined with him this day at the house of my friends, Messieurs Edward and Charles Dilly, booksellers in the Poultry: there were present, Dr. Goldsmith, Mr. Langton, Mr. Claxton, Rev. Dr. Mayo, a dissenting minister, the Rev. Mr. Toplady, and my friend the Rev. Mr. Temple.

I introduced the subject of toleration. JOHNSON. "Every society has a right to preserve public peace and order, and therefore has a good right to prohibit the propagation of opinions which have a dangerous tendency. To say the *magistrate* has this right, is using an inadequate word: it is the *society* for which the magistrate is agent. He may be morally or theologically wrong in restraining the propagation of opinions which he thinks dangerous, but he is politically right." MAYO. "I am of opinion, Sir, that every man is entitled to liberty of conscience in religion; and that the magistrate cannot restrain that right." JOHNSON. "Sir, I agree with you. Every man has a right to liberty of conscience, and with that the magistrate cannot interfere. People confound liberty of thinking with liberty of talking; nay, with liberty of preaching. Every man has a physical right to think as he pleases; for it cannot be discovered how he thinks. He has not a moral right, for he ought to inform himself, and think justly. But, Sir, no member of a society has a right to *teach* any doctrine contrary to what the society holds to be true. The magistrate, I say, may be wrong in what he thinks: but while he thinks himself right, he may and ought to enforce what he thinks." MAYO. "Then, Sir, we are to remain always in error, and truth never can prevail; and the magistrate was right in persecuting the first Christians." JOHNSON. "Sir, the only method by which religious truth can be established is by martyrdom. The magistrate has a right to enforce what he thinks; and he who is conscious of the truth has a right to suffer. I am afraid there is no other way of ascertaining the truth, but by persecution on the one hand and enduring it on the other." GOLD-SMITH. "But how is a man to act, Sir? Though firmly convinced of the truth of his doctrine, may he not think it wrong to expose himself to persecution? Has he a right to do so? Is it not, as it were, committing voluntary suicide?" JOHNSON. "Sir, as to voluntary suicide, as you call it, there are twenty thousand men in an army who will go without scruple to be shot at, and mount a breach for fivepence a day." GOLDSMITH. "But have they a moral right to do this?" JOHNSON. "Nay, Sir, if you will not take the universal opinion of mankind, I have nothing to say. If mankind cannot defend their own way of thinking, I cannot defend it. Sir, if a man is in doubt whether it would be better for him to expose himself to martyrdom or not, he should not do it. He must be convinced that he has a delegation from heaven." GOLDSMITH. "I would consider whether there is the greater chance of good or evil upon the whole. If I see a man who has fallen into a well, I would wish to help him out; but if there is a greater probability that he shall pull me in, than that I shall pull him out, I would not attempt it. So, were I to go to Turkey, I might wish to convert the grand signior to the Christian faith; but when I considered that I should probably be put to death without effectuating my purpose in any degree, I should keep myself quiet." JOHNSON. "Sir, you must consider that we have perfect and imperfect obligations. Perfect obligations, which are generally not to do something, are clear and positive; as, 'Thou shall not kill.' But charity, for instance, is not definable by limits. It is a duty to give to the poor; but no man can say how much another should give to the poor, or when a man has given too little to save his soul. In the same manner it is a duty to instruct the ignorant, and of consequence to convert infidels to Christianity; but no man in the common course of things is obliged to carry this to such a degree as to incur the danger of martyrdom, as no man is obliged to strip himself to the shirt in order to give charity. I have said, that a man must be persuaded that he has a particular delegation from heaven." GOLDSMITH. "How is this to be known? Our first reformers, who were burnt for not believing bread and wine to be Christ——" JOHNSON (interrupting him). "Sir, they were not burnt for not believing bread and wine to be Christ, but for insulting those who did believe it. And, Sir, when the first reformers began, they did not intend to be martyred: as many of them ran away as could." BOSWELL. "But, Sir, there was your countryman Elwal, who you told me challenged King George with his black-guards, and his red-guards." JOHNSON. "My countryman, Elwal, Sir, should have been put in the stocks—a proper pulpit for him; and he'd have had a numerous audience. A man who preaches in the stocks will always have hearers enough." BOSWELL. "But Elwal thought himself in the right." JOHNSON. "We are not providing for mad people; there are places for them in the neighbourhood" (meaning Moorfields). MAYO. "But, Sir, is it not very hard that I should not be allowed to teach my children what I really believe to be the truth?" JOHNSON. "Why, Sir, you might contrive to teach your children *extra scandalum;* but, Sir, the magistrate, if he knows it, has a right to restrain you. Suppose you teach your children to be thieves?" MAYO. "This is making a joke of the subject." JOHNSON. "Nay, Sir, take it thus: that you teach them the community of goods; for which there are as many plausible arguments as for most erroneous doctrines. You teach them that all things at first were in common, and that no man had a right to any thing but as he laid his hands upon it; and that this still is, or ought to be, the rule amongst mankind. Here, Sir, you sap a great principle in society—property. And don't you think the magistrate would have a right to prevent you? Or, suppose you should teach your children the notion of the Adamites, and they shall run naked into the streets, would not the magistrate have a right to flog 'em into their doublets?" MAYO. "I think the magistrate has no right to interfere till there is some overt act." BOSWELL. "So, Sir, though he sees an enemy to the state charging a blunderbuss, he is not to interfere till it is fired off!" MAYO. "He must be sure of its direction against the state." JOHNSON. "The magistrate is to judge of that. He has no right to restrain your thinking, because the evil centres in yourself. If a man were sitting at this table, and chopping off his fingers, the magistrate, as guardian of the community, has no authority to restrain him, however he might do it from kindness as a parent. Though, indeed, upon more consideration, I think he may; as it is probable, that he who is chopping off his own fingers, may soon proceed to chop off those of other people. If I think it right to steal Mr. Dilly's plate, I am a bad man; but he can say nothing to me. If I make an open declaration that I think so, he will keep me out of his house. If I put forth my hand, I shall be sent to Newgate. This is the gradation of thinking, preaching, and acting: if a man thinks erroneously, he may keep his thoughts to himself, and nobody will trouble him; if he preaches erroneous doctrine, society may expel him; if he acts in consequence of it, the law takes place, and he is hanged." MAYO. "But, Sir, ought not Christians to have liberty of conscience?" JOHNSON. "I have

already told you so, Sir. You're coming back to where you were."
BOSWELL. "Dr. Mayo is always taking a return post-chaise, and
going the stage over again. He has it at half-price." JOHNSON.
"Dr. Mayo, like other champions for unlimited toleration, has got
a set of words.[1] Sir, it is no matter, politically, whether the magistrate be right or wrong. Suppose a club were to be formed, to
drink confusion to King George the Third, and a happy restoration
to Charles the Third, this would be very bad with respect to the
state; but every member of that club must either conform to its
rules, or be turned out of it. Old Baxter, I remember, maintains,
that the magistrate should 'tolerate all things that are tolerable.'
This is no good definition of toleration upon any principle; but it
shows that he thought some things were not tolerable." TOPLADY.
"Sir, you have untwisted this difficult subject with great dexterity."

During this argument, Goldsmith sat in restless agitation, from
a wish to get in and *shine*. Finding himself excluded, he had taken
his hat to go away, but remained for some time with it in his hand,
like a gamester, who, at the close of a long night, lingers for a little
while, to see if he can have a favourable opening to finish with success. Once, when he was beginning to speak, he found himself overpowered by the loud voice of Johnson, who was at the opposite end
of the table, and did not perceive Goldsmith's attempt. Thus disappointed of his wish to obtain the attention of the company,
Goldsmith in a passion threw down his hat, looking angrily at
Johnson, and exclaiming in a bitter tone, "*Take it.*" When Toplady
was going to speak, Johnson uttered some sound, which led Goldsmith to think that he was beginning again, and taking the words
from Toplady. Upon which, he seized this opportunity of venting
his own envy and spleen, under the pretext of supporting another
person: "Sir," said he to Johnson, "the gentleman has heard you
patiently for an hour: pray allow us now to hear him." JOHNSON
(sternly). "Sir, I was not interrupting the gentleman. I was only
giving him a signal of my attention. Sir, you are impertinent."
Goldsmith made no reply, but continued in the company for some
time.

Johnson and Mr. Langton and I went together to the Club,
where we found Mr. Burke, Mr. Garrick, and some other members,

---

[1] Dr. Mayo's calm temper and steady perseverance, rendered him an admirable subject for the exercise of Dr. Johnson's powerful abilities. He never flinched; but, after reiterated blows, remained seemingly unmoved as at the first. The scintillations of Johnson's genius flashed every time he was
struck, without his receiving any injury. Hence he obtained the epithet of *The Literary Anvil.—Boswell.*

and amongst them our friend Goldsmith, who sat silently brooding over Johnson's reprimand to him after dinner. Johnson perceived this, and said aside to some of us,—"I'll make Goldsmith forgive me"; and then called to him in a loud voice, "Dr. Goldsmith,—something passed to-day where you and I dined: I ask your pardon." Goldsmith answered placidly, "It must be much from you, Sir, that I take ill." And so at once the difference was over, and they were on as easy terms as ever, and Goldsmith rattled away as usual.

It may also be observed, that Goldsmith was sometimes content to be treated with an easy familiarity, but upon occasions would be consequential and important. An instance of this occurred in a small particular. Johnson had a way of contracting the names of his friends: as, Beauclerk, Beau; Boswell, Bozzy; Langton, Lanky; Murphy, Mur; Sheridan, Sherry. I remember one day, when Tom Davies was telling that Dr. Johnson said, "We are all in labour for a name to *Goldy's* play," Goldsmith seemed displeased that such a liberty should be taken with his name, and said, "I have often desired him not to call me *Goldy*." Tom was remarkably attentive to the most minute circumstance about Johnson. I recollect his telling me once, on my arrival in London, "Sir, our great friend has made an improvement on his appellation of old Mr. Sheridan: he calls him now *Sherry derry*."

On Monday, May 9, as I was to set out on my return to Scotland next morning, I was as desirous to see as much of Dr. Johnson as I could. But I first called on Goldsmith to take leave of him. The jealousy and envy, which, though possessed of many most amiable qualities, he frankly avowed, broke out violently at this interview. Upon another occasion, when Goldsmith confessed himself to be of an envious disposition, I contended with Johnson that we ought not to be angry with him, he was so candid in owning it. "Nay, Sir," said Johnson, "we must be angry that a man has such a superabundance of an odious quality, that he cannot keep it within his own breast, but it boils over." In my opinion, however, Goldsmith had not more of it than other people have, but only talked of it freely.

He now seemed very angry that Johnson was going to be a traveller; said "he would be a dead weight for me to carry, and that I should never be able to lug him along through the Highlands and Hebrides." Nor would he patiently allow me to enlarge upon Johnson's wonderful abilities; but exclaimed, "Is he like Burke, who winds into a subject like a serpent?" "But," said I, "Johnson is the Hercules who strangled serpents in his cradle."

I dined with Dr. Johnson at General Paoli's. He was obliged, by indisposition, to leave the company early; he appointed me, however, to meet him in the evening at Mr. (now Sir Robert) Chambers's, in the Temple, where he accordingly came, though he continued to be very ill. Chambers, as is common on such occasions, prescribed various remedies to him. JOHNSON (fretted by pain). "Pr'ythee don't tease me. Stay till I am well, and then you shall tell me how to cure myself." He grew better, and talked with a noble enthusiasm of keeping up the representation of respectable families. He maintained the dignity and propriety of male succession, in opposition to the opinion of one of our friends who had that day employed Mr. Chambers to draw his will, devising his estate to his three sisters, in preference to a remote heir male. Johnson called them "three *dowdies*," and said, with as high a spirit as the boldest baron in the most perfect days of the feudal system, "An ancient estate should always go to males. It is mighty foolish to let a stranger have it because he marries your daughter, and takes your name. As for an estate newly acquired by trade, you may give it, if you will, to the dog *Towser*, and let him keep his *own* name."

I have known him at times exceedingly diverted at what seemed to others a very small sport. He now laughed immoderately, without any reason that we could perceive, at our friend's making his will: called him the *testator*, and added, "I dare say he thinks he has done a mighty thing. He won't stay till he gets home to his seat in the country, to produce this wonderful deed: he'll call up the landlord of the first inn on the road; and, after a suitable preface upon mortality and the uncertainty of life, will tell him that he should not delay in making his will; and here, Sir, will he say, is my will, which I have just made, with the assistance of one of the ablest lawyers in the kingdom; and he will read it to him (laughing all the time). He believes he has made this will; but he did not make it; you, Chambers, made it for him. I trust you have had more conscience than to make him say, 'being of sound understanding!' ha, ha, ha! I hope he has left me a legacy. I'd have his will turned into verse, like a ballad."

In this playful manner did he run on, exulting in his own pleasantry. Mr. Chambers did not by any means relish this jocularity, and seemed impatient till he got rid of us. Johnson could not stop his merriment, but continued it all the way till he got without the Temple Gate. He then burst into such a fit of laughter, that he appeared to be almost in a convulsion; and, in order to support himself, laid hold of one of the posts at the side of the foot pavement, and sent forth peals so loud, that in the silence of the night his voice seemed to resound from Temple Bar to Fleet Ditch.

This most ludicrous exhibition of the awful, melancholy, and venerable Johnson happened well to counteract the feelings of sadness which I used to experience when parting with him for a considerable time. I accompanied him to his door, where he gave me his blessing.

In a letter from Edinburgh, dated the 29th of May, I pressed him to persevere in his resolution to make this year the projected visit to the Hebrides, of which he and I had talked for many years, and which I was confident would afford us much entertainment. I again wrote to him, informing him that the court of session rose on the 12th of August, hoping to see him before that time, and expressing, perhaps in too extravagant terms, my admiration of him, and my expectation of pleasure from our intended tour.

To James Boswell, Esq.

Aug. 3, 1773

DEAR SIR,
    I shall set out from London on Friday the 6th of this month, and purpose not to loiter much by the way. Which day I shall be at Edinburgh, I cannot exactly tell. I suppose I must drive to an inn, and send a porter to find you.
    I am afraid Beattie will not be at his college soon enough for us, and I shall be sorry to miss him; but there is no staying for the concurrence of all conveniences. We will do as well as we can. I am, Sir, your most humble servant,   SAM. JOHNSON

To the Same

Aug. 3, 1773

DEAR SIR,
    Not being at Mr. Thrale's when your letter came, I had written the enclosed paper and sealed it; bringing it hither for a frank, I found yours. If any thing could repress my ardour, it would be such a letter as yours. To disappoint a friend is unpleasing; and he that forms expectations like yours, must be disappointed. Think only, when you see me, that you see a man who

loves you, and is proud and glad that you love him. I am, Sir, your most affectionate,   SAM. JOHNSON

To the Same

Newcastle, Aug. 11, 1773

DEAR SIR,
    I came hither last night, and hope, but do not absolutely promise to be in Edinburgh on Saturday. Beattie will not come so soon. I am, Sir, your most humble servant,

SAM. JOHNSON

My compliments to your lady.

To the Same

Mr. Johnson sends his compliments to Mr. Boswell, being just arrived at Boyd's.
Saturday night.

His stay in Scotland was from the 18th of August, on which day he arrived, till the 22nd of November, when he set out on his return to London; and I believe ninety-four days were never passed by any man in a more vigorous exertion.

He came by the way of Berwick-upon-Tweed to Edinburgh, where he remained a few days, and then went by St. Andrew's, Aberdeen, Inverness, and Fort Augustus, to the Hebrides, to visit which was the principal object he had in view. He visited the isles of Sky, Rasay, Coll, Mull, Inchkenneth, and Icolmkill. He travelled through Argyleshire by Inverary, and from thence by Lochlomond and Dumbarton to Glasgow, then by Loudon to Auchinleck in Ayrshire, the seat of my family, and then by Hamilton, back to Edinburgh, where he again spent some time. He thus saw the four universities of Scotland, its three principal cities, and as much of the Highland and insular life as was sufficient for his philosophical contemplation. I had the pleasure of accompanying him during the whole of his journey. He was respectfully entertained by the great, the learned, and the elegant, wherever he went; nor was he less delighted with the hospitality which he experienced in humbler life.

His various adventures, and the force and vivacity of his mind, as exercised during this peregrination, upon innumerable topics, have been faithfully, and to the best of my abilities, displayed in

LETTING THE WAX DROP UPON THE CARPET

my "Journal of a Tour to the Hebrides," to which, as the public
has been pleased to honour it by a very extensive circulation, I beg
leave to refer, as to a separate and remarkable portion of his life.[1]

To James Boswell, Esq.

Nov. 27, 1773

Dear Sir,
    I came home last night, without any incommodity, danger,
or weariness, and am ready to begin a new journey. I shall go to
Oxford on Monday. I know Mrs. Boswell wished me well to go; [2]
her wishes have not been disappointed. . . .
    Let the box [3] be sent as soon as it can, and let me know when
to expect it. . . .
    I am, Sir, yours affectionately,   Sam. Johnson

He was seriously engaged in writing an account of our travels
in the Hebrides. On the 5th of March I wrote to him, requesting
his counsel whether I should this spring come to London. I stated
to him on the one hand some pecuniary embarrassments, which,
together with my wife's situation at that time, made me hesitate;
and on the other, the pleasure and improvement which my annual
visit to the metropolis always afforded me; and particularly mentioned a peculiar satisfaction which I experienced in celebrating
the festival of Easter in St. Paul's cathedral; that, to my fancy, it
appeared like going up to Jerusalem at the Feast of the Passover;
and that the strong devotion which I felt on that occasion diffused
its influence on my mind through the rest of the year.

To James Boswell, Esq.

[Not dated, but written about the 15th of March]

Dear Sir,
    I am ashamed to think that since I received your letter I
have passed so many days without answering it.
    I think there is no great difficulty in resolving your doubts.

---

[1] Boswell's "Tour to the Hebrides" is included in this volume, pp. 461 to 591.
[2] In this he showed a very acute penetration. My wife paid him the most assiduous and respectful
attention while he was our guest; so that I wonder how he discovered her wishing for his departure. The
truth is, that his irregular hours and uncouth habits, such as turning the candles with their heads
downwards, when they did not burn bright enough, and letting the wax drop upon the carpet, could
not but be disagreeable to a lady. Besides, she had not that high admiration of him which was felt by
most of those who knew him; and, what was very natural to a female mind, she thought he had too much
influence over her husband. She once, in a little warmth, made, with more point than justice, this remark upon that subject: "I have seen many a bear led by a man; but I never before saw a man led by
a bear."
[3] This was a box containing a number of curious things which he had picked up in Scotland, particularly some horn-spoons.

The reasons for which you are inclined to visit London are, I think, not of sufficient strength to answer the objections. That you should delight to come once a year to the fountain of intelligence and pleasure is very natural; but both information and pleasure must be regulated by propriety. Pleasure, which cannot be obtained but by unseasonable or unsuitable expense, must always end in pain; and pleasure, which must be enjoyed at the expense of another's pain, can never be such as a worthy mind can fully delight in.

What improvement you might gain by coming to London, you may easily supply, or easily compensate, by enjoining yourself some particular study at home, or opening some new avenue to information. Edinburgh is not yet exhausted; and I am sure you will find no pleasure here which can deserve either that you should anticipate any part of your future fortune, or that you should condemn yourself and your lady to penurious frugality for the rest of the year.

I need not tell you what regard you owe to Mrs. Boswell's entreaties; or how much you ought to study the happiness of her who studies yours with so much diligence, and of whose kindness you enjoy such good effects. Life cannot subsist in society but by reciprocal concessions. She permitted you to ramble last year; you must permit her now to keep you at home.

Your last reason is so serious, that I am unwilling to oppose it. Yet you must remember, that your image of worshipping once a year in a certain place, in imitation of the Jews, is but a comparison; and *simile non est idem;* if the annual resort to Jerusalem was a duty to the Jews, it was a duty because it was commanded; and you have no such command, therefore no such duty. It may be dangerous to receive too readily, and indulge too fondly, opinions, from which, perhaps, no pious mind is wholly disengaged, of local sanctity and local devotion. You know what strange effects they have produced over a great part of the Christian world. I am now writing, and you, when you read this, are reading under the eye of Omnipresence.

To what degree fancy is to be admitted into religious offices, it would require much deliberation to determine. I am far from intending totally to exclude it. Fancy is a faculty bestowed by our Creator, and it is reasonable that all his gifts should be used to his glory, that all our faculties should co-operate in his worship; but they are to co-operate according to the will of him that gave them, according to the order which his wisdom has established. As ceremonies prudential or convenient are less obligatory than positive ordinances, as bodily worship is only the token to others or ourselves of mental adoration, so fancy is always to act in subordination to reason. We may take fancy for a companion, but must follow reason as our guide. We may allow fancy to suggest certain ideas in certain places; but reason must always be heard, when she tells us, that those ideas and those places have no natural or necessary relation. When we enter a church we habitually recall to mind the duty of adoration, but we must not omit adoration for want of a temple: because we know, and ought to remember, that the Universal Lord is everywhere present; and that, therefore, to come to Iona, or to Jerusalem, though it may be useful, cannot be necessary.

Thus I have answered your letter, and have not answered it negligently. I love you too well to be careless when you are serious.

I think I shall be very diligent next week about our travels, which I have too long neglected. I am, dear Sir, your most, &c.

SAM. JOHNSON

Compliments to Madam and Miss.

To James Boswell, Esq.

Streatham, June 12, 1774

DEAR SIR,

Yesterday I put the first sheets of the "Journey to the Hebrides" to the press. I have endeavoured to do you some justice in the first paragraph. It will be one volume in octavo, not thick. . . .

I am, Sir, your, &c.   SAM. JOHNSON

Mr. Boswell to Dr. Johnson

Edinburgh, June 24, 1774

You do not acknowledge the receipt of the various packets which I have sent to you. Neither can I prevail with you to *answer* my letters, though you honour me with *returns*. You have said nothing to me about poor Goldsmith,[1] nothing about Langton. . . .

To James Boswell, Esq.

July 4, 1774

DEAR SIR,

I wish you could have looked over my book before the printer, but it could not easily be. I suspect some mistakes; but as I deal, perhaps, more in notions than in facts, the matter is not great; and the second edition will be mended, if any such there be. The press will go on slowly for a time, because I am going into Wales to-morrow. . . .

Of poor dear Dr. Goldsmith there is little to be told, more

[1] Dr. Goldsmith died April 4, this year.

than the papers have made public. He died of a fever, made, I am afraid, more violent by uneasiness of mind. His debts began to be heavy, and all his resources were exhausted. Sir Joshua is of opinion that he owed not less than two thousand pounds. Was ever poet so trusted before? . . .

Of your second daughter you certainly gave the account yourself, though you have forgotten it. While Mrs. Boswell is well, never doubt of a boy. Mrs. Thrale brought, I think, five girls running, but while I was with you she had a boy.

I am, dear Sir, your most affectionate servant,

SAM. JOHNSON

My compliments to all the three ladies.

To the Same

London, Oct. 1, 1774

DEAR SIR,

Yesterday I returned from my Welsh journey. I was sorry to leave my book suspended so long; but having an opportunity of seeing, with so much convenience, a new part of the island, I could not reject it. I have been in five of the six counties of North Wales; and have seen St. Asaph and Bangor, the two seats of their bishops; have been upon Penmanmaur and Snowdon, and passed over into Anglesea. But Wales is so little different from England, that it offers nothing to the speculation of the traveller. . . .

I purpose now to drive the book forward. Make my compliments to Mrs. Boswell, and let me hear often from you. I am, &c.

SAM. JOHNSON

This tour to Wales, which was made in company with Mr. and Mrs. Thrale, though it no doubt contributed to his health and amusement, did not give an occasion to such a discursive exercise of his mind as our tour to the Hebrides. All that I heard him say of it was, that, "instead of bleak and barren mountains, there were green and fertile ones; and that one of the castles in Wales would contain all the castles that he had seen in Scotland."

Parliament having been dissolved, and his friend Mr. Thrale, who was a steady supporter of government, having again to encounter the storm of a contested election, he wrote a short political pamphlet, entitled "The Patriot" addressed to the electors of Great Britain. It was written with energetic vivacity; and, except those passages in which it endeavours to vindicate the glaring outrage of the House of Commons in the case of the Middlesex election, and to justify the attempt to reduce our fellow-subjects in

America to unconditional submission, it contained an admirable display of the properties of a real patriot, in the original and genuine sense;—a sincere, steady, rational, and unbiassed friend to the interests and prosperity of his king and country. It must be acknowledged, however, that both in this and his two former pamphlets, there was, amidst many powerful arguments, not only a considerable portion of sophistry, but a contemptuous ridicule of his opponents, which was very provoking.

To James Boswell, Esq.

Nov. 26, 1774

DEAR SIR,
    Last night I corrected the last page of our "Journey to the Hebrides." . . . As soon as I can, I will take care that copies be sent to you, for I would wish that they might be given before they are bought: but I am afraid that Mr. Strahan will send to you and to the booksellers at the same time. Trade is as diligent as courtesy. I have mentioned all that you recommended. Pray make my compliments to Mrs. Boswell and the younglings. The club has, I think, not yet met. Tell me, and tell me honestly, what you think and what others say of our travels. Shall we touch the continent? [1] I am, dear Sir, your most humble servant,

SAM. JOHNSON

In his manuscript diary of this year, there is the following entry:

Nov. 27, Advent Sunday. I considered that this day, being the beginning of the ecclesiastical year, was a proper time for a new course of life. I began to read the Greek Testament regularly at one hundred and sixty verses every Sunday. This day I began the Acts.
    In this week I read Virgil's Pastorals. I learned to repeat the Pollio and Gallus. I read carelessly the first Georgic.

Such evidences of his unceasing ardour, both for "divine and human lore," when advanced into his sixty-fifth year, and notwithstanding his many disturbances from disease, must make us at once honour his spirit, and lament that it should be so grievously clogged by his material tegument. It is remarkable that he was very fond of the precision which calculation produces. Thus we find in one of his manuscript diaries, "12 pages in 4to. Gr. Test. and 30 pages in Beza's folio, comprise the whole in 40 days."

[1] We had projected a voyage together up the Baltic, and talked of visiting some of the more northern regions.

To James Boswell, Esq.

Jan. 14, 1775

DEAR SIR,

You never did ask for a book by the post till now, and I did not think on it. You see now it is done. I sent one to the King, and I hear he likes it. . . .

I am, Sir, your most humble servant,   SAM. JOHNSON

Mr. Boswell to Dr. Johnson

Edinburgh, Jan. 19, 1775

Be pleased to accept of my best thanks for your "Journey to the Hebrides," which came to me by last night's post. . . . Though ill of a bad cold, you kept me up the greatest part of last night: for I did not stop till I had read every word of your book. I looked back to our first talking of a visit to the Hebrides, which was many years ago, when sitting by ourselves in the Mitre tavern in London, I think about *witching time o' night;* and then exulted in contemplating our scheme fulfilled, and a *monumentum perenne* of it erected by your superior abilities. I shall only say, that your book has afforded me a high gratification. I shall afterwards give you my thoughts on particular passages. . . .

To James Boswell, Esq.

Jan. 21, 1775

DEAR SIR,

I long to hear how you like the book; it is, I think, much liked here. But Macpherson is very furious; can you give me any more intelligence about him, or his Fingal? [1] Do what you can, and do it quickly. . . . Pray let me know what I owed you when I left you, that I may send it to you.

I am going to write about the Americans. [2] If you have picked up any hints among your lawyers, who are great masters of the law of nations, or if your own mind suggests anything, let me know. But mum, it is a secret. . . .

Langton is here; we are all that ever we were. He is a worthy fellow, without malice, though not without resentment. . . . Make my compliments to dear Mrs. Boswell, and to Miss Veronica. I am, dear Sir, yours most faithfully,   SAM. JOHNSON

---

[1] The succeeding pages explain the controversy over the poems published by Macpherson as translations from Ossian. Johnson denied that they had authenticity or merit; remarking to Reynolds, "Sir, a man might write such stuff for ever, if he would *abandon* his mind to it."

[2] The pamphlet of Taxation no Tyranny.

Mr. Boswell to Dr. Johnson

Edinburgh, Jan. 27, 1775

. . . As for myself, I am ashamed to say I have read little and thought little on the subject of America. I will be much obliged to you, if you will direct me where I shall find the best information of what is to be said on both sides. It is a subject vast in its present extent and future consequences. The imperfect hints which now float in my mind tend rather to the formation of an opinion that our government has been precipitant and severe in the resolutions taken against the Bostonians. Well do you know that I have no kindness for that race. But nations, or bodies of men, should, as well as individuals, have a fair trial, and not be condemned on character alone. Have we not express contracts with our colonies, which afford a more certain foundation of judgment, than general political speculations on the mutual rights of states and their provinces or colonies? Pray let me know immediately what to read, and I shall diligently endeavour to gather for you any thing that I can find. Is Burke's speech on American taxation published by himself? Is it authentic? . . .

To the Same

Edinburgh, Feb. 2, 1775

. . . As to Macpherson, I am anxious to have from yourself a full and pointed account of what has passed between you and him. It is confidently told here, that before your book came out he sent to you, to let you know that he understood you meant to deny the authenticity of Ossian's poems; that the originals were in his possession; that you might have inspection of them, and might take the evidence of people skilled in the Erse language; and that he hoped, after this fair offer, you would not be so un-candid as to assert that he had refused reasonable proof. That you paid no regard to his message, but published your strong attack upon him; and then he wrote a letter to you, in such terms as he thought suited to one who had not acted as a man of veracity. You may believe it gives me pain to hear your conduct represented as unfavourable, while I can only deny what is said, on the ground that your character refutes it, without having any information to oppose. Let me, I beg of you, be furnished with a sufficient answer to any calumny upon this occasion. . . .

To James Boswell, Esq.

Feb. 7, 1775

MY DEAR BOSWELL,

I am surprised that, knowing as you do the disposition of your countrymen to tell lies in favour of each other, you can be at all affected by any reports that circulate among them. Macpherson never in his life offered me a sight of any original, or of any evidence of any kind; but thought only of intimidating me by noise and threats, till my last answer—that I would not be deterred from detecting what I thought a cheat, by the menaces of a ruffian—put an end to our correspondence.

The state of the question is this. He, and Dr. Blair, whom I consider as deceived, say, that he copied the poem from old manuscripts. His copies, if he had them, and I believe him to have none, are nothing. Where are the manuscripts? They can be shown if they exist, but they were never shown. *De non existentibus et non apparentibus*, says our law, *eadem est ratio*. No man has a claim to credit upon his own word, when better evidence, if he had it, may be easily produced. But so far as we can find, the Erse language was never written till very lately for the purposes of religion. A nation that cannot write, or a language that was never written, has no manuscripts.

But whatever he has he never offered to show. If old manuscripts should now be mentioned, I should, unless there were more evidence that can be easily had, suppose them another proof of Scotch conspiracy in national falsehood.

Do not censure the expression; you know it to be true. . . .

I am now engaged, but in a little time I hope to do all you would have. My compliments to Madam and Veronica. I am, Sir, your most humble servant,   SAM. JOHNSON

What words were used by Mr. Macpherson in his letter to the venerable sage, I have never heard; but they are generally said to have been of a nature very different from the language of literary contest. Dr. Johnson's answer appeared in the newspapers of the day, and has since been frequently republished; but not with perfect accuracy. I give it as dictated to me by himself, written down in his presence, and authenticated by a note in his own handwriting. "*This, I think, is a true copy.*"

To Mr. Macpherson

MR. JAMES MACPHERSON,

I received your foolish and impudent letter. Any violence offered me I shall do my best to repel;[1] and what I cannot do for myself, the law shall do for me. I hope I never shall be deterred from detecting what I think a cheat, by the menaces of a ruffian.

---

[1] The threats alluded to in this letter were never attempted to be put in execution. But Johnson, as a provision for defence, furnished himself with a large oaken plant, six feet in height, of the diameter of an inch at the lower end, increasing to three inches at the top, and terminating in a head (once the root) of the size of a large orange. This he kept in his bed-chamber, so near his chair as to be within his reach.—Anderson's *Life of Johnson*.

ATTACKED IN THE STREET BY FOUR MEN

What would you have me retract? I thought your book an imposture; I think it an imposture still. For this opinion I have given my reasons to the public, which I here dare you to refute. Your rage I defy. Your abilities, since your Homer,[1] are not so formidable; and what I hear of your morals inclines me to pay regard, not to what you shall say, but to what you shall prove. You may print this if you will.   SAM. JOHNSON

Mr. Macpherson little knew the character of Dr. Johnson, if he supposed that he could be easily intimidated; for no man was ever more remarkable for personal courage. He had, indeed, an awful dread of death, or rather, "of something after death": and what rational man, who seriously thinks of quitting all that he has ever known, and going into a new and unknown state of being, can be without that dread? But his fear was from reflection; his courage natural. His fear, in that one instance, was the result of philosophical and religious consideration. He feared death, but he feared nothing else, not even what might occasion death.

Many instances of his resolution may be mentioned. One day, at Mr. Beauclerk's house in the country, when two large dogs were fighting, he went up to them, and beat them till they separated; and at another time, when told of the danger there was that a gun might burst if charged with many balls, he put in six or seven, and fired it off against a wall. Mr. Langton told me, that when they were swimming together near Oxford, he cautioned Dr. Johnson against a pool, which was reckoned particularly dangerous; upon which Johnson directly swam into it. He told me himself that one night he was attacked in the street by four men, to whom he would not yield, but kept them all at bay, till the watch came up, and carried both him and them to the round-house. In the playhouse at Lichfield, as Mr. Garrick informed me, Johnson having for a moment quitted a chair which was placed for him between the side scenes, a gentleman took possession of it, and, when Johnson on his return civilly demanded his seat, rudely refused to give it up; upon which Johnson laid hold of it, and tossed him and the chair into the pit. Foote, who so successfully revived the old comedy, by exhibiting living characters, had resolved to imitate Johnson on the stage, expecting great profits from his ridicule of so celebrated a man. Johnson being informed of his intention, and being at dinner at Mr. Thomas Davies's, the bookseller, from whom I had the story, he asked Mr. Davies, "what was the common price of an

[1] Macpherson's translation of the Iliad, published in 1773.

oak stick?" and being answered sixpence, "Why then, Sir," said he, "give me leave to send your servant to purchase me a shilling one. I'll have a double quantity; for I am told Foote means *to take me off*, as he calls it, and I am determined the fellow shall not do it with impunity." Davies took care to acquaint Foote of this, which effectually checked the wantonness of the mimic. Mr. Macpherson's menaces made Johnson provide himself with the same implement of defence: and had he been attacked, I have no doubt that, old as he was, he would have made his corporal prowess be felt as much as his intellectual.

His "Journey to the Western Islands of Scotland" is a most valuable performance. It abounds in extensive philosophical views of society, and in ingenious sentiment and lively description. That he was to some degree of excess *a true born Englishman*, so as to have entertained an undue prejudice against both the country and the people of Scotland, must be allowed. But it was a prejudice of the head, and not of the heart. He had no ill-will to the Scotch; for, if he had been conscious of that, he never would have thrown himself into the bosom of their country, and trusted to the protection of its remote inhabitants with a fearless confidence. His remark upon the nakedness of the country, from its being denuded of trees, was made after having travelled two hundred miles along the eastern coast, where certainly trees are not to be found near the road; and he said it was "a map of the road" which he gave. His disbelief of the authenticity of the poems ascribed to Ossian, a Highland bard, was confirmed in the course of his journey, by a very strict examination of the evidence offered for it; and although their authenticity was made too much a national point by the Scotch, there were many respectable persons in that country, who did not concur in this: so that his judgment upon the question ought not to be decried, even by those who differ from him. As to myself, I can only say, upon a subject now become very uninteresting, that when the fragments of Highland poetry first came out, I was much pleased with their wild peculiarity, and was one of those who subscribed to enable their editor, Mr. Macpherson, then a young man, to make a search in the Highlands and Hebrides for a long poem in the Erse language, which was reported to be preserved somewhere in those regions. But when there came forth an Epic poem in six books, with all the common circumstances of former compositions of that nature; and when, upon an attentive examination of it, there was found a perpetual recurrence of the same images which appear in the fragments; and when no ancient manuscript, to authenticate the work, was deposited in any public library, though that was insisted on as a reasonable proof; *who could forbear to doubt?*

He expressed to his friend Mr. Windham, of Norfolk, his wonder at the extreme jealousy of the Scotch, and their resentment at having their country described by him as it really was; when to say that it was a country as good as England would have been a gross falsehood. "None of us," said he, "would be offended if a foreigner who has travelled here should say, that vines and olives don't grow in England." And as to his prejudice against the Scotch, which I always ascribed to that nationality which he observed in *them*, he said to the same gentleman, "When I find a Scotchman to whom an Englishman is as a Scotchman, that Scotchman shall be as an Englishman to me." His intimacy with many gentlemen of Scotland, and his employing so many natives of that country as his amanuenses, proves that his prejudice was not virulent; and I have deposited in the British Museum, amongst other pieces of his writing, the following note in answer to one from me, asking if he would meet me at dinner at the Mitre, though a friend of mine, a Scotchman, was to be there:

Mr. Johnson does not see why Mr. Boswell should suppose a Scotchman less acceptable than any other man. He will be at the Mitre.

Dr. Barnard having once expressed to him an apprehension, that if he should visit Ireland he might treat the people of that country more unfavourably than he had done the Scotch, he answered, with strong pointed double-edged wit, "Sir, you have no reason to be afraid of me. The Irish are not in a conspiracy to cheat the world by false representations of the merits of their countrymen. No, Sir: the Irish are a *fair people;*—they never speak well of one another."

All the miserable cavillings against his "Journey," in newspapers, magazines, and other fugitive publications, I can speak from certain knowledge, only furnished him with sport. At last there came out a scurrilous volume, larger than Johnson's own, filled with malignant abuse, under a name, real or fictitious, of some low man in an obscure corner of Scotland. The effect which it had upon Johnson was, to produce this pleasant observation: "This fellow must be a blockhead. They don't know how to go about their abuse. Who will read a five shilling book against me? No, Sir, if they had wit, they should have kept pelting me with pamphlets."

On Tuesday, 21st March, I arrived in London; and on repairing to Dr. Johnson's before dinner, found him in his study, sitting with Mr. Peter Garrick, the elder brother of David, strongly resembling him in countenance and voice, but of more sedate and placid manners.

The doubts which, in my correspondence with him, I had ventured to state as to the justice and wisdom of the conduct of Great Britain towards the American colonies, while I at the same time requested that he would enable me to inform myself upon that momentous subject, he had altogether disregarded; and had recently published a pamphlet, entitled "Taxation no Tyranny; an Answer to the Resolutions and Address of the American Congress."

He had long before indulged most unfavourable sentiments of our fellow-subjects in America. For as early as 1769, I was told by Dr. John Campbell, that he had said of them, "Sir, they are a race of convicts, and ought to be thankful for any thing we allow them short of hanging."

Of this performance I avoided to talk with him; for I had now formed a clear and settled opinion, that the people of America were well warranted to resist a claim that their fellow-subjects in the mother country should have the entire command of their fortunes, by taxing them without their own consent; and the extreme violence which it breathed appeared to me so unsuitable to the mildness of a Christian philosopher, and so directly opposite to the principles of peace which he had so beautifully recommended in his pamphlet respecting Falkland's Islands, that I was sorry to see him appear in so unfavourable a light. Besides, I could not perceive in it that ability of argument, or that felicity of expression, for which he was, upon other occasions, so eminent. Positive assertion, sarcastical severity, and extravagant ridicule, which he himself reprobated as a test of truth, were united in this rhapsody.

That this pamphlet was written at the desire of those who were then in power, I have no doubt, and indeed, he owned to me, that it had been revised and curtailed by some of them. After the paragraph which now concludes the pamphlet, there followed this:

Their numbers are, at present, not quite sufficient for the greatness which, in some form of government or other, is to rival the ancient

A LITTLE VAIN OF THE SOLICITATIONS OF THIS ELEGANT AND FASHIONABLE ACTRESS

monarchies; but by Dr. Franklin's rule of progression, they will, in a century and a quarter, be more than equal to the inhabitants of Europe. When the Whigs of America are thus multiplied, let the princes of the earth tremble in their palaces. If they should continue to double and to double, their own hemisphere would not contain them. But let not our boldest oppugners of authority look forward with delight to this futurity of Whiggism.

How it ended I know not, as it is cut off abruptly at the foot of the last of these proof pages.

His pamphlets in support of the measures of administration were published on his own account, and drew upon him numerous attacks.

On Friday, March 24, I met him at the LITERARY CLUB. Before he came in, we talked of his "Journey to the Western Islands," and of his coming away "willing to believe the second sight," which seemed to excite some ridicule. I was then so impressed with the truth of many of the stories of which I had been told, that I avowed my conviction, saying, "He is only *willing* to believe: I *do* believe. The evidence is enough for me, though not for his great mind. What will not fill a quart bottle will fill a pint bottle. I am filled with belief." "Are you?" said Colman; "then cork it up."

Johnson was in high spirits this evening at the club, and talked with great animation and success. He attacked Swift, as he used to do upon all occasions. I wondered to hear him say of "Gulliver's Travels,"—"When once you have thought of big men and little men, it is very easy to do all the rest."

On Monday, March 27, I breakfasted with him at Mr. Strahan's. He told us, that he was engaged to go that evening to Mrs. Abington's benefit. "She was visiting some ladies whom I was visiting, and begged that I would come to her benefit. I told her I could not hear: but she insisted so much on my coming, that it would have been brutal to have refused her." This was a speech quite characteristical. He loved to bring forward his having been in the gay circles of life; and he was, perhaps, a little vain of the solicitations of this elegant and fashionable actress. He told us the play was to be "The Hypocrite," altered from Cibber's "Nonjuror," so as to satirise the Methodists. "I do not think," said he, "the character of the Hypocrite justly applicable to the Methodists, but it was very applicable to the Nonjurors. I once said that perhaps a Nonjuror would have been less criminal in taking the oaths imposed by the ruling power, than refusing them; because refusing them necessarily laid him under almost an irresistible temptation to be more criminal; for a man *must* live, and if he precludes himself from the support furnished by the establishment will probably be reduced to very wicked shifts to maintain himself." Boswell. "I should think, Sir, that a man who took the oaths contrary to his principles was a determined wicked man, because he was sure he was committing perjury: whereas a Nonjuror might be insensibly led to do what was wrong without being so directly conscious of it." Johnson. "Why, Sir, a man who goes to bed to his patron's wife is pretty sure that he is committing wickedness." Boswell. "Did the nonjuring clergymen do so, Sir?" Johnson. "I am afraid many of them did."

I was startled at this argument, and could by no means think it convincing.

Mr. Strahan talked of launching into the great ocean of London, in order to have a chance for rising into eminence; and observing that many men were kept back from trying their fortunes there, because they were born to a competency, said, "Small certainties are the bane of men of talents"; which Johnson confirmed. Mr. Strahan put Johnson in mind of a remark which he had made to him: "There are few ways in which a man can be more innocently employed than in getting money." "The more one thinks of this," said Strahan, "the juster it will appear."

Mr. Strahan had taken a poor boy from the country as an apprentice, upon Johnson's recommendation. Johnson having inquired after him, said, "Mr. Strahan, let me have five guineas on account, and I'll give this boy one. Nay, if a man recommends a boy, and does nothing for him, it is sad work. Call him down."

I followed him into the court-yard, behind Mr. Strahan's house; and there I had a proof of what I heard him profess, that he talked alike to all. "Some people tell you that they let themselves down to the capacity of their hearers. I never do that. I speak uniformly, in as intelligible a manner as I can."

"Well, my boy, how do you go on?" "Pretty well, Sir; but they are afraid I ar' n't strong enough for some parts of the business." Johnson. "Why, I shall be sorry for it; for, when you consider with how little mental power and corporeal labour a printer can get a guinea a week, it is a very desirable occupation for you. Do you hear—take all the pains you can; and if this does not do, we must think of some other way of life for you. There's a guinea."

Here was one of the many, many instances of his active benevolence. At the same time, the slow and sonorous solemnity with which, while he bent himself down, he addressed a little thick short-legged boy, contrasted with the boy's awkwardness and awe, could not but excite some ludicrous emotions.

I met him at Drury Lane playhouse in the evening. Sir Joshua Reynolds, at Mrs. Abington's request, had promised to bring a body of wits to her benefit; and having secured forty places in the front boxes, had done me the honour to put me in the group. Johnson sat on the seat directly behind me; and as he could neither see nor hear at such a distance from the stage, he was wrapped up in grave abstraction, and seemed quite a cloud, amidst all the sunshine of glitter and gaiety. I wondered at his patience in sitting out a play of five acts, and a farce of two. He said very little; but after the prologue to "Bon Ton" had been spoken, which he could hear pretty well from the more slow and distinct utterance, he talked on prologue-writing, and observed, "Dryden has written prologues superior to any that David Garrick has written; but David Garrick has written more good prologues than Dryden has done. It is wonderful that he has been able to write such variety of them."

At Mr. Beauclerk's, where I supped, was Mr. Garrick, whom I made happy with Johnson's praise of his prologues. He imitated the manner of his old master with ludicrous exaggeration; repeating, with pauses and half-whistlings interjected,

> Os homini sublime dedit,—cælumque tueri
> Jussit,—et erectos ad sidera—tollere vultus,

looking *downwards* all the time, and, while pronouncing the four last words, absolutely touching the ground with a kind of contorted gesticulation.

Garrick, however, when he pleased, could imitate Johnson very exactly. He was always jealous that Johnson spoke lightly of him. I recollect his exhibiting him to me one day, as if saying, "Davy has some convivial pleasantry about him, but 'tis a futile fellow"; which he uttered perfectly with the tone and air of Johnson.

I cannot too frequently request of my readers, while they peruse my account of Johnson's conversation, to endeavour to keep in mind his deliberate and strong utterance. His mode of speaking was indeed very impressive;[1] and I wish it could be preserved as music is written.

---

[1] My noble friend Lord Pembroke said once "that Dr. Johnson's sayings would not appear so extraordinary, were it not for his *bow-wow way*."—*Boswell.*

Next day [March 28] I dined with Johnson at Mr. Thrale's. A young lady who had married a man much her inferior in rank being mentioned, a question arose how a woman's relations should behave to her in such a situation. While I contended that she ought to be treated with an inflexible steadiness of displeasure, Mrs. Thrale was all for mildness and forgiveness, and, according to the vulgar phrase, "making the best of a bad bargain." JOHNSON. "Madam, we must distinguish. Were I a man of rank, I would not let a daughter starve who had made a mean marriage; but having voluntarily degraded herself from the station which she was originally entitled to hold, I would support her only in that which she herself had chosen; and would not put her on a level with my other daughters. You are to consider, Madam, that it is our duty to maintain the subordination of civilized society; and when there is a gross and shameful deviation from rank, it should be punished so as to deter others from the same perversion."

On Friday, 31st March, I supped with him and some friends at a tavern. One of the company attempted, with too much forwardness, to rally him on his late appearance at the theatre; but had reason to repent of his temerity. "Why, Sir, did you go to Mrs. Abington's benefit? Did you see?" JOHNSON. "No, Sir." "Did you hear?" JOHNSON. "No, Sir." "Why then, Sir, did you go?" JOHNSON. "Because, Sir, she is a favourite of the public; and when the public cares a thousandth part for you that it does for her, I will go to your benefit too."

Next morning I won a small bet from Lady Diana Beauclerk, by asking him as to one of his particularities, which her Ladyship laid I durst not do. It seems he had been frequently observed at the club to put into his pocket the Seville oranges, after he had squeezed the juice of them into the drink which he made for himself. Beauclerk and Garrick talked of it to me, and seemed to think that he had a strange unwillingness to be discovered. We could not divine what he did with them; and this was the bold question to be put. I saw on his table, the spoils of the preceding night, some fresh peels nicely scraped and cut into pieces. "O, Sir," said I, "I now partly see what you do with the squeezed oranges which you put into your pocket at the club." JOHNSON. "I have a great love for them." BOSWELL. "And pray, Sir, what do you do with them? You scrape them it seems, very neatly, and what next?" JOHNSON. "Let them dry, Sir." BOSWELL. "And what next?" JOHNSON. "Nay, Sir, you shall know their fate no further." BOS-

WELL. "Then the world must be left in the dark. It must be said (assuming a mock solemnity) he scraped them, and let them dry, but what he did with them next he never could be prevailed upon to tell." JOHNSON. "Nay, Sir, you should say it more emphatically he could not be prevailed upon, even by his dearest friends, to tell."[1]

He had this morning received his diploma as Doctor of Laws from the University of Oxford. He did not vaunt of his new dignity, but I understood he was highly pleased with it.

I observed to him that there were very few of his friends so accurate as that I could venture to put down in writing what they told me as his sayings. JOHNSON. "Why should you write down *my* sayings?" BOSWELL. "I write them when they are good." JOHNSON. "Nay, you may as well write down the sayings of any one else that are good." But *where*, I might with great propriety have added, can I find such?

I visited him by appointment in the evening, and we drank tea with Mrs. Williams. His "Taxation no Tyranny" being mentioned, he said, "I think I have not been attacked enough for it. Attack is the re-action; I never think I have hit hard, unless it rebounds." BOSWELL. "I don't know, Sir, what you would be at. Five or six shots of small arms in every newspaper, and repeated cannonading in pamphlets, might, I think, satisfy you."

I talked of the cheerfulness of Fleet Street, owing to the constant quick succession of people which we perceive passing through it. JOHNSON. "Why, Sir, Fleet Street has a very animated appearance; but I think the full tide of human existence is at Charing Cross."

He made the common remark on the unhappiness which men who have led a busy life experience, when they retire in expectation of enjoying themselves at ease, and that they generally languish for want of their habitual occupation, and wish to return to it. He mentioned as strong an instance of this as can well be imagined. "An eminent tallowchandler in London who had acquired a considerable fortune, gave up the trade in favour of his foreman, and went to live at a country-house near town. He soon grew weary, and paid frequent visits to his old shop, where he desired

---

[1] The following extract of one of his letters to Miss Boothby probably explains the use to which he put these orange peels: "Give me leave, who have thought much on medicine, to propose to you an easy and, I think, very probable remedy for indigestion and lubricity of the bowels. Take an ounce of dried orange peel, finely powdered, divide it into scruples, and take one scruple at a time in any manner: the best way is, perhaps, to drink it in a glass of hot red port, or to eat it first, and drink the wine after it."

they might let him know their *melting-days*, and he would come and assist them; which he accordingly did. Here, Sir, was a man to whom the most disgusting circumstances in the business to which he had been used was a relief from idleness."

On Thursday, 6th April, I dined with him at Mr. Thomas Davies's, with Mr. Hickey, the painter, and my old acquaintance Mr. Moody, the player.

Dr. Johnson, as usual, spoke contemptuously of Colley Cibber. Davies said, he was the first dramatic writer who introduced genteel ladies upon the stage. Johnson refuted his observation by instancing several such characters in comedies before his time. DAVIES (trying to defend himself from a charge of ignorance). "I mean genteel moral characters." "I think," said Hickey, "gentility and morality are inseparable." BOSWELL. "By no means, Sir. The genteelest characters are often the most immoral. Does not Lord Chesterfield give precepts for uniting wickedness and the graces? A man, indeed, is not genteel when he gets drunk; but most vices may be committed very genteelly: a man may debauch his friend's wife genteelly: he may cheat at cards genteelly." HICKEY. "I do not think *that* is genteel." BOSWELL. "Sir, it may not be like a gentleman, but it may be genteel." JOHNSON. "You are meaning two different things. One means exterior grace; the other honour. It is certain that a man may be very immoral with exterior grace. Lovelace, in 'Clarissa,' is a very genteel and a very wicked character. Tom Hervey, who died t'other day, though a vicious man, was one of the genteelest men that ever lived." Tom Davies instances Charles the Second. JOHNSON (taking fire at an attack upon that Prince, for whom he had an extraordinary partiality). "Charles the Second was licentious in his practice; but he always had a reverence for what was good. Charles the Second knew his people, and rewarded merit. The church was at no time better filled than in his reign. He was the best king we have had from his time till the reign of our present Majesty, except James the Second, who was a very good king, but unhappily believed that it was necessary for the salvation of his subjects that they should be Roman Catholics. *He* had the merit of endeavouring to do what he thought was for the salvation of the souls of his subjects, till he lost a great empire. *We*, who thought that we should *not* be saved if we were Roman Catholics, had the merit of maintaining our religion, at the expense of submitting ourselves to the government of King William, (for it could not be done otherwise)—to the government of one of the most worthless scoundrels that ever existed. No, Charles the Second was not such a man as —— (naming another king). He did not destroy his father's will. He took money, indeed, from France: but he did not betray those over whom he ruled: he did not let the French fleet pass ours. George the First knew nothing, and desired to know nothing; did nothing, and desired to do nothing; and the only good thing that is told of him is, that he wished to restore the crown to its hereditary successor." He roared with prodigious violence against George the Second. When he ceased, Moody interjected, in an Irish tone, and with a comic look, "Ah! poor George the Second."

We got into an argument whether the judges who went to India might with propriety engage in trade. Johnson warmly maintained that they might; "For why," he urged, "should not judges get riches, as well as those who deserve them less?" I said, they should have sufficient salaries, and have nothing to take off their attention from the affairs of the public. JOHNSON. "No judge, Sir, can give his whole attention to his office; and it is very proper that he should employ what time he has to himself to his own advantage, in the most profitable manner." "Then, Sir," said Davies, who enlivened the dispute by making it somewhat dramatic, "he may become an insurer; and when he is going to the bench, he may be stopped,—'Your Lordship cannot go yet; here is a bunch of invoices; several ships are about to sail.'" JOHNSON. "Sir, you may as well say a judge should not have a house; for they may come and tell him, 'Your Lordship's house is on fire'; and so, instead of minding the business of his court, he is to be occupied in getting the engines with the greatest speed. There is no end of this. Every judge who has land trades to a certain extent in corn or in cattle, and in the land itself; undoubtedly his steward acts for him, and so do clerks for a great merchant. A judge may be a farmer, but he is not to feed his own pigs. A judge may play a little at cards for his amusement; but he is not to play at marbles, or chuck farthings in the Piazza. No, Sir, there is no profession to which a man gives a very great proportion of his time. It is wonderful, when a calculation is made, how little the mind is actually employed in the discharge of any profession. No man would be a judge, upon the condition of being totally a judge. The best employed lawyer has his mind at work but for a small proportion of his time; a great deal of his occupation is merely mechanical. I once wrote for a magazine: I made a calculation, that if I should write but a page a day, at the same rate, I should, in ten years, write nine volumes in folio, of an ordinary size and print. When a man writes from his own mind, he writes very rapidly. The greatest part of a writer's time is spent in reading, in order to write; a man will turn over half a library, to make one book."

While the dispute went on, Moody once tried to say something on our side. Tom Davies clapped him on the back, to encourage him. Beauclerk, to whom I mentioned this circumstance, said, "that he could not conceive a more humiliating situation than to be clapped on the back by Tom Davies."

We spoke of Rolt, to whose "Dictionary of Commerce" Dr. Johnson wrote the preface. JOHNSON. "Old Gardener, the bookseller, employed Rolt and Smart to write a monthly miscellany, called 'The Universal Visitor.' There was a formal written contract, which Allen the printer saw. Gardener thought as you do of the judge. They were bound to write nothing else; they were to have, I think, a third of the profits of his sixpenny pamphlet; and the contract was for ninety-nine years. I wish I had thought of giving this to Thurlow, in the cause about literary property. What an excellent instance would it have been of the oppression of booksellers towards poor authors!" smiling. Davies, zealous for the honour of *the trade*, said Gardener was not properly a bookseller. JOHNSON. "Nay, Sir; he certainly was a bookseller. He had served his time regularly, was a member of the Stationers' Company, kept a shop in the face of mankind, purchased copyright, and was a *bibliopole*, Sir, in every sense. I wrote for some months in 'The Universal Visitor' for poor Smart, while he was mad, not then knowing the terms on which he was engaged to write, and thinking I was doing him good. I hoped his wits would soon return to him. Mine returned to me, and I wrote in 'The Universal Visitor' no longer."

Friday, 7th April, I dined with him at a tavern, with a numerous company.[1] One of the company suggested an internal objection to the antiquity of the poetry said to be Ossian's, that we do not find the *wolf* in it, which must have been the case had it been of that age.

The mention of the wolf had led Johnson to think of other wild beasts; and while Sir Joshua Reynolds and Mr. Langton were carrying on a dialogue about something which engaged them earnestly, he, in the midst of it, broke out, " Pennant tells of bears." What he added I have forgotten. They went on, which he, being

[1] A meeting of the club. Fox, though president, was apparently absent. The following members were present: Beauclerk, Boswell, Chamier, Gibbon, Johnson, Langton, Percy, Reynolds, Steevens.—*Records of the Club.*

THE LITERARY CLUB

LANGTON   GIBBON   PERCY   REYNOLDS   JOHNSON   STEVENS   BOSWELL   CHAMIER

dull of hearing, did not perceive, or, if he did, was not willing to break off his talk; so he continued to vociferate his remarks, and *bear* ("like a word in a catch," as Beauclerk said) was repeatedly heard at intervals; which coming from him who, by those who did not know him, had been so often assimilated to that ferocious animal, while we who were sitting round could hardly stifle laughter, produced a very ludicrous effect.   Silence having ensued, he proceeded: "We are told, that the black bear is innocent, but I should not like to trust myself with him."   Mr. Gibbon muttered in a low tone of voice, "I should not like to trust myself with *you*." This piece of sarcastic pleasantry was a prudent resolution, if applied to a competition of abilities.

Patriotism having become one of our topics, Johnson suddenly uttered, in a strong determined tone, an apophthegm, at which many will start: "Patriotism is the last refuge of a scoundrel."

On Saturday, April 8, I dined with him at Mr. Thrale's.   Johnson had supped the night before at Mrs. Abington's with some fashionable people whom he named; and he seemed much pleased with having made one in so elegant a circle.   Nor did he omit to pique his *mistress* a little with jealousy of her housewifery; for he said, with a smile, "Mrs. Abington's jelly, my dear lady, was better than yours."

On Monday, April 10, I dined with him at General Oglethorpe's. He this day enlarged upon Pope's melancholy remark,

Man never *is*, but always *to be* blest.

He asserted, that *the present* was never a happy state to any human being; but that, as every part of life, of which we are conscious, was at some point of time a period yet to come, in which felicity was expected, there was some happiness produced by hope. Being pressed on this subject, and asked if he really was of opinion, that though, in general, happiness was very rare in human life, a man was not sometimes happy in the moment that was present, he answered, "Never, but when he is drunk." [1]

---

[1] Mr. Johnson did not like any one who said they were happy, or who said any one else was so. "It was all *cant*," he would cry; "the dog knows he is miserable all the time." A friend whom he loved exceedingly, told him on some occasion, notwithstanding, that his wife's sister was *really* happy, and called upon the lady to confirm his assertion, which she did somewhat roundly as we say, and with an accent and manner capable of offending Mr. Johnson, if her position had not been sufficient, without any thing more, to put him in a very ill humour.   "If your sister-in-law is really the contented being she professes herself, Sir," said he, "her life gives the lie to every research of humanity; for she is happy without health, without beauty, without money, and without understanding."   This story he told me himself; and when I expressed something of the horror I felt, "The same stupidity," said he, "which prompted her to extol felicity she never felt, hindered her from feeling what shocks you on repetition. I tell you, the woman is ugly, and sickly, and foolish, and poor; and would it not make a man hang himself to hear such a creature say it was happy?"—*Piozzi's Anecdotes.*

No more of his conversation for some days appears in my journal, except that when a gentleman told him he had bought a suit of lace for his lady, he said, "Well, Sir, you have done a good thing and a wise thing." "I have done a good thing," said the gentleman, "but I do not know that I have done a wise thing." JOHNSON. "Yes, Sir, no money is better spent than what is laid out for domestic satisfaction. A man is pleased that his wife is dressed as well as other people; and a wife is pleased that she is dressed."

On Friday, April 14, being Good Friday, I repaired to him in the morning, according to my usual custom on that day, and break-fasted with him. I observed that he fasted very strictly, that he did not even taste bread, and took no milk with his tea; I suppose because it is a kind of animal food.

As we walked to St. Clement's church, and saw several shops open upon this most solemn fast-day of the Christian world, I remarked, that one disadvantage arising from the immensity of London was, that nobody was heeded by his neighbour; there was no fear of censure for not observing Good Friday, as it ought to be kept, and as it is kept in country towns. He said, it was, upon the whole, very well observed even in London. He however owned that London was too large; but added, "It is nonsense to say the head is too big for the body. It would be as much too big, though the body were ever so large; that is to say, though the country were ever so extensive. It has no similarity to a head connected with a body."

After the evening service, he said, "Come, you shall go home with me, and sit just an hour." But he was better than his word; for after we had drunk tea with Mrs. Williams, he asked me to go up to his study with him, where we sat a long while together in a serene undisturbed frame of mind, sometimes in silence, and some-times conversing, as we felt ourselves inclined, or more properly speaking, as *he* was inclined; for during all the course of my long intimacy with him, my respectful attention never abated, and my wish to hear him was such, that I constantly watched every dawn-ing of communication from that great and illuminated mind.

He was pleased to say, "If you come to settle here, we will have one day in the week on which we will meet by ourselves. That is the happiest conversation where there is no competition, no vanity, but a calm quiet interchange of sentiments." In his private register this evening is thus marked, "Boswell sat with me till night; we had some serious talk." It also appears from the same

record, that after I left him he was occupied in religious duties, in
"giving Francis, his servant, some directions for preparation to
communicate; in reviewing his life, and resolving on better conduct." The humility and piety which he discovers on such occasions is truly edifying. No saint, however, in the course of his
religious warfare, was more sensible of the unhappy failure of pious
resolves than Johnson. He said one day, talking to an acquaintance
on the subject, "Sir, hell is paved with good intentions."

On Sunday, 16th April, being Easter-day, after having attended
the solemn service at St. Paul's, I dined with Dr. Johnson and Mrs.
Williams. I maintained that Horace was wrong in placing happiness in *Nil admirari*, for that I thought admiration one of the most
agreeable of all our feelings; and I regretted that I had lost much
of my disposition to admire, which people generally do as they
advance in life. JOHNSON. "Sir, as a man advances in life, he gets
what is better than *admiration,—judgment*, to estimate things at
their true value." I still insisted that admiration was more pleasing
than judgment, as love is more pleasing than friendship. The feeling of friendship is like that of being comfortably filled with roast
beef; love, like being enlivened with champagne. JOHNSON. "No,
Sir, admiration and love are like being intoxicated with champagne;
judgment and friendship like being enlivened. Waller has hit upon
the same thought with you: but I don't believe you have borrowed
from Waller. I wish you would enable yourself to borrow more."

To Bennet Langton, Esq.

April 17, 1775

DEAR SIR,

I have inquired more minutely about the medicine for the
rheumatism, which I am sorry to hear that you still want. The
receipt is this:

Take equal quantities of flour of sulphur and flour of mustard-
seed, make them an electuary with honey or treacle; and take
a bolus as big as a nutmeg several times a day, as you can bear it;
drinking after it a quarter of a pint of the infusion of the root of
lovage.

Lovage, in Ray's "Nomenclature," is levisticum: perhaps the
botanists may know the Latin name. Of this medicine I pretend
not to judge. There is all the appearance of its efficacy, which a
single instance can afford: the patient was very old, the pain very
violent, and the relief, I think, speedy and lasting.

My opinion of alterative medicine is not high, but *quid tentasse nocebit?* if it does harm, or does no good, it may be omitted; but that it may do good, you have, I hope, reason to think is desired by, Sir, your most affectionate, humble servant,

Sam. Johnson

On Tuesday, April 18, he and I were engaged to go with Sir Joshua Reynolds to dine with Mr. Cambridge, at his beautiful villa on the banks of the Thames, near Twickenham. Dr. Johnson's tardiness was such, that Sir Joshua, who had an appointment at Richmond early in the day, was obliged to go by himself on horseback, leaving his coach to Johnson and me. Johnson was in such good spirits, that every thing seemed to please him as we drove along.

Our conversation turned on a variety of subjects. He thought portrait-painting an improper employment for a woman. "Public practice of any art," he observed, "and staring in men's faces, is very indelicate in a female." I happened to start a question, whether when a man knows that some of his intimate friends are invited to the house of another friend, with whom they are all equally intimate, he may join them without an invitation. Johnson. "No, Sir; he is not to go when he is not invited. They may be invited on purpose to abuse him," smiling.

As a curious instance how little a man knows, or wishes to know, his own character in the world, or rather as a convincing proof that Johnson's roughness was only external, and did not proceed from his heart, I insert the following dialogue. Johnson. "It is wonderful, Sir, how rare a quality good-humour is in life. We meet with very few good-humoured men." I mentioned four of our friends, none of whom he would allow to be good-humoured. One was *acid*, another was *muddy*, and to others he had objections which have escaped me. Then shaking his head and stretching himself at ease in the coach, and smiling with much complacency, he turned to me and said, "I look upon *myself* as a good-humoured fellow." The epithet *fellow*, applied to the great lexicographer, the stately moralist, the masterly critic, as if it had been *Sam* Johnson, a mere pleasant companion, was highly diverting; and this light notion of himself struck me with wonder. I answered, also smiling, "No, no, Sir; that will *not* do. You are good-natured, but not good-humoured; you are irascible. You have not patience with folly and absurdity. I believe you would pardon them, if there were time to deprecate your vengeance; but punishment follows so quick after sentence, that they cannot escape."

I had brought with me a great bundle of Scotch magazines and newspapers, in which his "Journey to the Western Islands" was attacked in every mode; and I read a great part of them to him, knowing they would afford him entertainment. I wish the writers of them had been present; they would have been sufficiently vexed. He defended his remark upon the general insufficiency of education in Scotland; and confirmed to me the authenticity of his witty saying on the learning of the Scotch—"Their learning is like bread in a besieged town; every man gets a little, but no man gets a full meal."

No sooner had we made our bow to Mr. Cambridge, in his library, than Johnson ran eagerly to one side of the room, intent on poring over the backs of the books. Mr. Cambridge politely said, "Dr. Johnson, I am going, with your pardon, to accuse myself, for I have the same custom which I perceive you have. But it seems odd that one should have such a desire to look at the backs of books." Johnson, ever ready for contest, instantly started from his reverie, wheeled about and answered, "Sir, the reason is very plain. Knowledge is of two kinds. We know a subject ourselves, or we know where we can find information upon it. When we inquire into any subject, the first thing we have to do is to know what books have treated of it. This leads us to look at catalogues, and the backs of books in libraries."

The common remark as to the utility of reading history being made;—JOHNSON. "We must consider how very little history there is; I mean real authentic history. That certain kings reigned, and certain battles were fought, we can depend upon as true; but all the colouring, all the philosophy of history is conjecture." BOSWELL. "Then, Sir, you would reduce all history to no better than an almanac, a mere chronological series of remarkable events." Mr. Gibbon, who must at that time have been employed upon his history, of which he published the first volume in the following year, was present; but did not step forth in defence of that species of writing. He probably did not like to *trust* himself with Johnson.

"The Beggar's Opera," and the common question, whether it was pernicious in its effects, having been introduced;—JOHNSON. "As to this matter, which has been very much contested, I myself am of opinion, that more influence has been ascribed to 'The Beggar's Opera' than it in reality ever had; for I do not believe that any man was ever made a rogue by being present at its representation. At the same time I do not deny that it may have some influence, by making the character of a rogue familiar, and in some degree pleasing." Then collecting himself, as it were, to give a heavy stroke: "There is in it such a *labefactation* of all principles as may be injurious to morality."

While he pronounced this response, we sat in a comical sort of restraint, smothering a laugh, which we were afraid might burst out.

Somebody found fault with writing verses in a dead language, maintaining that they were merely arrangements of so many words, and laughed at the Universities of Oxford and Cambridge, for sending forth collections of them, not only in Greek and Latin, but even in Syriac, Arabic, and other more unknown tongues. JOHNSON. "I would have as many of these as possible; I would have verses in every language that there are the means of acquiring. Nobody imagines that an university is to have at once two hundred poets: but it should be able to show two hundred scholars. Pieresc's death was lamented, I think, in forty languages. And I would have had at every coronation, and every death of a king, every *Gaudium*, and every *Luctus*, university-verses, in as many languages as can be acquired. I would have the world be thus told, 'Here is a school where every thing may be learnt.'"

Having set out next day on a visit to the Earl of Pembroke, at Wilton, and to my friend Mr. Temple, at Mamhead, in Devonshire, and not having returned to town till the 2nd of May, I did not see Dr. Johnson for a considerable time, and during the remaining part of my stay in London kept very imperfect notes of his conversation, which had I according to my usual custom written out at large soon after the time, much might have been preserved, which is now irretrievably lost.

On Monday, May 8, we went together and visited the mansions of Bedlam.[1] There was nothing peculiarly remarkable this day; but the general contemplation of insanity was very affecting. I accompanied him home, and dined and drank tea with him.

On Friday, May 12, as he had been so good as to assign me a room in his house, where I might sleep occasionally, when I happened to sit with him to a late hour, I took possession of it this night, found every thing in excellent order, and was attended by honest Francis with a most civil assiduity.

---

[1] Old Bedlam was one of the sights of London, like the *Abbey* and the *Tower*. The public were admitted for a small fee to perambulate long galleries into which the cells opened, and even to converse with the maniacs. "To gratify the curiosity of a country friend, I accompanied him a few weeks ago to Bedlam. It was in the Easter week, when, to my great surprise, I found a hundred people at least, who, having paid their twopence apiece, were suffered, unattended, to run rioting up and down the wards, making sport and diversion of the miserable inhabitants." &c.—*The World*, June 7, 1753.

On Saturday, May 13, I breakfasted with him by invitation, accompanied by Mr. Andrew Crosbie, a Scotch advocate, and the Hon. Colonel (now General) Edward Stopford. His tea and rolls and butter, and whole breakfast apparatus, were all in such decorum, and his behaviour was so courteous, that Colonel Stopford was quite surprised, and wondered at his having heard so much said of Johnson's slovenliness and roughness. I have preserved nothing of what passed, except that Crosbie pleased him much by talking learnedly of alchymy, as to which Johnson was not a positive unbeliever, but rather delighted in considering what progress had actually been made in the transmutation of metals, what near approaches there had been to the making of gold; and told us that it was affirmed that a person in the Russian dominions had discovered the secret but died without revealing it, as imagining it would be prejudicial to society. He added, that it was not impossible but it might in time be generally known.

It being asked whether it was reasonable for a man to be angry at another whom a woman had preferred to him;—JOHNSON. "I do not see, Sir, that it is reasonable for a man to be angry at another whom a woman has preferred to him; but angry he is, no doubt; and he is loth to be angry at himself."

Before setting out for Scotland on the 23rd, I was frequently in his company at different places, but during this period have recorded only two remarks; one concerning Garrick: "He has not Latin enough. He finds out the Latin by the meaning, rather than the meaning by the Latin." And another concerning writers of travels, who, he observed, "were more defective than any other writers."

I passed many hours with him on the 17th, of which I find all my memorial is, "much laughing." It should seem he had that day been in a humour for jocularity and merriment, and upon such occasions I never knew a man laugh more heartily. Johnson's laugh was as remarkable as any circumstance in his manner. It was a kind of good-humoured growl. Tom Davies described it drolly enough: "He laughs like a rhinoceros."

To James Boswell, Esq.

May 27, 1775

DEAR SIR,

I make no doubt but you are now safely lodged in your own habitation, and have told all your adventures to Mrs. Boswell and Miss Veronica. Pray teach Veronica to love me. Bid her not mind mamma. . . .

I will not send compliments to my friends by name, because I would be loth to leave any out in the enumeration. Tell them, as you see them, how well I speak of Scotch politeness, and Scotch hospitality, and Scotch beauty, and of everything Scotch, but Scotch oat-cakes, and Scotch prejudices. . . .

I am, my dearest Sir, with great affection, &c.,

SAM. JOHNSON

To James Boswell, Esq.

London, August 27, 1775
DEAR SIR,

I am returned from the annual ramble into the middle counties. Having seen nothing I had not seen before, I have nothing to relate. Time has left that part of the island few antiquities; and commerce has left the people no singularities. I was glad to go abroad, and, perhaps, glad to come home; which is, in other words, I was, I am afraid, weary of being at home, and weary of being abroad. Is not this the state of life? But if we confess this weariness, let us not lament it; for all the wise and all the good say, that we may cure it.

For the black fumes which rise in your mind, I can prescribe nothing but that you disperse them by honest business or innocent pleasure, and by reading, sometimes easy and sometimes serious. Change of place is useful; and I hope that your residence at Auchinleck will have many good effects. . . .

Mrs. Thrale was so entertained with your "Journal," that she almost read herself blind.[1] She has a great regard for you.

Of Mrs. Boswell, though she knows in her heart that she does not love me, I am always glad to hear any good, and hope that she and the little dear ladies will have neither sickness nor any other affliction. But she knows that she does not care what becomes of me, and for that she may be sure that I think her very much to blame.

Never, my dear Sir, do you take it into your head to think that I do not love you; you may settle yourself in full confidence both of my love and esteem: I love you as a kind man, I value you as a worthy man, and hope in time to reverence you as a man of exemplary piety. I hold you, as Hamlet has it, "in my heart of hearts," and therefore, it is little to say, that I am, Sir, your affectionate humble servant,   SAM. JOHNSON

---

[1] My Journal of a Tour to the Hebrides, which that lady read in the original manuscript.—*Boswell.*

VERY BUSY IN LOOKING ABOUT US

To the Same

Sept. 14, 1775

MY DEAR SIR,

I now write to you, lest in some of your freaks and humours
you should fancy yourself neglected. Such fancies I must entreat
you never to admit, at least never to indulge; for my regard for
you is so radicated and fixed, that it is become part of my mind,
and cannot be effaced but by some cause uncommonly violent;
therefore, whether I write or not, set your thoughts at rest. I
now write to tell you that I shall not very soon write again, for
I am to set out to-morrow on another journey. . . . Your friends
are all well at Streatham, and in Leicester Fields.[1] Make my compliments to Mrs. Boswell, if she is in good humour with me. I am,
Sir, &c.,   SAM. JOHNSON

What he mentions in such light terms as, "I am to set out to-
morrow on another journey," I soon afterwards discovered was no
less than a tour to France with Mr. and Mrs. Thrale. This was the
only time in his life that he went upon the Continent.

To Mr. Robert Levett

Calais, Sept. 18, 1775

DEAR SIR,

We are here in France, after a very pleasing passage of no
more than six hours. I know not when I shall write again, and
therefore I write now, though you cannot suppose that I have
much to say. You have seen France yourself. From this place
we are going to Rouen, and from Rouen to Paris. . . . We think
to go one way and return another, and see as much as we can.
I will try to speak a little French; I tried hitherto but little, but
I spoke sometimes. If I heard better, I suppose I should learn
faster. I am, Sir, your humble servant,

SAM. JOHNSON

To the Same

Paris, Oct. 22, 1775

DEAR SIR,

We are still here, commonly very busy in looking about
us. We have been to-day at Versailles. You have seen it, and I
shall not describe it. We came yesterday from Fontainbleau,
where the court is now. We went to see the king and queen at

[1] Where Sir Joshua Reynolds lived.

dinner, and the queen was so impressed by Miss [Thrale], that she sent one of the gentlemen to inquire who she was. I find all true that you have ever told me of Paris. Mr. Thrale is very liberal, and keeps us two coaches, and a very fine table; but I think our cookery very bad. Mrs. Thrale got into a convent of English nuns, and I talked with her through the grate, and I am very kindly used by the English Benedictine friars. But upon the whole I cannot make much acquaintance here; and though the churches, palaces, and some private houses are very magnificent, there is no very great pleasure after having seen many, in seeing more; at least the pleasure, whatever it be, must some time have an end, and we are beginning to think when we shall come home. Mr. Thrale calculates that as we left Streatham on the 15th of September, we shall see it again about the 15th of November.

I think I had not been on this side of the sea five days before I found a sensible improvement in my health. I ran a race in the rain this day, and beat Baretti. Baretti is a fine fellow, and speaks French, I think, quite as well as English.

Make my compliments to Mrs. Williams; and give my love to Francis; and tell my friends that I am not lost. I am, dear Sir, your affectionate humble, &c.,   SAM. JOHNSON

To Dr. Samuel Johnson

Edinburgh, Oct. 24, 1775

MY DEAR SIR,

If I had not been informed that you were at Paris, you should have had a letter from me by the earliest opportunity, announcing the birth of my son, on the 9th instant; I have named him Alexander, after my father. . . .

What a different scene have you viewed this autumn, from that which you viewed in autumn 1773! I ever am, my dear Sir, your much obliged and affectionate humble servant,

JAMES BOSWELL

To James Boswell, Esq.

London, Nov. 16, 1775

DEAR SIR,

I am glad that the young laird is born, and an end, as I hope, put to the only difference that you can ever have with Mrs. Boswell. . . .

Among all the congratulations that you may receive, I hope you believe none more warm or sincere than those of, dear Sir, your most affectionate,   SAM. JOHNSON

During his visit, which lasted about two months, he wrote notes or minutes of what he saw. He promised to show me them, but I neglected to put him in mind of it; and the greatest part of them has been lost, or perhaps destroyed in a precipitate burning of his papers a few days before his death, which must ever be lamented: one small paper book, however, entitled "France II.," has been preserved, and is in my possession. It is a diurnal register of his life and observations, from the 10th of October to the 4th of November, inclusive, being twenty-six days, and shows an extraordinary attention to various minute particulars.

"*Tuesday, Oct.* 10.—We saw the *Ecole Militaire*, in which 150 young boys are educated for the army. They have arms of different sizes, according to the age—flints of wood. The building is very large, but nothing fine except the council-room—The French have large squares in the windows. They make good iron palisades— Their meals are gross.

"We visited the Observatory, a large building of a great height. The upper stones of the parapet very large, but not cramped with iron—The flat on the top is very extensive; but on the insulated part there is no parapet—Though it was broad enough, I did not care to go upon it.

"*Thursday, Oct.* 12.—We went to the Gobelins—Tapestry makes a good picture—imitates flesh exactly—one piece with a gold ground—the birds not exactly coloured—Thence we went to the king's cabinet; very neat, not, perhaps, perfect—gold ore—candles of the candle-tree—seeds—woods—Thence to Gagnier's house, where I saw rooms nine, furnished with a profusion of wealth and elegance which I never had seen before—vases—pictures—the dragon china—The lustre is said to be of crystal, and to have cost 3,500*l.*—The whole furniture said to have cost 125,000*l.*— Damask hangings covered with pictures—Porphyry—this house struck me—Then we waited on the ladies to Monville's—Captain Irwin with us—Spain—County towns all beggars—Cross roads of France very bad—Five soldiers—Woman—Soldiers escaped—The colonel would not lose five men for the death of one woman—The magistrate cannot seize a soldier but by the colonel's permission— Good inn at Nismes—Moors of Barbary fond of Englishmen— Gibraltar eminently healthy; it has beef from Barbary—There is a large garden—Soldiers sometimes fall from the rock.

"*Saturday, Oct.* 14.—Much disturbed; hope no ill will be.

"In the afternoon I visited Mr. Fréron the journalist. He spoke

Latin very scantily, but seemed to understand me. His house not splendid, but of commodious size. His family, wife, son, and daughter, not elevated, but decent. I was pleased with my reception. He is to translate my books, which I am to send him with notes.

"*Monday, Oct.* 16.—The Palais Royal, very grand, large and lofty—I thought the pictures of Raphael fine.

"Austin Nuns—Grate—Mrs. Fermor, abbess—She knew Pope, and thought him disagreeable—Mrs. —— has many books—has seen life—Their frontlet disagreeable—Their hood—Their life easy—Rise about five; hour and half in chapel—Dine at ten—Another hour and half in chapel: half an hour about three, and half an hour more at seven—four hours in chapel—A large garden—Thirteen pensioners—Teachers complained.

"At the Boulevards saw nothing, yet was glad to be there—Rope-dancing and farce—Egg dance—*N.B.* Near Paris, whether on week-days or Sundays, the roads empty.

"*Tuesday, Oct.* 17.—At the *Palais Marchand* I bought—

A snuff box	. . . .	24 *livres*
——————	. . . .	6
Table book	. . . .	15
Scissors 3 p [pair].	. .	18

[*Livres*] 63—£2 12*s.* 6*d.* sterling.

"The sight of palaces, and other great buildings, leaves no very distinct images, unless to those who talk of them—As I entered, my wife was in my mind; she would have been pleased. Having now nobody to please, I am little pleased.

"*Wednesday, Oct.* 18.—We went to Fontainbleau, which we found a large mean town, crowded with people—The forest thick with woods, very extensive.

"*N.* Nobody but mean people walk in Paris.

"*Thursday, Oct.* 19.—At court we saw the apartments—The king's bed-chamber and council-chamber extremely splendid—Persons of all ranks in the external rooms through which the family passes—servants and masters—Brunet with us the second time.

"The introductor came to us—civil to me—Presenting—I had scruples—Not necessary—We went and saw the king and queen at dinner.

"*Friday, Oct.* 20.—We saw the queen mount in the forest—

Brown habit; rode aside: one lady rode aside—The queen's horse light gray—martingale—She galloped—We then went to the apartments, and admired them—Then wandered through the palace—In the passages, stalls and shops—Painting in fresco by a great master, worn out—We saw the king's horses and dogs—The dogs almost all English—degenerate.

"The horses not much commended—The stables cool; the kennel filthy.

"At night the ladies went to the opera—I refused, but should have been welcome.

"The king fed himself with his left hand as we.

"*Saturday*, *Oct.* 21.—We came home to Paris—.

"Faggots in the palace—Everything slovenly, except in the chief rooms.

"*Sunday*, *Oct.* 22.—To Versailles, a mean town—Our way lay through Sêve, where the China manufacture—Wooden bridge at Sêve, in the way to Versailles—The palace of great extent—The front long; I saw it not perfectly.

"Trianon is a kind of retreat appendant to Versailles—It has an open portico; the pavement, and, I think, the pillars, of marble —There are many rooms, which I do not distinctly remember—A table of porphyry, about five feet long, and between two and three broad, given to Louis XIV. by the Venetian state—In the council-room almost all that was not door or window was, I think, looking-glass—In the front of Versailles are small basins of water on the terrace, and other basins, I think, below them—There are little courts—The great gallery is wainscotted with mirrors not very large, but joined by frames—I suppose the large plates were not yet made—The play-house was very large—The dinner half a louis each, and—I think, a louis over—Money given at menagerie, three livres; at palace, six livres.

"*Monday*, *Oct.* 23.—Last night I wrote to Levett.—We went to see the looking-glasses wrought—They came from Normandy in cast plates, perhaps the third of an inch thick—At Paris they are ground upon a marble table, by rubbing one plate upon another with grit between them—The various sands, of which there are said to be five, I could not learn—The handle, by which the upper glass is moved, has the form of a wheel, which may be moved in all directions—The plates are sent up with their surfaces ground, but not polished, and so continue till they are bespoken, lest time should spoil the surface, as we were told—Those that are to be polished are laid on a table covered with several thick cloths, hard strained, that the resistance may be equal: they are then rubbed with a hand rubber, held down hard by a contrivance which I did not well understand—The powder which is used last seemed to me to be iron dissolved in aquafortis; they called it, as Baretti said, *marc de l'eau forte*, which he thought was dregs—They mentioned vitriol and saltpetre—The cannon ball swam in the quicksilver— To silver them, a leaf of beaten tin is laid, and rubbed with quicksilver, to which it unites—Then more quicksilver is poured upon it, which, by its mutual [attraction] rises very high—Then a paper is laid at the nearest end of the plate, over which the glass is slided till it lies upon the plate, having driven much of the quicksilver before it—It is then, I think, pressed upon cloth, and then set sloping to drop the superfluous mercury: the slope is daily heightened towards a perpendicular.

"*Tuesday, Oct. 24.*—We visited the king's library. Thence to the Sorbonne—The library very large, not in lattices like the king's— The prior and librarian dined with us—I waited on them home— their garden pretty, with covered walks, but small; yet may hold many students—The doctors of the Sorbonne are all equal—choose those who succeed to vacancies—Profit little.

"*Saturday, Oct. 28.*—I visited the Grand Chartreux built by St. Louis—The friar that spoke to us had a pretty apartment— His books seemed to be French—His garden was neat; he gave me grapes.

"Hotel—a guinea a day—Coach, three guineas a week—Valet de place, three l. a day—*Avantcoureur*, a guinea a week—Ordinary dinner six l. a head—Our ordinary [expense] seems to be about five guineas a day—Our extraordinary expenses, as diversions, gratuities, clothes, I cannot reckon—Our travelling is ten guineas a day.

"White stockings, 18 l.—Wig—hat.

"*Tuesday, Oct. 31.*—I lived at the Benedictines; meagre day; soup meagre, herrings, eels, both with sauce; fried fish; lentils, tasteless in themselves—I parted very tenderly from the prior and Friar Wilkes.

"*Wednesday, Nov. 1.*—We left Paris.

"*Thursday, Nov. 2.*—We came this day to Chantilly, a seat belonging to the Prince of Condé. This place is eminently beautified by all varieties of waters starting up in fountains, falling in cascades, running in streams, and spread in lakes. The water seems

SHE BADE THE FOOTMAN BLOW INTO IT

to be too near the house. All this water is brought from a source or river three leagues off, by an artificial canal, which for one league is carried under ground—The house is magnificent—The cabinet seems well stocked; what I remember was, the jaws of a hippopotamus, and a young hippopotamus preserved, which, however, is so small, that I doubt its reality—Nothing was [preserved] in spirits; all was dry—The dog; the deer; the ant-bear with long snout—The toucan, long broad beak—The stables were of very great length—The kennel had no scents—There was a mockery of a village—The menagerie had few animals—Two faussans, or Brazilian weasels, spotted, very wild—There is a forest, and, I think, a park—I walked till I was very weary, and next morning felt my feet battered, and with pains in the toes."

When I met him in London the following year, the account which he gave me of his French tour was, "Sir, I have seen all the visibilities of Paris, and around it: but to have formed an acquaintance with the people there would have required more time than I could stay. The great in France live very magnificently, but the rest very miserably. There is no happy middle state, as in England. The shops of Paris are mean; the meat in the markets is such as would be sent to a gaol in England; and Mr. Thrale justly observed, that the cookery of the French was forced upon them by necessity; for they could not eat their meat, unless they added some taste to it. The French are an indelicate people; they will spit upon any place. At Madame [Du Bocage's], a literary lady of rank, the footman took the sugar in his fingers, and threw it into my coffee. I was going to put it aside; but hearing it was made on purpose for me, I e'en tasted Tom's fingers. The same lady would needs make tea à l'Angloise. The spout of the teapot did not pour freely; she bade the footman blow into it. France is worse than Scotland in every thing but climate. Nature has done more for the French; but they have done less for themselves than the Scotch have done."

It happened that Foote was at Paris at the same time with Dr. Johnson, and his description of my friend while there was abundantly ludicrous. He told me, that the French were quite astonished at his figure and manner, and at his dress, which he obstinately continued exactly as in London;—his brown clothes, black stockings, and plain shirt.

While Johnson was in France, he was generally very resolute in speaking Latin. It was a maxim with him that a man should not let himself down by speaking a language which he speaks imperfectly.

Here let me not forget a curious anecdote. "When Madame de Boufflers was first in England," said Beauclerk, "she was desirous to see Johnson. I accordingly went with her to his chambers in the Temple, where she was entertained with his conversation for some time. When our visit was over, she and I left him, and were got into Inner Temple Lane, when all at once I heard a noise like thunder. This was occasioned by Johnson, who, it seems, upon a little reflection, had taken it into his head that he ought to have done the honours of his literary residence to a foreign lady of quality, and, eager to show himself a man of gallantry, was hurrying down the staircase in violent agitation. He overtook us before we reached the Temple-gate, and, brushing in between me and Madame de Boufflers, seized her hand, and conducted her to her coach. His dress was a rusty brown morning suit, a pair of old shoes by way of slippers, a little shrivelled wig sticking on the top of his head, and the sleeves of his shirt and the knees of his breeches hanging loose. A considerable crowd of people gathered round, and were not a little struck by this singular appearance."

I wrote to Dr. Johnson on the 20th of February, complaining of melancholy, and expressing a strong desire to be with him.

To James Boswell, Esq.

March 5, 1776

DEAR SIR,

I have not had your letter half an hour; as you lay so much weight upon my notions, I should think it not just to delay my answer. I am very sorry that your melancholy should return, and should be sorry likewise if it could have no relief but from my company. My counsel you may have when you please to require it; but of my company you cannot in the next month have much, for Mr. Thrale will take me to Italy, he says, on the 1st of April. . . . If you will come to me, you must come very quickly; and even then I know not but we may scour the country together, for I have a mind to see Oxford and Lichfield before I set out on this long journey. To this I can only add that I am, dear Sir, your most affectionate humble servant,

SAM. JOHNSON

Having arrived in London late on Friday, the 15th of March, I hastened next morning to wait on Dr. Johnson, at his house; but found he was removed from Johnson's Court, No. 7, to Bolt Court, No. 8, still keeping to his favourite Fleet Street. My reflection at the time upon this change, as marked in my journal, is as follows: "I felt a foolish regret that he had left a court which bore his name; but it was not foolish to be affected with some tenderness of regard for a place in which I had seen him a great deal, from whence I had often issued a better and a happier man than when I went in, and which had often appeared to my imagination, while I trod its pavement in the solemn darkness of the night, to be sacred to wisdom and piety." Being informed that he was at Mr. Thrale's in the Borough, I hastened thither, and found Mrs. Thrale and him at breakfast. I was kindly welcomed. In a moment he was in a full glow of conversation, and I felt myself elevated as if brought into another state of being. Mrs. Thrale and I looked to each other while we talked, and our looks expressed our congenial admiration and affection for him. I shall ever recollect this scene with great pleasure. I exclaimed to her, "I am now intellectually, *Hermippus redivivus;* I am quite restored by him, by transfusion of mind." "There are many," she replied, "who admire and respect Mr. Johnson; but you and I *love* him."

He seemed very happy in the near prospect of going to Italy with Mr. and Mrs. Thrale. "But," said he, "before leaving England, I am to take a jaunt to Oxford, Birmingham, my native city Lichfield, and my old friend Dr. Taylor's at Ashbourne, in Derbyshire. I shall go in a few days, and you, Boswell, shall go with me." I was ready to accompany him; being willing even to leave London to have the pleasure of his conversation.

I mentioned with much regret the extravagance of the representative of a great family in Scotland, by which there was danger of its being ruined; and as Johnson respected it for its antiquity, he joined with me in thinking it would be happy if this person should die. Mrs. Thrale seemed shocked at this, as feudal barbarity, and said, "I do not understand this preference of the estate to its owner; of the land to the man who walks upon that land." JOHNSON. "Nay, Madam, it is not a preference of the land to its owner; it is the preference of a family to an individual. Here is an establishment in a country, which is of importance for ages, not only to the chief but to his people; an establishment which extends upwards and downwards; that this should be destroyed by one idle fellow is a sad thing."

I mentioned Dr. Adam Smith's book on "The Wealth of Nations," which was just published, and that Sir John Pringle had observed to me, that Dr. Smith, who had never been in trade, could not be expected to write well on that subject, any more than a lawyer upon physic. JOHNSON. "He is mistaken, Sir; a man who has never been engaged in trade himself may undoubtedly write well upon trade, and there is nothing which requires more to be illustrated by philosophy than trade does. As to mere wealth, that is to say, money, it is clear that one nation or one individual cannot increase its store but by making another poorer; but trade procures what is more valuable, the reciprocation of the peculiar advantages of different countries. A merchant seldom thinks but of his own particular trade. To write a good book upon it, a man must have extensive views. It is not necessary to have practised, to write well upon a subject."

We got into a boat to cross over to Blackfriars; and as we moved along the Thames, I talked to him of a little volume, which, altogether unknown to him, was advertised to be published in a few days, under the title of "Johnsoniana, or Bon-mots of Dr. Johnson." JOHNSON. "Sir, it is a mighty impudent thing." BOSWELL. "Pray, Sir, could you have no redress if you were to prosecute a publisher for bringing out, under your name, what you never said, and ascribing to you dull stupid nonsense, or making you swear profanely, as many ignorant relaters of your *bon-mots* do?" JOHNSON. "No, Sir; there will always be some truth mixed with the falsehood, and how can it be ascertained how much is true and how much is false? Besides, Sir, what damages would a jury give me for having been represented as swearing?" BOSWELL. "I think, Sir, you should at least disavow such a publication, because the world and posterity might with much plausible foundation say, 'Here is a volume which was publicly advertised and came out in Dr. Johnson's own name, and, by his silence, was admitted by him to be genuine.'" JOHNSON. "I shall give myself no trouble about the matter."

Johnson was known to be so rigidly attentive to strict and scrupulous veracity, that even in his common conversation the slightest circumstance was mentioned with exact precision.

The knowledge of his having such a principle and habit made his friends have a perfect reliance on the truth of every thing that he told. As an instance of this, I may mention an odd incident which he related as having happened to him one night in Fleet Street. "A gentlewoman," said he, "begged I would give her my

"I PERCEIVED THAT SHE WAS SOMEWHAT IN LIQUOR"

arm to assist her in crossing the street, which I accordingly did; upon which she offered me a shilling, supposing me to be the watch- man. I perceived that she was somewhat in liquor." This, if told by most people, would have been thought an invention.

We landed at the Temple Stairs, where we parted. I found him in the evening in Mrs. Williams's room. We talked of religious orders. He said, "It is as unreasonable for a man to go into a Carthusian convent for fear of being immoral, as for a man to cut off his hands for fear he should steal. Their silence, too, is absurd. We read in the Gospel of the apostles being sent to preach, but not to hold their tongues. All severity that does not tend to increase good, or prevent evil, is idle. I said to the Lady Abbess of a con- vent, 'Madam, you are here, not for the love of virtue, but the fear of vice.' She said, 'She would remember this as long as she lived.'" I thought it hard to give her this view of her situation, when she could not help it.

Finding him still persevering in his abstinence from wine, I ventured to speak to him of it. JOHNSON. "Sir, I have no objection to a man's drinking wine, if he can do it in moderation. I found myself apt to go to excess in it, and therefore, after having been for some time without it, on account of illness, I thought it better not to return to it. Every man is to judge for himself, accord- ing to the effects which he experiences. One of the fathers tells us, he found fasting made him so peevish that he did not prac- tise it."

Though he often enlarged upon the evil of intoxication, he was by no means harsh and unforgiving to those who indulged in occasional excess in wine. One of his friends, I well remember, came to sup at a tavern with him and some other gentlemen, and too plainly discovered that he had drunk too much at dinner. When one who loved mischief, thinking to produce a severe censure, asked Johnson, a few days afterwards, "Well, Sir, what did your friend say to you, as an apology for being in such a situation?" Johnson answered, "Sir, he said all that a man *should* say: he said he was sorry for it."

I heard him once give a very judicious practical advice upon the subject: "A man who has been drinking wine at all freely should never go into a new company. With those who have partaken of wine with him, he may be pretty well in unison; but he will probably be offensive, or appear ridiculous, to other people."

I again visited him on Monday. He took occasion to enlarge, as he often did, upon the wretchedness of a sea-life. "A ship is worse than a gaol. There is, in a gaol, better air, better company, better conveniency of every kind; and a ship has the additional disadvantage of being in danger. When men come to like a sea-life, they are not fit to live on land." "Then," said I, "it would be cruel in a father to breed his son to the sea." JOHNSON. "It would be cruel in a father who thinks as I do. Men go to sea, before they know the unhappiness of that way of life; and when they have come to know it, they cannot escape from it, because it is then too late to choose another profession; as indeed is generally the case with men, when they have once engaged in any particular way of life."

On Tuesday, 19th March, which was fixed for our proposed jaunt, we met in the morning at the Somerset Coffee-house in the Strand, where we were taken up by the Oxford coach. Upon our arrival at Oxford, Dr. Johnson and I put up at the Angel inn, and passed the evening by ourselves in easy and familiar conversation. Talking of constitutional melancholy, he observed,—"A man so afflicted, Sir, must divert distressing thoughts, and not combat with them." BOSWELL. "May not he think them down, Sir?" JOHNSON. "No, Sir. To attempt to *think them down* is madness. He should have a lamp constantly burning in his bed-chamber during the night, and if wakefully disturbed, take a book, and read, and compose himself to rest. To have the management of the mind is a great art, and it may be attained in a considerable degree by experience and habitual exercise." BOSWELL. "Should not he provide amusement for himself? Would it not, for instance, be right for him to take a course of chemistry?" JOHNSON. "Let him take a course of chemistry, or a course of rope-dancing, or a course of any thing to which he is inclined at the time. Let him contrive to have as many retreats for his mind as he can, as many things to which it can fly from itself."

Next morning [Wednesday, March 20] we visited Dr. Wetherell, master of University College, with whom Dr. Johnson conferred on the most advantageous mode of disposing of the books printed at the Clarendon press. I often had occasion to remark, Johnson loved business, loved to have his wisdom actually operate on real life.

We then went to Pembroke College, and waited on his old friend Dr. Adams, the master of it. Dr. Adams had distinguished himself by an able Answer to David Hume's "Essay on Miracles." He told me he had once dined in company with Hume in London: that Hume shook hands with him, and said, "You have treated me much better than I deserve"; and that they exchanged visits. I took the liberty to object to treating an infidel writer with smooth civility. If a man firmly believes that religion is an invaluable treasure, he will consider a writer who endeavours to deprive mankind of it as a *robber;* he will look upon him as *odious,* though the infidel might think himself in the right. An abandoned profligate may think that it is not wrong to debauch my wife; but shall I, therefore, not detest him? And if I catch him in making an attempt, shall I treat him with politeness? No, I will kick him downstairs, or run him through the body; that is, if I really love my wife, or have a true rational notion of honour. An infidel then should not be treated handsomely by a Christian, merely because he endeavours to rob with ingenuity. Johnson coincided with me, and said, "When a man voluntarily engages in an important controversy, he is to do all he can to lessen his antagonist, because authority from personal respect has much weight with most people, and often more than reasoning. If my antagonist writes bad language, though that may not be essential to the question, I will attack him for his bad language." ADAMS. "You would not jostle a chimney-sweeper." JOHNSON. "Yes, Sir, if it were necessary to jostle him *down.*"

Dr. Adams told us, that in some of the colleges at Oxford, the fellows had excluded the students from social intercourse with them in the common room. JOHNSON. "They are in the right, Sir: there can be no real conversation, no fair exertion of mind amongst them, if the young men are by: for a man who has a character does not choose to stake it in their presence." BOSWELL. "But, Sir, may there not be very good conversation without a contest for superiority?" JOHNSON. "No animated conversation, Sir; for it cannot be but one or other will come off superior. I do not mean that the victor must have the better of the argument, for he may take the weak side; but his superiority of parts and knowledge will necessarily appear; and he to whom he thus shows himself superior is lessened in the eyes of the young men."

We walked with Dr. Adams into the master's garden, and into the common room. JOHNSON (after a reverie of meditation). "Ay! here I used to play at draughts with Phil. Jones and Fludyer. Jones loved beer, and did not get very forward in the church. Fludyer turned out a scoundrel, a whig, and said he was ashamed of having been bred at Oxford. He had a living at Putney; and got under the eye of some retainers to the court at that time, and so became a violent whig; but he had been a scoundrel all along, to be sure." BOSWELL. "Was he a scoundrel, Sir, in any other way than that of being a political scoundrel? Did he cheat at draughts?" JOHNSON. "Sir, we never played for *money*."

We then went to Trinity College, where he introduced me to Mr. Thomas Warton, with whom we passed a part of the evening. We talked of a work much in vogue at that time,[1] written in a very mellifluous style, but which, under pretext of another subject, contained much artful infidelity. I said it was not fair to attack us unexpectedly; he should have warned us of our danger, before we entered his garden of flowery eloquence, by advertising, "Spring-guns and men-traps set here."

I censured some ludicrous fantastic dialogues. He joined with me, and said, "Nothing odd will do long. 'Tristram Shandy' did not last." I expressed a desire to be acquainted with a lady who had been universally celebrated for extraordinary address and insinuation.[2] JOHNSON. "Never believe extraordinary characters which you hear of people. Depend upon it, Sir, they are exaggerated. You do not see one man shoot a great deal higher than another." I mentioned Mr. Burke. JOHNSON. "Yes, Burke *is* an extraordinary man. His stream of mind is perpetual." It is very pleasing to me to record, that Johnson's high estimation of the talents of this gentleman was uniform from their early acquaintance. And once, when Johnson was ill, and unable to exert himself as much as usual without fatigue, Mr. Burke having been mentioned, he said, "That fellow calls forth all my powers. Were I to see Burke now it would kill me." So much was he accustomed to consider conversation as a contest, and such was his notion of Burke as an opponent.

Next morning, Thursday, 21st March, we set out in a post-chaise to pursue our ramble. It was a delightful day, and we rode through Blenheim park. When I looked at the magnificent bridge built by John, Duke of Marlborough, over a small rivulet, and recollected the epigram made upon it—

> The lofty arch his high ambition shows,
> The stream an emblem of his bounty flows;

and saw that now, by the genius of Brown, a magnificent body of water was collected, I said, "They have *drowned* the epigram."

[1] The first volume of Gibbon's *Decline and Fall of the Roman Empire* was published Feb. 1, 1776. Its success was immediate.

[2] Margaret Caroline Rudd, a woman who lived with one of the brothers Perreau, who were about this time executed for a forgery. She betrayed her accomplices; they, in return, alleged that they were dupes and instruments in her hands, and exaggerated, to the highest degree, Mrs. Rudd's supposed powers of address and fascination.

"LIFE HAS NOT MANY THINGS BETTER THAN THIS"

I observed to him, while in the midst of the noble scene around us, "You and I, Sir, have, I think, seen together the extremes of what can be seen in Britain—the wild rough island of Mull, and Blenheim park."

We dined at an excellent inn at Chapel-house, where he expatiated on the felicity of England in its taverns and inns, and triumphed over the French for not having, in any perfection, the tavern life. "There is no private house," said he, "in which people can enjoy themselves so well as at a capital tavern. Let there be ever so great plenty of good things, ever so much grandeur, ever so much elegance, ever so much desire that every body should be easy; in the nature of things it cannot be: there must always be some degree of care and anxiety. The master of the house is anxious to entertain his guests; the guests are anxious to be agreeable to him; and no man, but a very impudent dog indeed, can as freely command what is in another man's house, as if it were his own. Whereas, at a tavern there is a general freedom from anxiety. You are sure you are welcome: and the more noise you make, the more trouble you give, the more good things you call for, the welcomer you are. No servants will attend you with the alacrity which waiters do, who are incited by the prospect of an immediate reward in proportion as they please. No, Sir; there is nothing which has yet been contrived by man, by which so much happiness is produced as by a good tavern or inn." [1] He then repeated, with great emotion, Shenstone's lines:

> Whoe'er has travell'd life's dull round,
> Where'er his stages may have been,
> May sigh to think he still has found
> The warmest welcome at an inn.

In the afternoon, as we were driven rapidly along in the post-chaise, he said to me, "Life has not many things better than this." [2]

[1] "In contradiction to those who, having a wife and children, prefer domestic enjoyments to those which a tavern affords, I have heard him assert, *that a tavern chair was the throne of human felicity.* 'As soon,' said he, 'as I enter the door of a tavern, I experience an oblivion of care, and a freedom from solicitude: when I am seated, I find the master courteous, and the servants obsequious to my call; anxious to know and ready to supply my wants: wine there exhilarates my spirits, and prompts me to free conversation and an interchange of discourse with those whom I most love: I dogmatise and am contradicted, and in this conflict of opinion and sentiments I find delight.'"—Sir John Hawkins, *Life of Johnson.*

[2] "He loved the very act of travelling, and I cannot tell how far one might have taken him in a carriage before he would have wished for refreshment. He was therefore in some respects an admirable companion on the road, as he piqued himself upon feeling no inconvenience, and on despising no accommodations. On the other hand, however, he expected no one else to feel any, and felt exceedingly inflamed with anger if any one complained of the rain, the sun, or the dust. 'How,' said he, 'do other people bear them?' "—*Mrs. Piozzi, Anecdotes.*

On Friday, 22nd March, having set out early from Henley [in Arden], where we had lain the preceding night, we arrived at Birmingham about nine o'clock, and after breakfast went to call on his old schoolfellow, Mr. Hector.[1] A very stupid maid, who opened the door, told us that "her master was gone out; he was gone to the country; she could not tell when he would return." In short, she gave us a miserable reception; and Johnson observed, "She would have behaved no better to people who wanted him in the way of his profession." He said to her, "My name is Johnson; tell him I called. Will you remember the name?" She answered with rustic simplicity, in the Warwickshire pronunciation, "I don't understand you, Sir." "Blockhead," said he, "I'll write." I never heard the word *blockhead* applied to a woman before, though I do not see why it should not, when there is evident occasion for it. He, however, made another attempt to make her understand him, and roared loud in her ear, "*Johnson,*" and then she catched the sound.

We next called on Mr. Lloyd, one of the people called quakers. He too was not at home, but Mrs. Lloyd was, and received us courteously, and asked us to dinner. Johnson said to me, "After the uncertainty of all human things at Hector's, this invitation came very well." We walked about the town, and were pleased to see it increasing.

Mr. Lloyd joined us in the street; and in a little while we met *friend Hector*, as Mr. Lloyd called him. It gave me pleasure to observe the joy which Johnson and he expressed on seeing each other again. At Mr. Lloyd's we were entertained with great hospitality. Mr. and Mrs. Lloyd had a numerous family of fine children. Johnson said, "Marriage is the best state for man in general; and every man is a worse man, in proportion as he is unfit for the married state."

As Dr. Johnson had said to me in the morning, while we walked together, that he liked individuals among the quakers, but not the sect; when we were at Mr. Lloyd's, I kept clear of introducing any questions concerning the peculiarities of their faith. But I having asked to look at Baskerville's edition of "Barclay's Apology," Johnson laid hold of it; and the chapter on baptism happening to open, Johnson remarked, "He says there is neither precept nor practice for baptism in the scriptures; that is false." Here he was the aggressor, by no means in a gentle manner; and the good

[1] Mr. Hector was a surgeon (see p. 9).

quakers had the advantage of him; for he had read negligently, and had not observed that Barclay speaks of *infant* baptism; which they calmly made him perceive.

Dr. Johnson said to me in the morning, "You will see, Sir, at Mr. Hector's, his sister, Mrs. Careless, a clergyman's widow. She was the first woman with whom I was in love. It dropped out of my head imperceptibly; but she and I shall always have a kindness for each other." He laughed at the notion that a man can never be really in love but once, and considered it as a mere romantic fancy.

When Mr. Hector took me to his house, we found Johnson sitting placidly at tea, with his *first love;* who, though now advanced in years, was a genteel woman, very agreeable and well-bred.

When he again talked of Mrs. Careless to-night, he seemed to have his affection revived; for he said, "If I had married her, it might have been as happy for me." BOSWELL. "Pray, Sir, do you not suppose that there are fifty women in the world, with any one of whom a man may be as happy, as with any one woman in particular?" JOHNSON. "Ay, Sir, fifty thousand." BOSWELL. "Then, Sir, you are not of opinion with some who imagine that certain men and certain women are made for each other; and that they cannot be happy if they miss their counterparts." JOHNSON. "To be sure not, Sir. I believe marriages would in general be as happy, and often more so, if they were all made by the lord chancellor, upon a due consideration of the characters and circumstances, without the parties having any choice in the matter."

I wished to have staid at Birmingham to-night, to have talked more with Mr. Hector; but my friend was impatient to reach his native city; so we drove on that stage in the dark, and were long pensive and silent. When we came within the focus of the Lichfield lamps, "Now," said he, "we are getting out of a state of death." We put up at the Three Crowns, not one of the great inns, but a good old-fashioned one, which was the very next house to that in which Johnson was born and brought up, and which was still his own property. We had a comfortable supper, and got into high spirits. I felt all my toryism glow in this old capital of Staffordshire. I could have offered incense *genio loci;* and I indulged in libations of that ale, which Boniface, in "The Beaux' Stratagem," recommends with such an eloquent jollity.

Next morning he introduced me to Mrs. Lucy Porter, his stepdaughter. She was now an old maid, with much simplicity of manner. She had never been in London. Her brother had left her a fortune of ten thousand pounds; about a third of which she had laid out in building a stately house, and making a handsome garden, in an elevated situation in Lichfield. Johnson, when here by himself, used to live at her house. She reverenced him, and he had a parental tenderness for her.

We dined at our inn. I saw here, for the first time, *oat ale;* and oat-cakes, not hard as in Scotland, but soft like a Yorkshire cake, were served at breakfast. It was pleasant to me to find, that "*oats,*" the "*food of horses,*" were so much used as the *food of the people* in Dr. Johnson's own town. He expatiated in praise of Lichfield and its inhabitants, who, he said, were "the most sober, decent people in England, the genteelest in proportion to their wealth, and spoke the purest English." I doubted as to the last article of this eulogy; for they had several provincial sounds; as, *there,* pronounced like *fear,* instead of like *fair; once* pronounced *woonse,* instead of *wunse* or *wonse.* Johnson himself never got entirely free of those provincial accents. Garrick sometimes used to take him off, squeezing a lemon into a punch-bowl, with uncouth gesticulations, looking round the company, and calling out, "Who's for *poonsh?*"

Very little business appeared to be going forward in Lichfield. I found, however, two strange manufactures for so inland a place, sail-cloth and streamers for ships; and I observed them making some saddle-cloths, and dressing sheep-skins; but upon the whole, the busy hand of industry seemed to be quite slackened. "Surely, Sir," said I, "you are an idle set of people." "Sir," said Johnson, "we are a city of philosophers; we work with our heads, and make the boobies of Birmingham work for us with their hands." There was at this time a company of players performing at Lichfield. He told me, "Forty years ago, Sir, I was in love with an actress here, Mrs. Emmet, who acted Flora, in 'Hob in the Well.'" What merit this lady had as an actress, or what was her figure, or her manner, I have not been informed; but, if we may believe Mr. Garrick, his old master's taste in theatrical merit was by no means refined. Garrick used to tell, that Johnson said of an actor, who played Sir Harry Wildair at Lichfield, "There is a courtly vivacity about the fellow"; when, in fact, according to Garrick's account, "he was the most vulgar ruffian that ever went upon *boards.*"

We had promised Mr. Stanton [1] to be at his theatre on Monday. Dr. Johnson jocularly proposed to me to write a prologue for the

---

[1] The manager, who had "sent his compliments, and begged leave to wait on Dr. Johnson."

occasion: "A Prologue, by James Boswell, Esqr., from the Hebrides." I was really inclined to take the hint. Methought, "Prologue, spoken before Dr. Samuel Johnson, at Lichfield, 1776," would have sounded as well as "Prologue spoken before the Duke of York at Oxford," in Charles the Second's time. But I found he was averse to it.

On Monday, March 25, we breakfasted at Mrs. Lucy Porter's. While we sat at breakfast, Dr. Johnson received a letter by the post, which seemed to agitate him very much. When he had read it, he exclaimed, "One of the most dreadful things that has happened in my time." The phrase *my time*, like the word *age*, is usually understood to refer to an event of a public or general nature. I imagined something like an assassination of the king—like a gunpowder plot carried into execution—or like another fire of London. When asked, "What is it, Sir?" he answered, "Mr. Thrale has lost his only son!" This was, no doubt, a very great affliction to Mr. and Mrs. Thrale, which their friends would consider accordingly; but from the manner in which the intelligence of it was communicated by Johnson, it appeared for the moment to be comparatively small. I, however, soon felt a sincere concern, and was curious to observe how Dr. Johnson would be affected. He said, "This is a total extinction to their family, as much as if they were sold into captivity." Upon my mentioning that Mr. Thrale had daughters, who might inherit his wealth: "Daughters!" said Johnson, warmly, "he'll no more value his daughters than——." I was going to speak. "Sir," said he, "don't you know how you yourself think? Sir, he wishes to propagate his name." In short, I saw male succession strong in his mind, even where there was no name, no family of any long standing. I said, it was lucky he was not present when this misfortune happened. JOHNSON. "It was lucky for *me*. People in distress never think you feel enough." BOSWELL. "And, Sir, they will have the hope of seeing you, which will be a relief in the mean time; and when you get to them, the pain will be so far abated, that they will be capable of being consoled by you, which, in the first violence of it, I believe, would not be the case." JOHNSON. "No, Sir; violent pain of mind, like violent pain of body, *must* be severely felt." BOSWELL. "I own, Sir, I have not so much feeling for the distress of others, as some people have, or pretend to have: but I know this, that I would do all in my power to relieve them." JOHNSON. "Sir, it is affectation to pretend to feel the distress of others as much as they do themselves. It is equally so, as if one should pretend to feel as much pain while a friend's leg is cutting off, as he does. No, Sir; you have expressed the rational and just nature of sympathy. I would have gone to the extremity of the earth to have preserved this boy."

He was soon quite calm. The letter was from Mr. Thrale's clerk, and concluded, "I need not say how much they wish to see you in London." He said, "We shall hasten back from Taylor's."

After dinner Dr. Johnson wrote a letter to Mrs. Thrale on the death of her son.

In the evening we went to the Town-hall, which was converted into a temporary theatre, and saw "Theodosius," with "The Stratford Jubilee." I was happy to see Dr. Johnson sitting in a conspicuous part of the pit, and receiving affectionate homage from all his acquaintance. We were quite gay and merry. I afterwards mentioned to him that I condemned myself for being so, when poor Mr. and Mrs. Thrale were in such distress. JOHNSON. "You are wrong, Sir; twenty years hence Mr. and Mrs. Thrale will not suffer much pain from the death of their son. Now, Sir, you are to consider, that distance of place, as well as distance of time, operates upon the human feelings. I would not have you be gay in the presence of the distressed, because it would shock them; but you may be gay at a distance. Pain for the loss of a friend, or of a relation, whom we love, is occasioned by the want which we feel. In time the vacuity is filled with something else; or sometimes the vacuity closes up of itself."

On Tuesday, March 26, there came for us an equipage properly suited to a wealthy, well-beneficed clergyman: Dr. Taylor's large roomy post-chaise, drawn by four stout plump horses, and driven by two steady jolly postilions, which conveyed us to Ashbourne; where I found my friend's schoolfellow living upon an establishment perfectly corresponding with his substantial creditable equipage: his house, garden, pleasure-ground, table, in short every thing good, and no scantiness appearing. Dr. Taylor, though the schoolfellow and friend of Johnson, was a Whig. I could not perceive in his character much congeniality of any sort with that of Johnson, who, however, said to me, "Sir, he has a very strong understanding."

Dr. Johnson and Dr. Taylor met with great cordiality. Johnson gave him a sad account of their schoolfellow, Congreve, adding a remark of such moment to the rational conduct of a man in the decline of life, that it deserves to be imprinted upon every mind:

"There is nothing against which an old man should be so much upon his guard as putting himself to nurse." Innumerable have been the melancholy instances of men once distinguished for firmness, resolution, and spirit, who in their later days have been governed like children, by interested female artifice.

Next day [Wednesday, March 27], as Dr. Johnson had acquainted Dr. Taylor of the reason for his returning speedily to London, it was resolved that we should set out after dinner.

Dr. Johnson talked with approbation of one who had attained to the state of the philosophical wise man, that is, to have no want of any thing. "Then, Sir," said I, "the savage is a wise man." "Sir," said he, "I do not mean simply being without,—but not having a want." I maintained, against this proposition, that it was better to have fine clothes, for instance, than not to feel the want of them. JOHNSON. "No, Sir; fine clothes are good only as they supply the want of other means of procuring respect. Was Charles the Twelfth, think you, less respected for his coarse blue coat and black stock? And you find the King of Prussia dresses plain, because the dignity of his character is sufficient." I here brought myself into a scrape, for I heedlessly said, "Would not *you*, Sir, be the better for velvet embroidery?" JOHNSON. "Sir, you put an end to all argument when you introduce your opponent himself. Have you no better manners? There is *your want.*"

Having left Ashbourne in the evening, we stopped to change horses at Derby. We lay this night at Loughborough.

On Thursday, March 28, we pursued our journey. He said, "It is commonly a weak man who marries for love." We then talked of marrying women of fortune; and I mentioned a common remark, that a man may be, upon the whole, richer by marrying a woman with a very small portion, because a woman of fortune will be proportionally expensive; whereas a woman who brings none will be very moderate in expenses. JOHNSON. "Depend upon it, Sir, this is not true. A woman of fortune, being used to the handling of money, spends it judiciously; but a woman who gets the command of money for the first time upon her marriage, has such a gust in spending it, that she throws it away with great profusion."

Having lain at St. Alban's on Thursday, March 28, we breakfasted the next morning at Barnet. I expressed to him a weakness of mind which I could not help; an uneasy apprehension that my wife and children, who were at a great distance from me, might, perhaps, be ill. "Sir," said he, "consider how foolish you would think it in *them* to be apprehensive that *you* are ill." This sudden turn relieved me for the moment.

I enjoyed the luxury of our approach to London, that metropolis which we both loved so much, for the high and varied intellectual pleasures which it furnishes. I experienced immediate happiness while whirled along with such a companion, and said to him, "Sir, you observed one day at General Oglethorpe's that a man is never happy for the present, but when he is drunk. Will you not add—or when driving rapidly in a post-chaise?" JOHNSON. "No, Sir, you are driving rapidly *from* something, or *to* something."

We stopped at Messieurs Dillys, booksellers in the Poultry; from whence he hurried away, in a hackney coach, to Mr. Thrale's in the Borough. I called at his house in the evening, having promised to acquaint Mrs. Williams of his safe return; when, to my surprise, I found him sitting with her at tea, and, as I thought, not in a very good humour: for, it seems, when he had got to Mr. Thrale's, he found the coach was at the door waiting to carry Mrs. and Miss Thrale, and Signor Baretti, their Italian master, to Bath. This was not showing the attention which might have been expected to the "guide, philosopher, and friend," who had hastened from the country to console a distressed mother, who he understood was very anxious for his return. They had, I found, without ceremony, proceeded on their journey. I was glad to understand from him that it was still resolved that his tour to Italy with Mr. and Mrs. Thrale should take place, of which he had entertained some doubt, on account of the loss which they had suffered.

On Wednesday, April 3, in the morning, I found him very busy putting his books in order, and, as they were generally very old ones, clouds of dust were flying around him. He had on a pair of large gloves, such as hedgers use. His present appearance put me in mind of my uncle Dr. Boswell's description of him, "A robust genius, born to grapple with whole libraries."

I gave him an account of a conversation which had passed between me and Captain Cook, the day before, at dinner at Sir John Pringle's; and he was much pleased with the conscientious accuracy of that celebrated circumnavigator, who set me right as to many of the exaggerated accounts given by Dr. Hawkesworth of his voyages. I told him that while I was with the captain I catched the enthusiasm of curiosity and adventure, and felt a

VERY BUSY PUTTING HIS BOOKS IN ORDER

strong inclination to go with him on his next voyage. JOHNSON. "Why, Sir, a man *does* feel so, till he considers how very little he can learn from such voyages." BOSWELL. "But one is carried away with the general, grand, and indistinct notion of A VOYAGE ROUND THE WORLD." JOHNSON. "Yes, Sir, but a man is to guard himself against taking a thing in general." I said I was certain that a great part of what we are told by the travellers to the South Sea must be conjecture, because they had not enough of the language of those countries to understand so much as they have related. Dr. Johnson was of the same opinion. He upon another occasion, when a friend mentioned to him several extraordinary facts, as communicated to him by the circumnavigators, slyly observed, "Sir, I never before knew how much I was respected by these gentlemen; they told me none of these things."

We agreed to dine to-day at the Mitre tavern. I brought with me Mr. Murray, solicitor-general of Scotland. Mr. Murray praised the ancient philosophers for the candour and good humour with which those of different sects disputed with each other. JOHNSON. "Sir, they disputed with good humour, because they were not in earnest as to religion. Had the ancients been serious in their belief we should not have had their gods exhibited in the manner we find them represented in the poets. The people would not have suffered it. They disputed with good humour upon their fanciful theories, because they were not interested in the truth of them: when a man has nothing to lose, he may be in good humour with his opponent. Accordingly you see, in Lucian, the Epicurean, who argues only negatively, keeps his temper; the Stoic, who has something positive to preserve, grows angry. Being angry with one who controverts an opinion which you value, is a necessary consequence of the uneasiness which you feel. Every man who attacks my belief, diminishes in some degree my confidence in it, and therefore makes me uneasy; and I am angry with him who makes me uneasy. Those only who believed in revelation have been angry at having their faith called in question; because they only had something upon which they could rest as matter of fact." MURRAY. "But, Sir, truth will always bear an examination." JOHNSON. "Yes, Sir, but it is painful to be forced to defend it. Consider, Sir, how should you like, though conscious of your innocence, to be tried before a jury for a capital crime, once a week."

I mentioned Mr. Maclaurin's uneasiness on account of a degree of ridicule carelessly thrown on his deceased father, in Goldsmith's

"History of Animated Nature." [1] This led us to agitate the question, whether legal redress could be obtained, even when a man's deceased relation was calumniated in a publication. Mr. Murray maintained there should be reparation, unless the author could justify himself by proving the fact; but Johnson firmly and resolutely opposed any restraint whatever, as adverse to a free investigation of the characters of mankind.

On Friday, 5th April, being Good Friday, after having attended the morning service at St. Clement's church, I walked home with Johnson. We talked of the Roman Catholic religion. JOHNSON. "In the barbarous ages, Sir, priests and people were equally deceived: but afterwards there were gross corruptions introduced by the clergy, such as indulgences to priests to have concubines, and the worship of images: not, indeed, inculcated, but knowingly permitted." He strongly censured the licensed stews at Rome. BOSWELL. "So then, Sir, you would allow of no irregular intercourse whatever between the sexes?" JOHNSON. "To be sure I would not, Sir. I would punish it much more than it is done, and so restrain it. In all countries there has been fornication, as in all countries there has been theft; but there may be more or less of the one, as well as of the other, in proportion to the force of the law. All men will naturally commit fornication, as all men will naturally steal. And, Sir, it is very absurd to argue, as has been often done, that prostitutes are necessary to prevent the violent effects of appetite from violating the decent order of life; nay, should be permitted, in order to preserve the chastity of our wives and daughters. Depend upon it, Sir, severe laws, steadily enforced, would be sufficient against those evils, and would promote marriage."

I stated to him this case: "Suppose a man has a daughter, who he knows has been seduced, but her misfortune is concealed from the world, should he keep her in his house? Would he not, by doing so, be accessory to imposition? And, perhaps, a worthy, unsuspecting man, might come and marry this woman, unless the father informed him of the truth." JOHNSON. "Sir, he is accessory to no

[1] "Every one knows . . . that for one person to yawn, it is sufficient to set all the company a-yawning. A ridiculous instance of this was commonly practised on the famous Maclaurin, one of the professors of Edinburgh. He was very subject to have his jaw dislocated; so that when he opened his mouth wider than ordinary, or when he yawned, he could not shut it again. In the midst of his harangues, therefore, if any of his pupils begun to be tired of his lecture, he had only to gape or yawn, and the professor instantly caught the sympathetic affection; so that he thus continued to stand speechless with his mouth wide open, till his servant from the next room was called in to set his jaw again." Goldsmith's *History of the Earth and Animated Nature*. After the first edition a footnote was added denying the truth of the story.

imposition. His daughter is in his house; and if a man courts her, he takes his chance. If a friend, or indeed if any man, asks his opinion whether he should marry her, he ought to advise him against it, without telling why, because his real·opinion is then required. Or, if he has other daughters who know of her frailty, he ought not to keep her in his house. You are to consider the state of life is this; we are to judge of one another's characters as well as we can; and a man is not bound in honesty or honour to tell us the faults of his daughter or of himself."

Mr. Thrale called upon him, and appeared to bear the loss of his son with a manly composure. There was no affectation about him; and he talked, as usual, upon indifferent subjects. He seemed to me to hesitate as to the intended Italian tour. I pressed it as much as I could. JOHNSON. "Mr. Thrale is to get a plan for seeing the most that can be seen in the time that we have to travel. We must, to be sure, see Rome, Naples, Florence, and Venice, and as much more as we can." (Speaking with a tone of animation.)

When I expressed an earnest wish for his remarks on Italy, he said, "I do not see that I could make a book upon Italy; yet I should be glad to get two hundred pounds, or five hundred pounds, by such a work." This showed both that a journal of his tour upon the continent was not wholly out of his contemplation, and that he uniformly adhered to that strange opinion which his indolent disposition made him utter: "No man but a blockhead ever wrote except for money."

He gave us one of the many sketches of character which were treasured in his mind, and which he was wont to produce quite unexpectedly in a very entertaining manner. Volumes would be required to contain a list of his numerous and various acquaintance, none of whom he ever forgot; and could describe and discriminate them all with precision and vivacity. He associated with persons the most widely different in manners, abilities, rank, and accomplishments. He was at once the companion of the brilliant Colonel Forrester of the Guards, who wrote "The Polite Philosopher," and of the awkward and uncouth Robert Levett; of Lord Thurlow, and Mr. Sastres, the Italian master; and has dined one day with the beautiful, gay, and fascinating Lady Craven, and the next with good Mrs. Gardiner, the tallow-chandler, on Snow-hill.

I mentioned a new gaming club,[1] of which Mr. Beauclerk had

[1] Almack's. Fox said that the deepest play he had ever known was about this period, between the year 1772 and the beginning of the American war: £5000 being staked on a single card at faro, and £70,000 lost and won in a night.

given me an account, where the members played to a desperate extent. JOHNSON. "Depend upon it, Sir, this is mere talk. *Who* is ruined by gaming? You will not find six instances in an age. There is a strange rout made about deep play; whereas you have many more people ruined by adventurous trade, and yet we do not hear such an outcry against it." THRALE. "There may be few absolutely ruined by deep play; but very many are much hurt in their circumstances by it." JOHNSON. "Yes, Sir, and so are very many by other kinds of expense." I had heard him talk once before in the same manner; and at Oxford he said, "he wished he had learned to play at cards." The truth, however, is, that he loved to display his ingenuity in argument; and therefore would sometimes in conversation maintain opinions which he was sensible were wrong, but in supporting which, his reasoning and wit would be most conspicuous. He would begin thus: "Why, Sir, as to the good or evil of card playing—" "Now," said Garrick, "he is thinking which side he shall take." He appeared to have a pleasure in contradiction, especially when any opinion whatever was delivered with an air of confidence; so that there was hardly any topic, if not one of the great truths of religion and morality, that he might not have been incited to argue either for or against.

On Sunday, April 7th, Easter-day, after having been at St. Paul's cathedral, I came to Dr. Johnson, according to my usual custom. I repeated to him an argument of a lady of my acquaintance, who maintained, that her husband's having been guilty of numberless infidelities, released her from conjugal obligations, because they were reciprocal. JOHNSON. "This is miserable stuff, Sir. To the contract of marriage, besides the man and wife, there is a third party—society; and if it be considered as a vow—God: and, therefore, it cannot be dissolved by their consent alone. Laws are not made for particular cases, but for men in general. A woman may be unhappy with her husband; but she cannot be freed from him without the approbation of the civil and ecclesiastical power. A man may be unhappy, because he is not so rich as another; but he is not to seize upon another's property with his own hand." BOSWELL. "But, Sir, this lady does not want that the contract should be dissolved; she only argues that she may indulge herself in gallantries with equal freedom as her husband does, provided she takes care not to introduce a spurious issue into his family." JOHNSON. "This lady of yours, Sir, I think, is very fit for a brothel."

Mr. Macbean, author of the "Dictionary of Ancient Geography," came in. He mentioned that he had been forty years absent from Scotland. "Ah, Boswell!" said Johnson smiling, "what would you give to be forty years from Scotland!"

This gentleman, Mrs. Williams, and Mr. Levett dined with us. Mrs. Williams was very peevish; and I wondered at Johnson's patience with her now, as I had often done on similar occasions. The truth is, that his humane consideration of the forlorn and indigent state in which this lady was left by her father induced him to treat her with the utmost tenderness, and even to be desirous of procuring her amusement, so as sometimes to incommode many of his friends, by carrying her with him to their houses, where, from her manner of eating, in consequence of her blindness, she could not but offend the delicacy of persons of nice sensations.

On Wednesday, 10th April, I dined with him at Mr. Thrale's. Before dinner, Dr. Johnson and I passed some time by ourselves. I was sorry to find it was now resolved that the proposed journey to Italy should not take place this year. He said, "I am disappointed, to be sure; but it is not a great disappointment." I wondered to see him bear, with a philosophical calmness, what would have made most people peevish and fretful. I perceived that he had so warmly cherished the hope of enjoying classical scenes, that he could not easily part with the scheme; for he said, "I shall probably contrive to get to Italy some other way. But I won't mention it to Mr. and Mrs. Thrale, as it might vex them." I suggested that going to Italy might have done Mr. and Mrs. Thrale good. JOHNSON. "I rather believe not, Sir. While grief is fresh, every attempt to divert only irritates. You must wait till grief be *digested*, and then amusement will dissipate the remains of it."

I said, I disliked the custom which some people had of bringing their children into company, because it in a manner forced us to pay foolish compliments to please their parents. JOHNSON. "You are right, Sir. We may be excused for not caring much about other people's children, for there are many who care very little about their own children. It may be observed, that men who, from being engaged in business, or from their course of life in whatever way, seldom see their children, do not care much about them. I myself should not have had much fondness for a child of my own." MRS. THRALE. "Nay, Sir, how can you talk so?" JOHNSON. "At least, I never wished to have a child."

On Thursday, April 11, I dined with him at General Paoli's, in whose house I now resided, and where I had ever afterwards the honour of being entertained with the kindest attention as his constant guest, while I was in London, till I had a house of my own there. A journey to Italy was still in his thoughts. He said, "A man who has not been in Italy is always conscious of an inferiority, from his not having seen what it is expected a man should see. The grand object of travelling is to see the shores of the Mediterranean. On those shores were the four great empires of the world; the Assyrian, the Persian, the Grecian, and the Roman. All our religion, almost all our law, almost all our arts, almost all that sets us above savages, has come to us from the shores of the Mediterranean."

On Friday, April 12, Johnson and I supped at the Crown and Anchor tavern, in company with Sir Joshua Reynolds, Mr. Langton, Mr. Nairne, and Sir William Forbes, of Pitsligo.

We discussed the question, whether drinking improved conversation and benevolence. Sir Joshua maintained, it did. JOHNSON. "No, Sir: before dinner men meet with great inequality of understanding; and those who are conscious of their inferiority have the modesty not to talk. When they have drunk wine every man feels himself happy, and loses that modesty, and grows impudent and vociferous: but he is not improved: he is only not sensible of his defects." Sir Joshua said the Doctor was talking of the effects of excess in wine; but that a moderate glass enlivened the mind, by giving a proper circulation to the blood. "I am," said he, "in very good spirits when I get up in the morning. By dinner-time I am exhausted; wine puts me in the same state as when I get up: and I am sure that moderate drinking makes people talk better." JOHNSON. "No, Sir: wine gives not light, gay, ideal hilarity; but tumultuous, noisy, clamorous merriment. I have heard none of those drunken,—nay, drunken is a coarse word,—none of those *vinous* flights." SIR JOSHUA. "Because you have sat by, quite sober, and felt an envy of the happiness of those who were drinking." JOHNSON. "Perhaps, contempt. And, Sir, it is not necessary to be drunk one's self, to relish the wit of drunkenness. Do we not judge of the drunken wit of the dialogue between Iago and Cassio, the most excellent in its kind, when we are quite sober? Wit is wit, by whatever means it is produced; and, if good, will appear so at all times. I admit that the spirits are raised by drinking, as by the common participation of any pleasure: cock-fighting or bear-baiting will

THEY WERE GONE TO THE ROOMS

raise the spirits of a company, as drinking does, though surely they will not improve conversation. I also admit, that there are some sluggish men who are improved by drinking; as there are fruits which are not good till they are rotten. There are such men, but they are medlars. I indeed allow that there have been a very few men of talents who were improved by drinking; but I maintain that I am right as to the effects of drinking in general: and let it be considered, that there is no position, however false in its universality, which is not true of some particular man." Sir William Forbes said, "Might not a man warmed with wine be like a bottle of beer, which is made brisker by being set before the fire." "Nay," said Johnson, laughing, "I cannot answer that: that is too much for me."

I observed, that wine did some people harm, by inflaming, confusing, and irritating their minds; but that the experience of mankind had declared in favour of moderate drinking. JOHNSON. "Sir, I do not say it is wrong to produce self-complacency by drinking; I only deny that it improves the mind. When I drank wine, I scorned to drink it when in company. I have drunk many a bottle by myself; in the first place, because I had need of it to raise my spirits; in the second place, because I would have nobody to witness its effects upon me."

Soon after this day, he went to Bath with Mr. and Mrs. Thrale. I had never seen that beautiful city, and wished to take the opportunity of visiting it while Johnson was there. Having written to him, on the 26th April I went; and on my arrival at the Pelican inn, found lying for me an obliging invitation from Mr. and Mrs. Thrale, by whom I was agreeably entertained almost constantly during my stay. They were gone to the rooms: but there was a kind note from Dr. Johnson, that he should sit at home all the evening. I went to him directly; and before Mr. and Mrs. Thrale returned, we had by ourselves some hours of tea-drinking and talk.

It having been mentioned, I know not with what truth, that a certain female political writer [Mrs. Macaulay], whose doctrines he disliked, had of late become very fond of dress, sat hours together at her toilet, and even put on rouge:—JOHNSON. "She is better employed at her toilet, than using her pen. It is better she should be reddening her own cheeks, than blackening other people's characters."

A literary lady of large fortune [Mrs. Montagu] was mentioned, as one who did good to many, but by no means "by stealth";

and instead of "blushing to find it fame," acted evidently from vanity. JOHNSON. "I have seen no beings who do as much good from benevolence, as she does, from whatever motive. If there are such under the earth, or in the clouds, I wish they would come up, or come down. No, Sir; to act from pure benevolence is not possible for finite beings. Human benevolence is mingled with vanity, interest, or some other motive."

He would not allow me to praise a lady then at Bath; observing, "She does not gain upon me, Sir; I think her empty-headed." He was, indeed, a stern critic upon characters and manners. Even Mrs. Thrale did not escape his friendly animadversion at times. When he and I were one day endeavouring to ascertain, article by article, how one of our friends could possibly spend as much money in his family as he told us he did, she interrupted us by a lively extravagant sally, on the expense of clothing his children, describing it in a very ludicrous and fanciful manner. Johnson looked a little angry, and said, "Nay, Madam, when you are declaiming, declaim; and when you are calculating, calculate."

On Monday, April 29, he and I made an excursion to Bristol, where I was entertained with seeing him inquire upon the spot into the authenticity of "Rowley's poetry," as I had seen him inquire upon the spot into the authenticity of "Ossian's poetry." George Catcot, the pewterer, who was zealous for Rowley, attended us at our inn, and with a triumphant air of lively simplicity, called out, "I'll make Dr. Johnson a convert." Dr. Johnson, at his desire, read aloud some of Chatterton's fabricated verses; while Catcot stood at the back of his chair, moving himself like a pendulum, and beating time with his feet, and now and then looking into Dr. Johnson's face, wondering that he was not yet convinced. We saw some of the *originals*, as they were called, which were executed very artificially; but from a careful inspection of them, and a consideration of the circumstances with which they were attended, we were quite satisfied of the imposture, which, indeed, has been clearly demonstrated from internal evidence, by several able critics.

Honest Catcot seemed to pay no attention whatever to any objections, but insisted, as an end of all controversy, that we should go with him to the tower of the church of St. Mary, Redcliff, and *view with our own eyes* the ancient chest in which the manuscripts were found. To this Dr. Johnson good-naturedly agreed; and, though troubled with a shortness of breathing, laboured up a long flight of steps, till we came to the place where the wondrous chest stood. "*There*," said Catcot, with a bouncing confident credulity, "*there* is the very chest itself." After this *ocular demonstration*, there was no more to be said.

Johnson said of Chatterton, "This is the most extraordinary young man that has encountered my knowledge. It is wonderful how the whelp has written such things."

We were by no means pleased with our inn at Bristol. "Let us see now," said I, "how we should describe it." Johnson was ready with his raillery. "Describe it, Sir? why, it was so bad, that—Boswell wished to be in Scotland!"

After Dr. Johnson's return to London, I was several times with him at his house, where I occasionally slept, in the room that had been assigned for me. I shall group together what I have preserved of his conversation during this period, without specifying each scene where it passed, except one, which will be found so remarkable as certainly to deserve a very particular relation.

"Lord Chesterfield's Letters to his Son, I think, might be made a very pretty book. Take out the immorality, and it should be put into the hands of every young gentleman. An elegant manner and easiness of behaviour are acquired gradually and imperceptibly. No man can say, 'I'll be genteel.' There are ten genteel women for one genteel man, because they are more restrained. A man without some degree of restraint is insufferable; but we are all less restrained than women. Were a woman sitting in company to put out her legs before her as most men do, we should be tempted to kick them in."

Lord Eliot informs me, that one day when Johnson and he were at dinner in a gentleman's house in London, upon Lord Chesterfield's Letters being mentioned, Johnson surprised the company by this sentence: "Every man of any education would rather be called a rascal, then accused of deficiency in *the graces*." Mr. Gibbon, who was present, turned to a lady who knew Johnson well, and lived much with him, and in his quaint manner, tapping his box, addressed her thus: "Don't you think, Madam (looking towards Johnson), that among *all* your acquaintance, you could find *one* exception?" The lady smiled, and seemed to acquiesce.

When I complained of having dined at a splendid table without hearing one sentence of conversation worthy of being remembered, he said, "Sir, there seldom is any such conversation." BOSWELL. "Why then meet at table?" JOHNSON. "Why, to eat and drink together, and to promote kindness; and, Sir, this is better done when there is no solid conversation: for when there is, people differ in opinion, and get into bad humour, or some of the company, who are not capable of such conversation, are left out, and feel themselves uneasy. It was for this reason Sir Robert Walpole said, he always talked grossly at his table, because in that all could join."

Being irritated by hearing a gentleman ask Mr. Levett a variety of questions concerning him, when he was sitting by, he broke out, "Sir, you have but two topics, yourself and me. I am sick of both." "A man," said he, "should not talk of himself, nor much of any particular person. He should take care not to be made a proverb; and, therefore, should avoid having any one topic of which people can say, 'We shall hear him upon it.'

"Every man is to take existence on the terms on which it is given to him. To some men it is given on condition of not taking liberties, which other men may take without much harm. One may drink wine, and be nothing the worse for it: on another, wine may have effects so inflammatory as to injure him both in body and mind, and perhaps make him commit something for which he may deserve to be hanged."

I am now to record a very curious incident in Dr. Johnson's life, which fell under my own observation. My desire of being acquainted with celebrated men of every description had made me, much about the same time, obtain an introduction to Dr. Samuel Johnson and to John Wilkes, Esq. Two men more different could perhaps not be selected out of all mankind. They had even attacked one another with some asperity in their writings; yet I lived in habits of friendship with both. I conceived an irresistible wish, if possible, to bring Dr. Johnson and Mr. Wilkes together. How to manage it, was a nice and difficult matter.

My worthy booksellers and friends, Messieurs Dilly in the Poultry, at whose hospitable and well-covered table I have seen a greater number of literary men than at any other, except that of Sir Joshua Reynolds, had invited me to meet Mr. Wilkes and some more gentlemen on Wednesday, May 15. "Pray," said I, "let us have Dr. Johnson." "What, with Mr. Wilkes? not for the world," said Mr. Edward Dilly: "Dr. Johnson would never forgive me." "Come," said I, "if you'll let me negotiate for you, I will be answerable that all shall go well." DILLY. "Nay, if you will take it upon you, I am sure I shall be very happy to see them both here."

Notwithstanding the high veneration which I entertained for Dr. Johnson, I was sensible that he was sometimes a little actuated by the spirit of contradiction, and by means of that I hoped I should gain my point. I was persuaded that if I had come upon him with a direct proposal, "Sir, will you dine in company with Jack Wilkes?" he would have flown into a passion, and would probably have answered, "Dine with Jack Wilkes, Sir! I'd as soon dine with Jack Ketch." I, therefore, while we were sitting quietly by ourselves at his house in an evening, took occasion to open my plan thus: "Mr. Dilly, Sir, sends his respectful compliments to you, and would be happy if you would do him the honour to dine with him on Wednesday next along with me, as I must soon go to Scotland." JOHNSON. "Sir, I am obliged to Mr. Dilly. I will wait upon him——" BOSWELL. "Provided, Sir, I suppose, that the company which he is to have is agreeable to you?" JOHNSON. "What do you mean, Sir? What do you take me for? Do you think I am so ignorant of the world as to imagine that I am to prescribe to a gentleman what company he is to have at his table?" BOSWELL. "I beg your pardon, Sir, for wishing to prevent you from meeting people whom you might not like. Perhaps he may have some of what he calls his patriotic friends with him." JOHNSON. "Well, Sir, and what then? What care *I* for his *patriotic friends?* Poh!" BOSWELL. "I should not be surprised to find Jack Wilkes there." JOHNSON. "And if Jack Wilkes *should* be there, what is that to *me,* Sir? My dear friend, let us have no more of this. I am sorry to be angry with you; but really it is treating me strangely to talk to me as if I could not meet any company whatever, occasionally." BOSWELL. "Pray forgive me, Sir: I meant well. But you shall meet whoever comes, for me." Thus I secured him, and told Dilly that he would find him very well pleased to be one of his guests on the day appointed.

Upon the much expected Wednesday, I called on him about half an hour before dinner, as I often did when we were to dine out together, to see that he was ready in time, and to accompany him. I found him buffeting his books, as upon a former occasion, covered with dust, and making no preparation for going abroad. "How is this, Sir?" said I. "Don't you recollect that you are to dine at Mr. Dilly's?" JOHNSON. "Sir, I did not think of going to Dilly's: it went out of my head. I have ordered dinner at home with Mrs. Williams." BOSWELL. "But, my dear Sir, you know you were engaged to Mr. Dilly, and I told him so. He will expect you, and will be much disappointed if you don't come. JOHNSON. "You must talk to Mrs. Williams about this."

Here was a sad dilemma. I feared that what I was so confident I had secured would yet be frustrated. He had accustomed himself to show Mrs. Williams such a degree of humane attention, as frequently imposed some restraint upon him; and I knew that if she should be obstinate, he would not stir. I hastened downstairs to the blind lady's room, and told her I was in great uneasiness, for Dr. Johnson had engaged to me to dine this day at Mr. Dilly's; but that he had told me he had forgotten his engagement, and had ordered dinner at home. "Yes, Sir," said she, pretty peevishly, "Dr. Johnson is to dine at home." "Madam," said I, "his respect for you is such, that I know he will not leave you, unless you absolutely desire it. But as you have so much of his company, I hope you will be good enough to forego it for a day, as Mr. Dilly is a very worthy man, has frequently had agreeable parties at his house for Dr. Johnson, and will be vexed if the Doctor neglects him to-day. And then, Madam, be pleased to consider my situation; I carried the message, and I assured Mr. Dilly that Dr. Johnson was to come; and no doubt he has made a dinner, and invited a company, and boasted of the honour he expected to have. I shall be quite disgraced if the Doctor is not there." She gradually softened to my solicitations, which were certainly as earnest as most entreaties to ladies upon any occasion, and was graciously pleased to empower me to tell Dr. Johnson, "That, all things considered, she thought he should certainly go." I flew back to him, still in dust, and careless of what should be the event, "indifferent in his choice to go or stay"; but as soon as I had announced to him Mrs. Williams's consent, he roared, "Frank, a clean shirt!" and was very soon dressed. When I had him fairly seated in a hackney-coach with me, I exulted as much as a fortune-hunter who has got an heiress into a post-chaise with him to set out for Gretna Green.

When we entered Mr. Dilly's drawing-room, he found himself in the midst of a company he did not know. I kept myself snug and silent, watching how he would conduct himself. I observed him whispering to Mr. Dilly, "Who is that gentleman, Sir?"— "Mr. Arthur Lee." JOHNSON. "Too, too, too" (under his breath), which was one of his habitual mutterings. Mr. Arthur Lee could not but be very obnoxious to Johnson, for he was not only a *patriot*, but an *American*. "And who is the gentleman in lace?"—

"Mr. Wilkes, Sir." This information confounded him still more; he had some difficulty to restrain himself, and, taking up a book, sat down upon a window-seat and read, or at least kept his eye upon it intently for some time, till he composed himself. His feelings, I dare say, were awkward enough. But he no doubt recollected having rated me for supposing that he could be at all disconcerted by any company, and he therefore resolutely set himself to behave quite as an easy man of the world, who could adapt himself at once to the disposition and manners of those whom he might chance to meet.

The cheering sound of "Dinner is upon the table," dissolved his reverie, and we *all* sat down without any symptom of ill humour. There were present, beside Mr. Wilkes and Mr. Arthur Lee, who was an old companion of mine when he studied physic at Edinburgh, Mr. (now Sir John) Miller, Dr. Lettsom, and Mr. Slater, the druggist. Mr. Wilkes placed himself next to Dr. Johnson, and behaved to him with so much attention and politeness, that he gained upon him insensibly. No man eat more heartily than Johnson, or loved better what was nice and delicate. Mr. Wilkes was very assiduous in helping him to some fine veal. "Pray give me leave, Sir—It is better here—A little of the brown—Some fat, Sir—A little of the stuffing—Some gravy—Let me have the pleasure of giving you some butter—Allow me to recommend a squeeze of this orange; or the lemon, perhaps, may have more zest."—"Sir; sir, I am obliged to you, Sir," cried Johnson, bowing, and turning his head to him with a look for some time of "surly virtue," but, in a short while, of complacency.

Foote being mentioned, Johnson said, "One species of wit he has in an eminent degree, that of escape. You drive him into a corner with both hands; but he's gone, Sir, when you think you have got him—like an animal that jumps over your head. Then he has a great range for wit; he never lets truth stand between him and a jest, and he is sometimes mighty coarse. Garrick is under many restraints from which Foote is free." WILKES. "Garrick's wit is more like Lord Chesterfield's. Garrick is now leaving the stage; but he will play *Scrub* all his life." I knew that Johnson would let nobody attack Garrick but himself, and I had heard him praise his liberality; so to bring out his commendation of his celebrated pupil, I said, loudly, "I have heard Garrick is liberal." JOHNSON. "Yes, Sir, I know that Garrick has given away more money than any man in England that I am acquainted with, and that not from ostentatious views. Garrick was very poor when he began life; so when he came to have money, he probably was very unskilful in giving away, and saved when he should not. But Garrick began to be liberal as soon as he could; and I am of opinion, the reputation of avarice which he has had has been very lucky for him, and prevented his having made enemies. You despise a man for avarice, but do not hate him. Garrick might have been much better attacked for living with more splendour than is suitable to a player; if they had had the wit to have assaulted him in that quarter, they might have galled him more. But they have kept clamouring about his avarice, which has rescued him from much obloquy and envy."

Mr. Wilkes remarked, that "among all the bold flights of Shakspeare's imagination, the boldest was making Birnam wood march to Dunsinane; creating a wood where there never was a shrub! a wood in Scotland! ha! ha! ha!"

Mr. Arthur Lee mentioned some Scotch who had taken possession of a barren part of America, and wondered why they should choose it. JOHNSON. "Why, Sir, all barrenness is comparative. The *Scotch* would not know it to be barren." BOSWELL. "Come, come, he is flattering the English. You have now been in Scotland, Sir, and say if you did not see meat and drink enough there." JOHNSON. "Why, yes, Sir; meat and drink enough to give the inhabitants sufficient strength to run away from home." All these quick and lively sallies were said sportively, quite in jest, and with a smile, which showed that he meant only wit. Upon this topic he and Mr. Wilkes could perfectly assimilate; here was a bond of union between them, and I was conscious that as both had visited Caledonia, both were fully satisfied of the strange narrow ignorance of those who imagine that it is a land of famine. But they amused themselves with persevering in the old jokes. When I claimed a superiority for Scotland over England in one respect, that no man can be arrested there for a debt merely because another swears it against him; but there must first be the judgment of a court of law ascertaining its justice; and that a seizure of the person, before judgment is obtained, can take place only if his creditors should swear that he is about to fly from the country. WILKES. "That, I should think, may be safely sworn of all the Scotch nation." JOHNSON (to Mr. Wilkes). "You must know, Sir, I lately took my friend Boswell, and showed him genuine civilised life in an English provincial town. I turned him loose at Lichfield,

THE FINGER OF AN ARCH CONNOISSEUR

my native city, that he might see for once real civility; for you
know he lives among savages in Scotland, and among rakes in
London." WILKES. "Except when he is with grave, sober, decent
people like you and me." JOHNSON (smiling). "And we ashamed
of him."

They were quite frank and easy. Johnson told the story of his
asking Mrs. Macaulay to allow her footman to sit down with them,
to prove the ridiculousness of the argument for the equality of
mankind; and he said to me afterwards, with a nod of satisfaction,
"You saw Mr. Wilkes acquiesced." Wilkes talked with all imaginable freedom of the ludicrous title given to the attorney-general,
Diabolus regis; adding, "I have reason to know something about
that officer; for I was prosecuted for a libel." Johnson, who many
people would have supposed must have been furiously angry at
hearing this talked of so lightly, said not a word. He was now,
indeed, "a good-humoured fellow."

After dinner we had an accession of Mrs. Knowles, the Quaker
lady, well known for her various talents, and of Mr. Alderman Lee.
Amidst some patriotic groans, somebody (I think the Alderman)
said, "Poor old England is lost." JOHNSON. "Sir, it is not so
much to be lamented that old England is lost, as that the Scotch
have found it."

Mr. Wilkes held a candle to show a fine print of a beautiful
female figure which hung in the room, and pointed out the elegant
contour of the bosom with the finger of an arch connoisseur. He
afterwards in a conversation with me waggishly insisted, that all
the time Johnson showed visible signs of a fervent admiration of the
corresponding charms of the fair Quaker.

This record, though by no means so perfect as I could wish, will
serve to give a notion of a very curious interview, which was not
only pleasing at the time, but had the agreeable and benignant
effect of reconciling any animosity, and sweetening any acidity,
which, in the various bustle of political contest, had been produced
in the minds of two men, who, though widely different, had so
many things in common—classical learning, modern literature, wit
and humour, and ready repartee—that it would have been much
to be regretted if they had been for ever at a distance from each
other.

Mr. Burke gave me much credit for this successful *negotiation;*
and pleasantly said, "that there was nothing equal to it in the
whole history of the *corps diplomatique.*"

I attended Dr. Johnson home, and had the satisfaction to hear him tell Mrs. Williams how much he had been pleased with Mr. Wilkes's company, and what an agreeable day he had passed.

I mentioned a scheme which I had of making a tour to the Isle of Man, and giving a full account of it; and that Mr. Burke had playfully suggested as a motto,

The proper study of mankind is MAN.

JOHNSON. "Sir, you will get more by the book than the jaunt will cost you; so you will have your diversion for nothing, and add to your reputation."

On the evening of the next day [16th May] I took leave of him, being to set out for Scotland. I thanked him, with great warmth, for all his kindness. "Sir," said he, "you are very welcome. Nobody repays it with more."

Concerning an Epitaph which he wrote for the monument of Dr. Goldsmith, in Westminster Abbey, it was, I think, after I had left London in this year, that this gave occasion to a remonstrance to the *Monarch of Literature.*

That my readers may have the subject more fully and clearly before them, I shall first insert the Epitaph: [1]

OLIVARII GOLDSMITH,

Poetæ, Physici, Historici,
Qui nullum ferè scribendi genus
Non tetigit,
Nullum quod tetigit non ornavit:

[1] OF OLIVER GOLDSMITH—
A Poet, Naturalist, and Historian,
Who left scarcely any style of writing
untouched,
And touched nothing that he did not adorn;
Of all the passions,
Whether smiles were to be moved
or tears,
A powerful yet gentle master;
In genius, sublime, vivid, versatile,
In style, elevated, clear, elegant—
The love of companions,
The fidelity of friends,
And the veneration of readers,
Have by this monument honoured the memory.

He was born in Ireland,
At a place called Pallas,
[in the parish] of Forney, [and county] of Longford,
On the 29th Nov. 1731,
Educated at [the University of] Dublin,
And died in London,
4th April, 1774.—*Croker.*

Sive risus essent movendi,
Sive lacrymæ,
Affectuum potens at lenis dominator:
Ingenio sublimis, vividus, versatilis,
Oratione grandis, nitidus, venustus:
Hoc monumento memoriam coluit
Sodalium amor,
Amicorum fides,

Lectorum veneratio.
Natus in Hiberniâ Forniæ Longfordiensis,
In loco cui nomen Pallas,
Nov XXIX. MDCCXXXI.; [1]
Eblanæ literis institutus;
Obiit Londini,
April IV. MDCCLXXIV.

Sir William Forbes writes to me thus:

I enclose the *Round Robin*. This *jeu d'esprit* took its rise one day at dinner at our friend Sir Joshua Reynolds's. All the company present, except myself, were friends and acquaintance of Dr. Goldsmith. The Epitaph written for him by Dr. Johnson became the subject of conversation, and various emendations were suggested, which it was agreed should be submitted to the Doctor's consideration. But the question was, who should have the courage to propose them to him? At last it was hinted, that there could be no way so good as that of a *Round Robin*, as the sailors call it, which they make use of when they enter into a conspiracy, so as not to let it be known who puts his name first or last to the paper. This proposition was instantly assented to; and Dr. Barnard, Dean of Derry, now Bishop of Killaloe, drew up an address to Dr. Johnson on the occasion, replete with wit and humour, but which it was feared the Doctor might think treated the subject with too much levity. Mr. Burke then proposed the address as it stands in the paper in writing, to which I had the honour to officiate as clerk.

Sir Joshua agreed to carry it to Dr. Johnson, who received it with much good humour,[2] and desired Sir Joshua to tell the gentle-

---

[1] This mistake was not discovered till after Goldsmith's monument was put up in Westminster Abbey. He was born Nov. 10, 1728; and therefore, when he died, was in his forty-sixth year.

[2] He, however, upon seeing Dr. Warton's name to the suggestion, that the epitaph should be in English, observed to Sir Joshua, "I wonder that Joe Warton, a scholar by profession, should be such a fool." He said too, "I should have thought Mund Burke would have had more sense." Mr. Langton, who was one of the company at Sir Joshua's, like a sturdy scholar, resolutely refused to sign the *Round Robin*. The epitaph is engraved upon Dr. Goldsmith's monument without any alteration. At another time, when somebody endeavoured to argue in favour of its being in English, Johnson said, "The language of the country of which a learned man was a native is not the language fit for his epitaph, which should be in ancient and permanent language. Consider, Sir, how you should feel, were you to find at Rotterdam an epitaph upon Erasmus *in Dutch!*"

men, that he would alter the Epitaph in any manner they pleased, as to the sense of it, but *he would never consent to disgrace the walls of Westminster Abbey with an English inscription.*

Mr. Boswell to Dr. Johnson

Edinburgh, June 25, 1776

You have formerly complained that my letters were too long. There is no danger of that complaint being made at present; for I find it difficult for me to write to you at all. [Here an account of having been afflicted with a return of melancholy or bad spirits.]

The boxes of books [1] which you sent to me are arrived; but I have not yet examined the contents.

Dr. Johnson to Mr. Boswell

July 2, 1776

DEAR SIR,

These black fits of which you complain, perhaps hurt your memory, as well as your imagination. When did I complain that your letters were too long? Your last letter, after a very long delay, brought very bad news. [Here a series of reflections upon melancholy, and—what I could not help thinking strangely unreasonable in him who had suffered so much from it himself—a good deal of severity and reproof, as if it were owing to my own fault, or that I was, perhaps, affecting it from a desire of distinction.]

To hear that you have not opened your boxes of books is very offensive. The examination and arrangement of so many volumes might have afforded you an amusement very seasonable at present, and useful for the whole of life. I am, I confess, very angry that you manage yourself so ill. . . .

I do not now say any more, than that I am, with great kindness and sincerity, dear Sir, your humble Servant,

SAM. JOHNSON

Dr. Johnson to Mr. Boswell

July 16, 1776

DEAR SIR,

I make haste to write again, lest my last letter should give you too much pain. If you are really oppressed with overpowering and involuntary melancholy, you are to be pitied rather than reproached. . . .

---

[1] Upon a settlement of our account of expenses on a tour to the Hebrides, there was a balance due to me, which Dr. Johnson chose to discharge by sending books.—*Boswell.*

I KNOW NOT THAT IT DOES ME ANY GOOD

Now, my dear Bozzy, let us have done with quarrels and with censure. Let me know whether I have not sent you a pretty library. There are, perhaps, many books among them which you never need read through; but there are none which it is not proper for you to know, and sometimes to consult. . . .

It vexes me to tell you, that on the evening of the 29th of May I was seized by the gout, and am not quite well. The pain has not been violent, but the weakness and tenderness were very troublesome; and what is said to be very uncommon, it has not alleviated my other disorders. Make use of youth and health while you have them. Make my compliments to Mrs. Boswell. I am, my dear Sir, your most affectionate,   SAM. JOHNSON

Mr. Boswell to Dr. Johnson

Edinburgh, July 18, 1776

MY DEAR SIR,

Your letter of the 2nd of this month was rather a harsh medicine; but I was delighted with that spontaneous tenderness, which, a few days afterwards, sent forth such balsam as your next brought me. I found myself for some time so ill that all I could do was to preserve a decent appearance, while all within was weakness and distress. Like a reduced garrison that has some spirit left, I hung out flags, and planted all the force I could muster, upon the walls. I am now much better, and I sincerely thank you for your kind attention and friendly counsel. . . .

To Mr. Robert Levett

Brighthelmstone, Oct. 21, 1776

DEAR SIR,

Having spent about six weeks at this place, we have at length resolved on returning. I expect to see you all in Fleet Street on the 30th of this month.

I did not go into the sea till last Friday; but think to go most of this week, though I know not that it does me any good. My nights are very restless and tiresome, but I am otherwise well. I have written word of my coming to Mrs. Williams.

Remember me kindly to Francis and Betsey. I am, Sir, &c.,
SAM. JOHNSON

In 1777, it appears from his "Prayers and Meditations," that Johnson suffered much from a state of mind "unsettled and perplexed," and from that constitutional gloom, which, together with his extreme humility and anxiety with regard to his religious state, made him contemplate himself through too dark and unfavourable a medium. It may be said of him, that he "saw God in clouds." Certain we may be of his injustice to himself in the following lamentable paragraph:

When I survey my past life, I discover nothing but a barren waste of time, with some disorders of body, and disturbances of the mind very near to madness, which I hope He that made me will suffer to extenuate many faults, and excuse many deficiencies.

But we find his devotions in this year eminently fervent; and we are comforted by observing intervals of quiet composure and gladness.

To James Boswell, Esq.

Feb. 18, 1777

DEAR SIR,

It is so long since I heard anything from you, that I am not easy about it: write something to me next post. When you sent your last letter, every thing seemed to be mending; I hope nothing has lately grown worse. I suppose young Alexander continues to thrive, and Veronica is now very pretty company. I do not suppose the lady is yet reconciled to me; yet let her know that I love her very well, and value her very much. . . .

Poor Beauclerk still continues very ill. Langton lives on as he used to do. His children are very pretty, and, I think, his lady loses her Scotch. Paoli I never see.

I have been so distressed by difficulty of breathing, that I lost, as was computed, six-and-thirty ounces of blood in a few days. I am better, but not well. . . .

Mrs. Williams sends her compliments, and promises that when you come hither she will accommodate you as well as ever she can in the old room. . . . My dear Boswell, do not neglect to write to me; for your kindness is one of the pleasures of my life, which I should be sorry to lose. I am, &c.,

SAM. JOHNSON

To Dr. Samuel Johnson

Edinburgh, Feb. 24, 1777

DEAR SIR,

Your letter dated the 18th instant, I had the pleasure to receive last post. . . . You are pleased to show me that my kindness is of some consequence to you. My heart is elated at the thought. Be assured, my dear Sir, that my affection and reverence for you are exalted and steady. I do not believe that a more perfect attachment ever existed in the history of mankind. And it is a noble attachment; for the attractions are genius, learning, and piety.

Your difficulty of breathing alarms me, and brings into my imagination an event, which, although in the natural course of things, I must expect at some period, I cannot view with composure. . . .

My wife is much honoured by what you say of her. She begs you may accept of her best compliments. She is to send you some marmalade of oranges of her own making. I ever am, my dear Sir, &c.,   JAMES BOSWELL

To James Boswell, Esq.

May 3, 1777

DEAR SIR,

Tell Mrs. Boswell that I shall taste her marmalade cautiously at first. *Timeo Danaos et dona ferentes.* Beware, says the Italian proverb, of a reconciled enemy. But when I find it does me no harm, I shall then receive it, and be thankful for it, as a pledge of firm, and, I hope, of unalterable kindness. She is, after all, a dear, dear lady. . . .

My health is very bad, and my nights are very unquiet. What can I do to mend them? I have for this summer nothing better in prospect than a journey into Staffordshire and Derbyshire, perhaps with Oxford and Birmingham in my way.

Make my compliments to Miss Veronica; I must leave it to *her* philosophy to comfort you for the loss of little David.[1] You must remember, that to keep three out of four is more than your share. Mrs. Thrale has but four out of eleven.

I am engaged to write little Lives, and little Prefaces, to a little edition of the English Poets. I think I have persuaded the booksellers to insert something of Thomson; and if you could give me some information about him, for the life which we have is very scanty, I should be glad.

I am, dear Sir, &c.,   SAM. JOHNSON

To those who delight in tracing the progress of works of literature, it will be an entertainment to compare the limited design with the ample execution of that admirable performance, "The Lives of the English Poets."

---

[1] Boswell's second son, who died in infancy.

To Dr. Samuel Johnson

Edinburgh, July 15, 1777

MY DEAR SIR,

The fate of poor Dr. Dodd [1] made a dismal impression upon my mind. . . .

Be so kind as to let me know how your time is to be distributed next autumn. I will meet you at Manchester, or where you please; but I wish you would complete your tour of the cathedrals, and come to Carlisle, and I will accompany you a part of the way homewards. I am ever, &c.,   JAMES BOSWELL

To James Boswell, Esq.

July 22, 1777

DEAR SIR,

Your notion of the necessity of an early interview is very pleasing to both my vanity and tenderness. I shall, perhaps, come to Carlisle another year; but my money has not held out so well as it used to do. I shall go to Ashbourne, and I purpose to make Dr. Taylor invite you. If you live a while with me at his house, we shall have much time to ourselves, and our stay will be no expense to us or him. I shall leave London the 28th; and, after some stay at Oxford and Lichfield, shall probably come to Ashbourne about the end of your session; but of all this you shall have notice. Be satisfied we will meet somewhere. What passed between me and poor Dr. Dodd, you shall know more fully when we meet. . . .

I have dined lately with poor dear Langton. I do not think he goes on well. His table is rather coarse, and he has his children too much about him.[2] But he is a very good man.

Mrs. Williams is in the country, to try if she can improve her health: she is very ill. Matters have come so about, that she is in the country with very good accommodation: but age, and sickness, and pride, have made her so peevish, that I was forced to bribe the maid to stay with her by a secret stipulation of half-a-crown a week over her wages. . . .

I am, dear Sir, &c.,   SAM. JOHNSON

---

[1] See p. 301, following.

[2] This very just remark I hope will be constantly held in remembrance by parents, who are in general too apt to indulge their own fond feelings for their children at the expense of their friends. The common custom of introducing them after dinner is highly injudicious. It is agreeable enough that they should appear at any other time; but they should not be suffered to poison the moments of festivity by attracting the attention of the company, and in a manner compelling them from politeness to say what they do not think.—*Boswell.*

Dr. Johnson to Mrs. Boswell

July 22, 1777

MADAM,

Though I am well enough pleased with the taste of sweet-meats, very little of the pleasure which I received at the arrival of your jar of marmalade arose from eating it. I received it as a token of friendship, as a proof of reconciliation, things much sweeter than sweetmeats; and upon this consideration I return you, dear Madam, my sincerest thanks. By having your kindness I think I have a double security for the continuance of Mr. Boswell's, which it is not to be expected that any man can long keep, when the influence of a lady so highly and so justly valued operates against him. Mr. Boswell will tell you that I was always faithful to your interest, and always endeavoured to exalt you in his estimation. You must now do the same for me. We must all help one another, and you must now consider me as, dear Madam, your, &c.,   SAM. JOHNSON

To James Boswell, Esq.

Ashbourne, Sept. 1, 1777

DEAR SIR,

On Saturday I wrote a very short letter, immediately upon my arrival hither, to show you that I am not less desirous of the interview than yourself. . . . If you and I live to be much older, we shall take great delight in talking over the Hebridean Journey. In the mean time it may not be amiss to contrive some other little adventure, but what it can be I know not; leave it, as Sydney says,

"To *virtue*, fortune, *time*, and woman's breast";

for I believe Mrs. Boswell must have some part in the consultation. One thing you will like. The doctor, so far as I can judge, is likely to leave us enough to ourselves. He was out to-day before I came down, and, I fancy, will stay out to dinner. I have brought the papers about poor Dodd, to show you, but you will soon have despatched them.

Write to me, and let us know when we may expect you. I am, dear Sir, your most humble servant,   SAM. JOHNSON

Mr. Boswell to Dr. Johnson

Edinburgh, Sept. 9, 1777

(After informing him that I was to set out next day, in order to meet him at Ashbourne):

I have, like yourself, a wonderful pleasure in recollecting our travels in those islands. The pleasure is, I think, greater than it reasonably should be, considering that we had not much either of beauty or elegance to charm our imaginations, or of rude novelty to astonish. Let us, by all means, have another expedition. I shrink a little from our scheme of going up the Baltic.[1] I am sorry you have already been in Wales: for I wish to see it. Shall we go to Ireland, of which I have seen but little? We shall try to strike out a plan when we are at Ashbourne. I am ever your most faithful servant,   JAMES BOSWELL

On Sunday evening, Sept. 14, I drove up to Dr. Taylor's door. Dr. Johnson and he appeared before I had got out of the post-chaise, and welcomed me cordially.

I told them that I had travelled all the preceding night, and gone to bed at Leek, in Staffordshire; and that when I rose to go to church in the afternoon, I was informed there had been an earthquake, of which, it seems, the shock had been felt in some degree at Ashbourne. JOHNSON. "Sir, it will be much exaggerated in public talk: for, in the first place, the common people do not accurately adapt their thoughts to the objects; nor, secondly, do they accurately adapt their words to their thoughts: they do not mean to lie; but, taking no pains to be exact, they give you very false accounts. A great part of their language is proverbial. If any thing rocks at all, they say *it rocks like a cradle*; and in this way they go on."

The subject of grief for the loss of relations and friends being introduced, I observed that it was strange to consider how soon it in general wears away. JOHNSON. "All grief for what cannot in the course of nature be helped soon wears away; in some sooner indeed, in some later; but it never continues very long, unless where there is madness, such as will make a man have pride so fixed in his

---

[1] Johnson, now in his sixty-eighth year, was seriously inclined to realise the project of our going up the Baltic, which I had started when we were in the Isle of Sky; he thus writes to Mrs. Thrale:

"Ashbourne, 13th Sept., 1777.—Boswell, I believe, is coming. He talks of being here to-day: I shall be glad to see him; but he shrinks from the Baltic expedition, which, I think, is the best scheme in our power: what we shall substitute, I know not. He wants to see Wales; but, except the woods of *Bachycraigh*, what is there in Wales that can fill the hunger of ignorance, or quench the thirst of curiosity? We may, perhaps, form some scheme or other; but, in the phrase of *Hockley in the Hole*, it is pity he has not a *better bottom*."

Such an ardour of mind, and vigour of enterprise, is admirable at any age; but more particularly so at the advanced period at which Johnson was then arrived. I am sorry now that I did not insist on our executing that scheme. Besides the other objects of curiosity and observation, to have seen my illustrious friend received, as he probably would have been, by a prince so eminently distinguished for his variety of talents and acquisitions as the late King of Sweden, and by the Empress of Russia, whose extraordinary abilities, information and magnanimity, astonish the world, would have afforded a noble subject of contemplation and record. This reflection may possibly be thought too visionary by the more sedate and cold-blooded part of my readers; yet I own I frequently indulge it with an earnest, unavailing regret.—*Boswell.*

mind as to imagine himself a king; or any other passion in an un-reasonable way: for all unnecessary grief is unwise, and therefore will not be long retained by a sound mind. If, indeed, the cause of our grief is occasioned by our own misconduct, if grief is mingled with remorse of conscience, it should be lasting." BOSWELL. "But, Sir, we do not approve of a man who very soon forgets the loss of a wife, or a friend." JOHNSON. "Sir, we disapprove of him, not because he soon forgets his grief, for the sooner it is forgotten the better; but because we suppose, that if he forgets his wife or his friend soon, he has not had much affection for them."

I was somewhat disappointed in finding that the edition of the "English Poets," for which he was to write prefaces and lives, was not an undertaking directed by him, but that he was to furnish a preface and life to any poet the booksellers pleased. I asked him if he would do this to any dunce's works, if they should ask him. JOHNSON. "Yes, Sir; and *say* he was a dunce." My friend seemed now not much to relish talking of this edition.

On Monday, Sept. 15, after breakfast, Johnson carried me to see the garden belonging to the school of Ashbourne, which is very prettily formed upon a bank, rising gradually behind the house. We sat basking in the sun upon a seat here.

And here is a proper place to give an account of Johnson's humane and zealous interference in behalf of the Reverend Dr. William Dodd, formerly prebendary of Brecon, and chaplain in ordinary to his majesty; celebrated as a very popular preacher, an encourager of charitable institutions, and author of a variety of works, chiefly theological. Having unhappily contracted expensive habits of living, partly occasioned by licentiousness of manners, he in an evil hour, when pressed by want of money, and dreading an exposure of his circumstances, forged a bond, of which he attempted to avail himself to support his credit, flattering himself with hopes that he might be able to repay its amount without being detected. The person whose name he thus rashly and criminally presumed to falsify was the Earl of Chesterfield, to whom he had been tutor, and who he perhaps, in the warmth of his feelings, flattered himself would have generously paid the money in case of an alarm being taken, rather than suffer him to fall a victim to the dreadful con-sequences of violating the law against forgery, the most dangerous crime in a commercial country: but the unfortunate divine had the mortification to find that he was mistaken. His noble pupil ap-peared against him, and he was capitally convicted.

Johnson told me that Dr. Dodd was very little acquainted with him, having been but once in his company, many years previous to this period; but in his distress he bethought himself of Johnson's persuasive power of writing, if haply it might avail to obtain for him the royal mercy. He did not apply to him directly, but through the late Countess of Harrington, who wrote a letter to Johnson, asking him to employ his pen in favour of Dodd. Johnson read it, walking up and down his chamber, and seemed much agitated, after which he said, "I will do what I can"; and certainly he did make extraordinary exertions.

He this evening, as he had obligingly promised in one of his letters, put into my hands the whole series of his writings upon this melancholy occasion.

I found a letter to Dr. Johnson from Dr. Dodd, May 23, 1777:

Dr. Dodd to Dr. Johnson

I am so penetrated, my ever dear Sir, with a sense of your extreme benevolence towards me, that I cannot find words equal to the sentiments of my heart. . . .

You are too conversant in the world to need the slightest hint from me of what infinite utility the speech [1] on the awful day has been to me. I experience, every hour, some good effect from it. I am sure that effects still more salutary and important must follow from *your kind and intended favour*. I will labour—God being my helper—to do justice to it from the pulpit. I am sure, had I your sentiments constantly to deliver from thence, in all their mighty force and power, not a soul could be left unconvinced and unpersuaded. . . .

May God Almighty bless and reward, with his choicest comforts, your philanthropic actions, and enable me at all times to express what I feel of the high and uncommon obligations which I owe to the *first man* in our times!

On Sunday, June 22, he writes, begging Dr. Johnson's assistance in framing a supplicatory letter to his majesty:

If his majesty could be moved of his royal clemency to spare me and my family the horrors and ignominy of a *public death*, which the *public* itself is solicitous to wave, and to grant me in some silent distant corner of the globe to pass the remainder of my days in penitence and prayer, I would bless his clemency and be humbled.

[1] Johnson wrote numerous letters and petitions on Dr. Dodd's behalf. The speech referred to here was one Johnson wrote for Dodd to read at the Old Bailey, when sentence was about to be pronounced. The "kind and intended favour" was "The Convict's Address to his unhappy Brethren," also provided by Johnson.

This letter was brought to Dr. Johnson when in church. He stooped down and read it; and wrote, when he went home, the following letter for Dr. Dodd to the king:

SIR,

May it not offend your majesty, that the most miserable of men applies himself to your clemency, as his last hope and his last refuge; that your mercy is most earnestly and humbly implored by a clergyman whom your laws and judges have condemned to the horror and ignominy of a public execution.

I confess the crime, and own the enormity of its consequences, and the danger of its example. Nor have I the confidence to petition for impunity; but humbly hope, that public security may be established, without the spectacle of a clergyman dragged through the streets, to a death of infamy, amidst the derision of the profligate and profane; and that justice may be satisfied with irrevocable exile, perpetual disgrace, and hopeless penury.

My life, Sir, has not been useless to mankind. I have benefited many. But my offences against God are numberless, and I have had little time for repentance. Preserve me, Sir, by your prerogative of mercy, from the necessity of appearing unprepared at that tribunal, before which kings and subjects must stand at last together. Permit me to hide my guilt in some obscure corner of a foreign country, where, if I can ever attain confidence to hope that my prayers will be heard, they shall be poured with all the fervour of gratitude, for the life and happiness of your majesty. I am, Sir, your majesty's, &c.

Subjoined to it was written as follows:

Dr. Johnson to Dr. Dodd

SIR,

I most seriously enjoin you not to let it be at all known that I have written this letter, and to return the copy to Mr. Allen in a cover to me. I hope I need not tell you that I wish it success. But do not indulge hope. Tell nobody.

It happened luckily that Mr. Allen was pitched on to assist in this melancholy office, for he was a great friend of Mr. Akerman, the keeper of Newgate. Dr. Johnson never went to see Dr. Dodd. He said to me, "It would have done *him* more harm than good to Dodd."

All applications for the royal mercy having failed, Dr. Dodd prepared himself for death; and, with a warmth of gratitude, wrote to Dr. Johnson as follows:

Dr. Dodd to Dr. Johnson

June 25, midnight

Accept, thou *great* and *good* heart, my earnest and fervent thanks and prayers for all thy benevolent and kind efforts in my behalf.—Oh! Dr. Johnson! as I sought your knowledge at an early hour in life, would to Heaven I had cultivated the love and acquaintance of so excellent a man!—I pray God most sincerely to bless you with the highest transports—the in-felt satisfaction of *humane* and benevolent exertions!—And admitted, as I trust I shall be, to the realms of bliss before you, I shall hail *your* arrival there with transports, and rejoice to acknowledge that you were my comforter, my advocate, and my *friend!* God *be ever* with *you!*

Dr. Johnson lastly wrote to Dr. Dodd this solemn and soothing letter:

To the Reverend Dr. Dodd

June 26, 1777

Dear Sir,

That which is appointed to all men is now coming upon you. Outward circumstances, the eyes and the thoughts of men, are below the notice of an immortal being about to stand the trial for eternity, before the Supreme Judge of heaven and earth. Be comforted: your crime, morally or religiously considered, has no very deep dye of turpitude. It corrupted no man's principles; it attacked no man's life. It involved only a temporary and reparable injury. Of this, and of all other sins, you are earnestly to repent; and may God, who knoweth our frailty, and desireth not our death, accept your repentance, for the sake of his Son Jesus Christ, our Lord!

In requital of those well-intended offices which you are pleased so emphatically to acknowledge, let me beg that you make in your devotions one petition for my eternal welfare. I am, dear Sir, your most affectionate servant,   Sam. Johnson

Under the copy of this letter I found written, in Johnson's own hand, "Next day, June 27, he was executed."

Johnson gave us this evening, in his happy discriminative manner, a portrait of the late Mr. Fitzherbert of Derbyshire. "There was," said he, "no sparkle, no brilliancy in Fitzherbert; but I never knew a man who was so generally acceptable. People were willing to think well of every thing about him. A gentleman was making an affecting rant, as many people do, of great feelings about 'his dear son,' who was at school near London; how anxious he was lest he might be ill, and what he would give to see him. 'Can't you,' said Fitzherbert, 'take a post-chaise and go to him?' This, to be sure, *finished* the affected man, but there was not much in it. However, this was circulated as wit for a whole winter, and I believe part of a summer too; a proof that he was no very witty man. He was an instance of the truth of the observation, that a man will please more upon the whole by negative qualities than by positive; by never offending, than by giving a great deal of delight. In the first place, men hate more steadily than they love; and if I have said something to hurt a man once, I shall not get the better of this by saying many things to please him."

Tuesday, September 16, Dr. Johnson having mentioned to me the extraordinary size and price of some cattle reared by Dr. Taylor, I rode out with our host. Taylor thus described to me his old schoolfellow and friend, Johnson: "He is a man of a very clear head, great power of words, and a very gay imagination; but there is no disputing with him. He will not hear you, and, having a louder voice than you, must roar you down."

In the evening Dr. Taylor's nose happening to bleed, he said it was because he had omitted to have himself blooded four days after a quarter of a year's interval. Dr. Johnson, who was a great dabbler in physic, disapproved much of periodical bleeding. "For," said he, "you accustom yourself to an evacuation which nature cannot perform of herself, and therefore she cannot help you, should you from forgetfulness or any other cause omit it; so you may be suddenly suffocated. You may accustom yourself to other periodical evacuations, because, should you omit them, nature can supply the omission; but nature cannot open a vein to blood you." "I do not like to take an emetic," said Taylor, "for fear of breaking some small vessel." "Poh!" said Johnson, "if you have so many things that will break, you had better break your neck at once, and there's an end on't. You will break no small vessels " (blowing with high derision).

The horror of death, which I had always observed in Dr. Johnson, appeared strong to-night. I ventured to tell him, that I had been, for moments in my life, not afraid of death; therefore I could suppose another man in that state of mind for a considerable space of time. He said, "he never had a moment in which death was not terrible to him." He added, that it had been observed, that scarce any man dies in public but with apparent resolution; from that desire of praise which never quits us. I said, Dr. Dodd seemed to be willing to die, and full of hopes of happiness. "Sir," said he, "Dr. Dodd would have given both his hands and both his legs to have lived. The better a man is, the more afraid is he of death, having a clearer view of infinite purity." He owned, that our being in an unhappy uncertainty as to our salvation was mysterious; and said, "Ah! we must wait till we are in another state of being to have many things explained to us."

On Wednesday, September 17, Dr. Butter, physician at Derby, drank tea with us; and it was settled that Dr. Johnson and I should go on Friday and dine with him. Johnson said, "I am glad of this." He seemed weary of the uniformity of life at Dr. Taylor's.

Talking of biography, I said, in writing a life, a man's peculiarities should be mentioned, because they mark his character. JOHNSON. "Sir, there is no doubt as to peculiarities: the question is, whether a man's vices should be mentioned; for instance, whether it should be mentioned that Addison and Parnell drank too freely; for people will probably more easily indulge in drinking from knowing this; so that more ill may be done by the example, than good by telling the whole truth." Here was an instance of his varying from himself in talk; for I well remember that Dr. Johnson maintained, that, if a man is to write a *Panegyric*, he may keep vices out of sight; but if he professes to write a *Life*, he must represent it really as it was: and when I objected to the danger of telling that Parnell drank to excess, he said that "it would produce an instructive caution to avoid drinking, when it was seen that even the learning and genius of Parnell could be debased by it."

He had this evening, partly, I suppose, from the spirit of contradiction to his Whig friend, a violent argument with Dr. Taylor, as to the inclinations of the people of England at this time towards the Royal Family of Stuart. He grew so outrageous as to say, "that if England were fairly polled, the present king would be sent away to-night, and his adherents hanged to-morrow." Taylor, who was as violent a Whig as Johnson was a Tory, was roused by this to a pitch of bellowing. He denied loudly what Johnson said; and maintained that there was an abhorrence against the Stuart family.

Thursday, Sept. 18.—Last night Dr. Johnson had proposed that the crystal lustre, or chandelier, in Dr. Taylor's large room, should be lighted up some time or other. Taylor said it should be lighted up next night. "That will do very well," said I, "for it is Dr. Johnson's birthday." He did not seem pleased that I mentioned it, and said (somewhat sternly), "he would *not* have the lustre lighted the next day."

Some ladies, who had been present yesterday when I mentioned his birth-day, came to dinner to-day, and plagued him, unintentionally, by wishing him joy. I know not why he disliked having his birth-day mentioned, unless it were that it reminded him of his approaching nearer to death, of which he had a constant dread.

I mentioned to him a friend of mine who was formerly gloomy from low spirits, and much distressed by the fear of death, but was now uniformly placid, and contemplated his dissolution without any perturbation. "Sir," said Johnson, "this is only a disordered imagination taking a different turn."

We talked of a collection being made of all the English poets who had published a volume of poems. He observed, that a gentleman of eminence in literature had got into a bad style of poetry of late. "He puts," said he, "a very common thing in a strange dress, till he does not know it himself, and thinks other people do not know it." BOSWELL. "That is owing to his being so much versant in old English poetry." JOHNSON. "What is that to the purpose, Sir? If I say a man is drunk, and you tell me it is owing to his taking much drink, the matter is not mended. No, Sir, —— has taken to an odd mode. For example, he'd write thus:

> Hermit hoar, in solemn cell,
>   Wearing out life's evening gray.

Gray evening is common enough; but *evening gray* he'd think fine.— Stay; we'll make out the stanza:

> Hermit hoar, in solemn cell,
>   Wearing out life's evening gray:
> Smite thy bosom, sage, and tell,
>   What is bliss? and which the way?

BOSWELL. "But why smite his bosom, Sir?" JOHNSON. "Why, to show he was in earnest" (smiling). He at an after period added the following stanza:

> Thus I spoke; and speaking sigh'd;
>   —Scarce repress'd the starting tear;—
> When the smiling sage replied—
>   —Come, my lad, and drink some beer.

I cannot help thinking the first stanza good solemn poetry, as also the first three lines of the second. Its last line is an excellent burlesque surprise on gloomy sentimental inquiries. And perhaps the advice is as good as can be given to a low-spirited, dissatisfied being: "Don't trouble your head with sickly thinking; take a cup, and be merry."

Friday, September 19, after breakfast, Dr. Johnson and I set out in Dr. Taylor's chaise to go to Derby. The day was fine, and we resolved to go by Keddlestone, the seat of Lord Scarsdale, that I might see his lordship's fine house. I was struck with the magnificence of the building; and the extensive park, with the finest verdure, covered with deer, and cattle, and sheep, delighted me. The number of old oaks, of an immense size, filled me with a sort of respectful admiration; for one of them sixty pounds was offered. The excellent smooth gravel roads; the large piece of water formed by his lordship from some small brooks, with a handsome barge upon it; the venerable Gothic church, now the family chapel, just by the house; in short, the grand group of objects agitated and distended my mind in a most agreeable manner. "One should think," said I, "that the proprietor of all this *must* be happy." "Nay, Sir," said Johnson, "all this excludes but one evil—poverty." [1]

In our way, Johnson strongly expressed his love of driving fast in a post-chaise. "If," said he, "I had no duties, and no reference to futurity, I would spend my life in driving briskly in a post-chaise with a pretty woman; but she should be one that could understand me, and would add something to the conversation."

I felt a pleasure in walking about Derby, such as I always have in walking about any town to which I am not accustomed. There is an immediate sensation of novelty; and one speculates on the way in which life is passed in it, which, although there is a sameness every where upon the whole, is yet minutely diversified. The minute diversities in every thing are wonderful. Talking of shaving the other night at Dr. Taylor's, Dr. Johnson said, "Sir, of a thousand shavers, two do not shave so much alike as not to be distinguished." I thought this not possible, till he specified so many of the varieties in shaving;—holding the razor more or less perpen-

---

[1] When I mentioned Dr. Johnson's remark to a lady of admirable good sense and quickness of understanding, she observed, "It is true all this excludes only one evil; but how much good does it let in!" To this observation much praise has been justly given. Let me then now do myself the honour to mention, that the lady who made it was the late Margaret Montgomerie, my very valuable wife, and the very affectionate mother of my children, who, if they inherit her good qualities, will have no reason to complain of their lot. *Dos magna parentum virtus.—Boswell.*

dicular; drawing long or short strokes; beginning at the upper part of the face, or the under—at the right side or the left side. Indeed, when one considers what variety of sounds can be uttered by the windpipe, in the compass of a very small aperture, we may be convinced how many degrees of difference there may be in the application of a razor.

We dined with Dr. Butter. Johnson and he had a good deal of medical conversation. I mentioned that Lord Monboddo told me, he awaked every morning at four, and then for his health got up and walked in his room naked, with the window open, which he called taking *an air bath;* after which he went to bed again, and slept two hours more. Johnson, who was always ready to beat down any thing that seemed to be exhibited with disproportionate importance, thus observed: "I suppose, Sir, there is no more in it than this; he wakes at four, and cannot sleep till he chills himself, and makes the warmth of the bed a grateful sensation."

I talked of the difficulty of rising in the morning. Dr. Johnson told me, "that the learned Mrs. Carter, at that period when she was eager in study, did not awake as early as she wished, and she therefore had a contrivance, that, at a certain hour, her chamber light should burn a string to which a heavy weight was suspended, which then fell with a strong sudden noise: this roused her from sleep, and then she had no difficulty in getting up." But I said *that* was my difficulty; and wished there could be some medicine invented which would make one rise without pain, which I never did, unless after lying in bed a very long time. Perhaps there may be something in the stores of Nature which could do this. I have thought of a pulley to raise me gradually; but that would give me pain, as it would counteract my internal inclination. I would have something that can dissipate the *vis inertiæ,* and give elasticity to the muscles. As I imagine that the human body may be put, by the operation of other substances, into any state in which it has ever been; and as I have experienced a state in which rising from bed was not disagreeable, but easy, nay, sometimes agreeable; I suppose that this state may be produced, if we knew by what. We can heat the body, we can cool it; we can give it tension or relaxation; and surely it is possible to bring it into a state in which rising from bed will not be a pain.

Johnson advised me to-night not to *refine* in the education of my children. "Life," said he, "will not bear refinement: you must do as other people do."

As we drove back to Ashbourne, Dr. Johnson recommended to me, as he had often done, to drink water only: "For," said he, "you are then sure not to get drunk; whereas, if you drink wine, you are never sure." I said, drinking wine was a pleasure which I was unwilling to give up. "Why, Sir," said he, "there is no doubt that not to drink wine is a great deduction from life; but it may be necessary."

By the time when we returned to Ashbourne, Dr. Taylor was gone to bed. Johnson and I sat up a long time by ourselves.

He was much diverted with an article which I showed him in the "Critical Review" giving an account of a curious publication, entitled "A Spiritual Diary and Soliloquies, by John Rutty, M.D." Dr. Rutty was one of the people called quakers, a physician of some eminence in Dublin. This Diary, which was kept from 1753 to 1775, the year in which he died, exhibited, in the simplicity of his heart, a minute and honest register of the state of his mind; which, though frequently laughable enough, was not more so than the history of many men would be, if recorded with equal fairness. The following specimens were extracted by the reviewers:

Tenth month, 1753, 23.—Indulgence in bed an hour too long.
Twelfth month, 17.—An hypochondriac obnubilation from wind and indigestion.
Ninth month, 28.—An over-dose of whisky.
29.—A dull, cross, choleric day.
First month, 1757, 22.—A little swinish at dinner and repast.
31.—Dogged on provocation.
Second month, 5.—Very dogged or snappish.
14.—Snappish on fasting.
26.—Cursed snappishness to those under me, on a bodily indisposition.
Third month, 11.—On a provocation, exercised a dumb resentment for two days, instead of scolding.
22.—Scolded too vehemently.
23.—Dogged again.
Fourth month, 29.—Mechanically and sinfully dogged.

Johnson laughed heartily at this good Quietist's self-condemning minutes.

On Saturday, September 20, after breakfast, when Taylor was gone out to his farm, Dr. Johnson and I had a serious conversation by ourselves on melancholy and madness; which he was, I always thought, erroneously inclined to confound together. When he talked of madness, he was to be understood as speaking of those who were in any great degree disturbed, or, as is commonly expressed, "troubled in mind."

Johnson said, "A madman loves to be with people whom he fears; not as the dog fears the lash, but of whom he stands in awe." He added, "Madmen are all sensual in the lower stages of the distemper. They are eager for gratification to soothe their minds, and divert their attention from the misery which they suffer; but when they grow very ill, pleasure is too weak for them, and they seek for pain. Employment, Sir, and hardships, prevent melancholy. I suppose, in all our army in America, there was not one man who went mad."

We entered seriously upon a question of much importance to me, which Johnson was pleased to consider with friendly attention. I had long complained to him that I felt myself discontented in Scotland, as too narrow a sphere, and that I wished to make my chief residence in London, the great scene of ambition, instruction, and amusement; a scene which was to me, comparatively speaking, a heaven upon earth. JOHNSON. "Why, Sir, I never knew any one who had such a *gust* for London as you have; and I cannot blame you for your wish to live there; yet, Sir, were I in your father's place, I should not consent to your settling there; for I have the old feudal notions, and I should be afraid that Auchinleck would be deserted."

I suggested a doubt, that if I were to reside in London, the exquisite zest with which I relished it in occasional visits might go off, and I might grow tired of it. JOHNSON. "Why, Sir, you find no man, at all intellectual, who is willing to leave London. No, Sir, when a man is tired of London, he is tired of life; for there is in London all that life can afford."

To obviate his apprehension, that by settling in London I might desert the seat of my ancestors, I assured him that I had old feudal principles to a degree of enthusiasm; and that I felt all the *dulcedo* of the *natale solum*. I reminded him, that the Laird of Auchinleck had an elegant house, in front of which he could ride ten miles forward upon his own territories, upon which he had upwards of six hundred people attached to him; that the family seat was rich in natural romantic beauties of rock, wood, and water; and that in my "morn of life" I had appropriated the finest descriptions in the ancient classics to certain scenes there, which were thus associated in my mind. That when all this was considered, I should certainly pass a part of the year at home, and enjoy it the more from variety, and from bringing with me a share of the intellectual stores of the metropolis. He listened to all this, and kindly "hoped it might be as I now supposed."

We talked of employment being absolutely necessary to preserve the mind from wearying and growing fretful, especially in those who have a tendency to melancholy; and I mentioned to him a saying which somebody had related of an American savage, who, when an European was expatiating on all the advantages of money, put this question: "Will it purchase *occupation?*" JOHNSON. "Depend upon it, Sir, this saying is too refined for a savage. And, Sir, money *will* purchase occupation; it will purchase all the conveniences of life; it will purchase variety of company; it will purchase all sorts of entertainment."

I talked to him of Forster's "Voyage to the South Seas", which pleased me; but I found he did not like it. "Sir," said he, "there is a great affectation of fine writing in it." BOSWELL. "But he carries you along with him." JOHNSON. "No, Sir; he does not carry *me* along with him; he leaves me behind him; or rather, indeed, he sets me before him; for he makes me turn over many leaves at a time."

On Sunday, September 21, we went to the church of Ashbourne, which is one of the largest and most luminous that I have seen in any town of the same size. I felt great satisfaction in considering that I was supported in my fondness for solemn public worship by the general concurrence and munificence of mankind.

Johnson and Taylor were so different from each other, that I wondered at their preserving an intimacy. Their having been at school and college together might, in some degree, account for this: but Sir Joshua Reynolds has furnished me with a stronger reason; for Johnson mentioned to him, that he had been told by Taylor he was to be his heir. I shall not take upon me to animadvert upon this; but certain it is that Johnson paid great attention to Taylor. He now, however, said to me, "Sir, I love him; but I do not love him more; my regard for him does not increase. As it is said in the Apocrypha, 'his talk is of bullocks.' I do not suppose he is very fond of my company. His habits are by no means sufficiently clerical: this he knows that I see; and no man likes to live under the eye of perpetual disapprobation."

I have no doubt that a good many sermons were composed for Taylor by Johnson. At this time I found upon his table a part of

one which he had newly begun to write.   Johnson was by no means
of opinion that every man of a learned profession should consider
it as incumbent upon him, or as necessary to his credit, to appear as
an author.   When, in the ardour of ambition for literary fame, I
regretted to him one day that an eminent judge had nothing of it,
and therefore would leave no perpetual monument of himself to
posterity; "Alas! Sir," said Johnson, "what a mass of confusion
should we have, if every bishop, and every judge, every lawyer,
physician, and divine, were to write books!"

I mentioned to Johnson a respectable person of a very strong
mind,[1] who had little of that tenderness which is common to human
nature; as an instance of which, when I suggested to him that he
should invite his son, who had been settled ten years in foreign
parts, to come home and pay him a visit, his answer was, "No, no,
let him mind his business."   JOHNSON.   "I do not agree with him,
Sir, in this. Getting money is not all a man's business: to cultivate
kindness is a valuable part of the business of life."

In the evening, Johnson, being in very good spirits, entertained
us with several characteristical portraits.   "Colley Cibber once
consulted me as to one of his birthday odes a long time before it
was wanted.   I objected very freely to several passages.   Cibber
lost patience, and would not read his ode to an end. When we had
done with criticism we walked over to Richardson's, the author of
'Clarissa,' and I wondered to find Richardson displeased that I
'did not treat Cibber with more *respect*.' Now, Sir, to talk of *respect*
for a *player!*" (smiling disdainfully).   BOSWELL.   "There, Sir, you
are always heretical: you never will allow merit to a player."
JOHNSON.   "Merit, Sir! what merit? Do you respect a rope-dancer
or a ballad-singer?"   BOSWELL.   "No, Sir; but we respect a great
player, as a man who can conceive lofty sentiments, and can express
them gracefully."   JOHNSON.   "What! Sir, a fellow who claps a
hump on his back, and a lump on his leg, and cries, '*I am Richard
the Third*'? Nay, Sir, a ballad-singer is a higher man, for he does
two things; he repeats and he sings: there is both recitation and
music in his performance; the player only recites."   BOSWELL.
"My dear Sir, you may turn any thing into ridicule. I allow, that a
player of farce is not entitled to respect; he does a little thing; but
he who can represent exalted characters, and touch the noblest
passions, has very respectable powers; and mankind have agreed

[1] Boswell's father, Lord Auchinleck; the absent son was David Boswell, who spent many years in
Spain.

in admiring great talents for the stage. We must consider, too, that a great player does what very few are capable to do; his art is a very rare faculty. *Who* can repeat Hamlet's soliloquy, 'To be, or not to be,' as Garrick does it?" JOHNSON. "Any body may. Jemmy, there (a boy about eight years old, who was in the room), will do as well in a week." BOSWELL. "No, no, Sir: and as a proof of the merit of great acting, and of the value which mankind set upon it, Garrick has got a hundred thousand pounds." JOHNSON. "Is getting a hundred thousand pounds a proof of excellence? That has been done by a scoundrel commissary." [1]

This was most fallacious reasoning. I was *sure* for once, that I had the best side of the argument.

On Monday, September 22, when at breakfast, I unguardedly said to Dr. Johnson, "I wish I saw you and Mrs. Macaulay together." He grew very angry; and, after a pause, while a cloud gathered on his brow, he burst out, "No, Sir; you would not see us quarrel, to make you sport. Don't you know that it is very uncivil to *pit* two people against one another?" Then, checking himself, and wishing to be more gentle, he added, "I do not say you should be hanged or drowned for this; but it *is* very uncivil." Dr. Taylor thought him in the wrong, and spoke to him privately of it; but I afterwards acknowledged to Johnson that I was to blame, for I candidly owned that I meant to express a desire to see a contest between Mrs. Macaulay and him; but then I knew how the contest would end; so that I was to see him triumph. JOHNSON. "Sir, you cannot be sure how a contest will end; and no man has a right to engage two people in a dispute by which their passions may be inflamed, and they may part with bitter resentment against each other. I would sooner keep company with a man from whom I must guard my pockets, than with a man who contrives to bring me into a dispute with somebody that he may hear it. Whatever the motive be, Sir, the man who does so, does very wrong. He has no more right to instruct himself at such risk, than he has to make two people fight a duel, that he may learn how to defend himself."

Dr. Johnson obligingly proposed to carry me to see Ilam, a romantic scene, now belonging to a family of the name of Port, but formerly the seat of the Congreves. Johnson described it distinctly and vividly; at which I could not but express to him my

---

[1] "The fact was," says Murphy, "that Johnson could not see the passions as they rose and chased one another in the varied features of the expressive face of Garrick." Murphy remembered being in conversation with Johnson near the side of the scenes, during the tragedy of King Lear: when Garrick came off the stage, he said, "You two talk so loud, you destroy all my feelings."—"Prithee," replied Johnson, "do not talk of feelings; Punch has no feelings."

wonder; because, though my eyes, as he observed, were better than his, I could not by any means equal him in representing visible objects. I said, the difference between us in this respect was as that between a man who has a bad instrument, but plays well on it, and a man who has a good instrument, on which he can play very imperfectly.

In the evening, a gentleman farmer, who was on a visit at Dr. Taylor's, attempted to dispute with Johnson in favour of Mungo Campbell, who shot Alexander, Earl of Eglintoune, upon his having fallen, when retreating from his lordship, who he believed was about to seize his gun, as he had threatened to do. He said he should have done just as Campbell did. JOHNSON. "Whoever would do as Campbell did, deserves to be hanged; not that I could, as a juryman, have found him legally guilty of murder; but I am glad they found means to convict him." The gentleman farmer said, "A poor man has as much honour as a rich man; and Campbell had *that* to defend." Johnson exclaimed, "A poor man has no honour." The English yeoman, not dismayed, proceeded: "Lord Eglintoune was a damned fool to run on upon Campbell, after being warned that Campbell would shoot him if he did." Johnson, who could not bear any thing like swearing, angrily replied, "He was *not* a *damned* fool: he only thought too well of Campbell. He did not believe Campbell would be such a *damned* scoundrel, as to do so *damned* a thing." His emphasis on *damned*, accompanied with frowning looks, reproved his opponent's want of decorum in *his* presence.

During this interview at Ashbourne, Johnson seemed to be more uniformly social, cheerful, and alert, than I had almost ever seen him. He was prompt on great occasions and on small. Taylor, who praised every thing of his own to excess, in short, "whose geese were all swans," as the proverb says, expatiated on the excellence of his bull-dog, which he told us was "perfectly well shaped." Johnson, after examining the animal attentively, thus repressed the vain-glory of our host: "No, Sir, he is *not* well shaped; for there is not the quick transition from the thickness of the fore-part, to the *tenuity*—the thin part—behind, which a bull-dog ought to have." This *tenuity* was the only *hard word* that I heard him use during this interview, and it will be observed, he instantly put another expression in its place.

One morning after breakfast, when the sun shone bright, we walked out together, and "pored" for some time with placid indolence upon an artificial waterfall, which Dr. Taylor had made by building a strong dyke of stone across the river behind the garden. It was now somewhat obstructed by branches of trees and other rubbish, which had come down the river, and settled close to it. Johnson, partly from a desire to see it play more freely, and partly from that inclination to activity which will animate at times the most inert and sluggish mortal, took a long pole which was lying on a bank, and pushed down several parcels of this wreck with painful assiduity, while I stood quietly by, wondering to behold the sage thus curiously employed, and smiling with a humorous satisfaction each time when he carried his point. He worked till he was quite out of breath; and having found a large dead cat so heavy that he could not move it after several efforts, "Come," said he (throwing down the pole), "*you* shall take it now"; which I accordingly did, and being a fresh man, soon made the cat tumble over the cascade. This may be laughed at as too trifling to record; but it is a small characteristic trait in the Flemish picture which I give of my friend, and in which, therefore, I mark the most minute particulars.

I mentioned an old gentleman of our acquaintance whose memory was beginning to fail. JOHNSON. "There must be a diseased mind where there is a failure of memory at seventy. A man's head, Sir, must be morbid if he fails so soon."

Dr. Johnson advised me to-day to have as many books about me as I could; that I might read upon any subject upon which I had a desire for instruction at the time. "What you read *then*," said he, "you will remember; but if you have not a book immediately ready, and the subject moulds in your mind, it is a chance if you have again a desire to study it." He added, "If a man never has an eager desire for instruction, he should prescribe a task for himself. But it is better when a man reads from immediate inclination."

On Tuesday, September 23, Johnson was remarkably cordial to me. It being necessary for me to return to Scotland soon, I had fixed on the next day for my setting out, and I felt a tender concern at the thought of parting with him. He had, at this time, frankly communicated to me many particulars, which are inserted in this work in their proper places; and once, when I happened to mention that the expense of my jaunt would come to much more than I had computed, he said, "Why, Sir, if the expense were to be an inconvenience, you would have reason to regret it; but, if you have had the money to spend, I know not that you could have purchased as much pleasure with it in any other way."

During this interview at Ashbourne, Johnson and I frequently talked with wonderful pleasure of mere trifles which had occurred in our tour to the Hebrides; for it had left a most agreeable and lasting impression upon his mind.

He found fault with me for using the phrase to *make* money. "Don't you see," said he, "the impropriety of it? To *make* money is to *coin* it; you should say *get* money." The phrase, however, is, I think, pretty current. But Johnson was at all times jealous of infractions upon the genuine English language, and prompt to repress colloquial barbarisms; such as *pledging myself* for *undertaking; line* for *department* or *branch*, as the *civil line*, the *banking line*. He was particularly indignant against the almost universal use of the word *idea*, in the sense of *notion* or *opinion*, when it is clear that *idea* can only signify something of which an image can be formed in the mind. We may have an *idea* or *image* of a mountain, a tree, a building; but we cannot surely have an *idea* or *image* of an *argument* or *proposition*. Yet we hear the sages of the law "delivering their *ideas* upon the question under consideration"; and the first speakers in parliament "entirely coinciding in the *idea* which has been ably stated by an honourable member"; or "reprobating an *idea* as unconstitutional, and fraught with the most dangerous consequences to a great and free country." Johnson called this "modern cant."

I perceived that he pronounced the word *heard*, as if spelt with a double *e*, *heerd*, instead of sounding it *herd*, as is most usually done. He said, his reason was, that if it were pronounced *herd*, there would be a single exception from the English pronunciation of the syllable *ear*, and he thought it better not to have that exception.

In the evening our gentleman-farmer, and two others, entertained themselves and the company with a great number of tunes on the fiddle. Johnson desired to have "Let Ambition fire thy Mind" played over again, and appeared to give a patient attention to it; though he owned to me that he was very insensible to the power of music. I told him that it affected me to such a degree, as often to agitate my nerves painfully, producing in my mind alternate sensations of pathetic dejection, so that I was ready to shed tears; and of daring resolution, so that I was inclined to rush into the thickest part of the battle. "Sir," said he, "I should never hear it, if it made me such a fool."

Much of the effect of music, I am satisfied, is owing to the association of ideas. I know from my own experience, that Scotch reels, though brisk, make me melancholy, because I used to hear them in my early years, at a time when Mr. Pitt called for soldiers, "from the mountains of the north," and numbers of brave High-landers were going abroad, never to return. Whereas the airs in "The Beggar's Opera," many of which are very soft, never fail to render me gay, because they are associated with the warm sensa-tions and high spirits of London. This evening, while some of the tunes of ordinary composition were played with no great skill, my frame was agitated, and I was conscious of a generous attachment to Dr. Johnson, as my preceptor and friend, mixed with an affec-tionate regret that he was an old man, whom I should probably lose in a short time. I thought I could defend him at the point of my sword. My reverence and affection for him were in full glow. I said to him, "My dear Sir, we must meet every year, if you don't quarrel with me." JOHNSON. "Nay, Sir, you are more likely to quarrel with me, than I with you. My regard for you is greater almost than I have words to express; but I do not choose to be always repeating it: write it down in the first leaf of your pocket-book, and never doubt of it again."

I talked to him of misery being "the doom of man" in this life, as displayed in his "Vanity of Human Wishes."

> Yet hope not life from grief or danger free,
> Nor think the doom of man revers'd for thee.

Yet I observed that things were done upon the supposition of hap-piness; grand houses were built, fine gardens were made, splendid places of public amusement were contrived, and crowded with company. JOHNSON. "Alas, Sir, these are only struggles for hap-piness. When I first entered Ranelagh, it gave an expansion and gay sensation to my mind, such as I never experienced any where else. But, as Xerxes wept when he viewed his immense army, and considered that not one of that great multitude would be alive a hundred years afterwards, so it went to my heart to consider that there was not one in all that brilliant circle that was not afraid to go home and think; but that the thoughts of each individual there would be distressing when alone."

I suggested, that being in love, and flattered with hopes of suc-cess; or having some favourite scheme in view for the next day, might prevent that wretchedness of which we had been talking. JOHNSON. "Why, Sir, it may sometimes be so as you suppose; but my conclusion is in general but too true."

While Johnson and I stood in calm conference by ourselves in Dr. Taylor's garden, at a pretty late hour in a serene autumn night, looking up to the heavens, I directed the discourse to the subject of a future state. My friend was in a placid and most benignant frame of mind. "Sir," said he, "I do not imagine that all things will be made clear to us immediately after death, but that the ways of Providence will be explained to us very gradually." I ventured to ask him whether, although the words of some texts of Scripture seemed strong in support of the dreadful doctrine of an eternity of punishment, we might not hope that the denunciation was figurative, and would not literally be executed. JOHNSON. "Sir, you are to consider the intention of punishment in a future state. We have no reason to be sure that we shall then be no longer liable to offend against God. We do not know that even the angels are quite in a state of security; nay, we know that some of them have fallen. It may therefore, perhaps, be necessary, in order to preserve both men and angels in a state of rectitude, that they should have continually before them the punishment of those who have deviated from it; but we hope that by some other means a fall from rectitude may be prevented. Some of the texts of Scripture upon this subject are, as you observe, indeed strong; but they may admit of a mitigated interpretation." He talked to me upon this awful and delicate question in a gentle tone, and as if afraid to be decisive.

After supper I accompanied him to his apartment, and at my request he dictated to me an argument in favour of the negro who was then claiming his liberty, in an action in the court of session in Scotland. He had always been very zealous against slavery in every form, in which I with all deference thought that he discovered "a zeal without knowledge." Upon one occasion, when in company with some very grave men at Oxford, his toast was, "Here's to the next insurrection of the negroes in the West Indies." His violent prejudice against our West Indian and American settlers appeared whenever there was an opportunity. Towards the conclusion of his "Taxation no Tyranny," he says, "How is it that we hear the loudest *yelps* for liberty among the drivers of negroes?"

But I beg leave to enter my most solemn protest against his general doctrine with respect to the slave trade. For I will resolutely say, that his unfavourable notion of it was owing to prejudice, and imperfect or false information. The wild and dangerous attempt which has for some time been persisted in to obtain an act of our legislature, to abolish so very important and necessary a branch of commercial interest, must have been crushed at once, had not the insignificance of the zealots who vainly took the lead in it made the vast body of planters, merchants, and others, whose immense properties are involved in that trade, reasonably enough suppose that there could be no danger. The encouragement which the attempt has received excites my wonder and indignation; and though some men of superior abilities have supported it, whether from a love of temporary popularity when prosperous, or a love of general mischief when desperate, my opinion is unshaken. To abolish a *status* which in all ages God has sanctioned, and man has continued, would not only be *robbery* to an innumerable class of our fellow-subjects, but it would be extreme cruelty to the African savages, a portion of whom it saves from massacre, or intolerable bondage in their own country, and introduces into a much happier state of life; especially now when their passage to the West Indies and their treatment there is humanely regulated. To abolish that trade would be to

—— shut the gates of mercy on mankind.

Whatever may have passed elsewhere concerning it, the House of Lords is wise and independent.

When I said now to Johnson, that I was afraid I kept him too late up;—"No, Sir," said he, "I don't care though I sit all night with you." This was an animated speech from a man in his sixty-ninth year.[1]

Had I been as attentive not to displease him as I ought to have been, I know not but this vigil might have been fulfilled; but I unluckily entered upon the controversy concerning the right of Great Britain to tax America, and attempted to argue in favour of our fellow-subjects on the other side of the Atlantic. Johnson could not bear my thus opposing his avowed opinion, which he had exerted himself with an extreme degree of heat to enforce; and the

---

[1] Dr. Johnson loved late hours extremely, or, more properly, hated early ones. Nothing was more terrifying to him than the idea of retiring to bed, which he never would call going to rest, or suffer another to call so. "I lie down," said he, "that my acquaintance may sleep; but I lie down to endure oppressive misery, and soon rise again to pass the night in anxiety and pain." By this pathetic manner, which no one ever possessed in so eminent a degree, he used to shock me from quitting his company, till I hurt my own health not a little by sitting up with him when I was myself far from well: nor was it an easy matter to oblige him even by compliance, for he always maintained that no one forbore their own gratifications for the sake of pleasing another, and if one *did* sit up, it was probably to amuse one's self. Some right, however, he certainly had to say so, as he made his company exceedingly entertaining when he had once forced one, by his vehement lamentations and piercing reproofs, not to quit the room, but to sit quietly and make tea for him, as I often did in London till four o'clock in the morning. At Streatham I managed better, having always some friend who was kind enough to engage him in talk, and favour my retreat: and he rose in the morning as unwillingly as he went to bed.—*Piozzi, Anecdotes.*

violent agitation into which he was thrown, while answering, or
rather reprimanding me, alarmed me so, that I heartily repented
of my having unthinkingly introduced the subject.   I myself,
however, grew warm, and the change was great, from the calm
state of philosophical discussion in which we had a little before been
pleasingly employed.

We were fatigued by the contest, which was produced by my
want of caution; and he was not then in the humour to slide into
easy and cheerful talk.   It therefore so happened, that we were
after an hour or two very willing to separate and go to bed.

On Wednesday, September 24, I went into Dr. Johnson's room
before he got up, and finding that the storm of the preceding night
was quite laid, I sat down upon his bedside, and he talked with as
much readiness and good humour as ever. He recommended to me
to plant a considerable part of a large moorish farm which I had
purchased, and he made several calculations of the expense and
profit; for he delighted in exercising his mind on the science of
numbers. He pressed upon me the importance of planting at the
first in a very sufficient manner, quoting the saying, "*In bello non
licet bis errare*": and adding, "this is equally true in planting."

After breakfast I departed, and pursued my journey northwards.

To James Boswell, Esq.

London, Nov. 25, 1777

DEAR SIR,
        . . . I was not well when you left me at the doctor's, and
I grew worse; yet I staid on, and at Lichfield was very ill. Travelling, however, did not make me worse; and when I came to London,
I complied with a summons to go to Brighthelmstone, where I
saw Beauclerk, and stayed three days.

Our club has recommenced last Friday, but I was not there.
Langton has another wench.[1] Mrs. Thrale is in hopes of a young
brewer. They got by their trade last year a very large sum, and
their expenses are proportionate.

Mrs. Williams's health is very bad. And I have had for some
time a very difficult and laborious respiration; but I am better by
purges, abstinence, and other methods. I am yet, however, much
behind-hand in my health and rest. . . .

My dear friend, let me thank you once more for your visit; you
did me great honour, and I hope met with nothing that displeased

---

[1] A daughter born to him, to whom Johnson was godfather.

you. I staid long at Ashbourne, not much pleased, yet awkward at departing. I then went to Lichfield, where I found my friend at Stowhill [Mrs. Aston] very dangerously diseased. Such is life. Let us try to pass it well, whatever it be, for there is surely something beyond it.

Well, now, I hope all is well; write as soon as you can to, dear Sir, &c.,   SAM. JOHNSON

To Dr. Samuel Johnson

Edinburgh, Feb. 28, 1778

MY DEAR SIR,

You are at present busy amongst the English poets, preparing, for the public instruction and entertainment, prefaces biographical and critical. It will not, therefore, be out of season to appeal to you for the decision of a controversy which has arisen between a lady and me concerning a passage in Parnell. That poet tells us that his hermit quitted his cell

> "—— to know the world by sight,
> To find if *books* or *swains* report it right;
> (For yet by *swains alone* the world he knew,
> Whose feet came wand'ring o'er the nightly dew.)"

I maintain, that there is an inconsistency here; for as the hermit's notions of the world were formed from the reports both of *books* and *swains*, he could not justly be said to know by *swains alone*. Be pleased to judge between us, and let us have your reasons.

What do you say to "Taxation no Tyranny," now, after Lord North's declaration, or confession, or whatever else his conciliatory speech should be called? I never differed from you in politics but upon two points—the Middlesex election, and the taxation of the Americans by the British houses of representatives. There is a *charm* in the word *parliament*, so I avoid it. As I am a steady and a warm tory, I regret that the king does not see it to be better for him to receive constitutional supplies from his American subjects by the voice of their own assemblies, where his royal person is represented, than through the medium of his British subjects. I am persuaded that the power of the crown, which I wish to increase, would be greater when in contact with all its dominions, than if "the rays of regal bounty" were "to shine" upon America through that dense and troubled body, a modern British parliament. But enough of this subject; for your angry voice at Ashbourne upon it still sounds awful "in my mind's *ears*." I ever am, &c.,   JAMES BOSWELL

On Wednesday, March 18, I arrived in London, and was informed by good Mr. Francis, that his master was gone to Mr. Thrale's at Streatham, to which place I wrote to him, begging to know when he would be in town. He was not expected for some time; but next day, having called on Dr. Taylor, in Dean's-yard, Westminster, I found him there, and was told he had come to town for a few hours. He met me with his usual kindness, but instantly returned to the writing of something on which he was employed when I came in, and on which he seemed much intent. Finding him thus engaged, I made my visit very short, and had no more of his conversation.

On Friday, March 20, I found him at his own house, sitting with Mrs. Williams, and was informed that the room formerly allotted to me was now appropriated to a charitable purpose; Mrs. Desmoulins, and, I think, her daughter, and a Miss Carmichael, being also lodged in it. Such was his humanity, and such his generosity, that Mrs. Desmoulins herself told me he allowed her half a guinea a week. Let it be remembered, that this was above a twelfth part of his pension.[1]

We retired from Mrs. Williams to another room. Tom Davies soon after joined us. He had now unfortunately failed in his circumstances, and was much indebted to Dr. Johnson's kindness for obtaining for him many alleviations of his distress. After he went away, Johnson blamed his folly in quitting the stage, by which he and his wife got five hundred pounds a year. I said, I believed it was owing to Churchill's attack upon him, "He mouths a sentence as curs mouth a bone." JOHNSON. "I believe, so too, Sir. But what a man is he who is to be driven from the stage by a line? Another line would have driven him from his shop!"

In my interview with Dr. Johnson this evening, I was quite easy, as his companion; upon which I find in my journal the follow-

[1] Mrs. Desmoulins was a daughter of Dr. Swinfen, Johnson's godfather, and widow of a writing-master. Before her marriage she had lived for a time with Mrs. Johnson. Johnson took to Miss Carmichael (whom he called Poll) "very well at first, but she won't do upon a nearer examination." Mrs. Thrale asked how she joined the household. JOHNSON. "Why, I don't rightly remember, but we could spare her very well from among us. Poll is a stupid slut; I had some hopes of her at first: but when I talked to her tightly and closely, I could make nothing of her; she was wiggle-waggle, and I could never persuade her to be categorical."
Johnson sometimes suffered Boswell to call the group of females "his Seraglio." It was not always at peace. In a letter to Mrs. Thrale, Johnson remarks, "Williams hates every body; Levett hates Desmoulins, and does not love Williams; Desmoulins hates them both; Poll loves none of them." Mrs. Thrale adds that these dissensions "distressed and mortified him exceedingly. He really was sometimes afraid of going home, because he was so sure to be met at the door with numberless complaints; and he used to lament that they made his life miserable from the impossibility he found of making theirs happy, when every favour he bestowed on one was wormwood to the rest. If, however, I ventured to blame their ingratitude, and condemn their conduct, he would instantly set about softening the one and justifying the other; and finished commonly by telling me, that I knew not how to make allowances for situations I never experienced."

ing reflection: "So ready is my mind to suggest matter for dissatisfaction, that I felt a sort of regret that I was so easy. I missed that awful reverence with which I used to contemplate MR. SAMUEL JOHNSON, in the complex magnitude of his literary, moral, and religious character."

He returned next day to Mr. Thrale's. I went to Streatham on Monday, March 30. Before he appeared, Mrs. Thrale made a very characteristical remark: "I do not know for certain what will please Dr. Johnson: but I know for certain that it will displease him to praise any thing, even what he likes, extravagantly."

Next morning, while we were at breakfast, Johnson gave a very earnest recommendation of what he himself practised with the utmost conscientiousness: I mean a strict attention to truth even in the most minute particulars. "Accustom your children," said he, "constantly to this: if a thing happened at one window, and they, when relating it, say that it happened at another, do not let it pass, but instantly check them: you do not know where deviation from truth will end." BOSWELL. "It may come to the door: and when once an account is at all varied in one circumstance, it may by degrees be varied so as to be totally different from what really happened." Our lively hostess, whose fancy was impatient of the rein, fidgeted at this, and ventured to say, "Nay, this is too much. If Dr. Johnson should forbid me to drink tea, I would comply, as I should feel the restraint only twice a day; but little variations in narrative must happen a thousand times a day, if one is not perpetually watching." JOHNSON. "Well, Madam, and you *ought* to be perpetually watching. It is more from carelessness about truth, than from intentional lying, that there is so much falsehood in the world."

Talking of ghosts, he said, "It is wonderful that five thousand years have now elapsed since the creation of the world, and still it is undecided whether or not there has ever been an instance of the spirit of any person appearing after death. All argument is against it, but all belief is for it."

He said, "John Wesley's conversation is good, but he is never at leisure. He is always obliged to go at a certain hour. This is very disagreeable to a man who loves to fold his legs and have out his talk, as I do."

On Friday, April 3, I dined with him in London, in a company [1]

[1] The Club. It is recorded that Johnson was president for the evening, and Boswell, Burke, Fordyce, Gibbon, Reynolds, Lord Upper Ossory, and Richard Brinsley Sheridan were also present. It seems clear that E, below, stands for Edmund Burke; about the other letters there is less certainty.

where were present several eminent men, whom I shall not name, but distinguish their parts in the conversation by different letters. F. "I have been looking at this famous antique marble dog of Mr. Jennings, valued at a thousand guineas." E. "A thousand guineas! The representation of no animal whatever is worth so much. At this rate, a dead dog would, indeed, be better than a living lion." JOHNSON. "Sir, it is not the worth of the thing, but of the skill in forming it, which is so highly estimated. Every thing that enlarges the sphere of human powers, that shows man he can do what he thought he could not do, is valuable. The first man who balanced a straw upon his nose; Johnson, who rode upon three horses at a time; in short, all such men deserve the applause of mankind, not on account of the use of what they did, but of the dexterity which they exhibited." BOSWELL. "Yet a misapplication of time and assiduity is not to be encouraged. Addison commends the judgment of a king, who, as a suitable reward to a man that by long perseverance had attained to the art of throwing a barley-corn through the eye of a needle, gave him a bushel of barley." JOHNSON. "He must have been a king of Scotland, where barley is scarce."

E. "We hear prodigious complaints at present of emigration. I am convinced that emigration makes a country more populous." J. "That sounds very much like a paradox." E. "Exportation of men, like exportation of all other commodities, makes more be produced." JOHNSON. "But there would be more people were there not emigration, provided there were food for more." E. "No; leave a few breeders, and you'll have more people than if there were no emigration." JOHNSON. "Nay, Sir, it is plain there will be more people, if there are more breeders. Thirty cows in good pasture will produce more calves than ten cows, provided they have good bulls." E. "There are bulls enough in Ireland." JOHNSON (smiling). "So, Sir, I should think from your argument."

R. "Mr. E., I don't mean to flatter, but when posterity reads one of your speeches, in parliament, it will be difficult to believe that you took so much pains, knowing with certainty that it could produce no effect, that not one vote would be gained by it." E. "Waiving your compliment to me, I shall say, in general, that it is very well worth while for a man to take pains to speak well in parliament. A man, who has vanity, speaks to display his talents; and if a man speaks well, he gradually establishes a certain reputa-tion and consequence in the general opinion, which sooner or later will have its political reward. Besides, though not one vote is gained, a good speech has its effect. Though an act which has been ably opposed passes into a law, yet in its progress it is modelled, it is softened in such a manner, that we see plainly the minister has been told, that the members attached to him are so sensible of its injustice or absurdity from what they have heard, that it must be altered." JOHNSON. "And, Sir, there is a gratification of pride. Though we cannot out-vote them, we will out-argue them. They shall not do wrong, without its being shown both to themselves and to the world."

JOHNSON. "I have been reading Thicknesse's 'Travels,' which I think are entertaining." BOSWELL. "What, Sir, a good book?" JOHNSON. "Yes, Sir, to read once. I do not say you are to make a study of it, and digest it; and I believe it to be a true book in his intention. All travellers generally mean to tell truth; though Thicknesse observes, upon Smollett's account of his alarming a whole town in France by firing a blunderbuss, and frightening a French nobleman till he made him tie on his portmanteau, that he would be loth to say Smollett had told two lies in one page; but he had found the only town in France where these things could have happened. Travellers must often be mistaken. In every thing, except where mensuration can be applied, they may honestly differ. There has been, of late, a strange turn in travellers to be displeased."

E. "From the experience which I have had,—and I have had a great deal,—I have learnt to think *better* of mankind." JOHNSON. "From my experience I have found them worse in commercial dealings, more disposed to cheat, than I had any notion of; but more disposed to do one another good than I had conceived." J. "Less just and more beneficent." JOHNSON. "And, really, it is wonderful,—considering how much attention is necessary for men to take care of themselves, and ward off immediate evils which press upon them,—it is wonderful how much they do for others. As it is said of the greatest liar, that he tells more truth than falsehood; so it may be said of the worst man, that he does more good than evil." BOSWELL. "Perhaps from experience men may be found *happier* than we suppose." JOHNSON. "No, sir; the more we inquire, we shall find men the less happy." P. "As to thinking better or worse of mankind from experience, some cunning people will not be satisfied unless they have put men to the test, as they think. There is a very good story told of Sir Godfrey Kneller, in

ALARMING A WHOLE TOWN IN FRANCE

his character of a justice of the peace. A gentleman brought his servant before him, upon an accusation of having stolen some money from him; but it having come out that he had laid it purposely in the servant's way, in order to try his honesty, Sir Godfrey sent the master to prison." JOHNSON. "To resist temptation once is not a sufficient proof of honesty. If a servant, indeed, were to resist the continued temptation of silver lying in a window, as some people let it lie, when he is sure his master does not know how much there is of it, he would give a strong proof of honesty. But this is a proof to which you have no right to put a man. You know, humanly speaking, there is a certain degree of temptation which will overcome any virtue. Now, in so far as you approach temptation to a man, you do him an injury; and, if he is overcome, you share his guilt." P. "And, when once overcome, it is easier for him to be got the better of again." BOSWELL. "Yes, you are his seducer; you have debauched him. I have known a man resolved to put friendship to the test, by asking a friend to lend him money, merely with that view, when he did not want it." JOHNSON. "That is very wrong, Sir. Your friend may be a narrow man, and yet have many good qualities; narrowness may be his only fault. Now you are trying his general character as a friend by one particular singly, in which he happens to be defective, when, in truth, his character is composed of many particulars."

E. "I understand the hogshead of claret, which this society was favoured with by our friend the Dean, is nearly out; I think he should be written to, to send another of the same kind. Let the request be made with a happy ambiguity of expression, so that we may have the chance of his sending it also as a present." JOHNSON. "I am willing to offer my services as secretary on this occasion." P. "As many as are for Dr. Johnson being secretary, hold up your hands.—Carried unanimously." BOSWELL. "He will be our dictator." JOHNSON. "No, the company is to dictate to me. I am only to write for wine; and I am quite disinterested, as I drink none; I shall not be suspected of having forged the application. I am no more than humble *scribe*." E. "Then you shall *pre*-scribe." BOSWELL. "Very well. The first play of words to-day." J. "No, no; the *bulls* in Ireland." JOHNSON. "Were I your dictator, you should have no wine. It would be my business *cavere ne quid detrimenti Respublica caperet*, and wine is dangerous. Rome was ruined by luxury" (smiling). E. "If you allow no wine as dictator, you shall not have me for your master of horse."

On Saturday, April 4, I drank tea with Johnson at Dr. Taylor's, where he had dined. He was very silent this evening, and read in a variety of books; suddenly throwing down one, and taking up another.

He talked of going to Streatham that night. TAYLOR. "You'll be robbed, if you do; or you must shoot a highwayman. Now, I would rather be robbed than do that; I would not shoot a highwayman." JOHNSON. "But I would rather shoot him in the instant when he is attempting to rob me, than afterwards swear against him at the Old Bailey, to take away his life, after he has robbed me. I am surer I am right in the one case, than in the other. I may be mistaken as to the man when I swear; I cannot be mistaken if I shoot him in the act. Besides, we feel less reluctance to take away a man's life, when we are heated by the injury, than to do it at a distance of time by an oath, after we have cooled." BOSWELL. "So, Sir, you would rather act from the motive of private passion, than that of public advantage." JOHNSON. "Nay, Sir, when I shoot the highwayman, I act from both." BOSWELL. "Very well, very well. There is no catching him." JOHNSON. "At the same time, one does not know what to say. For perhaps one may, a year after, hang himself from uneasiness for having shot a highwayman. Few minds are fit to be trusted with so great a thing." BOSWELL. "Then, Sir, you would not shoot him?" JOHNSON. "But I might be vexed afterwards for that too."

On Tuesday, April 7, I breakfasted with him at his house. He said, "Nobody was content." I mentioned to him a respectable person in Scotland whom he knew; and I asserted, that I really believed he was always content. "He seems to amuse himself quite well; to have his attention fixed, and his tranquillity preserved, by very small matters. I have tried this; but it would not do with me." JOHNSON (laughing). "No, Sir; it must be born with a man to be contented to take up with little things. Women have a great advantage, that they may take up with little things without disgracing themselves; a man cannot, except with fiddling. Had I learnt to fiddle, I should have done nothing else." BOSWELL. "Pray, Sir, did you ever play on any musical instrument?" JOHNSON. "No, Sir. I once bought me a flageolet; but I never made out a tune." BOSWELL. "A flageolet, Sir!—so small an instrument? I should have liked to hear you play on the violoncello. *That* should have been *your* instrument." JOHNSON. "Sir, I might as well have played on the violoncello as another; but I should have done nothing else. No, Sir; a man would never undertake great things, could he be amused with small. I once tried knitting. Dempster's sister undertook to teach me; but I could not learn it." BOSWELL. "So, Sir; it will be related in pompous narrative, 'Once for his amusement he tried knitting; nor did this Hercules disdain the distaff.'" JOHNSON. "Knitting of stockings is a good amusement. As a freeman of Aberdeen, I should be a knitter of stockings."

He asked me to go down with him and dine at Mr. Thrale's, to which I agreed. He talked to me with serious concern of a certain female friend's "laxity of narration, and inattention to truth." "I am as much vexed," said he, "at the ease with which she hears it mentioned to her, as at the thing itself. I told her, 'Madam, you are contented to hear every day said to you, what the highest of mankind have died for, rather than bear.'— You know, Sir, the highest of mankind have died rather than bear to be told they had uttered a falsehood. Do talk to her of it; I am weary."

BOSWELL. "Was not Dr. John Campbell a very inaccurate man in his narrative, Sir? He once told me that he drank thirteen bottles of port at a sitting." JOHNSON. "Why, Sir, I do not know that Campbell ever lied with pen and ink." Talking of drinking wine, he said, "I did not leave off wine because I could not bear it; I have drunk three bottles of port without being the worse for it. University College has witnessed this." BOSWELL. "Why, then, Sir, did you leave it off?" JOHNSON. "Why, Sir, because it is so much better for a man to be sure that he is never to be intoxicated, never to lose the power over himself. I shall not begin to drink wine again till I grow old, and want it." BOSWELL. "I think, Sir, you once said to me, that not to drink wine was a great deduction from life." JOHNSON. "It is a diminution of pleasure, to be sure; but I do not say a diminution of happiness. There is more happiness in being rational." BOSWELL. "But if we could have pleasure always, should not we be happy? The greatest part of men would compound for pleasure." JOHNSON. "Supposing we could have pleasure always, an intellectual man would not compound for it. The greatest part of men would compound, because the greatest part of men are gross." BOSWELL. "I allow there may be greater pleasure than from wine. I have had more pleasure from your conversation. I have, indeed; I assure you I have." JOHNSON. "When we talk of pleasure, we mean sensual pleasure. When a man says he had pleasure with a woman, he does not mean conversation, but something of a different nature. Philosophers tell you, that pleasure is *contrary* to happiness. Gross men prefer animal pleasure. So there are men who have preferred living among savages. Now, what a wretch must he be, who is content with such conversation as can be had among savages!"

I mentioned to him that I had become very weary in company where I heard not a single intellectual sentence, except that "a man who had been settled ten years in Minorca was become a much inferior man to what he was in London, because a man's mind grows narrow in a narrow place." JOHNSON. "A man's mind grows narrow in a narrow place, whose mind is enlarged only because he has lived in a large place; but what is got by books and thinking is preserved in a narrow place as well as in a large place. A man cannot know modes of life as well in Minorca as in London; but he may study mathematics as well in Minorca." BOSWELL. "I don't know, Sir; if you had remained ten years in the Isle of Col, you would not have been the man that you now are." JOHNSON. "Yes, Sir, if I had been there from fifteen to twenty-five; but not if from twenty-five to thirty-five." BOSWELL. "I own, Sir, the spirits which I have in London make me do every thing with more readiness and vigour. I can talk twice as much in London as any where else."

Soon after our arrival at Thrale's, I heard one of the maids calling eagerly on another to go to Dr. Johnson. I wondered what this could mean. I afterwards learnt, that it was to give her a Bible, which he had brought from London as a present to her.

He was for a considerable time occupied in reading "Mémoires de Fontenelle," leaning and swinging upon the low gate into the court, without his hat.

At dinner Mrs. Thrale expressed a wish to go and see Scotland. JOHNSON. "Seeing Scotland, Madam, is only seeing a worse England. It is seeing the flower gradually fade away to the naked stalk. Seeing the Hebrides, indeed, is seeing quite a different scene."

He and I returned to town in the evening. Next day, talking of a man's resolving to deny himself the use of wine, from moral and religious considerations, he said, "He must not doubt about it. When one doubts as to pleasure, we know what will be the conclusion. I now no more think of drinking wine than a horse does. The wine upon the table is no more for me, than for the dog who is under the table."

On Thursday, April 9, I dined with him at Sir Joshua Reynolds's, with the Bishop of St. Asaph, Mr. Allan Ramsay, Mr. Gibbon, Mr. Cambridge, and Mr. Langton. Goldsmith being mentioned, Johnson observed, that it was long before his merit came to be acknowledged: that he once complained to him in ludicrous terms of distress, "Whenever I write any thing, the public *make a point* to know nothing about it": but that his "Traveller" brought him into high reputation. LANGTON. "There is not one bad line in that poem; not one of Dryden's careless verses." SIR JOSHUA. "I was glad to hear Charles Fox say, it was one of the finest poems in the English language." LANGTON. "Why were you glad? You surely had no doubt of this before." JOHNSON. "No; the merit of 'The Traveller' is so well established, that Mr. Fox's praise cannot augment it, nor his censure diminish it." SIR JOSHUA. "But his friends may suspect they had too great a partiality for him." JOHNSON. "Nay, Sir, the partiality of his friends was always against him. It was with difficulty we could give him a hearing. Goldsmith had no settled notions upon any subject; so he talked always at random. It seemed to be his intention to blurt out whatever was in his mind, and see what would become of it. He was angry, too, when catched in an absurdity; but it did not prevent him from falling into another the next minute. Chamier once asked him, what he meant by *slow*, the last word in the first line of 'The Traveller,'—

Remote, unfriended, melancholy, slow.

Did he mean tardiness of locomotion? Goldsmith, who would say something without consideration, answered, 'Yes.' I was sitting by, and said, 'No, Sir, you do not mean tardiness of locomotion: you mean that sluggishness of mind which comes upon a man in solitude.' Chamier believed then that I had written the line, as much as if he had seen me write it. Goldsmith, however, was a man, who, whatever he wrote, did it better than any other man could do. He deserved a place in Westminster Abbey; and every year he lived would have deserved it better. He had, indeed, been at no pains to fill his mind with knowledge. He transplanted it from one place to another, and it did not settle in his mind; so he could not tell what was in his own books."

We talked of living in the country. JOHNSON. "No wise man will go to live in the country, unless he has something to do which can be better done in the country. For instance; if he is to shut himself up for a year to study a science, it is better to look out to the fields than to an opposite wall. Then if a man walks out in the country, there is nobody to keep him from walking in again; but if a man walks out in London, he is not sure when he shall walk in again. A great city is, to be sure, the school for studying life; and 'the proper study of mankind is man,' as Pope observes." Bos- well. "I fancy London is the best place for society; though I have heard that the very first society of Paris is still beyond any thing that we have here." Johnson. "Sir, I question if in Paris such a com- pany as is sitting round this table could be got together in less than half a year. They talk in France of the felicity of men and women living together; the truth is, that there the men are not higher than the women, they know no more than the women do, and they are not held down in their conversation by the presence of women." Ramsay. "Literature is upon the growth, it is in its spring in France: here it is rather *passée*." Johnson. "No, Sir, if literature be in its spring in France, it is a second spring; it is after a winter. We are now before the French in literature: but we had it long after them. In England, any man who wears a sword and a pow- dered wig is ashamed to be illiterate. I believe it is not so in France. Yet there is, probably, a great deal of learning in France, because they have such a number of religious establishments; so many men who have nothing else to do but to study. I do not know this; but I take it upon the common principles of chance. Where there are many shooters, some will hit."

We talked of old age. Johnson (now in his seventieth year) said, "It is a man's own fault, it is from want of use, if his mind grows torpid in old age." The bishop asked if an old man does not lose faster than he gets. Johnson. "I think not, my Lord, if he exerts himself." One of the company rashly observed, that he thought it was happy for an old man that insensibility comes upon him. Johnson (with a noble elevation and disdain). "No, Sir, I should never be happy by being less rational."

When we went to the drawing-room, there was a rich assem- blage. Besides the company who had been at dinner, there were Mr. Garrick, Mr. Harris of Salisbury, Dr. Percy, Dr. Burney, the Honourable Mrs. Cholmondeley, Miss Hannah More, &c.

After wandering about in a kind of pleasing distraction for some time, I got into a corner, with Johnson, Garrick, and Harris. I mentioned the vulgar saying, that Pope's Homer was not a good representation of the original. Johnson. "Sir, it is the greatest

A RICH ASSEMBLAGE

work of the kind that has ever been produced." GARRICK. "Of all the translations that ever were attempted, I think Elphinston's Martial the most extraordinary. He consulted me upon it, who am a little of an epigrammatist myself, you know. I told him freely, 'You don't seem to have that turn,' and advised him against publishing." JOHNSON. "Sir, you have done what I had not courage to do. But he did not ask my advice, and I did not force it upon him, to make him angry with me." GARRICK. "But as a friend, Sir——" JOHNSON. "Why, such a friend as I am with him—no." GARRICK. "But if you see a friend going to tumble over a precipice?" JOHNSON. "That is an extravagant case, Sir. You are sure a friend will thank you for hindering him from tumbling over a precipice: but, in the other case, I should hurt his vanity, and do him no good. He would not take my advice." BOSWELL. "It is easy for you, Mr. Garrick, to talk to an author as you talked to Elphinston; you, who have been so long the manager of a theatre, rejecting the plays of poor authors. You are an old judge, who have often pronounced sentence of death. You are a practised surgeon, who have often amputated limbs; and though this may have been for the good of your patients, they cannot like you. Those who have undergone a dreadful operation are not very fond of seeing the operator again." GARRICK. "Yes, I know enough of that. There was a reverend gentleman who wrote a tragedy, the SIEGE of something, which I refused." HARRIS. "So the siege was raised." JOHNSON. "Ay, he came to me and complained; and told me, that Garrick said his play was wrong in the *concoction*. Now, what is the concoction of a play!" (Here Garrick started, and twisted himself, and seemed sorely vexed; for Johnson told me, he believed the story was true.) GARRICK. "I—I—I—said, *first* concoction." JOHNSON (smiling). "Well, he left out *first*. And Rich, he said, refused him *in false English;* he could show it under his hand." GARRICK. "He wrote to me in violent wrath, for having refused his play: 'Sir, this is growing a very serious and terrible affair. I am resolved to publish my play. I will appeal to the world; and how will your judgment appear?' I answered, 'Sir, notwithstanding all the seriousness and all the terrors I have no objection to your publishing your play: and, as you live at a great distance (Devonshire, I believe), if you will send it to me, I will convey it to the press.' I never heard more of it, ha! ha! ha!"

On Friday, April 10, I found Johnson at home in the morning. We resumed the conversation of yesterday. He put me in mind of some of it which had escaped my memory, and enabled me to record it more perfectly than I otherwise could have done. He was much pleased with my paying so great attention to his recommendation in 1763, the period when our acquaintance began, that I should keep a journal; and I could perceive he was secretly pleased to find so much of the fruit of his mind preserved; and as he had been used to imagine and say, that he always laboured when he said a good thing,—it delighted him, on a review, to find that his conversation teemed with point and imagery.

I said to him, "You were, yesterday, Sir, in remarkably good humour; but there was nothing to offend you, nothing to produce irritation or violence. There was no bold offender. There was not one capital conviction. It was a maiden assize. You had on your white gloves."

He found fault with our friend Langton for having been too silent. "Sir," said I, "you will recollect that he very properly took up Sir Joshua for being glad that Charles Fox had praised Goldsmith's 'Traveller,' and you joined him." JOHNSON. "Yes, Sir, I knocked Fox on the head, without ceremony."

We dined together with Mr. Scott (now Sir William Scott, his majesty's advocate-general), at his chambers in the Temple, nobody else there. The company being small, Johnson was not in such spirits as he had been the preceding day, and for a considerable time little was said. At last he burst forth: "Subordination is sadly broken down in this age. No man, now, has the same authority which his father had—except a gaoler. No master has it over his servants: it is diminished in our colleges; nay, in our grammar-schools. My hope is, that as anarchy produces tyranny, this extreme relaxation will produce *freni strictio*."

Talking of fame, for which there is so great a desire, I observed, how little there is of it in reality, compared with the other objects of human attention. I slily introduced Mr. Garrick's fame and his assuming the airs of a great man. JOHNSON. "Sir, it is wonderful how *little* Garrick assumes. No, Sir, Garrick *fortunam reverenter habet*. Consider, Sir; celebrated men, such as you have mentioned, have had their applause at a distance; but Garrick had it dashed in his face, sounded in his ears, and went home every night with the plaudits of a thousand in his *cranium*. Then, Sir, Garrick did not *find*, but *made* his way to the tables, the levees, and almost the bed-chambers of the great. Then, Sir, Garrick had under him a numerous body of people; who from fear of his power, and hopes of his favour, and admiration of his talents, were constantly submissive to him. And here is a man who has advanced the dignity of his profession. Garrick has made a player a higher character." SCOTT. "And he is a very sprightly writer too." JOHNSON. "Yes, Sir; and all this supported by great wealth of his own acquisition. If all this had happened to me, I should have had a couple of fellows with long poles walking before me, to knock down every body that stood in the way. Consider, if all this had happened to Cibber or Quin, they'd have jumped over the moon. Yet Garrick speaks to *us*" (smiling). BOSWELL. "And Garrick is a very good man, a charitable man." JOHNSON. "Sir, a liberal man. He has given away more money than any man in England. There may be a little vanity mixed: but he has shown that money is not his first object." BOSWELL. "Yet Foote used to say of him, that he walked out with an intention to do a generous action; but, turning the corner of a street, he met with the ghost of a halfpenny, which frightened him." JOHNSON. "Why, Sir, that is very true too; for I never knew a man of whom it could be said with less certainty to-day, what he will do to-morrow, than Garrick; it depends so much on his humour at the time." SCOTT. "I am glad to hear of his liberality. He has been represented as very saving." JOHNSON. "With his domestic saving we have nothing to do. I remember drinking tea with him long ago, when Peg Woffington made it, and he grumbled at her for making it too strong. He had then begun to feel money in his purse, and did not know when he should have enough of it."

We talked of war. JOHNSON. "Every man thinks meanly of himself for not having been a soldier, or not having been at sea. Were Socrates and Charles the Twelfth of Sweden both present in any company, and Socrates to say, 'Follow me and hear a lecture in philosophy'; and Charles, laying his hand on his sword, to say, 'Follow me, and dethrone the Czar,' a man would be ashamed to follow Socrates. Sir, the impression is universal; yet it is strange. As to the sailor, when you look down from the quarter-deck to the space below, you see the utmost extremity of human misery; such crowding, such filth, such stench!" BOSWELL. "Yet sailors are happy." JOHNSON. "They are happy as brutes are happy, with a piece of fresh meat—with the grossest sensuality. But, Sir, the profession of soldiers and sailors has the dignity of danger. Mankind reverence those who have got over fear, which is so general a weakness." SCOTT. "But is not courage mechanical, and to be acquired?" JOHNSON. "Why yes, Sir, in a collective sense. Soldiers consider themselves only as part of a great machine." SCOTT. "We find people fond of being sailors." JOHNSON. "I cannot account for that, any more than I can account for other strange perversions of imagination." His abhorrence of the profession of a sailor was uniformly violent; but in conversation he always exalted the profession of a soldier. And yet I have, in my collection of his writings, a letter to an eminent friend, in which he expresses himself thus: "My godson called on me lately. He is weary, and rationally weary, of a military life. If you can place him in some other state, I think you may increase his happiness and secure his virtue. A soldier's time is passed in distress or danger, or in idleness and corruption." Such was his cool reflection in his study; but whenever he was warmed and animated by the presence of company, he caught the common enthusiasm for splendid renown.

He talked of Mr. Charles Fox, of whose abilities he thought highly, but observed, that he did not talk much at our Club. I have heard Mr. Gibbon remark, "that Mr. Fox could not be afraid of Dr. Johnson; yet he certainly was very shy of saying any thing in Dr. Johnson's presence."

He expressed great indignation at the imposture of the Cock-lane ghost, and related, with much satisfaction, how he had assisted in detecting the cheat, and had published an account of it in the newspapers. Upon this subject I incautiously offended him, by pressing him with too many questions, and he showed his displeasure. He sometimes could not bear being teased with questions. I was once present when a gentleman asked so many, as, "What did you do, Sir?" "What did you say, Sir?" that he at last grew enraged, and said, "I will not be put to the *question*. Don't you consider, Sir, that these are not the manners of a gentleman? I will not be baited with *what* and *why*; what is this? what is that? why is a cow's tail long? why is a fox's tail bushy?" The gentleman, who was a good deal out of countenance, said, "Why, Sir, you are so good, that I venture to trouble you." JOHNSON. "Sir, my being so good is no reason why you should be so *ill*."

He talked with an uncommon animation of travelling into distant countries; that the mind was enlarged by it, and that an acquisition of dignity of character was derived from it. He expressed a particular enthusiasm with respect to visiting the wall of China. I catched it for the moment, and said I really believed I should go and see the wall of China had I not children, of whom it was my duty to take care. "Sir," said he, "by doing so, you

would do what would be of importance in raising your children to
eminence. There would be a lustre reflected upon them from your
spirit and curiosity. They would be at all times regarded as the
children of a man who had gone to view the wall of China. I am
serious, Sir."

When we had left Mr. Scott's he said, "Will you go home with
me?" "Sir," said I, "it is late; but I'll go with you for three
minutes." JOHNSON. "Or *four*." We went to Mrs. Williams's
room. I this evening boasted, that although I did not write what
is called stenography, or short-hand, in appropriated characters
devised for the purpose, I had a method of my own of writing half-
words, and leaving out some altogether, so as yet to keep the substance and language of any discourse which I had heard so much in
view, that I could give it very completely soon after I had taken it
down. He defied me, as he had once defied an actual short-hand
writer; and he made the experiment by reading slowly and distinctly a part of Robertson's "History of America," while I
endeavoured to write it in my way of taking notes. It was found
that I had it very imperfectly.

On Sunday, April 12, he, and I, and Mrs. Williams went to dine
with the Reverend Dr. Percy. Books of travels having been
mentioned, Johnson praised Pennant very highly. Dr. Percy, the
heir male of the ancient Percies, and having the warmest and
most dutiful attachment to the noble house of Northumberland,
could not sit quietly and hear a man praised, who had spoken
disrespectfully of Alnwick Castle and the duke's pleasure-grounds,
especially as he thought meanly of his travels. He therefore
opposed Johnson eagerly. JOHNSON. "Pennant, in what he has
said of Alnwick, has done what he intended; he has made you very
angry." PERCY. "He has said the garden is trim, which is representing it like a citizen's parterre, when the truth is, there is a very
large extent of fine turf and gravel walks." JOHNSON. "According
to your own account, Sir, Pennant is right. It *is* trim. Here is
grass cut close, and gravel rolled smooth. Is not that trim? The
extent is nothing against that; a mile may be as trim as a square
yard. Your extent puts me in mind of the citizen's enlarged dinner,
two pieces of roast beef and two puddings. There is no variety,
no mind exerted in laying out the ground, no trees." PERCY. "He
pretends to give the natural history of Northumberland, and yet
takes no notice of the immense number of trees planted there of
late." JOHNSON. "That, Sir, has nothing to do with the *natural*

history; that is *civil* history. A man who gives the natural history of the oak, is not to tell how many oaks have been planted in this place or that. A man who gives the natural history of the cow, is not to tell how many cows are milked at Islington. The animal is the same whether milked in the Park or at Islington." PERCY. "Pennant does not describe well; a carrier who goes along the side of Lochlomond would describe it better." JOHNSON. "I think he describes very well." PERCY. "I travelled after him." JOHNSON. "And *I* travelled after him." PERCY. "But, my good friend, you are short-sighted, and do not see so well as I do." I wondered at Dr. Percy's venturing thus. Dr. Johnson said nothing at the time; but inflammable particles were collecting for a cloud to burst. In a little while Dr. Percy said something more in disparagement of Pennant. JOHNSON (pointedly). "This is the resentment of a narrow mind, because he did not find every thing in Northumber-land." PERCY (feeling the stroke). "Sir, you may be as rude as you please." JOHNSON. "Hold, Sir! Don't talk of rudeness: remember, Sir, you told me," puffing hard with passion struggling for a vent, "I was short-sighted. We have done with civility. We are to be as rude as we please." PERCY. "Upon my honor, Sir, I did not mean to be uncivil." JOHNSON. "I cannot say so, Sir; for I *did* mean to be uncivil, thinking *you* had been uncivil." Dr. Percy rose, ran up to him, and taking him by the hand, assured him affectionately that his meaning had been misunderstood; upon which a reconciliation instantly took place. JOHNSON. "My dear Sir, I am willing you shall *hang* Pennant."

We had a calm after the storm, staid the evening, and supped, and were pleasant and gay. But Dr. Percy told me he was very uneasy at what had passed, for there was a gentleman there who was acquainted with the Northumberland family, to whom he hoped to have appeared more respectable, by showing how intimate he was with Dr. Johnson, and who might now, on the contrary, go away with an opinion to his disadvantage. He begged I would mention this to Dr. Johnson, which I afterwards did. His observa-tion upon it was, "This comes of *stratagem;* had he told me that he wished to appear to advantage before that gentleman, he should have been at the top of the house all the time." He spoke of Dr. Percy in the handsomest manner. "Then, Sir," said I, "may I be allowed to suggest a mode by which you may effectually counter-act any unfavourable report of what passed? I will write a letter to you upon the subject of the unlucky contest of that day, and you will be kind enough to put in writing, as an answer to that letter, what you have now said, and as Lord Percy is to dine with us at General Paoli's soon, I will take an opportunity to read the correspondence in his lordship's presence." This friendly scheme was accordingly carried into execution without Dr. Percy's knowledge. Johnson's letter placed Dr. Percy's unquestionable merit in the fairest point of view; and I contrived that Lord Percy should hear the correspondence, by introducing it at General Paoli's as an instance of Dr. Johnson's kind disposition towards one in whom his lordship was interested. Thus every unfavourable impression was obviated that could possibly have been made on those by whom he wished most to be regarded. I breakfasted the day after with him, and informed him of my scheme, and its happy completion, for which he thanked me in the warmest terms, and was highly delighted with Dr. Johnson's letter in his praise, of which I gave him a copy. He said, "I would rather have this than degrees from all the universities in Europe. It will be for me, and my children, and grandchildren." Dr. Johnson having afterwards asked me if I had given him a copy of it, and being told I had, was offended, and insisted that I should get it back, which I did.

On Monday, April 13, I dined with Johnson at Mr. Langton's. He was at first in a very silent mood. Before dinner he said nothing but "Pretty baby," to one of the children. Langton said very well to me afterwards, that he could repeat Dr. Johnson's conversation before dinner, as Johnson had said that he could repeat a complete chapter of "The Natural History of Iceland," from the Danish of *Horrebow*, the whole of which was exactly thus:

Chap. LXXII.—*Concerning Snakes.*

There are no snakes to be met with throughout the whole island.

On Wednesday, April 15, I dined with Dr. Johnson at Mr. Dilly's, and was high in spirits, for I had been a good part of the morning with Mr. Orme, the able and eloquent historian of Hindostan, who expressed a great admiration of Johnson. "I do not care," said he, "on what subject Johnson talks; but I love better to hear him talk than any body. He either gives you new thoughts, or a new colouring. It is a shame to the nation that he has not been more liberally rewarded. Had I been George the Third, and thought as he did about America, I would have given Johnson three hundred a year for his 'Taxation no Tyranny,' alone." I repeated this, and Johnson was much pleased.

At Mr. Dilly's to-day were Mrs. Knowles, the ingenious quaker lady, Miss Seward, the poetess of Lichfield, the Reverend Dr. Mayo, and the Rev. Mr. Beresford, tutor to the Duke of Bedford. Before dinner Dr. Johnson seized upon Mr. Charles Sheridan's "Account of the late Revolution in Sweden," and seemed to read it ravenously, as if he devoured it, which was to all appearance his method of studying. "He knows how to read better than any one," says Mrs. Knowles; "he gets at the substance of a book directly; he tears out the heart of it." He kept it wrapped up in the table-cloth in his lap during the time of dinner, from an avidity to have one entertainment in readiness, when he should have finished another; resembling (if I may use so coarse a simile) a dog who holds a bone in his paws in reserve, while he eats something else which has been thrown to him.

The subject of cookery having been very naturally introduced at a table where Johnson, who boasted of the niceness of his palate, owned that "he always found a good dinner," he said, "I could write a better book of cookery than has ever yet been written; it should be a book upon philosophical principles. Pharmacy is now made much more simple. Cookery may be made so too. A prescription which is now compounded of five ingredients, had formerly fifty in it. So in cookery, if the nature of the ingredients be well known, much fewer will do. Then, as you cannot make bad meat good, I would tell what is the best butcher's meat, the best beef, the best pieces; how to choose young fowls; the proper seasons of different vegetables; and then how to roast and boil and compound. But you shall see what a book of cookery I shall make: I shall agree with Mr. Dilly for the copyright." Miss SEWARD. "That would be Hercules with the distaff indeed." JOHNSON. "No, Madam. Women can spin very well; but they cannot make a good book of cookery."

Mrs. Knowles affected to complain that men had much more liberty allowed them than women. JOHNSON. "Why, Madam, women have all the liberty they should wish to have. We have all the labour and the danger, and the women all the advantage. We go to sea, we build houses, we do everything, in short, to pay our court to the women." MRS. KNOWLES. "The Doctor reasons very wittily, but not very convincingly. Now, take the instance of building: the mason's wife, if she is ever seen in liquor, is ruined:

the mason may get himself drunk as often as he pleases, with little loss of character; nay, may let his wife and children starve." JOHNSON. "Madam, you must consider, if the mason does get himself drunk, and let his wife and children starve, the parish will oblige him to find security for their maintenance. We have different modes of restraining evil. Stocks for the men, a ducking-stool for women, and a pound for beasts. If we require more perfection from women than from ourselves, it is doing them honour. And women have not the same temptations that we have; they may always live in virtuous company; men must mix in the world indiscriminately. If a woman has no inclination to do what is wrong, being secured from it is no restraint to her. I am at liberty to walk into the Thames; but if I were to try it, my friends would restrain me in Bedlam, and I should be obliged to them." MRS. KNOWLES. "Still, Doctor, I cannot help thinking it a hardship that more indulgence is allowed to men than to women. It gives a superiority to men, to which I do not see how they are entitled." JOHNSON. "It is plain, Madam, one or other must have the superiority. As Shakspeare says, 'If two men ride on a horse, one must ride behind.'" DILLY. "I suppose, Sir, Mrs. Knowles would have them ride in panniers, one on each side." JOHNSON. "Then, Sir, the horse would throw them both." MRS. KNOWLES. "Well, I hope that in another world the sexes will be equal." BOSWELL. "That is being too ambitious, Madam. *We* might as well desire to be equal with the angels. We shall all, I hope, be happy in a future state, but we must not expect to be all happy in the same degree. It is enough, if we be happy according to our several capacities. A worthy carman will get to heaven as well as Sir Isaac Newton. Yet, though equally good, they will not have the same degrees of happiness." JOHNSON. "Probably not."

Dr. Mayo having asked Johnson's opinion of Soame Jenyns's "View of the Internal Evidence of the Christian Religion,"— JOHNSON. "I think it a pretty book; not very theological, indeed; and there seems to be an affectation of ease and carelessness, as if it were not suitable to his character to be very serious about the matter." BOSWELL. "*You* should like his book, Mrs. Knowles, as it maintains, as you *friends* do, that courage is not a Christian virtue." MRS. KNOWLES. "Yes, indeed, I like him there; but I cannot agree with him that friendship is not a Christian virtue." JOHNSON. "Why, Madam, strictly speaking, he is right. All friendship is preferring the interest of a friend to the neglect, or, perhaps, against the interest, of others; so that an old Greek said, 'He that has *friends* has no *friend.*' Now, Christianity recommends universal benevolence; to consider all men as our brethren; which is contrary to the virtue of friendship, as described by the ancient philosophers. Surely, Madam, your sect must approve of this; for you call all men *friends*." MRS. KNOWLES. "We are commanded to do good to all men, 'but especially to them who are of the household of faith.' " JOHNSON. "Well, Madam; the household of faith is wide enough." MRS. KNOWLES. "But, Doctor, our Saviour had twelve apostles, yet there was *one* whom he *loved*. John was called 'the disciple whom Jesus loved.' " JOHNSON (with eyes sparkling benignantly). "Very well indeed, Madam. You have said very well." BOSWELL. "A fine application. Pray, Sir, had you ever thought of it?" JOHNSON. "I had not, Sir."

From this pleasing subject he, I know not how or why, made a sudden transition to one upon which he was a violent aggressor; for he said, "I am willing to love all mankind, *except an American*"; and his inflammable corruption bursting into horrid fire, he "breathed out threatenings and slaughter"; calling them "rascals, robbers, pirates," and exclaiming, he'd "burn and destroy them." Miss Seward, looking to him with mild but steady astonishment, said, "Sir, this is an instance that we are always most violent against those whom we have injured." He was irritated still more by this delicate and keen reproach; and roared out another tremendous volley, which one might fancy could be heard across the Atlantic. During this tempest I sat in great uneasiness, lamenting his heat of temper, till, by degrees, I diverted his attention to other topics.

Talking of Miss [Hannah More], a literary lady, he said, "I was obliged to speak to Miss Reynolds, to let her know that I desired she would not flatter me so much." Somebody now observed, "She flatters Garrick." JOHNSON. "She is in the right to flatter Garrick. She is in the right for two reasons; first, because she has the world with her, who have been praising Garrick these thirty years; and, secondly, because she is rewarded for it by Garrick. Why should she flatter *me?* I can do nothing for her. Let her carry her praise to a better market." Then, turning to Mrs. Knowles, "You, Madam, have been flattering me all the evening; I wish you would give Boswell a little now. If you knew his merit as well as I do, you would say a great deal: he is the best travelling companion in the world."

I expressed a horror at the thought of death. MRS. KNOWLES. "Nay, thou shouldst not have a horror for what is the gate of life." JOHNSON (standing upon the hearth, rolling about, with a serious, solemn, and somewhat gloomy air). "No rational man can die without uneasy apprehension." MRS. KNOWLES. "The Scriptures tell us, 'The righteous shall have *hope* in his death.'" JOHNSON. "Yes, Madam, that is, he shall not have despair. But, consider, his hope of salvation must be founded on the terms on which it is promised that the mediation of our Saviour shall be applied to us,— namely, obedience; and where obedience has failed, then, as suppletory to it, repentance. But what man can say that his obedience has been such as he would approve of in another, or even in himself, upon close examination, or that his repentance has not been such as to require being repented of? No man can be sure that his obedience and repentance will obtain salvation." MRS. KNOWLES. "But divine intimation of acceptance may be made to the soul." JOHNSON. "Madam, it may; but I should not think the better of a man who should tell me on his death-bed, he was sure of salvation. A man cannot be sure himself that he has divine intimation of acceptance: much less can he make others sure that he has it." BOSWELL. "Then, Sir, we must be contented to acknowledge that death is a terrible thing." JOHNSON. "Yes, Sir. I have made no approaches to a state which can look on it as not terrible." MRS. KNOWLES (seeming to enjoy a pleasing serenity in the persuasion of benignant divine light). "Does not St. Paul say, 'I have fought the good fight of faith, I have finished my course; henceforth is laid up for me a crown of life'"? JOHNSON. "Yes, Madam; but here was a man inspired, a man who had been converted by supernatural interposition." BOSWELL. "In prospect death is dreadful; but in fact we find that people die easy." JOHNSON. "Why, Sir, most people have not *thought* much of the matter, so cannot *say* much, and it is supposed they die easy. Few believe it certain they are then to die; and those who do set themselves to behave with resolution, as a man does who is going to be hanged;— he is not the less unwilling to be hanged." MISS SEWARD. "There is one mode of the fear of death, which is certainly absurd; and that is the dread of annihilation, which is only a pleasing sleep without a dream." JOHNSON. "It is neither pleasing nor sleep; it is nothing. Now, mere existence is so much better than nothing, that one would rather exist even in pain, than not exist." BOSWELL. "If annihilation be nothing, then existing in pain is not a comparative state, but is a positive evil, which I cannot think we should choose. I must be allowed to differ here." JOHNSON. "The lady confounds annihilation, which is nothing, with the apprehension of it, which is dreadful. It is in the apprehension of it that the horror of annihilation consists."

Mrs. Knowles mentioned, as a proselyte to Quakerism, a young lady, well known to Dr. Johnson, for whom he had shown much affection. Mrs. Knowles at the same time took an opportunity of letting him know "that the amiable young creature was sorry at finding that he was offended at her leaving the Church of England, and embracing a simpler faith"; and, in the gentlest and most persuasive manner, solicited his kind indulgence for what was sincerely a matter of conscience. JOHNSON (frowning very angrily). "Madam, she is an odious wench. She could not have any proper conviction that it was her duty to change her religion, which is the most important of all subjects, and should be studied with all care, and with all the helps we can get. She knew no more of the church which she left, and that which she embraced, than she did of the difference between the Copernican and Ptolemaic systems." MRS. KNOWLES. "She had the New Testament before her." JOHNSON. "Madam, she could not understand the New Testament, the most difficult book in the world, for which the study of a life is required." MRS. KNOWLES. "It is clear as to essentials." JOHNSON. "But not as to controversial points. The heathens were easily converted, because they had nothing to give up; but we ought not, without very strong conviction indeed, to desert the religion in which we have been educated." He then rose again into passion, and attacked the young proselyte in the severest terms of reproach, so that both the ladies seemed to be much shocked.

We remained together till it was pretty late. Notwithstanding occasional explosions of violence, we were all delighted upon the whole with Johnson. I compared him at this time to a warm West Indian climate, where you have a bright sun, quick vegetation, luxuriant foliage, luscious fruits; but where the same heat sometimes produces thunder, lightning, and earthquakes in a terrible degree.

April 17, being Good Friday, I waited on Johnson, as usual. I observed at breakfast, that although it was a part of his abstemious discipline, on this most solemn fast, to take no milk in his tea, yet when Mrs. Desmoulins inadvertently poured it in, he did not reject it.

I expressed some inclination to publish an account of my travels upon the continent of Europe, for which I had a variety of materials collected. JOHNSON. "I do not say, Sir, you may not publish your travels; but I give you my opinion, that you would lessen yourself by it. What can you tell of countries so well known as those upon the continent of Europe, which you have visited?" BOSWELL. "But I can give an entertaining narrative, with many incidents, anecdotes, *jeux d'esprit*, and remarks, so as to make very pleasant reading." JOHNSON. "Why, Sir, most modern travellers in Europe who have published their travels have been laughed at: I would not have you added to the number. Now some of my friends asked me, why I did not give some account of my travels in France. The reason is plain: intelligent readers had seen more of France than I had. *You* might have liked my travels in France, and THE CLUB might have liked them; but, upon the whole, there would have been more ridicule than good produced by them." BOSWELL. "I cannot agree with you, Sir. People would like to read what you say of any thing. Suppose a face has been painted by fifty painters before; still we love to see it done by Sir Joshua." JOHNSON. "True, Sir; but Sir Joshua cannot paint a face when he has not time to look on it." BOSWELL. "Sir, a sketch of any sort by him is valuable. And, Sir, to talk to you in your own style, (raising my voice and shaking my head), you *should* have given us your travels in France. I am *sure* I am right, and *there's an end on't.*"

I said to him that a great part of what was in his "Journey to the Western Islands of Scotland" had been in his mind before he left London. JOHNSON. "Why, yes, Sir, the topics were; and books of travels will be good in proportion to what a man has previously in his mind; his knowing what to observe; his power of contrasting one mode of life with another. As the Spanish proverb says, 'He who would bring home the wealth of the Indies must carry the wealth of the Indies with him.' So it is in travelling; a man must carry knowledge with him, if he would bring home knowledge."

It was a delightful day: as we walked to St. Clement's church, I again remarked that Fleet Street was the most cheerful scene in the world. "Fleet Street," said I, "is in my mind more delightful than Tempé." JOHNSON. "Ay, Sir, but let it be compared with Mull!"

And now I am to give a pretty full account of one of the most curious incidents in Johnson's life, of which he himself has made the following minute on this day:

In my return from church, I was accosted by Edwards, an old fellow-collegian, who had not seen me since 1729. He knew me, and asked if I remembered one Edwards; I did not at first recollect the name, but gradually, as we walked along, recovered it, and told him a conversation that had passed at an alehouse between us. My purpose is to continue our acquaintance.

It was in Butcher-row that this meeting happened. Mr. Edwards, who was a decent-looking, elderly man, in gray clothes, and a wig of many curls, accosted Johnson with familiar confidence, knowing who he was, while Johnson returned his salutation with a courteous formality, as to a stranger. But as soon as Edwards had brought to his recollection their having been at Pembroke College together nine-and-forty years ago, he seemed much pleased, asked where he lived, and said he should be glad to see him in Bolt Court. EDWARDS. "Ah, Sir! we are old men now." JOHNSON (who never liked to think of being old). "Don't let us discourage one another." EDWARDS. "Why, doctor, you look stout and hearty. I am happy to see you so; for the newspapers told us you were very ill." JOHNSON. "Ay, Sir, they are always telling lies of *us old fellows*."

Wishing to be present at more of so singular a conversation as that between two fellow-collegians, who had lived forty years in London without ever having chanced to meet, I whispered to Mr. Edwards that Dr. Johnson was going home, and that he had better accompany him now. So Edwards walked along with us, I eagerly assisting to keep up the conversation. Mr. Edwards informed Dr. Johnson that he had practised long as a solicitor in Chancery, but that he now lived in the country upon a little farm, about sixty acres, just by Stevenage, in Hertfordshire, and that he came to London (to Barnard's Inn, No. 6) generally twice a week. Johnson appearing to be in a reverie, Mr. Edwards addressed himself to me, and expatiated on the pleasure of living in the country. BOSWELL. "I have no notion of this, Sir. What you have to entertain you is, I think, exhausted in half an hour." EDWARDS. "What! don't you love to have hope realised? I see my grass, and my corn, and my trees growing. Now, for instance, I am curious to see if this frost has not nipped my fruit trees." JOHNSON (who we did not imagine was attending). "You find, Sir, you have fears as well as hopes." So well did he see the whole when another saw but the half of a subject.

When we got to Dr. Johnson's house, and were seated in his library, the dialogue went on admirably. EDWARDS. "Sir, I re-

MR. EDWARDS . . . LIVED IN THE COUNTRY UPON A LITTLE FARM

member you would not let us say *prodigious* at college. For even then, Sir (turning to me), he was delicate in language, and we all feared him." JOHNSON (to Edwards). "From your having practised the law long, Sir, I presume you must be rich." EDWARDS. "No, Sir; I got a good deal of money; but I had a number of poor relations, to whom I gave a great part of it." JOHNSON. "Sir, you have been rich in the most valuable sense of the word." EDWARDS. "But I shall not die rich." JOHNSON. "Nay, sure, Sir, it is better to *live* rich, than to *die* rich." EDWARDS. "I wish I had continued at college." JOHNSON. "Why do you wish that, Sir?" EDWARDS. "Because I think I should have had a much easier life than mine has been. I should have been a parson, and had a good living, and lived comfortably." JOHNSON. "Sir, the life of a parson, of a conscientious clergyman, is not easy. I have always considered a clergyman as the father of a larger family than he is able to maintain. I would rather have Chancery suits upon my hands than the cure of souls. No, Sir, I do not envy a clergyman's life as an easy life, nor do I envy the clergyman who makes it an easy life." Here taking himself up all of a sudden, he exclaimed, "O! Mr. Edwards, I'll convince you that I recollect you. Do you remember our drinking together at an alehouse near Pembroke Gate? At that time, you told me of the Eton boy, who, when verses on our Saviour's turning water into wine were prescribed as exercise, brought up a single line, which was highly admired:

'Joann. 2.
'Aquæ in vinum versæ.
'Vidit et erubuit lympha pudica Deum';

and I told you of another fine line in 'Camden's Remains'; an eulogy upon one of our kings, who was succeeded by his son, a prince of equal merit:

'Mira cano, Sol occubuit, nox nulla secuta est.'"

EDWARDS. "You are a philosopher, Dr. Johnson. I have tried too in my time to be a philosopher; but, I don't know how, cheerfulness was always breaking in." Mr. Burke, Sir Joshua Reynolds, Mr. Courtenay, Mr. Malone, and, indeed, all the eminent men to whom I have mentioned this, have thought it an exquisite trait of character.

EDWARDS. "I have been twice married, doctor. You, I suppose, have never known what it was to have a wife." JOHNSON. "Sir,

I have known what it was to have a wife, and (in a solemn, tender, faltering tone) I have known what it was to *lose a wife*. It had almost broke my heart."

EDWARDS. "How do you live, Sir? For my part, I must have my regular meals, and a glass of good wine. I find I require it." JOHNSON. "I now drink no wine, Sir. Early in life I drank wine; for many years I drank none. I then for some years drank a great deal." EDWARDS. "Some hogsheads, I warrant you." JOHNSON. "I then had a severe illness, and left it off, and I have never begun it again. I never felt any difference upon myself from eating one thing rather than another, nor from one kind of weather rather than another. There are people, I believe, who feel a difference; but I am not one of them. And as to regular meals, I have fasted from the Sunday's dinner to the Tuesday's dinner without any inconvenience. I believe it is best to eat just as one is hungry: but a man who is in business, or a man who has a family, must have stated meals. I am a straggler. I may leave this town and go to Grand Cairo, without being missed here, or observed there." EDWARDS. "Don't you eat supper, Sir?" JOHNSON. "No, Sir." EDWARDS. "For my part, now, I consider supper as a turnpike through which one must pass in order to go to bed."

JOHNSON. "You are a lawyer, Mr. Edwards. Lawyers know life practically. A bookish man should always have them to converse with. They have what he wants." EDWARDS. "I am grown old: I am sixty-five." JOHNSON. "I shall be sixty-eight next birth-day. Come, Sir, drink water, and put in for a hundred."

Mr. Edwards, when going away, again recurred to his consciousness of senility, and, looking full in Johnson's face, said to him, "You'll find in Dr. Young,

'O my coevals! remnants of yourselves.'"

Johnson did not relish this at all; but shook his head with impatience. Edwards walked off seemingly highly pleased with the honour of having been thus noticed by Dr. Johnson. When he was gone, I said to Johnson, I thought him but a weak man. JOHNSON. "Why yes, Sir. Here is a man who has passed through life without experience: yet I would rather have him with me than a more sensible man who will not talk readily. This man is always willing to say what he has to say."

Mr. Edwards had said to me aside, that Dr. Johnson should have been of a profession. I repeated the remark to Johnson, that I might have his own thoughts on the subject. JOHNSON. "Sir, it *would* have been better that I had been of a profession. I ought to have been a lawyer." BOSWELL. "I do not think, Sir, it would have been better, for we should not have had the English Dictionary. Suppose you had been lord chancellor; you would have delivered opinions with more extent of mind, and in a more ornamented manner, than perhaps any chancellor ever did, or ever will do. But, I believe, causes have been as judiciously decided as you could have done." JOHNSON. "Yes, Sir. Property has been as well settled."

Johnson had, undoubtedly, often speculated on the possibility of his super-eminent powers being rewarded in this great and liberal country by the highest honours of the state. Sir William Scott, upon the death of the late Lord Lichfield, said to Johnson, "What a pity it is, Sir, that you did not follow the profession of the law! You might have been lord chancellor of Great Britain, and attained to the dignity of the peerage; and now that the title of Lichfield, your native city, is extinct, you might have had it." Johnson, upon this seemed much agitated; and, in an angry tone, exclaimed, "Why will you vex me by suggesting this, when it is too late?"

But he did not repine at the prosperity of others. When Mr. Edmund Burke showed Johnson his fine house and lands near Beaconsfield, Johnson coolly said, *"Non equidem invideo; miror magis."*

Yet no man had a higher notion of the dignity of literature than Johnson, or was more determined in maintaining the respect which he justly considered as due to it. Once when he dined in a numerous company of booksellers, where the room, being small, the head of the table, at which he sat, was almost close to the fire, he persevered in suffering a great deal of inconvenience from the heat, rather than quit his place, and let one of them sit above him.

Goldsmith, in his diverting simplicity, complained one day, in a mixed company, of Lord Camden. "I met him," said he, "at Lord Clare's house in the country, and he took no more notice of me than if I had been an ordinary man." The company having laughed heartily, Johnson stood forth in defence of his friend. "Nay, gentlemen," said he, "Dr. Goldsmith is in the right. A nobleman ought to have made up to such a man as Goldsmith; and I think it is much against Lord Camden that he neglected him."

Having fallen into a very serious frame of mind, in which mutual expressions of kindness passed between us, such as would be thought too vain in me to repeat, I talked with regret of the sad inevitable certainty that one of us must survive the other. JOHNSON. "Yes, Sir, that is an affecting consideration. I remember Swift, in one of his letters to Pope, says, 'I intend to come over, that we may meet once more; and when we must part, it is what happens to all human beings.' "

On Saturday, 18th April, I drank tea with him. The gentleman who had dined with us at Dr. Percy's came in. Johnson attacked the Americans with intemperate vehemence of abuse. I said something in their favour; and added, that I was always sorry when he talked on that subject. This, it seems, exasperated him; though he said nothing at the time. The cloud was charged with sulphureous vapour, which was afterwards to burst in thunder. We talked of a gentleman [Mr. Langton], who was running out his fortune in London; and I said, "We must get him out of it. All his friends must quarrel with him, and that will soon drive him away." JOHNSON. "Nay, Sir, we'll send *you* to him. If your company does not drive a man out of his house, nothing will." This was a horrible shock, for which there was no visible cause. I afterwards asked him, why he had said so harsh a thing. JOHNSON. "Because, Sir, you made me angry about the Americans." BOSWELL. "But why did you not take your revenge directly?" JOHNSON (smiling). "Because, Sir, I had nothing ready. A man cannot strike till he has his weapons."

He showed me to-night his drawing-room, very genteelly fitted up, and said, "Mrs. Thrale sneered, when I talked of my having asked you and your lady to live at my house. I was obliged to tell her, that you would be in as respectable a situation in my house as in hers. Sir, the insolence of wealth will creep out." BOSWELL. "She has a little both of the insolence of wealth and the conceit of parts." JOHNSON. "The insolence of wealth is a wretched thing; but the conceit of parts has some foundation. To be sure, it should not be. But who is without it?" BOSWELL. "Yourself, Sir." JOHNSON. "Why, I play no tricks: I lay no traps." BOSWELL. "No, Sir. You are six feet high, and you only do not stoop."

We talked of the numbers of people that sometimes have composed the household of great families. I mentioned that there were a hundred in the family of the present Earl of Eglintoune's father. Dr. Johnson seeming to doubt it, I began to enumerate; "Let us see: my lord and my lady, two." JOHNSON. "Nay, Sir, if you are to count by twos, you may be long enough." BOSWELL. "Well, but now I add two sons and seven daughters, and a servant for each; that will make twenty; so we have the fifth part already." JOHNSON. "Very true. You get at twenty pretty readily; but you will not so easily get further on. We grow to five feet pretty readily; but it is not so easy to grow to seven."

On Sunday, 19th April, being Easter-day, after the solemnities of the festival in St. Paul's church, I visited him, but could not stay to dinner.

On Monday, 20th April, I found him at home in the morning. We talked of a gentleman [Mr. Langton] who we apprehended was gradually involving his circumstances by bad management. JOHNSON. "Wasting a fortune is evaporation by a thousand imperceptible means. If it were a stream, they'd stop it. You must speak to him. It is really miserable. Were he a gamester, it could be said he had hopes of winning. Were he a bankrupt in trade, he might have grown rich; but he has neither spirit to spend, nor resolution to spare. He does not spend fast enough to have pleasure from it. He has the crime of prodigality, and the wretchedness of parsimony. If a man is killed in a duel, he is killed as many a one has been killed; but it is a sad thing for a man to lie down and die; to bleed to death, because he has not fortitude enough to sear the wound, or even to stitch it up." [1]

On Saturday, 25th April, I dined with him at Sir Joshua Reynolds's, with the learned Dr. Musgrave; Counsellor Leland of Ireland; Mrs. Cholmondeley, and some more ladies. JOHNSON. "Demosthenes Taylor, as he was called (that is, the editor of Demosthenes), was the most silent man, the merest statue of a man, that I have ever seen. I once dined in company with him, and all he said during the whole time was no more than *Richard*. How a man should say only *Richard*, it is not easy to imagine. But it was thus: Dr. Douglas was talking of Dr. Zachary Grey, and ascribing to him something that was written by Dr. Richard Grey. So, to correct him, Taylor said (imitating his affected sententious emphasis and nod), '*Richard*.'"

We talked of a lady's verses on Ireland. MISS REYNOLDS. "Have you seen them, Sir?" JOHNSON. "No, Madam; I have seen a translation from Horace, by one of her daughters. She showed it

---

[1] Of Langton, Johnson said elsewhere: "It is a sad thing to pass through the quagmire of parsimony to the gulf of ruin. To pass over the flowery path of extravagance is very well."

me." MISS REYNOLDS. "And how was it, Sir?" JOHNSON. "Why, very well, for a young miss's verses; that is to say, compared with excellence, nothing; but very well, for the person who wrote them. I am vexed at being shown verses in that manner." MISS REYNOLDS. "But if they should be good, why not give them hearty praise?" JOHNSON. "Why, Madam, because I have not then got the better of my bad humour from having been shown them. You must consider, Madam, beforehand, they may be bad as well as good. Nobody has a right to put another under such a difficulty, that he must either hurt the person by telling the truth, or hurt himself by telling what is not true." BOSWELL. "A man often shows his writings to people of eminence, to obtain from them, either from their good-nature, or from their not being able to tell the truth firmly, a commendation, of which he may afterwards avail himself." JOHNSON. "Very true, Sir. Therefore, the man who is asked by an author, what he thinks of his work, is put to *the torture*, and is not obliged to speak the truth; so that what he says is not considered as his opinion; yet he has said it, and cannot retract it; and this author, when mankind are hunting him with a canister at his tail, can say, 'I would not have published, had not Johnson, or Reynolds, or Musgrave, or some other good judge, commended the work.' Yet I consider it as a very difficult question in conscience, whether one should advise a man not to publish a work, if profit be his object; for a man may say, 'Had it not been for you, I should have had the money.' Now you cannot be sure; for you have only your own opinion, and the public may think very differently." SIR JOSHUA REYNOLDS. "You must upon such an occasion have two judgments; one as to the real value of the work, the other as to what may please the general taste at the time." JOHNSON. "But you can be *sure* of neither; and therefore I should scruple much to give a suppressive vote." SIR JOSHUA REYNOLDS. "'The Beggar's Opera' affords a proof how strangely people will differ in opinion about a literary performance. Burke thinks it has no merit." JOHNSON. "It was refused by one of the houses; but I should have thought it would succeed, not from any great excellence in the writing, but from the novelty, and the general spirit and gaiety of the piece, which keeps the audience always attentive, and dismisses them in good humour."

It was observed, that avarice was inherent in some dispositions. JOHNSON. "No man was born a miser, because no man was born to possession. Every man is born *cupidus*—desirous of getting;

THIS CEREMONY WAS PERFORMED EVERY DAY

but not *avarus*—desirous of keeping." BOSWELL. "I have heard old Mr. Sheridan maintain, with much ingenuity, that a complete miser is a happy man: a miser who gives himself wholly to the one passion of saving." JOHNSON. "That is flying in the face of all the world, who have called an avaricious man a *miser*, because he is miserable. No, Sir; a man who both spends and saves money is the happiest man, because he has both enjoyments."

On Tuesday, April 28, he was engaged to dine at General Paoli's, where I was still entertained in elegant hospitality. I called on him, and accompanied him in a hackney-coach. We stopped first at the bottom of Hedge Lane, into which he went to leave a letter, "with good news for a poor man in distress," as he told me. I did not question him particularly as to this. He loved to keep things floating in conjecture. We stopped again at Wirgman's, the well-known *toy-shop* in St. James's Street, at the corner of St. James's Place, to which he had been directed, but not clearly, for he searched about some time, and could not find it at first; and said, "To direct one only to a corner shop is *toying* with one." I suppose he meant this as a play upon the word *toy:* it was the first time that I knew him stoop to such sport. After he had been some time in the shop, he sent for me to come out of the coach, and help him to choose a pair of silver buckles, as those he had were too small. Probably this alteration in dress had been suggested by Mrs. Thrale, by associating with whom, his external appearance was much improved. He got better clothes; and the dark colour, from which he never deviated, was enlivened by metal buttons. His wigs, too, were much better; and, during their travels in France, he was furnished with a Paris-made wig, of handsome construction.[1]

This choosing of silver buckles was a negotiation: "Sir," said he, "I will not have the ridiculous large ones now in fashion; and I will give no more than a guinea for a pair." Such were the *principles* of the business; and, after some examination, he was fitted. As we drove along, I found him in a talking humour, of which I availed myself. BOSWELL. "I drank chocolate, Sir, this morning with Mr. Eld; and, to my no small surprise, found him to be a *Staffordshire Whig*, a being which I did not believe had existed." JOHNSON. "Sir, there are rascals in all countries." BOSWELL. "Eld said, a *Tory* was a creature generated between a non-juring parson

---

[1] In general his wigs were very shabby, and their fore parts were burned away by the near approach of the candle, which his short-sightedness rendered necessary in reading. At Streatham, Mr. Thrale's butler always kept a better wig in his own hands, with which he met Johnson at the parlour-door, when the bell had called him down to dinner; this ceremony was performed every day.

and one's grandmother." JOHNSON. "And I have always said, the first *Whig* was the Devil."

At General Paoli's were Sir Joshua Reynolds, Mr. Langton, Marchese Gherardi of Lombardy, and Mr. John Spottiswoode the younger. At this time fears of an invasion were circulated; to obviate which Mr. Spottiswoode observed, that the French had the same fear of us. JOHNSON. "It is thus that mutual cowardice keeps us in peace. Were one half of mankind brave, and one half cowards, the brave would be always beating the cowards. Were all brave, they would lead a very uneasy life; all would be continually fighting: but being all cowards, we go on very well."

We talked of drinking wine. JOHNSON. "I require wine only when I am alone. I have then often wished for it, and often taken it." SPOTTISWOODE. "What, by way of a companion, Sir?" JOHNSON. "To get rid of myself, to send myself away. Wine gives great pleasure; and every pleasure is of itself a good. It is a good, unless counterbalanced by evil. A man may have a strong reason not to drink wine; and that may be greater than the pleasure. Wine makes a man better pleased with himself. I do not say that it makes him more pleasing to others. Sometimes it does. But the danger is, that while a man grows better pleased with himself, he may be growing less pleasing to others. Wine gives a man nothing. It neither gives him knowledge nor wit; it only animates a man, and enables him to bring out what a dread of the company has repressed. It only puts in motion what has been locked up in frost. But this may be good, or it may be bad." SPOTTISWOODE. "So, Sir, wine is a key which opens a box; but this box may be either full or empty?" JOHNSON. "Nay, Sir, conversation is the key: wine is a picklock, which forces open the box, and injures it. A man should cultivate his mind so as to have that confidence and readiness without wine, which wine gives." BOSWELL. "The great difficulty of resisting wine is from benevolence. For instance, a good worthy man asks you to taste his wine, which he has had twenty years in his cellar." JOHNSON. "Sir, all this notion about benevolence arises from a man's imagining himself to be of more importance to others than he really is. They don't care a farthing whether he drinks wine or not." SIR JOSHUA REYNOLDS. "Yes, they do for the time." JOHNSON. "For the time! If they care this minute, they forget it the next. And as for the good worthy man, how do you know he is good and worthy? No good and worthy man will insist upon another man's drinking wine. As to the wine twenty years in the cellar,—of ten men, three say this, merely because they must say something; three are telling a lie, when they say they have had the wine twenty years; three would rather save the wine; one, perhaps, cares."

I was at this time myself a water-drinker, upon trial, by Johnson's recommendation. JOHNSON. "Boswell is a bolder combatant than Sir Joshua: he argues for wine without the help of wine; but Sir Joshua with it." SIR JOSHUA REYNOLDS. "But to please one's company is a strong motive." JOHNSON (who, from drinking only water, supposed every body who drank wine to be elevated). "I won't argue any more with you, Sir. You are too far gone." SIR JOSHUA. "I should have thought so indeed, Sir, had I made such a speech as you have now done." JOHNSON (drawing himself in, and, I really thought, blushing). "Nay, don't be angry. I did not mean to offend you." SIR JOSHUA. "At first the taste of wine was disagreeable to me; but I brought myself to drink it, that I might be like other people. The pleasure of drinking wine is so connected with pleasing your company, that altogether there is something of social goodness in it." JOHNSON. "Sir, this is only saying the same thing over again." SIR JOSHUA. "No, this is new." JOHNSON. "You put it in new words, but it is an old thought. This is one of the disadvantages of wine, it makes a man mistake words for thoughts." BOSWELL. "I think it is a new thought; at least it is in a new *attitude*." JOHNSON. "Nay, Sir, it is only in a new coat; or an old coat with a new facing." Then, laughing heartily: "It is the old dog in a new doublet. An extraordinary instance, however, may occur, where a man's patron will do nothing for him, unless he will drink: *there* may be a good reason for drinking."

On Wednesday, April 29, I dined with him at Mr. Allan Ramsay's, where were Lord Binning, Dr. Robertson the historian, Sir Joshua Reynolds, and the Honourable Mrs. Boscawen, widow of the Admiral. Before Johnson came, we talked a good deal of him. Ramsay said, he had always found him a very polite man, and that he treated him with great respect, which he did very sincerely. I said, I worshipped him. ROBERTSON. "But some of you spoil him: you should not worship him; you should worship no man." BOSWELL. "I cannot help worshipping him, he is so much superior to other men." ROBERTSON. "In criticism, and in wit and conversation, he is, no doubt, very excellent; but in other respects he is not above other men: he will believe any thing, and will strenuously defend the most minute circumstance connected with the church of England." BOSWELL. "Believe me, Doctor, you are much mistaken as to this; for when you talk with him calmly in private, he is very liberal in his way of thinking." ROBERTSON. "He and I have been always very gracious: the first time I met him was one evening at Strahan's, when he had just had an unlucky altercation with Adam Smith, to whom he had been so rough, that Strahan, after Smith was gone, had remonstrated with him, and told him that I was coming soon, and that he was uneasy to think that he might behave in the same manner to me. 'No, no, Sir (said Johnson), I warrant you, Robertson and I shall do very well.' Accordingly he was gentle and good-humoured and courteous with me, the whole evening; and he has been so upon every occasion that we have met since. I have often said (laughing), that I have ʋeen in a great measure indebted to Smith for my good reception."

No sooner did he, of whom we had been thus talking so easily, arrive, than we were all as quiet as a school upon the entrance of the head-master; and we very soon sat down to a table covered with such a variety of good things, as contributed not a little to dispose him to be pleased.

RAMSAY. "I am old enough to have been a contemporary of Pope. His poetry was highly admired in his life-time, more a great deal than after his death." JOHNSON. "Sir, it has not been less admired since his death; no authors ever had so much fame in their own life-time as Pope and Voltaire; and Pope's poetry has been as much admired since his death as during his life: it has only not been as much talked of; but that is owing to its being now more distant, and people having other writings to talk of. Virgil is less talked of than Pope, and Homer is less talked of than Virgil; but they are not less admired. We must read what the world reads at the moment. It has been maintained that this superfœtation, this teeming of the press in modern times, is prejudicial to good literature, because it obliges us to read so much of what is of inferior value, in order to be in the fashion; so that better works are neglected for want of time, because a man will have more gratification of his vanity in conversation, from having read modern books, than from having read the best works of antiquity. But it must be considered, that we have now more knowledge generally diffused: all our ladies read now, which is a great extension. Modern writers are the moons of literature; they shine with reflected light, with light borrowed from the ancients. Greece appears to me to be the fountain of knowledge; Rome of elegance."

Dr. Robertson expatiated on the character of a certain nobleman [Lord Clive]; that he was one of the strongest-minded men that ever lived; that he would sit in company quite sluggish, while there was nothing to call forth his intellectual vigour; but the moment that any important subject was started, for instance, how this country is to be defended against a French invasion, he would rouse himself, and show his extraordinary talents, with the most powerful ability and animation. JOHNSON. "Yet this man cut his own throat. The true strong and sound mind is the mind that can embrace equally great things and small. Now, I am told the King of Prussia will say to a servant, 'Bring me a bottle of such a wine, which came in such a year; it lies in such a corner of the cellars.' I would have a man great in great things, and elegant in little things." He said to me afterwards, when we were by ourselves, "Robertson was in a mighty romantic humour; he talked of one whom he did not know; but I *downed* him with the King of Prussia." "Yes, Sir," said I, "you threw a *bottle* at his head."

Johnson harangued against drinking wine. "A man," said he, "may choose whether he will have abstemiousness and knowledge, or claret and ignorance." Dr. Robertson (who is very companionable) was beginning to dissent as to the proscription of claret. JOHNSON (with a placid smile). "Nay, Sir, you shall not differ with me; as I have said that the man is most perfect who takes in the most things, I am for knowledge and claret." ROBERTSON (holding a glass of generous claret in his hand). "Sir, I can only drink your health." JOHNSON. "Sir, I should be sorry if *you* should be ever in such a state as to be able to do nothing more." ROBERTSON. "Dr. Johnson, allow me to say, that in one respect I have the advantage of you: when you were in Scotland you would not come to hear any of our preachers; whereas, when I am here, I attend your public worship without scruple, and, indeed, with great satisfaction." JOHNSON. "Why, Sir, that is not so extraordinary: the King of Siam sent ambassadors to Louis the Fourteenth, but Louis the Fourteenth sent none to the King of Siam."

Here my friend for once discovered a want of knowledge or forgetfulness; for Louis the Fourteenth did send an embassy to the King of Siam, and the Abbé Choisi, who was employed in it, published an account of it in two volumes.

Next day, Thursday, April 30, I found him at home by himself.

JOHNSON. "Well, Sir, Ramsay gave us a splendid dinner. I love Ramsay. You will not find a man in whose conversation there is more instruction, more information, and more elegance, than in Ramsay's." BOSWELL. "What I admire in Ramsay, is his continuing to be so young." JOHNSON. "Why, yes, Sir, it is to be admired. I value myself upon this, that there is nothing of the old man in my conversation. I am now sixty-eight, and I have no more of it than at twenty-eight." BOSWELL. "But, Sir, would not you wish to know old age? He who is never an old man, does not know the whole of human life; for old age is one of the divisions of it." JOHNSON. "Nay, Sir, what talk is this?" BOSWELL. "I mean, Sir, the Sphinx's description of it:—morning, noon, and night. I would know night, as well as morning and noon." JOHNSON. "What, Sir, would you know what it is to feel the evils of old age? Would you have the gout? Would you have decrepitude?" Seeing him heated, I would not argue any farther; but I was confident that I was in the right. I would, in due time, be a Nestor, an elder of the people; and there *should* be some difference between the conversation of twenty-eight and sixty-eight. JOHNSON. "Mrs. Thrale's mother said of me what flattered me much. A clergyman was complaining of want of society in the country where he lived; and said, 'They talk of *runts* (that is, young cows).' 'Sir, (said Mrs. Salusbury), Mr. Johnson would learn to talk of runts'; meaning that I was a man who would make the most of my situation, whatever I was." He added, "I think myself a very polite man."

On Saturday, May 2, I dined with him at Sir Joshua Reynolds's, where there was a very large company, and a great deal of conversation. There were several people there by no means of the Johnsonian school; so that less attention was paid to him than usual, which put him out of humour: and upon some imaginary offence from me, he attacked me with such rudeness, that I was vexed and angry, because it gave those persons an opportunity of enlarging upon his supposed ferocity, and ill treatment of his best friends. I was so much hurt, and had my pride so much roused, that I kept away from him for a week; and, perhaps, might have kept away much longer, nay, gone to Scotland without seeing him again, had not we fortunately met and been reconciled. To such unhappy chances are human friendships liable.

On Friday, May 8, I dined with him at Mr. Langton's. I was reserved and silent, which I suppose he perceived, and might recollect the cause. After dinner, when Mr. Langton was called out

CAREFULLY SENT TO HER FROM THE TAVERN READY DREST

of the room, and we were by ourselves, he drew his chair near to mine, and said in a tone of conciliating courtesy, "Well, how have you done?" BOSWELL. "Sir, you have made me very uneasy by your behaviour to me when we were last at Sir Joshua Reynolds's. You know, my dear Sir, no man has a greater respect and affection for you, or would sooner go to the end of the world to serve you. Now, to treat me so—." He insisted that I had interrupted, which I assured him was not the case; and proceeded—"But why treat me so before people who neither love you nor me?" JOHNSON. "Well, I am sorry for it. I'll make it up to you twenty different ways, as you please." BOSWELL. "I said to-day to Sir Joshua, when he observed that you *tossed* me sometimes, I don't care how often or how high he tosses me, when only friends are present, for then I fall upon soft ground; but I do not like falling on stones, which is the case when enemies are present. I think this a pretty good image, Sir." JOHNSON. "Sir, it is one of the happiest I have ever heard. I shall be at home to-morrow." BOSWELL. "Then let us dine by ourselves at the Mitre, to keep up the old custom— 'custom of the manor,' custom of the Mitre." JOHNSON. "Sir, so it shall be."

On Saturday, May 9, we fulfilled our purpose of dining by ourselves at the Mitre, according to the old custom. There was, on these occasions, a little circumstance of kind attention to Mrs. Williams, which must not be omitted. Before coming out, and leaving her to dine alone, he gave her her choice of a chicken, a sweetbread, or any other little nice thing, which was carefully sent to her from the tavern ready drest.

Our conversation to-day, I know not how, turned, I think, for the only time at any length, during our long acquaintance, upon the sensual intercourse between the sexes, the delight of which he ascribed chiefly to imagination. "Were it not for imagination, Sir," said he, "a man would be as happy in the arms of a chambermaid as of a duchess. But such is the adventitious charm of fancy, that we find men who have violated the best principles of society, and ruined their fame and their fortune, that they might possess a woman of rank."

On Tuesday, May 12, I waited on the Earl of Marchmont, to know if his lordship would favour Dr. Johnson with information concerning Pope, whose Life he was about to write. Johnson had not flattered himself with the hopes of receiving any civility from this nobleman; for he said to me, when I mentioned Lord Marchmont as one who could tell him a great deal about Pope,—"Sir, he will tell *me* nothing." I had the honour of being known to his lordship, and applied to him of myself, without being commissioned by Johnson. His lordship behaved in the most polite and obliging manner, promised to tell all he recollected about Pope, and was so very courteous as to say, "Tell Dr. Johnson I have a great respect for him, and am ready to show it in any way I can. I am to be in the city to-morrow, and will call at his house as I return." His lordship however asked, "Will he write the 'Lives of the Poets' impartially? He was the first that brought Whig and Tory into a dictionary. And what do you think of the definition of Excise?" I proposed to Lord Marchmont, that he should revise Johnson's Life of Pope: "So," said his lordship, "you would put me in a dangerous situation. You know he knocked down Osborne, the bookseller."

Elated with the success of my spontaneous exertion to procure material and respectable aid to Johnson for his very favourite work, the "Lives of the Poets," I hastened down to Mr. Thrale's, at Streatham, where he now was, that I might insure his being at home next day; and after dinner, when I thought he would receive the good news in the best humour, I announced it eagerly: "I have been at work for you to-day, Sir. I have been with Lord March-mont. He bade me tell you he has a great respect for you, and will call on you to-morrow at one o'clock, and communicate all he knows about Pope." Here I paused, in full expectation that he would be pleased with this intelligence, would praise my active merit, and would be alert to embrace such an offer from a nobleman. But whether I had shown an over exultation, which provoked his spleen; or whether he was seized with a suspicion that I had ob-truded him on Lord Marchmont, and humbled him too much, or whether there was any thing more than an unlucky fit of ill humour, I know not; but to my surprise the result was,—JOHNSON. "I shall not be in town to-morrow. I don't care to know about Pope." MRS. THRALE (surprised, as I was, and a little angry). "I suppose, Sir, Mr. Boswell thought, that as you are to write Pope's Life, you would wish to know about him." JOHNSON. "Wish! why yes. If it rained knowledge, I'd hold out my hand; but I would not give myself the trouble to go in quest of it." There was no arguing with him at the moment. Mrs. Thrale was uneasy at this unaccountable caprice; and told me, that if I did not take care to bring about a meeting between Lord Marchmont and him, it would never take place, which would be a great pity.

I sent a card to his lordship, to be left at Johnson's house, acquainting him, that Dr. Johnson could not be in town next day, but would do himself the honour of waiting on him at another time. I give this account fairly, as a specimen of that unhappy temper with which this great and good man had occasionally to struggle, from something morbid in his constitution. It will be seen that in the following year he had a very agreeable interview with Lord Marchmont at his lordship's house.

After Mrs. Thrale was gone to bed, Johnson and I sat up late. We resumed Sir Joshua Reynolds's argument on the preceding Sunday, that a man would be virtuous, though he had no other motive than to preserve his character. JOHNSON. "Sir, it is not true; for, as to this world, vice does not hurt a man's character." BOSWELL. "Yes, Sir, debauching a friend's wife will." JOHNSON. "No, Sir. Who thinks the worse of [Beauclerk] for it?" BOSWELL. "Lord [Bolingbroke] was not his friend." JOHNSON. "That is only a circumstance, Sir, a slight distinction. He could not get into the house but by Lord [Bolingbroke]. A man is chosen knight of the shire not the less for having debauched ladies." BOSWELL. "What, Sir, if he debauched the ladies of gentlemen in the county, will not there be a general resentment against him?" JOHNSON. "No, Sir. He will lose those particular gentlemen; but the rest will not trouble their heads about it" (warmly). BOSWELL. "Well, Sir; I cannot think so." JOHNSON. "Nay, Sir, there is no talking with a man who will dispute what every body knows (angrily). Don't you know this?" BOSWELL. "No, Sir; and I wish to think better of your country than you represent it. I knew in Scotland a gentleman obliged to leave it for debauching a lady; and in one of our counties an earl's brother lost his election because he had debauched the lady of another earl in that county, and destroyed the peace of a noble family."

Still he would not yield. He proceeded: "Will you not allow, Sir, that vice does not hurt a man's character so as to obstruct his prosperity in life, when you know that [Lord Clive] was loaded with wealth and honours? a man who had acquired his fortune by such crimes, that his consciousness of them impelled him to cut his own throat." BOSWELL. "You will recollect, Sir, that Dr. Robertson said he cut his throat because he was weary of still life; little things not being sufficient to move his great mind." JOHNSON (very angry). "Nay, Sir, what stuff is this! You had no more this opinion after Robertson said it than before. I know nothing more offensive than repeating what one knows to be foolish things, by way of continuing a dispute, to see what a man will answer,—to make him your butt!" (angrier still). BOSWELL. "My dear Sir, I had no such intention as you seem to suspect; I had not indeed. Might not this nobleman have felt everything 'weary, stale, flat, and unprofitable,' as Hamlet says?" JOHNSON. "Nay, if you are to bring in *gabble*, I'll talk no more. I will not, upon my honour." My readers will decide upon this dispute.

Next morning [13th May] I staid all day with him at Streatham. He talked a great deal in very good humour.

He censured Lord Kames's "Sketches of the History of Man." He added, "In this book it is maintained that virtue is natural to man, and that if we would but consult our own hearts we should be virtuous. Now after consulting our own hearts all we can, and with all the helps we have, we find how few of us are virtuous. This is saying a thing which all mankind knows not to be true." BOSWELL. "Is not modesty natural?" JOHNSON. "I cannot say, Sir, as we find no people quite in a state of nature; but, I think, the more they are taught, the more modest they are. The French are a gross, ill-bred, untaught people; a lady there will spit on the floor and rub it with her foot. What I gained by being in France was, learning to be better satisfied with my own country. Time may be employed to more advantage from nineteen to twenty-four, almost in any way than in travelling. When you set travelling against mere negation, against doing nothing, it is better to be sure; but how much more would a young man improve were he to study during those years! Indeed, if a young man is wild, and must run after women and bad company, it is better this should be done abroad, as, on his return, he can break off such connections, and begin at home a new man, with a character to form, and acquaint-ance to make."

On Saturday, May 16, I dined with him at Mr. Beauclerk's. The disaster of General Burgoyne's army [1] was then the common topic of conversation. It was asked why piling their arms was insisted upon as a matter of such consequence, when it seemed to be a circumstance so inconsiderable in itself. JOHNSON. "Why, Sir, a French author says, '*Il y a beaucoup de puérilités dans la guerre.*'"

On Tuesday, May 19, I was to set out for Scotland in the evening. I waited upon him; he gave me some salutary counsel, and recom-mended vigorous resolution against any deviation from moral duty.

[1] Its surrender at Saratoga, October, 1777.

BOSWELL. "But you would not have me to bind myself by a solemn obligation?" JOHNSON (much agitated). "What! a vow!—O, no, Sir; a vow is a horrible thing! it is a snare for sin. The man who cannot go to heaven without a vow,—may go——." Here, standing erect in the middle of his library, and rolling grand, his pause was truly a curious compound of the solemn and the ludicrous; he half-whistled in his usual way when pleasant, and he paused as if checked by religious awe. Methought he would have added, *to hell,* but was restrained.

This year, Johnson gave the world a luminous proof that the vigour of his mind in all its faculties was not in the least abated; for this year came out the first four volumes of his "Prefaces, biographical and critical, to the most eminent of the English Poets," published by the booksellers of London. The remaining volumes came out in the year 1780. Of this work I shall speak more particularly hereafter.

Mr. Boswell to Dr. Johnson

Edinburgh, Feb. 2, 1779

MY DEAR SIR,

Garrick's death is a striking event; [1] not that we should be surprised with the death of any man who has lived sixty-two years; but because there was a *vivacity* in our late celebrated friend, which drove away the thoughts of *death* from any association with *him.* I am sure you will be tenderly affected with his departure; and I would wish to hear from you upon the subject. I was obliged to him in my days of effervescence in London, when poor Derrick was my governor; and since that time I received many civilities from him. Do you remember how pleasing it was, when I received a letter from him at Inverary, upon our first return to civilised living after our Hebridean journey? I shall always remember him with affection as well as admiration.

Any fresh instance of the uncertainty of life makes one embrace more closely a valuable friend. My dear and much respected Sir, may God preserve you long in this world while I am in it. I am ever, your much obliged, and affectionate humble servant,

JAMES BOSWELL

On the 23rd of February I wrote to him again, complaining of his silence, as I had heard he was ill, and had written to Mr. Thrale for information concerning him: and I announced my intention of soon being again in London.

[1] He died on January 20.

I arrived on Monday, March 15, and next morning, at a late hour found Dr. Johnson sitting over his tea, attended by Mrs. Desmoulins, Mr. Levett, and a clergyman, who had come to submit some poetical pieces to his revision. My arrival interrupted, for a little while, the important business; upon its being resumed, a printed "Ode to the War-like Genius of Britain" came in review. The bard was a lank bony figure, with short black hair; he was writhing himself in agitation, while Johnson read, and, showing his teeth in a grin of earnestness, exclaimed in broken sentences, and in a keen sharp tone, "Is that poetry, Sir?—Is it Pindar?" Then, turning to me, the poet cried, "My muse has not been long upon the town, and (pointing to the Ode) it trembles under the hand of the great critic." Johnson, in a tone of displeasure, proceeded: "Here is an error, Sir: you have made Genius feminine." "Palpable, Sir (cried the enthusiast); I know it. But (in a lower tone) it was to pay a compliment to the Duchess of Devonshire, with which her grace was pleased. She is walking across Coxheath in the military uniform, and I suppose her to be the Genius of Britain." JOHNSON. "Sir, you are giving a reason for it; but that will not make it right. You may have a reason why two and two should make five; but they will still make but four."

Although I was several times with him in the course of the following days, I have preserved no memorial of his conversation till Friday, March 26, when I visited him. He said he expected to be attacked on account of his "Lives of the Poets." "However," said he, "I would rather be attacked than unnoticed. For the worst thing you can do to an author is to be silent as to his works. An assault upon a town is a bad thing; but starving it is still worse; an assault may be unsuccessful, you may have more men killed than you kill; but if you starve the town, you are sure of victory."

During my stay in London this spring, I find I was unaccountably negligent in preserving Johnson's sayings, more so than at any time when I was happy enough to have an opportunity of hearing his wisdom and wit. There is no help for it now. I must content myself with presenting such scraps as I have.

On Wednesday, March 31, when I visited him, and confessed an excess of which I had seldom been guilty,—that I had spent a whole night in playing at cards, and that I could not look back on it with satisfaction,—instead of a harsh animadversion, he mildly said, "Alas, Sir, on how few things can we look back with satisfaction!"

On Thursday, April 1, he said, "London is nothing to some people; but to a man whose pleasure is intellectual, London is the place. And there is no place where economy can be so well practised as in London: more can be had here for the money, even by ladies, than any where else. You cannot play tricks with your fortune in a small place; you must make an uniform appearance. Here a lady may have well-furnished apartments, and elegant dress, without any meat in her kitchen."

I was amused by considering with how much ease and coolness he could write or talk to a friend, exhorting him not to suppose that happiness was not to be found as well in other places as in London; when he himself was at all times sensible of its being, comparatively speaking, a heaven upon earth. The truth is, that by those who from sagacity, attention, and experience, have learnt the full advantage of London, its pre-eminence over every other place, not only for variety of enjoyment, but for comfort, will be felt with a philosophical exultation. The freedom from remark and petty censure, with which life may be passed there, is a circumstance which a man who knows the teasing restraint of a narrow circle must relish highly. In London, a man may live in splendid society at one time, and in frugal retirement at another, without animadversion. There, and there alone, a man's own house is truly his *castle*, in which he can be in perfect safety from intrusion whenever he pleases. I never shall forget how well this was expressed to me one day by Mr. Meynell: "The chief advantage of London," said he, "is, that a man is always *so near his burrow*."

On Friday, April 2, being Good Friday, in the interval between morning and evening service, he endeavoured to employ himself earnestly in devotional exercise; and gave me "Les Pensées de Pascal," that I might not interrupt him. I preserve the book with great reverence.

On Wednesday, April 7, I dined with him at Sir Joshua Reynolds's. Johnson harangued upon the qualities of different liquors; and spoke with great contempt of claret, as so weak, that "a man would be drowned by it before it made him drunk." He was persuaded to drink one glass of it, that he might judge, not from recollection, which might be dim, but from immediate sensation. He shook his head, and said, "Poor stuff! No, Sir, claret is the liquor for boys; port for men; but he who aspires to be a hero (smiling) must drink brandy. In the first place, the flavour of brandy is most grateful to the palate; and then brandy will do soonest for a man what drinking *can* do for him. There are, indeed, few who are able to drink brandy. That is a power rather to be wished for than attained. And yet," proceeded he, "as in all pleasure hope plays a considerable part, I know not but fruition comes too quick by brandy. Florence wine I think the worst; it is wine only to the eye; it is wine neither while you are drinking it, nor after you have drunk it; it neither pleases the taste, nor exhilarates the spirits." I reminded him how heartily he and I used to drink wine together, when we were first acquainted; and how I used to have a head-ache after sitting up with him. He did not like to have this recalled; or, perhaps, thinking that I boasted improperly, resolved to have a witty stroke at me: "Nay, Sir, it was not the *wine* that made your head ache, but the *sense* that I put into it." BOSWELL. "What, Sir! will sense make the head ache?" JOHNSON. "Yes, Sir (with a smile), when it is not used to it."

On Thursday, April 8, I dined with him at Mr. Allan Ramsay's, with Lord Graham and some other company.

Lord Graham commended Dr. Drummond at Naples as a man of extraordinary talents; and added, that he had a great love of liberty. JOHNSON. "He is *young*, my lord (looking to his lordship with an arch smile); all *boys* love liberty, till experience convinces them they are not so fit to govern themselves as they imagined. We are all agreed as to our own liberty; we would have as much of it as we can get; but we are not agreed as to the liberty of others: for in proportion as we take, others must lose. I believe we hardly wish that the mob should have liberty to govern us. When that was the case some time ago, no man was at liberty not to have candles in his windows." RAMSAY. "The result is, that order is better than confusion." JOHNSON. "The result is, that order cannot be had but by subordination."

On Friday, April 16, I had been present at the trial of the unfortunate Mr. Hackman, who, in a fit of frantick jealous love, had shot Miss Ray, the favourite of a nobleman.

This day a violent altercation arose between Johnson and Beauclerk,[1] which having made much noise at the time, I think it proper, in order to prevent any future misrepresentation, to give a minute account of it.

In talking of Hackman, Johnson argued, as Judge Blackstone

---

[1] At a meeting of the Club. Johnson was president, and the following members were present: Lord Althorp, Bunbury, Beauclerk, Boswell, Joseph Banks, Reynolds, and Steevens. The young nobleman and eminent traveller mentioned in this anecdote, were Lord Althorp and Joseph Banks, with neither of whom had Johnson dined before at the Club. They had been elected members in December of the preceding year.

had done, that his being furnished with two pistols was a proof that he meant to shoot two persons. Mr. Beauclerk said, "No; for that every wise man who intended to shoot himself took two pistols, that he might be sure of doing it at once. Lord ——'s cook shot himself with one pistol, and lived ten days in great agony. Mr. ——, who loved buttered muffins, but durst not eat them because they disagreed with his stomach, resolved to shoot himself; and then he eat three buttered muffins for breakfast, before shooting himself, knowing that he should not be troubled with indigestion; *he* had two charged pistols; one was found lying charged upon the table by him, after he had shot himself with the other."—"Well," said Johnson, with an air of triumph, "you see here one pistol was sufficient." Beauclerk replied smartly, "Because it happened to kill him." And either then or a very little afterwards, being piqued at Johnson's triumphant remark, added, "This is what you don't know, and I do." There was then a cessation of the dispute; and some minutes intervened, during which, dinner and the glass went on cheerfully; when Johnson suddenly and abruptly exclaimed, "Mr. Beauclerk, how came you to talk so petulantly to me, as 'This is what you don't know, but what I know'? One thing *I* know which *you* don't seem to know, that you are very uncivil." BEAUCLERK. "Because *you* began by being uncivil (which you always are)." The words in parenthesis were, I believe, not heard by Dr. Johnson. Here again there was a cessation of arms. Johnson told me, that the reason why he waited at first some time without taking any notice of what Mr. Beauclerk said, was because he was thinking whether he should resent it. But when he considered that there were present a young lord and an eminent traveller, two men of the world, with whom he had never dined before, he was apprehensive that they might think they had a right to take such liberties with him as Beauclerk did, and therefore resolved he would not let it pass; adding, "that he would not appear a coward." A little while after this, the conversation turned on the violence of Hackman's temper. Johnson then said, "It was his business to *command* his temper, as my friend, Mr. Beauclerk, should have done some time ago." BEAUCLERK. "I should learn of *you*, Sir." JOHNSON. "Sir, you have given *me* opportunities enough of learning, when I have been in *your* company. No man loves to be treated with contempt." BEAU-CLERK (with a polite inclination towards Johnson). "Sir, you have known me twenty years, and however I may have treated others, you may be sure I could never treat you with contempt." JOHNSON. "Sir, you have said more than was necessary." Thus it ended: and Beauclerk's coach not having come for him till very late, Dr. Johnson and another gentleman sat with him a long time after the rest of the company were gone; and he and I dined at Beauclerk's on the Saturday se'nnight following.

After this tempest had subsided, I recollect the following particulars of his conversation:

"I am always for getting a boy forward in his learning; for that is a sure good. I would let him at first read *any* English book which happens to engage his attention; because you have done a great deal, when you have brought him to have entertainment from a book. He'll get better books afterwards."

"To be contradicted in order to force you to talk is mighty unpleasing. You *shine*, indeed; but it is by being *ground*."

On Saturday, April 24, I dined with him at Mr. Beauclerk's. I mentioned that Mr. Wilkes had attacked Garrick to me. JOHNSON. "Garrick was a very good man, the cheerfullest man of his age; a decent liver in a profession which is supposed to give indulgence to licentiousness; and a man who gave away freely money acquired by himself. He began the world with a great hunger for money; the son of a half-pay officer, bred in a family whose study was to make fourpence do as much as others made fourpence-half-penny do. But when he had got money, he was very liberal." I presumed to animadvert on his eulogy on Garrick, in his "Lives of the Poets." "You say, Sir, his death eclipsed the gaiety of nations." JOHNSON. "I could not have said more or less. It is the truth; *eclipsed*, not *extinguished;* and his death *did* eclipse; it was like a storm." BOSWELL. "But why nations? Did his gaiety extend further than his own nation?" JOHNSON. "Why, Sir, some exaggeration must be allowed. Besides, nations may be said, if we allow the Scotch to be a nation, and to have gaiety—which they have not. *You* are an exception, though. Come, gentlemen, let us candidly admit that there is one Scotchman who is cheerful." BEAUCLERK. "But he is a very unnatural Scotchman." I, however, continued to think the compliment to Garrick hyperbolically untrue. I objected, also, to what appears an anti-climax of praise, when contrasted with the preceding panegyric "and diminished the public stock of harmless pleasure!" "Is not *harmless pleasure* very tame?" JOHNSON. "Nay, Sir, harmless pleasure is the highest praise. Pleasure is a word of dubious import; pleasure is in general dangerous, and pernicious to virtue; to be able, therefore, to furnish pleasure that is harmless, pleasure pure and unalloyed, is as great a power as man can possess." This was, perhaps, as ingenious a defence as could be made; still, however, I was not satisfied.

Soon after this time a little incident occurred, which I will not suppress.

To Dr. Johnson

South Audley Street, Monday, April 26
MY DEAR SIR,
      I am in great pain with an inflamed foot, and obliged to keep my bed, so am prevented from having the pleasure to dine at Mr. Ramsay's to-day, which is very hard; and my spirits are sadly sunk. Will you be so friendly as to come and sit an hour with me in the evening? I am ever yours, &c.,   JAMES BOSWELL

To Mr. Boswell

Harley Street [1]
MR. JOHNSON laments the absence of Mr. Boswell, and will come to him.

He came to me in the evening, and brought Sir Joshua Reynolds. I need scarcely say, that their conversation, while they sat by my bedside, was the most pleasing opiate to pain that could have been administered.

Johnson being now better disposed to obtain information concerning Pope than he was last year, sent by me to my Lord Marchmont a present of those volumes of his "Lives of the Poets" which were at this time published, with a request to have permission to wait on him; and his lordship, who had called on him twice, obligingly appointed Saturday, the 1st of May, for receiving us.

On that morning Johnson came to me from Streatham, and after drinking chocolate at General Paoli's in South Audley Street, we proceeded to Lord Marchmont's in Curzon Street. His lordship met us at the door of his library, and with great politeness said to Johnson, "I am not going to make an encomium upon *myself*, by telling you the high respect I have for *you*, Sir." Johnson was exceedingly courteous; and the interview, which lasted about two

[1] Allan Ramsay's residence, No. 67, Harley Street.

hours, during which the earl communicated his anecdotes of Pope, was as agreeable as I could have wished. When we came out, I said to Johnson, "that, considering his lordship's civility, I should have been vexed if he had again failed to come." "Sir," said he, "I would rather have given twenty pounds than not have come." I accompanied him to Streatham, where we dined, and returned to town in the evening.

On Monday, May 3, I dined with him at Mr. Dilly's. I pressed him this day for his opinion on the passage in Parnell, concerning which I had in vain questioned him in several letters, and at length obtained it *in due form of law*.

CASE FOR DR. JOHNSON'S OPINION:

May 3, 1779

Parnell, in his "Hermit," has the following passage:

> To clear this doubt, to know the world by sight,
> To find if *books* and *swains* report it right
> (For yet by *swains alone* the world he knew,
> Whose feet came wand'ring o'er the nightly dew).

Is there not a contradiction in its being *first* supposed that the Hermit knew *both* what books and swains reported of the world; yet *afterwards* said, that he knew it by swains *alone?*"

I think it an inaccuracy. He mentions two instructors in the first line, and says he had only one in the next.

This evening I set out for Scotland.

I did not write to Johnson, as usual, upon my return to my family; but tried how he would be affected by my silence.

To James Boswell, Esq.

July 13, 1779

DEAR SIR,

What can possibly have happened, that keeps us two such strangers to each other? I expected to have heard from you when you came home; I expected afterwards. I went into the country and returned; and yet there is no letter from Mr. Boswell. No ill, I hope, has happened; and if ill should happen, why should it be concealed from him who loves you? Is it a fit of humour, that has disposed you to try who can hold out longest without writing?

If it be, you have the victory. But I am afraid of something bad; set me free from my suspicions.

My thoughts are at present employed in guessing the reason of your silence: you must not expect that I should tell you any thing, if I had any thing to tell. Write, pray write to me, and let me know what is or what has been the cause of this long interruption. I am, dear Sir, your most affectionate humble servant,

SAM. JOHNSON

To Dr. Samuel Johnson

Edinburgh, July 17, 1779

MY DEAR SIR,

What may be justly denominated a supine indolence of mind has been my state of existence since I last returned to Scotland. In a livelier state I had often suffered severely from long intervals of silence on your part; and I had even been chid by you for expressing my uneasiness. I was willing to take advantage of my insensibility, and while I could bear the experiment, to try whether your affection for me would, after an unusual silence on my part, make you write first. This afternoon I have had a very high satisfaction by receiving your kind letter of inquiry, for which I most gratefully thank you. I am doubtful if it was right to make the experiment; though I have gained by it. I was beginning to grow tender, and to upbraid myself, especially after having dreamt two nights ago that I was with you. I and my wife, and my four children, are all well. I would not delay one post to answer your letter; but as it is late, I have not time to do more. You shall soon hear from me, upon many and various particulars; and I shall never again put you to any test. I am, with veneration, my dear Sir, your, &c.,   JAMES BOSWELL

On the 22nd of July, I wrote to him again. My letter was a pretty long one, and contained a variety of particulars; but he, it should seem, had not attended to it; for his next to me was as follows:

To James Boswell, Esq.

Streatham, Sept. 9, 1779

MY DEAR SIR,

Are you playing the same trick again, and trying who can keep silence longest? Remember that all tricks are either knavish or childish; and that it is as foolish to make experiments upon the constancy of a friend, as upon the chastity of a wife.

What can be the cause of this second fit of silence, I cannot conjecture; but after one trick, I will not be cheated by another, nor will harass my thoughts with conjectures about the motives of a man who, probably, acts only by caprice. I therefore suppose you are well, and that Mrs. Boswell is well too, and that the fine summer has restored Lord Auchinleck. I am much better than you left me; I think I am better than when I was in Scotland.

I forgot whether I informed you that poor Thrale has been in great danger. Mrs. Thrale likewise has miscarried, and been much indisposed. Every body else is well.

Mr. Thrale goes to Brighthelmstone, about Michaelmas, to be jolly and ride a-hunting. I shall go to town, or perhaps to Oxford. Exercise and gaiety, or rather carelessness, will, I hope, dissipate all remains of his malady; and I likewise hope, by the change of place, to find some opportunities of growing yet better myself. I am, dear Sir, your &c.,   SAM. JOHNSON

My readers will not be displeased at being told every slight circumstance of the manner in which Dr. Johnson contrived to amuse his solitary hours. He sometimes employed himself in chemistry, sometimes in watering and pruning a vine, sometimes in small experiments, at which those who may smile should recollect that there are moments which admit of being soothed only by trifles.[1]

My friend, Colonel James Stuart, having been in Scotland recruiting, obligingly asked me to accompany him to London for a short time. Such an offer, at a time of the year when I had full leisure, was very pleasing.

On Monday, October 4, I called at Dr. Johnson's house before he was up. He sent for me to his bedside, and expressed his satisfaction at this incidental meeting, with as much vivacity as if he had been in the gaiety of youth. He called briskly, "Frank, go and get coffee, and let us breakfast *in splendour*."

On Sunday, October 10, we dined together at Mr. Strahan's.

---

[1] In one of his manuscript Diaries, there is the following entry, which marks his curious minute attention: "July 26, 1768.—I have shaved my nail by accident in whetting the knife, about an eighth of an inch from the bottom, and about a fourth from the top. This I measure that I may know the growth of nails; the whole is about five eighths of an inch."

And, "August 15, 1783.—I cut from my vine forty-one leaves, which weighed five ounces and a half, and eight scruples: I lay them upon my bookcase, to see what weight they will lose by drying."

"Dr. Johnson was always exceeding fond of chemistry; and we made up a sort of laboratory at Streatham one summer, and diverted ourselves with drawing essences and colouring liquors. But the danger in which Mr. Thrale found his friend one day, when I had driven to London, and he had got the children and servants assembled round him to see some experiments performed, put an end to all our entertainment; as Mr. Thrale was persuaded that his short sight would have occasioned his destruction in a moment by bringing him close to a fierce and violent flame. Indeed, it was a perpetual miracle that he did not set himself on fire reading abed, as was his constant custom, when quite unable even to keep clear of mischief with our best help; and accordingly the foretops of all his wigs were burned by the candle down to the very network. Future experiments in chemistry, however, were too dangerous, and Mr. Thrale insisted that we should do no more towards finding the philosopher's stone."—*Piozzi, Anecdotes*.

TO SEE SOME EXPERIMENTS PERFORMED

The conversation having turned on the prevailing practice of going to the East Indies in quest of wealth;—JOHNSON. "A man had better have ten thousand pounds at the end of ten years passed in England, than twenty thousand pounds at the end of ten years passed in India, because you must compute what you *give* for money; and the man who has lived ten years in India has given up ten years of social comfort, and all those advantages which arise from living in England."

We left Mr. Strahan's at seven, as Johnson had said he intended to go to evening prayers. As we walked along, he complained of a little gout in his toe, and said, "I sha'n't go to prayers to-night: I shall go to-morrow: whenever I miss church on a Sunday, I resolve to go another day. But I do not always do it." This was a fair exhibition of vibration between pious resolutions and indolence.

I went home with him, and we had a long quiet conversation.

BOSWELL. "Why, Sir, do people play this trick which I observe now, when I look at your grate, putting the shovel against it to make the fire burn?" JOHNSON. "They play the trick, but it does not make the fire burn. *There* is a better (setting the poker perpendicularly up at right angles with the grate). In days of superstition they thought, as it made a cross with the bars, it would drive away the witch."

BOSWELL. "By associating with you, Sir, I am always getting an accession of wisdom. But perhaps a man, after knowing his own character—the limited strength of his own mind—should not be desirous of having too much wisdom, considering how little he can carry." JOHNSON. "Sir, be as wise as you can. Every man is to take care of his own wisdom and his own virtue, without minding too much what others think."

He said, "Dodsley first mentioned to me the scheme of an English Dictionary; but I had long thought of it." BOSWELL. "You did not know what you were undertaking." JOHNSON. "Yes, Sir, I knew very well what I was undertaking, and very well how to do it, and have done it very well." BOSWELL. "An excellent climax!"

I mentioned to him a dispute between a friend of mine and his lady, concerning conjugal infidelity, which my friend had maintained was by no means so bad in the husband as in the wife. JOHNSON. "Your friend was in the right, Sir. Between a man and his Maker it is a different question: but between a man and his wife, a husband's infidelity is nothing. They are connected by children, by fortune, by serious considerations of community. Wise married women don't trouble themselves about infidelity in their husbands." BOSWELL. "To be sure there is a great difference between the offence of infidelity in a man and that of his wife." JOHNSON. "The difference is boundless. The man imposes no bastards upon his wife."

Here let it be kept in remembrance, that he was very careful not to give any encouragement to irregular conduct. A gentleman, not adverting to the distinction made by him upon this subject, supposed a case of singular perverseness in a wife, and heedlessly said, "That then he thought a husband might do as he pleased with a safe conscience." JOHNSON. "Nay, Sir, this is wild indeed (smiling); you must consider that fornication is a crime in a single man, and you cannot have more liberty by being married."

He this evening expressed himself strongly against the Roman Catholics, observing, "In everything in which they differ from us, they are wrong." He was even against the invocation of saints; in short, he was in the humour of opposition.

He, I know not why, showed upon all occasions an aversion to go to Ireland, where I proposed to him that we should make a tour. JOHNSON. "It is the last place where I should wish to travel." BOSWELL. "Should you not like to see Dublin, Sir?" JOHNSON. "No, Sir; Dublin is only a worse capital." BOSWELL. "Is not the Giant's Causeway worth seeing?" JOHNSON. "Worth seeing? yes, but not worth going to see."

Yet he had a kindness for the Irish nation; and thus generously expressed himself to a gentleman from that country, on the subject of an UNION which artful politicians have often had in view: "Do not make an union with us, Sir. We should unite with you only to rob you. We should have robbed the Scotch, if they had had any thing of which we could have robbed them."

I left London on Monday, October 18.

To James Boswell, Esq.

April 8, 1780

DEAR SIR,

. . . Poor dear Beauclerk—*nec, ut. soles, dabis joca.* His wit and his folly, his acuteness and maliciousness, his merriment and reasoning, are now over.[1] Such another will not often be found

---

[1] He died on March 11.

among mankind. He directed himself to be buried by the side of his mother; an instance of tenderness which I hardly expected. . . .

Poor Mr. Thrale has been in extreme danger from an apoplectical disorder, and recovered, beyond the expectation of his physicians: he is now at Bath, that his mind may be quiet, and Mrs. Thrale and Miss are with him. . . .

Please to make my compliments to your lady and to the young ladies. I should like to see them, pretty loves! I am, dear Sir, yours affectionately,   SAM. JOHNSON

Mrs. Thrale being now at Bath with her husband, the correspondence between Johnson and her was carried on briskly.

Mrs. Thrale to Dr. Johnson

Bath, Friday, April 28
I had a very kind letter from you yesterday, dear Sir, with a most circumstantial date. . . .

Yesterday's evening was passed at Mrs. Montagu's. There was Mr. Melmoth. . . . Mrs. Montagu flattered him finely; so he had a good afternoon on't. This evening we spent at a concert. Poor Queeny's [1] sore eyes have just released her; she had a long confinement, and could neither read nor write, so my master treated her, very good-naturedly, with the visits of a young woman in this town, a tailor's daughter, who professes music, and teaches so as to give six lessons a day to ladies, at five and threepence a lesson. Miss Burney says she is a great performer; and I respect the wench for getting her living so prettily. She is very modest and pretty-mannered, and not seventeen years old.

You live in a fine whirl indeed. If I did not write regularly, you would half forget me, and that would be very wrong, for I *felt* my regard for you in my *face* last night, when the criticisms were going on.

This morning it was all connoisseurship. We went to see some pictures painted by a gentleman-artist, Mr. Taylor, of this place. My master makes one, every where, and has got a good dawdling companion to ride with him now. . . . He looks well enough, but I have no notion of health for a man whose mouth cannot be sewed up. Burney and I and Queeny tease him every meal he eats, and Mrs. Montagu is quite serious with him; but what *can* one do? He will eat, I think; and if he does eat, I know he will not live. It makes me very unhappy, but I must bear it. Let me always have your friendship. I am, most sincerely, dear Sir, your faithful servant,   H. L. T.

[1] Mrs. Thrale's eldest daughter, Esther.

Dr. Johnson to Mrs. Thrale

London, May 1, 1780

DEAREST MADAM,

Mr. Thrale never will live abstinently, till he can persuade himself to live by rule. . . . Encourage, as you can, the musical girl. . . .

Never let criticisms operate on your face or your mind; it is very rarely that an author is hurt by his critics. The blaze of reputation cannot be blown out, but it often dies in the socket. A very few names may be considered as perpetual lamps that shine unconsumed. From the author of "Fitzosborne's Letters" I cannot think myself in much danger. I met him only once about thirty years ago, and in some small dispute reduced him to whistle. Having not seen him since, that is the last impression. . . .

While Johnson was engaged in preparing a delightful literary entertainment for the world, the tranquillity of the metropolis of Great Britain was unexpectedly disturbed by the most horrid series of outrage that ever disgraced a civilised country. A relaxation of some of the severe penal provisions against our fellow-subjects of the Catholic communion had been granted by the legislature, with an opposition so inconsiderable, that the genuine mildness of Christianity, united with liberal policy, seemed to have become general in this island. But a dark and malignant spirit of persecution soon showed itself, in an unworthy petition for the repeal of the wise and humane statute. That petition was brought forward by a mob, with the evident purpose of intimidation, and was justly rejected. But the attempt was accompanied and followed by such daring violence as is unexampled in history. Of this extraordinary tumult, Dr. Johnson has given the following concise, lively, and just account in his "Letters to Mrs. Thrale":

On Friday [June 2], the good protestants met in Saint George's Fields at the summons of Lord George Gordon; and marching to Westminster, insulted the lords and commons, who all bore it with great tameness. At night the outrages began by the demolition of the mass-house by Lincoln's Inn.

An exact journal of a week's defiance of government I cannot give you. On Monday Mr. Strahan, who had been insulted, spoke to Lord Mansfield, who had I think been insulted too, of the licentiousness of the populace; and his lordship treated it as a very slight irregularity. On Tuesday night, they pulled down Fielding's house [in Bow Street] and burnt his goods in the street. They had gutted on Monday Sir George Savile's house [in Leicester Square], but the building was saved. On Tuesday evening, leaving Fielding's ruins, they went to Newgate to demand their companions, who had been seized demolishing the chapel. The keeper could not release them but by the mayor's permission, which he went to ask; at his return he found all the prisoners released, and Newgate in a blaze. They then went to Bloomsbury [Square], and fastened upon Lord Mansfield's house, which they pulled down; and as for his goods, they totally burnt them. They have since gone to Caenwood, but a guard was there before them. They plundered some papists, I think, and burnt a mass-house, in Moorfields, the same night.

On Wednesday I walked with Dr. Scott, to look at Newgate, and found it in ruins, with the fire yet glowing. As I went by the protestants were plundering the sessions-house at the Old Bailey. There were not, I believe, a hundred; but they did their work at leisure, in full security, without sentinels, without trepidation, as men lawfully employed in full day. Such is the cowardice of a commercial place. On Wednesday they broke open the Fleet, and the King's Bench, and the Marshalsea, and Wood-street Compter, and Clerkenwell Bridewell, and released all the prisoners.

At night they set fire to the Fleet, and to the King's Bench, and I know not how many other places; and one might see the glare of conflagration fill the sky from many parts. The sight was dreadful. Some people were threatened: Mr. Strahan advised me to take care of myself. Such a time of terror you have been happy in not seeing.

The King said in Council, "that the magistrates had not done their duty, but that he would do his own"; and a proclamation was published, directing us to keep our servants within doors, as the peace was now to be preserved by force. The soldiers were sent out to different parts, and the town is now [June 9] at quiet.

The soldiers are stationed so as to be every where within call. There is no longer any body of rioters, and the individuals are hunted to their holes, and led to prison. Lord George was last night sent to the Tower. Mr. John Wilkes was this day in my neighbourhood, to seize the publisher of a seditious paper.

Several chapels have been destroyed, and several inoffensive papists have been plundered; but the high sport was to burn the gaols. This was a good rabble trick. The debtors and the criminals were all set at liberty; but of the criminals, as has always happened, many are already retaken; and two pirates have surrendered themselves, and it is expected that they will be pardoned.

Government now acts again with its proper force; and we are all under the protection of the king and the law. I thought that it would be agreeable to you and my master to have my testimony to the public security; and that you would sleep more quietly when I told you that you are safe.

There has, indeed, been an universal panic, from which the King was the first that recovered. Without the concurrence of his ministers, or the assistance of the civil magistrates, he put the soldiers in motion, and saved the town from calamities, such as a rabble's government must naturally produce.

The public has escaped a very heavy calamity. The rioters attempted the Bank on Wednesday night, but in no great number; and, like other thieves, with no great resolution. Jack Wilkes headed the party that drove them away. It is agreed, that if they had seized the Bank on Tuesday, at the height of the panic, when no resistance had been prepared, they might have carried irrecoverably away whatever they had found. Jack, who was always zealous for order and decency, declares, that if he be trusted with power, he will not leave a rioter alive. There is, however, now no longer any need of heroism or bloodshed; no blue riband [1] is any longer worn."

Such was the end of this miserable sedition, from which London was delivered by the magnanimity of the sovereign himself.

To James Boswell, Esq.

London, Aug. 21, 1780

DEAR SIR,

I find you have taken one of your fits of taciturnity, and have resolved not to write till you are written to: it is but a peevish humour, but you shall have your way.

I have sat at home in Bolt Court all the summer, thinking to write the *Lives*, and a great part of the time only thinking. Several of them, however, are done, and I still think to do the rest.

Mr. Thrale and his family have, since his illness, passed their time first at Bath, and then at Brighthelmstone; but I have been at neither place. I would have gone to Lichfield if I could have had time, and I might have had time if I had been active; but I have missed much, and done little.

In the late disturbances, Mr. Thrale's house and stock were in great danger. The mob was pacified at their first invasion with about fifty pounds in drink and meat; and at their second, were driven away by the soldiers. Mr. Strahan got a garrison into his house, and maintained them a fortnight: he was so frighted, that

---

[1] Lord George Gordon and his followers wore blue ribands in their hats.

he removed part of his goods. Mrs. Williams took shelter in the country.

I know not whether I shall get a ramble this autumn. It is now about the time when we were travelling. I have, however, better health than I had then, and hope you and I may yet show ourselves on some part of Europe, Asia, or Africa. In the mean time let us play no trick, but keep each other's kindness by all means in our power. . . .

I suppose your little ladies are grown tall; and your son has become a learned young man. I love them all, and I love your naughty lady, whom I never shall persuade to love me. When the *Lives* are done, I shall send them to complete her collection, but must send them in paper, as, for want of a pattern, I cannot bind them to fit the rest.[1] I am, Sir, yours most affectionately,

SAM. JOHNSON

On his birthday, Johnson has this note:

I am now beginning the seventy-second year of my life, with more strength of body and greater vigour of mind than I think is common at that age.

But still he complains of sleepless nights and idle days, and forgetfulness, or neglect of resolutions. He thus pathetically expresses himself:

Surely I shall not spend my whole life with my own total disapprobation.

To James Boswell, Esq.

Oct. 17, 1780

DEAR SIR,
I am sorry to write you a letter that will not please you, and yet it is at last what I resolve to do. This year must pass without an interview; the summer has been foolishly lost, like many other of my summers and winters. I hardly saw a green field, but staid in town to work, without working much.

Mr. Thrale . . . is now going to Brighthelmstone, and expects me to go with him; and how long I shall stay, I cannot tell. I do not much like the place, but yet I shall go, and stay while my stay is desired. We must, therefore, content ourselves with knowing what we know as well as man can know the mind of man, that we love one another, and that we wish each other's happiness, and that the lapse of a year cannot lessen our mutual kindness. I am, dear Sir, yours, most affectionately,   SAM. JOHNSON

[1] Johnson had sent the first four volumes to Mrs. Boswell in March 1779, "elegantly bound and gilt," in acknowledgment of her marmalade.

Being disappointed in my hopes of meeting Johnson this year, so that I could hear none of his admirable sayings, I shall compensate for this want by inserting a collection, for which I am indebted to Mr. Langton.

"Having asked Mr. Langton if his father and mother had sat for their pictures, which he thought it right for each generation of a family to do, and being told they had opposed it, he said, 'Sir, among the anfractuosities of the human mind, I know not if it may not be one, that there is a superstitious reluctance to sit for a picture.'

"His affection for Topham Beauclerk was so great, that when Beauclerk was labouring under that severe illness which at last occasioned his death, Johnson said (with a voice faltering with emotion), 'Sir, I would walk to the extent of the diameter of the earth to save Beauclerk.'

"He used to quote, with great warmth, the saying of Aristotle that there was the same difference between one learned and unlearned, as between the living and the dead.

"An eminent foreigner, when he was shown the British Museum, was very troublesome with many absurd inquiries. 'Now there, Sir,' said he, 'is the difference between an Englishman and a Frenchman. A Frenchman must be always talking, whether he knows any thing of the matter or not; an Englishman is content to say nothing, when he has nothing to say.'

"His unjust contempt for foreigners was, indeed, extreme. One evening at Old Slaughter's Coffee-house, when a number of them were talking loud about little matters, he said, 'Does not this confirm old Meynell's observation, *For any thing I see, foreigners are fools?*'

"There was formerly a rude custom for those who were sailing upon the Thames to accost each other as they passed in the most abusive language they could invent; generally, however, with as much satirical humour as they were capable of producing. Johnson was once eminently successful in this species of contest. A fellow having attacked him with some coarse raillery, Johnson answered him thus, 'Sir, your wife, *under pretence of keeping a bawdy-house*, is a receiver of stolen goods.'

"As Johnson always allowed the extraordinary talents of Mr. Burke, so Mr. Burke was fully sensible of the wonderful powers of Johnson. Mr. Langton recollects having passed an evening with both of them, when Mr. Burke repeatedly entered upon topics

THE MOST ABUSIVE LANGUAGE THEY COULD INVENT

which it was evident he would have illustrated with extensive knowledge and richness of expression; but Johnson always seized upon the conversation, in which, however, he acquitted himself in a most masterly manner. As Mr. Burke and Mr. Langton were walking home, Mr. Burke observed that Johnson had been very great that night: Mr. Langton joined in this, but added he could have wished to hear more from Mr. Burke. 'O, no,' said Mr. Burke, 'it is enough for me to have rung the bell to him.'

"Beauclerk having observed to him of one of their friends, that he was awkward at counting money; 'Why, Sir,' said Johnson, 'I am likewise awkward at counting money. But then, Sir, the reason is plain; I have had very little money to count.'

"When Mr. Vesey was proposed as a member of the Literary Club, Mr. Burke began saying that he was a man of gentle manners. 'Sir,' said Johnson, 'you need say no more. When you have said a man of gentle manners, you have said enough.'

"'My dear friend, Dr. Bathurst,' said he, with a warmth of approbation, 'declared he was glad that his father, who was a West India planter, had left his affairs in total ruin, because, having no estate, he was not under the temptation of having slaves.'

"'Depend upon it,' said he, 'that if a man *talks* of his misfortunes, there is something in them that is not disagreeable to him; for where there is nothing but pure misery, there never is any recourse to the mention of it.'

"'The applause of a single human being is of great consequence.' This he said to me with great earnestness of manner, very near the time of his decease."

In 1781, Johnson at last completed his "Lives of the Poets," of which he gives this account: "Some time in March I finished the 'Lives of the Poets,' which I wrote in my usual way, dilatorily and hastily, unwilling to work, and working with vigour and haste." In a memorandum previous to this, he says of them: "Written, I hope, in such a manner as may tend to the promotion of piety."

This is the work which, of all Dr. Johnson's writings, will perhaps be read most generally, and with most pleasure. Philology and biography were his favourite pursuits, and those who lived most in intimacy with him, heard him upon all occasions, when there was a proper opportunity, take delight in expatiating upon the various merits of the English poets: upon the niceties of their characters, and the events of their progress through the world which they contributed to illuminate. His mind was so full of that kind of information, and it was so well arranged in his memory, that in performing what he had undertaken in this way, he had little more to do than to put his thoughts upon paper; exhibiting first each poet's life, and then subjoining a critical examination of his genius and works. But when he began to write, the subject swelled in such a manner, that instead of prefaces to each poet, of no more than a few pages, as he had originally intended, he produced an ample, rich, and most entertaining view of them in every respect. The booksellers, justly sensible of the great additional value of the copyright, presented him with another hundred pounds, over and above two hundred, for which his agreement was to furnish such prefaces as he thought fit.

I wrote to him in February, complaining of having been troubled by a recurrence of the perplexing question of Liberty and Necessity; and mentioning that I hoped soon to meet him again in London.

To James Boswell, Esq.

March 14, 1781

DEAR SIR,

I hoped you had got rid of all this hypocrisy of misery. What have you to do with Liberty and Necessity? Or what more than to hold your tongue about it? Do not doubt but I shall be most heartily glad to see you here again, for I love every part about you but your affectation of distress.

I have at last finished my Lives, and have laid up for you a load of copy, all out of order, so that it will amuse you a long time to set it right. Come to me, my dear Bozzy, and let us be as happy as we can. We will go again to the Mitre, and talk old times over. I am, dear Sir, yours affectionately,   SAM. JOHNSON

On Monday, March 19, I arrived in London, and on Tuesday, the 20th, met him in Fleet Street, walking or rather moving along: for his peculiar march is thus described: "When he walked the streets, what with the constant roll of his head, and the concomitant motion of his body, he appeared to make his way by that motion, independent of his feet." That he was often much stared at while he advanced in this manner may easily be believed; but it was not safe to make sport of one so robust as he was. Mr. Langton saw him one day, in a fit of absence, by a sudden start, drive the load off a porter's back, and walk forward briskly, without being conscious of what he had done. The porter was very angry,

TO WHIP A TOP IN GROSVENOR SQUARE

but stood still, and eyed the huge figure with much earnestness, till he was satisfied that his wisest course was to be quiet, and take up his burthen again.

Our accidental meeting in the street after a long separation was a pleasing surprise to us both. He stepped aside with me into Falcon Court, and made kind inquiries about my family; and as we were in a hurry, I promised to call on him next day. He said he was engaged to go out in the morning. "Early, Sir?" said I. JOHNSON. "Why, Sir, a London morning does not go with the sun."

I found on visiting his friend, Mr. Thrale, that he was now very ill, and had removed to a house in Grosvenor Square. I was sorry to see him sadly changed in his appearance.

He told me I might now have the pleasure to see Dr. Johnson drink wine again, for he had lately returned to it. When I mentioned this to Johnson, he said, "I drink it now sometimes, but not socially." The first evening that I was with him at Thrale's, I observed he poured a large quantity of it into a glass, and swallowed it greedily. Every thing about his character and manners was forcible and violent; there never was any moderation. Many a day did he fast, many a year did he refrain from wine; but when he did eat, it was voraciously; when he did drink wine, it was copiously. He could practise abstinence, but not temperance.

Johnson's profound reverence for the hierarchy made him expect from bishops the highest degree of decorum; he was offended even at their going to taverns: "A bishop," said he, "has nothing to do at a tippling-house. It is not indeed immoral in him to go to a tavern; neither would it be immoral in him to whip a top in Grosvenor Square: but, if he did, I hope the boys would fall upon him, and apply the whip to *him*. There are gradations in conduct; there is morality,—decency,—propriety. None of these should be violated by a bishop. A bishop should not go to a house where he may meet a young fellow leading out a wench." BOSWELL. "But, Sir, every tavern does not admit women." JOHNSON. "Depend upon it, Sir, any tavern will admit a well-dressed man and a well-dressed woman: they will not perhaps admit a woman whom they see every night walking by their door, in the street. But a well-dressed man may lead in a well-dressed woman to any tavern in London. Taverns sell meat and drink, and will sell them to any body who can eat and can drink. You may as well say that a mercer will not sell silks to a woman of the town."

He also disapproved of bishops going to routs; at least of their staying at them longer than their presence commanded respect. He mentioned a particular bishop. "Poh!" said Mrs. Thrale, "the Bishop of —— is never minded at a rout." BOSWELL. "When a bishop places himself in a situation where he has no distinct character, and is of no consequence, he degrades the dignity of his order." JOHNSON. "Mr. Boswell, Madam, has said it as correctly as it could be."

On Friday, March 30, I dined with him at Sir Joshua Reynolds's, with the Earl of Charlemont, Sir Annesley Stewart, Mr. Eliot of Port-Eliot, Mr. Burke, Dean Marlay, Mr. Langton; a most agreeable day, of which I regret that every circumstance is not preserved; but it is unreasonable to require such a multiplication of felicity.

Mr. Eliot mentioned a curious liquor peculiar to his country, which the Cornish fishermen drink. They call it *mahogany*, and it is made of two parts gin and one part treacle, well beaten together. I begged to have some of it made, which was done with proper skill by Mr. Eliot. I thought it very good liquor; and said it was a counterpart of what is called *Athol porridge* in the Highlands of Scotland, which is a mixture of whisky and honey. Johnson said, "that must be a better liquor than the Cornish, for both its component parts are better." He also observed, "*Mahogany* must be a modern name; for it is not long since the wood called mahogany was known in this country." I mentioned his scale of liquors: claret for boys,—port for men,—brandy for heroes. "Then," said Mr. Burke, "let me have claret: I love to be a boy; to have the careless gaiety of boyish days." JOHNSON. "I should drink claret too, if it would give me that; but it does not: it neither makes boys men, nor men boys. You'll be drowned by it before it has any effect upon you."

I ventured to mention a ludicrous paragraph in the newspapers, that Dr. Johnson was learning to dance of Vestris. Lord Charlemont, wishing to excite him to talk, proposed in a whisper, that he should be asked whether it was true. We were, by a great majority, clear for the experiment. Upon which his lordship very gravely, and with a courteous air, said, "Pray, Sir, is it true that you are taking lessons of Vestris?" This was risking a good deal, and required the boldness of a general of Irish volunteers to make the attempt. Johnson was at first startled, and in some heat answered, "How can your lordship ask so simple a question?" But immediately recovering himself, whether from unwillingness to be deceived or to appear deceived, or whether from real good humour, he kept up the joke: "Nay, but if any body were to answer the paragraph, and contradict it, I'd have a reply, and would say, that he who contradicted it was no friend either to Vestris or me. For why should not Doctor Johnson add to his other powers a little corporeal agility?"

On Sunday, April 1, I dined with him at Mr. Thrale's, with Sir Philip Jennings Clerk and Mr. Perkins, who had the superintendence of Mr. Thrale's brewery, with a salary of five hundred pounds a year. Sir Philip had the appearance of a gentleman of ancient family, well advanced in life. He wore his own white hair in a bag of goodly size, a black velvet coat, with an embroidered waistcoat, and very rich laced ruffles; which Mrs. Thrale said were old-fashioned, but which, for that reason, I thought the more respectable, more like a Tory; yet Sir Philip was then in opposition in parliament. "Ah! Sir," said Johnson, "ancient ruffles and modern principles do not agree." Sir Philip defended the opposition to the American war ably and with temper, and I joined him. He said the majority of the nation was against the ministry. JOHNSON. "*I*, Sir, am against the ministry; but it is for having too little of that of which opposition thinks they have too much. Were I minister, if any man wagged his finger against me, he should be turned out; for that which it is in the power of government to give at pleasure to one or to another should be given to the supporters of government. If you will not oppose at the expense of losing your place, your opposition will not be honest, you will feel no serious grievance; and the present opposition is only a contest to get what others have. Sir Robert Walpole acted as I would do. As to the American war, the *sense* of the nation is *with* the ministry. The majority of those who can *understand* is with it; the majority of those who can only *hear* is against it; and as those who can only hear are more numerous than those who can understand, and opposition is always loudest, a majority of the rabble will be for opposition."

This boisterous vivacity entertained us; but the truth in my opinion was, that those who could understand the best were against the American war, as almost every man now is, when the question has been coolly considered.

Mrs. Thrale gave high praise to Mr. Dudley Long (now North). JOHNSON. "Nay, my dear lady, don't talk so. Mr. Long's character is very *short*. It is nothing. I know nobody who blasts by praise

as you do: for whenever there is exaggerated praise, every body is
set against a character. They are provoked to attack it. Now there
is Pepys:[1] you praised that man with such disproportion, that I
was incited to lessen him, perhaps more than he deserves. His
blood is upon your head. By the same principle, your malice de-
feats itself; for your censure is too violent. And yet (looking to
her with a leering smile) she is the first woman in the world, could
she but restrain that wicked tongue of hers;—she would be the
only woman, could she but command that little whirligig."

Mr. Thrale appeared very lethargic to-day. I saw him again
on Monday evening, at which time he was not thought to be in
immediate danger; but early in the morning of Wednesday the
4th he expired. Johnson was in the house and thus mentions the
event: "I felt almost the last flutter of his pulse, and looked for the
last time upon the face that for fifteen years had never been turned
upon me but with respect and benignity." Upon that day there
was a *call* of the Literary Club, but Johnson apologised for his
absence by the following note:

Wednesday (4th April)

Mr. Johnson knows that Sir Joshua Reynolds and the other
gentlemen will excuse his incompliance with the call, when they
are told that Mr. Thrale died this morning.

Mr. Thrale's death was a very essential loss to Johnson, who,
although he did not foresee all that afterwards happened, was
sufficiently convinced that the comforts which Mr. Thrale's family
afforded him would now in a great measure cease. He, however,
continued to show a kind attention to his widow and children as
long as it was acceptable; and he took upon him, with a very
earnest concern, the office of one of his executors; the importance of
which seemed greater than usual to him, from his circumstances
having been always such that he had scarcely any share in the real
business of life. His friends of the Club were in hopes that Mr.
Thrale might have made a liberal provision for him for his life,
which, as Mr. Thrale left no son and a very large fortune, it would
have been highly to his honour to have done; and, considering
Dr. Johnson's age, could not have been of long duration; but he
bequeathed him only two hundred pounds, which was the legacy
given to each of his executors. I could not but be somewhat

---

[1] William Weller Pepys, Esq., one of the Masters in the High Court of Chancery, and well known in
polite circles.— *Boswell.*

diverted by hearing Johnson talk in a pompous manner of his new office, and particularly of the concerns of the brewery, which it was at last resolved should be sold. Lord Lucan tells a very good story, which, if not precisely exact, is certainly characteristical; that when the sale of Thrale's brewery was going forward, Johnson appeared bustling about, with an ink-horn and pen in his button-hole, like an exciseman; and on being asked what he really considered to be the value of the property, which was to be disposed of, answered, "We are not here to sell a parcel of boilers and vats, but the potentiality of growing rich beyond the dreams of avarice."

On Friday, April 13, being Good Friday, I went to St. Clement's church with him as usual. There I saw again his old fellow-collegian, Edwards, to whom I said, "I think, Sir, Dr. Johnson and you meet only at church." "Sir," said he, "it is the best place we can meet in, except heaven, and I hope we shall meet there too." Dr. Johnson told me that there was very little communication between Edwards and him after their unexpected renewal of acquaintance. "But," said he, smiling, "he met me once and said, 'I am told you have written a very pretty book called "The Rambler."'" I was unwilling that he should leave the world in total darkness, and sent him a set."

Mr. Berenger visited him to-day, and was very pleasing. We talked of an evening society for conversation at a house in town, of which we were all members, but of which Johnson said, "It will never do, Sir. There is nothing served about there; neither tea, nor coffee, nor lemonade, nor anything whatever; and depend upon it, Sir, a man does not love to go to a place from whence he comes out exactly as he went in." I endeavoured, for argument's sake, to maintain that men of learning and talents might have very good intellectual society, without the aid of any little gratifications of the senses. Berenger joined with Johnson, and said that without these any meeting would be dull and insipid. "Sir," said Johnson to me, with an air of triumph, "Mr. Berenger knows the world. Everybody loves to have good things furnished to them without any trouble. I told Mrs. Thrale once, that, as she did not choose to have card-tables, she should have a profusion of the best sweetmeats, and she would be sure to have company enough come to her."

On Sunday, April 15, being Easter-day, after solemn worship in St. Paul's church, I found him alone. Dr. Scott, of the Commons, came in. He talked of its having been said, that Addison wrote some of his best papers in "The Spectator" when warm with wine. Dr. Johnson did not seem willing to admit this. Dr. Scott, as a confirmation of it, related that Blackstone, a sober man, composed his "Commentaries" with a bottle of port before him; and found his mind invigorated and supported in the fatigue of his great work, by a temperate use of it.

We talked of the difference between the mode of education at Oxford and that in those colleges where instruction is chiefly conveyed by lectures. JOHNSON. "Lectures were once useful; but now, when all can read, and books are so numerous, lectures are unnecessary. If your attention fails, and you miss a part of the lecture, it is lost; you cannot go back as you do upon a book."

Dr. Scott left us, and soon afterwards we went to dinner. Our company consisted of Mrs. Williams, Mrs. Desmoulins, Mr. Levett, Mr. Allen, the printer, [Mr. Macbean], and Mrs. Hall, sister of the Reverend Mr. John Wesley, and resembling him, as I thought, both in figure and manner. Johnson produced now, for the first time, some handsome silver salvers, which he told me he had bought fourteen years ago; so it was a great day. I was not a little amused by observing Allen perpetually struggling to talk in the manner of Johnson, like the little frog in the fable blowing himself up to resemble the stately ox.

I mentioned a kind of religious Robin-Hood society, which met every Sunday evening at Coachmakers'-Hall for free debate; and that the subject for this night was, the text which relates, with other miracles which happened at our Saviour's death, "And the graves were opened, and many bodies of the saints which slept arose, and came out of the graves after his resurrection, and went into the holy city, and appeared unto many." Mrs. Hall said it was a very curious subject, and she should like to hear it discussed. JOHNSON (somewhat warmly). "One would not go to such a place to hear it,—one would not be seen in such a place, to give countenance to such a meeting." I, however, resolved that I would go. "But, Sir," said she to Johnson, "I should like to hear *you* discuss it." He seemed reluctant to engage in it, and left the question in obscurity.

He mentioned a thing as not unfrequent, of which I had never heard before,—being *called*, that is, hearing one's name pronounced by the voice of a known person at a great distance, far beyond the possibility of being reached by any sound uttered by human organs. An acquaintance, on whose veracity I can depend, told me, that walking home one evening to Kilmarnock, he heard himself *called* from a wood, by the voice of a brother who had gone to America: and the next packet brought accounts of that brother's death. Macbean asserted that this inexplicable *calling* was a thing very well known. Dr. Johnson said, that one day at Oxford, as he was turning the key of his chamber, he heard his mother distinctly call—*Sam*. She was then at Lichfield; but nothing ensued.

Some time after this, upon his making a remark which escaped my attention, Mrs. Williams and Mrs. Hall were both together striving to answer him. He grew angry, and called out loudly, "Nay, when you both speak at once, it is intolerable." But checking himself, and softening, he said, "This one may say, though, you *are* ladies." Then he brightened into gay humour, and addressed them in the words of one of the songs in "The Beggar's Opera,"

But two at a time there's no mortal can bear.

"What, Sir," said I, "are you going to turn Captain Macheath?" There was something as pleasantly ludicrous in this scene as can be imagined. The contrast between Macheath, Polly, and Lucy—and Dr. Samuel Johnson, blind, peevish Mrs. Williams, and lean, lank, preaching Mrs. Hall, was exquisite.

I stole away to Coachmakers'-Hall, and heard the difficult text of which we had talked, discussed with great decency, and some intelligence, by several speakers.

On Friday, April 20, I spent with him one of the happiest days that I remember to have enjoyed in the whole course of my life. Mrs. Garrick, whose grief for the loss of her husband was sincere, had this day, for the first time since his death, a select party of his friends to dine with her. The company was, Miss Hannah More, who lived with her, and whom she called her chaplain; Mrs. Boscawen, Mrs. Elizabeth Carter, Sir Joshua Reynolds, Dr. Burney, Dr. Johnson, and myself. We found ourselves very elegantly entertained at her house in the Adelphi, where I have passed many a pleasing hour with him "who gladdened life." She looked well, talked of her husband with complacency, and while she cast her eyes on his portrait, which hung over the chimney-piece, said, that "death was now the most agreeable object to her." The very semblance of David Garrick was cheering. Mr. Beauclerk, with happy propriety, inscribed under that fine portrait of him the following passage from his beloved Shakspeare:

—————— A merrier man,
Within the limit of becoming mirth,
I never spent an hour's talk withal.
His eye begets occasion for his wit;
For every object that the one doth catch
The other turns to a mirth-moving jest;
Which his fair tongue (Conceit's expositor)
Delivers in such apt and gracious words,
That aged ears play truant at his tales,
And younger hearings are quite ravished
So sweet and voluble is his discourse.

We were all in fine spirits; and I whispered to Mrs. Boscawen, "I believe this is as much as can be made of life." In addition to a splendid entertainment, we were regaled with Lichfield ale, which had a peculiar appropriate value. Sir Joshua, and Dr. Burney, and I drank cordially of it to Dr. Johnson's health; and though he would not join us, he as cordially answered, "Gentlemen, I wish you all as well as you do me."

One of the company mentioned Mr. Thomas Hollis, the strenuous Whig, who used to send over Europe presents of democratical books, with their boards stamped with daggers and caps of liberty. Mrs. Carter said, "He was a bad man: he used to talk uncharitably." JOHNSON. "Poh! poh! Madam; who is the worse for being talked of very uncharitably?" Mrs. Carter said, "I doubt he was an atheist":—JOHNSON. "I don't know that. He might, perhaps, have become one, if he had had time to ripen (smiling). He might have *exuberated* into an atheist."

In the evening we had a large company in the drawing-room. Somebody said, the life of a mere literary man could not be very entertaining. JOHNSON. "But it certainly may. This is a remark which has been made, and repeated, without justice. Why should the life of a literary man be less entertaining than the life of any other man? Are there not as interesting varieties in such a life? As *a literary life* it may be very entertaining." BOSWELL. "But it must be better surely when it is diversified with a little active variety—such as his having gone to Jamaica;—or—his having gone to the Hebrides." Johnson was not displeased at this.

Talking of a very respectable author, he told us a curious circumstance in his life, which was, that he had married a printer's

GLANCED STERNLY AROUND

devil. REYNOLDS. "A printer's devil, Sir! why, I thought a printer's devil was a creature with a black face and in rags." JOHNSON. "Yes, Sir. But I suppose he had her face washed, and put clean clothes on her." Then, looking very serious, and very earnest, "And she did not disgrace him;—the woman had a bottom of good sense." The word *bottom* thus introduced was so ludicrous when contrasted with his gravity, that most of us could not forbear tittering and laughing; though I recollect that the Bishop of Killaloe kept his countenance with perfect steadiness, while Miss Hannah More slily hid her face behind a lady's back who sat on the same settee with her. His pride could not bear that any expression of his should excite ridicule, when he did not intend it: he therefore resolved to assume and exercise despotic power, glanced sternly around, and called out in a strong tone, "Where's the merriment?" Then collecting himself, and looking awful, to make us feel how he could impose restraint, and as it were searching his mind for a still more ludicrous word, he slowly pronounced, "I say the *woman* was *fundamentally* sensible"; as if he had said, "Hear this now, and laugh if you dare." We all sat composed as at a funeral.

He and I walked away together: we stopped a little while by the rails of the Adelphi, looking on the Thames, and I said to him with some emotion, that I was now thinking of two friends we had lost, who once lived in the buildings behind us, Beauclerk and Garrick. "Ay, Sir, (said he, tenderly) and two such friends as cannot be supplied."

On Tuesday, May 8, I had the pleasure of again dining with him and Mr. Wilkes, at Mr. Dilly's. No *negotiation* was now required to bring them together; for Johnson was so well satisfied with the former interview, that he was very glad to meet Wilkes again, who was this day seated between Dr. Beattie and Dr. Johnson (between *Truth* and *Reason*, as General Paoli said, when I told him of it). Johnson and Wilkes joined in extravagant sportive raillery upon the supposed poverty of Scotland, which Dr. Beattie and I did not think it worth our while to dispute.

He gave us an entertaining account of Bet Flint, a woman of the town, who, with some eccentric talents and much effrontery, forced herself upon his acquaintance. "Bet," said he, "wrote her own Life in verse, which she brought to me, wishing that I would furnish her with a preface to it (laughing). I used to say of her, that she was generally slut and drunkard; occasionally whore and thief. She had,

however, genteel lodgings, a spinnet on which she played, and a
boy that walked before her chair. Poor Bet was taken up on a
charge of stealing a counterpane, and tried at the Old Bailey.
Chief Justice ——, who loved a wench, summed up favourably,
and she was acquitted. After which, Bet said, with a gay and
satisfied air, 'Now that the counterpane is *my own*, I shall make a
petticoat of it.' "

The company gradually dropped away. Mr. Dilly himself was
called downstairs upon business; I left the room for some time;
when I returned, I was struck with observing Dr. Samuel Johnson
and John Wilkes, Esq., literally *tête-à-tête;* for they were reclined
upon their chairs, with their heads leaning almost close to each
other, and talking earnestly, in a kind of confidential whisper, of
the personal quarrel between George the Second and the King of
Prussia. Such a scene of perfectly easy sociality presented to my
mind the happy days foretold in the scripture, when the lion shall
lie down with the kid.

After this there was another pretty long interval, during which
Dr. Johnson and I did not meet. When I mentioned it to him with
regret, he was pleased to say, "Then, Sir, let us live double."

About this time it was much the fashion for several ladies to have
evening assemblies, where the fair sex might participate in conversation with literary and ingenious men, animated by a desire
to please. These societies were denominated *Blue-stocking Clubs*.

Johnson was prevailed with to come sometimes into these
circles, and did not think himself too grave even for the lively
Miss Monckton, who used to have the finest *bit of blue* at the house
of her mother, Lady Galway. Her vivacity enchanted the sage,
and they used to talk together with all imaginable ease. A singular
instance happened one evening when she insisted that some of
Sterne's writings were very pathetic. Johnson bluntly denied it.
"I am sure," said she, "they have affected me." "Why," said
Johnson, smiling and rolling himself about, "that is because,
dearest, you're a dunce." When she some time afterwards mentioned this to him, he said, with equal truth and politeness,
"Madam, if I had thought so, I certainly should not have said it."

Another evening Johnson's kind indulgence towards me had a
pretty difficult trial. I had dined at the Duke of Montrose's with
a very agreeable party; and his grace, according to his usual custom,
had circulated the bottle very freely. Lord Graham and I went
together to Miss Monckton's, where I certainly was in extraordi-

nary spirits, and above all fear or awe. In the midst of a great number of persons of the first rank, amongst whom I recollect, with confusion, a noble lady of the most stately decorum, I placed myself next to Johnson, and thinking myself now fully his match, talked to him in a loud and boisterous manner, desirous to let the company know how I could contend with *Ajax*. I particularly remember pressing him upon the value of the pleasures of the imagination, and, as an illustration of my argument, asking him, "What, Sir, supposing I were to fancy that the —— (naming the most charming duchess in his majesty's dominions) were in love with me, should I not be very happy?" My friend with much address evaded my interrogatories, and kept me as quiet as possible; but it may easily be conceived how he must have felt. However, when a few days afterwards I waited upon him and made an apology, he behaved with the most friendly gentleness.

I asked him if he was not dissatisfied with having so small a share of wealth, and none of those distinctions in the state which are the objects of ambition. He had only a pension of three hundred a year. Why was he not in such circumstances as to keep his coach? Why had he not some considerable office? JOHNSON. "Sir, I have never complained of the world; nor do I think that I have reason to complain. It is rather to be wondered at that I have so much. My pension is more out of the usual course of things than any instance that I have known. Here, Sir, was a man avowedly no friend to government at the time, who got a pension without asking for it. I never courted the great; they sent for me; but I think they now give me up. They are satisfied: they have seen enough of me." Upon my observing that I could not believe this, for they must certainly be highly pleased by his conversation; conscious of his own superiority, he answered, "No, Sir; great lords and great ladies don't love to have their mouths stopped."

On Saturday, June 2, I set out for Scotland, and had promised to pay a visit, in my way, as I sometimes did, at Southill, in Bedfordshire, at the hospitable mansion of Squire Dilly, the elder brother of my worthy friends, the booksellers, in the Poultry. Dr. Johnson agreed to be of the party this year. He talked little to us in the carriage, being chiefly occupied in reading Dr. Watson's second volume of "Chemical Essays," which he liked very well, and his own "Prince of Abyssinia," on which he seemed to be intensely fixed; having told us, that he had not looked at it since it was first finished. I happened to take it out of my pocket this day, and he seized upon it with avidity. He pointed out to me the following remarkable passage:

"By what means (said the prince) are the Europeans thus powerful? or why, since they can so easily visit Asia and Africa for trade or conquest, cannot the Asiatics and Africans invade their coasts, plant colonies in their ports, and give laws to their natural princes? The same wind that carried them back would bring us thither." "They are more powerful, Sir, than we (answered Imlac), because they are wiser. Knowledge will always predominate over ignorance, as man governs the other animals. But why their knowledge is more than ours, I know not what reason can be given but the unsearchable will of the Supreme Being."

He said, "This, Sir, no man can explain otherwise."

Upon the road we talked of the uncertainty of profit with which authors and booksellers engage in the publication of literary works. JOHNSON. "My judgment I have found is no certain rule as to the sale of a book." BOSWELL. "Pray, Sir, have you been much plagued with authors sending you their works to revise?" JOHNSON. "No, Sir; I have been thought a sour surly fellow."

He found himself very happy at Squire Dilly's. On Sunday, June 3, we all went to Southill church. Being in a frame of mind which I hope, for the felicity of human nature, many experience,—in fine weather,—at the country-house of a friend,—consoled and elevated by pious exercises,—I expressed myself with an unrestrained fervour to my "Guide, Philosopher, and Friend." "My dear Sir, I would fain be a good man; and I am very good now. I fear God, and honour the king; I wish to do no ill, and to be benevolent to all mankind." He looked at me with a benignant indulgence; but took occasion to give me wise and salutary caution. "Do not, Sir, accustom yourself to trust to *impressions*. Favourable impressions at particular moments, as to the state of our souls, may be deceitful and dangerous."

The opinion as to there being merit in religious faith, being mentioned:—JOHNSON. "Why, yes, Sir, the most licentious man, were hell open before him, would not take the most beautiful strumpet to his arms. We must, as the apostle says, live by faith, not by sight."

Although upon most occasions I never heard a more strenuous advocate for the advantages of wealth than Dr. Johnson, he this day, I know not from what caprice, took the other side. "I have not observed," said he, "that men of very large fortunes, enjoy

"I WOULD PREFER A PRETTY WOMAN"

any thing extraordinary that makes happiness. What has the
Duke of Bedford? What has the Duke of Devonshire? The only
great instance that I have ever known of the enjoyment of wealth
was that of Jamaica Dawkins, who going to visit Palmyra, and
hearing that the way was infested by robbers, hired a troop of
Turkish horse to guard him."

When I observed that a housebreaker was in general very timorous;—JOHNSON. "No wonder, Sir; he is afraid of being shot getting
into a house, or hanged when he has got *out* of it."

On Monday, June 4, we all went to Luton-Hoe, to see Lord
Bute's magnificent seat, for which I had obtained a ticket. As we
entered the park, I talked in a high style of my old friendship with
Lord Mountstuart, and said, "I shall probably be much at this
place." The sage, aware of human vicissitudes, gently checked me:
"Don't you be too sure of that." He made two or three peculiar
observations; as, when shown the botanical garden, "Is not *every*
garden a botanical garden?" When told that there was a shrubbery to the extent of several miles;—"That is making a very
foolish use of the ground; a little of it is very well." When it was
proposed that we should walk on the pleasure-ground; "Don't let
us fatigue ourselves. Why should we walk there? Here's a fine
tree, let's get to the top of it." But upon the whole, he was very
much pleased.

It happened that we visited the seat of Lord Bute upon the
king's birthday; we dined and drank his majesty's health at an
inn in the village of Luton.

In the evening I put him in mind of his promise to favour me
with a copy of his celebrated Letter to the Earl of Chesterfield, and
he was at last pleased to comply with this earnest request, by
dictating it to me from his memory; for he believed that he himself
had no copy. There was an animated glow in his countenance
while he thus recalled his high-minded indignation.

On Tuesday, June 5, Johnson was to return to London. He was
very pleasant at breakfast: I mentioned a friend of mine having
resolved never to marry a pretty woman. JOHNSON. "Sir, it is a
very foolish resolution to resolve not to marry a pretty woman.
Beauty is of itself very estimable. No, Sir, I would prefer a pretty
woman, unless there are objections to her. A pretty woman may
be foolish; a pretty woman may be wicked; a pretty woman may
not like me. But there is no such danger in marrying a pretty
woman as is apprehended; she will not be persecuted if she does

not invite persecution. A pretty woman, if she has a mind to be wicked, can find a readier way than another; and that is all."

I accompanied him in Mr. Dilly's chaise to Shefford, where, talking of Lord Bute's never going to Scotland, he said, "As an Englishman, I should wish all the Scotch gentlemen should be educated in England; Scotland would become a province; they would spend all their rents in England." This is a subject of much consequence, and much delicacy. The advantage of an English education is unquestionably very great to Scotch gentlemen of talents and ambition; and regular visits to Scotland, and perhaps other means, might be effectually used to prevent them from being totally estranged from their native country.

At Shefford I had another affectionate parting from my revered friend, who was taken up by the Bedford coach and carried to the metropolis. I went to see some friends at Bedford; dined with the officers of the militia of the county, and next day proceeded on my journey.

The following anecdote I insert in Dr. Burney's words:

Dr. Burney related to Dr. Johnson the partiality which his writings had excited in Mr. Bewley, well known in Norfolk by the name of the *Philosopher of Massingham;* who had conceived such a reverence for him, that he earnestly begged Dr. Burney to give him the cover of the first letter he had received from him, as a relic of so estimable a writer. This was in 1755. In 1760, when Dr. Burney visited Dr. Johnson at the Temple, in London, where he had then chambers, he happened to arrive there before he was up; and being shown into the room where he was to breakfast, finding himself alone, he examined the contents of the apartment, to try whether he could, undiscovered, steal anything to send to his friend Bewley,[1] as another relic of the admirable Dr. Johnson. But finding nothing better to his purpose, he cut some bristles off his hearth-broom, and enclosed them in a letter to his country enthusiast, who received them with due reverence. The Doctor was so sensible of the honour done to him by a man of genius and science, to whom he was an utter stranger, that he said to Dr. Burney, "Sir, there is no man possessed of the smallest portion of modesty, but must be flattered with the admiration of such a man. I'll give him a set of my Lives, if he will do me the honour to accept of them." In this he kept his word.

In one of his little memorandum-books is the following minute:

---

[1] "The humble but devoted preserver of the bristly tuft of the Bolt Court hearth-broom." So Madame D'Arblay describes Bewley, but is rebuked by Croker for the inaccuracy. The broom belonged to the Temple.

August 9, 3 P.M., ætat. 72, in the summer-house at Streatham. After innumerable resolutions formed and neglected, I have retired hither, to plan a life of greater diligence, in hope that I may yet be useful, and be daily better prepared to appear before my Creator and my Judge, from whose infinite mercy I humbly call for assistance and support.

My purpose is,—To pass eight hours every day in some serious employment.

Having prayed, I purpose to employ the next six weeks upon the Italian language for my settled study.

How venerably pious does he appear in these moments of solitude! and how spirited are his resolutions for the improvement of his mind, even in elegant literature, at a very advanced period of life, and when afflicted with many complaints!

In 1782 his complaints increased, and the history of his life this year is little more than a mournful recital of the variations of his illness.

To James Boswell, Esq.

Jan. 5, 1782

DEAR SIR,

I sit down to answer your letter on the same day in which I received it, and am pleased that my first letter of the year is to you. No man ought to be at ease while he knows himself in the wrong; and I have not satisfied myself with my long silence. . . .

My health has been tottering this last year; and I can give no very laudable account of my time. I am always hoping to do better than I have ever hitherto done. My journey to Ashbourne and Staffordshire was not pleasant; for what enjoyment has a sick man visiting the sick? Shall we ever have another frolic like our journey to the Hebrides?

I hope that dear Mrs. Boswell will surmount her complaints: in losing her you will lose your anchor, and be tossed, without stability, by the waves of life.[1] I wish both you and her very many years, and very happy.

For some months past I have been so withdrawn from the world, that I can send you nothing particular. All your friends however, are well, and will be glad of your return to London. I am, dear Sir, &c.,   SAM. JOHNSON

At a time when he was less able than he had once been to sustain a shock, he was suddenly deprived of Mr. Levett; which event he thus communicated to Dr. Lawrence.

---

[1] The truth of this has been proved by sad experience.—*Boswell.* Mrs. Boswell died June 4. 1789.

Jan. 17, 1782

SIR,

Our old friend, Mr. Levett, who was last night eminently cheerful, died this morning. The man who lay in the same room, hearing an uncommon noise, got up and tried to make him speak, but without effect. He then called Mr. Holder, the apothecary, who, though when he came he thought him dead, opened a vein, but could draw no blood. So has ended the long life of a very useful and very blameless man. I am, Sir, your most humble servant,   SAM. JOHNSON

To Mrs. Lucy Porter, in Lichfield

London, March 2, 1782

DEAR MADAM,

I went away from Lichfield ill, and have had a troublesome time with my breath. For some weeks I have been disordered by a cold, of which I could not get the violence abated till I had been let blood three times. I have not, however, been so bad but that I could have written, and am sorry that I neglected it.

My dwelling is but melancholy. Both Williams and Desmoulins and myself, are very sickly; Frank is not well; and poor Levett died in his bed the other day by a sudden stroke. I suppose not one minute passed between health and death. So uncertain are human things.

Such is the appearance of the world about me; I hope your scenes are more cheerful. But whatever befalls us, though it is wise to be serious, it is useless and foolish, and perhaps sinful, to be gloomy. Let us, therefore, keep ourselves as easy as we can; though the loss of friends will be felt, and poor Levett had been a faithful adherent for thirty years. . . . I am, &c.,

SAM. JOHNSON

On March 19, he thus feelingly mentions Dr. Lawrence:

Poor Lawrence has almost lost the sense of hearing; and I have lost the conversation of a learned, intelligent, and communicative companion, and a friend whom long familiarity has much endeared. Lawrence is one of the best men whom I have known.— *Nostrum omnium miserere Deus.*[1]

---

[1] Dr. Lawrence had long been his friend and confidant. The conversation I saw them hold together in Essex Street, one day in the year 1781 or 1782, was a melancholy one, and made a singular impression on my mind. He was himself exceedingly ill, and I accompanied him thither for advice. The physician was, however, in some respects, more to be pitied than the patient: Johnson was panting under an asthma and dropsy; but Lawrence had been brought home that very morning struck with the palsy, from which he had two hours before we came, strove to awaken himself by blisters: they were both deaf, and scarce able to speak besides; one from difficulty of breathing, the other from paralytic debility. To give and receive medical counsel, therefore, they fairly sat down on each side a table in the doctor's

It was Dr. Johnson's custom, when he wrote to Dr. Lawrence concerning his own health, to use the Latin language. I have been favoured with a specimen:

T. Lawrencio, Medico S.

Maiis Calendis, 1782

Novum frigus, nova tussis, nova spirandi difficultas, novam sanguinis missionem suadent, quam tamen te inconsulto nolim fieri. Ad te venire vix possum, nec est cur ad me venias. Licere vel non licere uno verbo dicendum est; cætera mihi et Holdero [1] reliqueris. Si per te licet, imperatur nuncio Holderum ad me deducere.

Post tu discesseris, quò me vertam? [2]

In one of Johnson's registers of this year there occurs the following curious passage: "*March 20. The ministry is dissolved. I prayed with Francis, and gave thanks.*" [3] His mean opinion of that ministry is strongly confirmed by what he said on the subject to Mr. Seward: "I am glad the ministry is removed. Such a bunch of imbecility never disgraced a country. If they sent a messenger into the city to take up a printer, the messenger was taken up instead of the printer, and committed by the sitting alderman. If they sent one army to the relief of another, the first army was defeated and taken before the second arrived. I will not say that what they did was always wrong; but it was always done at a wrong time."

I wrote to him that I could not come to London this spring, but hoped we should meet somewhere in the summer.

To James Boswell, Esq.

London, March 28, 1782

DEAR SIR,

The pleasure which we used to receive from each other on Good-Friday and Easter-day, we must be this year content to miss. Let us, however, pray for each other, and hope to see one another yet from time to time with mutual delight. My disorder

gloomy apartment, adorned with skeletons, preserved monsters, and agreed to write Latin billets to each other. Such a scene did I never see. "You," said Johnson, "are *timidè* and *gelidè*"; finding that his friend had prescribed palliative not drastic remedies. "It is not *me*," replies poor Lawrence, in an interrupted voice; " 'tis nature that is *gelidè* and *timidè*." In fact he lived but a few months after, I believe, and retained his faculties a still shorter time.—*Piozzi, Anecdotes.*

[1] Mr. Holder, in the Strand, Dr. Johnson's apothecary.
[2] Soon after the above letter, Dr. Lawrence left London.
[3] Lord North's administration was superseded by that of Lord Rockingham on the 9th of March.

has been a cold, which impeded the organs of respiration, and kept me many weeks in a state of great uneasiness; but by repeated phlebotomy it is now relieved: and next to the recovery of Mrs. Boswell, I flatter myself, that you will rejoice at mine.

What we shall do in the summer, it is yet too early to consider. You want to know what you shall do now; I do not think this time of bustle and confusion like to produce any advantage to you. Every man has those to reward and gratify who have contributed to his advancement. To come hither with such expectations at the expense of borrowed money, which I find you know not where to borrow, can hardly be considered prudent. I am sorry to find, what your solicitations seem to imply, that you have already gone the whole length of your credit. This is to set the quiet of your whole life at hazard. If you anticipate your inheritance, you can at last inherit nothing; all that you receive must pay for the past. You must get a place, or pine in penury, with the empty name of a great estate. Poverty, my dear friend, is so great an evil, and pregnant with so much temptation, and so much misery, that I cannot but earnestly enjoin you to avoid it. Live on what you have; live if you can on less; do not borrow either for vanity or pleasure; the vanity will end in shame, and the pleasure in regret: stay therefore at home, till you have saved money for your journey hither. . . . I am, dear Sir, &c.,   SAM. JOHNSON

A clergyman at Bath wrote to him, that a passage in "The Beauties of Johnson" had been pointed out as supposed by some readers to recommend suicide, the words being, "To die is the fate of man; but to die with lingering anguish is generally his folly." Johnson answered:

To the Rev. Mr. ——

At Bath

May 15, 1782

SIR,

Being now in the country in a state of recovery, as I hope, from a very oppressive disorder, I cannot neglect the acknowledgment of your Christian letter. The book called "The Beauties of Johnson" is the production of I know not whom; I never saw it but by casual inspection, and considered myself as utterly disengaged from its consequences. Of the passage you mention, I remember some notice in some paper; but knowing that it must be misrepresented, I thought of it no more, nor do I know where to find it in my own books. I am accustomed to think little of newspapers; but an opinion so weighty and serious as yours has determined me to do, what I should without your seasonable admonition have omitted: and I will direct my thought to be shown in its true state. If I could find the passage, I would direct you to it.[1] I suppose the tenor is this: "Acute diseases are the immediate and inevitable strokes of Heaven; but of them the pain is short, and the conclusion speedy; chronical disorders, by which we are suspended in tedious torture between life and death, are commonly the effect of our own misconduct and intemperance. To die, &c."—This, Sir, you see, is all true and all blameless. I hope some time in the next week to have all rectified. My health has been lately much shaken; if you favour me with any answer, it will be a comfort to me to know that I have your prayers. I am, &c.,   SAM. JOHNSON

This letter, as might be expected, had its full effect, and the clergyman acknowledged it in grateful and pious terms.

The following letter requires no extract to introduce it:

To Mr. Perkins [2]

July 28, 1782

DEAR SIR,

I am much pleased that you are going a very long journey, which may by proper conduct restore your health and prolong your life.

Observe these rules:

1. Turn all care out of your head as soon as you mount the chaise.

2. Do not think about frugality; your health is worth more than it can cost.

3. Do not continue any day's journey to fatigue.

4. Take now and then a day's rest.

5. Get a smart sea-sickness, if you can.

6. Cast away all anxiety, and keep your mind easy.

This last direction is the principal; with an unquiet mind, neither exercise, nor diet, nor physic, can be of much use.

I wish you, dear Sir, a prosperous journey, and a happy recovery. I am, dear Sir, your most affectionate humble servant,

SAM. JOHNSON

---

[1] The original passage (*Rambler*, No. 85) reads:

"Exercise cannot secure us from that dissolution to which we are decreed; but while the soul and body continue united, it can make the association pleasing, and give probable hopes that they shall be disjoined by an easy separation. It was a principle among the ancients, that acute diseases are from Heaven, and chronical from ourselves; the dart of death, indeed, falls from Heaven; but we poison it by our own misconduct: to die is the fate of man; but to die with lingering anguish is generally his folly."

[2] Mr. Thrale's successor in the brewery.

On the 30th August, I informed him that my honoured father had died that morning; a complaint under which he had long laboured having suddenly come to a crisis.

To James Boswell, Esq.

London, Sept. 7, 1782

DEAR SIR,

I have struggled through this year with so much infirmity of body, and such strong impressions of the fragility of life, that death, whenever it appears, fills me with melancholy; and I cannot hear without emotion of the removal of any one, whom I have known, into another state.

Your father's death had every circumstance that could enable you to bear it; it was at a mature age, and it was expected; and as his general life had been pious, his thoughts had doubtless for many years past been turned upon eternity. That you did not find him sensible must doubtless grieve you; his disposition towards you was undoubtedly that of a kind, though not of a fond father. Kindness, at least actual, is in our power, but fondness is not; and if by negligence or imprudence you had extinguished his fondness, he could not at will rekindle it. Nothing then remained between you but mutual forgiveness of each other's faults, and mutual desire of each other's happiness. I shall long to know his final disposition of his fortune.

You, dear Sir, have now a new station, and have therefore new cares and employments. Life, as Cowley seems to say, ought to resemble a well-ordered poem; of which one rule generally received is, that the exordium should be simple, and should promise little. Begin your new course of life with the least show and the least expense possible; you may at pleasure increase both, but you cannot diminish them. Do not think your estate your own, while any man can call upon you for money which you cannot pay: therefore, begin with timorous parsimony. Let it be your first care not to be in any man's debt.

When the thoughts are extended to a future state, the present life seems hardly worthy of all those principles of conduct and maxims of prudence which one generation of men has transmitted to another; but upon a closer view, when it is perceived how much evil is produced and how much good is impeded by embarrassment and distress, and how little room the expedients of poverty leave for the exercise of virtue, it grows manifest that the boundless importance of the next life enforces some attention to the interests of this.

Be kind to the old servants, and secure the kindness of the agents and factors. Do not disgust them by asperity, or unwelcome gaiety, or apparent suspicion. From them you must learn the real state of your affairs, the characters of your tenants, and the value of your lands.

Make my compliments to Mrs. Boswell. I think her expectations from air and exercise are the best that she can form. I hope she will live long and happily. . . .

I am, &c.,   SAM. JOHNSON

In answer to my next letter I received one from him, dissuading me from hastening to him as I had proposed. What is proper for publication is the following paragraph, equally just and tender:

One expense, however, I would not have you to spare: let nothing be omitted that can preserve Mrs. Boswell, though it should be necessary to transplant her for a time into a softer climate. She is the prop and stay of your life. How much must your children suffer by losing her!

My wife was now so much convinced of his sincere friendship for me, and regard for her, that without any suggestion on my part, she wrote him a very polite and grateful letter.

Dr. Johnson to Mrs. Boswell

London, Sept. 7, 1782

DEAR LADY,

I have not often received so much pleasure as from your invitation to Auchinleck. The journey thither and back is, indeed, too great for the latter part of the year; but if my health were fully recovered, I would suffer no little heat and cold, nor a wet or a rough road, to keep me from you. I am, indeed, not without hope of seeing Auchinleck again; but to make it a pleasant place I must see its lady well, and brisk, and airy. For my sake, therefore, among many greater reasons, take care, dear Madam, of your health; spare no expense, and want no attendance, that can procure ease or preserve it. Be very careful to keep your mind quiet; and do not think it too much to give an account of your recovery to, Madam, yours, &c.,   SAM. JOHNSON

To James Boswell, Esq.

London, Dec. 7, 1782

DEAR SIR,

Having passed almost this whole year in a succession of disorders, I went in October to Brighthelmstone, whither I came in a state of so much weakness, that I rested four times in walking between the inn and the lodging. By physic and abstinence I grew better, and am now reasonably easy, though at a great distance from health.   I am afraid, however, that health begins, after seventy, and long before, to have a meaning different from that which it had at thirty.   But it is culpable to murmur at the established order of the creation, as it is vain to oppose it.   He that lives must grow old; and he that would rather grow old than die has God to thank for the infirmities of old age.

At your long silence I am rather angry.   You do not, since now you are at the head of your house, think it worth your while to try whether you or your friend can live longer without writing; nor suspect, after so many years of friendship, that when I do not write to you I forget you.   Put all such useless jealousies out of your head, and disdain to regulate your own practice by the practice of another, or by another principle than the desire of doing right.

Your economy, I suppose, begins now to be settled; your expenses are adjusted to your revenue, and all your people in their proper places.   Resolve not to be poor.   Whatever you have, spend less.   Poverty is a great enemy to human happiness: it certainly destroys liberty; and it makes some virtues impracticable, and others extremely difficult.

Let me know the history of your life since your accession to your estate;—how many houses, how many cows, how much land in your own hand, and what bargains you make with your tenants. . . .

The death of Mr. Thrale had made a very material alteration with respect to Johnson's reception in that family.   The manly authority of the husband no longer curbed the lively exuberance of the lady; and as her vanity had been fully gratified, by having the Colossus of Literature attached to her for many years, she gradually became less assiduous to please him.   Whether her attachment to him was already divided by another object, I am unable to ascertain; but it is plain that Johnson's penetration was alive to her neglect or forced attention; for on the 6th of October this year we find him making a "parting use of the library" at Streatham, and pronouncing a prayer which he composed on leaving Mr. Thrale's family.

Almighty God, Father of all mercy, help me by thy grace, that I may, with humble and sincere thankfulness, remember the comforts and conveniences which I have enjoyed at this place; and that I may resign them with holy submission, equally trusting in thy protection when thou givest and when thou takest away. Have mercy upon me, O Lord! have mercy upon me!

To thy fatherly protection, O Lord, I commend this family. Bless, guide, and defend them, that they may so pass through this world, as finally to enjoy in thy presence everlasting happiness, for Jesus Christ's sake. Amen.

One cannot read this prayer without some emotions not very favourable to the lady whose conduct occasioned it.[1]

He met Mr. Philip Metcalfe often at Sir Joshua Reynolds's and other places, and was a good deal with him at Brighthelmstone this autumn, being pleased at once with his excellent table and animated conversation. Mr. Metcalfe showed him great respect, and sent him a note that he might have the use of his carriage whenever he pleased. Johnson returned this polite answer: "Mr. Johnson is very much obliged by the kind offer of the carriage, but he has no desire of using Mr. Metcalfe's carriage except when he can have the pleasure of Mr. Metcalfe's company." They went together to Chichester, and they visited Petworth, and Cowdray, the venerable seat of the Lords Montacute. "Sir," said Johnson, "I should like to stay here four-and-twenty hours. We see here how our ancestors lived."

In 1783 he was more severely afflicted than ever, as will appear in the course of his correspondence; but still the same ardour for literature, the same constant piety, the same kindness for his friends, and the same vivacity, both in conversation and writing, distinguished him.

On Friday, March 21, having arrived in London the night before, I was glad to find him at Mrs. Thrale's house, in Argyll Street, appearances of friendship between them being still kept up. I was shown into his room; and after the first salutation he said, "I am glad you are come; I am very ill." He looked pale, and was distressed with a difficulty of breathing; but after the common inquiries, he assumed his usual strong animated style of conversation. Seeing me now for the first time as a *laird*, or proprietor of land, he began thus: "Sir, the superiority of a country gentleman over the people upon his estate is very agreeable; and he who says he does not feel it to be agreeable, lies; for it must be agreeable to have a casual superiority over those who are by nature equal with us."

---

[1] The next day he made the following memorandum:

"October 7.—I was called early. I packed up my bundles, and used the foregoing prayer, with my morning devotions somewhat, I think, enlarged. Being earlier than the family, I read St. Paul's farewell in the Acts, and then read fortuitously in the Gospels,—which was my parting use of the library."

BOSWELL. "Yet, Sir, we see great proprietors of land who prefer living in London." JOHNSON. "Why, Sir, the pleasure of living in London, the intellectual superiority that is enjoyed there, may counterbalance the other. Besides, Sir, a man may prefer the state of the country gentleman upon the whole, and yet there may never be a moment when he is willing to make the change, to quit London for it."

He was pleased to say, "You must be as much with me as you can. You have done me good. You cannot think how much better I am since you came in."

He sent a message to acquaint Mrs. Thrale that I was arrived. I had not seen her since her husband's death. She soon appeared, and favoured me with an invitation to stay to dinner, which I accepted. There was no other company but herself and three of her daughters, Dr. Johnson, and I. She too said she was very glad I was come; for she was going to Bath, and should have been sorry to leave Dr. Johnson before I came. This seemed to be attentive and kind; and I, who had not been informed of any change, imagined all to be as well as formerly. He was little inclined to talk at dinner, and went to sleep after it; but when he joined us in the drawing-room he seemed revived, and was again himself.

Talking of conversation, he said, "There must, in the first place, be knowledge—there must be materials; in the second place, there must be a command of words; in the third place, there must be imagination, to place things in such views as they are not commonly seen in; and, in the fourth place, there must be presence of mind, and a resolution that is not to be overcome by failures; this last is an essential requisite; for want of it many people do not excel in conversation. Now *I* want it; I throw up the game upon losing a trick." I wondered to hear him talk thus of himself, and said, "I don't know, Sir, how this may be; but I am sure you beat other people's cards out of their hands." I doubt whether he heard this remark. While he went on talking triumphantly, I was fixed in admiration, and said to Mrs. Thrale, "O for short-hand to take this down!"—"You'll carry it all in your head," said she: "a long head is as good as short-hand."

It has been observed and wondered at, that Mr. Charles Fox never talked with any freedom in the presence of Dr. Johnson; though it is well known, and I myself can witness, that his conversation is various, fluent, and exceedingly agreeable. Johnson's own experience, however, of that gentleman's reserve, was a sufficient reason for his going on thus: "Fox never talks in private company; not from any determination not to talk, but because he has not the first motion. A man who is used to the applause of the House of Commons has no wish for that of a private company. A man accustomed to throw for a thousand pounds, if set down to throw for sixpence, would not be at the pains to count his dice. Burke's talk is the ebullition of his mind. He does not talk from a desire of distinction, but because his mind is full."

After musing for some time, he said, "I wonder how I should have any enemies; for I do harm to nobody." BOSWELL. "In the first place, Sir, you will be pleased to recollect that you set out with attacking the Scotch; so you got a whole nation for your enemies." JOHNSON. "Why, I own that by my definition of *oats* [1] I meant to vex them." BOSWELL. "Pray, Sir, can you trace the cause of your antipathy to the Scotch?" JOHNSON. "I cannot, Sir." BOSWELL. "Old Mr. Sheridan says it was because they sold Charles the First." JOHNSON. "Then, Sir, old Mr. Sheridan has found out a very good reason."

Next day, Saturday, 22nd March, I found him still at Mrs. Thrale's, but he told me that he was to go to his own house in the afternoon. He was better, but I perceived he was but an unruly patient; for Sir Lucas Pepys, who visited him while I was with him, said, "If you were *tractable*, Sir, I should prescribe for you."

I had paid a visit to General Oglethorpe in the morning, and was told by him that Dr. Johnson saw company on Saturday evenings, and he would meet me at Johnson's that night. When I mentioned this to Johnson, not doubting that it would please him, as he had a great value for Oglethorpe, the fretfulness of his disease unexpectedly showed itself; his anger suddenly kindled, and he said with vehemence, "Did not you tell him not to come? Am I to be *hunted* in this manner?" I satisfied him that I could not divine that the visit would not be convenient, and that I certainly could not take it upon me of my own accord to forbid the General.

I found Dr. Johnson in the evening in Mrs. Williams's room, at tea and coffee with her and Mrs. Desmoulins, who were also both ill; it was a sad scene, and he was not in a very good humour. He said of a performance that had lately come out, "Sir, if you should search all the madhouses in England, you would not find ten men who would write so, and think it sense." [2]

---

[1] See p. 63, *note*.
[2] Probably Annus Mirabilis; or, the Eventful Year 1782, an Historical Poem, by the Rev. W. Tasker.

I was glad when General Oglethorpe's arrival was announced, and we left the ladies. Dr. Johnson attended him in the parlour, and was as courteous as ever.

On Sunday, 23rd March, I breakfasted with Dr. Johnson, who seemed much relieved, having taken opium the night before. He however protested against it, as a remedy that should be given with the utmost reluctance, and only in extreme necessity. I mentioned how commonly it was used in Turkey, and that therefore it could not be so pernicious as he apprehended. He grew warm, and said, "Turks take opium, and Christians take opium; but Russel, in his account of Aleppo, tells us, that it is as disgraceful in Turkey to take too much opium, as it is with us to get drunk. Sir, it is amazing how things are exaggerated. A gentleman was lately telling in a company where I was present, that in France as soon as a man of fashion marries, he takes an opera girl into keeping; and this he mentioned as a general custom. 'Pray, Sir,' said I, 'how many opera girls may there be?' He answered, 'About fourscore.' 'Well then, Sir,' said I, 'you see there can be no more than fourscore men of fashion who can do this.' "

Mrs. Desmoulins made tea; and she and I talked before him upon a topic which he had once borne patiently from me when we were by ourselves,—his not complaining of the world, because he was not called to some great office, nor had attained to great wealth. He flew into a violent passion, I confess with some justice, and commanded us to have done. "Nobody," said he, "has a right to talk in this manner, to bring before a man his own character, and the events of his life, when he does not choose it should be done. I never have sought the world; the world was not to seek me. It is rather wonderful that so much has been done for me. All the complaints which are made of the world are unjust. I never knew a man of merit neglected; it was generally by his own fault that he failed of success. A man may hide his head in a hole; he may go into the country, and publish a book now and then, which nobody reads, and then complain he is neglected. There is no reason why any person should exert himself for a man who has written a good book; he has not written it for any individual. I may as well make a present to the postman who brings me a letter. When patronage was limited, an author expected to find a Mæcenas, and complained if he did not find one. Why should he complain? This Mæcenas has others as good as he, or others who have got the start of him."

On the subject of the right employment of wealth, Johnson observed,—"A man cannot make a bad use of his money, so far as regards society, if he does not hoard it; for if he either spends it or lends it out, society has the benefit. It is in general better to spend money than to give it away; for industry is more promoted by spending money than by giving it away. A man who spends his money is sure he is doing good with it; he is not so sure when he gives it away. A man who spends ten thousand a year will do more good than a man who spends two thousand and gives away eight."

In the evening I came to him again. He was somewhat fretful from his illness. A gentleman asked him whether he had been abroad to-day. "Don't talk so childishly," said he. "You may as well ask if I hanged myself to-day." I mentioned politics. Johnson. "Sir, I'd as soon have a man to break my bones as talk to me of public affairs, internal or external. I have lived to see things all as bad as they can be."

Soon after this time I had an opportunity of seeing, by means of one of his friends, a proof that his talents, as well as his obliging service to authors, were ready as ever. He had revised "The Village," an admirable poem, by the Reverend Mr. Crabbe. Its sentiments as to the false notions of rustic happiness and virtue were quite congenial with his own; and he had taken the trouble not only to suggest slight corrections and variations, but to furnish some lines when he thought he could give the writer's meaning better than in the words of the manuscript.

On Sunday, March 30, I found him at home in the evening, and had the pleasure to meet with Dr. Brocklesby. He mentioned a respectable gentleman, who became extremely penurious near the close of his life. Johnson said there must have been a degree of madness about him. "Not at all, Sir," said Dr. Brocklesby, "his judgment was entire." Unluckily, however, he mentioned that although he had a fortune of twenty-seven thousand pounds, he denied himself many comforts, from an apprehension that he could not afford them. "Nay, Sir," cried Johnson, "when the judgment is so disturbed that a man cannot count, that is pretty well."

I praised the accuracy of an account-book of a lady whom I mentioned. Johnson. "Keeping accounts, Sir, is of no use when a man is spending his own money, and has nobody to whom he is to account. You won't eat less beef to-day, because you have written down what it cost yesterday." I mentioned another lady who thought as he did, so that her husband could not get her to keep an account of the expense of the family, as she thought it enough that she never exceeded the sum allowed her. JOHNSON. "Sir, it is fit she should keep an account, because her husband wishes it; but I do not see its use."

It is remarkable, that notwithstanding their congeniality in politics, he never was acquainted with a late eminent noble judge, whom I have heard speak of him as a writer with great respect. Johnson entertained no exalted opinion of his lordship's intellectual character. Talking of him to me one day, he said, "It is wonderful, Sir, with how little real superiority of mind men can make an eminent figure in public life."

I told him I should send him some "Essays" which I had written, which I hoped he would be so good as to read, and pick out the good ones. JOHNSON. "Nay, Sir, send me only the good ones: don't make *me* pick them."

As a small proof of his kindliness and delicacy of feeling, the following circumstance may be mentioned: One evening, when we were in the street together, and I told him I was going to sup at Mr. Beauclerk's he said, "I'll go with you." After having walked part of the way, seeming to recollect something, he suddenly stopped and said, "I cannot go,—but *I do not love Beauclerk the less.*"

He said, "How few of his friends' houses would a man choose to be at when he is sick!" He mentioned one or two. I recollect only Thrale's.

He observed, "There is a wicked inclination in most people to suppose an old man decayed in his intellects. If a young or middle-aged man, when leaving a company, does not recollect where he laid his hat, it is nothing; but if the same inattention is discovered in an old man, people will shrug up their shoulders, and say, 'His memory is going.'"

I am very sorry that I did not take a note of an eloquent argument, in which he maintained that the situation of Prince of Wales was the happiest of any person's in the kingdom, even beyond that of the sovereign. I recollect only—the enjoyment of hope—the high superiority of rank, without the anxious cares of government—and a great degree of power, both from natural influence wisely used, and from the sanguine expectations of those who look forward to the chance of future favour.

Sir Joshua Reynolds communicated to me the following particular:

He said, "A man should pass a part of his time with *the laughers,* by which means any thing ridiculous or particular about him might be presented to his view, and corrected." I observed, he must have been a bold laugher who would have ventured to tell Dr. Johnson of any of his particularities.[1]

Johnson's dexterity in retort, when he seemed to be driven to an extremity by his adversary, was very remarkable. However unfavourable to Scotland, he uniformly gave liberal praise to George Buchanan, as a writer. In a conversation concerning the literary merits of the two countries, in which Buchanan was introduced, a Scotchman, imagining that on this ground he should have an undoubted triumph over him, exclaimed, "Ah, Dr. Johnson, what would you have said of Buchanan had he been an Englishman?" "Why, Sir," said Johnson, after a little pause, "I should *not* have said of Buchanan, had he been an *Englishman,* what I will now say of him as *Scotchman,*—that he was the only man of genius his country ever produced."

Though his usual phrase for conversation was *talk,* yet he made a distinction; for when he once told me that he dined the day before at a friend's house, with "a very pretty company"; and I asked him if there was good conversation, he answered, "No, Sir; we had *talk* enough, but no *conversation;* there was nothing *discussed.*"

Mr. Hoole told him he was born in Moorfields, and had received part of his early instruction in Grub Street. "Sir," said Johnson, smiling, "you have been *regularly* educated." Having asked who was his instructor, and Mr. Hoole having answered, "My uncle, Sir, who was a tailor"; Johnson, recollecting himself, said, "Sir, I knew him: we called him the *metaphysical tailor.* He was of a club in Old Street, with me and George Psalmanazar, and some others: but pray, Sir, was he a good tailor?" Mr. Hoole having answered that he believed he was too mathematical, and used to draw squares and triangles on his shopboard, so that he did not excel in the cut of a coat. "I am sorry for it," said Johnson, "for I would have every man to be master of his own business."

In pleasant reference to himself and Mr. Hoole, as brother authors, he often said, "Let you and I, Sir, go together, and eat a beefsteak in Grub Street."

He said to Sir William Scott, "The age is running mad after

[1] I am happy, however, to mention a pleasing instance of his enduring with great gentleness to hear one of his most striking particularities pointed out: Miss Hunter, a niece of his friend, Christopher Smart, when a very young girl, struck by his extraordinary motions, said to him, "Pray, Dr. Johnson, why do you make such strange gestures?" "From bad habit," he replied: "do you, my dear, take care to guard against bad habits."—*Boswell.*

innovation; and all the business of the world is to be done in a new way; men are to be hanged in a new way; Tyburn itself is not safe from the fury of innovation." It having been argued that this was an improvement.—"No, Sir," said he, eagerly, "it is *not* an improvement: they object, that the old method drew together a number of spectators. Sir, executions are intended to draw spectators. If they do not draw spectators, they don't answer their purpose. The old method was most satisfactory to all parties; the public was gratified by a procession; the criminal was supported by it. Why is all this to be swept away?" I perfectly agree with Dr. Johnson upon this head, and am persuaded that executions now, the solemn procession being discontinued, have not nearly the effect which they formerly had.

Johnson's attention to precision and clearness in expression was very remarkable. He disapproved of a parenthesis; and I believe, in all his voluminous writings, not half a dozen of them will be found. He never used the phrases the *former* and the *latter*, having observed, that they often occasioned obscurity; he therefore contrived to construct his sentences so as not to have occasion for them, and would even rather repeat the same words, in order to avoid them. Nothing is more common than to mistake surnames, when we hear them carelessly uttered for the first time. To prevent this, he used not only to pronounce them slowly and distinctly, but to take the trouble of spelling them; a practice which I have often followed, and which I wish were general.

Such was the heat and irritability of his blood, that not only did he pare his nails to the quick, but scraped the joints of his fingers with a penknife, till they seemed quite red and raw.

The heterogeneous composition of human nature was remarkably exemplified in Johnson. His liberality in giving his money to persons in distress was extraordinary. Yet there lurked about him a propensity to paltry saving. One day I owned to him, that "I was occasionally troubled with a fit of *narrowness*." "Why, Sir," said he, "so am I. *But I do not tell it.*" He has now and then borrowed a shilling of me; and when I asked him for it again, seemed to be rather out of humour. A droll little circumstance once occurred; as if he meant to reprimand my minute exactness as a creditor, he thus addressed me;—"Boswell, *lend* me sixpence—*not to be repaid.*"

This great man's attention to small things was very remarkable. As an instance of it, he one day said to me, "Sir, when you get silver in change for a guinea, look carefully at it; you may find some curious piece of coin."

Though a stern, *true-born Englishman*, and fully prejudiced against all other nations, he had discernment enough to see, and candour enough to censure, the cold reserve too common among Englishmen towards strangers: "Sir," said he, "two men of any other nation who are shown into a room together, at a house where they are both visitors, will immediately find some conversation. But two Englishmen will probably go each to a different window, and remain in obstinate silence. Sir, we as yet do not enough understand the common rights of humanity."

Maurice Morgann, Esq., had once an opportunity of entertaining Johnson a day or two at Wycombe, and by him I have been favoured with two anecdotes.

One is not a little to the credit of Johnson's candour. Mr. Morgann and he had a dispute pretty late at night, in which Johnson would not give up, though he had the wrong side; and, in short, both kept the field. Next morning, when they met in the break-fasting-room, Dr. Johnson accosted Mr. Morgann thus: "Sir, I have been thinking on our dispute last night;—*You were in the right.*" [1]

The other was as follows: Johnson, for sport perhaps, or from the spirit of contradiction, eagerly maintained that Derrick had merit as a writer. Mr. Morgann argued with him directly, in vain. At length he had recourse to this device. "Pray, Sir," said he, "whether do you reckon Derrick or Smart the best poet?" Johnson at once felt himself roused; and answered, "Sir, there is no settling the point of precedency between a louse and a flea."

Once, when checking my boasting too frequently of myself in company, he said to me, "Boswell, you often vaunt so much as to provoke ridicule. You put me in mind of a man who was standing in the kitchen of an inn with his back to the fire, and thus accosted the person next him. 'Do you know, Sir, who I am?' 'No, Sir,' said the other, 'I have not that advantage.' 'Sir,' said he, 'I am the *great* Twalmley, who invented the New Floodgate Iron.'" [2]

He was pleased to say to me one morning when we were left

---

[1] A friend was one day, about two years before his death, struck with some instance of Dr. Johnson's great candour. "Well, Sir," said he, "I will always say that you are a very candid man." "Will you?" replied the doctor; "I doubt then you will be very singular. But, indeed, Sir," continued he, "I look upon myself to be a man very much misunderstood. I am not an uncandid, nor am I a severe man. I sometimes say more than I mean, in jest; and people are apt to believe me serious: however, I am more candid than I was when I was younger. As I know more of mankind, I expect less of them, and am ready now to call a man *a good man* upon easier terms than I was formerly."

[2] A kind of box-iron for smoothing linen.

alone in his study, "Boswell, I think I am easier with you than with almost any body."

His acute observation of human life made him remark, "Sir, there is nothing by which a man exasperates most people more than by displaying a superior ability of brilliancy in conversation. They seem pleased at the time; but their envy makes them curse him at their hearts."

Johnson's love of little children, which he discovered upon all occasions, calling them "pretty dears," and giving them sweetmeats, was an undoubted proof of the real humanity and gentleness of his disposition.

His uncommon kindness to his servants, and serious concern, not only for their comfort in this world, but their happiness in the next, was another unquestionable evidence of what all, who were intimately acquainted with him, knew to be true.

Nor would it be just, under this head, to omit the fondness which he showed for animals which he had taken under his protection. I shall never forget the indulgence with which he treated Hodge, his cat; for whom he himself used to go out and buy oysters, lest the servants, having that trouble, should take a dislike to the poor creature. I am, unluckily, one of those who have an antipathy to a cat, so that I am uneasy when in the room with one; and I own that I frequently suffered a good deal from the presence of this same Hodge. I recollect him one day scrambling up Dr. Johnson's breast, apparently with much satisfaction, while my friend, smiling and half-whistling, rubbed down his back, and pulled him by the tail; and when I observed he was a fine cat, saying, "Why, yes, Sir, but I have had cats whom I liked better than this"; and then, as if perceiving Hodge to be out of countenance, adding, "But he is a very fine cat, a very fine cat indeed."

This reminds me of the ludicrous account which he gave of the despicable state of a young gentleman of good family. "Sir, when I heard of him last, he was running about town shooting cats." And then, in a sort of kindly reverie, he bethought himself of his own favourite cat, and said, "But Hodge shan't be shot; no, no, Hodge shall not be shot."

On Saturday, April 12, I visited him, in company with Mr. Windham, of Norfolk, whom, though a Whig, he highly valued. He talked to-day a good deal of the wonderful extent and variety of London, and observed, that men of curious enquiry might see in it such modes of life as very few could even imagine. He in

"HE IS A VERY FINE CAT"

particular recommended to us to *explore Wapping*, which we resolved to do.[1]

On April 18 (being Good Friday), I found him at breakfast, in his
usual manner upon that day, drinking tea without milk, and eating
a cross bun to prevent faintness; we went to St. Clement's church, as
formerly. When we came home from church, he placed himself on
one of the stone seats at his garden door, and I took the other, and
thus in the open air, and in a placid frame of mind, he talked away
very easily. JOHNSON. "Were I a country gentleman, I should
not be very hospitable; I should not have crowds in my house."
BOSWELL. "Sir Alexander Dick tells me that he remembers having
a thousand people in a year to dine at his house; that is, reckoning
each person as one, each time that he dined there." JOHNSON.
"That, Sir, is about three a day." BOSWELL. "How your statement
lessens the idea!" JOHNSON. "That, Sir, is the good of counting.
It brings every thing to a certainty, which before floated in the
mind indefinitely." BOSWELL. "But *Omne ignotum pro magnifico
est:* one is sorry to have this diminished." JOHNSON. "Sir, you
should not allow yourself to be delighted with error." BOSWELL.
"Three a day seem but few." JOHNSON. "Nay, Sir, he who entertains three a day does very liberally. And if there is a large family,
the poor entertain those three, for they eat what the poor would
get; there must be superfluous meat; it must be given to the poor, or
thrown out." BOSWELL. "I observe in London, that the poor go
about and gather bones, which I understand are manufactured."
JOHNSON. "Yes, Sir; they boil them, and extract a grease from them
for greasing wheels and other purposes. Of the best pieces they make
a mock ivory, which is used for hafts to knives, and various other
things; the coarser pieces they burn and pound, and sell the ashes."
BOSWELL. "For what purpose, Sir?" JOHNSON. "Why, Sir, for
making a furnace for the chemists for melting iron. A paste made
of burnt bones will stand a stronger heat than any thing else.
Consider, Sir, if you are to melt iron, you cannot line your pot
with brass, because it is softer than iron, and would melt sooner;
nor with iron, for though malleable iron is harder than cast-iron,
yet it would not do; but a paste of burnt bones will not melt."
BOSWELL. "Do you know, Sir, I have discovered a manufacture

[1] We accordingly carried our scheme into execution, in October, 1782; but whether from that uniformity which has in modern times, in a great degree, spread through every part of the metropolis, or
from our want of sufficient exertion, we were disappointed.—*Boswell.*
  This is also recorded by Windham in his Diary.—"Oct. 23. I let myself foolishly be drawn by Boswell
to explore, as he called it, Wapping, instead of going, when everything was prepared, to see the battle
between Ward and Stanyard, which turned out a very good one and which would have served as a **very**
good introduction to Boswell."

to a great extent, of what you only piddle at—scraping and drying the peel of oranges? At a place in Newgate Street there is a prodigious quantity prepared, which they sell to the distillers." JOHNSON. "Sir, I believe they make a higher thing out of them than a spirit; they make what is called orange-butter, the oil of the orange inspissated, which they mix perhaps with common pomatum, and make it fragrant. The oil does not fly off in the drying." BOSWELL. "I wish to have a good walled garden." JOHNSON. "I don't think it would be worth the expense to you. We compute, in England, a park wall at a thousand pounds a mile: now a garden wall must cost at least as much. You intend your trees should grow higher than a deer will leap. Now let us see; for a hundred pounds you could only have forty-four square yards,[1] which is very little; for two hundred pounds you may have eighty-four square yards, which is very well. But when will you get the value of two hundred pounds of walls, in fruit, in your climate? No, Sir; such contention with nature is not worth while. I would plant an orchard, and have plenty of such fruit as ripen well in your country. My friend, Dr. Madden, of Ireland, said, that 'In an orchard there should be enough to eat, enough to lay up, enough to be stolen, and enough to rot upon the ground.' Cherries are an early fruit; you may have them; and you may have the early apples and pears." BOSWELL. "We cannot have nonpareils." JOHNSON. "Sir, you can no more have nonpareils than you can have grapes." BOSWELL. "We have them, Sir; but they are very bad." JOHNSON. "Nay, Sir, never try to have a thing merely to show that you *cannot* have it. From ground that would let for forty shillings you may have a large orchard; and you see it costs you only forty shillings. Nay, you may graze the ground when the trees are grown up; you cannot, while they are young." BOSWELL. "Is not a good garden a very common thing in England, Sir?" JOHNSON. "Not so common, Sir, as you imagine. In Lincolnshire there is hardly an orchard; in Staffordshire, very little fruit." BOSWELL. "Has Langton no orchard?" JOHNSON. "No, Sir." BOSWELL. "How so, Sir?" JOHNSON. "Why, Sir, from the general negligence of the country. He has it not, because nobody else has it." BOSWELL. "A hothouse is a certain thing; I may have that." JOHNSON. "A hothouse is pretty certain; but you must first build it, then you must keep fires in it, and you must have a gardener to take care of it." BOSWELL. "But if I have a gardener at any rate?——" JOHNSON.

[1] A slip, for forty-four yards square.

"Why, yes." Boswell. "I'd have it near my house; there is no need to have it in the orchard." Johnson. "Yes, I'd have it near my house. I would plant a great many currants; the fruit is good, and they make a pretty sweetmeat."

Talking of the origin of language:—Johnson. "It must have come by inspiration. A thousand, nay a million of children could not invent a language. While the organs are pliable, there is not understanding enough to form a language; by the time that there is understanding enough, the organs are become stiff. We know that after a certain age we cannot learn to pronounce a new language. No foreigner, who comes to England when advanced in life, ever pronounces English tolerably well; at least such instances are very rare. When I maintain that language must have come by inspiration, I do not mean that inspiration is required for rhetoric, and all the beauties of language; for when once man has language, we can conceive that he may gradually form modifications of it. I mean only that inspiration seems to me to be necessary to give man the faculty of speech; to inform him that he may have speech; which I think he could no more find out without inspiration, than cows or hogs would think of such a faculty."

Mrs. Burney, wife of his friend, Dr. Burney, came in, and he seemed to be entertained with her conversation.

Garrick's funeral was talked of as extravagantly expensive. Johnson, from his dislike to exaggeration, would not allow that it was distinguished by an extraordinary pomp. "Were there not six horses to each coach?" said Mrs. Burney. Johnson. "Madam, there were no more six horses than six phœnixes."

Mrs. Burney wondered that some very beautiful new buildings should be erected in Moorfields, in so shocking a situation as between Bedlam and St. Luke's Hospital; and said she could not live there. Johnson. "Nay, Madam, you see nothing there to hurt you. You no more think of madness by having windows that look to Bedlam, than you think of death by having windows that look to a churchyard." Mrs. Burney. "We may look to a churchyard, Sir; for it is right that we should be kept in mind of death." Johnson. "Nay, Madam, if you go to that, it is right that we should be kept in mind of madness, which is occasioned by too much indulgence of imagination. I think a very moral use may be made of these new buildings; I would have those who have heated imaginations live there, and take warning."

Time passed on in conversation till it was too late for the service of the church at three o'clock. I took a walk, and left him alone for some time; then returned, and we had coffee and conversation again by ourselves. We went to evening prayers at St. Clement's, at seven, and then parted.

On Sunday, April 20, being Easter-day, after attending solemn service at St. Paul's, I came to Dr. Johnson, and found Mr. Lowe, the painter, sitting with him. Mr. Lowe mentioned the great number of new buildings of late in London, yet that Dr. Johnson had observed, that the number of inhabitants was not increased. JOHNSON. "Why, Sir, the bills of mortality prove that no more people die now than formerly; so it is plain no more live. The register of births proves nothing, for not one-tenth of the people of London are born there." BOSWELL. "I believe, Sir, a great many of the children born in London, die early." JOHNSON. "Why, yes, Sir." BOSWELL. "But those who do live are as stout and strong people as any. Dr. Price says, they must be naturally strong to get through." JOHNSON. "That is system, Sir. A great traveller observes, that it is said there are no weak or deformed people among the Indians; but he, with much sagacity, assigns the reason of this, which is, that the hardship of their life as hunters and fishers does not allow weak or diseased children to grow up. Now, had I been an Indian, I must have died early; my eyes would not have served me to get food. I, indeed, now could fish, give me English tackle; but had I been an Indian, I must have starved, or they would have knocked me on the head, when they saw I could do nothing." BOSWELL. "Perhaps, they would have taken care of you; we are told they are fond of oratory,—you would have talked to them." JOHNSON. "Nay, Sir, I should not have lived long enough to be fit to talk; I should have been dead before I was ten years old. Depend upon it, Sir, a savage, when he is hungry, will not carry about with him a looby of nine years old, who cannot help himself. They have no affection, Sir." BOSWELL. "I believe natural affection, of which we hear so much, is very small." JOHNSON. "Sir, natural affection is nothing: but affection from principle and established duty is sometimes wonderfully strong." LOWE. "A hen, Sir, will feed her chickens in preference to herself." JOHNSON. "But we don't know that the hen is hungry; let the hen be fairly hungry, and I'll warrant she'll peck the corn herself. A cock, I believe, will feed hens instead of himself: but we don't know that the cock is hungry." BOSWELL. "And that, Sir, is not from affection, but gallantry. But some of the Indians have affection."

JOHNSON. "Sir, that they help some of their children is plain; for some of them live, which they could not do without being helped."

I dined with him; the company were Mrs. Williams, Mrs. Desmoulins, and Mr. Lowe. He seemed not to be well, talked little, grew drowsy soon after dinner, and retired; upon which I went away.

Having next day gone to Mr. Burke's seat in the country, from whence I was recalled by an express, that a near relation of mine had killed his antagonist in a duel, and was himself dangerously wounded, I saw little of Dr. Johnson till Monday, April 28, when I spent a considerable part of the day with him, and introduced the subject which then chiefly occupied my mind. JOHNSON. "I do not see, Sir, that fighting is absolutely forbidden in Scripture; I see revenge forbidden, but not self-defence." BOSWELL. "The Quakers say it is. 'Unto him that smiteth thee on one cheek, offer him also the other.'" JOHNSON. "But stay, Sir; the text is meant only to have the effect of moderating passion; it is plain that we are not to take it in a literal sense. We see this from the context, where there are other recommendations; which, I warrant you, the Quaker will not take literally; as, for instance, 'From him that would borrow of thee turn thou not away.' Let a man whose credit is bad come to a Quaker, and say, 'Well, Sir, lend me a hundred pounds'; he'll find him as unwilling as any other man. No, Sir; a man may shoot the man who invades his character, as he may shoot him who attempts to break into his house.[1] So, in 1745, my friend, Tom Cumming, the Quaker, said he would not fight, but he would drive an ammunition cart: and we know that the Quakers have sent flannel waistcoats to our soldiers, to enable them to fight better." BOSWELL. "When a man is the aggressor, and by ill usage forces on a duel in which he is killed, have we not little ground to hope that he is gone to a state of happiness?" JOHNSON. "Sir, we are not to judge determinately of the state in which a man leaves this life. He may in a moment have repented effectually, and it is possible may have been accepted of God. There is in 'Camden's Remains' an epitaph upon a very wicked man, who was killed by a fall from his horse, in which he is supposed to say,

'Between the stirrup and the ground
I mercy ask'd, I mercy found.'"

[1] I think it necessary to caution my readers against concluding that, in this or any other conversation of Dr. Johnson, they have his serious and deliberate opinion on the subject of duelling. In my Journal of a Tour to the Hebrides he made this frank confession: "Nobody, at times, talks more laxly than I do"; and "He fairly owned he could not explain the rationality of duelling." We may therefore infer that he could not think that justifiable, which seems so inconsistent with the spirit of the Gospel. At the same time, it must be confessed, that, from the prevalent notions of honour, a gentleman who receives a challenge is reduced to a dreadful alternative.—*Boswell.*

BOSWELL. "Is not the expression in the burial-service—'in the *sure* and *certain* hope of a *blessed* resurrection'—too strong to be used indiscriminately, and, indeed, sometimes when those over whose bodies it is said have been notoriously profane?" JOHNSON. "It is sure and certain *hope*, Sir, not *belief*."

I mentioned the very liberal payment which had been received for reviewing; and as evidence of this, that it had been proved in a trial, that Dr. Shebbeare had received six guineas a sheet for that kind of literary labour. JOHNSON. "Sir, he might get six guineas for a particular sheet, but not *communibus sheetibus*." BOSWELL. "Pray, Sir, by a sheet of review, is it meant that it shall be all of the writer's own composition? or are extracts, made from the book reviews, deducted?" JOHNSON. "No, Sir; it is a sheet, no matter of what." BOSWELL. "I think that is not reasonable." JOHNSON. "Yes, Sir, it is. A man will more easily write a sheet all his own, than read an octavo volume to get extracts." To one of Johnson's wonderful fertility of mind, I believe writing was really easier than reading and extracting; but with ordinary men the case is very different.

Upon being told that old Mr. Sheridan, indignant at the neglect of his oratorical plans, had threatened to go to America: JOHNSON. "I hope he will go to America." BOSWELL. "The Americans don't want oratory." JOHNSON. "But we can want Sheridan."

On Monday, April 28, I found him at home in the morning, and Mr. Seward with him. Horace having been mentioned: BOSWELL. "There is a great deal of thinking in his works. One finds there almost every thing but religion. There are, I am afraid, many people who have no religion at all." SEWARD. "And sensible people, too." JOHNSON. "Why, Sir, not sensible in that respect. There must be either a natural or a moral stupidity, if one lives in a total neglect of so very important a concern." SEWARD. "I wonder that there should be people without religion." JOHNSON. "Sir, you need not wonder at this, when you consider how large a proportion of almost every man's life is passed without thinking of it. I myself was for some years totally regardless of religion. It had dropped out of my mind. It was at an early part of my life. Sickness brought it back, and I hope I have never lost it since." BOSWELL. "My dear Sir, what a man must you have been without religion! Why you must have gone on drinking, and swearing, and——" JOHNSON (with a smile). "I drank enough, and swore enough, to be sure." SEWARD. "One should think that sickness and the view of death would make more men religious." JOHNSON. "Sir, they do not know how to go about it: they have not the first notion. A man who has never had religion before, no more grows religious when he is sick, than a man who has never learnt figures can count when he has need of calculation."

On Thursday, 1st May, I visited him in the evening along with young Mr. Burke.[1] He said, "It is strange that there should be so little reading in the world, and so much writing. People in general do not willingly read, if they can have any thing else to amuse them. There must be an external impulse; emulation, or vanity, or avarice. The progress which the understanding makes through a book has more pain than pleasure in it. Language is scanty and inadequate to express the nice gradations and mixtures of our feelings. No man reads a book of science from pure inclination. The books that we do read with pleasure are light compositions, which contain a quick succession of events. However, I have this year read all Virgil through. I read a book of the Æneid every night, so it was done in twelve nights, and I had a great delight in it. The Georgics did not give me so much pleasure, except the fourth book. The Eclogues I have almost all by heart. I do not think the story of the Æneid interesting. I like the story of the Odyssey much better; and this not on account of the wonderful things which it contains; for there are wonderful things enough in the Æneid;—the ships of the Trojans turned to sea-nymphs,—the tree at Polydorus's tomb dropping blood. The story of the Odyssey is interesting, as a great part of it is domestic. It has been said there is pleasure in writing, particularly in writing verses. I allow you may have pleasure from writing after it is over, if you have written well; but you don't go willingly to it again. I know, when I have been writing verses, I have run my finger down the margin, to see how many I had made, and how few I had to make."

He seemed to be in a very placid humour; and although I have no note of the particulars of young Mr. Burke's conversation, it was such that Dr. Johnson said to me afterwards, "He did very well indeed; I have a mind to tell his father."

I have no minute of any interview with Johnson till Thursday, May 15th, when I find what follows: BOSWELL. "I wish much to be in parliament, Sir." JOHNSON. "Why, Sir, unless you come resolved to support any administration, you would be the worse for being in parliament, because you would be obliged to live more

[1] Richard Burke, who died Aug. 2, 1794, in his thirty-fifth year.

expensively." BOSWELL. "Perhaps, Sir, I should be the less happy for being in parliament. I never would sell my vote, and I should be vexed if things went wrong." JOHNSON. "That's cant, Sir. It would not vex you more in the House than in the gallery: public affairs vex no man." BOSWELL. "Have not they vexed yourself a little, Sir? Have not you been vexed by all the turbulence of this reign, and by that absurd vote of the House of Commons, 'That the influence of the crown has increased, is increasing, and ought to be diminished'?" JOHNSON. "Sir, I have never slept an hour less, nor eat an ounce less meat. I would have knocked the factious dogs on the head, to be sure; but I was not *vexed*." BOSWELL. "I declare, Sir, upon my honour, I did imagine I was vexed, and took a pride in it; but it *was*, perhaps, cant; for I own I neither eat less nor slept less." JOHNSON. "My dear friend, clear your *mind* of cant. You may *talk* as other people do; you may say to a man, 'Sir, I am your humble servant.' You are *not* his most humble servant. You may say, 'These are bad times; it is a melancholy thing to be reserved to such times.' You don't mind the times. You tell a man, 'I am sorry you had such bad weather the last day of your journey, and were so much wet.' You don't care sixpence whether he is wet or dry. You may *talk* in this manner; it is a mode of talking in society; but don't *think* foolishly."

I talked of living in the country. JOHNSON. "Don't set up for what is called hospitality; it is a waste of time, and a waste of money: you are eaten up, and not the more respected for your liberality. If your house be like an inn, nobody·cares for you. A man who stays a week with another makes him a slave for a week." BOSWELL. "But there are people, Sir, who make their houses a home to their guests, and are themselves quite easy." JOHNSON. "Then, Sir, home must be the same to the guests, and they need not come."

Another day I mentioned my expectations from the interest of an eminent person then in power; adding, "But I have no claim but the claim of friendship; however, some people will go a great way from that motive." JOHNSON. "Sir, they will go all the way from that motive." A gentleman talked of retiring;—"Never think of that," said Johnson. The gentleman urged, "I should then do no ill." JOHNSON. "Nor no good either. Sir, it would be a civil suicide."

On Monday, May 26, I found him at tea, and the celebrated Miss Burney, the author of "Evelina" and "Cecilia," with him.

I asked if there would be any speakers in parliament, if there were no places to be obtained. JOHNSON. "Yes, Sir. Why do you speak here? Either to instruct and entertain, which is a benevolent motive; or for distinction, which is a selfish motive." I mentioned "Cecilia." JOHNSON (with an air of animated satisfaction). "Sir, if you talk of 'Cecilia,' talk on."

I asked, whether a man naturally virtuous, or one who has over-come wicked inclinations, is the best. JOHNSON. "Sir, to *you*, the man who has overcome wicked inclinations is not the best. He has more merit to *himself*. I would rather trust my money to a man who has no hands, and so a physical impossibility to steal, than to a man of the most honest principles. There is a witty satirical story of Foote. He had a small bust of Garrick placed upon his bureau. 'You may be surprised,' said he, 'that I allow him to be so near my gold;—but you will observe he has no hands.' "

On Friday, May 29, being to set out for Scotland next morning, I passed a part of the day with him in more than usual earnestness, as his health was in a more precarious state than at any time when I had parted from him.

He said, "Get as much force of mind as you can. Live within your income. Always have something saved at the end of the year. Let your imports be more than your exports, and you'll never go far wrong."

I assured him, that in the extensive and various range of his ac-quaintance there never had been any one who had a more sincere respect and affection for him than I had. He said, "I believe it, Sir. Were I in distress, there is no man to whom I should sooner come than to you. I should like to come and have a cottage in your park, toddle about, live mostly on milk, and be taken care of by Mrs. Boswell. She and I are good friends now; are we not?"

He embraced me, and gave me his blessing, as usual, when I was leaving him for any length of time. I walked from his door to-day with a fearful apprehension of what might happen before I re-turned.

My anxious apprehensions at parting with him this year proved to be but too well founded; for not long afterwards he had a dread-ful stroke of the palsy, of which there are very full and accurate accounts in letters written by himself, to show with what compo-sure of mind and resignation to the Divine will his steady piety enabled him to behave.

To Mr. Edmund Allen

June 17, 1783

It has pleased God this morning to deprive me of the powers of speech; and as I do not know but that it may be his further good pleasure to deprive me soon of my senses, I request you will, on the receipt of this note, come to me, and act for me as the exigencies of my case may require. I am, &c.,   Sam. Johnson

To the Reverend Dr. John Taylor

June 17, 1783

Dear Sir,

It has pleased God, by a paralytic stroke in the night, to deprive me of speech. I am very desirous of Dr. Heberden's assistance, as I think my case is not past remedy. Let me see you as soon as it is possible. Bring Dr. Heberden with you, if you can; but come yourself at all events. I am glad you are so well when I am so dreadfully attacked.

I think that by a speedy application of stimulants much may be done. I question if a vomit, vigorous and rough, would not rouse the organs of speech to action. As it is too early to send, I will try to recollect what I can that can be suspected to have brought on this dreadful distress.

I have been accustomed to bleed frequently for an asthmatic complaint; but have forborne for some time by Dr. Pepys's persuasion, who perceived my legs beginning to swell. I sometimes alleviate a painful, or, more properly, an oppressive constriction of my chest, by opiates; and have lately taken opium frequently; but the last, or two last times, in smaller quantities. My largest dose is three grains, and last night I took but two. You will suggest these things (and they are all that I can call to mind) to Dr. Heberden. I am, &c.,   Sam. Johnson

Two days after he wrote thus to Mrs. Thrale:

On Monday, the 16th, I sat for my picture and walked a considerable way with little inconvenience. In the afternoon and evening I felt myself light and easy, and began to plan schemes of life. Thus I went to bed, and in a short time waked and sat up, as has been long my custom, when I felt a confusion and indistinctness in my head, which lasted, I suppose, about half a minute. I was alarmed, and prayed God, that however he might afflict my body, he would spare my understanding. This prayer, that I might try the integrity of my faculties, I made in Latin verse.

The lines were not very good, but I knew them not to be very good: I made them easily, and concluded myself to be unimpaired in my faculties.

Soon after I perceived that I had suffered a paralytic stroke, and that my speech was taken from me. I had no pain, and so little dejection in this dreadful state, that I wondered at my own apathy, and considered that perhaps death itself, when it should come, would excite less horror than seems now to attend it.

In order to rouse the vocal organs, I took two drams. Wine has been celebrated for the production of eloquence. I put myself into violent motion, and I think repeated it; but all was vain. I then went to bed; and, strange as it may seem, I think slept. When I saw light, it was time to contrive what I should do. Though God stopped my speech, he left me my hand: I enjoyed a mercy which was not granted to my dear friend Lawrence, who now perhaps overlooks me as I am writing, and rejoices that I have what he wanted. My first note was necessarily to my servant, who came in talking, and could not immediately comprehend why he should read what I put into his hands.

I then wrote a card to Mr. Allen, that I might have a discreet friend at hand to act as occasion should require. In penning this note I had some difficulty: my hand, I knew not how or why, made wrong letters. I then wrote to Dr. Taylor to come to me, and bring Dr. Heberden; and I sent to Dr. Brocklesby, who is my neighbour. My physicians are very friendly, and give me great hopes; but you may imagine my situation. I have so far recovered my vocal powers, as to repeat the Lord's Prayer with no imperfect articulation. My memory, I hope, yet remains as it was; but such an attack produces solicitude for the safety of every faculty.

Such was the general vigour of his constitution, that he recovered from this alarming and severe attack with wonderful quickness: so that in July he was able to make a visit to Mr. Langton at Rochester, where he passed about a fortnight, and made little excursions as easily as at any time of his life.

In August he went as far as the neighbourhood of Salisbury, to Heale, the seat of William Bowles, Esq. While he was here, he had a letter from Dr. Brocklesby, acquainting him of the death of Mrs. Williams,[1] which affected him a good deal. Though for several years her temper had not been complacent, she had valuable qualities, and her departure left a blank in his house. Upon this

---

[1] "Mrs. Williams, from mere inanition, has at length paid the great debt to nature, about three o'clock this morning [Sept. 6th]. She died without a struggle, retaining her faculties entire to the very last; and, as she expressed it, having set her house in order, was prepared to leave it at the last summons of nature."—*Extract from Dr. Brocklesby's letter.*

occasion he, according to his habitual course of piety, composed a prayer.

On his return from Heale he wrote to Dr. Burney:

I came home on the 18th of September, at noon, to a very disconsolate house. . . . My domestic companion is taken from me. She is much missed, for her acquisitions were many, and her curiosity universal; so that she partook of every conversation. I am not well enough to go much out; and to sit, and eat or fast alone, is very wearisome.

His fortitude and patience met with severe trials during this year. The stroke of the palsy has been related circumstantially; but he was also afflicted with the gout, and was besides troubled with a complaint which not only was attended with immediate inconvenience, but threatened him with a chirurgical operation, from which most men would shrink. The complaint was a *sarcocele*, which Johnson bore with uncommon firmness. Happily the complaint abated without his being put to the torture of amputation.

He this autumn received a visit from the celebrated Mrs. Siddons. Mr. Kemble has favoured me with the following minute of what passed at this visit:—

When Mrs. Siddons came into the room, there happened to be no chair ready for her, which he observing said, with a smile, "Madam, you who so often occasion a want of seats to other people, will the more easily excuse the want of one yourself."

Having placed himself by her, he, with great good humour, entered upon a consideration of the English drama; and, among other inquiries, particularly asked her which of Shakspeare's characters she was most pleased with. Upon her answering that she thought the character of Queen Catharine, in Henry the Eighth, the most natural: "I think so too, Madam," said he; "and whenever you perform it, I will once more hobble out to the theatre myself." . . .

I find in this, as in former years, notices of his kind attention to Mrs. Gardiner, who, though in the humble station of a tallowchandler upon Snow Hill, was a woman of excellent good sense, pious, and charitable.

I consulted him on two questions of a very different nature: one, Whether the unconstitutional influence exercised by the peers of Scotland in the election of the representatives of the commons, by means of fictitious qualifications, ought not to be resisted; the

other, What in propriety and humanity should be done with old
horses unable to labour. I gave him some account of my life at
Auchinleck; and expressed my satisfaction that the gentlemen of
the county had, at two public meetings, elected me their chairman.

To James Boswell, Esq.

London, Dec. 24, 1783

DEAR SIR,

Like all other men who have great friends, you begin to feel
the pangs of neglected merit; and all the comfort that I can give
you is, by telling you that you have probably more pangs to feel,
and more neglect to suffer. You have, indeed, begun to complain
too soon; and I hope I am the only confidant of your discontent.
Your friends have not yet had leisure to gratify personal kindness;
they have hitherto been busy in strengthening their ministerial
interest. If a vacancy happens in Scotland, give them early intelligence: and as you can serve government as powerfully as any
of your probable competitors, you may make in some sort a war-
rantable claim.

Of the exaltations and depressions of your mind you delight to
talk, and I hate to hear. Drive all such fancies from you.

On the day when I received your letter, I think, the foregoing
page was written; to which one disease or another has hindered
me from making any additions. I am now a little better. But sickness and solitude press me very heavily. I could bear sickness
better, if I were relieved from solitude.

The present dreadful confusion of the public ought to make
you wrap yourself up in your hereditary possessions, which, though
less than you may wish, are more than you can want; and in an
hour of religious retirement return thanks to God, who has exempted you from any strong temptation to faction, treachery,
plunder, and disloyalty.

As your neighbours distinguish you by such honours as they
can bestow, content yourself with your station, without neglecting
your profession. Your estate and the courts will find you full
employment, and your mind well occupied will be quiet.

The usurpation of the nobility, for they apparently usurp all
the influence they gain by fraud and misrepresentation, I think
it certainly lawful, perhaps your duty, to resist. What is not their
own, they have only by robbery.

Your question about the horses gives me more perplexity. I
know not well what advice to give you. I can only recommend a
rule which you do not want: give as little pain as you can. I sup-

pose that we have a right to their service while their strength lasts; what we can do with them afterwards, I cannot so easily determine. But let us consider. Nobody denies that man has a right first to milk the cow, and to shear the sheep, and then to kill them for his table. May he not, by parity of reason, first work a horse, and then kill him the easiest way, that he may have the means of another horse, or food for cows and sheep? Man is influenced in both cases by different motives of self-interest. He that rejects the one must reject the other. I am, &c.,   SAM. JOHNSON

A happy and pious Christmas; and many happy years to you, your lady, and children.

Notwithstanding the complication of disorders under which Johnson now laboured, he did not resign himself to despondency and discontent, but with wisdom and spirit endeavoured to console and amuse his mind with as many innocent enjoyments as he could procure. He insisted that such of the members of the old club in Ivy Lane as survived should meet again and dine together, which they did, twice at a tavern, and once at his house, and in order to ensure himself society in the evening for three days in the week, he instituted a club at the Essex Head, in Essex Street, then kept by Samuel Greaves, an old servant of Mr. Thrale's.[1] Johnson himself, like his namesake Old Ben, composed the rules of his club.[2]

---

[1] I was in Scotland when this club was founded, and during all the winter. Johnson, however, declared I should be a member, and invented a word upon the occasion: "Boswell," said he, "is a very *clubable* man." When I came to town I was proposed by Mr. Barrington, and chosen. I believe there are few societies where there is better conversation or more decorum. Several of us resolved to continue it after our great founder was removed by death. Other members were added; and now, about eight years since that loss, we go on happily.—*Boswell.*

[2] "RULES.

"To-day deep thoughts with me resolve to drench
In mirth, which after no repenting draws.—MILTON.

"The club shall consist of four and twenty.
"The meetings shall be on the Monday, Thursday, and Saturday of every week; but in the week before Easter there shall be no meeting.
"Every member is at liberty to introduce a friend once a week, but not oftener.
"Two members shall oblige themselves to attend in their turn every night from eight to ten, or procure two to attend in their room.
"Every member present at the club shall spend at least sixpence; and every member who stays away shall forfeit threepence (*sic*).
"The master of the house shall keep an account of the absent members; and deliver to the president of the night a list of the forfeits incurred.
"When any member returns after absence, he shall immediately lay down his forfeits; which if he omits to do, the president shall require.
"There shall be no general reckoning, but every man shall adjust his own expenses.
"The night of indispensable attendance will come to every member once a month. Whoever shall for three months together omit to attend himself, or by substitution, nor shall make any apology in the fourth month, shall be considered as having abdicated the club.
"When a vacancy is to be filled, the name of the candidate, and of the member recommending him, shall stand in the club-room three nights. On the fourth he may be chosen by ballot; six members at

In the end of this year he was seized with a spasmodic asthma of such violence, that he was confined to the house in great pain, being sometimes obliged to sit all night in his chair, a recumbent posture being so hurtful to his respiration, that he could not endure lying in bed; and there came upon him at the same time that oppressive and fatal disease, a dropsy. It was a very severe winter, which probably aggravated his complaints; and the solitude in which Mr. Levett and Mrs. Williams had left him rendered his life very gloomy. Mrs. Desmoulins, who still lived, was herself so very ill, that she could contribute very little to his relief. He, however, had none of that unsocial shyness which we commonly see in people afflicted with sickness. He did not hide his head from the world, in solitary abstraction; he did not deny himself to the visits of his friends and acquaintances; but at all times when he was not overcome by sleep, was as ready for conversation as in his best days.

And now I am arrived at the last year of the life of SAMUEL JOHNSON; a year in which, although passed in severe indisposition, he nevertheless gave many evidences of the continuance of those wondrous powers of mind which raised him so high in the intellectual world. His conversation and his letters of this year were in no respect inferior to those of former years.

On the 8th of January I wrote to him, anxiously inquiring as to his health, and enclosing my "Letter to the People of Scotland on the Present State of the Nation."

To James Boswell, Esq.

Feb. 11, 1784

DEAR SIR,

I hear of many inquiries which your kindness has disposed you to make after me. I have long intended you a long letter, which perhaps the imagination of its length hindered me from beginning. I will, therefore, content myself with a shorter.

Having promoted the institution of a new club in the neighbourhood, at the house of an old servant of Thrale's, I went thither to meet the company, and was seized with a spasmodic asthma,

least being present, and two-thirds of the ballot being in his favour; or the majority, should the numbers not be divisible by three.

"The master of the house shall give notice, six days before, to each of those members whose turn of necessary attendance is come.

"The notice may be in these words: 'Sir, On—— the —— of ——, will be your turn of presiding at the Essex Head. Your company is therefore earnestly requested.'

"One penny shall be left by each member for the waiter."

Johnson's definition of a club, in this sense, in his Dictionary, is, "An assembly of good fellows, meeting under certain conditions."

so violent, that with difficulty I got to my own house, in which I have been confined eight or nine weeks, and from which I know not when I shall be able to go even to church. The asthma, however, is not the worst. A dropsy gains ground upon me: my legs and thighs are very much swollen with water, which I should be content if I could keep there; but I am afraid that it will soon be higher. My nights are very sleepless and very tedious, and yet I am extremely afraid of dying.

My physicians try to make me hope that much of my malady is the effect of cold, and that some degree at least of recovery is to be expected from vernal breezes and summer suns. If my life is prolonged to autumn, I should be glad to try a warmer climate; though how to travel with a diseased body, without a companion to conduct me, and with very little money, I do not well see. Ramsay has recovered his limbs in Italy; and Fielding was sent to Lisbon, where, indeed, he died; but he was, I believe, past hope when he went. Think for me what I can do.

I received your pamphlet, and when I write again may perhaps tell you some opinion about it; but you will forgive a man struggling with disease his neglect of disputes, politics, and pamphlets. Let me have your prayers. My compliments to your lady and young ones. Ask your physicians about my case: and desire Sir Alexander Dick to write me his opinion. I am, dear Sir, &c., SAM. JOHNSON

To Mrs. Lucy Porter in Lichfield

Feb. 23, 1784

MY DEAREST LOVE,

I have been extremely ill of an asthma and dropsy, but received by the mercy of God sudden and unexpected relief last Thursday by the discharge of twenty pints of water. Whether I shall continue free, or shall fill again, cannot be told. Pray for me. Death, my dear, is very dreadful; let us think nothing worth our care but how to prepare for it; what we know amiss in ourselves let us make haste to amend, and put our trust in the mercy of God and the intercession of our Saviour. I am, &c.,

SAM. JOHNSON

To James Boswell, Esq.

London, Feb. 27, 1784

DEAR SIR,

I have just advanced so far towards recovery as to read a pamphlet; and you may reasonably suppose that the first pamphlet which I read was yours. I am very much of your opinion, and, like you, feel great indignation at the indecency with which the king is every day treated. Your paper contains very considerable knowledge of history and of the constitution, very properly produced and applied. It will certainly raise your character, though perhaps it may not make you a minister of state. . . . I am, dear Sir, &c.,   SAM. JOHNSON

To James Boswell, Esq.

London, March 18, 1784

DEAR SIR,

I am too much pleased with the attention which you and your dear lady show to my welfare, not to be diligent in letting you know the progress which I make towards health. The dropsy, by God's blessing, has now run almost totally away by natural evacuation: and the asthma, if not irritated by cold, gives me little trouble. While I am writing this I have not any sensation of debility or disease. But I do not yet venture out, having been confined to the house from the 13th of December, now a quarter of a year.

When it will be fit for me to travel as far as Auchinleck I am not able to guess; but such a letter as Mrs. Boswell's might draw any man not wholly motionless a great way. Pray tell the dear lady how much her civility and kindness have touched and gratified me. . . .

I wish you an easy and happy journey, and hope I need not tell you that you will be welcome to, dear Sir, your, &c.,

SAM. JOHNSON

I wrote to him, March 28, from York, informing him that I was thus far on my way to him, but that news of the dissolution of parliament having arrived, I was to hasten back to my own county, where I had some intention of being a candidate to represent the county in parliament.

To James Boswell, Esq.

LONDON, March 30, 1784

DEAR SIR,

You could do nothing so proper as to hasten back when you found the parliament dissolved. With the influence which your address must have gained you, it may reasonably be expected that your presence will be of importance, and your activity of effect. . . .

You are entering upon a transaction which requires much prudence. You must endeavour to oppose without exasperating; to practise temporary hostility, without producing enemies for life. This is, perhaps, hard to be done; yet it has been done by many, and seems most likely to be effected by opposing merely upon general principles, without descending to personal or particular censures or objections. One thing I must enjoin you, which is seldom observed in the conduct of elections; I must entreat you to be scrupulous in the use of strong liquors. One night's drunkenness may defeat the labours of forty days well employed. Be firm, but not clamorous; be active, but not malicious; and you may form such an interest, as may not only exalt yourself, but dignify your family.

We are, as you may suppose, all busy here. Mr. Fox resolutely stands for Westminster, and his friends say will carry the election. However that be, he will certainly have a seat. Mr. Hoole has just told me, that the city leans towards the king.

Let me hear, from time to time, how you are employed, and what progress you make. Make dear Mrs. Boswell, and all the young Boswells, the sincere compliments of, Sir, your affectionate humble servant, &c.,   SAM. JOHNSON

To Mr. Langton he wrote:

April 8. I am still disturbed by my cough; but what thanks have I not to pay, when my cough is the most painful sensation that I feel? and from that I expect hardly to be released, while winter continues to gripe us with so much pertinacity. The year has now advanced eighteen days beyond the equinox, and still there is very little remission of the cold. When warm weather comes, which surely must come at last, I hope it will help both me and your young lady.

The man so busy about addresses is neither more nor less than our own Boswell, who had come as far as York towards London, but turned back on the dissolution, and is said now to stand for some place. Whether to wish him success his best friends hesitate. . . .

What follows is a beautiful specimen of his gentleness and complacency to a young lady, his godchild, one of the daughters of his friend Mr. Langton, then, I think, in her seventh year. He took the trouble to write it in a large round hand, nearly resembling printed characters, that she might have the satisfaction of reading it herself.

To Miss Jane Langton

In Rochester, Kent

May 10, 1784

MY DEAREST MISS JENNY,

I am sorry that your pretty letter has been so long without being answered; but, when I am not pretty well, I do not always write plain enough for young ladies. I am glad, my dear, to see that you write so well, and hope that you mind your pen, your book and your needle, for they are all necessary. Your books will give you knowledge, and make you respected; and your needle will find you useful employment when you do not care to read. When you are a little older, I hope you will be very diligent in learning arithmetic; and, above all, that through your whole life you will carefully say your prayers and read your Bible. I am, my dear, your most humble servant,   SAM. JOHNSON

On Wednesday, May 5, I arrived in London, and next morning had the pleasure to find Dr. Johnson greatly recovered. I but just saw him; for a coach was waiting to carry him to Islington, to the house of his friend the Reverend Mr. Strahan, where he went sometimes for the benefit of good air, which, notwithstanding his having formerly laughed at the general opinion upon the subject, he now acknowledged was conducive to health.

One morning afterwards, when I found him alone, he communicated to me, with solemn earnestness, the very remarkable circumstance which had happened in the course of his illness, when he was much distressed by the dropsy. He had shut himself up, and employed a day in particular exercises of religion, fasting, humiliation, and prayer. On a sudden he obtained extraordinary relief, for which he looked up to Heaven with grateful devotion. He made no direct inference from this fact; but from his manner of telling it, I could perceive that it appeared to him as something more than an incident in the common course of events. For my own part, I have no difficulty to avow that cast of thinking, which, by many modern pretenders to wisdom, is called *superstitious*. But here I think even men of dry rationality may believe, that there was an intermediate interposition of Divine Providence, and that the "fervent prayer of this righteous man" availed.

On Saturday, May 15, I dined with him at Dr. Brocklesby's. Of these days I have no memorials, except the general recollection of his being able and animated in conversation, and appearing to relish society as much as the youngest man. I find only these three small particulars: When a person was mentioned, who said, "I have lived fifty-one years in the world without having had ten minutes of uneasiness"; he exclaimed, "The man who says so lies: he attempts to impose on human credulity." The Bishop of Exeter in vain observed that men were very different. His lordship's manner was not impressive; and I learnt afterwards, that Johnson did not find out that the person who talked to him was a prelate; if he had, I doubt not that he would have treated him with more respect; for, once talking of George Psalmanazar, whom he reverenced for his piety, he said, "I should as soon think of contradicting a bishop." [1] One of the company provoked him greatly by doing what he could least of all bear, which was, quoting something of his own writing, against what he then maintained. "What, Sir," cried the gentleman, "do you say to—

> 'The busy day, the peaceful night,
> Unfelt, uncounted, glided by'?"

Johnson, finding himself thus presented as giving an instance of a man who had lived without uneasiness, was much offended, for he looked upon such a quotation as unfair: his anger burst out in an unjustifiable retort, insinuating that the gentleman's remark was a sally of ebriety: "Sir, there is one passion I would advise you to command; when you have drunk out that glass, don't drink another."

Another was this: when a gentleman of eminence in the literary world was violently censured for attacking people by anonymous paragraphs in newspapers, he, from the spirit of contradiction, as I thought, took up his defence, and said, "Come, come, this is not so terrible a crime; he means only to vex them a little. I do not say that I should do it; but there is a great difference between him and me: what is fit for Hephæstion is not fit for Alexander." Another, when I told him that a young and handsome countess had said to me, "I should think that to be praised by Dr. Johnson would make one a fool all one's life"; and that I answered, "Madam, I shall make him a fool to-day, by repeating this to him"; he said, "I am too old to be made a fool: but if you say I am made a fool, I shall not deny it. I am much pleased with a compliment, especially from a pretty woman."

---

[1] Boswell mentions elsewhere an instance of Johnson's respect for the dignitaries of the church: "Mr. Seward saw him presented to the Archbishop of York, and described his *bow to an* ARCHBISHOP as such a studied elaboration of homage, such an extension of limb, such a flexion of body, as have seldom or ever been equalled."

JOHNSON'S "BOW TO AN ARCHBISHOP"

On the evening of Saturday, May 15, he was in fine spirits at our
Essex Head Club. He told us, "I dined yesterday at Mrs. Garrick's,
with Mrs. Carter, Miss Hannah More, and Miss Fanny Burney.
Three such women are not to be found: I know not where I could
find a fourth, except Mrs. Lennox, who is superior to them all."
BOSWELL. "What! had you them all to yourself, Sir?" JOHNSON.
"I had them all, as much as they were had; but it might have been
better had there been more company there."

He called to us with a sudden air of exultation, as the thought
started into his mind, "O! Gentlemen, I must tell you a very great
thing. The Empress of Russia has ordered the 'Rambler' to be
translated into the Russian language; [1] so I shall be read on the
banks of the Wolga. Horace boasts that his fame would extend as
far as the banks of the Rhone; now the Wolga is farther from me
than the Rhone was from Horace." BOSWELL. "You must certainly be pleased with this, Sir." JOHNSON. "I am pleased, Sir,
to ·be sure. A man is pleased to find he has succeeded in that which
he has endeavoured to do."

One of the company mentioned his having seen a noble person
driving in his carriage, and looking exceedingly well, notwithstanding his great age. JOHNSON. "Ah, Sir, that is nothing. Bacon
observes, that a stout healthy old man is like a tower undermined."

On Sunday, May 16, I found him alone: he talked of Mrs. Thrale
with much concern, saying, "Sir, she has done every thing wrong
since Thrale's bridle was off her neck"; and was proceeding to
mention some circumstances which have since been the subject of
public discussion, when he was interrupted.

In one of his little manuscript diaries about this time I find a
short notice, which marks his amiable disposition more certainly
than a thousand studied declarations. "Afternoon spent cheerfully
and elegantly, I hope without offence to God or man; though in no
holy duty, yet in the general exercise and cultivation of benevolence."

On Monday, May 17, I dined with him at Mr. Dilly's. Johnson
was very quiescent to-day. Perhaps, too, I was indolent. I find
nothing more of him in my notes, but that when I mentioned that
I had seen in the king's library sixty-three editions of my favourite
Thomas à Kempis, he said he thought it unnecessary to collect
many editions of a book, which were all the same, except as to the

---

[1] I have since heard that the report was not well founded; but the elation discovered by Johnson, in
the belief that it was true, showed a noble ardour for literary fame.—*Boswell.*

paper and print; he would have the original, and all the translations, and all the editions which had any variations in the text, and
he added, "every man should try to collect one book in that manner, and present it to a public library."

On Tuesday, May 18, I saw him for a short time in the morning.
I told him that the mob had called out, as the king passed,[1] "No
Fox, no Fox!" which I did not like. He said, "They were right,
Sir." I said, I thought not; for it seemed to be making Mr. Fox the
king's competitor. There being no audience, so that there could be
no triumph in a victory, he fairly agreed with me.

On Wednesday, May 19, I sat a part of the evening with him,
by ourselves. I observed, that the death of our friends might be a
consolation against the fear of our own dissolution, because we
might have more friends in the other world than in this. He perhaps felt this as a reflection upon his apprehension as to death, and
said, with heat, "How can a man know *where* his departed friends
are, or whether they will be his friends in the other world? How
many friendships have you known formed upon principles of
virtue? Most friendships are formed by caprice or by chance—
mere confederacies in vice or leagues in folly."

We talked of our worthy friend Mr. Langton. He said, "I know
not who will go to heaven if Langton does not. Sir, I could almost
say *Sit anima mea cum Langtono.*"

He however charged Mr. Langton with what he thought want of
judgment upon an interesting occasion. "When I was ill," said
he, "I desired he would tell me sincerely in what he thought my life
was faulty. Sir, he brought me a sheet of paper, on which he had
written down several texts of Scripture recommending Christian
charity. And when I questioned him what occasion I had given
for such an animadversion, all that he could say amounted to this,
—that I sometimes contradicted people in conversation. Now
what harm does it do to any man to be contradicted?" BOSWELL.
"I suppose he meant the *manner* of doing it; roughly and harshly."
JOHNSON. "And who is the worse for that?" BOSWELL. "It hurts
people of weaker nerves." JOHNSON. "I know no such weak-
nerved people." Mr. Burke, to whom I related this conference,
said, "It is well if, when a man comes to die, he has nothing heavier
upon his conscience than having been a little rough in conversation."

---

[1] To open parliament. The Westminster election had concluded the day before in favour of Fox,
whose return, however, was delayed by the requisition for a scrutiny.

Johnson, at the time when the paper was presented to him, though at first pleased with the attention of his friend, whom he thanked in an earnest manner, soon exclaimed in a loud angry tone, "What is your drift, Sir?" Sir Joshua Reynolds pleasantly observed, that it was a scene for a comedy, to see a penitent get into a violent passion and belabour his confessor.

I have preserved no more of his conversation at the times when I saw him during the rest of this month, till Sunday, the 30th of May, when I met him in the evening at Mr. Hoole's. Sir James Johnston happened to say that he paid no regard to the arguments of counsel at the bar of the House of Commons, because they were paid for speaking. JOHNSON. "Nay, Sir, argument is argument. You cannot help paying regard to their arguments if they are good. If it were testimony, you might disregard it, if you knew that it were purchased. There is a beautiful image in Bacon upon this subject. Testimony is like an arrow shot from a long-bow; the force of it depends on the strength of the hand that draws it. Argument is like an arrow from a cross-bow, which has equal force though shot by a child."

He had dined that day at Mr. Hoole's, and Miss Helen Maria Williams being expected in the evening, Mr. Hoole put into his hands her beautiful "Ode on the Peace." Johnson read it over, and when this elegant and accomplished young lady was presented to him, he took her by the hand in the most courteous manner, and repeated the finest stanza of her poem. This was the most delicate and pleasing compliment he could pay.

Miss Williams told me, that the only other time she was fortunate enough to be in Dr. Johnson's company, he asked her to sit down by him, which she did; and upon her inquiring how he was, he answered, "I am very ill indeed, Madam. I am very ill even when you are near me; what should I be were you at a distance?"

He had now a great desire to go to Oxford, as his first jaunt after his illness. We talked of it for some days, and I had promised to accompany him. He was impatient and fretful to-night, because I did not at once agree to go with him on Thursday. When I considered how ill he had been, and what allowance should be made for the influence of sickness upon his temper, I resolved to indulge him, though with some inconvenience to myself, as I wished to attend the musical meeting in honour of Handel, in Westminster Abbey, on the following Saturday.

In the midst of his own diseases and pains, he was ever com-

passionate to the distresses of others, and actively earnest in procuring them aid, as appears from a note to Sir Joshua Reynolds:

I am ashamed to ask for some relief for a poor man, to whom
I hope I have given what I can be expected to spare. The man
importunes me, and the blow goes round. I am going to try another
air on Thursday.

On Thursday, June 3, the Oxford post coach took us up in the
morning at Bolt Court. The other two passengers were Mrs. Beresford and her daughter, two very agreeable ladies from America;
they were going to Worcestershire, where they then resided. Frank
had been sent by his master the day before to take places for us;
and I found from the way-bill that Dr. Johnson had made our
names be put down. Mrs. Beresford, who had read it, whispered
me, "Is this the great Dr. Johnson?" I told her it was; so she was
then prepared to listen. As she soon happened to mention, in a
voice so low that Johnson did not hear it, that her husband had been
a member of the American Congress, I cautioned her to beware of
introducing that subject, as she must know how very violent Johnson was against the people of that country. He talked a great deal;
Miss Beresford was so much charmed, that she said to me aside,
"How he does talk! Every sentence is an essay." She amused herself in the coach with knotting. He would scarcely allow this
species of employment any merit. "Next to mere idleness," said he,
"I think knotting is to be reckoned in the scale of insignificance;
though I once attempted to learn knotting: Dempster's sister (looking to me) endeavoured to teach me it, but I made no progress."

I was surprised at his talking without reserve in the public post
coach of the state of his affairs: "I have," said he, "about the
world, I think, above a thousand pounds, which I intend shall
afford Frank an annuity of seventy pounds a year." Indeed, his
openness with people at a first interview was remarkable. He said
once to Mr. Langton, "I think I am like Squire Richard in 'The
Journey to London,' *I'm never strange in a strange place.*" He was
truly *social*.

At the inn where we stopped he was exceedingly dissatisfied
with some roast mutton which we had for dinner. The ladies, I
saw, wondered to see the great philosopher, whose wisdom and wit
they had been admiring all the way, get into ill-humour from such
a cause. He scolded the waiter, saying, "It is as bad as bad can be:
it is ill-fed, ill-killed, ill-kept, and ill-drest."

HE SCOLDED THE WAITER

He bore the journey very well, and seemed to feel himself elevated as he approached Oxford, that magnificent and venerable seat of learning, orthodoxy, and Toryism. Frank came in the heavy coach, in readiness to attend him; and we were received with the most polite hospitality at the house of his old friend Dr. Adams. Before we were set down, I communicated to Johnson my having engaged to return to London directly for the reason I have mentioned, but that I would hasten back to him again. He was pleased that I had made this journey merely to keep him company. He was easy and placid, with Dr. Adams, Mrs. and Miss Adams, and Mrs. Kennicott, widow of the learned Hebræan, who was here on a visit. I fulfilled my intention by going to London, and returned to Oxford on Wednesday the 9th of June. Johnson welcomed my return with more than ordinary glee.

He made a remark this evening which struck me a good deal. "I never," said he, "knew a nonjuror who could reason."

Mrs. Kennicott spoke of her brother, the Reverend Mr. Chamberlayne, who had given up great prospects in the Church of England on his conversion to the Roman Catholic faith. Johnson, who warmly admired every man who acted from a conscientious regard to principle, erroneous or not, exclaimed fervently, "God bless him."

On the Roman Catholic religion he said, "If you join the papists externally, they will not interrogate you strictly as to your belief in their tenets. No reasoning papist believes every article of their faith. There is one side on which a good man might be persuaded to embrace it. A good man of a timorous disposition, in great doubt of his acceptance with God, and pretty credulous, may be glad to be of a church where there are so many helps to get to heaven. I would be a papist if I could. I have fear enough; but an obstinate rationality prevents me. I shall never be a papist, unless on the near approach of death, of which I have a very great terror. I wonder that women are not all papists." Boswell. "They are not more afraid of death than men are." Johnson. "Because they are less wicked." Dr. Adams. "They are more pious." Johnson. "No, hang 'em, they are not more pious. A wicked fellow is the most pious when he takes to it. He'll beat you all at piety."

After dinner, when one of us talked of there being a great enmity between Whig and Tory:—Johnson. "Why, not so much, I think, unless when they come into competition with each other. There is none when they are only common acquaintance, none when they are of different sexes. A Tory will marry into a Whig family, and a Whig into a Tory family, without any reluctance. But, indeed, in a matter of much more concern than political tenets, and that is religion, men and women do not concern themselves much about difference of opinion; and ladies set no value on the moral character of men who pay their addresses to them: the greatest profligate will be as well received as the man of the greatest virtue, and this by a very good woman, by a woman who says her prayers three times a day." Our ladies endeavoured to defend their sex from this charge; but he roared them down! "No, no, a lady will take Jonathan Wild as readily as St. Austin, if he has threepence more; and, what is worse, her parents will give her to him. Women have a perpetual envy of our vices: they are less vicious than we, not from choice, but because we restrict them; they are the slaves of order and fashion; their virtue is of more consequence to us than our own, so far as concerns this world."

Miss Adams mentioned a gentleman of licentious character, and said, "Suppose I had a mind to marry that gentleman, would my parents consent?" JOHNSON. "Yes, they'd consent, and you'd go. You'd go, though they did not consent." MISS ADAMS. "Perhaps their opposing might make me go." JOHNSON. "Oh, very well; you'd take one whom you think a bad man, to have the pleasure of vexing your parents. You put me in mind of Dr. Barrowby, the physician, who was very fond of swine's flesh. One day, when he was eating it, he said, 'I wish I was a Jew.'—'Why so?' said somebody; 'the Jews are not allowed to eat your favourite meat.'— 'Because,' said he, 'I should then have the gust of eating it, with the pleasure of sinning.' "

Miss Adams soon afterwards made an observation that I do not recollect, which pleased him much: he said with a good-humoured smile, "That there should be so much excellence united with so much *depravity*, is strange."

Indeed this lady's good qualities, merit, and accomplishments, and her constant attention to Dr. Johnson, were not lost upon him. She happened to tell him that a little coffeepot, in which she had made him coffee, was the only thing she could call her own. He turned to her with a complacent gallantry:—"Don't say so, my dear: I hope you don't reckon my heart as nothing."

I asked him if it was true, as reported, that he had said lately, "I am for the King against Fox: but I am for Fox against Pitt."

JOHNSON. "Yes, Sir; the King is my master; but I do not know Pitt; and Fox is my friend."

"Fox," added he, "is a most extraordinary man: here is a man who has divided the kingdom with Cæsar; so that it was a doubt whether the nation should be ruled by the sceptre of George the Third, or the tongue of Fox."

Dr. Wall, physician at Oxford, drank tea with us. Johnson had in general a peculiar pleasure in the company of physicians. Johnson said, "It is wonderful how little good Radcliffe's travelling fellowships have done. I know nothing that has been imported by them; yet many additions to our medical knowledge might be got in foreign countries. Inoculation, for instance, has saved more lives than war destroys; and the cures performed by the Peruvian bark are innumerable. But it is in vain to send our travelling physicians to France and Italy and Germany, for all that is known there is known here. I'd send them out of Christendom; I'd send them among barbarous nations."

On Friday, June 11, we talked at breakfast of forms of prayer. JOHNSON. "I know of no good prayers but those in the 'Book of Common Prayer.'" DR. ADAMS (in a very earnest manner). "I wish, Sir, you would compose some family prayers." JOHNSON. "I will not compose prayers for you, Sir, because you can do it for yourself. But I have thought of getting together all the books of prayers which I could, selecting those which should appear to me the best, putting out some, inserting others, adding some prayers of my own, and prefixing a discourse on prayer." We all now gathered about him, and two or three of us at a time joined in pressing him to execute this plan. He seemed to be a little displeased at the manner of our importunity, and in great agitation called out, "Do not talk thus of what is so awful. I know not what time GOD will allow me in this world. There are many things which I wish to do." Some of us persisted, and Dr. Adams said, "I never was more serious about any thing in my life." JOHNSON. "Let me alone—let me alone—I am overpowered." And then he put his hands before his face, and reclined for some time upon the table.

Dr. Johnson and I went in Dr. Adams's coach to dine with Dr. Nowell, Principal of St. Mary Hall, at his villa at Iffley, on the banks of the Isis, about two miles from Oxford. While we were upon the road, I had the resolution to ask Johnson whether he thought that the roughness of his manner had been an advantage or not, and if he would not have done more good if he had been more gentle. I proceeded to answer myself thus: "Perhaps it has been of advantage, as it has given weight to what you said; you could not, perhaps, have talked with such authority without it." JOHNSON. "No, Sir; I have done more good as I am. Obscenity and impiety have always been repressed in my company." BOSWELL. "True, Sir; and that is more than can be said of every bishop. Greater liberties have been taken in the presence of a bishop, though a very good man, from his being milder, and therefore not commanding such awe. Yet, Sir, many people who might have been benefited by your conversation have been frightened away. A worthy friend of ours has told me, that he has often been afraid to talk to you." JOHNSON. "Sir, he need not have been afraid, if he had any thing rational to say. If he had not, it was better he did not talk."

We were well entertained and very happy at Dr. Nowell's, where was a very agreeable company; and we drank "Church and King" after dinner, with true Tory cordiality.

We talked of a certain clergyman of extraordinary character, who, by exerting his talents in writing on temporary topics, and displaying uncommon intrepidity, had raised himself to affluence. I maintained that we ought not to be indignant at his success; for merit of every sort was entitled to reward. JOHNSON. "Sir, I will not allow this man to have merit. No, Sir; what he has is rather the contrary: I will, indeed, allow him courage; and on this account we so far give him credit. We have more respect for a man who robs boldly on the highway, than for a fellow who jumps out of a ditch, and knocks you down behind your back. Courage is a quality so necessary for maintaining virtue, that it is always respected, even when it is associated with vice."

I censured the coarse invectives which were become fashionable in the House of Commons, and said, that if members of parliament must attack each other personally in the heat of debate, it should be done more genteelly. JOHNSON. "No, Sir; that would be much worse. Abuse is not so dangerous when there is no vehicle of wit and delicacy, no subtle conveyance. The difference between coarse and refined abuse is as the difference between being bruised by a club, and wounded by a poisoned arrow."

On Saturday, June 12, there drank tea with us at Dr. Adams's, Mr. John Henderson, student of Pembroke College, celebrated for his wonderful acquirements in alchymy, judicial astrology, and other abstruse and curious learning. Dr. Johnson surprised him not a little, by acknowledging with a look of horror, that he was much oppressed by the fear of death. The amiable Dr. Adams suggested that GOD was infinitely good:—JOHNSON. "That he is infinitely good, so far as the perfection of his nature will allow, I certainly believe; but it is necessary for good upon the whole, that individuals should be punished. As to an *individual*, therefore, he is not infinitely good; and as I cannot be *sure* that I have fulfilled the conditions on which salvation is granted, I am afraid I may be one of those who shall be damned." (Looking dismally.) DR. ADAMS. "What do you mean by damned?" JOHNSON (passionately and loudly). "Sent to hell, Sir, and punished everlastingly." DR. ADAMS. "I don't believe that doctrine." JOHNSON. "Hold, Sir: do you believe that some will be punished at all?" DR. ADAMS. "Being excluded from heaven will be a punishment; yet there may be no great positive suffering." JOHNSON. "Well, Sir, but if you admit any degree of punishment, there is an end of your argument for infinite goodness simply considered; for infinite goodness would inflict no punishment whatever. There is not infinite goodness physically considered: morally there is." BOSWELL. "But may not a man attain to such a degree of hope as not to be uneasy from the fear of death?" JOHNSON. "A man may have such a degree of hope as to keep him quiet. You see I am not quiet, from the vehemence with which I talk; but I do not despair." MRS. ADAMS. "You seem, Sir, to forget the merits of our Redeemer." JOHNSON. "Madam, I do not forget the merits of my Redeemer; but my Redeemer has said that he will set some on his right hand and some on his left."—He was in gloomy agitation, and said, "I'll have no more on't."

From the subject of death we passed to discourse of life, whether it was upon the whole more happy or miserable. Johnson was decidedly for the balance of misery: in confirmation of which I maintained that no man would choose to lead over again the life which he had experienced. Johnson acceded to that opinion in the strongest terms. It was observed to Dr. Johnson, that it seemed strange that he, who has so often delighted his company by his lively and brilliant conversation, should say he was miserable. JOHNSON. "Alas! it is all outside; I may be cracking my joke, and cursing the sun. *Sun, how I hate thy beams!*"

On Sunday, 13th June, our philosopher was calm at breakfast. There was something exceedingly pleasing in our leading a college life, without restraint and with superior elegance, in consequence of our living in the master's house, and having the company of ladies. Mrs. Kennicott related, in his presence, a lively saying of Dr. Johnson to Miss Hannah More, who had expressed a wonder that the poet who had written "Paradise Lost," should write such poor sonnets: "Milton, Madam, was a genius that could cut a Colossus from a rock, but could not carve heads upon cherry stones."

We talked of the casuistical question, "Whether it was allowable at any time to depart from *truth?*" JOHNSON. "The general rule is, that truth should never be violated, because it is of the utmost importance to the comfort of life that we should have a full security by mutual faith; and occasional inconveniences should be willingly suffered, that we may preserve it. There must, however, be some exceptions. If, for instance, a murderer should ask you which way a man is gone, you may tell him what is not true, because you are under a previous obligation not to betray a man to a murderer." BOSWELL. "Supposing the person who wrote 'Junius' were asked whether he was the author, might he deny it?" JOHNSON. "I don't know what to say to this. If you were *sure* that he wrote 'Junius,' would you, if he denied it, think as well of him afterwards? Yet it may be urged that what a man has no right to ask, you may refuse to communicate; and there is no other effectual mode of preserving a secret, and an important secret, the discovery of which may be very hurtful to you, but a flat denial; for if you are silent, or hesitate, or evade, it will be held equivalent to a confession. But stay, Sir, here is another case. Supposing the author had told me confidentially that he had written 'Junius,' and I were asked if he had, I should hold myself at liberty to deny it, as being under a previous promise, express or implied, to conceal it. Now what I ought to do for the author, may I not do for myself? But I deny the lawfulness of telling a lie to a sick man, for fear of alarming him. You have no business with consequences; you are to tell the truth. Besides, you are not sure what effect your telling him that he is in danger may have. It may bring his distemper to a crisis, and that may cure him. Of all lying, I have the greatest abhorrence of this, because I believe it has been frequently practised on myself."

In the morning of Tuesday, 15th of June, while we sat at Dr. Adams's, we talked of a printed letter from the Reverend Herbert Croft, to a young gentleman who had been his pupil, in which he advised him to read to the end of whatever books he should begin to read. JOHNSON. "This is surely a strange advice; you may as well resolve that whatever men you happen to get ac-

quainted with, you are to keep to them for life. A book may be good
for nothing; or there may be only one thing in it worth knowing;
are we to read it all through? These Voyages (pointing to the three
large volumes of 'Voyages to the South Sea' which were just come
out) *who* will read them through? A man had better work his way
before the mast than read them through: they will be eaten by
rats and mice, before they are read through. There can be little
entertainment in such books; one set of savages is like another."
BOSWELL. "I do not think the people of Otaheite can be reckoned
savages." JOHNSON. "Don't cant in defence of savages." BOS-
WELL. "They have the art of navigation." JOHNSON. "A dog or
cat can swim." BOSWELL. "They carve very ingeniously."
JOHNSON. "A cat can scratch, and a child with a nail can scratch."
I perceived this was none of the *mollia tempora fandi;* so desisted.

On Wednesday, June 16th, Dr. Johnson and I returned to
London: he was not well to-day, and said very little, employing
himself chiefly in reading Euripides. He expressed some displeasure
at me for not observing sufficiently the various objects upon the
road. "If I had your eyes, Sir," said he, "I should count the
passengers."

After his return to London from this excursion, I saw him frequently, but have few memorandums; I shall therefore here insert
some particulars which I collected at various times.

It having been mentioned to Dr. Johnson, that a gentleman who
had a son whom he imagined to have an extreme degree of timidity,
resolved to send him to a public school, that he might acquire confidence: "Sir," said Johnson, "this is a preposterous expedient for
removing his infirmity; such a disposition should be cultivated in
the shade. Placing him at a public school is forcing an owl upon
day."

A dull country magistrate gave Johnson a long, tedious account
of his exercising his criminal jurisdiction, the result of which was
his having sentenced four convicts to transportation. Johnson, in
an agony of impatience to get rid of such a companion, exclaimed,
"I heartily wish, Sir, that I were a fifth."

Johnson was present when a tragedy was read, in which there
occurred this line:

Who rules o'er freemen should himself be free.

The company having admired it much, "I cannot agree with you,"
said Johnson: "it might as well be said,

"Who drives fat oxen should himself be fat."

Johnson having argued for some time with a pertinacious gentleman; his opponent, who had talked in a very puzzling manner, happened to say, "I don't understand you, Sir"; upon which Johnson observed, "Sir, I have found you an argument, but I am not obliged to find you an understanding."

Here it may be observed, that his frequent use of the expression, *No, Sir*, was not always to intimate contradiction: for he would do so when he was about to enforce an affirmative proposition which had not been denied. I used to consider it as a kind of flag of defiance; as if he had said, "Any argument you may offer against this is not just. No, Sir, it is not." It was like Falstaff's "I deny your major."

Sir Joshua Reynolds having said that he took the attitude of a man's taste by his stories and his wit, and of his understanding by the remarks which he repeated; being always sure that he must be a weak man who quotes common things with an emphasis as if they were oracles;—Johnson agreed with him; and Sir Joshua having also observed that the real character of a man was found out by his amusements, Johnson added, "Yes, Sir; no man is a hypocrite in his pleasures."

I have mentioned Johnson's general aversion to a pun. He once, however, endured one of mine. When we were talking of a numerous company in which he had distinguished himself highly, I said, "Sir, you were a cod surrounded by smelts. Is not this enough for you? at a time too when you were not *fishing* for a compliment?" He laughed at this with a complacent approbation. Old Mr. Sheridan observed, upon my mentioning it to him, "He liked your compliment so well, he was willing to take it with *pun sauce*." For my own part, I think no innocent species of wit or pleasantry should be suppressed; and that a good pun may be admitted among the smaller excellencies of lively conversation.

It may be worth remarking, among the *minutiæ* of my collection, that Johnson was once drawn to serve in the militia, the trained bands of the city of London, and that Mr. Rackstrow, of the museum in Fleet Street, was his colonel. It may be believed he did not serve in person; but the idea, with all its circumstances, is certainly laughable. He upon that occasion provided himself with a musket, and with a sword and belt, which I have seen hanging in his closet.

He was very constant to those whom he once employed, if they gave him no reason to be displeased. When somebody talked of being imposed on in the purchase of tea and sugar, and such articles: "That will not be the case," said he, "if you go to a *stately shop*, as I always do. In such a shop it is not worth their while to take a petty advantage."

The difference, he observed, between a well-bred and an ill-bred man is this: "One immediately attracts your liking, the other your aversion. You love the one till you find reason to hate him; you hate the other till you find reason to love him."

The wife of one of his acquaintance had fraudulently made a purse for herself out of her husband's fortune. Feeling a proper compunction in her last moments, she confessed how much she had secreted; but before she could tell where it was placed, she was seized with a convulsive fit and expired. Her husband said, he was more hurt by her want of confidence in him, than by the loss of his money. "I told him," said Johnson, "that he should console himself; for *perhaps* the money might be *found*, and he was *sure* that his wife was *gone*."

He seemed to take a pleasure in speaking in his own style; for when he had carelessly missed it, he would repeat the thought translated into it. Talking of the comedy of "The Rehearsal," he said, "It has not wit enough to keep it sweet." This was easy;— he therefore caught himself, and pronounced a more round sentence: "It has not vitality enough to preserve it from putrefaction."

No man was more ready to make an apology when he had censured unjustly than Johnson. When a proof-sheet of one of his works was brought to him, he found fault with the mode in which a part of it was arranged, refused to read it, and in a passion, desired that the compositor might be sent to him. The compositor was Mr. Manning, a decent sensible man, who had composed about one half of his "Dictionary," a great part of his "Lives of the Poets," and who (in his seventy-seventh year) composed a part of the first edition of this work. By producing the manuscript, he at once satisfied Dr. Johnson that he was not to blame. Upon which Johnson candidly and earnestly said to him, "Mr. Compositor, I ask your pardon; Mr. Compositor, I ask your pardon, again and again."

His generous humanity to the miserable was almost beyond example. The following instance is well attested: coming home late one night, he found a poor woman lying in the street, so much exhausted that she could not walk; he took her upon his back and carried her to his house, where he discovered that she was one of those wretched females who had fallen into the lowest state of vice, poverty, and disease. Instead of harshly upbraiding her, he had her taken care of with all tenderness for a long time, at a considerable expense, till she was restored to health, and endeavoured to put her into a virtuous way of living.

He once in his life was known to have uttered what is called a *bull:* Sir Joshua Reynolds, when they were riding together in Devonshire, complained that he had a very bad horse, for that even when going down hill he moved slowly step by step. "Ay," says Johnson, "and when he *goes* up hill he *stands still.*"

He had a great aversion to gesticulating in company. He called once to a gentleman who offended him in that point, "Don't *attitudinise.*" And when another gentleman thought he was giving additional force to what he uttered by expressive movements of his hands, Johnson fairly seized them, and held them down.

A gentleman having said that a *congé d'élire* has not, perhaps, the force of a command, but may be considered only as a strong recommendation:—"Sir," replied Johnson, who overheard him, "it is such a recommendation, as if I should throw you out of a two-pair-of-stairs window, and recommend to you to fall soft."

Mr. Steevens, who passed many a social hour with him, has been pleased to favour me with the following:

Dr. Johnson once assumed a character in which perhaps even Mr. Boswell never saw him. His curiosity having been excited by the praises bestowed on the celebrated Torré's fireworks at Marybone Gardens, he desired Mr. Steevens to accompany him thither. The evening had proved showery, and soon after the few people present were assembled, public notice was given that the conductors of the wheels, suns, stars, &c., were so thoroughly watersoaked that it was impossible any part of the exhibition should be made. "This is a mere excuse," says the doctor, "to save their crackers for a more profitable company. Let us both hold up our sticks and threaten to break those coloured lamps that surround the orchestra, and we shall soon have our wishes gratified. The core of the fireworks cannot be injured; let the different pieces be touched in their respective centres, and they will do their offices as well as ever." Some young men, who overheard him, immediately began the violence he had recommended, and an attempt was speedily made to fire some of the wheels which appeared to have received the smallest damage; but to little purpose were they lighted, for most of them completely failed. The author of "The Rambler," however, may be considered on this occasion as the ringleader of a successful riot, though not as a skilful pyrotechnist.

It has been supposed that Dr. Johnson, so far as fashion was concerned, was careless of his appearance in public. But this is not altogether true, as the following slight instance may show: Goldsmith's last comedy was to be represented during some court-mourning, and Mr. Steevens appointed to call on Dr. Johnson, and carry him to the tavern where he was to dine with other of the poet's friends. The doctor was ready dressed, but in coloured clothes; yet being told that he would find every one else in black, received the intelligence with a profusion of thanks, hastened to change his attire, all the while repeating his gratitude for the information that had saved him from an appearance so improper in the front row of a front box. "I would not," added he, "for ten pounds have seemed so retrograde to any general observance."

On Tuesday, June 22, I dined with him at the Literary Club, the last time of his being in that respectable society. He looked ill, but had such a manly fortitude, that he did not trouble the company with melancholy complaints. They all showed evident marks of kind concern about him, with which he was much pleased, and he exerted himself to be as entertaining as his indisposition allowed him.

The anxiety of his friends to preserve so estimable a life as long as human means might be supposed to have influence, made them plan for him a retreat from the severity of a British winter to the mild climate of Italy. This scheme was at last brought to a serious resolution at General Paoli's, where I had often talked of it. One essential matter, however, I understood, was necessary to be previously settled, which was obtaining such an addition to his income as would be sufficient to enable him to defray the expense in a manner becoming the first literary character of a great nation, and, independent of all his other merits, the author of the "Dictionary of the English Language." The person to whom I above all others thought I should apply to negotiate this business was the Lord Chancellor, because I knew that he highly valued Johnson, and that Johnson highly valued his lordship, so that it was no degradation of my illustrious friend to solicit for him the favour of such a man.

I first consulted with Sir Joshua Reynolds, who perfectly coincided in opinion with me; and I therefore, though personally very little known to his lordship, wrote to him, stating the case, and requesting his good offices for Dr. Johnson. I mentioned that I was obliged to set out for Scotland early in the following week, so that if his lordship should have any commands for me as to this pious negotiation, he would be pleased to send them before that time, otherwise Sir Joshua Reynolds would give all attention to it.

This application was made not only without any suggestion on the part of Johnson himself, but was utterly unknown to him, nor had he the smallest suspicion of it. Any insinuations, therefore, which since his death have been thrown out, as if he had stooped to ask what was superfluous, are without any foundation. But, had he asked it, it would not have been superfluous; for though the money he had saved proved to be more than his friends imagined, or than I believe he himself, in his carelessness concerning worldly matters, knew it to be, had he travelled upon the continent, an augmentation of his income would by no means have been unnecessary.

On Wednesday, June 23, I visited him in the morning, after having been present at the shocking sight of fifteen men executed before Newgate. Talking of the religious discipline proper for unhappy convicts, he said, "Sir, one of our regular clergy will probably not impress their minds sufficiently: they should be attended by a methodist preacher, or a popish priest."

On Thursday, June 24, I dined with him at Mr. Dilly's. At my desire old Mr. Sheridan [1] was invited, as I was earnest to have Johnson and him brought together again by chance, that a reconciliation might be effected. Mr. Sheridan happened to come early, and having learnt that Dr. Johnson was to be there, went away; so I found, with sincere regret, that my friendly intentions were hopeless. I recollect nothing that passed this day, except Johnson's quickness, who, when Dr. Beattie observed, as something remarkable which had happened to him, that he had chanced to see both No. 1 and No. 1000 of the hackney-coaches, the first and the last—"Why, Sir," said Johnson, "there is an equal chance for one's seeing those two numbers as any other two." He was clearly right; yet the seeing of the two extremes, each of which is in some degree more conspicuous than the rest, could not but strike one in a stronger manner than the sight of any other two numbers.

On Friday, June 25, I dined with him at General Paoli's, where, he says in one of his letters to Mrs. Thrale, "I love to dine."

1 See p. 79.

There was a variety of dishes much to his taste, of all which he
seemed to me to eat so much, that I was afraid he might be hurt
by it; and I whispered to the General my fear, and begged he
might not press him. "Alas!" said the General, "see how very ill
he looks; he can live but a very short time. Would you refuse any
slight gratifications to a man under sentence of death?"

On Sunday, June 27, we dined at Sir Joshua Reynolds's, with
General Paoli, Lord Eliot, Dr. Beattie, and some other company.
He entered upon a curious discussion of the difference between
intuition and sagacity; one being immediate in its effect, the other
requiring a circuitous process; one, he observed, was the *eye* of the
mind, the other the *nose* of the mind. A young gentleman present
took up the argument against him, and maintained that no man
ever thinks of the *nose of the mind.* He persisted much too long,
and appeared to Johnson as putting himself forward as his antagonist with too much presumption; upon which he called to him
in a loud tone, "What is it you are contending for, if you *be* contending?"—And afterwards, imagining that the gentleman retorted upon him with a kind of smart drollery, he said, "Mr.*****,
it does not become you to talk so to me. Besides, ridicule is not
your talent; you have *there* neither intuition nor sagacity."—The
gentleman protested that he intended no improper freedom, but
had the greatest respect for Dr. Johnson. After a short pause,
during which we were somewhat uneasy;—JOHNSON. "Give me
your hand, Sir, you were too tedious, and I was too short." MR.
*****. "Sir, I am honoured by your attention in any way." JOHN-
SON. "Come, Sir, let's have no more of it. We offended one another by our contention; let us not offend the company by our
compliments."

He now said, he wished much to go to Italy, and that he dreaded
passing the winter in England. I said nothing; but enjoyed a
secret satisfaction in thinking that I had taken the most effectual
measures to make such a scheme practicable.

On Monday, June 28, I had the honour to receive from the
Lord Chancellor the following letter:

> *To James Boswell, Esq.*
>
> SIR,
>
> I should have answered your letter immediately, if (being
> much engaged when I received it) I had not put it in my pocket,
> and forgot to open it till this morning.

I am much obliged to you for the suggestion; and I will adopt and press it as far as I can. The best argument, I am sure, and I hope it is not likely to fail, is Dr. Johnson's merit. But it will be necessary, if I should be so unfortunate as to miss seeing you, to converse with Sir Joshua on the sum it will be proper to ask,—in short, upon the means of setting him out. It would be a reflection on us all if such a man should perish for want of the means to take care of his health. Yours, &c.,

THURLOW

This letter gave me very high satisfaction; I next day went and showed it to Sir Joshua Reynolds, who was exceedingly pleased with it. He thought that I should now communicate the negotiation to Dr. Johnson, who might afterwards complain if the attention with which he had been honoured should be too long concealed from him. I intended to set out for Scotland next morning; but Sir Joshua cordially insisted that I should stay another day, that Johnson and I might dine with him, that we three might talk of his Italian tour, and, as Sir Joshua expressed himself, "have it all out."

I hastened to Johnson, and was told by him that he was rather better to-day. BOSWELL. "I am very anxious about you, Sir, and particularly that you should go to Italy for the winter, which I believe is your own wish." JOHNSON. "It is, Sir." BOSWELL. "You have no objection, I presume, but the money it would require." JOHNSON. "Why, no, Sir." Upon which I gave him a particular account of what had been done, and read to him the Lord Chancellor's letter. He listened with much attention; then warmly said, "This is taking prodigious pains about a man." "O, Sir," said I, with most sincere affection, "your friends would do every thing for you." He paused,—grew more and more agitated,—till tears started into his eyes, and he exclaimed with fervent emotion, "GOD bless you all!" I was so affected that I also shed tears. After a short silence, he renewed and extended his grateful benediction, "God bless you all, for JESUS CHRIST's sake." We both remained for some time unable to speak. He rose suddenly, and quitted the room, quite melted in tenderness. He staid but a short time, till he had recovered his firmness; soon after he returned I left him, having first engaged him to dine at Sir Joshua Reynolds's next day.

I never was again under that roof which I had so long reverenced.

On Wednesday, June 30, the friendly confidential dinner with Sir Joshua Reynolds took place, no other company being present.

Had I known that this was the last time that I should enjoy in this world the conversation of a friend whom I so much respected, and from whom I derived so much instruction and entertainment, I should have been deeply affected. When I now look back to it, I am vexed that a single word should have been forgotten.

Both Sir Joshua and I were so sanguine in our expectations, that we expatiated with confidence on the liberal provision which we were sure would be made for him, conjecturing whether munificence would be displayed in one large donation, or in an ample increase of his pension. He himself catched so much of our enthusiasm as to allow himself to suppose it not impossible that our hopes might in one or other be realised. He said that he would rather have his pension doubled than a grant of a thousand pounds. "For," said he, "though probably I may not live to receive as much as a thousand pounds, a man would have the consciousness that he should pass the remainder of his life in splendour, how long soever it might be." Considering what a moderate proportion an income of six hundred pounds a-year bears to innumerable fortunes in this country, it is worthy of remark, that a man so truly great should think it splendour.

As an instance of extraordinary liberality of friendship he told us that Dr. Brocklesby had upon this occasion offered him a hundred a year for his life. A grateful tear started into his eye, as he spoke in a faltering tone.

Sir Joshua and I endeavoured to flatter his imagination with agreeable prospects of happiness in Italy. "Nay," said he, "I must not expect much of that; when a man goes to Italy merely to feel how he breathes the air, he can enjoy very little."

I accompanied him in Sir Joshua Reynolds's coach to the entry of Bolt Court. He asked me whether I would not go with him to his house; I declined it, from an apprehension that my spirits would sink. We bade adieu to each other affectionately in the carriage. When he had got down upon the foot pavement, he called out, "Fare you well!" and, without looking back, sprang away with a kind of pathetic briskness, if I may use that expression, which seemed to indicate a struggle to conceal uneasiness, and impressed me with a foreboding of our long, long separation.

I remained one day more in town, to have the chance of talking over my negotiation with the Lord Chancellor; but the multiplicity of his lordship's important engagements did not allow of it; so I left the management of the business in the hands of Sir Joshua Reynolds.

Soon after this time Dr. Johnson had the mortification of being informed by Mrs. Thrale, that "what she supposed he never believed" was true: namely, that she was actually going to marry Signor Piozzi, an Italian music-master. He endeavoured to prevent it; but in vain. If she would publish the whole of the correspondence that passed between Dr. Johnson and her on the subject, we should have a full view of his real sentiments. As it is, our judgment must be biassed by that characteristic specimen which Sir John Hawkins has given us:

Poor Thrale! I thought that either her virtue or her vice would have restrained her from such a marriage. She is now become a subject for her enemies to exult over, and for her friends, if she has any left, to forget or pity.

It must be admitted that Johnson derived a considerable portion of happiness from the comforts and elegancies which he enjoyed in Mr. Thrale's family; but Mrs. Thrale assures us he was indebted for these to her husband alone, who certainly respected him sincerely. Her words are, "*Veneration for his virtue, reverence for his talents,* delight *in his conversation, and* habitual endurance of a yoke *my husband first put upon me, and of which he contentedly bore his share for sixteen or seventeen years, made me go on so long with* Mr. Johnson; *but the perpetual confinement I will own to have been* terrifying *in the first years of our friendship, and* irksome *in the last; nor could I pretend to support it without help, when my coadjutor was no more.*" Alas! how different is this from the declarations which I have heard Mrs. Thrale make in his lifetime, without a single murmur against any peculiarities, or against any one circumstance which attended their intimacy!

Having left the *pious negotiation,* as I called it, in the best hands, I shall here insert what relates to it. Johnson wrote to Sir Joshua Reynolds, on July 6, as follows:

I am going, I hope, in a few days, to try the air of Derbyshire, but hope to see you before I go. Let me, however, mention to you what I have much at heart. If the Chancellor should continue his attention to Mr. Boswell's request, and confer with you on the means of relieving my languid state, I am very desirous to avoid the appearance of asking for money upon false pretences. I desire you to represent to his lordship, what, as soon as it is suggested, he will perceive to be reasonable,—that, if I grow much worse, I shall be afraid to leave my physicians, to suffer the inconveniences of travel, and pine in the solitude of a foreign country;—that if I grow much better, of which indeed there is now little appearance, I shall not wish to leave my friends and my domestic comforts, for I do not travel for pleasure or curiosity; yet if I should recover, curiosity would revive. In my present state I am desirous to make a struggle for a little longer life, and to hope to obtain some help from a softer climate. Do for me what you can.

He wrote to me July 26:

I wish your affairs could have permitted a longer and continued exertion of your zeal and kindness. They that have your kindness may want your ardour. In the meantime I am very very feeble and very dejected.

By a letter from Sir Joshua Reynolds I was informed that the Lord Chancellor had called on him, and acquainted him that the application had not been successful; but that his lordship, after speaking highly in praise of Johnson, as a man who was an honour to his country, desired Sir Joshua to let him know, that on granting a mortgage of his pension, he should draw on his lordship to the amount of five or six hundred pounds, and that his lordship explained the meaning of the mortgage to be, that he wished the business to be conducted in such a manner, that Dr. Johnson should appear to be under the least possible obligation. Sir Joshua mentioned that he had by the same post communicated all this to Dr. Johnson.

How Johnson was affected upon the occasion will appear from what he wrote to Sir Joshua Reynolds [1]:

Ashbourne, Sept. 9

Many words I hope are not necessary between you and me, to convince you what gratitude is excited in my heart by the Chancellor's liberality, and your kind offices.

I have enclosed a letter to the Chancellor, which, when you have read it, you will be pleased to seal with a head, or any other general seal, and convey it to him: had I sent it directly to him, I should have seemed to overlook the favour of your intervention.

[1] See p. 484.

To The Lord High Chancellor

September, 1784

MY LORD,

After a long and not inattentive observation of mankind, the generosity of your lordship's offer raises in me not less wonder than gratitude. Bounty, so liberally bestowed, I should gladly receive, if my condition made it necessary; for, to such a mind, who would not be proud to own his obligations? But it has pleased God to restore me to so great a measure of health, that if I should now appropriate so much of a fortune destined to do good, I could not escape from myself the charge of advancing a false claim. My journey to the Continent, though I once thought it necessary, was never much encouraged by my physicians; and I was very desirous that your lordship should be told of it by Sir Joshua Reynolds as an event very uncertain; for if I grew much better, I should not be willing, if much worse, not able, to migrate. Your lordship was first solicited without my knowledge; but, when I was told that you were pleased to honour me with your patronage, I did not expect to hear of a refusal; yet, as I have had no long time to brood hope, and have not rioted in imaginary opulence, this cold reception has been scarce a disappointment; and, from your lordship's kindness, I have received a benefit, which only men like you are able to bestow. I shall now live *mihi carior*, with a higher opinion of my own merit. I am, my Lord, &c.,   SAM. JOHNSON

Upon this unexpected failure I abstain from presuming to make any remarks, or to offer any conjectures.

Let us now contemplate Johnson thirty years after the death of his wife, still retaining for her all the tenderness of affection.

To the Rev. Mr. Bagshaw

At Bromley

July 12, 1784

SIR,

Perhaps you may remember, that in the year 1752 you committed to the ground my dear wife. I now entreat your permission to lay a stone upon her; and have sent the inscription, that, if you find it proper, you may signify your allowance.

You will do me a great favour by showing the place where she lies, that the stone may protect her remains.

Mr. Ryland will wait on you for the inscription, and procure it to be engraved. You will easily believe that I shrink from this mournful office. When it is done, if I have strength remaining, I will visit Bromley once again, and pay you part of the respect to which you have a right from, reverend Sir, your most humble servant, SAM. JOHNSON

Next day he set out on a jaunt to Staffordshire and Derbyshire, flattering himself that he might be in some degree relieved.

To Dr. Brocklesby he writes:

Aug. 14.—I have hitherto sent you only melancholy letters: you will be glad to hear some better account. Yesterday the asthma remitted, perceptibly remitted, and I moved with more ease than I have enjoyed for many weeks. May God continue his mercy! This account I would not delay, because I am not a lover of complaints or complainers; and yet I have, since we parted, uttered nothing till now but terror and sorrow. Write to me, dear Sir.

Aug. 16.—Better, I hope, and better. My respiration gets more and more ease and liberty. I went to church yesterday, after a very liberal dinner, without any inconvenience; it is indeed no long walk, but I never walked it without difficulty, since I came, before. . . . I am favoured with a degree of ease that very much delights me, and do not despair of another race up the stairs of the Academy. . . .

Sept. 11.—I think nothing grows worse, but all rather better, except sleep, and that of late has been at its old pranks. Last evening, I felt what I had not known for a long time, an inclination to walk for amusement; I took a short walk, and came back again neither breathless nor fatigued. This has been a gloomy, frigid, ungenial summer; but of late it seems to mend; I hear the heat sometimes mentioned, but I do not feel it. . . .

Lichfield, Sept. 29.—On one day I had three letters about the air-balloon: [1] yours was far the best, and has enabled me to impart to my friends in the country an idea of this species of amusement. In amusement, mere amusement, I am afraid it must end. . . .

Oct. 6.—The fate of the balloon I do not much lament: to make new balloons is to repeat the jest again. We now know a method of mounting into the air, and I think, are not likely to know more. The vehicles can serve no use till we can guide them; and they can gratify no curiosity till we mount with them to greater heights than we can reach without; till we rise above the tops of the highest mountains, which we have yet not done. We know the state of the air in all its regions, to the top of Teneriffe, and therefore learn nothing from those who navigate a balloon below the clouds. The first experiment, however, was bold, and

[1] Lunardi had ascended from the Artillery Ground on the 15th; the first balloon ascent in England.

deserved applause and reward: but since it has been performed, and its event is known, I had rather now find a medicine that can ease an asthma.

Oct. 25.—You write to me with a zeal that animates and a tenderness that melts me. I am not afraid either of a journey to London, or a residence in it. I came down with little fatigue, and am now not weaker. In the smoky atmosphere I was delivered from the dropsy, which I consider as the original and radical disease. The town is my element: there are my friends, there are my books, to which I have not yet bid farewell, and there are my amusements. Sir Joshua told me long ago, that my vocation was to public life; and I hope still to keep my station, till God shall bid me *Go in peace.*[1]

To Dr. Burney

August 2

The weather, you know, has not been balmy. I am now reduced to think, and am at least content to talk, of the weather. Pride must have a fall. I have lost dear Mr. Allen; and wherever I turn, the dead or the dying meet my notice, and force my attention upon misery and mortality.[2] Mrs. Burney's escape from so much danger, and her ease after so much pain, throws, however, some radiance of hope upon the gloomy prospect. May her recovery be perfect, and her continuance long! I struggle hard for life. I take physic and take air: my friend's chariot is always ready. We have run this morning twenty-four miles, and could run forty-eight more. *But who can run the race with death?*

To Sir Joshua Reynolds

Sept. 9.—I could not answer your letter before this day, because I went on the sixth to Chatsworth, and did not come back till the post was gone. Many words, I hope, are not necessary between you and me to convince you what gratitude is excited in my heart by the chancellor's liberality and your kind offices. I did not indeed expect that what was asked by the chancellor would have been refused; but since it has, we will not tell that anything has been asked.—I have enclosed a letter to the chancellor, which, when you have read it, you will be pleased to seal with a head or other general seal, and convey it to him. Had I sent it directly to him, I should have seemed to overlook the favour of your intervention.—My last letter told you of my advance in

---

[1] His love of London continually appears. Once upon reading that line in the curious epitaph quoted in "The Spectator"—"Born in New England, did in London die," he laughed, and said, "I do not wonder at this. It would have been strange if, born in London, he had died in New England."

[2] His thoughts in the latter part of his life were frequently employed on his deceased friends. He often muttered these or such like sentences: "Poor man! and then he died."

health, which, I think, in the whole still continues. Of the hydropic tumour there is now very little appearance: the asthma is much less troublesome, and seems to remit something day after day. I do not despair of supporting an English winter.—At Chatsworth, I met young Mr. Burke, who led me very commodiously into conversation with the duke and duchess. We had a very good morning. The dinner was public.

Oct. 2.—I am always proud of your approbation, and therefore was much pleased that you liked my letter. When you copied it, you invaded the chancellor's right rather than mine.—The refusal I did not expect, but I had never thought much about it, for I doubted whether the chancellor had so much tenderness for me as to ask. He, being keeper of the king's conscience, ought not to be supposed capable of an improper petition.—All is not gold that glitters, as we have often been told; and the adage is verified in your place and my favour; but if what happens does not make us richer, we must bid it welcome if it makes us wiser.— I do not at present grow better, nor much worse. My hopes, however, are somewhat abated, and a very great loss is the loss of hope; but I struggle on as I can.

We now behold Johnson for the last time in his native city, for which he ever retained a warm affection, and which by a sudden apostrophe, under the word *Lich*, he introduces with reverence into his immortal work, "The English Dictionary": "*Salve magna parens!*"

To Mr. Henry White, a young clergyman, with whom he now formed an intimacy, he mentioned that he could not in general accuse himself of having been an undutiful son. "Once, indeed," said he, "I was disobedient: I refused to attend my father to Uttoxeter market. Pride was the source of that refusal, and the remembrance of it was painful. A few years ago I desired to atone for this fault. I went to Uttoxeter in very bad weather, and stood for a considerable time bare-headed in the rain, on the spot where my father's stall used to stand. In contrition I stood, and I hope the penance was expiatory."

As Johnson had now very faint hopes of recovery, and as Mrs. Thrale was no longer devoted to him, it might have been supposed that he would naturally have chosen to remain in the comfortable house of his beloved wife's daughter, and end his life where he began it. But there was in him an animated and lofty spirit; and however complicated diseases might depress ordinary mortals, all who saw him beheld and acknowledged the *invictum animum*

Catonis. Such was his intellectual ardour even at this time, that he said to one friend, "Sir, I look upon every day to be lost in which I do not make a new acquaintance"; and to another, when talking of his illness, "I will be conquered; I will not capitulate." And such was his love of London, so high a relish had he of its magnificent extent and variety of intellectual entertainment, that he languished when absent from it, his mind having become quite luxurious from the long habit of enjoying the metropolis; and, therefore, although at Lichfield, surrounded with friends who loved and revered him, and for whom he had a very sincere affection, he still found that such conversation as London affords could be found nowhere else. These feelings, joined probably to some flattering hopes of aid from the eminent physicians and surgeons in London, who kindly and generously attended him without accepting fees, made him resolve to return to the capital.

From Lichfield he came to Birmingham, where he passed a few days with his worthy old school-fellow, Mr. Hector. Johnson then proceeded to Oxford, where he was again kindly received by Dr. Adams, who was pleased to give me the following account:

We had much serious talk together, for which I ought to be the better as long as I live. You will remember some discourse which we had in the summer upon the subject of prayer, and the difficulty of this sort of composition. He reminded me of this, and of my having wished him to try his hand, and to give us a specimen of the style and manner that he approved. He added that he was now in a right frame of mind; and as he could not possibly employ his time better, he would in earnest set about it.

Various prayers, composed by him at different periods, which, intermingled with pious resolutions and some short notes of his life, were entitled by him "Prayers and Meditations," have been published by the Reverend Mr. Strahan, to whom he delivered them. This admirable collection, to which I have frequently referred in the course of this work, evinces, beyond all his compositions for the public, and all the eulogies of his friends and admirers, the sincere virtue and piety of Johnson.

His correspondence with me, after his letter on the subject of my settling in London, shall now, so far as is proper, be produced in one series. Having written to him in bad spirits a letter filled with dejection and fretfulness, and at the same time expressing anxious apprehensions concerning him on account of a dream which had disturbed me; his answer was chiefly in terms of reproach, for a supposed charge of "affecting discontent, and indulging the vanity of complaint." It, however, proceeded:

Write to me often, and write like a man. I consider your fidelity and tenderness as a great part of the comforts which are yet left me, and sincerely wish we could be nearer to each other. . . . My dear friend, life is very short and very uncertain; let us spend it as well as we can. My worthy neighbour, Allen, is dead. Love me as well as you can. Pay my respects to dear Mrs. Boswell. Nothing ailed me at that time; let your superstition at last have an end.

Feeling very soon that the manner in which he had written might hurt me, he two days afterwards wrote to me again:

Before this letter you will have had one which I hope you will not take amiss; for it contains only truth, and that truth kindly intended. *Spartam quam nactus es orna;* make the most and best of your lot, and compare yourself not with the few that are above you, but with the multitudes which are below you. Go steadily forwards with lawful business or honest diversions. "Be," as Temple says of the Dutchman, "well when you are not ill, and pleased when you are not angry." This may seem but an ill return for your tenderness; but I mean it well, for I love you with great ardour and sincerity. . . .

I unfortunately was so much indisposed during a considerable part of the year, that it was not, or at least I thought it was not, in my power to write to my illustrious friend as formerly, or without expressing such complaints as offended him. Having conjured him not to do me the injustice of charging me with affectation, I was with much regret long silent. His last letter to me then came, and affected me very tenderly:

To James Boswell, Esq.

Lichfield, Nov. 5, 1784

DEAR SIR,
    I have this summer sometimes amended, and sometimes relapsed, but, upon the whole, have lost ground very much. My legs are extremely weak, and my breath very short, and the water is now increasing upon me. In this uncomfortable state your letters used to relieve; what is the reason that I have them no longer? Are you sick, or are you sullen? Whatever be the reason, if it be less than necessity, drive it away; and of the short life that we

have, make the best use for yourself and for your friends. . . .
I am sometimes afraid that your omission to write has some real
cause, and shall be glad to know that you are not sick, and that
nothing ill has befallen dear Mrs. Boswell, or any of your family.
I am, &c.,   SAM. JOHNSON

Yet it was not a little painful to me to find that in a paragraph of
this letter, which I have omitted, he still persevered in arraigning
me as before, which was strange in him who had so much experience
of what I suffered. I, however, wrote to him two as kind letters as
I could; the last of which came too late to be read by him, for his
illness increased more rapidly upon him than I had apprehended;
but I had the consolation of being informed that he spoke of me on
his death-bed with affection, and I look forward with humble hope
of renewing our friendship in a better world.

I now relieve the readers of this work from any farther personal
notice of its author; who, if he should be thought to have obtruded
himself too much upon their attention, requests them to consider
the peculiar plan of his biographical undertaking.

Soon after Johnson's return to the metropolis [November 16th,]
both the asthma and dropsy became more violent and distressful.
He had for some time kept a journal in Latin of the state of his
illness, and the remedies which he used, under the title of *Ægri
Ephemeris*, which he began on the 6th of July, but continued it no
longer than the 8th of November; finding, I suppose, that it was a
mournful and unavailing register. It is in my possession; and is
written with great care and accuracy.

Still his love of literature did not fail. During his sleepless
nights he amused himself by translating into Latin verse, from the
Greek, many of the epigrams in the "Anthologia." These translations, with some other poems by him in Latin, he gave to his friend
Mr. Langton, who, having added a few notes, sold them to the
booksellers for a small sum to be given to some of Johnson's relations.

My readers are now, at last, to behold SAMUEL JOHNSON preparing himself for that doom, from which the most exalted powers
afford no exemption to man. Death had always been to him an
object of terror: so that, though by no means happy, he still clung
to life with an eagerness at which many have wondered. At any
time when he was ill, he was very much pleased to be told that he
looked better. Upon one occasion, when some one said to him that
he saw health returning to his cheek, Johnson seized him by the

hand and exclaimed, "Sir, you are one of the kindest friends I ever had."

His great fear of death, and the strange dark manner in which Sir John Hawkins imparts the uneasiness which he expressed on account of offences with which he charged himself, may give occasion to injurious suspicions, as if there had been something of more than ordinary criminality weighing upon his conscience. On that account, therefore, as well as from the regard to truth which he inculcated, I am to mention (with all possible respect and delicacy, however), that his conduct, after he came to London, and had associated with Savage and others, was not so strictly virtuous, in one respect, as when he was a younger man. It was well known that his amorous inclinations were uncommonly strong and impetuous. He owned to many of his friends, that he used to take women of the town to taverns, and hear them relate their history. In short, it must not be concealed, that like many other good and pious men, among whom we may place the apostle Paul upon his own authority, Johnson was not free from propensities which were ever "warring against the law of his mind,"—and that in his combats with them, he was sometimes overcome.

Here let the profane and licentious pause; let them not thoughtlessly say that Johnson was an *hypocrite*, or that his *principles* were not firm, because his *practice* was not uniformly conformable to what he professed. I heard Dr. Johnson once observe, "There is something noble in publishing truth, though it condemns one's self." And one who said in his presence, "he had no notion of people being in earnest in their good professions, whose practice was not suitable to them," was thus reprimanded by him: "Sir, are you so grossly ignorant of human nature as not to know that a man may be very sincere in good principles, without having good practice?"

But let no man encourage or soothe himself in "presumptuous sin," from knowing that Johnson was sometimes hurried into indulgences which he thought criminal. I have exhibited this circumstance as a shade in so great a character, both from my sacred love of truth, and to show that he was not so weakly scrupulous as he has been represented by those who imagine that the sins, of which a deep sense was upon his mind, were merely such little venial trifles as pouring milk into his tea on Good-Friday. His understanding will be defended by my statement, if his consistency of conduct be in some degree impaired. But what wise man would, for momentary gratifications, deliberately subject himself to suffer such uneasiness as we find was experienced by Johnson in reviewing his conduct as compared with his notion of the ethics of the Gospel? Let the following passages be kept in remembrance:

O God, giver and preserver of all life, by whose power I was created, and by whose providence I am sustained, look down upon me with tenderness and mercy; grant that I may not have been created to be finally destroyed; that I may not be preserved to add wickedness to wickedness. (*Pr. and Med.*, p. 41.)

O Lord, let me not sink into total depravity; look down upon me, and rescue me at last from the captivity of sin. (p. 62.)

Almighty and most merciful Father, who hast continued my life from year to year, grant that by longer life I may become less desirous of sinful pleasures, and more careful of eternal happiness. (p. 78.)

Let not my years be multiplied to increase my guilt; but as my age advances, let me become more pure in my thoughts, more regular in my desires, and more obedient to thy laws. (p. 114.)

Forgive, O merciful Lord, whatever I have done contrary to thy laws. Give me such a sense of my wickedness as may produce true contrition and effectual repentance: so that when I shall be called into another state, I may be received among the sinners to whom sorrow and reformation have obtained pardon, for Jesus Christ's sake. Amen. (p. 223.)

Such was the distress of mind, such the penitence of Johnson, in his hours of privacy, and in his devout approaches to his Maker. His *sincerity*, therefore, must appear to every candid mind unquestionable.

It is of essential consequence to keep in view that there was in this excellent man's conduct no false principle of *commutation*, no *deliberate* indulgence in sin, in consideration of a counterbalance of duty. His offending and his repenting were distinct and separate: and when we consider his almost unexampled attention to truth, his inflexible integrity, his constant piety, who will dare to "cast a stone at him"? Besides, let it never be forgotten that he cannot be charged with any offence indicating badness of *heart*, any thing dishonest, base, or malignant; but that, on the contrary, he was charitable in an extraordinary degree.

I am conscious that this is the most difficult and dangerous part of my biographical work, and I cannot but be very anxious concerning it. I trust that I have got through it, preserving at once my regard to truth,—to my friend,—and to the interests of virtue and religion. Nor can I apprehend that more harm can ensue from the knowledge of the irregularities of Johnson, guarded as I have stated it, than from knowing that Addison and Parnell were intemperate in the use of wine; which he himself, in his Lives of those celebrated writers and pious men, has not forborne to record.

It is not my intention to give a very minute detail of the particulars of Johnson's remaining days, of whom it was now evident that the crisis was fast approaching, when he must *"die like men, and fall like one of the princes."* Dr. Heberden, Dr. Brocklesby, Dr. Warren, and Dr. Butter, physicians, generously attended him, without accepting any fees, as did Mr. Cruikshank, surgeon; and all that could be done from professional skill and ability was tried. He himself, indeed, having been perpetually applying himself to medical inquiries, united his own efforts with those of the gentlemen who attended him; and imagining that the dropsical collection of water which oppressed him might be drawn off by making incisions in his body, he, with his usual resolute defiance of pain, cut deep, when he thought that his surgeon had done it too tenderly.

About eight or ten days before his death, when Dr. Brocklesby paid him his morning visit, he seemed very low and desponding, and said, "I have been as a dying man all night." On another day after this, when talking on the subject of prayer, Dr. Brocklesby repeated from Juvenal,—

Orandum est, ut sit mens sana in corpore sano,

and so on to the end of the tenth satire; but in running it quickly over, he happened, in the line,

Qui spatium vitæ extremum inter munera ponat,

to pronounce *supremum* for *extremum;* at which Johnson's critical ear instantly took offence, and discoursing vehemently on the unmetrical effect of such a lapse, he showed himself as full as ever of the spirit of the grammarian.

Having no other relations, it had been for some time Johnson's intention to make a liberal provision for his faithful servant, Mr. Francis Barber, whom he looked upon as particularly under his protection, and whom he had all along treated truly as an humble friend. Having asked Dr. Brocklesby what would be a proper annuity to a favourite servant, and being answered that in the case of a nobleman fifty pounds a year was considered as an adequate reward for many years' faithful service;—"Then," said Johnson, "shall I be *nobilissimus*, for I mean to leave Frank seventy pounds a year, and I desire you to tell him so." It is strange, however, to think, that Johnson was not free from that general weakness of being averse to execute a will, so that he delayed it from time to time; and had it not been for Sir John Hawkins's repeatedly urging it, I think it is probable that his kind resolution would not have been fulfilled.[1]

The consideration of numerous papers of which he was possessed seems to have struck Johnson's mind with a sudden anxiety; and as they were in great confusion, it is much to be lamented that he had not intrusted some faithful and discreet person with the care and selection of them; instead of which he, in a precipitate manner, burnt large masses of them, with little regard, as I apprehend, to discrimination. Two very valuable articles, I am sure,

[1] The will read: "In the name of God. Amen. I, Samuel Johnson, being in full possession of my faculties, but fearing this night may put an end to my life, do ordain this my last will and testament. I bequeath to God a soul polluted by many sins, but I hope purified by Jesus Christ. I leave seven hundred and fifty pounds in the hands of Bennet Langton, Esq.: three hundred pounds in the hands of Mr. Barclay and Mr. Perkins, brewers; one hundred and fifty pounds in the hands of Dr. Percy, bishop of Dromore; one thousand pounds, three per cent. annuities in the public funds; and one hundred pounds now lying by me in ready money; all these before-mentioned sums and property I leave, I say, to Sir Joshua Reynolds, Sir John Hawkins, and Dr. William Scott, of Doctors' Commons, in trust, for the following uses:—That is to say, to pay to the representatives of the late William Innys, bookseller, in St. Paul's Churchyard, the sum of two hundred pounds; to Mrs. White, my female servant, one hundred pounds stock in the three per cent. annuities aforesaid. The rest of the aforesaid sums of money and property, together with my books, plate, and household furniture, I leave to the before-mentioned Sir Joshua Reynolds, Sir John Hawkins, and Dr. William Scott, also in trust, to be applied, after paying my debts, to the use of Francis Barber, my man-servant, a negro, in such manner as they shall judge most fit and available to his benefit. And I appoint the aforesaid Sir Joshua Reynolds, Sir John Hawkins, and Dr. William Scott, sole executors of this my last will and testament, hereby revoking all former wills and testaments whatever. In witness whereof I hereunto subscribe my name, and affix my seal, this eighth day of December, 1784.

"SAM. JOHNSON. (L.S.)

"Signed, sealed, published, declared, and delivered, by the said testator, as his last will and testament, in the presence of us, the word *two* being first inserted in the opposite page.
"GEORGE STRAHAN.
"JOHN DESMOULINS."

To this was attached a codicil mentioning certain individual bequests (among them various books to different friends), and arranging for the annuity to Barber. Boswell added some notes when printing these documents.

"The amount of his property proved to be considerably more than he had supposed it to be. Sir John Hawkins estimates the bequest of Francis Barber at a sum little short of fifteen hundred pounds, including an annuity of seventy pounds to be paid to him by Mr. Langton, in consideration of seven hundred and fifty pounds which Johnson had lent to that gentleman. Sir John seems not a little angry at this bequest, and mutters 'a caveat against ostentatious bounty and favour to negroes.' But surely, when a man has money entirely of his own acquisition, when he has no near relations, he may, without blame, dispose of it as he pleases, and with great propriety to a faithful servant. Mr. Barber, on the recommendation of his master, retired to Lichfield, where he might pass the rest of his days in comfort. [He died in 1801.]

"It has been objected that Johnson omitted many of his best friends, when leaving books to several as tokens of his last remembrance. The names of Dr. Adams, Dr. Taylor, Dr. Burney, Mr. Hector, Mr. Murphy, the author of this work, and others who were intimate with him, are not to be found in his will. This may be accounted for by considering, that as he was very near his dissolution at the time, he probably mentioned such as happened to occur to him; and that he may have recollected that he had formerly shown others such proofs of his regard, that it was not necessary to crowd his will with their names. Mrs. Lucy Porter was much displeased that nothing was left to her; but besides what I have now stated, she should have considered that she had left nothing to Johnson by her will, which was made during his lifetime, as appeared at her decease.

"His library, though by no means handsome in its appearance, was sold by Mr. Christie for two hundred and forty-seven pounds nine shillings; many people being desirous to have a book which had belonged to Johnson. In many of them he had written little notes: sometimes tender memorials of his departed wife; as, 'This was dear Tetty's book.' "

we have lost, which were two quarto volumes, containing a full, fair, and most particular account of his own life, from his earliest recollection. I owned to him, that having accidentally seen them, I had read a great deal in them; and apologising for the liberty I had taken, asked him if I could help it. He placidly answered, "Why, Sir, I do not think you could have helped it." I said that I had, for once in my life, felt half an inclination to commit theft. It had come into my mind to carry off those two volumes, and never see him more. Upon my inquiring how this would have affected him, "Sir," said he, "I believe I should have gone mad."

During his last illness Johnson experienced the steady and kind attachment of his numerous friends. Nobody was more attentive to him than Mr. Langton,[1] to whom he tenderly said, *Te teneam moriens deficiente manu.* Mr. Langton informs me, that "one day he found Mr. Burke and four or five more friends sitting with Johnson. Mr. Burke said to him, 'I am afraid, Sir, such a number of us may be oppressive to you.'—'No, Sir,' said Johnson, 'it is not so; and I must be in a wretched state indeed when your company would not be a delight to me.' Mr. Burke, in a tremulous voice, expressive of being very tenderly affected, replied, 'My dear Sir, you have always been too good to me.' Immediately afterwards he went away. This was the last circumstance in the acquaintance of these two eminent men."

Amidst the melancholy clouds which hung over the dying Johnson, his characteristical manner showed itself on different occasions.

He said, three or four days only before his death, speaking of the little fear he had of undergoing a chirurgical operation, "I would give one of these legs for a year more of life, I mean of comfortable life, not such as that which I now suffer";—and lamented much his inability to read during his hours of restlessness. "I used formerly," he added, "when sleepless in bed, *to read like a Turk.*"

When Dr. Warren, in his usual style, hoped that he was better, his answer was, "No, Sir; you cannot conceive with what acceleration I advance towards death."

A man whom he had never seen before was employed one night to sit up with him. Being asked next morning how he liked his attendant, his answer was, "Not at all, Sir; the fellow's an idiot; he is as awkward as a turnspit when first put into the wheel, and as sleepy as a dormouse."

---

[1] Langton took a lodging in Fleet Street, to be near Johnson during his illness.

Mr. Windham having placed a pillow conveniently to support him, he thanked him for his kindness, and said, "That will do—all that a pillow can do."

He repeated with great spirit a poem, which he said he had composed some years before, on occasion of a rich, extravagant young gentleman's coming of age: saying he had never repeated it but once since he composed it, and had given but one copy of it.

As he opened a note which his servant brought to him, he said, "An odd thought strikes me:—we shall receive no letters in the grave."

He requested three things of Sir Joshua Reynolds:—To forgive him thirty pounds which he had borrowed of him;—to read the Bible;—and never to use his pencil on a Sunday. Sir Joshua readily acquiesced.

Indeed he showed the greatest anxiety for the religious improvement of his friends, to whom he discoursed of its infinite consequence. He begged of Mr. Hoole to think of what he had said, and to commit it to writing; and Dr. Brocklesby having attended him with the utmost assiduity and kindness as his physician and friend, he was peculiarly desirous that this gentleman should not entertain any loose speculative notions, but be confirmed in the truths of Christianity, and insisted on his writing down in his presence, as nearly as he could collect it, the import of what passed on the subject.

Johnson, with that native fortitude which, amidst all his bodily distress and mental sufferings, never forsook him, asked Dr. Brocklesby to tell him plainly whether he could recover. "Give me," said he, "a direct answer." The doctor, having first asked him if he could bear the whole truth, which way soever it might lead, and being answered that he could, declared that, in his opinion, he could not recover without a miracle. "Then," said Johnson, "I will take no more physic, not even my opiates; for I have prayed that I may render up my soul to God unclouded." In this resolution he persevered, and, at the same time, used only the weakest kinds of sustenance. Being pressed to take somewhat more generous nourishment, lest too low a diet should have the very effect which he dreaded, by debilitating his mind, he said, "I will take any thing but inebriating sustenance."

The Reverend Mr. Strahan has given me the agreeable assurance, that after being in much agitation, Johnson became quite composed, and continued so till his death. Having in his mind the true

"GOD BLESS YOU, MY DEAR!"

Christian scheme, at once rational and consolatory, uniting justice and mercy in Divinity, with the improvement of human nature, previous to receiving the Holy Sacrament in his apartment, he composed and fervently uttered this prayer:

Almighty and most merciful Father, I am now as to human eyes it seems, about to commemorate for the last time, the death of Thy Son Jesus Christ, our Saviour and Redeemer. Grant, O Lord, that my whole hope and confidence, may be in His merits, and Thy mercy; enforce and accept my imperfect repentance; make this commemoration available to the confirmation of my faith, the establishment of my hope, and the enlargement of my charity; and make the death of Thy Son Jesus Christ effectual to my redemption. Have mercy upon me, and pardon the multitude of my offences. Bless my friends; have mercy upon all men. Support me by Thy Holy Spirit, in the days of weakness, and at the hour of death; and receive me, at my death, to everlasting happiness, for the sake of Jesus Christ. Amen.

Having made his will on the 8th and 9th of December, and settled all his worldly affairs, he languished till Monday, the 13th of that month, when he expired, about seven o'clock in the evening, with so little apparent pain, that his attendants hardly perceived when his dissolution took place.

Of his last moments, my brother, Thomas David, has furnished me with the following particulars:

The Doctor, from the time that he was certain his death was near, appeared to be perfectly resigned, was seldom or never fretful or out of temper, and often said to his faithful servant, "Attend, Francis, to the salvation of your soul, which is the object of greatest importance": he also explained to him passages in the Scripture, and seemed to have pleasure in talking upon religious subjects.

On Monday, the 13th of December, the day on which he died, a Miss Morris, daughter to a particular friend of his, called, and said to Francis, that she begged to be permitted to see the Doctor, that she might earnestly request him to give her his blessing. Francis went into the room, followed by the young lady, and delivered the message. The Doctor turned himself in the bed, and said, "God bless you, my dear!" These were the last words he spoke. His difficulty of breathing increased till about seven o'clock in the evening, when Mr. Barber and Mrs. Desmoulins, who were sitting in the room, observing that the noise he had made in breathing had ceased, went to the bed, and found he was dead.

A few days before his death, he had asked Sir John Hawkins, as one of his executors, where he should be buried, and on being answered, "Doubtless, in Westminster Abbey," seemed to feel a satisfaction, very natural to a poet; and indeed in my opinion very natural to every man of any imagination, who has no family sepulchre in which he can be laid with his fathers. Accordingly, upon Monday, December 20, his remains were deposited in that noble and renowned edifice; and over his grave was placed a large blue flagstone, with this inscription:

SAMUEL JOHNSON, LL.D.
Obiit XIII. die Decembris,
Anno Domini
M. DCC. LXXXIV.
Ætatis suæ LXXV.

His funeral was attended by a respectable number of his friends, particularly such of the members of The Literary Club as were in town. Mr. Burke, Sir Joseph Banks, Mr. Windham, Mr. Langton, Sir Charles Bunbury, and Mr. Colman bore his pall. His school-fellow, Dr. Taylor, performed the mournful office of reading the burial service.

I trust I shall not be accused of affectation when I declare that I find myself unable to express all that I felt upon the loss of such a "Guide, Philosopher, and Friend." I shall, therefore, not say one word of my own, but adopt those of an eminent friend: "He has made a chasm, which not only nothing can fill up, but which nothing has a tendency to fill up. Johnson is dead. Let us go to the next best: there is nobody; no man can be said to put you in mind of Johnson."

The character of SAMUEL JOHNSON has, I trust, been so developed in the course of this work, that they who have honoured it with a perusal may be considered as well acquainted with him. As, how-ever, it may be expected that I should collect into one view the capital and distinguishing features of this extraordinary man, I shall endeavour to acquit myself of that part of my biographical undertaking, however difficult it may be to do that which many of my readers will do better for themselves.

His figure was large and well formed, and his countenance of the cast of an ancient statue; yet his appearance was rendered strange and somewhat uncouth, by convulsive cramps, by the scars of that distemper which it was once imagined the royal touch could cure, and by a slovenly mode of dress. He had the use only of one eye; yet so much does mind govern, and even supply the deficiency of organs, that his visual perceptions, as far as they extended, were uncommonly quick and accurate. So morbid was his temperament, that he never knew the natural joy of a free and vigorous use of his limbs: when he walked, it was like the struggling gait of one in fetters; when he rode, he had no command or direction of his horse, but was carried as if in a balloon. That with his constitution and habits of life he should have lived seventy-five years, is a proof that an inherent *vivida vis* is a powerful preservative of the human frame.

Man is, in general, made up of contradictory qualities; and these will ever show themselves in strange succession, where a consistency in appearance at least, if not reality, has not been attained by long habits of philosophical discipline. In proportion to the native vigour of the mind, the contradictory qualities will be the more prominent, and more difficult to be adjusted; and, therefore, we are not to wonder that Johnson exhibited an eminent example of this remark which I have made upon human nature. At different times he seemed a different man in some respects; not, however, in any great or essential article, upon which he had fully employed his mind, and settled certain principles of duty, but only in his manners, and in the display of argument and fancy in his talk. He was prone to superstition, but not to credulity. Though his imagination might incline him to a belief of the marvellous and the mysterious, his vigorous reason examined the evidence with jealousy. He was a sincere and zealous Christian, of high Church of England and monarchical principles, which he would not tamely suffer to be questioned; and had, perhaps, at an early period, narrowed his mind somewhat too much, both as to religion and politics. His being impressed with the danger of extreme latitude in either, though he was of a very independent spirit, occasioned his appearing somewhat unfavourable to the prevalence of that noble freedom of sentiment which is the best possession of man. Nor can it be denied that he had many prejudices; which, however, frequently suggested many of his pointed sayings, that rather show a playfulness of fancy than any settled malignity. He was steady and inflexible in maintaining the obligations of religion and morality, both from a regard for the order of society and from a veneration for the Great Source of all order; correct, nay stern, in his taste; hard to please, and easily offended; impetuous and irritable in his temper, but of a most humane and benevolent heart, which showed itself not only in a most liberal charity, as far as his circumstances would allow, but in a thousand instances of active benevolence. He was afflicted with a bodily disease, which made him often restless and fretful, and with a constitutional melancholy, the clouds of which darkened the brightness of his fancy, and gave a gloomy cast to his whole course of thinking; we, therefore, ought not to wonder at his sallies of impatience and passion at any time, especially when provoked by obtrusive ignorance or presuming petulance; and allowance must be made for his uttering hasty and satirical sallies even against his best friends. And, surely, when it is considered, that "amidst sickness and sorrow" he exerted his faculties in so many works for the benefit of mankind, and particularly that he achieved the great and admirable Dictionary of our language, we must be astonished at his resolution. The solemn text, "Of him to whom much is given much will be required," seems to have been ever present to his mind, in a rigorous sense, and to have made him dissatisfied with his labours and acts of goodness, however comparatively great; so that the unavoidable consciousness of his superiority was, in that respect, a cause of disquiet. He suffered so much from this, and from the gloom which perpetually haunted him, and made solitude frightful, that it may be said of him, "If in this life only he had hope, he was of all men most miserable." He loved praise when it was brought to him; but was too proud to seek for it. He was somewhat susceptible of flattery. As he was general and unconfined in his studies, he cannot be considered as master of any one particular science; but he had accumulated a vast and various collection of learning and knowledge, which was so arranged in his mind as to be ever in readiness to be brought forth. But his superiority over other learned men consisted chiefly in what may be called the art of thinking, the art of using his mind; a certain continual power of seizing the useful substance of all that he knew, and exhibiting it in a clear and forcible manner; so that knowledge, which we often see to be no better than lumber in men of dull understanding, was in him true, evident, and actual wisdom. His moral precepts are practical, for they are drawn from an intimate acquaintance with human nature. His maxims carry conviction: for they are founded on the basis of common sense, and a very attentive and minute survey of real life. His mind was so full of imagery that he might have been perpetually a poet; yet it is remarkable, that however rich his prose is in this respect, his poetical pieces in general have not much of that splendour, but are rather distinguished by strong sentiment and acute observation, conveyed in harmonious and energetic verse, particularly in heroic couplets. Though usually grave, and even awful in his deportment, he possessed uncommon and peculiar powers of wit and humour; he frequently indulged himself in colloquial pleasantry; and the heartiest merriment was often enjoyed in his company; with this great advantage, that, as it was entirely free from any poisonous tincture of vice or impiety, it was salutary to those who shared in it. He had accustomed himself to such accuracy in his common conversation, that he at all times expressed his thoughts with great force, and an elegant choice of language, the effect of which was aided by his having a loud voice, and a slow deliberate utterance. In him were united a most logical head with a most fertile imagination, which gave him an extraordinary advantage in arguing: for he could reason close or wide, as he saw best for the moment. Exulting in his intellectual strength and dexterity, he could, when he pleased, be the greatest sophist that ever contended in the lists of declamation; and, from a spirit of contradiction, and a delight in showing his powers, he would often maintain the wrong side with equal warmth and ingenuity; so that, when there was an audience, his real opinions could seldom be gathered from his talk; though when he was in company with a single friend, he would discuss a subject with genuine fairness; but he was too conscientious to make error permanent and pernicious by deliberately writing it; and, in all his numerous works, he earnestly inculcated what appeared to him to be the truth; his piety being constant, and the ruling principle of all his conduct.

Such was SAMUEL JOHNSON: a man whose talents, acquirements, and virtues, were so extraordinary, that the more his character is considered, the more he will be regarded by the present age, and by posterity, with admiration and reverence.

THE JOURNAL OF A TOUR TO THE HEBRIDES

WITH

SAMUEL JOHNSON, LL.D.

A TOUR TO THE HEBRIDES

Dr. Johnson had for many years given me hopes that we should go together, and visit the Hebrides. Martin's account of those islands had impressed us with a notion, that we might there contemplate a system of life almost totally different from what we had been accustomed to see; and to find simplicity and wildness, and all the circumstances of remote time or place, so near to our native great island, was an object within the reach of reasonable curiosity. We reckoned there would be some inconveniences and hardships, and perhaps a little danger; but these, we were persuaded, were magnified in the imagination of every body. When I was at Ferney, in 1764, I mentioned our design to Voltaire. He looked at me, as if I had talked of going to the North Pole, and said, "You do not insist on my accompanying you?"—"No, sir." "Then I am very willing you should go." I was not afraid that our curious expedition would be prevented by such apprehensions; but I doubted that it would not be possible to prevail on Dr. Johnson to relinquish, for some time, the felicity of a London life.

He had disappointed my expectations so long, that I began to despair; but, in spring, 1773, he talked of coming to Scotland that year with so much firmness, that I hoped he was at last in earnest. I knew that, if he were once launched from the metropolis, he would go forward very well; and I got our common friends there to assist in setting him afloat.

Luckily Mr. Justice Chambers, who was about to sail for the East Indies, was going to take leave of his relations at Newcastle, and he conducted Dr. Johnson to that town. Mr. Scott, of Oxford, accompanied him from thence to Edinburgh. With such propitious convoys did he proceed to my native city. He travelled in post-chaises, of which the rapid motion was one of his most favourite amusements.

He wore a full suit of plain brown clothes, with twisted hair-buttons of the same colour, a large bushy greyish wig, a plain shirt, black worsted stockings, and silver buckles. Upon this tour, when journeying, he wore boots, and a very wide brown cloth great coat, with pockets which might have almost held the two volumes

505

of his folio Dictionary; and he carried in his hand a large English oak stick. Let me not be censured for mentioning such minute particulars. Everything relative to so great a man is worth observing.

On Saturday, the 14th of August, 1773, late in the evening, I received a note from him, that he was arrived at Boyd's inn,[1] at the head of the Canongate. I went to him directly. He embraced me cordially; and I exulted in the thought that I now had him actually in Caledonia. Mr. Scott told me that, before I came in, the Doctor had unluckily had a bad specimen of Scottish cleanliness. He then drank no fermented liquor. He asked to have his lemonade made sweeter; upon which the waiter, with his greasy fingers, lifted a lump of sugar, and put it into it. The Doctor, in indignation, threw it out of the window. Scott said he was afraid he would have knocked the waiter down. Mr. Johnson told me that such another trick was played him at the house of a lady in Paris.

He was to do me the honour to lodge under my roof. Mr. Johnson and I walked arm-in-arm, up the High Street, to my house in James's Court; it was a dusky night: I could not prevent his being assailed by the evening effluvia of Edinburgh. I heard a late baronet of some distinction observe, that "walking the streets of Edinburgh at night was pretty perilous, and a good deal odoriferous." The peril is much abated, by the care which the magistrates have taken to enforce the city laws against throwing foul water from the windows; but, from the structure of the houses in the old town, which consist of many stories, in each of which a different family lives, and there being no covered sewers, the odour still continues. A zealous Scotsman would have wished Mr. Johnson to be without one of his five senses upon this occasion. As we marched slowly along, he grumbled in my ear, "I smell you in the dark!"

My wife had tea ready for him, which he delighted to drink at all hours, particularly when sitting up late. He showed much complacency upon finding that the mistress of the house was so attentive to his singular habit; and as no man could be more polite when he chose to be so, his address to her was most courteous and engaging; and his conversation soon charmed her into a forgetfulness of his external appearance.

We sat till near two in the morning, having chatted a good while

---

[1] The sign of the White Horse. It was a base hovel.—*Walter Scott.*
It was the best of the only three inns in Edinburgh.—*Chambers.*

after my wife left us. She had insisted, that, to show all respect to the sage, she would give up her own bedchamber to him, and take a worse. This I cannot but gratefully mention as one of a thousand obligations which I owe her, since the great obligation of her being pleased to accept of me as her husband.

Sunday, Aug. 15.—Mr. Scott came to breakfast, at which I introduced to Dr. Johnson, and him, my friend Sir William Forbes. Mr. Johnson was pleased with my daughter Veronica, then a child about four months old. She had the appearance of listening to him. His motions seemed to her to be intended for her amusement; and when he stopped she fluttered, and made a little infantine noise, and a kind of signal for him to begin again. She would be held close to him, which was a proof from simple nature, that his figure was not horrid. Her fondness for him endeared her still more to me, and I declared she should have five hundred pounds of additional fortune.

We talked of the practice of the law. Sir William Forbes said, he thought an honest lawyer should never undertake a cause which he was satisfied was not a just one. "Sir," said Mr. Johnson, "a lawyer has no business with the justice or injustice of the cause which he undertakes, unless his client asks his opinion, and then he is bound to give it honestly. The justice or injustice of the cause is to be decided by the judge. Consider, Sir, what is the purpose of courts of justice? It is, that every man may have his cause fairly tried, by men appointed to try causes. A lawyer is not to tell what he knows to be a lie: he is not to produce what he knows to be a false deed; but he is not to usurp the province of the jury and of the judge, and determine what shall be the effect of evidence,—what shall be the result of legal argument. As it rarely happens that a man is fit to plead his own cause, lawyers are a class of the community who, by study and experience, have acquired the art and power of arranging evidence, and of applying to the points at issue what the law has settled. A lawyer is to do for his client all that his client might fairly do for himself, if he could. If, by a superiority of attention, of knowledge, of skill, and a better method of communication, he has the advantage of his adversary, it is an advantage to which he is entitled. There must always be some advantage, on one side or other; and it is better that advantage should be had by talents than by chance. If lawyers were to undertake no causes till they were sure they were just, a man might be precluded altogether from a trial of his claim, though, were it judicially examined, it might be found a very just claim." This was sound practical doctrine, and rationally repressed a too refined scrupulosity of conscience.

Sir William Forbes, Mr. Scott, and I, accompanied Mr. Johnson to the chapel for the service of the Church of England. I was sorry to think Mr. Johnson did not attend to the sermon, Mr. Carr's low voice not being strong enough to reach his hearing.

When we got home, Dr. Johnson desired to see my books. He took down Ogden's "Sermons on Prayer," and retired with them to his room. He did not stay long, but soon joined us in the drawing-room.

Of Dr. Beattie, Mr. Johnson said, "Sir, he has written like a man conscious of the truth, and feeling his own strength. Treating your adversary with respect, is giving him an advantage to which he is not entitled. The greatest part of men cannot judge of reasoning, and are impressed by character; so that, if you allow your adversary a respectable character, they will think, that though you differ from him, you may be in the wrong. Sir, treating your adversary with respect, is striking soft in a battle. And as to Hume, a man who has so much conceit as to tell all mankind that they have been bubbled for ages, and he is the wise man who sees better than they—a man who has so little scrupulosity as to venture to oppose those principles which have been thought necessary to human happiness—is he to be surprised if another man comes and laughs at him? If he is the great man he thinks himself, all this cannot hurt him; it is like throwing peas against a rock." He added "something much too rough," both as to Mr. Hume's head and heart, which I suppress. Violence is, in my opinion, not suitable to the Christian cause.

While we were talking, there came a note to me from Dr. William Robertson.

DEAR SIR,

I have been expecting every day to hear from you of Dr. Johnson's arrival. Pray, what do you know about his motions? I long to take him by the hand. I write this from the college, where I have only this scrap of paper. Ever yours,

W. R.

Sunday.

It pleased me to find Dr. Robertson thus eager to meet Dr. Johnson. I was glad I could answer that he was come; and I begged Dr. Robertson might be with us as soon as he could.

Sir William Forbes, Mr. Scott, Mr. Arbuthnot, and another gentleman dined with us. "Come, Dr. Johnson," said I, "it is commonly thought that our veal in Scotland is not good. But here is some which I believe you will like." There was no catching him. JOHNSON. "Why, Sir, what is commonly thought, I should take to be true. *Your* veal may be good; but that will only be an exception to the general opinion, not a proof against it."

Dr. Robertson, according to the custom of Edinburgh at that time, dined in the interval between the forenoon and afternoon service, which was then later than now; so we had not the pleasure of his company till dinner was over, when he came and drank wine with us; and then began some animated dialogue.

We talked of Mr. Burke. Dr. Johnson said, he had great variety of knowledge, store of imagery, copiousness of language. ROBERTSON. "He has wit too." JOHNSON. "No, Sir; he never succeeds there. 'Tis low; 'tis conceit. I used to say, Burke never once made a good joke. What I most envy Burke for is, his being constantly the same. He is never what we call hum-drum; never unwilling to begin to talk, nor in haste to leave off." BOSWELL. "Yet he can listen." JOHNSON. "No; I cannot say he is good at that. So desirous is he to talk, that if one is speaking at this end of the table, he'll speak to somebody at the other end. Burke, Sir, is such a man, that if you met him for the first time in the street, where you were stopped by a drove of oxen, and you and he stepped aside to take shelter but for five minutes, he'd talk to you in such a manner, that, when you parted, you would say, This is an extraordinary man. Now, you may be long enough with me, without finding anything extraordinary." He said, he believed Burke was intended for the law; but either had not money enough to follow it, or had not diligence enough. He said, he could not understand how a man could apply to one thing and not to another. Robertson said, one man had more judgment, another more imagination. JOHNSON. "No, Sir; it is only, one man has more mind than another. He may direct it differently; he may, by accident, see the success of one kind of study, and take a desire to excel in it. I am persuaded that had Sir Isaac Newton applied to poetry, he would have made a very fine epic poem. I could as easily apply to law as to tragic poetry." BOSWELL. "Yet, Sir, you did apply to tragic poetry, not to law." JOHNSON. "Because, Sir, I had not money to study law. Sir, the man who has vigour may walk to the east, just as well as to the west, if he happens to turn his head that way." BOSWELL. "But,

Sir, 'tis like walking up and down a hill; one man may naturally do the one better than the other. A hare will run up a hill best, from her fore-legs being short; a dog down." JOHNSON. "Nay, Sir; that is from mechanical powers. If you make mind mechanical, you may argue in that manner. One mind is a vice, and holds fast; there's a good memory. Another is a file; and he is a disputant, a controversialist. Another is a razor; and he is sarcastical."

Dr. Johnson said, a certain eminent political friend of ours was wrong in his maxim of sticking to a certain set of men on all occasions. "I can see that a man may do right to stick to a party," said he, "that is to say, he is a Whig, or he is a Tory, and he thinks one of those parties upon the whole the best, and that to make it prevail, it must be generally supported, though, in particulars, it may be wrong. He takes its faggot of principles, in which there are fewer rotten sticks than in the other, though some rotten sticks to be sure; and they cannot well be separated. But, to bind one's self to one man, or one set of men (who may be right to-day, and wrong to-morrow), without any general preference of system, I must disapprove."

In the evening Dr. Johnson displayed another of his heterodox opinions—a contempt of tragic acting. He said, the action of all players in tragedy is bad. It should be a man's study to repress those signs of emotion and passion, as they are called. When I asked him "Would not you, Sir, start as Mr. Garrick does, if you saw a ghost?" he answered, "I hope not. If I did, I should frighten the ghost."

Monday, August 16th.—Dr. William Robertson came to breakfast. Dr. Johnson said, "I remember I was once on a visit at the house of a lady for whom I had a high respect. There was a good deal of company in the room. When they were gone, I said to this lady, 'What foolish talking have we had!'—'Yes,' said she, 'but while they talked, you said nothing.' I was struck with the reproof. How much better is the man who does any thing that is innocent, than he who does nothing! Besides, I love anecdotes. I fancy mankind may come, in time, to write all aphoristically, except in narrative; grow weary of preparation, and connection, and illustration, and all those arts by which a big book is made. If a man is to wait till he weaves anecdotes into a system, we may be long in getting them, and get but few, in comparison of what we might get."

We walked out, that Dr. Johnson might see some of the things we have to show at Edinburgh. We went to the Parliament House,[1] to the Advocates' Library, and then to what is called the Laigh (or under) Parliament House, where the records of Scotland are deposited, till the great register office be finished. I was pleased to behold Dr. Samuel Johnson rolling about in this old magazine of antiquities. There was by this time, a pretty numerous circle of us attending upon him. Somebody talked of happy moments for composition, and how a man can write at one time and not at another. "Nay," said Dr. Johnson, "a man may write at any time, if he will set himself *doggedly* to it."

I here began to indulge old Scottish sentiments, and to express a warm regret, that, by our union with England, we were no more; our independent kingdom was lost. JOHNSON. "Sir, never talk of your independency, who could let your queen remain twenty years in captivity, and then be put to death, without even a pretence of justice, without your ever attempting to rescue her; and such a queen too! as every man of any gallantry of spirit would have sacrificed his life for." Worthy MR. JAMES KERR, keeper of the records. "Half our nation was bribed by English money." JOHNSON. "Sir, that is no defence: that makes you worse." Good MR. BROWN, keeper of the Advocates' Library. "We had better say nothing about it." BOSWELL. "You would have been glad, however, to have had us last war, Sir, to fight your battles!" JOHNSON. "We should have had you for the same price, though there had been no union, as we might have had Swiss, or other troops. No, no, I shall agree to a separation. You have only to *go home*." Just as he had said this, I, to divert the subject, showed him the signed assurances of the three successive kings of the Hanover family, to maintain the presbyterian establishment in Scotland. "We'll give you that," said he, "into the bargain."

We next went to the great church of St. Giles, which has lost its original magnificence in the inside, by being divided into four places of presbyterian worship. "Come," said Dr. Johnson jocularly to Principal Robertson, "let me see what was once a church!" We entered that division which was formerly called the New Church, and of late the High Church, so well known by the eloquence of Dr. Hugh Blair. It is now very elegantly fitted up; but it was then shamefully dirty. Dr. Johnson said nothing at the time; but when we came to the great door of the Royal Infirmary,

---

[1] It was on this visit to the parliament-house, that Mr. Henry Erskine, after being presented to Dr. Johnson by Mr. Boswell, and having made his bow, slipped a shilling into Boswell's hand, whispering that it was for the sight of his *bear.—Walter Scott.*

where, upon a board, was this inscription, "Clean your feet!" he turned about slyly, and said, "There is no occasion for putting this at the doors of your churches!"

We then conducted him down the Post-house Stairs, Parliament Close, and made him look up from the Cowgate to the highest building in Edinburgh (from which he had just descended), being thirteen floors or stories from the ground upon the back elevation; the front wall being build upon the edge of the hill, and the back wall rising from the bottom of the hill several stories before it comes to a level with the front wall. We proceeded to the college, with the Principal at our head. As the college buildings are indeed very mean, the Principal said to Dr. Johnson, that he must give them the same epithet that a Jesuit did when showing a poor college abroad: "*Hæ miseriæ nostræ.*" Dr. Johnson was, however, much pleased with the library. We talked of Kennicott's edition of the Hebrew Bible, and hoped it would be quite faithful. JOHNSON. "Sir, I know not any crime so great that a man could contrive to commit, as poisoning the sources of eternal truth."

I pointed out to him where there formerly stood an old wall enclosing part of the college, which I remember bulged out in a threatening manner, and of which there was a common tradition similar to that concerning Bacon's study at Oxford, that it would fall upon some very learned man. It had some time before this been taken down, that the street might be widened. Dr. Johnson, glad of an opportunity to have a pleasant hit at Scottish learning, said, "They have been afraid it never would fall."

We showed him the Royal Infirmary, and were too proud not to carry him to the abbey of Holyrood House, that beautiful piece of architecture, but, alas! deserted mansion of royalty. We surveyed that part of the palace appropriated to the Duke of Hamilton, as keeper, in which our beautiful Queen Mary lived, and in which David Rizzio was murdered, and also the state rooms. Dr. Johnson was a great reciter of all sorts of things, serious or comical. I overheard him repeating here in a kind of muttering tone, a line of the old ballad, "Johnny Armstrong's Last Good Night."

And ran him through the fair body![1]

---

[1] The stanza from which he took this line is—
"But then rose up all Edinburgh,
They rose up by thousands three;
A cowardly Scot came John behind,
And ran him through the fair body!"

We returned to my house. Before dinner, he told us of a curious conversation between the famous George Faulkner and him. George said, that England had drained Ireland of fifty thousand pounds in specie, annually, for fifty years. "How so, Sir?" said Dr. Johnson: "you must have very great trade?"—"No trade." —"Very rich mines?"—"No mines."—"From whence, then, does all this money come?"—"Come! why out of the blood and bowels of the poor people of Ireland!"

We gave him as good a dinner as we could. Our Scotch muir-fowl, or grouse, were then abundant, and quite in season; and so far as wisdom and wit can be aided by administering agreeable sensations to the palate, my wife took care that our great guest should not be deficient.

At supper we had Dr. Cullen, Dr. Adam Fergusson, and Mr. Crosbie, advocate. Witchcraft was introduced. Mr. Crosbie said he thought it the greatest blasphemy to suppose evil spirits counteracting the Deity, and raising storms, for instance, to destroy his creatures. JOHNSON. "Why, Sir, if moral evil be consistent with the government of the Deity, why may not physical evil be also consistent with it? It is not more strange that there should be evil spirits than evil men: evil unembodied spirits, than evil embodied spirits. And as to storms, we know there are such things; and it is no worse that evil spirits raise them than that they rise." CROSBIE. "But it is not credible that witches should have effected what they are said in stories to have done." JOHNSON. "Sir, I am not defending their credibility. I am only saying that your arguments are not good, and will not overturn the belief of witchcraft.—(Dr. Fergusson said to me aside, 'He is right.')—And then, Sir, you have all mankind rude and civilized, agreeing in the belief of the agency of preternatural powers. You must take evidence; you must consider that wise and great men have condemned witches to die." CROSBIE. "But an act of parliament put an end to witchcraft." JOHNSON. "No, Sir, witchcraft had ceased; and, therefore, an act of parliament was passed to prevent persecution for what was not witchcraft. Why it ceased we cannot tell, as we cannot tell the reason of many other things." Dr. Cullen talked in a very entertaining manner, of people walking and conversing in their sleep. We talked of the ouran-outang, and of Lord Monboddo's thinking that he might be taught to speak. Dr. Johnson treated this with ridicule. Mr. Crosbie said that Lord Monboddo believed the existence of every thing possible; in short, that all which is *in posse* might be found *in esse.* JOHNSON. "But, Sir, it is as possible that the ouran-outang does not speak, as that he speaks. However, I shall not contest the point. I should have thought it not possible to find a Monboddo; yet *he* exists." I again mentioned the stage. JOHNSON. "The appearance of a player, with whom I have drunk tea, counter-acts the imagination that he is the character he represents. Nay, you know, nobody imagines that he is the character he represents. They say, 'See Garrick! how he looks to-night! See how he'll clutch the dagger!' That is the buzz of the theater."

Tuesday, Aug. 17.—Sir William Forbes came to breakfast, and brought with him Dr. Blacklock, whom he introduced to Dr. John-son, who received him with a most humane complacency; "Dear Dr. Blacklock, I am glad to see you!" Blacklock seemed to be much surprised when Dr. Johnson said, "it was easier to him to write poetry than to compose his Dictionary. His mind was less on the stretch in doing the one than the other. Besides, composing a dictionary requires books and a desk: you can make a poem walking in the fields, or lying in bed." Dr. Blacklock spoke of scepticism in morals and religion with apparent uneasiness, as if he wished for more certainty. Dr. Johnson, who had thought it all over, and whose vigorous understanding was fortified by much experience, thus encouraged the blind bard: "Why, Sir, the greatest concern we have in this world, the choice of our profession, must be de-termined without demonstrative reasoning. Human life is not yet so well known, as that we can have it: and take the case of a man who is ill. I call two physicians: they differ in opinion. I am not to lie down, and die between them: I must do something." The conversation then turned on atheism, and on the supposition of an eternal necessity without design, without a governing mind. JOHN-SON. "If it were so, why has it ceased? Why don't we see men thus produced around us now? Why, at least, does it not keep pace, in some measure, with the progress of time? If it stops because there is now no need of it, then it is plain there is, and ever has been, an all-powerful intelligence. But stay! (said he, with one of his satiric laughs). Ha! ha! ha! I shall suppose Scotchmen made necessarily, and Englishmen by choice."

At dinner this day we had Sir Alexander Dick, whose amiable character and ingenious and cultivated mind are so generally known (he was then on the verge of seventy, and is now (1785) eighty-one, with his faculties entire, his heart warm, and his temper gay); Sir David Dalrymple, Lord Hailes; Mr. Maclaurin, advocate; Dr. Gregory, who now worthily fills his father's medical chair; and my uncle, Dr. Boswell. This was one of Dr. Johnson's best days. He was quite in his element. All was literature and taste, without any interruption.

Wednesday, Aug. 18.—On this day we set out from Edinburgh. I have given a sketch of Dr. Johnson: my readers may wish to know a little of his fellow-traveller. Think, then, of a gentleman of ancient blood, the pride of which was his predominant passion. He was then in his thirty-third year, and had been about four years happily married. His inclination was to be a soldier, but his father, a respectable judge, had pressed him into the profession of the law. He had travelled a good deal, and seen many varieties of human life. He had thought more than any body had supposed, and had a pretty good stock of general learning and knowledge. He had all Dr. Johnson's principles, with some degree of relaxation. He had rather too little than too much prudence; and, his imagination being lively, he often said things of which the effect was very different from the intention. He resembled sometimes

The best good man, with the worst-natured muse.

He cannot deny himself the vanity of finishing with the encomium of Dr. Johnson, whose friendly partiality to the companion of his tour represents him as one, "whose acuteness would help my inquiry, and whose gaiety of conversation, and civility of manners, are sufficient to counteract the inconveniences of travel, in countries less hospitable than we have passed." [1]

Dr. Johnson thought it unnecessary to put himself to the additional expense of bringing with him Francis Barber, his faithful black servant; so we were attended only by my man, Joseph Ritter, a Bohemian, a fine stately fellow above six feet high, who had been over a great part of Europe, and spoke many languages. He was the best servant I ever saw. Let not my readers disdain his introduction; for Dr. Johnson gave him this character: "Sir, he is a civil man and a wise man."

From an erroneous apprehension of violence, Dr. Johnson had provided a pair of pistols, some gunpowder, and a quantity of bullets; but upon being assured we should run no risk of meeting any robbers, he left his arms and ammunition in an open drawer,

[1] Previous to this public eulogium of his travelling companion, Johnson wrote to Mrs. Thrale: "Boswell will praise my resolution and perseverance, and I shall in return celebrate his good humour and perpetual cheerfulness. He has better faculties than I had imagined; more justice of discernment, and more fecundity of images. It is very convenient to travel with him; for there is no house where he is not received with kindness and respect."

of which he gave my wife the charge. He also left in that drawer one volume of a pretty full and curious Diary of his Life, of which I have a few fragments; but the book has been destroyed. I wish female curiosity had been strong enough to have had it all transcribed, which might easily have been done, and I should think the theft, being *pro bono publico*, might have been forgiven. But I may be wrong. My wife told me she never once looked into it. She did not seem quite easy when we left her: but away we went!

Mr. Nairne, advocate, was to go with us as far as St. Andrew's. When we came to Leith, I talked with perhaps too boasting an air, how pretty the Frith of Forth looked; as indeed, after the prospect from Constantinople, of which I have been told, and that from Naples which I have seen, I believe the view of that Frith and its environs, from the Castle-hill of Edinburgh, is the finest prospect in Europe. "Ay," said Dr. Johnson, "that is the state of the world. Water is the same everywhere."

I told him the port here was the mouth of the river or water of *Leith.* "Not *Lethe*," said Mr. Nairne. "Why, Sir," said Dr. Johnson, "when a Scotchman sets out from this port for England, he forgets his native country." NAIRNE. "I hope, Sir, you will forget England here." JOHNSON. "Then 't will be still more *Lethe*." He observed of the pier or quay, "You have no occasion for so large a one; your trade does not require it: but you are like a shopkeeper who takes a shop, not only for what he has to put into it, but that it may be believed he has a great deal to put into it." It is very true, that there is now, comparatively, little trade upon the eastern coast of Scotland. The riches of Glasgow show how much there is in the west; and, perhaps, we shall find trade travel westward on a great scale as well as a small.

We talked of a man's drowning himself. JOHNSON. "I should never think it time to make away with myself." I put the case of Eustace Budgell, who was accused of forging a will, and sunk himself in the Thames, before the trial of its authenticity came on. "Suppose, Sir," said I, "that a man is absolutely sure, that, if he lives a few days longer, he shall be detected in a fraud, the consequence of which will be utter disgrace and expulsion from society." JOHNSON. "Then, Sir, let him go abroad to a distant country; let him go to some place where he is *not* known. Don't let him go to the devil, where he *is* known!"

He then said, "I see a number of people barefooted here: I suppose you all went so before the Union. Boswell, your ancestors

went so when they had as much land as your family has now. Yet
Auchinleck is the field of stones; there would be bad going bare-
footed there. The lairds however did it." I bought some speldings,
fish (generally whitings) salted and dried in a particular manner,
being dipped in the sea and dried in the sun, and eaten by the
Scots by way of a relish. He had never seen them though they are
sold in London. I insisted on scottifying his palate; but he was very
reluctant. With difficulty I prevailed with him to let a bit of one
of them lie in his mouth. He did not like it.

In crossing the Frith, Dr. Johnson determined that we should
land upon Inch Keith. On approaching it, we first observed a high
rocky shore. We coasted about and put into a little bay on the
north-west. We clambered up a very steep ascent, on which was
very good grass, but rather a profusion of thistles. There were sixteen head of black cattle grazing upon the island. Brantôme calls
it L'isle des Chevaux, and it was probably "a *safer* stable" than
many others in his time. The fort, with an inscription on it,
Maria Re: 1564, is strongly built. Dr. Johnson examined it with
much attention. He stalked like a giant among the luxuriant
thistles and nettles. He said, "I'd have this island. I'd build a
house, make a good landing-place, have a garden, and vines, and all
sorts of trees. A rich man of a hospitable turn, here, would have
many visitors from Edinburgh." When we had got into our boat
again, he called to me, "Come, now, pay a classical compliment
to the island on quitting it." I happened luckily, in allusion to the
beautiful Queen Mary, whose name is upon the fort, to think of
what Virgil makes Æneas say, on having left the country of his
charming Dido:

Invitus, regina, tuo de littore cessi. [1]

"Very well hit off!" said he.

We dined at Kinghorn, and then got into a post-chaise. Mr.
Nairne and his servant, and Joseph, rode by us. We stopped at
Cupar, and drank tea. We talked of Parliament; and I said, I
suppose very few of the members knew much of what was going on,
as indeed very few gentlemen know much of their own private
affairs. JOHNSON. "Why, Sir, if a man is not of a sluggish mind, he
may be his own steward. If he will look into his affairs, he will soon
learn. So it is as to public affairs. There must always be a certain

[1] Æn., vi. 460.
      "Unhappy queen!
      Unwilling I forsook your friendly *state*."—*Dryden.*

number of men of business in parliament." BOSWELL. "But consider, Sir, what is the House of Commons? Is not a great part of it chosen by peers? Do you think, Sir, they ought to have such an influence?" JOHNSON. "Yes, Sir. Influence must ever be in proportion to property; and it is right it should." BOSWELL. "But is there not reason to fear that the common people may be oppressed?" JOHNSON. "No, Sir. Our great fear is from want of power in government. Such a storm of vulgar force has broken in." BOSWELL. "It has only roared." JOHNSON. "Sir, it has roared, till the judges in Westminster Hall have been afraid to pronounce sentence in opposition to the popular cry. You are frightened by what is no longer dangerous, like presbyterians by popery." He then repeated a passage, I think, in Butler's Remains, which ends, "and would cry fire! fire! in Noah's flood." [1]

We had a dreary drive, in a dusky night, to St. Andrew's, where we arrived late. We found a good supper at Glass's inn, and Dr. Johnson revived agreeably. After supper, we made a procession to Saint Leonard's college, the landlord walking before us with a candle, and the waiter with a lantern.

Thursday, Aug. 19.—We rose much refreshed. I had with me a map of Scotland, a Bible which was given me by Lord Mountstuart when we were together in Italy, and Ogden's "Sermons on Prayer." Mr. Nairne introduced us to Dr. Watson. His daughter, a very pleasing young lady, made breakfast. Dr. Watson observed, that Glasgow University had fewer home students since trade increased, as learning was rather incompatible with it. JOHNSON. "Why, Sir, as trade is now carried on by subordinate hands, men in trade have as much leisure as others; and now learning itself is a trade. A man goes to a bookseller, and gets what he can. We have done with patronage. In the infancy of learning, we find some great man praised for it. This diffused it among others. When it becomes general, an author leaves the great, and applies to the multitude." BOSWELL. "It is a shame that authors are not now better patronised." JOHNSON. "No, Sir. If learning cannot support a man, if he must sit with his hands across till somebody feeds him, it is as to him a bad thing, and it is better as it is. With patronage, what flattery! what falsehood! While a man is in equilibrio, he throws truth among the multitude, and lets them take it as they please: in patronage, he must say what pleases his

---

[1] "He preaches, indeed, both in season and out of season; for he rails at Popery, when the land is almost lost in Presbytery; and would cry fire! fire! in Noah's flood."—*Butler's Remains.*

patron, and it is an equal chance whether that be truth or false-hood." WATSON. "But is it not the case now, that, instead of flattering one person, we flatter the age?" JOHNSON. "No, Sir. The world always lets a man tell what he thinks his own way. I wonder, however, that so many people have written, who might have let it alone. That people should endeavour to excel in con-versation, I do not wonder; because in conversation praise is instantly reverberated."

We talked of change of manners. Dr. Johnson observed, that our drinking less than our ancestors was owing to the change from ale to wine. "I remember," said he, "when all the *decent* people in Lichfield got drunk every night, and were not the worse thought of. Ale was cheap, so you pressed strongly. When a man must bring a bottle of wine, he is not in such haste. Smoking has gone out. To be sure, it is a shocking thing, blowing smoke out of our mouths into other people's mouths, eyes, and noses, and having the same thing done to us. Yet I cannot account, why a thing which requires so little exertion, and yet preserves the mind from total vacuity, should have gone out. Every man has something by which he calms himself; beating with his feet or so." [1]

After what Dr. Johnson had said of St. Andrew's, which he had long wished to see, as our oldest university, and the seat of our primate in the days of episcopacy, I can say little. Dr. Johnson's veneration for the hierarchy is well known. There is no wonder then, that he was affected with a strong indignation, while he beheld the ruins of religious magnificence. I happened to ask where John Knox was buried. Dr. Johnson burst out, "I hope in the highway. I have been looking at his reformations."

It was a very fine day. Dr. Johnson seemed quite wrapt up in the contemplation of the scenes which were now presented to him. He kept his hat off while he was upon any part of the ground where the cathedral had stood. He said well, that "Knox had set on a mob, without knowing where it would end; and that differing from a man in doctrine was no reason why you should pull his house about his ears." As we walked in the cloisters, there was a solemn echo, while he talked loudly of a proper retirement from the world. "In general, as every man is obliged not only to 'love God, but his neighbour as himself,' he must bear his part in active life; yet there are exceptions. Those who are exceedingly scrupulous (which I do not approve, for I am no friend to scruples), and find their scrupu-

---

[1] Dr Johnson used to practise this himself very much.—*Boswell*.

losity invincible, so that they are quite in the dark, and know not what they shall do,—or those who cannot resist temptations, and find they make themselves worse by being in the world, without making it better,—may retire. I never read of a hermit, but in imagination I kiss his feet: never of a monastery, but I could fall on my knees, and kiss the pavement. But I think putting young people there, who know nothing of life, nothing of retirement, is dangerous and wicked. It is a saying as old as Hesiod—

"Ἔργα νεῶν, βουλαί τε μέσων, εὐχαί τε γερόντων.¹

That is a very noble line: not that young men should not pray, or old men not give counsel, but that every season of life has its proper duties. I have thought of retiring, and have talked of it to a friend; but I find my vocation is rather to active life."

He wanted to mount the steeples, but it could not be done. One of the steeples, which he was told was in danger, he wished not to be taken down; "for," said he, "it may fall on some of the posterity of John Knox; and no great matter!" Dinner was mentioned. JOHNSON. "Ay, ay, amidst all these sorrowful scenes, I have no objection to dinner."

The professors entertained us with a very good dinner. Present: Murison, Shaw, Cooke, Hill, Haddo, Watson, Flint, Brown. I observed, that I wondered to see him eat so well, after viewing so many sorrowful scenes of ruined religious magnificence. "Why," said he, "I am not sorry, after seeing these gentlemen, for they are not sorry." Murison said, all sorrow was bad as it was murmuring against the dispensations of Providence. JOHNSON. "Sir, sorrow is inherent in humanity. As you cannot judge two and two to be either five or three, but certainly four, so, when comparing a worse present state, with a better which is past, you cannot but feel sorrow. It is not cured by reason, but by the incursion of present objects, which wear out the past. You need not murmur, though you are sorry."

I was much pleased to see Dr. Johnson actually in St. Andrew's, of which we had talked so long. We observed two occupations united in the same person, who had hung out two signposts. Upon one was "James Hood, White Iron Smith" (i.e. tin-plate worker). Upon another, "The Art of Fencing Taught, by James Hood." Upon this last were painted some trees, and two men fencing, one of

¹ "Let youth in deeds, in counsel man engage:
Prayer is the proper duty of old age."

whom had hit the other in the eye, to show his great dexterity; so that the art was well taught. JOHNSON. "Were I studying here, I should go and take a lesson."

Friday, Aug. 20.—Dr. Shaw, the professor of divinity, breakfasted with us. I took out my "Ogden on Prayer," and read some of it to the company. Dr. Johnson praised him. Dr. Johnson enforced the strict observance of Sunday. "It should be different (he observed) from another day. People may walk, but not throw stones at birds. There may be relaxation, but there should be no levity."

We left St. Andrew's about noon, and some miles from it, observing, at Leuchars, a church with an old tower, we stopped to look at it. The manse, as the parsonage-house is called in Scotland, was close by. I waited on the minister, mentioned our names, and begged he would tell us what he knew about it. He was a very civil old man; but could only inform us, that it was supposed to have stood eight hundred years. He told us there was a colony of Danes in his parish; that they had landed at a remote period of time, and still remained a distinct people. Dr. Johnson shrewdly inquired, whether they had brought women with them. We were not satisfied as to this colony.

We saw, this day, Dundee and Aberbrothick. Upon the road he said, our judges had not gone deep in the question concerning literary property. I mentioned Lord Monboddo's opinion, that if a man could get a work by heart, he might print it, as by such an act the mind is exercised. JOHNSON. "No, Sir; a man's repeating it no more makes it his property, than a man may sell a cow which he drives home." I said, printing an abridgment of a work was allowed, which was only cutting the horns and tail off the cow. JOHNSON. "No, Sir; 'tis making the cow have a calf."

About eleven at night we arrived at Montrose. We found but a sorry inn, where I myself saw another waiter put a lump of sugar with his fingers into Dr. Johnson's lemonade, for which he called him "rascal!" It put me in great glee that our landlord was an Englishman. I rallied the Doctor upon this, and he grew quiet.

He was angry at me for proposing to carry lemons with us to Sky, that he might be sure to have his lemonade. "Sir," said he, "I do not wish to be thought that feeble man who cannot do without any thing. Sir, it is very bad manners to carry provisions to any man's house, as if he could not entertain you. To an inferior, it is oppressive; to a superior, it is insolent."

Having taken the liberty, this evening, to remark to Dr. Johnson, that he very often sat quite silent for a long time, even when in company with only a single friend, which I myself had sometimes sadly experienced, he smiled and said, "It is true, Sir. Tom Tyers described me the best. He once said to me, 'Sir, you are like a ghost: you never speak till you are spoken to.'"

Montrose, Saturday, Aug. 21st.—Before breakfast, we went and saw the town-hall, where is a good dancing room, and other rooms for tea-drinking. When we came down from it, I met Mr. Gleig, a merchant here. He went with us to see the English chapel. Dr. Johnson gave a shilling extraordinary to the clerk, saying, "He belongs to an honest church." I put him in mind, that episcopals were but *dissenters* here; they were only *tolerated*. "Sir," said he, "we are here, as Christians in Turkey." He afterwards went into an apothecary's shop, and ordered some medicine for himself, and wrote the prescription in technical characters. The boy took him for a physician.

I doubted much which road to take, whether to go by the coast, or by Lawrence Kirk and Monboddo. I knew Lord Monboddo and Dr. Johnson did not love each other; yet I was unwilling not to visit his lordship; and was also curious to see them together.[1] I mentioned my doubts to Dr. Johnson, who said he would go two miles out of his way to see Lord Monboddo. I therefore sent Joseph forward.

As we travelled onwards from Montrose, we had the Grampian hills in our view, and some good land around us, but void of trees and hedges. Dr. Johnson has said ludicrously, in his "Journey," that the *hedges* were of *stone;* for, instead of the verdant *thorn* to refresh the eye, we found the bare *wall* or *dike* intersecting the prospect. He observed, that it was wonderful to see a country so divested, so denuded of trees.

About a mile from Monboddo, where you turn off the road, Joseph was waiting to tell us my lord expected us to dinner. We drove over a wild moor. It rained, and the scene was somewhat dreary. Dr. Johnson repeated, with solemn emphasis, Macbeth's speech on meeting the witches. As we travelled on, he told me, "Sir, you got into our Club by doing what a man can do.[2] Several of the members wished to keep you out. Burke told me, he doubted

[1] Johnson described Lord Monboddo to Mrs. Thrale: "He is a Scotch judge, who has lately written a strange book about the origin of language, in which he traces monkeys up to men, and says that in some countries the human species have tails like other beasts. He inquired for these long-tailed men from Banks, and was not pleased that they had not been found in all his peregrinations. He talked nothing of this to *me*."
[2] This, I find, is considered obscure. I suppose Dr. Johnson meant, that I assiduously and earnestly recommended myself to some of the members, as in a canvass for an election into parliament.—*Boswell*.

if you were fit for it: but, now you are in, none of them are sorry. Burke says, that you have so much good-humour naturally, it is scarce a virtue." BOSWELL. "They were afraid of you, Sir, as it was you who proposed me." JOHNSON. "Sir, they knew, that if they refused you, they'd probably never have got in another. I'd have kept them all out. Beauclerk was very earnest for you." BOSWELL. "Beauclerk has a keenness of mind which is very uncommon." JOHNSON. "Yes, Sir; and every thing comes from him so easily. It appears to me that I labour, when I say a good thing."

Monboddo is a wretched place, wild and naked, with a poor old house, though, if I recollect right, there are two turrets, which mark an old baron's residence. Lord Monboddo received us at his gate most courteously; pointed to the Douglas arms upon his house, and told us that his great-grandmother was of that family. "In such houses," said he, "our ancestors lived, who were better men than we." "No, no, my lord," said Dr. Johnson; "we are as strong as they, and a great deal wiser." This was an assault upon one of Lord Monboddo's capital dogmas, and I was afraid there would have been a violent altercation in the very close, before we got into the house. But his lordship is distinguished for ancient *politesse*, "*la vieille cour*," and he made no reply.

His lordship was drest in a rustic suit, and wore a little round hat; he told us, we now saw him as Farmer Burnet, and we should have his family dinner, a farmer's dinner. He said, "I should not have forgiven Mr. Boswell, had he not brought you here, Dr. Johnson." He produced a very long stalk of corn, as a specimen of his crop, and said, "You see here the *lætas segetes*": he added, that Virgil seemed to be as enthusiastic a farmer as he, and was certainly a practical one. JOHNSON. "It does not always follow, my lord, that a man, who has written a good poem on an art, has practised it."

I started the subject of emigration. JOHNSON. "To a man of mere animal life, you can urge no argument against going to America, but that it will be some time before he will get the earth to produce. But a man of any intellectual enjoyment will not easily go and immerse himself and his posterity for ages in barbarism."

He and my lord spoke highly of Homer. JOHNSON. "He had all the learning of his age. The shield of Achilles shows a nation in war, a nation in peace: harvest sport, nay stealing." MONBODDO. "Ay, and what we (looking to me) would call a parliament-house scene; a cause pleaded." JOHNSON. "That is part of the life of a nation in peace. And there are in Homer such characters of heroes, and combinations of qualities of heroes, that the united powers of mankind ever since have not produced any but what are to be found there." MONBODDO. "The history of manners is the most valuable. I never set a high value on any other history." JOHNSON. "Nor I; and therefore I esteem biography, as giving us what comes near to ourselves, what we can turn to use." BOSWELL. "But in the course of general history we find manners. In wars, we see the dispositions of people, their degrees of humanity, and other particulars." JOHNSON. "Yes; but then you must take all the facts to get this, and it is but a little you get." MONBODDO. "And it is that little which makes history valuable." Bravo! thought I; they agree like two brothers. We talked of the decrease of learning in Scotland. JOHNSON. "Learning is much decreased in England, in my remembrance." MONBODDO. "You, Sir, have lived to see its decrease in England, I its extinction in Scotland." JOHNSON. "Learning has decreased in England, because learning will not do so much for a man as formerly. There are other ways of getting preferment. Few bishops are now made for their learning. To be a bishop, a man must be learned in a learned age, factious in a factious age, but always of eminence."

Dr. Johnson examined young Arthur, Lord Monboddo's son, in Latin. He answered very well. My lord and Dr. Johnson disputed a little, whether the savage or the London shopkeeper had the best existence; his lordship, as usual, preferring the savage. My lord was extremely hospitable, and I saw both Dr. Johnson and him liking each other better every hour.

Dr. Johnson having retired for a short time, his lordship spoke of his conversation as I could have wished. Dr. Johnson had said, "I have done greater feats with my knife than this"; though he had eaten a very hearty dinner. My lord, who affects or believes he follows an abstemious system, seemed struck with Dr. Johnson's manner of living. I had a particular satisfaction in being under the roof of Monboddo, my lord being my father's old friend, and having been always very good to me. We were cordial together. He asked Dr. Johnson and me to stay all night. When I said we must be at Aberdeen, he replied, "Well, I am like the Romans: I shall say to you, 'Happy to come; happy to depart!'" He thanked Dr. Johnson for his visit.

Gory, my lord's black servant, was sent as our guide, to conduct us to the high road. The circumstance of each of them having a

RIDING TOGETHER MOST CORDIALLY

black servant was another point of similarity between Johnson and Monboddo. I observed how curious it was to see an African in the north of Scotland, with little or no difference of manners from those of the natives. Dr. Johnson laughed to see Gory and Joseph riding together most cordially. "Those two fellows," said he, "one from Africa, the other from Bohemia, seem quite at home." He was much pleased with Lord Monboddo to-day. He said, he would have pardoned him for a few paradoxes, when he found that he had so much that was good: but that, from his appearance in London, he thought him all paradox; which would not do. He observed that his lordship had talked no paradoxes to-day. "And as to the savage and the London shopkeeper," said he, "I don't know but I might have taken the side of the savage equally, had any body else taken the side of the shopkeeper."

When Gory was about to part from us, Dr. Johnson called to him, "Mr. Gory, give me leave to ask you a question! are you baptized?" Gory told him he was—and confirmed by the Bishop of Durham. He then gave him a shilling.

We had a tedious driving this afternoon, and were somewhat drowsy. Last night I was afraid Dr. Johnson was beginning to faint in his resolution; for he said, "If we must ride much we shall not go; and there's an end on't." To-day, when he talked of Sky with spirit, I said, "Why Sir, you seemed to me to despond yesterday. You are a delicate Londoner; you are a maccaroni; you can't ride." JOHNSON. "Sir, I shall ride better than you. I was only afraid I should not find a horse able to carry me." I hoped then there would be no fear of getting through our wild Tour.

We came to Aberdeen at half an hour past eleven. The New Inn, we were told, was full. This was comfortless. The waiter, however, asked if one of our names was Boswell, and brought me a letter left at the inn; it was from Mr. Thrale, enclosing one to Dr. Johnson. Finding who I was, we were told they would contrive to lodge us by putting us for a night into a room with two beds. The waiter said to me in the broad strong Aberdeenshire dialect, "I thought I knew you, by your likeness to your father." My father puts up at the New Inn, when on his circuit. Little was said to-night. I was to sleep in a little press-bed in Dr. Johnson's room. I had it wheeled out into the dining-room, and there I lay very well.

Sunday, Aug. 22.—I sent a message to Professor Thomas Gordon, who came and breakfasted with us. He had secured seats for us at the English chapel. We found a respectable congregation, and an admirable organ.

We walked down to the shore. Dr. Johnson laughed to hear that Cromwell's soldiers taught the Aberdeen people to make shoes and stockings, and to plant cabbages. I was sensible to-day, to an extraordinary degree, of Dr. Johnson's excellent English pronunciation. I cannot account for its striking me more now than any other day; but it was as if new to me, and I listened to every sentence which he spoke, as to a musical composition.

At dinner, Dr. Johnson ate several platefuls of Scotch broth, with barley and peas in it, and seemed very fond of the dish. I said, "You never ate it before." JOHNSON. "No, Sir; but I don't care how soon I eat it again." My cousin, Miss Dallas, formerly of Inverness, was married to Mr. Riddoch, one of the ministers of the English chapel here. He was ill, and confined to his room; but she sent us a kind invitation to tea, which we all accepted. She was the same lively, sensible, cheerful woman, as ever. Dr. Johnson here threw out some jokes against Scotland. He said, "You go first to Aberdeen; then to *Embru* (the Scottish pronunciation of Edinburgh); then to Newcastle, to be polished by the colliers; then to York; then to London." And he laid hold of a little girl, Stuart Dallas, niece to Mrs. Riddoch, and, representing himself as a giant, said, he would take her with him! telling her, in a hollow voice, that he lived in a cave, and had a bed in the rock, and she should have a little bed cut opposite to it!

We went to our inn, and sat quietly. Dr. Johnson borrowed, at Mr. Riddoch's, a volume of Massillon's "Discourses on the Psalms"; but I found he read little in it. Ogden too he sometimes took up, and glanced at; but threw it down again. I then entered upon religious conversation. Never did I see him in a better frame: calm, gentle, wise, holy.

Monday, Aug. 23.—We went and saw the Marischal College, and at one o'clock we waited on the magistrates in the town-hall, as they had invited us, in order to present Dr. Johnson with the freedom of the town. Dr. Johnson was much pleased with this mark of attention, and received it very politely. There was a pretty numerous company assembled. It was striking to hear all of them drinking, "Dr. Johnson! Dr. Johnson!" in the town-hall of Aberdeen, and then to see him with his burgess-ticket, or diploma, in his hat, which he wore as he walked along the street, according to the usual custom. It gave me great satisfaction to observe the regard, and, indeed, fondness too, which every body here had for my father.

We dined at Sir Alexander Gordon's. The provost, Professor Ross, Professor Dunbar, Professor Thomas Gordon, were there. We had little or no conversation in the morning; now we were but barren. The professors seemed afraid to speak.

We sauntered after dinner in Sir Alexander's garden, and saw his little grotto, which is hung with pieces of poetry written in a fair hand. I was weary of this day, and began to think wishfully of being again in motion. I was uneasy to think myself too fastidious, whilst I fancied Dr. Johnson quite satisfied. But he owned to me, that he was fatigued and teased by Sir Alexander's doing too much to entertain him. I said, it was all kindness. JOHNSON. "True, Sir; but sensation is sensation."

We went and sat near an hour at Mr. Riddoch's. He could not tell distinctly how much education at the college here costs, which disgusted Dr. Johnson. I saw Mr. Riddoch did not please him. He said to me afterwards, "Sir, he has no vigour in his talk." But my friend should have considered, that he himself was not in good humour; so that it was not easy to talk to his satisfaction. We sat contentedly at our inn. He then became merry, and observed how little we had either heard or said at Aberdeen; that the Aberdonians had not started a single *mawkin* (the Scottish word for hare) for us to pursue.

Tuesday, August 24.—We set out about eight in the morning, and breakfasted at Ellon. The landlady said to me, "Is not this the great doctor that is going about through the country?" I said, "Yes." "Ay," said she, "we heard of him; I made an errand into the room on purpose to see him. There's something great in his appearance: it is a pleasure to have such a man in one's house; a man who does so much good. If I had thought of it, I would have shown him a child of mine, who has had a lump on his throat for some time." "But," said I, "he is not a doctor of physic." "Is he an oculist?" said the landlord. "No," said I; "he is only a very learned man." LANDLORD. "They say he is the greatest man in England, except Lord Mansfield." Dr. Johnson was highly entertained with this, and I do think he was pleased too. He said, "I like the exception. To have called me the greatest man in England, would have been an unmeaning compliment; but the exception marked that the praise was in earnest."

He told me a good story of Dr. Goldsmith. Graham, who wrote

"Telemachus, a Masque," was sitting one night with him and Dr. Johnson, and was half drunk. He rattled away to Dr. Johnson. "You are a clever fellow, to be sure; but you cannot write an essay like Addison, or verses like the 'Rape of the Lock.'" At last he said, "Doctor, I should be happy to see you at Eton." "I shall be glad to wait on you," answered Goldsmith. "No," said Graham, "'tis not you I mean, Dr. *Minor;* 'tis Dr. *Major,* there." Goldsmith was excessively hurt by this. He afterwards spoke of it himself. "Graham," said he, "is a fellow to make one commit suicide."

We had received a polite invitation to Slains Castle. We arrived there just at three o'clock, as the bell for dinner was ringing. Though, from its being just on the northeast ocean, no trees will grow here, Lord Errol has done all that can be done. He has cultivated his fields so as to bear rich crops of every kind, and he has made an excellent kitchen-garden, with a hot-house. I had never seen any of the family; but there had been a card of invitation written by the honourable Charles Boyd, the Earl's brother. We were conducted into the house, and at the dining-room door were met by that gentleman, whom both of us at first took to be Lord Errol; but he soon corrected our mistake. My lord was gone to dine in the neighbourhood. Lady Errol received us politely, and was very attentive to us during the time of dinner. There was nobody at table but her ladyship, Mr. Boyd, and some of the children, their governor and governess. After dinner, Lady Errol favoured us with a sight of her young family, whom she made stand up in a row: there were six daughters and two sons. It was a very pleasing sight.

Dr. Johnson proposed our setting out. Mr. Boyd said, he hoped we would stay all night; his brother would be at home in the evening, and would be very sorry if he missed us. Mr. Boyd was called out of the room. I was very desirous to stay in so comfortable a house, and I wished to see Lord Errol. Dr. Johnson, however, was right in resolving to go, if we were not asked again, as it is best to err on the safe side in such cases, and to be sure that one is quite welcome. To my great joy, when Mr. Boyd returned, he told Dr. Johnson that it was Lady Errol who had called him out, and said that she would never let Dr. Johnson into the house again, if he went away that night; and that she had ordered the coach, to carry us to view a great curiosity on the coast, after which we should see the house. We cheerfully agreed.

IT WAS A VERY PLEASING SIGHT

We got immediately into the coach, and drove to Dunbui, a rock near the shore, quite covered with sea-fowls: then to a circular basin of large extent, surrounded with tremendous rocks. On the quarter next the sea, there is a high arch in the rock, which the force of the tempest has driven out. This place is called Buchan's Buller, or the Buller of Buchan, and the country people call it the Pot. We walked round this monstrous cauldron. In some places, the rock is very narrow; and on each side there is a sea deep enough for a man-of-war to ride in; so that it is somewhat horrid to move along. However, there is earth and grass upon the rock, and a kind of road marked out by the print of feet; so that one makes it out pretty safely: yet it alarmed me to see Dr. Johnson striding irregularly along. He insisted on taking a boat, and sailing into the Pot. We did so. He was stout and wonderfully alert. As the entry into the Buller is so narrow that oars cannot be used as you go in, the method taken is, to row very hard when you come near it, and give the boat such a rapidity of motion that it glides in. Dr. Johnson observed what an effect this scene would have had, were we entering into an unknown place.

When we returned to the house, we found coffee and tea in the drawing-room. Lady Errol was not there, being, as I supposed, engaged with her young family. There is a bow-window fronting the sea. Dr. Johnson repeated the ode, " Jam satis terris."

This room is ornamented with a number of fine prints, and with a whole-length picture of Lord Errol, by Sir Joshua Reynolds. This led Dr. Johnson to talk of our amiable and elegant friend: "Sir Joshua Reynolds, Sir, is the most invulnerable man I know; the man with whom if you should quarrel, you will find the most difficulty how to abuse."

About nine the Earl [1] came home. His lordship put Dr. Johnson in mind of their having dined together in London, along with Mr. Beauclerk. I was exceedingly pleased with Lord Errol. His dignified person and agreeable countenance, with the most unaffected affability, gave me high satisfaction. From perhaps a weakness, or, as I rather hope, more fancy and warmth of feeling than is quite reasonable, my mind is ever impressed with admiration for persons of high birth, and I could, with the most perfect honesty, expatiate on Lord Errol's good qualities; but he stands in

[1] James, 14th Earl of Errol. "His stature was six feet four inches, and his countenance and deportment exhibited such a mixture of the sublime and the graceful, as I have never seen united in any other man. He often put me in mind of an ancient hero; and I remember Dr. Johnson was positive that he resembled Homer's character of Sarpedon."—*Beattie.*

no need of my praise. He talked very easily and sensibly with his learned guest. I observed that Dr. Johnson, though he showed that respect to his lordship, which, from principle, he always does to high rank, yet, when they came to argument, maintained that manliness which becomes the force and vigour of his understanding.

The Earl said grace both before and after supper, with much decency. I was afraid he might have urged drinking, as, I believe, he used formerly to do; but he drank port and water out of a large glass himself, and let us do as we pleased. He went with us to our rooms at night; said he took the visit very kindly; and told me my father and he were very old acquaintance; that I now knew the way to Slains, and he hoped to see me there again.

I had a most elegant room: but there was a fire in it which blazed; and the sea, to which my windows looked, roared; and the pillows were made of the feathers of some sea-fowl, which had to me a disagreeable smell: so that, by all these causes, I was kept awake a good while. I saw, in imagination, Lord Errol's father, Lord Kilmarnock (who was beheaded on Tower-Hill in 1746), and I was somewhat dreary. But the thought did not last long, and I fell asleep.

Wednesday, Aug. 25.—We got up between seven and eight, and found Mr. Boyd in the dining-room, with tea and coffee before him, to give us breakfast. We were in an admirable humour.

I regretted the decay of respect for men of family, and that a nabob now would carry an election from them. JOHNSON. "Why, Sir, the nabob will carry it by means of his wealth, in a country where money is highly valued, as it must be where nothing can be had without money; but, if it comes to personal preference, the man of family will always carry it. There is generally a *scoundrelism* about a low man." Mr. Boyd said, that was a good *ism*.

I said, I believed mankind were happier in the ancient feudal state of subordination, than they are in the modern state of independency. JOHNSON. "To be sure, the *chief* was: but we must think of the number of individuals. That *they* were less happy seems plain; for that state from which all escape as soon as they can, and to which none return after they have left it, must be less happy; and this is the case with the state of dependence on a chief or great man."

We set out about nine. Dr. Johnson was curious to see one of those structures, which northern antiquarians call a Druid's temple. I had a recollection of one at Strichen, which I had seen fifteen years ago; so we went four miles out of our road, after passing Old Deer, and went thither. But I had augmented it in my mind; for all that remains is two stones set up on end, with a long one laid upon them, as was usual, and one stone at a little distance from them.

I started a thought this afternoon which amused us a great part of the way. "If," said I, "our Club should come and set up in St. Andrew's, as a college, to teach all that each of us can in the several departments of learning and taste, we should rebuild the city: we should draw a wonderful concourse of students." Dr. Johnson entered fully into the spirit of this project. We immediately fell to distributing the offices. I was to teach civil and Scotch law; Burke, politics and eloquence; Garrick, the art of public speaking; Langton was to be our Grecian, Colman our Latin professor; Nugent, to teach physic; Lord Charlemont, modern history; Beauclerk, natural philosophy; Vesey, Irish antiquities, or Celtic learning; Jones, Oriental learning; Goldsmith, poetry and ancient history; Chamier, commercial politics; Reynolds, painting, and the arts which have beauty for their object; Chambers, the law of England. Dr. Johnson at first said, "I'll trust theology to nobody but myself." But upon due consideration, that Percy is a clergyman, it was agreed that Percy should teach practical divinity and British antiquities; Dr. Johnson himself, logic, metaphysics, and scholastic divinity. In this manner did we amuse ourselves, each suggesting, and each varying or adding, till the whole was adjusted. Dr. Johnson said we only wanted a mathematician since Dyer died, who was a very good one; but as to everything else we should have a very capital university.

We got at night to Banff. I sent Joseph on to Duff House: but Earl Fife was not at home, which I regretted much, as we should have had a very elegant reception from his lordship. We found here but an indifferent inn.[1] Dr. Johnson wrote a long letter to Mrs. Thrale. I wondered to see him write so much so easily.

Thursday, Aug. 26.—We got a fresh chaise here, a very good one, and very good horses. We breakfasted at Cullen. They set down dried haddocks broiled, along with our tea. I ate one: but Dr. Johnson was disgusted by the sight of them, so they were removed.

---

[1] Here, unluckily, the windows had no pulleys, and Dr. Johnson, who was constantly eager for fresh air, had much struggling to get one of them kept open. Thus he had a notion impressed upon him, that this wretched defect was general in Scotland, in consequence of which he has erroneously enlarged upon it in his "Journey."—*Boswell.*

Mr. Robertson sent a servant with us, to show us through Lord Findlater's wood, by which our way was shortened, and we saw some part of his domain, which is indeed admirably laid out. Dr. Johnson did not choose to walk through it. He always said that he was not come to Scotland to see fine places, of which there were enough in England; but wild objects—mountains—waterfalls —peculiar manners; in short, things which he had not seen before. I have a notion that he at no time has had much taste for rural beauties. I have myself very little.

Dr. Johnson said there was nothing more contemptible than a country gentleman living beyond his income, and every year growing poorer and poorer. He spoke strongly of the influence which a man has by being rich. "A man," said he, "who keeps his money, has in reality more use from it than he can have by spending it." I observed that this looked very like a paradox: but he explained it thus: "If it were certain that a man would keep his money locked up for ever, to be sure he would have no influence; but, as so many want money, and he has the power of giving it, and they know not but by gaining his favour they may obtain it, the rich man will always have the greatest influence. He, again, who lavishes his money, is laughed at as foolish, and in a great degree with justice, considering how much is spent from vanity. Even those who partake of a man's hospitality have but a transient kindness for him. If he has not the command of money, people know he cannot help them if he would: whereas the rich man always can, if he will, and for the chance of that, will have much weight." BOSWELL. "But philosophers and satirists have all treated a miser as contemptible." JOHNSON. "He is so philosophically; but not in the practice of life."

We dined at Elgin, and saw the noble ruins of the cathedral. Though it rained much, Dr. Johnson examined them with the most patient attention. We fared but ill at our inn here; and Dr. Johnson said, this was the first time he had seen a dinner in Scotland that he could not eat.

In the afternoon, we drove over the very heath where Macbeth met the witches, according to tradition. Dr. Johnson again solemnly repeated—

> How far is't called to Fores? What are these,
> So wither'd, and so wild in their attire?
> That look not like the inhabitants o' the earth,
> And yet are on't?

"HAIL TO THEE, LORD OF 'AUCHINLECK'!"

He repeated a good deal more of Macbeth. His recitation was grand and affecting.

He then parodied the "All hail" of the witches to Macbeth, addressing himself to me. I had purchased some land called Dalblair; and, as in Scotland it is customary to distinguish landed men by the name of their estates, I had thus two titles, Dalblair and young Auchinleck. So my friend, in imitation of

All hail, Macbeth! hail to thee, Thane of Cawdor!

condescended to amuse himself with uttering

All hail, *Dalblair!* hail to thee, Lord of *Auchinleck!* [1]

We got to Fores at night, and found an admirable inn, in which Dr. Johnson was pleased to meet with a landlord, who styled himself—"Wine-Cooper, from London."

Friday, Aug. 27.—We came to Nairn to breakfast. Though a county town and a royal burgh, it is a miserable place. Over the room where we sat, a girl was spinning wool with a great wheel, and singing an Erse song: "I'll warrant you," said Dr. Johnson, "one of the songs of Ossian." He then repeated these lines:

> Verse sweetens toil, however rude the sound.
> All at her work the village maiden sings;
> Nor, while she turns the giddy wheel around,
> Revolves the sad vicissitude of things.

I expected Mr. Kenneth M'Aulay, the minister of Calder, who published the History of St. Kilda, a book which Dr. Johnson liked, would have met us here, as I had written to him from Aberdeen. But I received a letter from him telling me that he could not leave home, as he was to administer the sacrament the following Sunday, and earnestly requesting to see us at his manse. "We'll go," said Dr. Johnson; which we accordingly did. Mrs. M'Aulay received us, and told us her husband was in the church distributing tokens. We arrived between twelve and one o'clock, and it was near three before he came to us.

Dr. Johnson thanked him for his book, and said "it is a very pretty piece of topography." M'Aulay did not seem much to mind the compliment. From his conversation, Dr. Johnson was persuaded that he had not written the book which goes under his name. He said privately to me, "There is a combination in it of

---

[1] Then, Boswell tells us, pronounced as a dissyllable, *Affleck*, but now, as it is written, *Auchinleck*.

which M'Aulay is not capable." [1]   However, he was exceedingly hospitable; and, as he obligingly promised us a route for our Tour through the Western Isles, we agreed to stay with him all night.

After dinner we walked to the old castle of Calder (pronounced Cawder), the Thane of Cawdor's seat. There were here some large venerable trees.

I was afraid of a quarrel between Dr. Johnson and Mr. M'Aulay, who talked slightingly of the lower English clergy. The Doctor gave him a frowning look, and said, "This is a day of novelties: I have seen old trees in Scotland, and I have heard the English clergy treated with disrespect."

Mr. M'Aulay began a rhapsody against creeds and confessions. Dr. Johnson showed, that "what he called *imposition*, was only a voluntary declaration of agreement in certain articles of faith, which a church has a right to require, just as any other society can insist on certain rules being observed by its members. Nobody is compelled to be of the church, as nobody is compelled to enter into a society." This was a very clear and just view of the subject; but M'Aulay could not be driven out of his track. Dr. Johnson said, "Sir, you are a *bigot to laxness.*"

Mr. M'Aulay and I laid the map of Scotland before us; and he pointed out a route which I wrote down. Dr. Johnson went up to the library, which consisted of a tolerable collection; but the Doctor thought it rather a lady's library, with some Latin books in it by chance, than the library of a clergyman. It had only two of the Latin fathers, and one of the Greek fathers in Latin. I doubted whether Dr. Johnson would be present at a presbyterian prayer. I told Mr. M'Aulay so, and said that the Doctor might sit in the library while we were at family worship. Mr. M'Aulay said, he would omit it, rather than give Dr. Johnson offence: but I would by no means agree that an excess of politeness, even to so great a man, should prevent what I esteem as one of the best pious regulations. I mentioned to Dr. Johnson the over-delicate scrupulosity of our host. He said, he had no objection to hear the prayer. This was a pleasing surprise to me; for he refused to go and hear Principal Robertson preach. "I will hear him," said he, "if he will get up into a tree and preach; but I will not give a sanction, by my presence, to a presbyterian assembly."

[1] "A decision, which to those who happen to have read the work, will give a very poor notion of my ancestor's abilities."—Trevelyan's Life of Lord Macaulay.

DINNER WITH THE 37TH AT FORT GEORGE

Saturday, Aug. 28.—Dr. Johnson had brought a Sallust with him in his pocket from Edinburgh. He gave it last night to Mr. M'Aulay's son, a smart young lad about eleven years old. Dr. Johnson had given an account of the education at Oxford, in all its gradations. The advantage of being a servitor to a youth of little fortune struck Mrs. M'Aulay much. I observed it aloud. Dr. Johnson very handsomely and kindly said, that, if they would send their boy to him, when he was ready for the university, he would get him made a servitor, and perhaps would do more for him. He could not promise to do more; but would undertake for the servitorship.

I should have mentioned that Mr. White, a Welshman, who has been many years factor (*i.e.* steward) on the estate of Calder, drank tea with us last night. He gave us a letter of introduction to Mr. Ferne, master of stores at Fort George. He showed it to me. It recommended "two celebrated gentlemen; no less than Dr. Johnson, *author of his Dictionary*, and Mr. Boswell, known at Edinburgh by the name of *Paoli.*" He said, he hoped I had no objection to what he had written; if I had, he would alter it. I thought it was a pity to check his effusions, and acquiesced; taking care, however, to seal the letter, that it might not appear that I had read it.

A conversation took place about saying grace at breakfast (as we do in Scotland), as well as at dinner and supper; in which Dr. Johnson said, "It is enough if we have stated seasons of prayer; no matter when. A man may as well pray when he mounts his horse, or a woman when she milks her cow, as at meals; and custom is to be followed."

We proceeded to Fort George. When we came into the square, I sent a soldier with the letter to Mr. Ferne. He came to us immediately, and carried us to wait on Sir Eyre Coote, whose regiment, the 37th, was lying here, and who then commanded the fort. He asked us to dine with him, which we agreed to do.

Before dinner we examined the fort. Dr. Johnson talked of the proportions of charcoal and saltpetre in making gun-powder, of granulating it, and of giving it a gloss. He made a very good figure upon these topics. He said to me afterwards, that "he had talked ostentatiously." We reposed ourselves a little in Mr. Ferne's house. He had every thing in neat order as in England; and a tolerable collection of books.

At three the drum beat for dinner. I, for a little while, fancied myself a military man, and it pleased me. We had a dinner of two complete courses, variety of wines, and the regimental band of music playing in the square, before the windows, after it. I enjoyed this day much. We were quite easy and cheerful. Dr. Johnson said, "I shall always remember this fort with gratitude." I could not help being struck with some admiration, at finding upon this barren sandy point such buildings, such a dinner, such company: it was like enchantment. Dr. Johnson, on the other hand, said to me more rationally, that "it did not strike *him* as anything extraordinary; because he knew, here was a large sum of money expended in building a fort; here was a regiment. If there had been less than what we found, it would have surprised him."

We left the fort between six and seven o'clock. We got safely to Inverness, and put up at Mackenzie's inn. Mr. Keith, the collector of excise here, my old acquaintance at Ayr, visited us in the evening, and engaged us to dine with him next day, promising to breakfast with us, and take us to the English chapel; so that we were at once commodiously arranged.

Not finding a letter here that I expected, I felt a momentary impatience to be at home. Transient clouds darkened my imagination, and in those clouds I saw events from which I shrunk: but a sentence or two of the Rambler's conversation gave me firmness, and I considered that I was upon an expedition for which I had wished for years, and the recollection of which would be a treasure to me for life.

Sunday, Aug. 29.—Mr. Keith breakfasted with us. Dr. Johnson expatiated rather too strongly upon the benefits derived to Scotland from the Union, and the bad state of our people before it. I am entertained with his copious exaggeration upon that subject; but I am uneasy when people are by, who do not know him as well as I do, and may be apt to think him narrow-minded.[1] I therefore diverted the subject.

The English chapel, to which we went this morning, was but mean. The altar was a bare fir table, with a coarse stool for kneeling on, covered with a piece of thick sail-cloth doubled, by way of cushion. The congregation was small. Mr. Tait, the clergyman, read prayers very well, though with much of the Scotch accent. It was remarkable that, when talking of the connections amongst men, he said, that some connected themselves with men of distinguished talents; and since they could not equal them, tried to

---

[1] It is remarkable that Dr. Johnson read this gentle remonstrance, and took no notice of it to me.
—*Boswell.*

deck themselves with their merit, by being their companions. It
had an odd coincidence with what might be said of my connecting
myself with Dr. Johnson.

After church, we walked down to the quay. We then went to
Macbeth's castle. I had a romantic satisfaction in seeing Dr. Johnson actually in it. It perfectly corresponds with Shakspeare's description. Just as we came out of it, a raven perched on one of the
chimney-pots, and croaked. Then I repeated

————The raven himself is hoarse,
That croaks the fatal entrance of Duncan
Under my battlements.

We dined at Mr. Keith's. Mrs. Keith was rather too attentive
to Dr. Johnson, asking him many questions about his drinking
only water. He repressed that observation by saying to me, "You
may remember that Lady Errol took no notice of this."

Dr. Johnson has the happy art of instructing himself, by making
every man he meets tell him something of what he knows best.
He led Keith to talk to him of the excise in Scotland.

After this there was little conversation that deserves to be
remembered. I shall, therefore, here again glean what I have
omitted on former days. Dr. Gerard, at Aberdeen, told us, that
when he was in Wales, he was shown a valley inhabited by Danes,
who still retain their own language, and are quite a distinct people.
Dr. Johnson thought it could not be true, or all the kingdom must
have heard of it. He said to me, as we travelled, "These people,
Sir, that Gerard talks of, may have somewhat of a *peregrinity* in
their dialect, which relation has augmented to a different language."
I asked him if *peregrinity* was an English word. He laughed, and
said, "No." I told him this was the second time that I had heard
him coin a word. When Foote broke his leg, I observed that it
would make him fitter for taking off George Faulkner, poor George
having a wooden leg. Dr. Johnson at that time said, "George will
rejoice at the *depeditation* of Foote"; and when I challenged that
word, laughed, and owned he had made it, and added that he had
not made above three or four in his Dictionary.

Having conducted Dr. Johnson to our inn, I begged permission
to leave him for a little, that I might run about and pay some short
visits to several good people of Inverness. He said to me, "You
have all the old-fashioned principles, good and bad." I acknowledge
I have. That of attention to relations in the remotest degree, or to

worthy persons in every state, whom I have once known, I inherit from my father. Mr. Keith and Mr. Grant supped with us at the inn. We had roasted kid, which Dr. Johnson had never tasted before. He relished it much.

Monday, Aug. 30.—This day we were to begin our *equitation,* as I said; for *I* would needs make a word too. We might have taken a chaise to Fort Augustus; but, had we not hired horses at Inverness, we should not have found them afterwards: so we resolved to begin here to ride. We had three horses, for Dr. Johnson, myself, and Joseph, and one which carried our portmanteaus, and two Highlanders who walked along with us, John Hay and Lauchland Vass. Dr. Johnson rode very well.

It was a delightful day. Loch Ness, and the road upon the side of it, shaded with birch trees, and the hills above it, pleased us much. The scene was as sequestered and agreeably wild as could be desired, and for a time engrossed all our attention.

To see Dr. Johnson in any new situation is always an interesting object to me; and, as I saw him now for the first time on horseback, jaunting about at his ease in quest of pleasure and novelty, the very different occupations of his former laborious life, his admirable productions, his "London," his "Rambler," &c., &c., immediately presented themselves to my mind, and the contrast made a strong impression on my imagination.

When we had advanced a good way by the side of Loch Ness, I perceived a little hut, with an old-looking woman at the door of it. I thought here might be a scene that would amuse Dr. Johnson; so I mentioned it to him. "Let's go in," said he. We dismounted, and we and our guides entered the hut. It was a wretched little hovel of earth only, I think, and for a window had only a small hole, which was stopped with a piece of turf, that was taken out occasionally, to let in light. In the middle of the room or space which we entered was a fire of peat, the smoke going out at a hole in the roof. She had a pot upon it, with goat's flesh, boiling. There was at one end under the same roof, but divided by a kind of partition made of wattles, a pen or fold in which we saw a good many kids.

Dr. Johnson was curious to know where she slept. I asked one of the guides, who questioned her in Erse. She answered with a tone of emotion, saying (as he told us), she was afraid we wanted to go to bed to her. This coquetry, or whatever it may be called, of so wretched a being, was truly ludicrous. Dr. Johnson and I afterwards were merry upon it. I said, it was he who alarmed the poor woman's virtue. "No, Sir," said he, "she'll say, 'There came a wicked young fellow, a wild dog, who, I believe, would have ravished me, had there not been with him a grave old gentleman, who repressed him: but when he gets out of the sight of his tutor, I'll warrant you he'll spare no woman he meets, young or old.' "— "No, Sir," I replied, "she'll say, 'There was a terrible ruffian who would have forced me, had it not been for a civil decent young man, who, I take it, was an angel sent from heaven to protect me.' "

Dr. Johnson would not hurt her delicacy by insisting on "seeing her bed-chamber." But my curiosity was more ardent; I lighted a piece of paper, and went into the place where the bed was. There was a little partition of wicker, rather more neatly done than that for the fold, and close by the wall was a kind of bedstead of wood, with heath upon it by way of bed; at the foot of which I saw some sort of blankets or covering rolled up in a heap. The woman's name was Fraser; so was her husband's. He was a man of eighty. Mr. Fraser, of Balnain, allows him to live in this hut, and keep sixty goats, for taking care of his woods, where he then was. They had five children, the eldest only thirteen. Two were gone to Inverness to buy meal; the rest were looking after the goats. This contented family had four stacks of barley, twenty-four sheaves in each. They had a few fowls. We were informed that they lived all the spring without meal, upon milk and curds and whey alone. What they get for their goats, kids, and fowls, maintains them during the rest of the year.

She asked us to sit down and take a dram. I saw one chair. She said she was as happy as any woman in Scotland. She could hardly speak any English except a few detached words. Dr. Johnson was pleased at seeing, for the first time, such a state of human life. She asked for snuff. It is her luxury, and she uses a great deal. We had none; but gave her sixpence apiece. She then brought out her whisky bottle. I tasted it; as did Joseph and our guides: so I gave her sixpence more. She sent us away with many prayers in Erse.

We dined at a public house called the *General's Hut*, from General Wade, who was lodged there when he commanded in the north. After dinner we passed through a good deal of mountainous country. I had known Mr. Trapaud, the deputy-governor of Fort-Augustus, twelve years ago, at a circuit at Inverness, where my father was judge. I sent forward one of our guides, and Joseph, with a card to him, that he might know Dr. Johnson and I were coming up, leaving it to him to invite us or not. It was dark when we arrived. The inn was wretched. Government ought to build one, or give the resident governor an additional salary; as in the present state of things, he must necessarily be put to a great expense in entertaining travellers. Joseph announced to us, when we alighted, that the governor waited for us at the gate of the fort. We walked to it. He met us, and with much civility conducted us to his house. It was comfortable to find ourselves in a well-built little square, and a neatly furnished house, in good company, and with a good supper before us; in short, with all the conveniencies of civilised life, in the midst of rude mountains. Mrs. Trapaud, and the governor's daughter, and her husband, Capt. Newmarsh, were all most obliging and polite. The governor had excellent animal spirits, the conversation of a soldier, and somewhat of a Frenchman, to which his extraction entitles him. We passed a very agreeable evening.

Tuesday, Aug. 31.—Between twelve and one we set out, and travelled eleven miles, through a wild country, till we came to a house in Glenmorison, called Anoch, kept by a M'Queen. Our landlord was a sensible fellow: he had learnt his grammar, and his pride seemed to be much piqued that we were surprised at his having books.

Near to this place we had passed a party of soldiers, under a sergeant's command, at work upon the road. We gave them two shillings to drink. They came to our inn, and made merry in the barn. We went and paid them a visit, Dr. Johnson saying, "Come, let's go and give 'em another shilling apiece." We did so; and he was saluted "My lord" by all of them. He is really generous, loves influence, and has the way of gaining it. He said, "I am quite feudal, Sir."

The poor soldiers got too much liquor. Some of them fought, and left blood upon the spot, and cursed whisky next morning.

I talked of the officers whom we had left to-day; how much service they had seen, and how little they got for it, even of fame. JOHNSON. "Sir, a soldier gets as little as any man can get." BOSWELL. "Goldsmith has acquired more fame than all the officers of the last war, who were not generals." JOHNSON. "Why, Sir, you will find ten thousand fit to do what they did, before you find one who does what Goldsmith has done. You must consider, that a thing is valued according to its rarity. A pebble that paves the street is in itself more useful than the diamond upon a lady's finger." I wish our friend Goldsmith had heard this.

I yesterday expressed my wonder that John Hay, one of our guides, who had been pressed aboard a man of war, did not choose to continue in it longer than nine months, after which time he got off. JOHNSON. "Why, Sir, no man will be a sailor who has contrivance enough to get himself into a jail; for being in a ship is being in a jail with the chance of being drowned."

We had tea in the afternoon, and our landlord's daughter, a modest, civil girl, very neatly dressed, made it for us. She told us she had been a year at Inverness, and learnt reading and writing, sewing, knotting, working lace, and pastry. Dr. Johnson made her a present of a book which he had bought at Inverness.[1]

The room had some deals laid across the joists, as a kind of ceiling. There were two beds in the room, and a woman's gown was hung on a rope to make a curtain of separation between them. Joseph had sheets, which my wife had sent with us, laid on them. We had much hesitation, whether to undress, or lie down with our clothes on. I said at last, "I'll plunge in! There will be less harbour for vermin about me when I am stripped." Dr. Johnson said, he was like one hesitating whether to go into the cold bath. At last he resolved too. I observed he might serve a campaign. JOHNSON. "I could do all that can be done by patience: whether I should have strength enough, I know not." He was in excellent humour. To see the Rambler as I saw him to-night, was really an amusement. I yesterday told him, I was thinking of writing a poetical letter to him, on his return from Scotland, in the style of Swift's humorous epistle in the character of Mary Gulliver to her husband, Captain Lemuel Gulliver, on his return to England from the country of the Houyhnhnms:

> At early morn I to the market haste,
> Studious in ev'ry thing to please thy taste.
> A curious *fowl* and *sparagrass* I chose;
> (For I remember you were fond of those:)
> Three shillings cost the first, the last seven groats;
> Sullen you turn from both, and call for OATS.

[1] This book has given rise to much inquiry, which has ended in ludicrous surprise. Several ladies, wishing to learn the kind of reading which the great and good Dr. Johnson esteemed most fit for a young woman, desired to know what book he had selected for this Highland nymph. "They never adverted," said he, "that I had no choice in the matter. I have said that I presented her with a book, which I happened to have about me." And what was this book? My readers, prepare your features for merriment. It was Cocker's Arithmetic! Wherever this was mentioned, there was a loud laugh, at which Dr. Johnson, when present, used sometimes to be a little angry. One day I ventured to interrogate him, "But, Sir, is it not somewhat singular that you should happen to have Cocker's Arithmetic about you on your journey? What made you buy such a book at Inverness?" He gave me a very sufficient answer. "Why, Sir, if you are to have but one book with you upon a journey, let it be a book of science. When you have read through a book of entertainment, you know it, and it can do no more for you; but a book of science is inexhaustible."—*Boswell*.

He laughed, and asked in whose name I would write it. I said in Mrs. Thrale's. He was angry. "Sir, if you have any sense of decency or delicacy, you won't do that." BOSWELL. "Then let it be in Cole's, the landlord of the Mitre tavern, where we have so often sat together." JOHNSON. "Ay, that may do."

After we had offered up our private devotions, and had chatted a little from our beds, Dr. Johnson said, "God bless us both, for Jesus Christ's sake! Good night." I pronounced "Amen." He fell asleep immediately. I was not so fortunate for a long time. I fancied myself bit by innumerable vermin under the clothes; and that a spider was travelling from the wainscot towards my mouth. At last I fell into insensibility.

Wednesday, Sept. 1.—I awaked very early. I began to imagine that the landlord, being about to emigrate, might murder us to get our money, and lay it upon the soldiers in the barn. Such groundless fears will arise in the mind, before it has resumed its vigour after sleep. Dr. Johnson had had the same kind of ideas; for he told me afterwards that he considered so many soldiers, having seen us, would be witnesses, should any harm be done, and that circumstance, I suppose, he considered as a security. When I got up, I found him sound asleep in his miserable sty, as I may call it, with a coloured handkerchief tied round his head. With difficulty could I awaken him.

We got away about eight. M'Queen walked some miles to give us a convoy. He had, in 1745, joined the Highland army at Fort Augustus, and continued in it till after the battle of Culloden. As he narrated the particulars of that ill-advised, but brave attempt, I could not refrain from tears. There is a certain association of ideas in my mind upon that subject, by which I am strongly affected. The very Highland names, or the sound of a bagpipe, will stir my blood, and fill me with a mixture of melancholy and respect for courage; with pity for an unfortunate and superstitious regard for antiquity, and thoughtless inclination for war; in short, with a crowd of sensations with which sober rationality has nothing to do. We passed through Glensheal, with prodigious mountains on each side. We saw where the battle was fought, in the year 1719. Dr. Johnson owned he was now in a scene of as wild nature as he could see; but he corrected me sometimes in my inaccurate observations. "There," said I, "is a mountain like a cone." JOHNSON. "No, Sir, it would be called so in a book; and when a man comes to look at it, he sees it is not so. It is indeed

HE FELL ASLEEP IMMEDIATELY

pointed at the top; but one side of it is larger than the other." Another mountain I called immense. JOHNSON. "No; it is no more than a considerable protuberance."

We came to a rich green valley, comparatively speaking, and stopped awhile to let our horses rest and eat grass. We soon afterwards came to Auchnasheal, a kind of rural village, a number of cottages being built together, as we saw all along in the Highlands. We passed many miles this day without seeing a house, but only little summer huts, called shielings. At Auchnasheal, we sat down on a green turf-seat at the end of a house; they brought us out two wooden dishes of milk, which we tasted. One of them was frothed like a syllabub. I saw a woman preparing it with such a stick as is used for chocolate, and in the same manner. We had a considerable circle about us, men, women, and children, all M'Craas, Lord Seaforth's people. Not one of them could speak English. I observed to Dr. Johnson, it was much the same as being with a tribe of Indians. JOHNSON. "Yes, Sir, but not so terrifying." I gave all who chose it snuff and tobacco. I also gave each person a piece of wheat bread, which they had never tasted before. I then gave a penny apiece to each child. I told Dr. Johnson of this: upon which he called to Joseph and our guides, for change for a shilling, and declared that he would distribute among the children. Upon this being announced in Erse, there was a great stir; not only did some children come running down from neighbouring huts, but I observed one black-haired man, who had been with us all along, had gone off, and returned, bringing a very young child. My fellow-traveller then ordered the children to be drawn up in a row, and he dealt about his copper, and made them and their parents all happy.

There was great diversity in the faces of the circle around us; some were as black and wild in their appearance as any American savages whatever. One woman was as comely almost as the figure of Sappho, as we see it painted. We asked the old woman, the mistress of the house where we had the milk (which, by the by, Dr. Johnson told me, for I did not observe it myself, was built not of turf, but of stone), what we should pay. She said what we pleased. One of our guides asked her, in Erse, if a shilling was enough. She said, "Yes." But some of the men bade her ask more. This vexed me; because it showed a desire to impose upon strangers, as they knew that even a shilling was high payment. The woman, however, honestly persisted in her first price; so I gave her half a crown. Thus we had one good scene of life uncommon to us. The people were very much pleased, gave us many blessings, and said they had not had such a day since the old Laird of Macleod's time.

Dr. Johnson was much refreshed by this repast. He was pleased when I told him he would make a good chief. He said, "Were I a chief, I would dress my servants better than myself, and knock a fellow down if he looked saucy to a Macdonald in rags; but I would not treat men as brutes. I would let them know why all of my clan were to have attention paid to them. I would tell my upper servants why, and make them tell the others."

We rode on well, till we came to the high mountain called the Rattakin, by which time both Dr. Johnson and the horses were a good deal fatigued. It is a terrible steep to climb, notwithstanding the road is formed slanting along it; however, we made it out. On the top of it we met Captain Macleod, of Balmenoch, riding with his sword slung across him. He asked, "Is this Mr. Boswell?" which was a proof that we were expected. Going down the hill on the other side was no easy task. As Dr. Johnson was a great weight, the two guides agreed that he should ride the horses alternately. Hay's were the two best, and the Doctor would not ride but upon one or other of them, a black or a brown. But, as Hay complained much, after ascending the Rattakin, the Doctor was prevailed with to mount one of Vass's grays. As he rode upon it down hill, it did not go well, and he grumbled. I walked on a little before, but was excessively entertained with the method taken to keep him in good humour. Hay led the horse's head, talking to Dr. Johnson as much as he could; and (having heard him, in the forenoon, express a pastoral pleasure on seeing the goats browsing) just when the Doctor was uttering his displeasure, the fellow cried, with a very Highland accent, "See, such pretty goats!" Then he whistled *whu!* and made them jump. Little did he conceive what Dr. Johnson was. Here now was a common ignorant Highland clown imagining that he could divert, as one does a child, Dr. Samuel Johnson! The ludicrousness, absurdity, and extraordinary contrast between what the fellow fancied, and the reality, was truly comic.

It grew dusky; and we had a very tedious ride for what was called five miles, but I am sure would measure ten. We had no conversation. I was riding forward to the inn at Glenelg, on the shore opposite to Sky, that I might take proper measures, before Dr. Johnson, who was now advancing in dreary silence, Hay leading his horse, should arrive. Vass also walked by the side of his horse, and Joseph followed behind. As, therefore, he was thus attended, and seemed to be in deep meditation, I thought there could be no harm in leaving him for a little while. He called me back with a tremendous shout, and was really in a passion with me for leaving him. I told him my intentions, but he was not satisfied, and said, "Do you know, I should as soon have thought of picking a pocket, as doing so." BOSWELL. "I am diverted with you, Sir." JOHNSON. "Sir, I could never be diverted with incivility. Doing such a thing makes one lose confidence in him who has done it, as one cannot tell what he may do next." His extraordinary warmth confounded me so much, that I justified myself but lamely to him; yet my intentions were not improper. I wished to get on, to see how we were to be lodged, and how we were to get a boat; all which I thought I could best settle myself, without his having any trouble. To apply his great mind to minute particulars is wrong: it is like taking an immense balance (such as is kept on quays for weighing cargoes of ships) to weigh a guinea. I knew I had neat little scales, which would do better; and that his attention to every thing which falls in his way, and his uncommon desire to be always in the right, would make him weigh, if he knew of the particulars: it was right, therefore, for me to weigh them, and let him have them only in effect. I, however, continued to ride by him, finding he wished I should do so.

As we passed the barracks at Bernéra, I looked at them wishfully, as soldiers have always every thing in the best order; but there was only a sergeant and a few men there. We came on to the inn at Glenelg. There was no provender for our horses; so they were sent to grass, with a man to watch them. A maid showed us up stairs into a room damp and dirty, with bare walls, a variety of bad smells, a coarse black greasy fir table, and forms of the same kind; and out of a wretched bed started a fellow from his sleep, like Edgar in King Lear, "*Poor Tom's a cold.*"

This inn was furnished with not a single article that we could either eat or drink; but Mr. Murchison, factor to the Laird of Macleod, in Glenelg, sent us a bottle of rum and some sugar, with a polite message. Such extraordinary attention from this gentleman, to entire strangers, deserves the most honourable commemoration.

Our bad accommodation here made me uneasy and almost fretful. Dr. Johnson was calm. I said he was so from vanity. JOHNSON. "No, Sir; it is from philosophy." I resumed the subject of my leaving him on the road, and endeavoured to defend it better. He was still violent upon that head, and said, "Sir, had you gone on, I was thinking that I should have returned with you to Edinburgh, and then have parted from you, and never spoken to you more."

I sent for fresh hay, with which we made beds for ourselves, each in a room equally miserable. Like Wolfe, we had "*a choice of difficulties.*" Dr. Johnson made things easier by comparison. At M'Queen's, last night, he observed, that few were so well lodged in a ship. To-night, he said, we were better than if we had been upon the hill. He lay down buttoned up in his great coat. I had my sheets spread on the hay, and my clothes and great coat laid over me, by way of blankets.[1]

Thursday, Sept. 2.—I had slept ill. Dr. Johnson's anger had affected me much. I considered that, without any bad intention, I might suddenly forfeit his friendship; and was impatient to see him this morning. I told him how uneasy he had made me by what he had said, and reminded him of his own remark at Aberdeen, upon old friendships being hastily broken off. He owned, he had spoken to me in passion; that he would not have done what he threatened; and that, if he had, he should have been ten times worse than I; that forming intimacies would indeed be "limning the water," were they liable to such sudden dissolution; and he added, "Let's think no more on't." BOSWELL. "Well then, Sir, I shall be easy. Remember, I am to have fair warning in case of any quarrel. You are never to spring a mine upon me. It was absurd in me to believe you." JOHNSON. "You deserved about as much, as to believe me from night to morning."

After breakfast, we got into a boat for Sky. It rained much when we set off, but cleared up as we advanced. We reached the shore of Armidale before one o'clock. Sir Alexander Macdonald came down to receive us. Armidale is situated on a pretty bay. In front there is a grand prospect of the rude mountains of Moidart and Knoidart. Behind are hills gently rising and covered with a finer verdure than I expected to see in this climate, and the scene is enlivened by a number of little clear brooks.

Sir Alexander Macdonald having been an Eton scholar, and being a gentleman of talents, Dr. Johnson had been very well

---

[1] Johnson describes this scene to Mrs. Thrale: "*I* ordered hay to be laid thick upon the bed, and slept upon it in my great coat: Boswell laid sheets upon his bed, and reposed in linen, *like a gentleman.* . . . Sept. 2nd. I rose rustling from the hay, and went to tea, which I forget whether we found or brought. We saw the island of Sky before us, darkening the horizon with its rocky coast. A boat was procured, and we launched into one of the straits of the Atlantic ocean. . . "

pleased with him in London. But my fellow-traveller and I were now full of the old Highland spirit, and were dissatisfied at hearing of racked rents, and emigration, and finding a chief not surrounded by his clan.[1]

Friday, Sept. 3.—This day proving wet, we should have passed our time very uncomfortably, had we not found in the house two chests of books, which we eagerly ransacked.

We were advised by some persons here to visit Rasay, in our way to Dunvegan, the seat of the Laird of Macleod. Being informed that the Rev. Mr. Donald M'Queen was the most intelligent man in Sky, and having been favoured with a letter of introduction to him, by the learned Sir James Foulis, I sent it to him by an express, and requested he would meet us at Rasay; and at the same time enclosed a letter to the Laird of Macleod, informing him that we intended in a few days to have the honour of waiting on him at Dunvegan.

Dr. Johnson this day endeavoured to obtain some knowledge of the state of the country; but complained that he could get no distinct information about any thing, from those with whom he conversed.

Saturday, Sept. 4.—My endeavours to rouse the English-bred chieftain, in whose house we were, to the feudal and patriarchal feelings, proving ineffectual, Dr. Johnson this morning tried to bring him to our way of thinking. JOHNSON. "Were I in your place, Sir, in seven years I would make this an independent island. I would roast oxen whole, and hang out a flag as a signal to the Macdonalds, to come and get beef and whisky." Sir Alexander was still starting difficulties. JOHNSON. "Nay, Sir; if you are born to object, I have done with you. Sir, I would have a magazine of arms." SIR ALEXANDER. "They would rust." JOHNSON. "Let there be men to keep them clean. Your ancestors did not use to let their arms rust."

We attempted in vain to communicate to him a portion of our enthusiasm. He bore with so polite a good-nature our warm, and what some might call Gothic, expostulations on this subject, that I should not forgive myself were I to record all that Dr. Johnson's ardour led him to say. This day was little better than a blank.

[1] "If he aspired to meanness, his retrograde ambition was completely gratified, but he did not succeed in escaping reproach. He had no cook nor, I suppose, much provision, nor had the lady the common decencies of her tea-table: we picked up our sugar with our fingers.' Boswell was very angry, and reproached him with his improper parsimony. I did not much reflect upon the conduct of a man with whom I was not likely to converse as long at any other time."—*Johnson to Mrs. Thrale.*

Sunday, Sept. 5.—This being a beautiful day, my spirits were cheered by the mere effect of climate. I had felt a return of spleen during my stay at Armidale, and had it not been that I had Dr. Johnson to contemplate, I should have sunk into dejection; but his firmness supported me. I looked at him, as a man whose head is turning giddy at sea looks at a rock, or any fixed object. I wondered at his tranquillity. He said, " Sir, when a man retires into an island, he is to turn his thoughts entirely to another world. He has done with this."

Monday, Sept. 6.—We set out, accompanied by Mr. Donald M'Leod as our guide. We rode for some time along the district of Slate, near the shore. The houses in general are made of turf, covered with grass. The country seemed well peopled. We came into the district of Strath, and passed along a wild moorish tract of land till we arrived at the shore. There we found good verdure, and some curious whin-rocks, or collections of stones, like the ruins of the foundations of old buildings. We saw also three cairns of considerable size.

About a mile beyond Broadfoot is Corrichatachin, a farm of Sir Alexander Macdonald's, possessed by Mr. M'Kinnon, who received us with a hearty welcome, as did his wife, who was what we call in Scotland a *lady-like* woman. Mr. Pennant in the course of his tour to the Hebrides, passed two nights at this gentleman's house. On its being mentioned that a present had here been made to him of a curious specimen of Highland antiquity, Dr. Johnson said, "Sir, it was more than he deserved; the dog is a Whig."

We here enjoyed the comfort of a table plentifully furnished, the satisfaction of which was heightened by a numerous and cheerful company; and we, for the first time, had a specimen of the joyous social manners of the inhabitants of the Highlands. They talked in their own ancient language, with fluent vivacity, and sung many Erse songs with such spirit, that though Dr. Johnson was treated with the greatest respect and attention, there were moments in which he seemed to be forgotten. For myself, though but a Low-lander, having picked up a few words of the language, I presumed to mingle in their mirth, and joined in the choruses with as much glee as any of the company. Dr. Johnson, being fatigued with his journey, retired early to his chamber.

Tuesday, Sept. 7.—Dr. Johnson was much pleased with his entertainment here. There were many good books in the house. It was a very wet stormy day. I employed a part of the forenoon in writing this journal. The rest of it was somewhat dreary, from the gloominess of the weather, and the uncertain state which we were in, as we could not tell but it might clear up every hour. Nothing is more painful to the mind than a state of suspense, especially when it depends upon the weather, concerning which there can be so little calculation. I was happy when tea came. Such, I take it, is the state of those who live in the country. Meals are wished for from the cravings of vacuity of mind, as well as from the desire of eating.

Wednesday, Sept. 8.—When I waked, the rain was much heavier than yesterday; but the wind had abated. By breakfast, the day was better, and in a little while it was calm and clear. I felt my spirits much elated.

We resolved to set out directly after breakfast. We had about two miles to ride to the sea side, and there we expected to get one of the boats belonging to the fleet of herring-busses then on the coast. But while we were preparing to set out, there arrived a man with the following card from the Rev. Mr. Donald M'Queen:

Mr. M'Queen's compliments to Mr. Boswell, and begs leave to acquaint him that, fearing the want of a proper boat, as much as the rain of yesterday, might have caused a stop, he is now at Skianwden with *Macgillichallum's* carriage, to convey him and Dr. Johnson to Rasay, where they will meet with a most hearty welcome, and where Macleod, being on a visit, now attends their motions.

Wednesday afternoon.

This card was most agreeable; it was a prologue to that hospitable and truly polite reception which we found at Rasay. In a little while arrived Mr. Donald M'Queen himself; a decent minister, an elderly man with his own black hair, courteous, and rather slow of speech, but candid, sensible, and well informed, nay learned. Along with him came, as our pilot, a gentleman whom I had a great desire to see, Mr. Malcolm Macleod, one of the Rasay family, celebrated in the year 1745-6. He was now sixty-two years of age, hale, and well proportioned,—with a manly countenance, tanned by the weather, yet having a ruddiness in his cheeks, over a great part of which his rough beard extended. His eye was quick and lively, yet his look was not fierce, but he appeared at once firm and good humoured. He wore a pair of brogues; tartan hose which came up only near to his knees, and left them bare; a purple camblet kilt; a black waistcoat; a short green cloth coat bound with gold cord; a yellowish bushy wig; a large blue bonnet with a gold thread button. I never saw a figure that gave a more perfect representation of a Highland gentleman.

The good family at Corrichatachin said they hoped to see us on our return. We rode down to the shore; but Malcolm walked with graceful agility.

We got into *Rasay's* carriage, which was a good strong open boat made in Norway. The wind had now risen pretty high, and was against us; but we had four stout rowers, particularly a Macleod, a robust, black-haired fellow, half naked, and bare-headed, something between a wild Indian and an English tar. Dr. Johnson sat high on the stern like a magnificent Triton. Malcolm sung an Erse song, the chorus of which was *"Hatyin foam foam eri,"* with words of his own. The boatmen and Mr. M'Queen chorused, and all went well. At length Malcolm himself took an oar, and rowed vigorously. We sailed along the coast of Scalpa, a rugged island, about four miles in length. Dr. Johnson proposed that he and I should buy it, and found a good school, and an episcopal church (Malcolm said he would come to it), and have a printing-press, where he would print all the Erse that could be found.

Here I was strongly struck with our long projected scheme of visiting the Hebrides being realized. I called to him, "We are contending with seas"; which I think were the words of one of his letters to me. "Not much," said he; and though the wind made the sea lash considerably upon us, he was not discomposed. After we were out of the shelter of Scalpa, and in the sound between it and Rasay, which extended about a league, the wind made the sea very rough. I did not like it. JOHNSON. "This now is the Atlantic. If I should tell, at a tea-table in London, that I have crossed the Atlantic in an open boat, how they'd shudder, and what a fool they'd think me to expose myself to such danger!" He then repeated Horace's Ode—

> Otium divos rogat in patenti
> Prensus Ægæo ———.

In the confusion and hurry of this boisterous sail, Dr. Johnson's spurs, of which Joseph had charge, were carried overboard into the sea, and lost. This was the first misfortune that had befallen us. Dr. Johnson was a little angry at first, observing that "there was something wild in letting a pair of spurs be carried into the sea

DR. JOHNSON SAT HIGH ON THE STERN

out of a boat"; but then he remarked "that, as Janes the naturalist had said upon losing his pocket-book, it was rather an inconvenience than a loss."

The approach to Rasay was very pleasing. We saw before us a
beautiful bay, well defended by a rocky coast; a good family
mansion; a fine verdure about it, with a considerable number of
trees; and beyond it hills and mountains in gradation of wildness.
Our boatmen sung with great spirit. Dr. Johnson, observed, that
naval music was very ancient. As we came near the shore, the
singing of our rowers was succeeded by that of reapers, who
were busy at work, and who seemed to shout as much as to sing,
while they worked with a bounding activity. Just as we landed,
I observed a cross, or rather the ruins of one, upon a rock, which
had to me a pleasing vestige of religion. I perceived a large company coming out from the house. We met them as we walked up.
There were *Rasay* himself; his brother Dr. Macleod, his nephew
the Laird of M'Kinnon; the Laird of Macleod; Colonel Macleod of
Talisker, an officer in the Dutch service, a very genteel man, and a
faithful branch of the family; Mr. Macleod of Muiravenside, best
known by the name of Sandie Macleod, who was long in exile on
account of the part which he took in 1745; and several other
persons. We were welcomed upon the green, and conducted into
the house, where we were introduced to Lady Rasay, who was
surrounded by a numerous family, consisting of three sons and ten
daughters.

It was past six o'clock when we arrived. Some excellent brandy
was served round immediately, according to the custom of the
Highlands, where a dram is generally taken every day. They call
it a *scalch*. On a sideboard was placed for us, who had come off the
sea, a substantial dinner, and a variety of wines. Then we had
coffee and tea. I observed in the room several elegantly bound
books 'and other marks of improved life. Soon afterwards a fiddler
appeared, and a little ball began. *Rasay* himself danced with as
much spirit as any man, and Malcolm bounded like a roe. Sandie
Macleod, who has at times an excessive flow of spirits, and had it
now, made much jovial noise. Dr. Johnson was so delighted with
this scene, that he said, "I know not how we shall get away." It
entertained me to observe him sitting by, while we danced, sometimes in deep meditation, sometimes smiling complacently, sometimes looking upon Hooke's Roman History, and sometimes talking
a little, amidst the noise of the ball, to Mr. Donald M'Queen, who

anxiously gathered knowledge from him. He was pleased with M'Queen, and said to me, "This is a critical man, Sir."

Thursday, Sept. 9.—At breakfast this morning, among a profusion of other things, there were oatcakes, made of what is called *graddaned* meal, that is, meal made of grain separated from the husks, and toasted by fire, instead of being threshed and kiln-dried. This seems to be bad management, as so much fodder is consumed by it. Mr. M'Queen however defended it, by saying, that the servants in Sky are a faithless pack, and steal what they can; so that much is saved by the corn passing but once through their hands, as at each time they pilfer some. There was also, what I cannot help disliking at breakfast, cheese: it is the custom over all the Highlands to have it; and it often smells very strong, and poisons to a certain degree the elegance of an *Indian* repast. The day was showery; however, *Rasay* and I took a walk, and had some cordial conversation. I conceived a more than ordinary regard for this worthy gentleman. His family has possessed this island above four hundred years. When we returned, Dr. Johnson walked with us to see the old chapel. He was in fine spirits. He said, "This is truly the patriarchal life: this is what we came to find."

Friday, Sept. 10.—Having resolved to explore the island of Rasay, which could be done only on foot, I last night obtained my fellow-traveller's permission to leave him for a day, he being unable to take so hardy a walk. Old Mr. Malcolm Macleod, who had obligingly promised to accompany me, was at my bedside between five and six. I sprang up immediately; and he and I, attended by two other gentlemen, traversed the country during the whole of this day. Though we had passed over not less than four and twenty miles of very rugged ground, and had a Highland dance on the top of Dun Can, the highest mountain in the island, we returned in the evening not at all fatigued, and piqued ourselves at not being outdone at the nightly ball by our less active friends, who had remained at home.

A little to the west of the house is an old ruinous chapel, unroofed. We here saw some human bones of an uncommon size. There was a heel-bone, in particular, which Dr. Macleod said was such, that if the foot was in proportion, it must have been twenty-seven inches long. Dr. Johnson would not look at the bones. He started back from them with a striking appearance of horror.

Saturday, Sept. 11.—It was a storm of wind and rain, so we could not set out. I wrote some of this journal, and talked a while with

Dr. Johnson in his room, and passed the day, I cannot well say how, but very pleasantly.

Dr. Johnson was now wishing to move. There was not enough of intellectual entertainment for him, after he had satisfied his curiosity, which he did, by asking questions, till he had exhausted the island; and where there was so numerous a company, mostly young people, there was such a flow of familiar talk, so much noise, and so much singing and dancing, that little opportunity was left for his energetic conversation. He seemed sensible of this; for when I told him how happy they were at having him there, he said, "Yet we have not been able to entertain them much." Dr. Johnson, however, had several opportunities of instructing the company; his discourse turned chiefly on mechanics, agriculture, and such subjects. Last night Lady Rasay showed him the operation of *wawking* cloth, that is, thickening it in the same manner as is done by a mill. Here it is performed by women, who kneel upon the ground, and rub it with both their hands, singing an Erse song all the time. He was asking questions while they were performing this operation, and, amidst their loud and wild howl, his voice was heard even in the room above.

They dance here every night. The queen of our ball was the eldest Miss Macleod, of Rasay, an elegant well-bred woman, and celebrated for her beauty over all those regions.

Sunday, Sept. 12.—It was a beautiful day, and although we did not approve of travelling on Sunday, we resolved to set out, as we were in an island from whence one must take occasion as it serves. *Rasay* himself went with us in a large boat, with eight oars, built in his island.

We spoke of Death. I mentioned Hawthornden's Cypress Grove, where it is said that the world is a mere show; and that it is unreasonable for a man to wish to continue in a show-room after he has seen it. Let him go cheerfully out, and give place to other spectators. JOHNSON. "Yes, Sir, if he is sure he is to be well, after he goes out of it. But if he is to grow blind after he goes out of the show-room, and never to see any thing again; or if he does not know whither he is to go next, a man will not go cheerfully out of a show-room. No wise man will be contented to die, if he thinks he is to go into a state of punishment. Nay, no wise man will be contented to die, if he thinks he is to fall into annihilation: for however unhappy any man's existence may be, he yet would rather have it than not exist at all. No; there is no rational principle by

which a man can die contented, but a trust in the mercy of God,
through the merits of Jesus Christ." This short sermon, delivered
with an earnest tone, in a boat upon the sea, which was perfectly
calm, on a day appropriated to religious worship, while every one
listened with an air of satisfaction, had a most pleasing effect upon
my mind.

We reached the harbour of Portree, in Sky; which is a large and
good one. There was here a tolerable inn. Dr. Johnson and I
resolved that we should treat the company, so I played the landlord, or master of the feast, having previously ordered Joseph to
pay the bill. When we were about to depart we found that *Rasay*
had been beforehand with us, and that all was paid; I would fain
have contested this matter with him, but seeing him resolved, I
declined it.

In the evening Dr. Johnson and I remounted our horses, accompanied by Mr. M'Queen and Dr. Macleod. It rained very
hard. We rode what they call six miles to Dr. Macleod's house.
On the road Dr. Johnson appeared to be somewhat out of spirits.
When I talked of our meeting Lord Elibank, he said, "I cannot
be with him much. I long to be again in civilized life." He said,
"Let us go to Dunvegan tomorrow."—"Yes," said I, "if it is not
a deluge." "At any rate," he replied. This showed a kind of fretful
impatience; nor was it to be wondered at, considering our disagreeable ride. I feared he would give up Mull and Icolmkill;
for he said something of his apprehensions of being detained by
bad weather. However, I hoped well. We had a dish of tea at
Dr. Macleod's, who had a pretty good house. His lady was a
polite agreeable woman. The doctor accompanied us to Kingsburgh, which is called a mile farther; but the computation of Sky
has no connection whatever with real distance.

I was highly pleased to see Dr. Johnson safely arrived at Kingsburgh, and received by the hospitable Mr. Macdonald, who, with
a most respectful attention, supported him into the house. *Kingsburgh* was completely the figure of a gallant Highlander,—exhibiting
"the graceful mien and manly looks," which our popular Scotch
song has justly attributed to that character. He had his tartan
plaid thrown about him, a large blue bonnet with a knot of black
riband like a cockade, a brown short coat of a kind of duffil, a
tartan waistcoat with gold buttons and gold button-holes, a bluish
philibeg, and tartan hose. He had jet black hair tied behind, and
was a large stately man, with a steady sensible countenance.

There was a comfortable parlour with a good fire, and a dram went round. By and by supper was served, at which there appeared the lady of the house, the celebrated Miss Flora Macdonald. She is a little woman, of a genteel appearance, and uncommonly mild and well bred. To see Dr. Samuel Johnson, the great champion of the English Tories, salute Miss Flora Macdonald in the isle of Sky, was a striking sight.

Miss Flora Macdonald (for so I shall call her) told me, she heard upon the main land, as she was returning home about a fortnight before, that Mr. Boswell was coming to Sky, and one Mr. Johnson, a young English *buck*, with him. He was highly entertained with this fancy. He was rather quiescent to-night, and went early to bed. I was in a cordial humour, and promoted a cheerful glass. The punch was excellent. Honest Mr. M'Queen observed that I was in high glee, "my *governor* being gone to bed."

Monday, Sept. 13.—The room where we lay was a celebrated one. Dr. Johnson's bed was the very bed in which the grandson of the unfortunate King James the Second lay, on one of the nights after the failure of his rash attempt in 1745–6, while he was eluding the pursuit of the emissaries of government, which had offered thirty thousand pounds as a reward for apprehending him. To see Dr. Samuel Johnson lying in that bed, in the Isle of Sky, in the house of Miss Flora Macdonald, struck me with such a group of ideas as it is not easy for words to describe, as they passed through the mind. He smiled, and said, "I have had no ambitious thoughts in it."

He had caught a cold a day or two ago, and the rain yesterday having made it worse, he was become very deaf. At breakfast he said, he would have given a good deal rather than not have lain in that bed. I owned he was the lucky man; and observed, that without doubt it had been contrived between Mrs. Macdonald and him. She seemed to acquiesce; adding, "You know young *bucks* are always favourites of the ladies." He spoke of Prince Charles being there, and asked Mrs. Macdonald, "*Who* was with him? We were told, Madam, in England, there was one Miss Flora Macdonald with him." She said, "they were very right"; and perceiving Dr. Johnson's curiosity, though he had delicacy enough not to question her, very obligingly entertained him with a recital of the particulars which she herself knew of that escape, which does so much honour to the humanity, fidelity, and generosity of the Highlanders. Dr. Johnson listened to her with placid attention, and said, "All this should be written down."

Kingsburgh conducted us in his boat across one of the lochs, as they call them, or arms of the sea, which flow in upon all the coasts of Sky, to a mile beyond a place called Grishinish. Our horses had been sent round by land to meet us. By this sail we saved eight miles of bad riding. Dr. Johnson said, "When we take into the computation what we have saved, and what we have gained, by this agreeable sail, it is a great deal." He observed, "It is very disagreeable riding in Sky. The way is so narrow, one only at a time can travel, so it is quite unsocial; and you cannot indulge in meditation by yourself, because you must be always attending to the steps which your horse takes."

During our sail, Dr. Johnson asked about the use of the dirk, with which he imagined the Highlanders cut their meat. He was told, they had a knife and fork besides to eat with. He asked, how did the women do? and was answered, some of them had a knife and fork too; but in general the men, when they had cut their meat, handed their knives and forks to the women, and they themselves eat with their fingers. The old *tutor* of Macdonald always eat fish with his fingers, alleging that a knife and fork gave it a bad taste. I took the liberty to observe to Dr. Johnson, that he did so. "Yes," said he, "but it is because I am short-sighted, and afraid of bones, for which reason I am not fond of eating many kinds of fish, because I must use my fingers."

As soon as we reached the shore, we took leave of *Kingsburgh*, and mounted our horses. We passed through a wild moor, in many places so soft that we were obliged to walk, which was very fatiguing to Dr. Johnson. Once he had advanced on horseback to a very bad step. There was a steep declivity on his left, to which he was so near, that there was not room for him to dismount in the usual way. He tried to alight on the other side, as if he had been a young buck indeed, but in the attempt he fell at his length upon the ground; from which, however, he got up immediately without being hurt. During this dreary ride, we were sometimes relieved by a view of branches of the sea, that universal medium of connection amongst mankind. A guide, who had been sent with us from Kingsburgh, explored the way (much in the same manner as, I suppose, is pursued in the wilds of America) by observing certain marks known only to the inhabitants. We arrived at Dunvegan late in the afternoon. The great size of the castle, which is partly old and partly new, and is built upon a rock close to the sea, while the land around it presents nothing but wild, moorish, hilly, and craggy appearances, gave a rude magnificence to the scene. Having dismounted, we ascended a flight of steps, which was made by the late Macleod, for the accommodation of persons coming to him by land, there formerly being, for security, no other access to the castle but from the sea; so that visitors who came by the land were under the necessity of getting into a boat, and sailed round to the only place where it could be approached. We were introduced into a stately dining-room, and received by Lady Macleod, mother of the Laird, who, with his friend *Talisker*, having been detained on the road, did not arrive till some time after us.

We found the lady of the house a very polite and sensible woman, who had lived for some time in London, and had there been in Dr. Johnson's company. After we had dined, we repaired to the drawing-room, where some of the young ladies of the family, with their mother, were at tea. This room had formerly been the bed-chamber of Sir Roderick Macleod, one of the old lairds: and he chose it, because behind it there was a considerable cascade, the sound of which disposed him to sleep. Above his bed was this inscription: "Sir Rorie Macleod of Dunvegan, Knight. God send good rest!" He was called *Rorie More*, that is, great Rorie, not from his size, but from his spirit. Our entertainment here was in so elegant a style, and reminded my fellow-traveller so much of England, that he became quite joyous. He laughed, and said, "Boswell, we came in at the wrong end of this island." "Sir," said I, "it was best to keep this for the last." He answered, "I would have it both first and last."

Tuesday, Sept. 14.—Dr. Johnson said in the morning, "Is not this a fine lady?" There was not a word now of his "impatience to be in civilized life"; though indeed I should beg pardon—he found it here. We had slept well, and lain long. After breakfast we surveyed the castle and the garden. Two substantial gentlemen of the clan dined with us. We had admirable venison, generous wine: in a word, all that a good table has. This was really the hall of a chief. Lady Macleod had been much obliged to my father, who had settled, by arbitration, a variety of perplexed claims, which she now repaid by particular attention to me. Macleod started the subject of making women do penance in the church for fornication. JOHNSON. "It is right, Sir. Infamy is attached to the crime, by universal opinion, as soon as it is known. I would not be the man who would discover it, if I alone knew it, for a woman may reform; nor would I commend a parson who divulges a woman's first

offence; but being once divulged, it ought to be infamous. Consider
of what importance to society the chastity of women is. Upon that
all the property in the world depends. We hang a thief for stealing
a sheep, but the unchastity of a woman transfers sheep, and farm,
and all, from the right owner. I have much more reverence for a
common prostitute than for a woman who conceals her guilt. The
prostitute is known. She cannot deceive. She cannot bring a
strumpet into the arms of an honest man, without his knowledge."
BOSWELL. "There is, however, a great difference between the
licentiousness of a single woman, and that of a married woman."
JOHNSON. "Yes, Sir; there is a great difference between stealing a
shilling and stealing a thousand pounds; between simply taking a
man's purse, and murdering him first, and then taking it. But
when one begins to be vicious, it is easy to go on. Where single
women are licentious, you rarely find faithful married women."
BOSWELL. "And yet we are told, that in some nations in India, the
distinction is strictly observed." JOHNSON. "Nay, don't give us
India. That puts me in mind of Montesquieu, who is really a fellow
of genius too in many respects; whenever he wants to support a
strange opinion, he quotes you the practice of Japan, or of some
other distant country, of which he knows nothing."

At supper, Lady Macleod mentioned Dr. Cadogan's book on the
gout. Lady Macleod objected that the author does not practise
what he teaches. JOHNSON. "I cannot help that, Madam. That
does not make his book the worse. People are influenced more by
what a man says, if his practice is suitable to it, because they are
blockheads. The more intellectual people are, the readier will they
attend to what a man tells them. If it is just, they will follow it, be
his practice what it will. No man practises as well as he writes. I
have, all my life long, been lying till noon; yet I tell all young men,
and tell them with great sincerity, that nobody who does not rise
early will ever do any good. Only consider! You read a book; you
are convinced by it; you do not know the author. Suppose you
afterwards know him, and find that he does not practise what he
teaches; are you to give up your former conviction? At this rate
you would be kept in a state of equilibrium, when reading every
book, till you knew how the author practised." "But," said Lady
Macleod, "you would think better of Dr. Cadogan, if he acted
according to his principles." JOHNSON. "Why, Madam, to be sure,
a man, who acts in the face of light is worse than a man who does
not know so much; yet I think no man should be the worse thought

of for publishing good principles. There is something noble in publishing truth, though it condemns one's self." I expressed some surprise at Cadogan's recommending good humour, as if it were quite in our own power to attain it. JOHNSON. "Why, Sir, a man grows better humoured as he grows older. He improves by experience. When young, he thinks himself of great consequence, and every thing of importance. As he advances in life, he learns to think himself of no consequence, and little things of little importance; and so he becomes more patient, and better pleased. All good humour and complaisance are acquired. Naturally a child seizes directly what it sees, and thinks of pleasing itself only. By degrees, it is taught to please others, and to prefer others; and that this will ultimately produce the greatest happiness. If a man is not convinced of that, he never will practise it. Common language speaks the truth as to this: we say, a person is *well bred.*" Lady Macleod asked, if no man was naturally good? JOHNSON. "No, Madam, no more than a wolf." BOSWELL. "Nor no woman, Sir?" JOHNSON. "No, Sir." Lady Macleod started at this, saying, in a low voice, "This is worse than Swift."

Macleod of Ulinish had come in the afternoon. We were a jovial company at supper. The Laird, surrounded by so many of his clan, was to me a pleasing sight. They listened with wonder and pleasure while Dr. Johnson harangued. I am vexed that I cannot take down his full strain of eloquence.

Wednesday, Sept. 15.—The gentlemen of the clan went away early in the morning to the harbour of Lochbraccadale, to take leave of some of their friends who were going to America. It was a very wet day. We looked at *Rorie More's* horn, which is a large cow's horn, with the mouth of it ornamented with silver curiously carved. It holds rather more than a bottle and a half. Every Laird of Macleod, it is said, must, as a proof of his manhood, drink it off full of claret without laying it down. We also saw his bow, which hardly any man now can bend, and his *glaymore*, which was wielded with both hands, and is of a prodigious size. We saw here some old pieces of iron armour, immensely heavy. The broad-sword used, though called the *glaymore* (*i.e.* the *great sword*), is much smaller than that used in *Rorie More's* time. There is hardly a target now to be found in the Highlands. After the disarming act, they made them serve as covers to their butter-milk barrels; a kind of change, like beating spears into pruning-hooks.

Sir George Mackenzie's Works happened to lie in a window in

the dining-room. In the sixty-fifth page of the first volume Dr. Johnson pointed out a paragraph, and told me there was an error in the text, which he bade me try to discover. I was lucky enough to hit it at once. As the passage is printed, it is said that the devil answers *even* in *engines*. I corrected it to—*ever in ænigmas*. "Sir," said he, "you are a good critic. This would have been a great thing to do in the text of an ancient author."

Thursday, Sept. 16.—Last night much care was taken of Dr. Johnson, who was still distressed by his cold. He had hitherto most strangely slept without a night-cap. Miss Macleod made him a large flannel one, and he was prevailed with to drink a little brandy when he was going to bed. He has great virtue in not drinking wine or any fermented liquor, because, as he acknowledged to us, he could not do it in moderation. Lady Macleod would hardly believe him, and said, "I am sure, Sir, you would not carry it too far." JOHNSON. "Nay, Madam, it carried me. I took the opportunity of a long illness to leave it off. It was then prescribed to me not to drink wine; and having broken off the habit, I have never returned to it."

In the argument on Tuesday night, about natural goodness, Dr. Johnson denied that any child was better than another, but by difference of instruction; though, in consequence of greater attention being paid to instruction by one child than another, and of a variety of imperceptible causes, such as instruction being counteracted by servants, a notion was conceived, that of two children, equally well educated, one was naturally much worse than another. He owned, this morning, that one might have a greater aptitude to learn than another, and that we inherit dispositions from our parents. "*I inherited,*" said he, "*a vile melancholy from my father, which has made me mad all my life, at least not sober.*" Lady Macleod wondered he should tell this. "Madam," said I, "he knows that with that madness he is superior to other men."

I was elated by the thought of having been able to entice such a man to this remote part of the world. A ludicrous, yet just image presented itself to my mind, which I expressed to the company. I compared myself to a dog who has got hold of a large piece of meat, and runs away with it to a corner, where he may devour it in peace, without any fear of others taking it from him. "In London, Reynolds, Beauclerk, and all of them, are contending who shall enjoy Dr. Johnson's conversation. We are feasting upon it, undisturbed, at Dunvegan."

It was still a storm of wind and rain. Dr. Johnson however walked out with Macleod, and saw *Rorie More's* cascade in full perfection. My fellow-traveller and I talked of going to Sweden; and, while we were settling our plan, I expressed a pleasure in the prospect of seeing the king. JOHNSON. "I doubt, Sir, if he would speak to us." Colonel Macleod said, "I am sure Mr. Boswell would speak to *him*." But seeing me a little disconcerted by his remark, he politely added, "and with great propriety." Here let me offer a short defence of that propensity in my disposition, to which this gentleman alluded. It has procured me much happiness. I hope it does not deserve so hard a name as either forwardness or impudence. If I know myself, it is nothing more than an eagerness to share the society of men distinguished either by their rank or their talents, and a diligence to attain what I desire. If a man is praised for seeking knowledge, though mountains and seas are in his way, may he not be pardoned, whose ardour, in the pursuit of the same object, leads him to encounter difficulties as great, though of a different kind?

After the ladies were gone from the table, we talked of the Highlanders not having sheets; and this led us to consider the advantage of wearing linen. JOHNSON. "All animal substances are less cleanly than vegetables. Wool, of which flannel is made, is an animal substance; flannel therefore is not so cleanly as linen. I remember I used to think tar dirty; but when I knew it to be only a preparation of the juice of the pine, I thought so no longer. It is not disagreeable to have the gum that oozes from a plum-tree upon your fingers, because it is vegetable; but if you have any candle-grease, any tallow upon your fingers, you are uneasy till you rub it off.—I have often thought that, if I kept a seraglio, the ladies should all wear linen gowns, or cotton—I mean stuffs made of vegetable substances. I would have no silk; you cannot tell when it is clean; it will be very nasty before it is perceived to be so. Linen detects its own dirtiness."

To hear the grave Dr. Samuel Johnson, "that majestic teacher of moral and religious wisdom," while sitting solemn in an arm-chair in the Isle of Sky, talk, *ex cathedrâ*, of his keeping a seraglio, and acknowledge that the supposition had *often* been in his thoughts, struck me so forcibly with ludicrous contrast, that I could not but laugh immoderately. He was too proud to submit, even for a moment, to be the object of ridicule, and instantly retaliated with such keen sarcastic wit, and such a variety of degrading images, of every one of which I was the object, that though I can bear such attacks as well as most men, I yet found myself so much the sport of all the company, that I would gladly expunge from my mind every trace of this severe retort.

Friday, Sept. 17.—The weather this day was rather better than any that we had since we came to Dunvegan. Mr. M'Queen had often mentioned a curious piece of antiquity near this, which he called a temple of the goddess Anaitis. Having often talked of going to see it, he and I set out after breakfast, attended by his servant, a fellow quite like a savage. I must observe here, that in Sky there seems to be much idleness; for men and boys follow you, as colts follow passengers upon a road. The usual figure of a Sky-boy is a *lown* with bare legs and feet, a dirty kilt, ragged coat and waistcoat, a bare head, and a stick in his hand, which, I suppose, is partly to help the lazy rogue to walk, partly to serve as a kind of defensive weapon. We walked what is called two miles, but is probably four, from the castle, till we came to the sacred place. The country round is a black dreary moor on all sides, except to the sea-coast, towards which there is a view through a valley; and the farm of Bay shows some good land. The place itself is green ground, being well drained, by means of a deep glen on each side, in both of which there runs a rivulet with a good quantity of water, forming several cascades, which make a considerable appearance and sound. The first thing we came to was an earthen mound, or dike, extending from the one precipice to the other. A little farther on was a strong stone wall, not high, but very thick, extending in the same manner. On the outside of it were the ruins of two houses, one on each side of the entry or gate to it. The wall is built all along of uncemented stones, but of so large a size as to make a very firm and durable rampart. It has been built all about the consecrated ground, except where the precipice is steep enough to form an enclosure of itself. The sacred spot contains more than two acres. There are within it the ruins of many houses, none of them large,—a cairn,—and many graves marked by clusters of stones. Mr. M'Queen insisted that the ruin of a small building, standing east and west, was actually the temple of the goddess Anaitis, where her statue was kept, and from whence processions were made to wash it in one of the brooks. There is, it must be owned, a hollow road visible for a good way from the entrance; but Mr. M'Queen, with the keen eye of an antiquary, traced it much farther than I could perceive it. There is not above a foot and a half in height of the walls now remaining; and the whole extent of the building was never, I imagine, greater than an ordinary Highland house.

After dinner I started the subject of the temple of Anaitis. Mr. M'Queen had laid stress on the name given to the place by the country people,—*Ainnit;* and added, "I knew not what to make of this piece of antiquity, till I met with the *Anaitidis delubrum* in Lydia, mentioned by Pausanias and the elder Pliny." Dr. Johnson, with his usual acuteness, examined Mr. M'Queen as to the meaning of the word *Ainnit,* in Erse; and it proved to be a water-place, or a place near water, "which," said Mr. M'Queen, "agrees with all the descriptions of the temples of that goddess, which were situated near rivers, that there might be water to wash the statue." JOHNSON. "Nay, Sir, the argument from the name is gone. The name is exhausted by what we see. We have no occasion to go to a distance for what we can pick up under our feet. Had it been an accidental name, the similarity between it and *Anaitis* might have had something in it; but it turns out to be a mere physiological name." Macleod said, Mr. M'Queen's knowledge of etymology had destroyed his conjecture. JOHNSON. "Yes, Sir; Mr. M'Queen is like the eagle mentioned by Waller, who was shot with an arrow feathered from his own wing."

Saturday, Sept. 18.—Before breakfast, Dr. Johnson came up to my room, to forbid me to mention that it was his birthday; but I told him I had done it already; at which he was displeased—I suppose from wishing to have nothing particular done on his account.[1] Lady Macleod and I got into a warm dispute. She wanted to build a house upon a farm which she has taken, about five miles from the castle, and to make gardens and other ornaments there; all of which I approved of; but insisted that the seat of the family should always be upon the rock of Dunvegan. The lady insisted that the rock was very inconvenient; that there was no place near it where a good garden could be made; that it must always be a rude place; that it was a *Herculean* labour to make a dinner here. I was vexed to find the alloy of modern refinement in a lady who had so much old family spirit. "Madam," said I, "if once you quit this rock, there is no knowing where you may settle.

[1] "Boswell, with some of his troublesome kindness, has informed this family, and reminded me, that the 18th of September is my birthday. The return of my birthday, if I remember it, fills me with thoughts which it seems to be the general care of humanity to escape. I can now look back upon three score and four years, in which little has been done, and little has been enjoyed, a life diversified by misery, spent part in the sluggishness of penury, and part under the violence of pain, in gloomy discontent or importunate distress. But, perhaps, I am better than I should have been, if I had been less afflicted. With this I will try to be content."—*Johnson to Mrs. Thrale.*

You move five miles first; then to St. Andrew's, as the late Laird did; then to Edinburgh; and so on till you end at Hampstead, or in France. No, no; keep to the rock; it is the very jewel of the estate. It looks as if it had been let down from heaven by the four corners, to be the residence of a chief. Have all the comforts and conveniences of life upon it, but never leave *Rorie More's* cascade." "But," said she, "is it not enough if we keep it? Must we never have more convenience than *Rorie More* had? he had his beef brought to dinner in one basket, and his bread in another. Why not as well be *Rorie More* all over, as live upon his rock? And should not we tire, in looking perpetually on this rock? It is very well for you who have a fine place, and every thing easy, to talk thus, and think of chaining honest folks to a rock. You would not live upon it yourself." "Yes, Madam," said I, "I would live upon it, were I the Laird of Macleod, and should be unhappy if I were not upon it." JOHNSON (with a strong voice and most determined manner). "Madam, rather than quit the old rock, Boswell would live in the pit; he would make his bed in the dungeon." I feel a degree of elation, at finding my resolute feudal enthusiasm thus confirmed by such a sanction. The lady was puzzled a little. She still returned to her pretty farm—rich ground—fine garden. "Madam," said Dr. Johnson, "were they in Asia, I would not leave the rock."

We were so comfortably situated at Dunvegan, that Dr. Johnson could hardly be moved from it. I proposed to him that we should leave it on Monday. "No, Sir," said he, "I will not go before Wednesday. I will have some more of this good." However, as the weather was at this season so bad, and so very uncertain, and we had a great deal to do yet, Mr. M'Queen and I prevailed with him to agree to set out on Monday, if the day should be good.

Sunday, Sept. 19.—It was rather worse weather than any that we had yet. At breakfast Dr. Johnson said, "Some cunning men choose fools for their wives, thinking to manage them, but they always fail. Depend upon it, no woman is the worse for sense and knowledge. Men know that women are an over-match for them, and therefore they choose the weakest or most ignorant. If they did not think so, they never could be afraid of women knowing as much as themselves." In a subsequent conversation he told me that he was serious in what he had said.

He came to my room this morning before breakfast, to read my Journal, which he has done all along. He often before said, "I take great delight in reading it." To-day he said, "You improve: it grows better and better." I observed, there was a danger of my getting a habit of writing in a slovenly manner. "Sir," said he, "it is not written in a slovenly manner. It might be printed, were the subject fit for printing." He asked me to-day, how it happened that we were so little together; I told him my Journal took up much time. Yet, on reflection, it appeared strange to me, that although I will run from one end of London to another, to pass an hour with him, I should omit to seize any spare time to be in his company, when I am settled in the same house with him. But my Journal is really a task of much time and labour, and he forbids me to contract it.

After supper he said, "I am sorry that prize-fighting is gone out; every art should be preserved, and the art of defence is surely important. Prize-fighting [1] made people accustomed not to be alarmed at seeing their own blood, or feeling a little pain from a wound. I think the heavy *glaymore* was an ill-contrived weapon. A man could only strike once with it. It employed both his hands, and he must of course be soon fatigued with wielding it; so that if his antagonist could only keep playing awhile, he was sure of him. I would fight with a dirk against *Rorie More's* sword. I could ward off a blow with a dirk, and then run in upon my enemy. When within that heavy sword, I have him; he is quite helpless, and I could stab him at my leisure, like a calf. It is thought by sensible military men, that the English do not enough avail themselves of their superior strength of body against the French; for that must always have a great advantage in pushing with bayonets. I have heard an officer say, that if women could be made to stand, they would do as well as men in mere interchange of bullets from a distance; but if a body of men should come close up to them, then to be sure they must be overcome; now," said he, "in the same manner the weaker-bodied French must be overcome by our strong soldiers."

Monday, Sept. 20.—When I awaked, the storm was higher still. It abated about nine, and the sun shone; but it rained again very soon, and it was not a day for travelling.

Macleod was too late in coming to breakfast. Dr. Johnson said, laziness was worse than the tooth-ache. BOSWELL. "I cannot agree with you, Sir; a basin of cold water, or a horsewhip will cure

[1] "Mr. Johnson was very conversant in the art of attack and defence by boxing, which science he had learned from his uncle Andrew, I believe; and I have heard him descant upon the age when people were received, and when rejected, in the schools once held for that brutal amusement, much to the admiration of those who had no expectation of his skill in such matters."—*Anecdotes.*

laziness." JOHNSON. "No, Sir; it will only put off the fit; it will not cure the disease. I have been trying to cure my laziness all my life, and could not do it." BOSWELL. "But if a man does in a shorter time what might be the labour of a life, there is nothing to be said against him." JOHNSON (perceiving at once that I alluded to him and his "Dictionary"). "Suppose that flattery to be true, the consequence would be, that the world would have no right to censure a man; but that will not justify him to himself."

Tuesday, Sept. 21.—The uncertainty of our present situation having prevented me from receiving any letters from home for some time, I could not help being uneasy. Dr. Johnson had an advantage over me in this respect, he having no wife or child to occasion anxious apprehensions in his mind.

It was a good morning; so we resolved to set out. Macleod and *Talisker* accompanied us. We got to Ulinish about six o'clock, and found a very good farm-house, of two stories.

Wednesday, Sept. 22.—In the morning I walked out, and saw a ship, the Margaret of Clyde, pass by with a number of emigrants on board. It was a melancholy sight. After breakfast, we went to see what was called a subterraneous house, about a mile off. It was upon the side of a rising ground. It was discovered by a fox's having taken up his abode in it, and in chasing him they dug into it. It was very narrow and low, and seemed about forty feet in length. Near it, we found the foundations of several small huts, built of stone. Mr. M'Queen, who is always for making everything as ancient as possible, boasted that it was the dwelling of some of the first inhabitants of the island, and observed, what a curiosity it was to find here a specimen of the houses of the *aborigines*, which he believed could be found nowhere else; and it was plain that they lived without fire. Dr. Johnson remarked, that they who made this were not in the rudest state; for that it was more difficult to make *it* than to build a house; therefore certainly those who made it were in possession of houses, and had this only as a hiding-place.

We had a very cheerful evening, and Dr. Johnson talked a good deal on the subject of literature. He told us he was well acquainted with Swift's Lord Orrery. Lord Orrery's unkind treatment of his son in his will led us to talk of the dispositions a man should have when dying. I said, I did not see why a man should act differently with respect to those of whom he thought ill when in health, merely because he was dying. JOHNSON. "I should not scruple to speak against a party, when dying; but should not do it against an individual. It is told of Sixtus Quintus, that on his death-bed, in the intervals of his last pangs, he signed death-warrants." Mr. M'Queen said, he should not do so; he would have more tenderness of heart. JOHNSON. "I believe I should not either; but Mr. M'Queen and I are cowards. It would not be from tenderness of heart; for the heart is as tender when a man is in health as when he is sick, though his resolution may be stronger. Sixtus Quintus was a sovereign as well as a priest; and, if the criminals deserved death, he was doing his duty to the last. You would not think a judge died ill, who should be carried off by an apoplectic fit while pronouncing sentence of death. Consider a class of men whose business it is to distribute death:—soldiers, who die scattering bullets. Nobody thinks they die ill on that account."

Talking of biography, he said, he did not think that the life of any literary man in England had been well written. Beside the common incidents of life, it should tell us his studies, his mode of living, the means by which he attained to excellence, and his opinion of his own works.

Thursday, Sept. 23.—We set out this morning on our way to Talisker, in *Ulinish's* boat, having taken leave of him and his family. Mr. Donald M'Queen still favoured us with his company. As we sailed along, Dr. Johnson got into one of his fits of railing at the Scots. He owned they had been a very learned nation for a hundred years, from about 1550 to about 1650; but that they afforded the only instance of a people among whom the arts of civil life did not advance in proportion with learning; that they had hardly any trade, any money, or any elegance, before the Union; that it was strange that, with all the advantages possessed by other nations, they had not any of those conveniences and embellishments which are the fruits of industry, till they came in contact with a civilized people. "We have taught you," said he, "and we'll do the same in time to all barbarous nations, to the Cherokees, and at last to the Ouran-Outangs," laughing with as much glee as if Monboddo had been present. BOSWELL. "We had wine before the Union." JOHNSON. "No, Sir; you had some weak stuff, the refuse of France, which would not make you drunk." BOSWELL. "I assure you, Sir, there was a great deal of drunkenness." JOHNSON. "No, Sir; there were people who died of dropsies, which they contracted in trying to get drunk."

I must here glean some of his conversation at Ulinish, which I have omitted. He repeated his remark, that a man in a ship was worse than a man in a jail. "The man in a jail," said he, "has more room, better food, and commonly better company, and is in safety." "Ay; but," said Mr. M'Queen, "the man in the ship has the pleasing hope of getting to shore." JOHNSON. "Sir, I am not talking of a man's getting to shore, but of a man while he is in a ship; and then, I say, he is worse than a man while he is in jail. A man in a jail *may* have the '*pleasing hope*' of getting out. A man confined for only a limited time actually *has* it." Macleod mentioned his schemes for carrying on fisheries with spirit, and that he would wish to understand the construction of boats. I suggested that he might go to a dock-yard and work, as Peter the Great did. JOHNSON. "Nay, Sir, he need not work. Peter the Great had not the sense to see that the mere mechanical work may be done by any body, and that there is the same art in constructing a vessel, whether the boards are well or ill wrought. Sir Christopher Wren might as well have served his time to a bricklayer, and first, indeed, to a brickmaker."

There is a beautiful little island in the Loch of Dunvegan, called Isa. Macleod said, he would give it to Dr. Johnson, on condition of his residing on it three months in the year; nay, one month. Dr. Johnson was highly amused with the fancy. I have seen him please himself with little things, even with mere ideas like the present. He talked a great deal of this island; how he would build a house there—how he would fortify it—how he would have cannon—how he would plant—how he would sally out, and *take* the Isle of Muck; and then he laughed with uncommon glee, and could hardly leave off. I have seen him do so at a small matter that struck him, and was a sport to no one else. Macleod encouraged the fancy of Dr. Johnson's becoming owner of an island; told him, that it was the practice in this country to name every man by his lands; and begged leave to drink to him in that mode: "*Island Isa*, your health!" *Ulinish, Talisker,* Mr. M'Queen, and I, all joined in our different manners, while Dr. Johnson bowed to each, with much good humour.

We had good weather and a fine sail this day. The shore was varied with hills, and rocks, and corn-fields, and bushes, which are here dignified with the name of natural *wood*. We landed near the house of Ferneley, a farm possessed by another gentleman of the name of Macleod, who, expecting our arrival, was waiting on the shore, with a horse for Dr. Johnson. The rest of us walked. At dinner, I expressed to Macleod the joy which I had in seeing him

RODE HARDER AT A FOX CHASE THAN ANY BODY

on such cordial terms with his clan. "Government," said he, "has deprived us of our ancient power; but it cannot deprive us of our domestic satisfactions. I would rather drink punch in one of their houses (meaning the houses of his people), than be enabled, by their hardships, to have claret in my own." This should be the sentiment of every chieftain.

We had a very good ride, for about three miles, to Talisker, where Colonel Macleod introduced us to his lady. We found here Mr. Donald M'Lean, the young Laird of Col. He was a little lively young man.

Talisker is a better place than one commonly finds in Sky. It is situated in a rich bottom. Before it is a wide expanse of sea, on each hand of which are immense rocks; and, at some distance in the sea, there are three columnal rocks rising to sharp points. The billows break with prodigious force and noise on the coast of Talisker. There are here a good many well-grown trees. Talisker is an extensive farm. The possessor of it has, for several generations, been the next heir to *Macleod*, as there has been but one son always in that family. The court before the house is most injudiciously paved with the round bluish-grey pebbles which are found upon the sea-shore; so that you walk as if upon cannon balls driven into the ground.

Friday, Sept. 24.—This was a good day. Dr. Johnson told us, at breakfast, that he rode harder at a fox chase than any body. "The English," said he, "are the only nation who ride hard a-hunting. A Frenchman goes out upon a managed horse, and capers in the field, and no more thinks of leaping a hedge than of mounting a breach. Lord Powerscourt laid a wager, in France, that he would ride a great many miles in a certain short time. The French academicians set to work, and calculated that, from the resistance of the air, it was impossible. His lordship, however, performed it."

Our money being nearly exhausted, we sent a bill for thirty pounds to Lochbraccadale, but our messenger found it very difficult to procure cash for it; at length, however, he got us value from the master of a vessel which was to carry away some emigrants. There is a great scarcity of specie in Sky. The people consume a vast deal of snuff and tobacco, for which they must pay ready money; and pedlars, who come about selling goods, as there is not a shop in the island, carry away the cash. I got one and twenty shillings in silver at Portree, which was thought a wonderful store.

Talisker, Mr. M'Queen, and I, walked out, and looked at no less than fifteen different waterfalls, near the house, in the space of about a quarter of a mile. We also saw Cuchillin's well, said to have been the favourite spring of that ancient hero. I drank of it. The water is admirable. On the shore are many stones full of crystallizations in the heart.

Though our obliging friend, Mr. M'Lean, was but the young laird, he had the title of *Col* constantly given him. After dinner he and I walked to the top of Prieshwell, a very high rocky hill, from whence there is a view of Barra—the Long Island—Bernera—the Loch of Dunvegan—part of Rum—part of Rasay—and a vast deal of the Isle of Sky. *Col*, though he had come into Sky with an intention to be at Dunvegan, and pass a considerable time in the island, most politely planned an expedition for us. He proposed we should see the islands of Egg, Muck, Col, and Tyr-yi. In all these islands he could show us every thing worth seeing; and in Mull he said he should be as if at home, his father having lands there, and he a farm.

Dr. Johnson did not talk much to-day, but seemed intent in listening to the schemes of future excursion, planned by *Col*.

Saturday, Sept. 25.—It was resolved that we should set out, in order to return to Slate, to be in readiness to take a boat whenever there should be a fair wind. Dr. Johnson remained in his chamber writing a letter, and it was long before we could get him into motion. He did not come to breakfast, but had it sent to him. When he had finished his letter, it was twelve o'clock, and we should have set out at ten. When I went up to him, he said to me, "Do you remember a song which begins—

> Every island is a prison
>   Strongly guarded by the sea;
> Kings and princes, for that reason,
>   Prisoners are as well as we?"

I suppose he had been thinking of our confined situation. He would fain have got in a boat from hence, instead of riding back to Slate. A scheme for it was proposed. He said, "We'll not be driven tamely from it": but it proved impracticable.

We took leave of Macleod and *Talisker*, from whom we parted with regret. Young *Col* was now our leader. Mr. M'Queen was to accompany us half a day more. We stopped at a little hut, where we saw an old woman grinding with the *quern*, the ancient Highland instrument, which it is said was used by the Romans; but which, being very slow in its operation, is almost entirely gone into disuse.

The walls of the cottages in Sky, instead of being one compacted mass of stones, are often formed by two exterior surfaces of stone, filled up with earth in the middle, which makes them very warm. The roof is generally bad. They are thatched, sometimes with straw, sometimes with heath, sometimes with fern. The thatch is secured by ropes of straw, or of heath; and, to fix the ropes, there is a stone tied to the end of each. These stones hang round the bottom of the roof, and make it look like a lady's hair in papers; but I should think that, when there is wind, they would come down, and knock people on the head.

We dined at the inn at Sconser, where I had the pleasure to find a letter from my wife. Here we parted from our learned companion, Mr. Donald M'Queen. Dr. Johnson took leave of him very affectionately, saying, "Dear Sir, do not forget me!" We settled, that he should write an account of the Isle of Sky, which Dr. Johnson promised to revise.

We sent our horses round a point of land, that we might shun some very bad road; and resolved to go forward by sea. It was seven o'clock when we got into our boat. We had many showers, and it soon grew pretty dark. Dr. Johnson sat silent and patient. Once he said, as he looked on the black coast of Sky,—black, as being composed of rocks seen in the dusk,—"This is very solemn." Our boatmen were rude singers, and seemed so like wild Indians, that a very little imagination was necessary to give one an impression of being upon an American river. We landed at Strolimus, from whence we got a guide to walk before us, for two miles, to Corrichatachin. Not being able to procure a horse for our baggage, I took one portmanteau before me, and Joseph another. We had but a single star to light us on our way. It was about eleven when we arrived. We were most hospitably received by the master and mistress, who were just going to bed, but, with unaffected ready kindness, made a good fire, and at twelve o'clock at night had supper on the table.

Dr. Johnson went to bed soon. When one bowl of punch was finished, I rose, and was near the door, in my way upstairs to bed; but *Corrichatachin* said it was the first time *Col* had been in his house, and he should have his bowl;—and would not I join in drinking it? The heartiness of my honest landlord, and the desire of doing social honour to our very obliging conductor, induced me to sit down again. *Col's* bowl was finished; and by that time we were well warmed. A third bowl was soon made, and that too was finished. We were cordial, and merry to a high degree; but of what passed I have no recollection, with any accuracy. I remember calling *Corrichatachin* by the familiar appellation of *Corri*, which his friends do. A fourth bowl was made, by which time *Col*, and young M'Kinnon, *Corrichatachin's* son, slipped away to bed. I continued a little with *Corri* and *Knockow;* but at last I left them. It was near five in the morning when I got to bed.

Sunday, Sept. 26.—I awaked at noon, with a severe headache. I was much vexed, that I should have been guilty of such a riot, and afraid of a reproof from Dr. Johnson. I thought it very inconsistent with that conduct which I ought to maintain, while the companion of the Rambler. About one he came into my room, and accosted me, "What, drunk yet?" His tone of voice was not that of severe upbraiding: so I was relieved a little. "Sir," said I, "they kept me up." He answered, "No, you kept them up, you drunken dog." This he said with good-humoured English pleasantry. Soon afterwards, *Corrichatachin, Col,* and other friends, assembled round my bed. *Corri* had a brandy-bottle and glass with him, and insisted I should take a dram. "Ay," said Dr. Johnson, "fill him drunk again. Do it in the morning, that we may laugh at him all day. It is a poor thing for a fellow to get drunk at night, and skulk to bed, and let his friends have no sport." Finding him thus jocular, I became quite easy; and when I offered to get up, he very good-naturedly said, "You need be in no such hurry now." I took my host's advice, and drank some brandy, which I found an effectual cure for my headache. When I rose, I went into Dr. Johnson's room, and taking up Mrs. M'Kinnon's Prayer-book, I opened it at the twentieth Sunday after Trinity, in the epistle for which I read, "And be not drunk with wine, wherein there is excess." Some would have taken this as divine interposition.

This was another day of wind and rain; but good cheer and good society helped to beguile the time. I felt myself comfortable enough in the afternoon. I then thought that my last night's riot was no more than such a social excess as may happen without much moral blame; and recollected that some physicians maintained, that a fever produced by it was, upon the whole, good for health: so different are our reflections on the same subject, at different periods; and such the excuses with which we palliate what we know to be wrong.

Monday, Sept. 27.—Mr. Donald Macleod, our original guide, who had parted from us at Dunvegan, joined us again to-day. The weather was still so bad that we could not travel. I found a closet here, with a good many books, besides those that were lying about. Dr. Johnson told me, he found a library in his room at Talisker; and observed, that it was one of the remarkable things of Sky, that there were so many books in it.

After dinner, Dr. Johnson was quite social and easy; and though he drank no fermented liquor, toasted Highland beauties with great readiness. His conviviality engaged them so much, that they seemed eager to show their attention to him, and vied with each other in crying out, with a strong Celtic pronunciation, "Toctor Shonson, Toctor Shonson, your health!"

This evening one of our married ladies, a lively pretty little woman, good humouredly sat down upon Dr. Johnson's knee, and, being encouraged by some of the company, put her arms round his neck and kissed him. "Do it again," said he, "and let us see who will tire first." He kept her on his knee some time, while he and she drank tea. He was now like a *buck* indeed. All the company were much entertained to find him so easy and pleasant. To me it was highly comic, to see the grave philosopher—the Rambler—toying with a Highland beauty! But what could he do? He must have been surly and weak too, had he not behaved as he did. He would have been laughed at, and not more respected, though less loved.

He read to-night, to himself, as he sat in company, a great deal of my Journal, and said to me, "The more I read of this, I think the more highly of you." The gentlemen sat a long time at their punch, after he and I had retired to our chambers. The manner in which they were attended struck me as singular. The bell being broken, a smart lad lay on a table in the corner of the room, ready to spring up and bring the kettle whenever it was wanted. They continued drinking, and singing Erse songs, till near five in the morning, when they all came into my room, where some of them had beds. Unluckily for me, they found a bottle of punch in a corner, which they drank; and *Corrichatachin* went for another, which they also drank. They made many apologies for disturbing me. I told them, that, having been kept awake by their mirth, I had once thoughts of getting up and joining them again. Honest *Corrichatachin* said, "To have had you done so, I would have given a cow."

Tuesday, Sept. 28.—The weather was worse than yesterday. I felt as if imprisoned. Dr. Johnson said it was irksome to be detained thus: yet he seemed to have less uneasiness, or more patience, than I had. What made our situation worse here was, that we had no rooms that we could command; for the good people had no notion that a man could have any occasion but for a mere sleeping place; so, during the day, the bed-chambers were common to all the house. Servants eat in Dr. Johnson's, and mine was a kind of general rendezvous of all under the roof, children and dogs not excepted. As the gentlemen occupied the parlour, the ladies had no place to sit in, during the day, but Dr. Johnson's room. I had always some quiet time for writing in it, before he was up; and, by degrees, I accustomed the ladies to let me sit in it after breakfast, at my Journal, without minding me.

Dr. Johnson was this morning for going to see as many islands as we could, not recollecting the uncertainty of the season, which might detain us in one place for many weeks. He said to me, "I have more the spirit of adventure than you." For my part, I was anxious to get to Mull, from whence we might almost any day reach the main land.

Happily the weather cleared up between one and two o'clock, and we got ready to depart; but our kind host and hostess would not let us go without taking a *snatch*, as they called it; which was in truth a very good dinner. While the punch went round, Dr. Johnson kept a close whispering conference with Mrs. M'Kinnon, which, however, was loud enough to let us hear that the subject of it was the particulars of Prince Charles's escape. The company were entertained and pleased to observe it. Upon that subject, there was something congenial between the soul of Dr. Samuel Johnson and that of an Isle of Sky farmer's wife. We were merry with *Corrichatachin*, on Dr. Johnson's whispering with his wife. She, perceiving this, humorously cried, "I am in love with him. What is it to live and not to love?" Upon her saying something, which I did not hear, or cannot recollect, he seized her hand eagerly, and kissed it.

As we were going, the Scottish phrase of "*honest man!*" which is an expression of kindness and regard, was again and again applied by the company to Dr. Johnson. I was also treated with much civility; and I must take some merit from my assiduous attention to him, and from my contriving that he shall be easy wherever he goes, that he shall not be asked twice to eat or drink any thing (which always disgusts him), that he shall be provided with water at his meals, and many such little things, which, if not attended to, would fret him. I also may be allowed to claim some merit in leading the conversation: I do not mean leading, as in an orchestra, by playing the first fiddle; but leading as one does in examining a witness—starting topics, and making him pursue them. He appears to me like a great mill, into which a subject is thrown to be ground. It requires, indeed, fertile minds to furnish materials for this mill. I regret whenever I see it unemployed; but sometimes I feel myself quite barren, and having nothing to throw in.

We set out about four. Young *Corrichatachin* went with us. We had a fine evening, and arrived in good time at Ostig, the residence of Mr. Martin M'Pherson, minister of Slate. We were received here with much kindness by Mr. and Mrs. M'Pherson, and his sister, Miss M'Pherson, who pleased Dr. Johnson much by singing Erse songs, and playing on the guitar.

Wednesday, Sept. 29.—After a very good sleep, I rose more refreshed than I had been for some nights. We were now at but a little distance from the shore, and saw the sea from our windows, which made our voyage seem nearer.

Col, who had gone yesterday to pay a visit at Camuscross, joined us this morning at breakfast. Some other gentlemen also came to enjoy the entertainment of Dr. Johnson's conversation. The day was windy and rainy, so that we had just seized a happy interval for our journey last night. We had good entertainment here, better accommodation than at Corrichatachin, and time enough to ourselves. The hours slipped along imperceptibly.

Dr. Johnson was this afternoon full of critical severity, and dealt about his censures on all sides. While he was in this mood, I was unfortunate enough, simply perhaps, but I could not help thinking undeservedly, to come within "the whiff and wind of his fell sword." I asked him, if he had ever been accustomed to wear a night-cap. He said, "No." I asked, if it was best not to wear one. JOHNSON. "Sir, I had this custom by chance, and perhaps no man shall ever know whether it is best to sleep with or without a night-cap." Soon afterwards he was laughing at some deficiency in the Highlands, and said, "One might as well go without shoes and stockings." Thinking to have a little hit at his own deficiency, I ventured to add, "or without a night-cap, Sir." But I had better have been silent, for he retorted directly, "I do not see the connection there (laughing). Nobody before was ever foolish enough to ask whether it was best to wear a night-cap or not. This comes of being a little wrong-headed." He carried the company along with him, and yet the truth is, that if he had always worn a night-cap, as is the common practice, and found the Highlanders did not wear one, he would have wondered at their barbarity; so that my hit was fair enough.

Thursday, Sept. 30.—There was as great a storm of wind and rain as I have almost ever seen, which necessarily confined us to the house; but we were fully compensated by Dr. Johnson's conversation.

There was something not quite serene in his humour to-night, after supper; for he spoke of hastening away to London, without stopping much at Edinburgh. I reminded him that he had General Oughton, and many others, to see. JOHNSON. "Nay, I shall neither go in jest, nor stay in jest. I shall do what is fit." BOSWELL. "Ay, Sir, but all I desire is, that you will let me tell you when it is fit." JOHNSON. "Sir, I shall not consult you." BOSWELL. "If you are to run away from us, as soon as you get loose, we will keep you confined in an island." He was, however, on the whole, very good company. Mr. Donald Macleod expressed very well the gradual impression made by Dr. Johnson on those who are so fortunate as to obtain his acquaintance. "When you see him first, you are struck with awful reverence; then you admire him; and then you love him cordially."

Friday, Oct. 1.—I showed to Dr. Johnson verses in a Magazine, on his Dictionary, composed of uncommon words taken from it;

Little of Anthropopathy has he, &c.

He read a few of them, and said, "I am not answerable for all the words in my Dictionary." I told him, that Garrick kept a book of all who had either praised or abused him. On the subject of his own reputation, he said, "Now that I see it has been so current a topic, I wish I had done so too; but it could not well be done now, as so many things are scattered in newspapers." He remarked, that attacks on authors did them much service. "A man who tells me my play is very bad, is less my enemy than he who lets it die in silence. A man, whose business is to be talked of, is much helped by being attacked. It was said to old Bentley, upon the attacks against him, 'Why, they'll write you down.' 'No, Sir,' he replied; 'depend upon it, no man was ever written down but by himself.'" He observed to me afterwards, that the advantages authors derived from attacks were chiefly in subjects of taste, where you cannot confute, as so much may be said on either side.

The weather being now somewhat better, Mr. James M'Donald, factor to Sir Alexander M'Donald, in Slate, insisted that all the company at Ostig should go to the house at Armidale, which Sir Alexander had left, having gone with his lady to Edinburgh, and be his guests, till we had an opportunity of sailing to Mull. We accordingly got there to dinner; and passed our day very cheerfully, being no less than fourteen in number.

Saturday, Oct. 2.—Dr. Johnson said, that "a chief and his lady should make their house like a court. They should have a certain number of the gentlemen's daughters to receive their education in the family, to learn pastry and such things from the housekeeper, and manners from my lady. That was the way in the great families in Wales; at Lady Salusbury's, Mrs. Thrale's grandmother, and at Lady Philips's. I distinguish the families by the ladies, as I speak of what was properly their province. There were always six young ladies at Sir John Philips's; when one was married, her place was filled up. There was a large schoolroom, where they learnt needlework and other things." I observed, that, at some courts in Germany, there were academies for the pages, who are the sons of gentlemen, and receive their education without expense to their parents. Dr. Johnson said, that manners were best learnt at those courts. "You are admitted with great facility to the prince's company, and yet must treat him with much respect. At a great court, you are at such a distance that you get no good." I said, "Very true: a man sees the court of Versailles, as if he saw it on a theatre." He said, "The best book that ever was written upon good breeding, 'Il Cortegiano,' by Castiglione, grew up at the little court of Urbino, and you should read it." I am glad always to have his opinion of books.

He said to-day, while reading my Journal, "This will be a great treasure to us some years hence."

We were very social and merry in his room this forenoon. In the evening the company danced as usual. We performed, with much activity, a dance which, I suppose, the emigration from Sky has occasioned. They call it *America.* Each of the couples, after the common *involutions* and *evolutions*, successively whirls round in a circle, till all are in motion; and the dance seems intended to show how emigration catches, till a whole neighbourhood is set afloat. Mrs. M'Kinnon told me, that last year, when a ship sailed from

Portree for America, the people on shore were almost distracted when they saw their relations go off; they lay down on the ground, tumbled, and tore the grass with their teeth. This year there was not a tear shed. The people on the shore seemed to think that they would soon follow. This indifference is a mortal sign for the country.

We danced to-night to the music of the bagpipe, which made us beat the ground with prodigious force. I thought it better to endeavour to conciliate the kindness of the people of Sky, by joining heartily in their amusements, than to play the abstract scholar. I looked on this tour to the Hebrides as a co-partnership between Dr. Johnson and me. Each was to do all he could to promote its success; and I have some reason to flatter myself, that my gayer exertions were of service to us. Dr. Johnson's immense fund of knowledge and wit was a wonderful source of admiration and delight to them; but they had it only at times; and they required to have the intervals agreeably filled up, and even little elucidations of his learned text. I was also fortunate enough frequently to draw him forth to talk, when he would otherwise have been silent. The fountain was at times locked up, till I opened the spring. It was curious to hear the Hebrideans, when any dispute happened while he was out of the room, saying, "Stay till Dr. Johnson comes; say that to *him!*"

Yesterday, Dr. Johnson said, "I cannot but laugh, to think of myself roving among the Hebrides at sixty. I wonder where I shall rove at fourscore!" This evening he disputed the truth of what is said as to the people of St. Kilda catching cold whenever strangers come. They said, it was annually proved by Macleod's steward, on whose arrival all the inhabitants caught cold. He jocularly remarked, "The steward always comes to demand something from them; and so they fall a coughing. I suppose the people in Sky all take a cold when ——[1] (naming a certain person) comes." They said, he came only in summer. Johnson. "That is out of tenderness to you. Bad weather and he, at the same time, would be too much."

Sunday, Oct. 3.—Joseph reported that the wind was still against us. Dr. Johnson said, "A wind, or not a wind? that is the question"; for he can amuse himself at times with a little play of words, or rather sentences. I remember when he turned his cup at Aberbrothick, where we drank tea, he muttered, *Claudite jam rivos, pueri.*

[1] Sir Alexander Macdonald.

WE DANCED TO-NIGHT TO THE MUSIC OF THE BAGPIPE

While we were chatting in the indolent style of men who were to stay here all this day at least, we were suddenly roused at being told that the wind was fair, that a little fleet of herring-busses were passing by for Mull, and that Mr. Simpson's vessel was about to sail. Hugh M'Donald, the skipper, came to us, and was impatient that we should get ready, which we soon did. Dr. Johnson, with composure and solemnity, repeated the observation of Epictetus, that, "as man has the voyage of death before him,—whatever may be his employment, he should be ready at the master's call; and an old man should never be far from the shore, lest he should not be able to get himself ready." He rode, and I and the other gentlemen walked, about an English mile to the shore, where the vessel lay. Dr. Johnson said he should never forget Sky, and returned thanks for all civilities. We were carried to the vessel in a small boat which she had, and we set sail very briskly about one o'clock. I was much pleased with the motion for many hours. Dr. Johnson grew sick, and retired under cover, as it rained a good deal. I kept above, that I might have fresh air, and finding myself not affected by the motion of the vessel, I exulted in being a stout seaman, while Dr. Johnson was quite in a state of annihilation. But I was soon humbled; for after imagining that I could go with ease to America or the East Indies, I became very sick, but kept above board though it rained hard.

As we had been detained so long in Sky by bad weather, we gave up the scheme that *Col* had planned for us of visiting several islands, and contented ourselves with the prospect of seeing Mull, and Icolmkill and Inch-kenneth, which lie near to it.

Mr. Simpson was sanguine in his hopes for awhile, the wind being fair for us. He said he would land us at Icolmkill that night. But when the wind failed, it was resolved we should make for the Sound of Mull, and land in the harbour of Tobermorie. We kept near the five herring vessels for some time; but afterwards four of them got before us, and one little wherry fell behind us. When we got in full view of the point of Ardnamurchan, the wind changed, and was directly against our getting into the Sound. We were then obliged to tack, and get forward in that tedious manner. As we advanced, the storm grew greater, and the sea very rough. *Col* then began to talk of making for Egg, or Canna, or his own island. Our skipper said, he would get us into the Sound. Having struggled for this a good while in vain, he said he would push forward till we were near the land of Mull, where we might cast anchor, and lie till the morning; for although, before this, there had been a good moon, and I had pretty distinctly seen not only the land of Mull, but up the Sound, and the country of Morven as at one end of it, the night was now grown very dark. Our crew consisted of M'Donald, our skipper, and two sailors, one of whom had but one eye; Mr. Simpson, himself, *Col*, and M'Donald his servant, all helped. Simpson said, he would willingly go for Col, if young *Col* or his servant would undertake to pilot us to a harbour; but, as the island is low land, it was dangerous to run upon it in the dark. *Col* and his servant appeared a little dubious. The scheme of running for Canna seemed then to be embraced; but Canna was ten leagues off, all out of our way; and they were afraid to attempt the harbour of Egg. All these different plans were successively in agitation. The old skipper still tried to make for the land of Mull; but then it was considered that there was no place there where we could anchor in safety. Much time was lost in striving against the storm. At last it became so rough, and threatened to be so much worse, that *Col* and his servant took more courage, and said they would undertake to hit one of the harbours in Col. "Then let us run for it in God's name," said the skipper; and instantly we turned towards it. The little wherry which had fallen behind us had hard work. The master begged that, if we made for Col, we should put out a light to him. Accordingly, one of the sailors waved a glowing peat for some time. The various difficulties that were started gave me a good deal of apprehension, from which I was relieved, when I found we were to run for a harbour before the wind. But my relief was but of short duration; for I soon heard that our sails were very bad, and were in danger of being torn in pieces, in which case we should be driven upon the rocky shore of Col. It was very dark, and there was a heavy and incessant rain. The sparks of the burning peat flew so much about, that I dreaded the vessel might take fire. Then, as *Col* was a sportsman, and had powder on board, I figured that we might be blown up. Simpson and he appeared a little frightened, which made me more so; and the perpetual talking, or rather shouting, which was carried on in Erse, alarmed me still more. A man is always suspicious of what is saying in an unknown tongue; and, if fear be his passion at the time, he grows more afraid. Our vessel often lay so much on one side, that I trembled lest she should be overset; and indeed they told me afterwards, that they had run her sometimes to within an inch of the water, so anxious were they to make what haste they could before the night should be worse. I now saw what I never saw before, a prodigious sea, with immense billows coming upon a vessel, so as that it seemed hardly possible to escape. There was something grandly horrible in the sight. I am glad I have seen it once. Amidst all these terrifying circumstances, I endeavoured to compose my mind. It was not easy to do it; for all the stories that I had heard of the dangerous sailing among the Hebrides, which is proverbial, came full upon my recollection. When I thought of those who were dearest to me, and would suffer severely, should I be lost, I upbraided myself, as not having a sufficient cause for putting myself in such danger.

It was half an hour after eleven before we set ourselves in the course for Col. As I saw them all busy doing something, I asked *Col*, with much earnestness, what I could do. He, with a happy readiness, put into my hand a rope, which was fixed to the top of one of the masts, and told me to hold it till he bade me pull. If I had considered the matter, I might have seen that this could not be of the least service; but his object was to keep me out of the way of those who were busy working the vessel, and at the same time to divert my fear, by employing me, and making me think that I was of use. Thus did I stand firm to my post, while the wind and rain beat upon me, always expecting a call to pull my rope.

The man with one eye steered; old M'Donald, and *Col* and his servant, lay upon the forecastle, looking sharp out for the harbour. It was necessary to carry much *cloth*, as they termed it, that is to say, much sail, in order to keep the vessel off the shore of Col. This made violent plunging in a rough sea. At last they spied the harbour of Lochiern, and *Col* cried, "Thank God, we are safe!" We ran up till we were opposite to it, and soon afterwards we got into it, and cast anchor.

Dr. Johnson had all this time been quiet and unconcerned. He had lain down on one of the beds, and having got free from sickness, was satisfied. The truth is, he knew nothing of the danger we were in;[1] but, fearless and unconcerned, might have said, in the words which he has chosen for the motto to his "Rambler,"

Quo me cunque rapit tempestas, deferor hospes.[2]

---

[1] He at least made light of it, in a letter to Mrs. Thrale. "After having been detained by storms many days at Sky, we left it, as we thought, with a fair wind; but a violent gust, which Boswell had a great mind to call a tempest, forced us into *Col*, an obscure island."

"Their risque, in a sea full of islands, was very considerable. Indeed, the whole expedition was highly perilous, considering the season of the year, the precarious chance of getting sea-worthy boats, and the ignorance of the Hebrideans, who, notwithstanding the opportunities, I may say the *necessities*, of their situation, are very careless and unskilful sailors."—*Walter Scott.*

[2] "For as the tempest drives, I shape my way."—Hor. 1, Ep. 1, 15.

Once, during the doubtful consultations, he asked whither we were going; and upon being told that it was not certain whether to Mull or Col, he cried, "Col for my money!" I now went down, with *Col* and Mr. Simpson, to visit him. He was lying in philosophic tranquillity with a greyhound of *Col's* at his back, keeping him warm. *Col* is quite the *Juvenis qui gaudet canibus.* He had, when we left Talisker, two greyhounds, two terriers, a pointer, and a large Newfoundland water-dog. He lost one of his terriers by the road, but had still five dogs with him. I was very ill, and very desirous to get to shore. When I was told that we could not land that night, as the storm had now increased, I looked so miserably, as *Col* afterwards informed me, that what Shakspeare has made the Frenchman say of the English soldiers, when scantily dieted, "Piteous they will look, like drowned mice!" might, I believe, have been well applied to me. There was in the harbour, before us, a Campbell-town vessel, the *Betty*, Kenneth Morison master, taking in kelp, and bound for Ireland. We sent our boat to beg beds for two gentlemen, and that the master would send his boat, which was larger than ours. He accordingly did so, and *Col* and I were accommodated in his vessel till the morning.

Monday, Oct. 4.—About eight o'clock we went in the boat to Mr. Simpson's vessel, and took in Dr. Johnson. He was quite well, though he had tasted nothing but a dish of tea since Saturday night. On our expressing some surprise at this, he said, that "when he lodged in the Temple, and had no regular system of life, he had fasted for two days at a time, during which he had gone about visiting, though not at the hours of dinner or supper; that he had drunk tea, but eaten no bread; that this was no intentional fasting, but happened just in the course of a literary life."

There was a little miserable public-house close upon the shore, to which we should have gone, had we landed last night: but this morning *Col* resolved to take us directly to the house of Captain Lauchlan M'Lean, a descendant of his family, who had acquired a fortune in the East Indies, and taken a farm in Col. We had about an English mile to go to it. *Col* and Joseph, and some others, ran to some little horses, called here *shelties*, that were running wild on a heath, and catched one of them. We had a saddle with us, which was clapped upon it, and a straw halter was put on its head. Dr. Johnson was then mounted, and Joseph very slowly and gravely led the horse. I said to Dr. Johnson, "I wish, Sir, *the club* saw you in this attitude."

It was a very heavy rain, and I was wet to the skin. Captain M'Lean had but a poor temporary house, or rather hut; however, it was a very good haven to us. There was a blazing peat fire, and Mrs. M'Lean, daughter of the minister of the parish, got us tea. I felt still the motion of the sea. Dr. Johnson said, it was not in the imagination, but a continuation of motion on the fluids, like that of the sea itself after the storm is over.

The day passed away pleasantly enough. The wind became fair for Mull in the evening, and Mr. Simpson resolved to sail next morning: but having been thrown into the island of Col, we were unwilling to leave it unexamined, especially as we considered that the Campbell-town vessel would sail for Mull in a day or two; and therefore we determined to stay.

Tuesday, Oct. 5.—I rose, and wrote my Journal till about nine, and then went to Dr. Johnson, who sat up in bed and talked and laughed. I said, it was curious to look back ten years, to the time when we first thought of visiting the Hebrides. How distant and improbable the scheme then appeared! Yet here we were actually among them. "Sir," said he, "people may come to do any thing almost, by talking of it. I really believe I could talk myself into building a house upon Island Isa, though I should probably never come back again to see it. I could easily persuade Reynolds to do it; and there would be no great sin in persuading him to do it. Sir, he would reason thus: 'What will it cost me to be there once in two or three summers? Why, perhaps, five hundred pounds; and what is that, in comparison of having a fine retreat, to which a man can go, or to which he can send a friend?' He would never find out that he may have this within twenty miles of London. Then I would tell him, that he may marry one of the Miss Macleods, a lady of great family. Sir, it is surprising, how people will go to a distance, for what they may have at home. I knew a lady who came up from Lincolnshire to Knightsbridge with one of her daughters, and gave five guineas a week for a lodging and a warm bath; that is, mere warm water. *That*, you know, could not be had in *Lincolnshire!* She said, it was made either too hot or too cold there."

After breakfast, Dr. Johnson and I, and Joseph, mounted horses, and *Col* and the captain walked with us about a short mile across the island. We paid a visit to the Rev. Mr. Hector M'Lean. His parish consists of the islands of Col and Tyr-yi. He was about seventy-seven years of age, a decent ecclesiastic, dressed in a full suit of black clothes, and a black wig. We were told that he had a valuable library, though but poor accommodation for it, being obliged to keep his books in large chests. It was curious to see him and Dr. Johnson together. Neither of them heard very distinctly; so each of them talked in his own way, and at the same time. Mr. M'Lean said, he had a confutation of Bayle, by Leibnitz. JOHNSON. "A confutation of Bayle, Sir! What part of Bayle do you mean? The greatest part of his writings is not confutable: it is historical and critical." Mr. M'Lean said, "the irreligious part"; and proceeded to talk of Leibnitz's controversy with Clarke, calling Leibnitz a great man. JOHNSON. "No, Sir; Leibnitz was as paltry a fellow as I know. Out of respect to Queen Caroline, who patronized him, Clarke treated him too well."

During the time that Dr. Johnson was thus going on, the old minister was standing with his back to the fire, cresting up erect, pulling down the front of his periwig, and talking what a great man Leibnitz was. To give an idea of the scene would require a page with two columns; but it ought rather to be represented by two good players. The old gentleman said, Clarke was very wicked, for going so much into the Arian system. "I will not say he was wicked," said Dr. Johnson; "he might be mistaken." M'LEAN. "He was wicked, to shut his eyes against the Scriptures; and worthy men in England have since confuted him to all intents and purposes." JOHNSON. "I know not *who* has confuted him to *all intents and purposes*." Here again there was a double talking, each continuing to maintain his own argument, without hearing exactly what the other said.

I regretted that Dr. Johnson did not practise the art of accommodating himself to different sorts of people. Had he been softer with this venerable old man, we might have had more conversation; but his forcible spirit and impetuosity of manner, may be said to spare neither sex nor age. I have seen even Mrs. Thrale stunned; but I have often maintained, that it is better he should retain his own manner. Pliability of address I conceive to be inconsistent with that majestic power of mind which he possesses, and which produces such noble effects. A lofty oak will not bend like a supple willow.

He told me afterwards, he liked firmness in an old man, and was pleased to see Mr. M'Lean so orthodox. "At his age, it is too late for a man to be asking himself questions as to his belief."

We rode to the northern part of the island, where we saw the ruins of a church or chapel. At Grissipol we found a good farm-house, belonging to the Laird of Col. We were entertained here with a primitive heartiness. Whisky was served round in a shell, according to the ancient Highland custom. Dr. Johnson would not partake of it; but being desirous to do honour to the modes "of other times," drank some water out of the shell.

In the forenoon Dr. Johnson said, "It would require great resignation to live in one of these islands." BOSWELL. "I don't know, Sir: I have felt myself at times in a state of almost mere physical existence, satisfied to eat, drink, and sleep, and walk about, and enjoy my own thoughts: and I can figure a continuation of this." JOHNSON. "Ay, Sir; but if you were shut up here, your own thoughts would torment you: you would think of Edinburgh, or of London, and that you could not be there."

We set out after dinner for Breacacha, the family seat of the Laird of Col. We found here a neat new-built gentleman's house, better than any we had been in since we were at Lord Errol's. Dr. Johnson relished it much at first, but soon remarked to me, that "there was nothing becoming a chief about it: it was a mere tradesman's box." He seemed quite at home, and no longer found any difficulty in using the Highland address; for as soon as we arrived, he said, with a spirited familiarity, "Now, *Col*, if you could get us a dish of tea." Dr. Johnson and I had each an excellent bed-chamber. We had a dispute which of us had the best curtains. His were rather the best, being of linen; but I insisted that my bed had the best posts, which was undeniable. "Well," said he, "if you *have* the best *posts*, we will have you tied to them and whipped." I mention this slight circumstance, only to show how ready he is, even in mere trifles, to get the better of his antagonist, by placing him in a ludicrous view.

Wednesday, Oct. 6.—After a sufficiency of sleep, we assembled at breakfast. We were just as if in barracks. Everybody was master. We went and viewed the old castle of Col, which is not far from the present house, near the shore, and founded on a rock. On the second story we saw a vault which was, and still is, the family prison. We were shown, in a corner of this vault, a hole into which *Col* said greater criminals used to be put. It was now filled up with rubbish of different kinds. He said, it was of a great depth. "Ay," said Dr. Johnson, smiling, "all such places that *are filled up* were of a great depth."

Thursday, Oct. 7.—There came on a dreadful storm of wind and rain, which continued all day, and rather increased at night. The wind was directly against our getting to Mull. We were in a strange state of abstraction from the world. *Col* had brought Burnet's "History of his own Times," from Captain M'Lean's; and he had of his own some books of farming, and Gregory's "Geometry." Dr. Johnson read a good deal of Burnet, and of Gregory, and I observed he made some geometrical notes in the end of his pocket-book.

Friday, Oct. 8.—Dr. Johnson appeared to-day very weary of our present confined situation. He said, "I want to be on the main land, and go on with existence. This is a waste of life."

Saturday, Oct. 9.—As, in our present confinement, any thing that had even the name of curious was an object of attention, I proposed that *Col* should show me a great stone, mentioned as having been thrown by a giant to the top of a mountain. Dr. Johnson, who did not like to be left alone, said he would accompany us as far as riding was practicable. We ascended a part of the hill on horseback, and *Col* and I scrambled up the rest. A servant held our horses, and Dr. Johnson placed himself on the ground, with his back against a large fragment of rock. The wind being high, he let down the cocks of his hat, and tied it with his handkerchief under his chin. While we were employed in examining the stone, which did not repay our trouble in getting to it, he amused himself with reading "Gataker on Lots and on the Christian Watch," a very learned book, of the last age, which had been found in the garret of *Col's* house, and which he said was a treasure here. When we descried him from above, he had a most eremitical appearance; and on our return told us, he had been so much engaged by Gataker, that he had never missed us. His avidity for variety of books, while we were in Col, was frequently expressed; and he often complained that so few were within his reach.

In our way we came to a strand of some extent, where we were glad to take a gallop, in which my learned friend joined with great alacrity. Dr. Johnson, mounted on a large bay mare without shoes, and followed by a foal, which had some difficulty in keeping up with him, was a singular spectacle.

Sunday, Oct. 10.—There was this day the most terrible storm of wind and rain that I ever remember. It made such an awful impression on us all, as to produce, for some time, a kind of dismal quietness in the house. The day was passed without much conversation.

Monday, Oct. 11.—We had some days ago engaged the Campbell-town vessel to carry us to Mull, from the harbour where she lay.

AMUSED HIMSELF WITH READING

The morning was fine, and the wind fair and moderate; so we hoped at length to get away.

Mrs. M'Sweyn, who officiated as our landlady here, had never been on the main land. On hearing this, Dr. Johnson said to me, before her, "That is rather being behindhand with life. I would at least go and see Glenelg." BOSWELL. "You yourself, Sir, have never seen, till now, any thing but your native island." JOHNSON. "But, Sir, by seeing London, I have seen as much of life as the world can show." BOSWELL. "You have not seen Pekin." JOHNSON. "What is Pekin? Ten thousand Londoners would *drive* all the people of Pekin: they would drive them like deer."

We set out about eleven for the harbour; but, before we reached it, so violent a storm came on, that we were obliged again to take shelter in the house of Captain M'Lean, where we dined, and passed the night.

Tuesday, Oct. 12.—After breakfast, we made a second attempt to get to the harbour; but another storm soon convinced us that it would be in vain. Captain M'Lean's house being in some confusion, on account of Mrs. M'Lean being expected to lie-in, we resolved to go to Mr. M'Sweyn's, where we arrived very wet, fatigued, and hungry. In this situation, we were somewhat disconcerted by being told that we should have no dinner till late in the evening; but should have tea in the mean time. Dr. Johnson opposed this arrangement; but they persisted, and he took the tea very readily. He said to me afterwards, "You must consider, Sir, a dinner here is a matter of great consequence. It is a thing to be first planned, and then executed. I suppose the mutton was brought some miles off, from some place where they knew there was a sheep killed."

There being little conversation to-night, I must endeavour to recollect what I may have omitted on former occasions. When I boasted, at Rasay, of my independency of spirit, and that I could not be bribed, he said, "Yes, you may be bribed by flattery." At the Rev. Mr. M'Lean's, Dr. Johnson asked him if the people of Col had any superstitions. He said "No." The cutting peats at the increase of the moon was mentioned as one; but he would not allow it, saying it was not a superstition, but a whim. Dr. Johnson would not admit the distinction. There were many superstitions, he maintained, not connected with religion; and this was one of them. On Monday we had a dispute at the Captain's whether sand-hills could be fixed down by art. Dr. Johnson said, "How *the devil* can you do it?" but instantly corrected himself, "How can you do it?" I never before heard him use a phrase of that nature.

He has particularities which it is impossible to explain. He never wears a night-cap, as I have already mentioned; but he puts a handkerchief on his head in the night. The day that we left Talisker, he bade us ride on. He then turned the head of his horse back towards Talisker, stopped for some time; then wheeled round to the same direction with ours, and then came briskly after us. He sets open a window in the coldest day or night, and stands before it. It may do with his constitution; but most people, among whom I am one, would say, with the frogs in the fable, "This may be sport to you; but it is death to us." It is in vain to try to find a meaning in every one of his particularities, which, I suppose, are mere habits, contracted by chance; of which every man has some that are more or less remarkable. His speaking to himself, or rather repeating, is a common habit with studious men accustomed to deep thinking; and, in consequence of their being thus rapt, they will even laugh by themselves, if the subject which they are musing on is a merry one. Dr. Johnson is often uttering pious ejaculations, when he appears to be talking to himself; for sometimes his voice grows stronger, and parts of the Lord's Prayer are heard. I have sat beside him with more than ordinary reverence on such occasions.[1]

In our tour, I observed that he was disgusted whenever he met with coarse manners. He said to me, "I know not how it is, but I cannot bear low life; and I find others, who have as good a right as I to be fastidious, bear it better, by having mixed more with different sorts of men. You would think that I have mixed pretty well too."

He read this day a good deal of my Journal, written in a small book with which he had supplied me, and was pleased, for he said, "I wish thy books were twice as big." He helped me to fill up blanks which I had left in first writing it, when I was not quite sure of what he had said, and he corrected any mistakes that I had made. "They call me a scholar," said he, "and yet how very little literature is there in my conversation." BOSWELL. "That, Sir, must be according to your company. You would not give literature to those who cannot taste it. Stay till we meet Lord Elibank."

---

[1] It is remarkable that Dr. Johnson should have read this account of some of his own peculiar habits, without saying anything on the subject, which I hoped he would have done.—*Boswell.*

We had at last a good dinner, or rather supper, and were very well satisfied with our entertainment.

Wednesday, Oct. 13.—*Col* called me up, with intelligence that it was a good day for a passage to Mull; and just as we rose, a sailor from the vessel arrived for us. We got all ready with despatch. Dr. Johnson was displeased at my bustling and walking quickly up and down. He said, "It does not hasten us a bit. It is getting on horseback in a ship. All boys do it; and you are longer a boy than others." He himself has no alertness, or whatever it may be called.

Before we reached the harbour, the wind grew high again. However, the small boat was waiting, and took us on board. We remained for some time in uncertainty what to do; at last it was determined, that, as a good part of the day was over, and it was dangerous to be at sea at night, in such a vessel and such weather, we should not sail till the morning tide, when the wind would probably be more gentle. We resolved not to go ashore again, but lie here in readiness. Dr. Johnson and I had each a bed in the cabin. *Col* sat at the fire in the forecastle, with the captain, and Joseph, and the rest. I eat some dry oatmeal, of which I found a barrel in the cabin. I had not done this since I was a boy. Dr. Johnson owned that he too was fond of it when a boy; a circumstance which I was highly pleased to hear from him, as it gave me an opportunity of observing that, notwithstanding his joke on the article of OATS, he was himself a proof that this kind of *food* was not peculiar to the people of Scotland.

Thursday, Oct. 14.—When Dr. Johnson awaked this morning, he called "*Lanky!*" having, I suppose, been thinking of Langton, but corrected himself instantly, and cried "*Bozzy!*"

Between six and seven we hauled our anchor, and set sail with a fair breeze; and, after a pleasant voyage, we got safely and agreeably into the harbour of Tobermorie, before the wind rose, which it always has done, for some days, about noon.

Tobermorie is an excellent harbour. An island lies before it, and it is surrounded by a hilly theatre. The island is too low, otherwise this would be quite a secure port; but, the island not being a sufficient protection, some storms blow very hard here. Not long ago, fifteen vessels were blown from their moorings. There are sometimes sixty or seventy sail here: to-day there were twelve or fourteen vessels. To see such a fleet was the next thing to seeing a town.

After having been shut up so long in Col, the sight of such an assemblage of moving habitations, containing such a variety of people, engaged in different pursuits, gave me much gaiety of spirit. When we had landed, Dr. Johnson said, "Boswell is now all alive. He is like Antæus; he gets new vigour whenever he touches the ground." I went to the top of a hill fronting the harbour, from whence I had a good view of it. We had here a tolerable inn. Dr. Johnson had owned to me this morning, that he was out of humour. Indeed, he showed it a good deal in the ship; for when I was expressing my joy on the prospect of our landing in Mull, he said, he had no joy, when he recollected that it would be five days before he should get to the main land. I was afraid he would now take a sudden resolution to give up seeing Icolmkill. A dish of tea, and some good bread and butter, did him service, and his bad humour went off. I told him, that I was diverted to hear all the people whom we had visited in our tour say, "*Honest man!* he's pleased with every thing; he's always content!" "Little do they know," said I. He laughed, and said, "You rogue!"

We sent to hire horses to carry us across the island of Mull to the shore opposite to Inch-kenneth, the residence of Sir Allan M'Lean, uncle to young *Col*, and chief of the M'Leans, to whose house we intended to go the next day. Our friend *Col* went to visit his aunt, who lives about a mile from Tobermorie.

Dr. Johnson and I sat by ourselves at the inn, and talked a good deal. The Sunday evening that we sat by ourselves at Aberdeen, I asked him several particulars of his life, from his early years, which he readily told me; and I wrote them down before him. This day I proceeded in my inquiries, also writing them in his presence. I have them on detached sheets. I shall collect authentic materials for The Life of Samuel Johnson, LL.D., and, if I survive him, I shall be one who will most faithfully do honour to his memory. I have now a vast treasure of his conversation, at different times, since the year 1762, when I first obtained his acquaintance; and, by assiduous inquiry, I can make up for not knowing him sooner.[1]

A Newcastle ship-master, who happened to be in the house, intruded himself upon us. He was much in liquor, and talked nonsense about his being a man for *Wilkes and Liberty*, and against the ministry. Dr. Johnson was angry, that "a fellow should come into *our* company, who was fit for *no* company." He left us soon.

[1] It is no small satisfaction to me to reflect, that Dr. Johnson read this, and after being apprised of my intentions, communicated to me, at subsequent periods, many particulars of his life, which probably could not otherwise have been preserved.—*Boswell*.

Col returned from his aunt, and told us, she insisted that we should come to her house that night. He introduced to us Mr. Campbell, the Duke of Argyle's factor in Tyr-yi. He was going to Inverary, and promised to put letters into the post-office for us. I now found that Dr. Johnson's desire to get on the main land arose from his anxiety to have an opportunity of conveying letters to his friends.

After dinner, we proceeded to Dr. M'Lean's, which was about a mile from our inn. He was not at home, but we were received by his lady and daughter, who entertained us so well, that Dr. Johnson seemed quite happy. When we had supped, he asked me to give him some paper to write letters. I begged he would write short ones, and not *expatiate*, as we ought to set off early. He was irritated by this, and said, "What must be done, must be done: the thing is past a joke."—"Nay, Sir," said I, "write as much as you please; but do not blame me, if we are kept six days before we get to the main land. You were very impatient in the morning: but no sooner do you find yourself in good quarters, than you forget that you are to move." I got him paper enough, and we parted in good humour.

When on Mull, I said, "Well, Sir, this is the fourth of the Hebrides that we have been upon." JOHNSON. "Nay, we cannot boast of the number we have seen. We thought we should see many more. We thought of sailing about easily from island to island; and so we should had we come at a better [1] season; but we, being wise men, thought it would be summer all the year where *we* were. However, Sir, we have seen enough to give us a pretty good notion of the system of insular life."

Friday, Oct. 15.—We this morning found that we could not proceed, there being a violent storm of wind and rain, and the rivers being impassable. When I expressed my discontent at our confinement, Dr. Johnson said, "Now that I have had an opportunity of writing to the main land, I am in no such haste." I was amused with his being so easily satisfied; for the truth was, that the gentleman who was to convey our letters, as I was now informed, was not to set out for Inverary for some time; so that it was probable we should be there as soon as he: however, I did not undeceive my friend, but suffered him to enjoy his fancy.

Dr. Johnson asked, in the evening, to see Dr. M'Lean's books.

---

[1] This observation is very just. The time for the Hebrides was too late by a month or six weeks. I have heard those who remembered their tour express surprise they were not drowned.—*Walter Scott.*

He took down "Willis de Anima Brutorum," and pored over it a good deal. Miss M'Lean gave us several tunes on a spinnet, which, though made so long ago as in 1667, was still very well toned. She sung along with it. Dr. Johnson seemed pleased with the music, though he owns he neither likes it, nor has hardly any perception of it. In Slate, he told us, that "he knew a drum from a trumpet, and a bagpipe from a guitar, which was about the extent of his knowledge of music."

We had the music of the bagpipe every day, at Armidale, Dunvegan, and Col. Dr. Johnson appeared fond of it, and used often to stand for some time with his ear close to the great drone.

He asked me if our jaunt had answered expectation. I said it had much exceeded it. I expected much difficulty with him, and had not found it. "And," he added, "wherever we have come, we have been received like princes in their progress."

He said, he would not wish not to be disgusted in the Highlands; for that would be to lose the power of distinguishing, and a man might then lie down in the middle of them. He wished only to conceal his disgust.

Saturday, Oct. 16.—This day there was a new moon, and the weather changed for the better. Dr. Johnson said of Miss M'Lean, "She is the most accomplished lady that I have found in the Highlands. She knows French, music, and drawing, sews neatly, makes shellwork, and can milk cows; in short, she can do every thing. She talks sensibly, and is the first person whom I have found that can translate Erse poetry literally." We set out, mounted on little Mull horses. Mull corresponded exactly with the idea which I had always had of it; a hilly country, diversified with heath and grass, and many rivulets. Dr. Johnson was not in very good humour. He said, it was a dreary country, much worse than Sky. I differed from him. "O, Sir," said he, "a most dolorous country!"

We had a very hard journey to-day. I had no bridle for my sheltie, but only a halter; and Joseph rode without a saddle. At one place, a loch having swelled over the road, we were obliged to plunge through pretty deep water. Dr. Johnson observed, how helpless a man would be, were he travelling here alone, and should meet with any accident; and said, "he longed to get to a *country of saddles and bridles*." He was more out of humour to-day than he has been in the course of our tour, being fretted to find that his little horse could scarcely support his weight; and having suffered a loss, which, though small in itself, was of some consequence to him, while travelling the rugged steeps of Mull, where he was at times obliged to walk. The loss that I allude to was that of the large oak-stick, which, as I formerly mentioned, he had brought with him from London. It was of great use to him in our wild peregrinations; for, ever since his last illness in 1766, he has had a weakness in his knees, and has not been able to walk easily. It had too the properties of a measure; for one nail was driven into it at the length of a foot; another at that of a yard. In return for the services it had done him, he said, this morning, he would make a present of it to some museum; but he little thought he was so soon to lose it. As he preferred riding with a switch, it was intrusted to a fellow to be delivered to our baggage-man, who followed us at some distance; but we never saw it more. I could not persuade him out of a suspicion that it had been stolen. "No, no, my friend," said he; "it is not to be expected that any man in Mull, who has got it, will part with it. Consider, Sir, the value of such a *piece of timber* here!"

We were in hopes to get to Sir Allan Maclean's at Inch-kenneth, to-night; but the eight miles of which our road was *said* to consist, were so very long, that we did not reach the opposite coast of Mull till seven at night, though we had set out about eleven in the forenoon; and when we did arrive there, we found the wind strong against us. *Col* determined that we should pass the night at M'Quarrie's, in the island of Ulva, which lies between Mull and Inch-kenneth; and a servant was sent forward to the ferry, to secure the boat for us: but the boat was gone to the Ulva side, and the wind was so high that the people could not hear him call; and the night so dark that they could not see a signal. We should have been in a very bad situation, had there not fortunately been lying in the little sound of Ulva an Irish vessel, the Bonnetta, of Londonderry, Captain M'Lure, master. He himself was at M'Quarrie's; but his men obligingly came with their long-boat, and ferried us over.

M'Quarrie's house was mean; but we were agreeably surprised with the appearance of the master, whom we found to be intelligent, polite, and much a man of the world. When Dr. Johnson and I were by ourselves at night, I observed of our host, "*aspectum generosum habet*"; " *et generosum animum*," he added. For fear of being overheard in the small Highland houses, I often talked to him in such Latin as I could speak, and with as much of the English accent as I could assume, so as not to be understood, in case our conversation should be too loud for the space.

We had each an elegant bed in the same room; and here it was that a circumstance occurred, as to which he has been strangely misunderstood. From his description of his chamber, it has erroneously been supposed, that his bed being too short for him, his feet, during the night, were in the mire; whereas he has only said, that when he undressed, he felt his feet in the mire: that is, the clay floor of the room, which he stood upon before he went into bed, was wet, in consequence of the windows being broken, which let in the rain.

Sunday, Oct. 17.—Being informed that there was nothing worthy of observation in Ulva, we took boat, and proceeded to Inchkenneth, where we were introduced by our friend *Col* to Sir Allan M'Lean, the chief of his clan, and to two young ladies, his daughters. Inch-kenneth is a pretty little island, a mile long, and about half a mile broad, all good land.

As we walked up from the shore, Dr. Johnson's heart was cheered by the sight of a road marked with cart-wheels, as on the main land; a thing which we had not seen for a long time. It gave us a pleasure similar to that which a traveller feels, when, whilst wandering on what he fears is a desert island, he perceives the print of human feet.

Dr. Johnson here showed so much of the spirit of a Highlander, that he won Sir Allan's heart: indeed, he has shown it during the whole of our tour. One night, in Col, he strutted about the room with a broad sword and target, and made a formidable appearance: and, another night, I took the liberty to put a large blue bonnet on his head. His age, his size, and his bushy gray wig, with this covering on it, presented the image of a venerable *Senachi:* and however unfavourable to the Lowland Scots, he seemed much pleased to assume the appearance of an ancient Caledonian. We only regretted that he could not be prevailed with to partake of the social glass. One of his arguments against drinking appears to me not convincing. He urged, that, " in proportion as drinking makes a man different from what he is before he has drunk, it is bad; because it has so far affected his reason." But may it not be answered, that a man may be altered by it *for the better;* that his spirits may be exhilarated, without his reason being affected? On the general subject of drinking, however, I do not mean positively to take the other side. I am *dubius non improbus.*

In the evening, Sir Allan informed us that it was the custom of the house to have prayers every Sunday; and Miss M'Lean read the evening service, in which we all joined. I then read Ogden's second and ninth Sermons on Prayer, which, with their other distinguished excellence, have the merit of being short. Dr. Johnson said, that it was the most agreeable Sunday he had ever passed.

Monday, Oct. 18*th.*—We agreed to pass the day with Sir Allan, and he engaged to have every thing in order for our voyage to-morrow.

Being now soon to be separated from our amiable friend young *Col*, his merits were all remembered. At Ulva, he had appeared in a new character, having given us a good prescription for a cold. On my mentioning him with warmth, Dr. Johnson said, "*Col* does every thing for us: we will erect a statue to *Col*." "Yes," said I, "and we will have him with his various attributes and characters, like Mercury, or any other of the heathen gods. We will have him as a pilot; we will have him as a fisherman, as a hunter, as a husbandman, as a physician."

I this morning took a spade, and dug a little grave in the floor of a ruined chapel,[1] near Sir Allan M'Lean's house, in which I buried some human bones I found there. Dr. Johnson praised me for what I had done, though he owned he could not have done it. He showed in the chapel at Rasay his horror at dead men's bones. He showed it again at *Col's* house. In the charter-room there was a remarkably large shin bone, which was said to have been a bone of John Garve, one of the lairds. Dr. Johnson would not look at it, but started away.

Having expressed a desire to have an island like Inch-kenneth, Dr. Johnson set himself to think what would be necessary for a man in such a situation.

"Sir, I should build me a fortification, if I came to live here; for, if you have it not, what should hinder a parcel of ruffians to land in the night, and carry off every thing you have in the house, which, in a remote country, would be more valuable than cows and sheep? add to all this the danger of having your throat cut." BOSWELL. "I would have a large dog." JOHNSON. "So you may, Sir; but a large dog is of no use but to alarm." He, however, I apprehend, thinks too lightly of the power of that animal. I have heard him say that he is afraid of no dog. "He would take him up by the hinder legs, which would render him quite helpless; and then knock his head against a stone, and beat out his brains." But few

---

[1] Mr. Boswell had visited this chapel the evening before; Johnson says to Mrs. Thrale, "Boswell, who is very pious, went into it at night to perform his devotions, but came back in haste *for fear of spectres.*"

men have his intrepidity, Herculean strength, or presence of mind. Most thieves or robbers would be afraid to encounter a mastiff.

Young *Col* told us he could run down a greyhound; "for," said he, "the dog runs himself out of breath, by going too quick, and then I get up with him." I accounted for his advantage over the dog, by remarking that *Col* had the faculty of reason, and knew how to moderate his pace, which the dog had not sense enough to do. Dr. Johnson said, "He is a noble animal. He is as complete an islander as the mind can figure. He is a farmer, a sailor, a hunter, a fisher: he will run you down a dog; if any man has a *tail*,[1] it is *Col*. He is hospitable; and he has an intrepidity of talk, whether he understands the subject or not. I regret that he is not more intellectual."

Tuesday, Oct. 19.—After breakfast we took leave of the young ladies, and of our excellent companion *Col*, to whom we had been so much obliged. He had now put us under the care of his chief; and was to hasten back to Sky. We parted from him with very strong feelings of kindness and gratitude, and we hoped to have had some future opportunity of proving to him the sincerity of what we felt; but in the following year he was unfortunately lost in the Sound between Ulva and Mull;[2] and this imperfect memorial, joined to the high honour of being tenderly and respectfully mentioned by Dr. Johnson, is the only return which the uncertainty of human events has permitted us to make to this deserving young man.

Sir Allan, who obligingly undertook to accompany us to Icolmkill, had a strong good boat, with four stout rowers. We coasted along Mull till we reached *Gribon*, where is what is called Mackinnon's cave. It is in a rock of great height close to the sea. Upon the left of its entrance there is a cascade, almost perpendicular from the top to the bottom of the rock. There is a tradition that it was conducted thither artificially, to supply the inhabitants of the cave with water. Dr. Johnson gave no credit to this tradition.

The height of this cave I cannot tell with any tolerable exactness; but it seemed to be very lofty, and to be a pretty regular arch. We penetrated by candle-light, a great way; by our measurement, no less than four hundred and eight-five feet. Tradition says, that a piper and twelve men once advanced into this cave, nobody can tell how far, and never returned. At the distance to which we proceeded the air was quite pure; for the candle burned freely, without

[1] In allusion to Monboddo's theory, that a perfect man would have a tail.
[2] Just opposite to M'Quarrie's house the boat was swamped by the intoxication of the sailors, who had partaken too largely of M'Quarrie's wonted hospitality.—*Walter Scott.*

the least appearance of the flame growing globular; but as we had only one, we thought it dangerous to venture farther, lest, should it have been extinguished, we should have had no means of ascertaining whether we could remain without danger. Dr. Johnson said, this was the greatest natural curiosity he had ever seen.

We saw the island of Staffa, at no very great distance, but could not land upon it, the surge was so high on its rocky coast.

Sir Allan, anxious for the honour of Mull, was still talking of its *woods*, and pointing them out to Dr. Johnson, as appearing at a distance on the skirts of that island, as we sailed along. JOHNSON. "Sir, I saw at Tobermorie what they called a wood, which I unluckily took for *heath*. If you show me what I shall take for *furze*, it will be something."

In the afternoon we went ashore on the coast of Mull, and partook of a cold repast, which we carried with us. We hoped to have procured some rum or brandy for our boatmen and servants, from a public-house near where we landed; but unfortunately a funeral a few days before had exhausted all their store.

We continued to coast along Mull, and passed by Nuns' Island, which, it is said, belonged to the nuns of Icolmkill, and from which, we were told, the stone for the buildings there was taken. As we sailed along by moonlight, in a sea somewhat rough, and often between black and gloomy rocks, Dr. Johnson said, "If this be not *roving among the Hebrides*, nothing is."

After a tedious sail, which, by our following various turnings of the coast of Mull, was extended to about forty miles, it gave us no small pleasure to perceive a light in the village at Icolmkill, in which almost all the inhabitants of the island live, close to where the ancient building stood. As we approached the shore, the tower of the cathedral, just discernible in the air, was a picturesque object.

When we had landed upon the sacred place, which, as long as I can remember, I had thought on with veneration, Dr. Johnson and I cordially embraced. We had long talked of visiting Icolmkill; and, from the lateness of the season, were at times very doubtful whether we should be able to effect our purpose. To have seen it, even alone, would have given me great satisfaction; but the venerable scene was rendered much more pleasing by the company of my great and pious friend, who was no less affected by it than I was; and who has described the impressions it should make on the mind, with such strength of thought, and energy of language, that I shall

THE RUINS OF ICOLMKILL

quote his words, as conveying my own sensations much more forcibly than I am capable of doing:

We were now treading that illustrious island, which was once the luminary of the Caledonian regions, whence savage clans and roving barbarians derived the benefits of knowledge, and the blessings of religion.   To abstract the mind from all local emotion would be impossible if it were endeavoured, and would be foolish if it were possible.   Whatever withdraws us from the power of our senses, whatever makes the past, the distant, or the future, predominate over the present, advances us in the dignity of thinking beings.   Far from me, and from my friends, be such frigid philosophy as may conduct us indifferent and unmoved over any ground which has been dignified by wisdom, bravery, or virtue.   That man is little to be envied, whose patriotism would not gain force upon the plain of *Marathon*, or whose piety would not grow warmer among the ruins of *Iona!* [1]

We were accommodated this night in a large barn, the island affording no lodging that we should have liked so well.   Some good hay was strewed at one end of it, to form a bed for us, upon which we lay with our clothes on; and we were furnished with blankets from the village.   Each of us had a portmanteau for a pillow.   When I awaked in the morning, and looked around me, I could not help smiling at the idea of the chief of the M'Leans, the great English moralist, and myself, lying thus extended in such a situation.

Wednesday, Oct. 20.—Early in the morning we surveyed the remains of antiquity at this place.   As I knew that many persons had already examined them, and as I saw Dr. Johnson inspecting and measuring several of the ruins, my mind was quiescent; and I resolved to stroll among them at my ease to take no trouble to investigate minutely, and only receive the general impression of solemn antiquity, and the particular ideas of such objects as should of themselves strike my attention.

We walked from the monastery of nuns to the great church or cathedral, as they call it, along an old broken causeway.   The convent of monks, the great church, Oran's chapel, and four other chapels, are still to be discerned.   But I must own that Icolmkill did not answer my expectations; for they were high, from what I had read of it, and still more from what I had heard and thought of it,

---

[1] Had our tour produced nothing else but this sublime passage, the world must have acknowledged that it was not made in vain. The present respectable President of the Royal Society [Sir Joseph Banks] told me, he was so much struck on reading it, that he clasped his hands together, and remained for some time in an attitude of silent admiration.—*Boswell.*

from my earliest years. Dr. Johnson said it came up to his expectations, because he had taken his impression from an account where it is said, there is not much to be seen here. We were both disappointed, when we were shown what are called the monuments of the kings of Scotland, Ireland, and Denmark, and of a king of France. There are only some grave-stones flat on the earth, and we could see no inscriptions. How far short was this of marble monuments, like those in Westminster Abbey, which I had imagined here!

I left him and Sir Allan at breakfast in our barn, and stole back again to the cathedral, to indulge in solitude and devout meditation. I hoped that ever after having been in this holy place, I should maintain an exemplary conduct. One has a strange propensity to fix upon some point of time from whence a better course of life may begin.

We set sail again about mid-day, and in the evening landed on Mull, near the house of the Rev. Mr. Neil Macleod, who came out to meet us. We were this night very agreeably entertained at his house. Dr. Johnson observed to me that he was the cleanest-headed man that he had met with in the Western Islands.

Thursday, Oct. 21.—This morning the subject of politics was introduced. BOSWELL. "The History of England is so strange, that, if it were not so well vouched as it is, it would hardly be credible." JOHNSON. "Sir, if it were told as shortly, and with as little preparation for introducing the different events, as the History of the Jewish Kings, it would be equally liable to objections of improbability." Mr. Macleod was much pleased with the justice and novelty of the thought. Dr. Johnson illustrated what he had said as follows: "Take, as an instance, Charles the First's concessions to his parliament, which were greater and greater, in proportion as the parliament grew more insolent, and less deserving of trust. Had these concessions been related nakedly, without any detail of the circumstances which generally led to them, they would not have been believed."

Sir Allan M'Lean bragged, that Scotland had the advantage of England by its having more water. JOHNSON. "Sir, we would not have your water, to take the vile bogs which produce it. You have too much! A man who is drowned has more water than either of us";—and then he laughed. (But this was surely robust sophistry; for the people of taste in England, who have seen Scotland, own that its variety of rivers and lakes makes it naturally more beautiful than England, in that respect.) Pursuing his victory over Sir

Allan, he proceeded: "Your country consists of two things, stone and water. There is, indeed, a little earth above the stone in some places, but a very little; and the stone is always appearing. It is like a man in rags—the naked skin is still peeping out."

He took leave of Mr. Macleod, saying, "Sir, I thank you for your entertainment, and your conversation."

Mr. Campbell very obligingly furnished us with horses to proceed on our journey to Mr. M'Lean's of Lochbuy, where we were to pass the night. We dined at the house of another physician at Mull, who was so much struck with the uncommon conversation of Dr. Johnson, that he observed to me, "This man is just a *hogshead* of sense."

After a very tedious ride, through what appeared to me the most gloomy and desolate country I had ever beheld, we arrived, between seven and eight o'clock, at Moy, the seat of the Laird of Lochbuy. He proved to be a bluff, comely, noisy, old gentleman, proud of his hereditary consequence, and a very hearty and hospitable landlord. Being told that Dr. Johnson did not hear well, *Lochbuy* bawled out to him, "Are you of the Johnstons of Glencro, or of Ardnamurchan?" Dr. Johnson gave him a significant look, but made no answer; and I told *Lochbuy* that he was not John*ston*, but John*son*, and that he was an Englishman.

Sir Allan, *Lochbuy*, and I, had the conversation chiefly to ourselves to-night. Dr. Johnson, being extremely weary, went to bed soon after supper.

Friday, Oct. 22.—Before Dr. Johnson came to breakfast, Lady *Lochbuy* said, "he was a *dungeon* of wit"; a very common phrase in Scotland to express a profoundness of intellect. She proposed that he should have some cold sheep's head for breakfast. Sir Allan seemed displeased at his sister's vulgarity, and wondered how such a thought should come into her head. From a mischievous love of sport, I took the lady's part; and very gravely said, "I think it is but fair to give him an offer of it. If he does not choose it, he may let it alone." "I think so," said the lady, looking at her brother with an air of victory. Sir Allan, finding the matter desperate, strutted about the room, and took snuff. When Dr. Johnson came in, she called to him, "Do you choose any cold sheep's head, Sir?" "No, Madam," said he, with a tone of surprise and anger.[1]

[1] Begging pardon of the Doctor and his conductor, I have often seen and partaken of cold sheep's head at as good breakfast-tables as ever they sat at. This protest is something in the manner of the late Culrosse, who fought a duel for the honour of Aberdeen butter. I have passed over all the Doctor's other reproaches upon Scotland, but the sheep's head I will defend *totis viribus*. Dr. Johnson himself must have forgiven my zeal on this occasion; for if, as he says, *dinner* be the thing of which a man thinks *oftenest during the day*, *breakfast* must be that of which he thinks *first in the morning.*—*Walter Scott.*

"It is here, Sir," said she, supposing he had refuse. it to save the trouble of bringing it in. They thus went on at cross purposes, till he confirmed his refusal in a manner not to be misunderstood; while I sat quietly by and enjoyed my success.

After breakfast, we set out for the ferry, by which we were to cross to the main land of Argyleshire. We bade adieu to *Lochbuy*, and to Sir Allan M'Lean, on the shore of Mull, and then got into the ferry-boat, the bottom of which was strewed with branches of trees or bushes, upon which we sat. We had a good day and a fine passage, and in the evening landed at Oban, where we found a tolerable inn. After having been so long confined at different times in islands, from which it was always uncertain when we could get away, it was comfortable to be now on the main land, and to know that, if in health, we might get to any place in Scotland or England in a certain number of days.

Here we discovered, from the conjectures which were formed, that the people of the main land were entirely ignorant of our motions.

Saturday, Oct. 23.—After a good night's rest, we breakfasted at our leisure. We talked of Goldsmith's "Traveller," of which Dr. Johnson spoke highly; and while I was helping him on with his great coat, he repeated from it the character of the British nation, which he did with such energy that the tear started into his eye:

> Stern o'er each bosom reason holds her state,
> With daring aims irregularly great,
> Pride in their port, defiance in their eye,
> I see the lords of humankind pass by,
> Intent on high designs, a thoughtful band,
> By forms unfashion'd, fresh from nature's hand;
> Fierce in their native hardiness of soul,
> True in imagined right, above controul,
> While even the peasant boasts these rights to scan,
> And learns to venerate himself as man.

We could get but one bridle here, which, according to the maxim *detur digniori*, was appropriated to Dr. Johnson's sheltie. I and Joseph rode with halters. We crossed in a ferry-boat a pretty wide lake, and on the farther side of it, close by the shore, found a hut for our inn. We were much wet. I changed my clothes in part, and was at pains to get myself well dried. Dr. Johnson resolutely kept on all his clothes, wet as they were, letting them steam before the smoky turf fire. I thought him in the wrong; but his firmness was, perhaps, a species of heroism.

It rained very hard as we journeyed on after dinner. We got at night to Inverary, where we found an excellent inn. Even here, Dr. Johnson would not change his wet clothes.

The prospect of good accommodation cheered us much. We supped well; and after supper, Dr. Johnson, whom I had not seen taste any fermented liquor during all our travels, called for a gill of whisky. "Come," said he, "let me know what it is that makes a Scotchman happy!" He drank it all but a drop, which I begged leave to pour into my glass, that I might say we had drunk whisky together. I proposed Mrs. Thrale should be our toast. He would not have *her* drunk in whisky, but rather "some insular lady"; so we drank one of the ladies whom we had lately left. He owned to-night, that he got as good a room and bed as at an English inn.

I had here the pleasure of finding a letter from home, which relieved me from the anxiety I had suffered, in consequence of not having received any account of my family for many weeks. I also found a letter from Mr. Garrick, which was a regale as agreeable as a pine-apple would be in a desert.

Sunday, Oct. 24.—We passed the forenoon calmly and placidly. I prevailed on Dr. Johnson to read aloud Ogden's sixth Sermon on Prayer, which he did with a distinct expression, and pleasing solemnity. He praised my favourite preacher, his elegant language, and remarkable acuteness; and said, he fought infidels with their own weapons.

In a Magazine I found a saying of Dr. Johnson's something to this purpose; that the happiest part of a man's life is what he passes lying awake in bed in the morning. I read it to him. He said, "I may, perhaps, have said this; for nobody, at times, talks more laxly than I do." I ventured to suggest to him, that this was dangerous from one of his authority.

I told Dr. Johnson I was in some difficulty how to act at Inverary. I had reason to think that the Duchess of Argyle disliked me, on account of my zeal in the Douglas cause; [1] but the Duke of Argyle had always been pleased to treat me with great civility. They were now at the castle, which is a very short walk from our inn; and the question was whether I should go and pay my respects

1 Elizabeth Gunning, celebrated for her personal charms, had been previously Duchess of Hamilton, and was mother of Douglas, Duke of Hamilton, the competitor for the Douglas property with the late Lord Douglas; she was, of course, prejudiced against Boswell, who had shown all the bustling importance of his character in the Douglas cause.—*Walter Scott.*

there. Dr. Johnson, to whom I had stated the case, was clear that I ought; but, in his usual way, he was very shy of discovering a desire to be invited there himself. He insisted that I should not go to the castle this day before dinner, as it would look like seeking an invitation. "But," said I, "if the duke invites us to dine with him to-morrow, shall we accept?" "Yes, sir;" I think he said, "to be sure." But he added, "He won't ask us." I mentioned, that I was afraid my company might be disagreeable to the duchess. He treated this objection with a manly disdain; "*That*, Sir, he must settle with his wife." We dined well. I went to the castle just about the time when I supposed the ladies would be retired from dinner. I sent in my name; and, being shown in, found the amiable duke sitting at the head of his table with several gentlemen. I was most politely received, and gave his grace some particulars of the curious journey which I had been making with Dr. Johnson. When we rose from table, the duke said to me, "I hope you and Dr. Johnson will dine with us to-morrow." I thanked his grace; but told him, my friend was in a great hurry to get back to London. The duke, with a kind complacency, said, "He will stay one day; and I will take care he shall see this place to advantage." I said, I should be sure to let him know his grace's invitation. As I was going away, the duke said, "Mr. Boswell, won't you have some tea?" I thought it best to get over the meeting with the duchess this night; so respectfully agreed. I was conducted to the drawing-room by the duke, who announced my name; but the duchess, who was sitting with her daughter, Lady Betty Hamilton, and some other ladies, took not the least notice of me. I should have been mortified at being thus coldly received by a lady of whom I, with the rest of the world, have always entertained a very high admiration, had I not been consoled by the obliging attention of the duke.

When I returned to the inn, I informed Dr. Johnson of the Duke of Argyle's invitation, with which he was much pleased, and readily accepted of it.

Monday, Oct. 25.—My acquaintance, the Rev. Mr. John M'Aulay, brother to our good friend at Calder, came to us this morning, and accompanied us to the castle, where I presented Dr. Johnson to the Duke of Argyle. We were shown through the house; and I never shall forget the impression made upon my fancy by some of the ladies' maids tripping about in neat morning dresses. After seeing for a long time little but rusticity, their lively manner, and gay inviting appearance, pleased me so much, that I thought for a moment I could have been a knight-errant for them.

We then got into a low one-horse chair, ordered for us by the duke, in which we drove about the place. Dr. Johnson was much struck by the grandeur and elegance of this princely seat. He thought, however, the castle too low, and wished it had been a story higher. He said, "What I admire here is the total defiance of expense." I had a particular pride in showing him a great number of fine old trees, to compensate for the nakedness which had made such an impression on him on the eastern coast of Scotland.

When we came in, before dinner, we found the duke and some gentlemen in the hall. Dr. Johnson took much notice of the large collection of arms, which are excellently disposed there. I told what he had said to Sir Alexander M'Donald, of his ancestors not suffering their arms to rust. "Well," said the doctor, "but let us be glad we live in times when arms *may* rust. We can sit to-day at his grace's table, without any risk of being attacked, and perhaps sitting down again wounded or maimed." The duke placed Dr. Johnson next himself at table. I was in fine spirits; and though sensible that I had the misfortune of not being in favour with the duchess, I was not in the least disconcerted, and offered her grace some of the dish that was before me. It must be owned that I was in the right to be quite unconcerned, if I could. I was the Duke of Argyle's guest; and I had no reason to suppose that he had adopted the prejudices and resentments of the Duchess of Hamilton.

I knew it was the rule of modern high life not to drink to any body; but, that I might have the satisfaction for once to look the duchess in the face, with a glass in my hand, I with a respectful air addressed her, "My Lady Duchess, I have the honour to drink your grace's good health." I repeated the words audibly, and with a steady countenance. This was, perhaps, rather too much; but some allowance must be made for human feelings.

The duchess was very attentive to Dr. Johnson. The subject of luxury having been introduced, Dr. Johnson defended it. "We have now," said he, "a splendid dinner before us; which of all these dishes is unwholesome?" The duke asserted, that he had observed the grandees of Spain diminished in their size by luxury. Dr. Johnson politely refrained from opposing directly an observation which the duke himself had made; but said, "Man must be very different from other animals, if he is diminished by good living; for the size of all other animals is increased by it." I made

I COULD HAVE BEEN A KNIGHT-ERRANT FOR THEM

some remark that seemed to imply a belief in *second sight*. The duchess said, "I fancy you will be a *methodist.*" This was the only sentence her grace deigned to utter to me; and I take it for granted, she thought it a good hit on my *credulity* in the Douglas cause.

A gentleman in company, after dinner, was desired by the duke to go to another room, for a specimen of curious marble, which his grace wished to show us. He brought a wrong piece, upon which the duke sent him back again. He could not refuse; but, to avoid any appearance of servility, he whistled as he walked out of the room, to show his independency. On my mentioning this afterwards to Dr. Johnson, he said, it was a nice trait of character.

Dr. Johnson talked a great deal, and was so entertaining, that Lady Betty Hamilton, after dinner, went and placed her chair close to his, leaned upon the back of it, and listened eagerly. It would have made a fine picture to have drawn the sage and her at this time in their several attitudes. He did not know, all the while, how much he was honoured. I told him afterwards, I never saw him so gentle and complaisant as this day.

We went to tea. The duke and I walked up and down the drawing-room, conversing. The duchess still continued to show the same marked coldness for me; for which, though I suffered from it, I made every allowance, considering the very warm part that I had taken for Douglas, in the cause in which she thought her son deeply interested. Had not her grace discovered some displeasure towards me, I should have suspected her of insensibility or dissimulation.

Her grace made Dr. Johnson come and sit by her, and asked him why he made his journey so late in the year. "Why, Madam," said he, "you know Mr. Boswell must attend the court of session, and it does not rise till the twelfth of August." She said, with some sharpness, "I *know nothing* of Mr. Boswell." Poor Lady Lucy Douglas,[1] to whom I mentioned this, observed, "She knew *too much* of Mr. Boswell." I shall make no remark on her grace's speech. I indeed felt it as rather too severe; but when I recollected that my punishment was inflicted by so dignified a beauty, I had that kind of consolation which a man would feel who is strangled by a silken cord. Dr. Johnson was all attention to her grace. He used afterwards a droll expression, upon her enjoying the three

[1] Lady Lucy Graham, wife of Mr. Douglas, the successful claimant: she died in 1780, whence Boswell calls her "poor Lady Lucy."

titles of Hamilton, Brandon, and Argyle. Borrowing an image from the Turkish empire, he called her a *duchess* with *three tails*.

He was much pleased with our visit at the castle of Inverary. The Duke of Argyle was exceedingly polite to him, and, upon his complaining of the shelties which he had hitherto ridden being too small for him, his grace told him he should be provided with a good horse to carry him next day.

Mr. John M'Aulay passed the evening with us at our inn. I recollect very little of this night's conversation. I am sorry that indolence came upon me towards the conclusion of our journey, so that I did not write down what passed with the same assiduity as during the greatest part of it.

Tuesday, Oct. 26.—Either yesterday morning, or this, I communicated to Dr. Johnson, from Mr. M'Aulay's information, the news that Dr. Beattie had got a pension of two hundred pounds a year. He sat up in his bed, clapped his hands, and cried, "O brave we!"—a peculiar exclamation of his when he rejoices.

While we were lamenting the number of ruined religious buildings which we had lately seen, I spoke with peculiar feeling of the miserable neglect of the chapel belonging to the palace of Holyrood-house, in which are deposited the remains of many of the kings of Scotland, and of many of our nobility. I particularly complained that my friend Douglas, the representative of a great house, and proprietor of a vast estate, should suffer the sacred spot where his mother lies interred to be unroofed, and exposed to all the inclemencies of the weather. Dr. Johnson, who, I knew not how, had formed an opinion on the Hamilton side, in the Douglas cause, slily answered, "Sir, Sir, don't be too severe upon the gentleman; don't accuse him of want of filial piety; Lady Jane Douglas was not *his* mother." He roused my zeal so much that I took the liberty to tell him he knew nothing of the cause; which I do most seriously believe was the case.

We were now "in a country of bridles and saddles," and set out fully equipped. The Duke of Argyle was obliging enough to mount Dr. Johnson on a stately steed from his grace's stable. My friend was highly pleased, and Joseph said, "He now looks like a bishop."

We dined at the inn at Tarbat, and at night came to Rosedow, the beautiful seat of Sir James Colquhoun, on the banks of Lochlomond, where I, and any friends whom I have introduced, have ever been received with kind and elegant hospitality.

Wednesday, Oct. 27.—When I went into Dr. Johnson's room this morning, I observed to him how wonderfully courteous he had been at Inverary, and said, "You were quite a fine gentleman when with the duchess." He answered, in good humour, "Sir, I look upon myself as a very polite man": and he was right, in a proper manly sense of the word. As an immediate proof of it, let me observe that he would not send back the Duke of Argyle's horse without a letter of thanks.

After breakfast, Dr. Johnson and I were furnished with a boat, and sailed about upon Lochlomond, and landed on some of the islands which are interspersed. He was much pleased with the scene.

I recollect none of his conversation, except that, when talking of dress, he said, "Sir, were I to have anything fine, it should be very fine. Were I to wear a ring, it should not be a bauble, but a stone of great value. Were I to wear a laced or embroidered waistcoat, it should be very rich. I had once a very rich laced waistcoat, which I wore the first night of my tragedy."

We were favoured with Sir James Colquhoun's coach to convey us in the evening to Cameron, the seat of Commissary Smollett. Our satisfaction of finding ourselves again in a comfortable carriage was very great. We had a pleasing conviction of the commodiousness of civilization, and heartily laughed at the ravings of those visionaries who have attempted to persuade us of the superior advantages of a state of nature.

Thursday, Oct. 28.—We had this morning a singular proof of Dr. Johnson's quick and retentive memory. Hay's translation of "Martial" was lying in a window; I said, I thought it was pretty well done, and showed him a particular epigram, I think of ten, but am certain of eight lines. He read it, and tossed away the book, saying, "No, it is *not* pretty well." As I persisted in my opinion, he said, "Why, Sir, the original is thus," and he repeated it, "and this man's translation is thus," and then he repeated that also, exactly, though he had never seen it before, and read it over only once, and that, too, without any intention of getting it by heart.

Here a post-chaise, which I had ordered from Glasgow, came for us, and we drove on in high spirits. We stopped at Dumbarton, and though the approach to the castle there is very steep, Dr. Johnson ascended it with alacrity, and surveyed all that was to be seen. During the whole of our Tour he showed uncommon spirit, could not bear to be treated like an old or infirm man, and was very unwilling to accept of any assistance, insomuch that at our landing at Icolmkill, when Sir Allan M'Lean and I submitted to be carried on men's shoulders from the boat to the shore, as it could not be brought quite close to land, he sprang into the sea, and waded vigorously out.

On our arrival at the Saracen's Head inn, at Glasgow, I was made happy by good accounts from home; and Dr. Johnson, who had not received a single letter since we left Aberdeen, found here a great many, the perusal of which entertained him much. He enjoyed in imagination the comforts which we could now command, and seemed to be in high glee. I remember, he put a leg upon each side of the grate, and said, with mock solemnity, by way of soliloquy, but loud enough for me to hear it, "Here am I, an *English*-man, sitting by a *coal* fire."

Friday, Oct. 29.—Professors Reid and Anderson, and the two Messieurs Foulis, the Elzevirs of Glasgow, dined and drank tea with us at our inn, after which the professors went away; and I, having a letter to write, left my fellow-traveller with Messieurs Foulis. Though good and ingenious men, they had that unsettled speculative mode of conversation which is offensive to a man regularly taught at an English school and university. I found that, instead of listening to the dictates of the sage, they had teased him with questions and doubtful disputations. He came in a flutter to me, and desired I might come back again, for he could not bear these men. "O ho! Sir," said I, "you are flying to me for refuge!" He never, in any situation, was at a loss for a ready repartee. He answered, with quick vivacity, "It is of two evils choosing the least." I was delighted with this flash bursting from the cloud which hung upon his mind, closed my letter directly, and joined the company.

We supped at Professor Anderson's. The general impression upon my memory is, that we had not much conversation at Glasgow, where the professors, like their brethren at Aberdeen, did not venture to expose themselves much to the battery of cannon which they knew might play upon them. Dr. Johnson, who was fully conscious of his own superior powers, afterwards praised Principal Robertson for his caution in this respect. He said to me, "Robertson, Sir, was in the right. Robertson is a man of eminence, and the head of a college at Edinburgh. He had a character to maintain, and did well not to risk its being lessened."

NOW IN HER EIGHTY-FIFTH YEAR

Saturday, Oct. 30.—We set out towards Ayrshire. I sent Joseph on to Loudoun, with a message, that if the earl was at home, Dr. Johnson and I would have the honour to dine with him. Joseph met us on the road, and reported that the earl *"jumped for joy,"* and said, "I shall be very happy to see them." We were received with a most pleasing courtesy by his lordship, and by the countess his mother, who, in her ninety-fifth year, had all her faculties quite unimpaired. This was a very cheering sight to Dr. Johnson, who had an extraordinary desire for long life.

At night, we advanced a few miles farther, to the house of Mr. Campbell, of Treesbank, who was married to one of my wife's sisters, and were entertained very agreeably by a worthy couple.

Sunday, Oct. 31.—We reposed here in tranquillity. Dr. Johnson was pleased to find a numerous and excellent collection of books.

Monday, Nov. 1.—Though Dr. Johnson was lazy and averse to move, I insisted that he should go with me, and pay a visit to the Countess of Eglintoune, mother of the late and present earl. I assured him he would find himself amply recompensed for the trouble; and he yielded to my solicitations, though with some unwillingness. We were well mounted, and had not many miles to ride. As we passed very near the castle of Dundonald, which was one of the many residences of the kings of Scotland, and in which Robert the Second lived and died, Dr. Johnson wished to survey it particularly. It has long been unroofed; and, though of considerable size, we could not, by any power of imagination, figure it as having been a suitable habitation for majesty. Dr. Johnson, to irritate my old Scottish enthusiasm, was very jocular on the homely accommodation of "King *Bob*," and roared and laughed till the ruins echoed.

Lady Eglintoune, though she was now in her eighty-fifth year, and had lived in the retirement of the country for almost half a century, was still a very agreeable woman. Her figure was majestic, her manners high bred, her reading extensive, and her conversation elegant. She had been the admiration of the gay circles of life, and the patroness of poets. Dr. Johnson was delighted with his reception here. Her principles in church and state were congenial with his. She knew all his merit, and had heard much of him from her son, Earl Alexander, who loved to cultivate the acquaintance of men of talents in every department.

In the course of our conversation it came out that Lady Eglintoune was married the year before Dr. Johnson was born: upon which she graciously said to him that she might have been his mother, and that she now adopted him; and when we were going away, she embraced him, saying, "My dear son, farewell!" My friend was much pleased with this day's entertainment, and owned that I had done well to force him out.

Tuesday, Nov. 2.—We were now in a country not only of "*saddles and bridles,*" but of post-chaises; and having ordered one from Kilmarnock, we got to Auchinleck before dinner.

My father was not quite a year and a half older than Dr. Johnson; but his conscientious discharge of his laborious duty as a judge in Scotland, where the law proceedings are almost all in writing,—a severe complaint which ended in his death,—and the loss of my mother, a woman of almost unexampled piety and goodness,—had before this time in some degree affected his spirits, and rendered him less disposed to exert his faculties: for he had originally a very strong mind, and cheerful temper. He assured me he never had felt one moment of what is called low spirits, or uneasiness, without a real cause. He had a great many good stories, which he told uncommonly well, and he was remarkable for "humour, *incolumi gravitate,*" as Lord Monboddo used to characterize it. His age, his office, and his character had long given him an acknowledged claim to great attention, in whatever company he was; and he could ill brook any diminution of it. He was as sanguine a Whig and presbyterian as Dr. Johnson was a Tory and Church-of-England man: and as he had not much leisure to be informed of Dr. Johnson's great merits by reading his works, he had a partial and unfavourable notion of him, founded on his supposed political tenets; which were so discordant to his own, that instead of speaking of him with that respect to which he was entitled, he used to call him "*a Jacobite fellow.*" Knowing all this, I should not have ventured to bring them together, had not my father, out of kindness to me, desired me to invite Dr. Johnson to his house.

I was very anxious that all should be well; and begged of my friend to avoid three topics, as to which they differed very widely; whiggism, presbyterianism, and—Sir John Pringle. He said courteously, "I shall certainly not talk on subjects which I am told are disagreeable to a gentleman under whose roof I am; especially, I shall not do so to *your father.*"

Our first day went off very smoothly. It rained, and we could not get out: but my father showed Dr. Johnson his library, which, in curious editions of the Greek and Roman classics, is, I suppose, not excelled by any private collection in Great Britain. My father had studied at Leyden; he was a sound scholar, and, in particular, had collated manuscripts and different editions of Anacreon, and others of the Greek lyric poets, with great care; so that my friend and he had much matter for conversation, without touching on the fatal topics of difference.

Dr. Johnson found here Baxter's "Anacreon," which he told me he had long inquired for in vain, and began to suspect there was no such book. My father has written many notes on this book, and Dr. Johnson and I talked of having it reprinted.

Wednesday, Nov. 3.—It rained all day, and gave Dr. Johnson an impression of that incommodiousness of climate in the west, of which he has taken notice in his "Journey"; but, being well accommodated, and furnished with a variety of books, he was not dissatisfied.

Some gentlemen of the neighbourhood came to visit my father; but there was little conversation. One of them asked Dr. Johnson how he like the Highlands. The question seemed to irritate him, for he answered, "How, Sir, can you ask me what obliges me to speak unfavourably of a country where I have been hospitably entertained? Who *can* like the Highlands? I like the inhabitants very well." The gentleman asked no more questions.

He this day, when we were by ourselves, observed, how common it was for people to talk from books; to retail the sentiments of others, and not their own; in short, to converse without any originality of thinking. He was pleased to say, "You and I do not talk from books."

Thursday, Nov. 4.—I was glad to have at length a very fine day, on which I could show Dr. Johnson the place of my family, which he has honoured with so much attention in his "Journey." The "sullen dignity of the old castle," as he has forcibly expressed it, delighted him exceedingly. On one side of the rock on which its ruins stand, runs the river Lugar, which is here of considerable breadth, and is bordered by other high rocks, shaded with wood. On the other side runs a brook, skirted in the same manner, but on a smaller scale. I cannot figure a more romantic scene.

I felt myself elated here, and expatiated to my illustrious Mentor on the antiquity and honourable alliances of my family, and on the merits of its founder, Thomas Boswell, who was highly favoured by his sovereign, James IV. of Scotland, and fell with him at the battle of Flodden-field. I have, in a former page, acknowledged my pride of ancient blood, in which I was encouraged by Dr. Johnson: my readers, therefore, will not be surprised at my having indulged it on this occasion.

Not far from the old castle is a spot of consecrated earth, on which may be traced the foundations of an ancient chapel. Dr. Johnson was pleased when I showed him some venerable old trees, under the shade of which my ancestors had walked. He exhorted me to plant assiduously, as my father had done to a great extent.

As I wandered with my reverend friend in the groves of Auchinleck, I told him, that, if I survived him, it was my intention to erect a monument to him here, among scenes which, in my mind, were all classical; for, in my youth, I had appropriated to them many of the descriptions of the Roman poets. He could not bear to have death presented to him in any shape; for his constitutional melancholy made the king of terrors more frightful. He turned off the subject, saying, "Sir, I hope to see your grand-children."

Friday, Nov. 5.—Our parish minister, who had dined with us yesterday, insisted that Dr. Johnson and I should dine with him to-day. This gave me an opportunity to show my friend the road to the church, made by my father at a great expense, for above three miles, on his own estate, through a range of well-enclosed farms, with a row of trees on each side of it. He called it the *via sacra,* and was very fond of it. Dr. Johnson, though he held notions far distant from those of the presbyterian clergy, yet could associate on good terms with them. He, indeed, occasionally attacked them. One of them discovered a narrowness of information concerning the dignitaries of the Church of England, among whom may be found men of the greatest learning, virtue, and piety, and of a truly apostolic character. He talked before Dr. Johnson of fat bishops and drowsy deans; and, in short, seemed to believe the illiberal and profane scoffings of professed satirists, or vulgar railers. Dr. Johnson was so highly offended, that he said to him, "Sir, you know no more of our church than a Hottentot." I was sorry that he brought this upon himself.

Saturday, Nov. 6.—I cannot be certain whether it was on this day, or a former, that Dr. Johnson and my father came in collision. If I recollect right, the contest began while my father was showing him his collection of medals; and Oliver Cromwell's coin unfortunately introduced Charles the First and Toryism. They became exceedingly warm and violent, and I was very much distressed by being present at such an altercation between two men, both of whom I reverenced; yet I durst not interfere. It would certainly be very unbecoming in me to exhibit my honoured father and my respected friend, as intellectual gladiators, for the entertainment of the public; and, therefore, I suppress what would, I dare say, make an interesting scene in this dramatic sketch, this account of the transit of Johnson over the Caledonian hemisphere.[1]

Yet I think I may, without impropriety, mention one circumstance, as an instance of my father's address. Dr. Johnson challenged him, as he did us all at Talisker, to point out any theological works of merit written by presbyterian ministers in Scotland. My father, whose studies did not lie much in that way, owned to me afterwards, that he was somewhat at a loss how to answer, but that luckily he recollected having read in catalogues the title of Durham on the Galatians; upon which he boldly said, "Pray, Sir, have you read Mr. Durham's excellent commentary on the Galatians?" "No, Sir," said Dr. Johnson. By this lucky thought my father kept him at bay, and for some time enjoyed his triumph; [2] but his antagonist soon made a retort, which I forbear to mention.

In the course of their altercation, Whiggism and presbyterianism, Toryism and episcopacy, were terribly buffeted. My worthy hereditary friend, Sir John Pringle, never having been mentioned, happily escaped without a bruise.

[1] "Old Lord Auchinleck was an able lawyer, a good scholar, after the manner of Scotland, and highly valued his own advantages as a man of good estate and ancient family; and, moreover, he was a strict presbyterian and Whig of the old Scottish cast. This did not prevent his being a terribly proud aristocrat; and great was the contempt he entertained and expressed for his son James, for the nature of his friendships and the character of the personages of whom he was *engoué* one after another. 'There's nae hope for Jamie, mon,' he said to a friend. 'Jamie is gaen clean gyte.—What do you think, mon? He's done wi' Paoli—he's off wi' the landlouping scoundrel of a Corsican; and whose tail do you think he has pinned himself to now, mon?' Here the old judge summoned up a sneer of most sovereign contempt. 'A *dominie*, mon—an auld dominie; he keeped a schûle, and cau'd it an acaadamy.' Probably if this had been reported to Johnson, he would have felt it more galling, for he never much liked to think of that period of his life; it would have aggravated his dislike of Lord Auchinleck's Whiggery and presbyterianism. These the old lord carried to such an unusual height, that once, when a countryman came in to state some justice business, and being required to make his oath, declined to do so before his lordship, because he was not a *covenanted* magistrate—'Is that a' your objection, mon?' said the judge; 'come your ways in here, and we'll baith of us tak the solemn league and covenant together.' The oath was accordingly agreed and sworn to by both, and I dare say it was the last time it ever received such homage. It may be surmised how far Lord Auchinleck, such as he is here described, was likely to suit a high Tory and episcopalian like Johnson. As they approached Auchinleck, Boswell conjured Johnson by all the ties of regard, and in requital of the services he had rendered him upon his tour, that he would spare two subjects in tenderness to his father's prejudices; the first related to Sir John Pringle, president of the Royal Society, about whom there was then some dispute current: the second concerned the general question of Whig and Tory. Sir John Pringle, as Boswell says, escaped, but the controversy between Tory and Covenanter raged with great fury, and ended in Johnson's pressing upon the old judge the question, what good Cromwell, of whom he had said something derogatory, had ever done to his country; when, after being much tortured, Lord Auchinleck at last spoke out, 'God, doctor! he gart kings ken that they had a *lith* in their neck'—he taught kings they had a *joint* in their necks. Jamie then set to mediating between his father and the philosopher, and availing himself of the judge's sense of hospitality, which was punctilious, reduced the debate to more order."—*Walter Scott.*

[2] The full enjoyment lies in the fact (according to Croker) that there is no such book as Durham on the Galatians.

My father's opinion of Dr. Johnson may be conjectured from the name he afterwards gave him, which was URSA MAJOR.

Sunday, Nov. 7.—My father and I went to public worship in our parish church, in which I regretted that Dr. Johnson would not join us. His reason for not joining in presbyterian worship has been recorded in a former page.

Monday, Nov. 8.—Notwithstanding the altercation that had passed, my father, who had the dignified courtesy of an old baron, was very civil to Dr. Johnson, and politely attended him to the post-chaise which was to convey us to Edinburgh.

Thus they parted. They are now in another, and a higher state of existence: and as they were both worthy Christian men, I trust they have met in happiness.

We came at night to a good inn at Hamilton.——I recollect no more.

Tuesday, Nov. 9.—We arrived this night at Edinburgh, after an absence of eighty-three days. For five weeks together, of the tempestuous season, there had been no account received of us. I cannot express how happy I was on finding myself again at home.

Wednesday, Nov. 10.—Old Mr. Drummond, the bookseller, came to breakfast. Dr. Johnson and he had not met for ten years. There was respect on his side, and kindness on Dr. Johnson's. Soon afterwards Lord Elibank came in, and was much pleased at seeing Dr. Johnson in Scotland. Mr. Nairne came in, and he and I accompanied Dr. Johnson to Edinburgh castle, which he owned was "a great place." But when Lord Elibank was some days after talking of it with the natural elation of a Scotchman, Dr. Johnson affected to despise it, observing, that "it would make a good *prison* in ENGLAND."

Thursday, Nov. 11.—Principal Robertson came to us as we sat at breakfast; he advanced to Dr. Johnson, repeating a line of Virgil, which I forget. Every body had accosted us with some studied compliment on our return. Dr. Johnson said, "I am really ashamed of the congratulations which we receive. We are addressed as if we had made a voyage to Nova Zembla, and suffered five persecutions in Japan." And he afterwards remarked, that "to see a man come up with a formal air, and a Latin line, when we had no fatigue and no danger, was provoking." I told him, he was not sensible of the danger, having lain under cover in the boat during the storm: he was like the chicken, that hides its head under its wing, and then thinks itself safe.

As I kept no journal of any thing that passed after this morning, I shall, from memory, group together this and the other days, till that on which Dr. Johnson departed for London. They were in all nine days; on which he dined at Lady Colvill's, Lord Hailes's, Sir Adolphus Oughton's, Sir Alexander Dick's, Principal Robertson's, Mr. M'Laurin's, and thrice at Lord Elibank's seat in the country, where we also passed two nights. He supped at the Hon. Alexander Gordon's, Lord Rockville; at Mr. Nairne's, now Lord Dunsinan; at Dr. Blair's and Mr. Tytler's; and at my house thrice, one evening with a numerous company, chiefly gentlemen of the law; another with Mr. Menzies of Culdares, and Lord Monboddo, who disengaged himself on purpose to meet him; and the evening on which we returned from Lord Elibank's, he supped with my wife and me by ourselves.

He breakfasted at Dr. Webster's, at old Mr. Drummond's, and at Dr. Blacklock's; and spent one forenoon at my uncle Dr. Boswell's, who showed him his curious museum.

On the mornings when he breakfasted at my house, he had, from ten o'clock till one or two, a constant levee of various persons, of very different characters and descriptions. I could not attend him, being obliged to be in the court of session; but my wife was so good as to devote the greater part of the morning to the endless task of pouring out tea for my friend and his visitors.

Such was the disposition of his time at Edinburgh. He said one evening to me, in a fit of languor, "Sir, we have been harassed by invitations." I acquiesced. "Ay, Sir," he replied; "but how much worse would it have been if we had been neglected?"

At Mr. Tytler's I happened to tell that one evening, a great many years ago, when Dr. Hugh Blair and I were sitting together in the pit of Drury-Lane playhouse, in a wild freak of youthful extravagance, I entertained the audience *prodigiously*, by imitating the lowing of a cow. A little while after I had told this story, I differed from Dr. Johnson, I suppose too confidently, upon some point, which I now forget. He did not spare me. "Nay, Sir," said he, "if you cannot talk better as a man, I'd have you bellow like a cow." [1]

---

[1] As I have been scrupulously exact in relating anecdotes concerning other persons, I shall not withhold any part of this story, however ludicrous. I was so successful in this boyish frolic, that the universal cry of the galleries was, "*Encore* the cow! *Encore* the cow!" In the pride of my heart I attempted imitations of some other animals, but with very inferior effect. My reverend friend, anxious for my *fame*, with an air of the utmost gravity and earnestness, addressed me thus: "My dear Sir, I would *confine* myself to the *cow!*"—*Boswell.*

"Blair's advice was expressed more emphatically, and with a peculiar *burr*—'*Stick to the cow, mon!*'"
—*Walter Scott.*

At Dr. Webster's, he said, that he believed hardly any man died without affectation. This remark appears to me to be well founded, and will account for many of the celebrated death-bed sayings which are recorded.

At Sir Alexander Dick's, from that absence of mind to which every man is at times subject, I told, in a blundering manner, Lady Eglintoune's complimentary adoption of Dr. Johnson as her son; for I unfortunately stated that her ladyship adopted him as her son, in consequence of her having been married the year *after* he was born. Dr. Johnson instantly corrected me. "Sir, don't you perceive that you are defaming the countess? For, supposing me to be her son, and that she was not married till the year after my birth, I must have been her *natural* son." A young lady of quality, who was present, very handsomely said, "Might not the son have justified the fault?" My friend was much flattered by this compliment, which he never forgot. When in more than ordinary spirits, and talking of his journey in Scotland, he has called to me, "Boswell, what was it that the young lady of quality said of me at Sir Alexander Dick's?" Nobody will doubt that I was happy in repeating it.

My illustrious friend being now desirous to be again in the great theatre of life and animated exertion, took a place in the coach, which was to set out for London on Monday the 22nd of November. Sir John Dalrymple pressed him to come on the Saturday before, to his house at Cranston, which being twelve miles from Edinburgh, it would make his journey easier, as the coach would take him up at a more seasonable hour than that at which it sets out. Sir John, I perceive, was ambitious of having such a guest; but as I was well assured, that at this very time he had joined with some of his prejudiced countrymen in railing at Dr. Johnson, and had said, he wondered how any gentleman of Scotland could keep company with him, I thought he did not deserve the honour; yet, as it might be a convenience to Dr. Johnson, I contrived that he should accept the invitation, and engaged to conduct him. I resolved that, on our way to Sir John's, we should make a little circuit by Roslin Castle and Hawthornden, and wished to set out soon after breakfast; but young Mr. Tytler came to show Dr. Johnson some essays which he had written; and my great friend who was exceedingly obliging when thus consulted, was detained so long, that it was, I believe, one o'clock before we got into our post-chaise. I found that we should be too late for dinner at Sir John Dalrymple's, to which we were engaged; but I would by no means lose the pleasure of seeing my friend at Hawthornden, of seeing *Sam Johnson* at the very spot where *Ben Jonson* visited the learned and poetical Drummond.

We surveyed Roslin Castle, the romantic scene around it, and the beautiful Gothic chapel, and dined and drank tea at the inn; after which we proceeded to Hawthornden and viewed the caves; and I all the while had *Rare Ben* in my mind, and was pleased to think that this place was now visited by another celebrated wit of England.

By this time "the waning night was growing old," and we were yet several miles from Sir John Dalrymple's. Dr. Johnson did not seem much troubled at our having treated the baronet with so little attention to politeness; but when I talked of the grievous disappointment it must have been to him that we did not come to the *feast* that he had prepared for us (for he told us he had killed a seven-year-old sheep on purpose), my friend got into a merry mood, and jocularly said, "I dare say, Sir, he has been very sadly distressed; nay, we do not know but the consequence may have been fatal. Let me try to describe his situation in his own historical style. I have as good a right to make him think and talk, as he has to tell us how people thought and talked a hundred years ago, of which he has no evidence. All history, so far as it is not supported by contemporary evidence, is romance.—Stay now—let us consider!" He then (heartily laughing all the while) proceeded in his imitation:

Dinner being ready, he wondered that his guests were not yet come. His wonder was soon succeeded by impatience. He walked about the room in anxious agitation; sometimes he looked at his watch, sometimes he looked out at the window with an eager gaze of expectation, and revolved in his mind the various accidents of human life. His family beheld him with mute concern. "Surely," said he, with a sigh, "they will not fail me." The mind of man can bear a certain pressure; but there is a point when it can bear no more. A rope was in his view, and he died a Roman death.

It was very late before we reached the seat of Sir John Dalrymple, who, certainly with some reason, was not in very good humour. Our conversation was not brilliant. We supped, and went to bed in ancient rooms, which would have better suited the climate of Italy in summer, than that of Scotland in the month of November.

I recollect no conversation of the next day worth preserving, except one saying of Dr. Johnson, which will be a valuable text for many decent old dowagers, and other good company, in various circles to descant upon. He said, "I am sorry I have not learnt to play cards. It is very useful in life: it generates kindness and consolidates society."

My friend and I thought we should be more comfortable at the inn at Blackshields, two miles farther on. We therefore went thither in the evening, and he was very entertaining. We breakfasted together next morning, and then the coach came and took him up.

I have now completed my account of our Tour to the Hebrides. I have brought Dr. Johnson down to Scotland, and seen him into the coach which in a few hours carried him back into England. He said to me often, that the time he had spent in this Tour was the pleasantest part of his life, and asked me if I would lose the recollection of it for five hundred pounds. I answered I would not; and he applauded my setting such a value on an accession of new images in my mind.

Before I conclude, I think it proper to say, that I have suppressed every thing which I thought could really hurt any one now living. Vanity and self-conceit indeed may sometimes suffer. With respect to what is related, I considered it my duty to "extenuate nothing, nor set down aught in malice"; and with those lighter strokes of Dr. Johnson's satire, proceeding from a warmth and quickness of imagination, not from any malevolence of heart, and which, on account of their excellence, could not be omitted, I trust that they who are the subject of them have good sense and good temper enough not to be displeased.

I have only to add, that I shall ever reflect with great pleasure on a Tour, which has been the means of preserving so much of the enlightened and instructive conversation of one whose virtues will, I hope, ever be an object of imitation, and whose powers of mind were so extraordinary, that ages may revolve before such a man shall again appear.

INDEX

INDEX

Abercrombie, James (of Philadelphia), his admiration for Johnson, 177.

Aberdeen, Boswell and Johnson at, 527–529.

Abington, Mrs. (actress), Johnson vain of her solicitations, 221; her benefit at Drury Lane, 223; Johnson sups with, 231; *alluded to*, 223, 224.

Adams, Rev. William, Master of Pembroke College, 10, 13; account of Johnson's arrival àt Oxford, 13; takes Johnson's bitterness for frolic, 16; converses with Johnson about his "Dictionary," 37; present at first night of *Irene*, 41; expostulates with Johnson about his letter to Lord Chesterfield, 60; his description of Johnson's melancholy, 114; Johnson and Boswell visit, 256–58; entertains Johnson on his last visits to Oxford, 465, 467, 468, 469, 470, 486; *alluded to*, 28, 59.

Adams, Miss, 465, 466.

Addison, Joseph, 306, 325, 403, 530.

Akerman, Mr., keeper of Newgate, 303.

Allen, E. (a printer, Johnson's friend and landlord), Johnson borrows from him when in trouble, 69, *n.*; his good dinner, 109; endeavours to talk like Johnson, 404; *alluded to*, 228, 303, 446.

America, Johnson's friends in, 177, 178, 179; Boswell asked for information about, 210, 211; Johnson's unfavourable sentiments towards, 218, 319, 346, 356; Johnson on the war with, 401; *alluded to*, 322, 442.

Anne, Queen, "touches" Johnson, 6.

Argyle, John, 5th Duke of, Boswell and Johnson visit at Inverary, 621–26; lends Johnson "a stately steed," 626.

Ashbourne (Derbyshire), Johnson and Boswell visit Dr. Taylor at, 300–21; *alluded to*, 251, 266, 267, 298, 322.

Aston, Mrs. (of Stowhill, Johnson's friend), 322.

Auchinleck (the Boswell estate), Johnson's delight in hearing of, 106; Johnson visits, 202; Boswell's feeling for, 311; Johnson invited to, by Mrs. Boswell, 423; Johnson's last visit to, 632–36; *alluded to*, 238, 449, 517, 539.

Auchinleck, Lord (father of James Boswell), account of, 632; Johnson's visit to, 632–36; his "collision" with Johnson, 634–35; his "whiggery," 635, *n.*; *alluded to*, 311, 382, 422.

Auchnasheal, Boswell and Johnson at, 553; wild inhabitants of, 553.

Bacon, Francis, 459, 461.

Bagpipes, Johnson "appears fond of," 610.

Bagshaw, Rev. Thomas, Johnson's letter to, regarding his wife's grave, 482–83.

Baltic, projected visit of Johnson and Boswell, 209, *n.*; 299.

Bankes, Mr. (of Dorsetshire), astonished by Johnson's gesticulations, 29.

Barber, Francis (Johnson's negro servant), 47; his history, 49, *n.*; his account of Johnson's acquaintances, 49–50; his interlude at sea, 72; now returned home, 158; his civil assiduity, 236; Johnson's provision for, 491, 492, *n.*; *alluded to*, 119, 180, 181, 233, 242, 284, 295, 418, 462, 515.

Baretti, Signor (writer), tried for his life, 139–41; his "furious quarrel" with Davies, 177; Johnson wins a race against, 242; Mrs. Thrale's Italian master, 268; *alluded to*, 131, 246.

Barnard (Mr.), the King's Librarian, 122–26, 217.

Barnard, Dr. (Dean of Derry, late Bishop of Killaloe), 291.

Barrowby, Dr., 466.

Barry, S. (actor), 42.

Bateman, Mr., tutor at Christchurch, 16.

Bath, Johnson and Boswell at, 279; *alluded to*, 268, 387.

Bathurst, Dr., 37, 49, *n.*, 50, 395.

Baxter, Richard, 198.

Bayle, his dictionary praised by Johnson, 93; Leibnitz's confutation of, 600.